P9-BZO-093

DICTIONARY OF CONTEMPORARY RELIGION IN THE WESTERN WORLD

Dictionary of Contemporary Religion in the Western World

Editor:
Christopher Partridge
Senior Lecturer in Theology and Contemporary Religion, Chester College

Consulting editor:
Douglas Groothuis
Associate Professor of Philosophy, Denver Seminary, USA

Editorial advisers:
David Burnett
Director of Studies, All Nations Christian College, Ware
John Drane
Head of Practical Theology, University of Aberdeen
Peter G. Riddell
Director, Centre of Islamic Studies, London Bible College

Organizing editor:
Steve Carter
Reference Books Editor, Inter-Varsity Press, Leicester

Inter-Varsity Press, Leicester, England
InterVarsity Press, Downers Grove, Illinois, USA

INTER-VARSITY PRESS
38 De Montfort Street, Leicester LE1 7GP, England
Email: ivp@uccf.org.uk
Website: www.ivpbooks.com

INTERVARSITY PRESS
PO Box 1400, Downers Grove, Illinois 60515, USA
Email: mail@ivpress.com
Website: http://www.ivpress.com

© Inter-Varsity Press 2002

All rights reserved. No part of this publication may be reproduced, stored in a retrieval system, or transmitted, in any form or by any means, electronic, mechanical, photocopying, recording or otherwise, without the prior permission of Inter-Varsity Press or the Copyright Licensing Agency.

Unless otherwise stated, Scripture quotations in this publication are from the Holy Bible, New International Version. Copyright © 1973, 1978, 1984 by International Bible Society. Used by permission of Hodder & Stoughton, a division of Hodder Headline Ltd. All rights reserved. 'NIV' is a registered trademark of International Bible Society. UK trademark number 1448790.

First published 2002

British Library Cataloguing in Publication Data
A catalogue record for this book is available from the British Library.

UK ISBN 0–85111–982–4

Library of Congress Cataloging-in-Publication
Data has been requested.

US ISBN 0–8308–1436–1

Set in Sabon 9.5/11pt

Typeset in Great Britain by Avocet Typeset, Brill, Aylesbury, Bucks
Printed in Great Britain by Creative Print and Design (Wales), Ebbw Vale

Inter-Varsity Press is the book-publishing division of the Universities and Colleges Christian Fellowship (formerly the Inter-Varsity Fellowship), a student movement linking Christian Unions in universities and colleges throughout Great Britain, and a member movement of the International Fellowship of Evangelical Students. For more information about local and national activities write to UCCF, 38 De Montfort Street, Leicester LE1 7GP, email us at email@uccf.org.uk, or visit the UCCF website at www.uccf.org.uk.

InterVarsity Press® is the book-publishing division of InterVarsity Christian Fellowship/USA®, a student movement active on campus at hundreds of universities, colleges and schools of nursing in the United States of America, and a member movement of the International Fellowship of Evangelical Students. For information about local and regional activities, write to Public Relations Dept., InterVarsity Christian Fellowship USA, 6400 Schroeder Road, PO Box 7895, Madison, WI 53707-7895.

CONTENTS

ABBREVIATIONS

BOOKS AND JOURNALS

ALJ — *Australian Law Journal*
AV — Authorized Version (King James'), 1611
ER — *Encyclopedia of Religion*, M. Eliade (ed.), 14 vols. (London and New York, 1987).
GES — Grove Ethical Studies
IBMR — *International Bulletin of Missionary Research*
JCQ — *Japan Christian Quarterly*
JCR — *Journal of Contemporary Religion*
JJRS — *Journal of Japanese Religious Studies*
MEQ — *Muslim Education Quarterly*
NIV — New International Version
NRSV — New Revised Standard Version
RPT — *Research in Philosophy and Technology*
SA — *Sociological Analysis*
SCB — *Science and Christian Belief*
SPP — *Social Philosophy and Policy*
TCP — *The Christian Parapsychologist*

BIBLICAL BOOKS

BOOKS OF THE OLD TESTAMENT

Gen., Exod., Lev., Num., Deut., Josh., Judg., Ruth, 1,2 Sam., 1,2 Kgs., 1,2 Chr., Ezra, Neh., Est., Job, Ps.(Pss.), Prov., Eccles., Song, Is., Jer., Lam., Ezek., Dan., Hos., Joel, Amos, Obad., Jonah, Mic., Nah., Hab., Zeph., Hag., Zech., Mal.

BOOKS OF THE NEW TESTAMENT

Matt., Mark, Luke, John, Acts, Rom., 1,2 Cor., Gal., Eph., Phil., Col., 1,2 Thess., 1,2 Tim., Titus, Philem., Heb., Jas., 1,2 Pet., 1,2,3 John, Jude, Rev.

GENERAL ABBREVIATIONS

ad loc.	at the place
b.	born
c.	about, approximately
cf.	compare
ch(s).	chapter(s)
d.	died
ed(s).	editor(s)
edn	edition
e.g.	for example
esp.	especially
est.	established
ET	English translation
et al.	and others
etc.	and so on
f., ff.	and the following
idem	the same author
i.e.	that is to say
lit.	literally
loc. cit.	in the place already quoted
mg.	margin
MS(S)	manuscript(s)
n.	note
n.d.	no date
no.	number
n.s.	new series
NT	New Testament
OT	Old Testament
p(p).	page(s)
par.	and parallel
pl.	plural
Q	Qurían
repr.	reprinted
sic.	thus
sing.	singular
tr.	translated, translation
v(v).	verse(s)
viz	namely
vol(s).	volume(s)
vs(s).	version(s)

LIST OF CONTRIBUTORS

John D. Allan, BA, Staff member, Belmont Chapel, Exeter

Allan H. Anderson, Hons BTh, MTh, DTh, Director, Research Unit for New Religions and Churches, Centre for Missiology and World Christianity, Department of Theology, University of Birmingham

David W. Bebbington, MA, PhD, FRHistS, Professor of History, University of Stirling

Francis J. Beckwith, PhD, MJS, MA, BA, Associate Professor of Philosophy, Culture and Law, Trinity International University, USA

Ruth A. C. Bradby, BA, MTh, PhD, Research Student, Chester College

Peter W. Brierley, BSc, DipTh, DLitt, Executive Director, Christian Research, London

David G. Burnett, BSc, PhD, MA, PhD, Director of Studies, All Nations Christian College, Ware

K. J. Clark, PhD, MA, BA, Professor of Philosophy, Calvin College, USA

E. David Cook, BA, MA, PhD, MA, DLitt, Director, Whitefield Institute, Oxford; Fellow and Chaplain, Green College, Oxford

Winfried Corduan, PhD, MA, BS, Professor of Philosophy and Religion, Taylor University, USA

Douglas E. Cowan, BA, MDiv, PhD, Lecturer, Department of Religious Studies, University of Calgary, Canada

Kenneth Cragg, BA, MA, DPhil, HonDD, formerly Anglican Bishop in Jerusalem

Celia E. Deane-Drummond, MA, PhD, BA, PhD, Professor in Theology and Biological Sciences, Chester College

John W. Drane, MA, PhD, DD, Head of Practical Theology, School of Divinity and Religious Studies, University of Aberdeen

Martyn A. Eden, BSc (Econ), MA, Public Affairs Director, Evangelical Alliance (UK), London

Craig M. Gay, BSc, MTS, PhD, Associate Professor of Interdisciplinary Studies, Regent College, Canada

Ram Gidoomal, BSc (Hons), Diploma in Theology, Chairman, South Asian Concern, Sutton; Honorary Member, Faculty of Divinity, University of Cambridge

Tim Grass, BA, PhD, Freelance Writer, Editor and Tutor

Douglas R. Groothuis, BS, MA, PhD, Associate Professor of Philosophy, Denver Seminary, USA

Harriet A. Harris, BA, MA, DPhil, Wadham College, Oxford; Honorary University Fellow of the University of Exeter

Paul Helm, MA, J. I. Packer Chair of Philosophical Theology, Regent College, Canada; Emeritus Professor, University of London

David J. Hesselgrave, BA, MA, DiplTh, PhD, Professor Emeritus, Trinity Evangelical Divinity School, USA

Irving Hexham, MA, PhD, Professor of Religious Studies, University of Calgary, Canada

James M. Houston, MA, BSc, DPhil, Professor of Spiritual Theology, Regent College, Canada

David T. Howell, MA, Director of the Centre for Youth Ministry, Swindon

William K. Kay, MA, MEd, PhD (Educ), PhD (Theol), Senior Lecturer in Religious and Theology Education, Kings College, London; Director of the Centre for Pentecostal and Charismatic Studies, University of Wales, Bangor

Graham A. Keith, MA, DPhil, Teacher in Religious Education, James Hamilton Academy, Kilmarnock

J. Andrew Kirk, BA, BD, MPhil, AKC, Director, Centre for Missiology and World Christianity, University of Birmingham

Richard G. Kyle, BS, MA, MDiv, ThM, PhD, Professor of History and Religion, Tabor College, USA

Ian D. Leigh, LLB, LLM, Solicitor of the Supreme Court, Professor of Law, University of Durham

David Lyon, BSc (Soc Sci), PhD, Professor of Sociology, Queen's University, Kingston, Canada

H. Newton Malony, MS, PhD, MDiv, Senior Professor, Graduate School of Psychology, Fuller Theological Seminary, USA

Clive Marsh, BA, DPhil, Secretary of the Faith and Order Committee of the Methodist Church (Great Britain)

Gillian E. McCulloch, BA, BD, PhD, Research Fellow

Donald E. M. Meek, MA, PhD, FRHistS, Professor of Scottish and Gaelic Studies, University of Edinburgh

I. David Miller, MA, BD, MTh, Lecturer in Mission Studies, International Christian College, Glasgow

Chawkat G. Moucarry, MA, PhD, Lecturer in Islamic Studies, All Nations Christian College, Ware

Michael J. Nazir-Ali, BA, BLitt, MLitt, PhD, Bishop of Rochester

Harold A. Netland, BA, MA, PhD, Associate Professor of Philosophy of Religion and Intercultural Studies, Trinity Evangelical Divinity School, USA

The late John P. Newport, PhD, formerly Special Consultant to the President for Academic Research, Vice President for Academic Affairs, Provost, and Distinguished Professor of Philosophy of Religion, Southwestern Baptist Theological Seminary, USA

Bruce J. Nicholls, MA, BD, ThM, DTChg, DD, Principal, Union Biblical Seminary, Pune, India

Christopher H. Partridge, BD, PhD, DipRS, Senior Lecturer in Theology and Contemporary Religion, Chester College

Michael C. Perry, MA, Editor of The Christian Parapsychologist; President of CFPSS; formerly Archdeacon of Durham and Canon Residentiary of Durham Cathedral

Michael W. Poole, BSc, MPhil, AKC, FRSA, Visiting Research Fellow, School of Education, King's College London, formerly Lecturer in Science Education, King's College London

Paul C. Reisser, MD, BA, Family Physician, Conejo Oaks Medical Group, Thousand Oaks, USA

Peter G. Riddell, BA, DipEd, GradDipDiv, PhD, Director, Centre for Islamic Studies, London Bible College (Brunel University)

Nigel A. D. Scotland, MA, MDiv, MLitt, PhD, Field Chair, School of Theology and Religious Studies, Cheltenham and Gloucester College of Higher Education

Basil J. M. Scott, MA, Trumpington, Cambridge

James W. Skillen, AB, MA, PhD, President, Center for Public Justice, USA

David W. Smith, MA, PhD, Co-Director, Whitefield Institute, Oxford

Charles R. Strohmer, author; minister

Iain R. Torrance, TD, MA, BD, DPhil, Professor in Patristics and Christian Ethics, University of Aberdeen; Editor, *Scottish Journal of Theology*

Garry W. Trompf, BA, MA, PhD, DipEd, Professor in the History of Ideas, University of Sydney, Australia

Carl R. Trueman, MA, PhD, Associate Professor of Church History and Historical Theology, Westminster Theological Seminary, USA

Gene E. Veith, BA, MA, PhD, Professor of English, Concordia University, USA

Andrew F. Walls, MA, BLitt, DD, FSA(Scot.), Honorary Professor, Centre for the Study of Christianity in the Non-Western World, and Centre of African Studies, University of Edinburgh

Keith Warrington, BA, MPhil, PhD, Lecturer in New Testament Studies and Director of Postgraduate Studies, Regents Theological College, Nantwich

Charles W. Weber, BA, MA, PhD, Professor of History, Wheaton College, USA

Ian G. Williams, BD, MA, MEd, PhD, AKC, DPS, PGCE, Post-Doctoral Research Fellow in Islamic Studies

David F. Wright, MA, DD, Professor of Patristic and Reformed Christianity, New College, University of Edinburgh

J. Isamu Yamamoto, BA, MA, General Editor, Publications International Ltd, USA

INTRODUCTION

CONTEMPORARY RELIGION IN THE WESTERN WORLD

During the past century, particularly in the years since the Second World War, the religious landscape has dramatically changed. For example, individuals and families have, for a variety of reasons, travelled from the countries in which they were born and settled in other countries and cultures. This has led to a situation in which many people in the world, certainly the Western world, live in religiously plural societies. Moreover, not only do modern methods of travel mean that the world's cultures are only a few hours away, but, thanks to radio, television, and the Internet, fewer and fewer people are able to avoid learning about other cultures and religious communities. As a result contemporary people are increasingly aware of and influenced by not only other faiths, but the very fact of religious plurality.

Of course, having said that, and although it is hard to overestimate its impact on contemporary belief and practice, religious plurality is actually nothing new. There has always been religious diversity in the world and it has always been difficult for even the most isolated of tribes to remain ignorant of the fact that other people exist who hold different religious beliefs from their own. What is new today is an increased exposure to, and, consequently, a greater understanding of, the beliefs of others. For example, whereas the majority of Westerners at the beginning of the twentieth century knew very little about non-Christian faiths and often regarded their devotees as deluded and possibly backward, this is not the case nowadays. Not only are people much more tolerant of and interested in the religious beliefs of others but also, in some cases, they adopt those beliefs in preference to the dominant beliefs in their own culture.

Furthermore, although some people clearly feel threatened by religious plurality, others celebrate it. Many, for example, will argue that no one culture is superior and no one religion possesses the whole truth about God, humanity and the world. Indeed, it is sometimes claimed that there are no absolute standards of good or bad, right or wrong, truth or error which are applicable to all people everywhere. Such 'relativism' holds that beliefs, morals and values are only relatively true, not universally or absolutely true. Hence the principal relativist response to other beliefs and practices is 'tolerance', 'live and let live'. Although there are philosophical problems with relativism, and although in practice many people actually believe that their own understanding of the world is correct and universally applicable, 'relativism' is popularly regarded as 'common sense'.

Although Western societies are increasingly characterized by religious plurality, it is often pointed out that in most industrial societies there has been a decline not only in the social significance of religion, but also in its appeal. The process by which a society becomes increasingly secular (non-religious) has been termed 'secularization' (see 'Secularization' and 'Religion and Sociology'). However, although it is popularly claimed that the declining significance of religion is a necessary feature of a modern educated society, arguably there is too much evidence to the contrary for this claim to be successfully defended. Indeed, some theorists have gone so far as to argue that the secularization thesis has been greatly overstated and that religion will always be a significant feature of human society. Such is the human mind that it will never be satisfied with a purely material explanation of the universe.

So, when mainstream religions lose their appeal and decline (as Christianity has done in the West), new forms of religion will emerge to satisfy this human religious need. As the variety of 'new religious movements' and new forms of spirituality discussed in this volume indicate, this certainly seems to be the case. Indeed, arguably the West is experiencing a process of 'sacralization' or re-enchantment. Whilst Christianity has gone into decline in the West, other religions, including smaller breakaway movements and the increasing number of new and alternative religions, are experiencing growth, often rapid and substantial growth. (It should also be noted that Christianity is experiencing massive and rapid growth in large areas of the non-Western world. In other words, it is important to understand that Christianity *per se* has not gone into decline, but rather that its centre of gravity has shifted to the southern hemisphere.)

The most prominent feature of the religious landscape in the West during the years since the Second World War is the massive proliferation of new and alternative forms of religion. If you were to carry out a survey of the beliefs of people living within a five-mile radius of where you are now sitting reading these words, you would almost certainly come across a multitude of diverse beliefs and practices, many of which will be new and eclectic. In particular, there has been a proliferation of eclectic belief systems (often grouped together under the umbrella term 'New Age') which tend to pick and mix from a variety of religious sources (see 'New Age Spiritualities' and 'New Age Therapies'). It is no accident that whilst traditional Christianity in the West has seen a decline in numbers, a non-dogmatic form of religion which has, in many cases, no binding creeds and no headquarters has seen a rise in numbers. New Age religion is particularly suited to contemporary consumer culture. With their emphasis on the individual and the personal search for spirituality, many Westerners treat religious beliefs like products in a spiritual supermarket. A person simply creates an individually tailored spirituality by picking and mixing from the variety on offer. From Hinduism to Islamic mysticism, from UFOs to Christianity, from Daoism to Witchcraft, from fairies to the religious significance of dolphins, almost any belief can be found in the spectrum of new, eclectic forms of spirituality emerging in the West.

In contrast to the often amorphous and eclectic spiritualities of the New Age, during the last few decades the West has also witnessed the emergence of increasingly conspicuous and active fundamentalisms (see 'Fundamentalisms'). Although, strictly speaking, the term 'fundamentalism' refers to an American Protestant Christian movement which arose in 1920s America, more recently it has been applied to movements in other faiths, many of which seek political goals and a few of which use violent means to achieve their particular religious and political ends.

Finally, another increasingly prominent feature to emerge on the religious landscape during the twentieth century is the irenic activity of those engaged in interfaith work (see 'Interfaith Dialogue'). In Chicago in 1893 the World Parliament of Religions (a gathering of representatives from the world religions) marked the beginning of the interfaith movement, the concern of which is to foster respectful and cooperative relationships between the religions of the world. From this gathering emerged the International Association for Religious Freedom, followed in 1936 by the World Congress of Faith. Since then there have been many interfaith initiatives including a second World Parliament of Religions in 1993. As a result, more than in any period in the history of religions, members of the world religions are reassessing their attitudes to other faiths. On a more practical level, motivated by a common sense of global responsibility, an effort has been made to work together to seek solutions to the common issues facing humanity (e.g. the ecological crisis, the threat of nuclear warfare, disparity between rich and poor, and human rights abuses).

THE DICTIONARY

This is the age of plurality: religious plurality, ethical plurality, cultural plurality, lifestyle plurality, philosophical plurality. Whether one understands Western culture to be modern, late-modern or postmodern (see 'Modern and Postmodern Culture' and 'Religion and Globalization'), it is increasingly characterized by a plurality which is often felt to undermine traditional, institutional religions. This plurality causes problems and raises important issues for those wanting to engage with Western religion and culture from the perspective of faith. Certainly if Christians are to minister to, communicate the Christian message to, or dialogue with those around them, they need to have at least some grasp of what such people might believe. One should not simply assume that a person who is white, professional and middle class is also atheist, agnostic, or Christian. Many such people are working, not with a Christian or Western rationalist view of the world, but with a Daoist, or Hindu, or Pagan worldview. Hence, if one is going to relate meaningfully to and engage with such persons, not only does there need to be a genuine respect for their beliefs and practices, and a willingness to listen, there also needs to be some understanding of the ideas informing these beliefs and practices. The problem is not only that this is often lacking, but also that some Christians (as well as some Muslims, Hindus, Pagans, atheists, etc.) approach those around them on the basis of offensive misinformation which breaks down rather than establishes and builds good relations. Similarly, the roots of intolerance, distrust and sometimes hatred of others can often be traced back to, among other things, a lack of empathetic understanding. The point is that, whilst reliable knowledge certainly is not everything in the establishing of meaningful personal relationships, it is important, just as meaningful relationships are, in turn, important for meaningful interpersonal communication.

Because it is of great importance that contemporary Westerners, not least Christians, have at least a basic grasp of the faiths, beliefs and issues that contribute to their religiously and culturally plural milieu, the aim of this dictionary is to provide a ready and accessible reference tool which will go some way to providing for this need. More specifically, it is hoped that the volume will be of use to busy scholars seeking brief but authoritative discussions, students writing essays or dissertations, pastors desiring a greater understanding of the beliefs they encounter and the contexts in which they minister, Christians engaged in interfaith dialogue, Christian workers seeking to communicate the Christian message to their contemporaries, and the lay person simply interested in furthering his or her general knowledge. More broadly, the aim of the volume is to contribute to an informed understanding of contemporary religious belief and practice in the West.

Because of the dictionary's deliberate focus on *contemporary religion*, although some necessary attention is given to the historical backgrounds and contexts of the particular faiths and ideologies discussed, the aim throughout is to outline *current* belief and practice. (Those requiring a more detailed treatment of a religion's historical development should consult the texts in the bibliography at the end of the article.)

Whilst another principal focus is *the West*, because of the growing and almost ubiquitous influence of modern and postmodern Western culture, and because many of the religions and spiritualities discussed operate outside Western culture and the northern hemisphere, the volume will prove to be a helpful resource in most areas of the world. (Those requiring a more detailed treatment of the beliefs and practices of a particular religion in the non-Western world should again consult the texts in the bibliography at the end of the article.)

As to the level of the dictionary, although the scholarship is of the highest order (many of the authors being acknowledged experts in the areas on which they have written), the aim throughout has been to provide an accessible volume. To this end an effort has been made to provide treatments which are as clear as possible, avoiding unnecessary technical shorthand and professional jargon.

Because these are necessarily concise discussions which do not pretend to offer comprehensive treatments, as indicated above, each article concludes with a short bibliography which includes both basic and more advanced studies. Hence those wishing to gain a detailed understanding of a particular religious tradition, whilst they will find the articles within this volume a useful place to begin, they are *encouraged* to make use of these lists of key texts.

Another important feature of the dictionary is its indexes. These, as might be expected, include many persons, religions, spiritualities, technical terms, concepts and practices which are discussed, but which do not have individual articles devoted to them. Because a religious term, concept or practice is adequately understood only in relation to other terms, concepts and practices within the respective faith, readers are encouraged to read whole articles, rather than simply the page referenced in the index, or the paragraph in which the word appears. Furthermore, it is always useful to consult other articles in which a term appears. To do so will give readers an overview of the different ways particular religious concepts are used in the West.

The dictionary is set out in two parts. In Part One the reader will find articles dealing with general and introductory issues. There are discussions of, for example, the approaches and issues involved in studying a religion; debates concerning the nature of religion; the impact of postmodernity on religion in the West; Christian attitudes to non-Christian faiths; non-Christian attitudes to Christianity; poverty and oppression; youth culture; the relationships between religion and the arts; sociology and religion; psychology and religion; technology and religion; and globalization and religion. The aim of Part One therefore is to provide readers with the necessary background information for a broad understanding of contemporary religion and culture in the West. Hence, whilst individual religions will be mentioned and discussed as case-studies, these articles are more concerned to identify key themes, patterns and issues in religion and culture in the contemporary Western world.

Part Two contains articles on a broad range of specific religions and spiritualities, from the major world faiths to small but significant alternative forms of spirituality. Whilst it would be impossible in a single volume to provide articles on every minor new religious movement or every contemporary expression of a major world faith in the West, it is hoped that many of the principal forms of religion have been discussed. Having said that, the number of entries has been restricted in order to provide scope for slightly more extended and informative treatments than might ordinarily be expected in a dictionary of this size. Moreover, in considering which traditions, spiritualities and movements should have articles devoted to them, the estimated numerical size of the faith was not the only consideration. For example, whereas some forms of religion, such as Rastafarianism, are numerically small, such has been their impact on contemporary popular culture in the West that an article was felt to be necessary.

Whilst all of the authors in this volume are practising Christians, every effort has been made to ensure that the discussions are, as far as possible, descriptive. In other words, whilst pure neutrality is arguably not a possibility (see 'The Study of Religion'), there has been a determined effort to avoid value judgments and, needless to say, misrepresentation. The editor's aim throughout has been to produce a broadly phenomenological reference work. That is to say, in order to produce a reliable and careful resource which is as fair as possible, the authors have taken seriously the self-understanding and self-presentation of the various religions discussed. Although one may find comparative comments which draw attention to 'family resemblances' between faiths in order to facilitate greater understanding, readers should not expect to find criticisms and explicit confessional bias. Rather they will find reliable treatments, the aim of which is to inform careful reflection and effective ministry in the contemporary Western world.

Christopher Partridge

Part 1

BLASPHEMY

Blasphemy as a libellous offence remained dormant on the British statute books for much of the twentieth century. Not a single case came before the courts in over fifty years. However, since the 1970s blasphemy has again become a live issue in British society, especially for Christians and Muslims. This renewal of interest is symptomatic of the paradigm shift in global cultures from modernity to postmodernity, the rediscovery of spiritual values and the contemporary return to religious fundamentalism. It has therefore become an important starting point for cross-cultural interfaith dialogue for those who are committed to mutual communal respect, the reducing of misunderstanding between religions and the search for peace and harmony in today's plural society.

Blasphemy derives from the Greek term *blasphemeō* which means 'to speak evil of' or 'to insult', often with reference to God and his works. Blasphemy 'constitutes a litmus test of the standards a society feels it must enforce to preserve its religious peace, order, morality and, above all, salvation' (Levy in *ER* 2, p. 238). In different contexts the term 'blasphemy' is identified with other concepts, such as idolatry, heresy and shame.

In monotheistic Judeo-Christian traditions blasphemy is always God-centred and with a particular focus on the Name of God. The concept is rooted in the Mosaic code. The third commandment of the Decalogue states, 'You shall not misuse the name of the Lord your God' (Exod. 20:7, NIV). To slander or insult the name of God is to detract from his glory and honour. For the Hebrew, idolatry was the ultimate blasphemy. The Mosaic law decreed that the punishment for blasphemy should be death by stoning (Lev. 24:10–23). Indeed, this practice was the usual form of execution in Hebrew society (Lev. 20:27; Luke 20:6; Acts 7:54–59 [the stoning of Stephen]). Over time, particularly during the New Testament era, the concept of blasphemy was widened to include slandering the works of God. Jesus was convicted of blasphemy for his claim to forgive sins and his implied claim to divine status, even though at his trial before the high priest he was careful to avoid using the divine name for himself (Matt. 26:65).

Throughout church history the relationship between blasphemy and heresy has varied. For Augustine (354–430) the concepts were virtually interchangeable. The honour of God was always at stake, but the doctrine of the Trinity increasingly became the focal point in heresy trials. The excesses of the Inquisition in the Middle Ages reflected the widening of 'heresy' to include all that the church decreed to be blasphemy. Heresy was punishable by torture or death. Without diminishing the seriousness of heresy, the Reformers emphasized that blasphemy dishonoured God. In Calvin's Geneva, Michael Servetus was executed by burning (1553) for his anti-trinitarian views. It was argued that his blasphemy endangered the salvation of the souls of the many. In the post-reformation era the focus shifted from blasphemy as a crime against the church to blasphemy as a crime punishable by the state. Under the influence of Enlightenment thinking, punishment by death for blasphemy steadily declined and the emphasis shifted from prosecution of false beliefs to that of malice or abusive criticism of religion. As the spirit of secular humanism gained momentum in Western society, attention shifted away from protection against intentional slander or offensive insults concerning God to protection of religious believers against ridicule and offence. Although there have been no prosecutions for the denial of Christian beliefs in Britain since 1833, blasphemy is still an offence on the law books. Because there is no agreed definition of 'religion', the definition of blasphemy is now debated. In 1985 the Law Commission Report on *Offences Against Religion and Public Worship* recommended 'that the common law offences of blasphemy and blasphemous libel should be abolished without replacement' (Simpson, *Blasphemy and the Law in a Plural Society*, p. 4). But it is also significant that two of the five commissioners in a *Note of Dissent* recommended the extension of the present blasphemy laws to protect other faiths as well as Christianity. In this present state of uncertainty Christian scholars, including evangelicals, are divided as to whether the blasphemy laws should be abolished altogether or extended to protect the rights of other faiths.

This renewal of concern over the state of blasphemy legislation arises from a succession of recent events. In 1979 Mary Whitehouse successfully prosecuted *Gay News* and its editor for publishing (in 1976) an illustrated poem concerning a homosexual fantasy about Christ on the cross. Since then public protests by Christians have been made against a number of films deemed to be blasphemous, the most notable being *The Last Temptation of Christ* (1987). However, the event that attracted the widest public attention was the publication of Salman Rushdie's *The Satanic Verses* by Penguin (1988), followed by Ayatollah Khomeini's *fatwa* of 14 February 1990 calling for Rushdie's death. Three years later Khomeini renewed the *fatwa*. The publication of this book resulted in outbursts of rage from many Muslims, particularly those living in Britain, and led to riots by white racists against Asians in Bradford, UK. These outbursts have raised issues regarding freedom of speech, and appeal has been made to Articles 19 and 20 of the Universal Declaration of Human Rights in support of such freedom. However, others have seen the need for legislation to make incitement to hatred on religious and racial grounds an offence and they have appealed to the restraint imposed in Article 29 of the Declaration. This confused and conflicting situation opens up new opportunities for Christians and Muslims to engage in open dialogue at all levels, with ordinary people as well as scholars taking part.

The relationship between blasphemy and heresy is now an international issue. Early in 1992 a Pakistani court in Lahore sentenced to death two Pakistani Christians, one aged 42 and the other aged only 14, on the sole evidence of one Muslim's word that they had blasphemed the prophet Muhammad. Later the Lahore High Court overturned the verdict for lack of evidence, but the blasphemy law remains in place; to insult Allah, the Prophet Muhammad or the Qur'an as divine revelation is a crime punishable by death. The general Islamic understanding of blasphemy not only includes insults against Allah, Muhammad, the Qur'an and the angels, but may also be extended to include certain dubious theological theses and claimed mystical experiences. However, blasphemy cannot be committed by insane persons, minors and those who are forced. Finally, whilst blasphemy is punishable by death, not only are a range of punishments available (execution usually being the last resort), but also repentance is generally taken seriously.

Other world religions understand blasphemy in different ways. Buddhist leaders have shown little interest in blasphemy laws. The office of the Western Buddhist Order has explicitly stated that Buddhists do not want the protection of any such law. Buddhists remain agnostic concerning the existence of God. Hinduism is an eclectic faith of multitudes of gods and goddesses and of irreconcilable beliefs and forms of worship. Hindus too have little interest in blasphemy laws as defined by Christian legislation. The broad concern of Eastern religions, including Hinduism, Buddhism and Confucianism (to mention three of the major religions), is to protect the sacredness of their temples and the images of their deities and of their cultic worship. This concern has been heightened with the renewal of fundamentalism across Asia, whether among Hindus in India or Buddhists in Sri Lanka. The prolonged outbreak of violence between Hindus and Muslims in Ayodhya in Bihar (North India) during the 1990s concerned the presence of a mosque built on the sacred site of the supposed birthplace of the *avatara* Ram. For these essentially pluralistic religions, the claim of Christians that Jesus Christ is the only way to God and to salvation arouses negative emotions and sometimes violent reactions comparable to those aroused over blasphemy. The sense of sacredness regarding temples, images of deities and holy places engenders concerns similar to those regarding the name of God in monotheistic faiths. Having said that, it is important to understand that the religions of Asia are primarily shame-cultures, rather than guilt-cultures, and that therefore the concept of the 'honour' of their gods and religious practices is paramount. For such faiths, religious truth transcends all verbal definition. There is no dichotomy between the sacred and the secular, between religion and daily life. The issue is not blasphemy or heresy, but the identity of religion and culture.

In secular Westernized society the use of the name of God or Christ as a profane or swear word is common practice. Such words may be used to express feelings of anger or frustration, or even be uttered in a spirit of joviality with little if any thought as to their sacred reference. To the hearer who has a strong religious faith, such language is dishonouring to God and may indicate the user's unconscious desire to manipulate God. To the user the words may be meaningless, but to the hearer they are blasphemy. Having said that, the sense of offence in the West, particularly within Christianity, has been considerably eroded and is often negligible.

Some occult practices are attempts to manipulate unseen spiritual beings and to personalize the forces of nature through astrology, channelling and other psychic methods, and so to control the future. More extreme forms of such practices are found in some Satanic groups which use symbols, some of which are Christian, in ceremonies designed to enhance psychic knowledge and power. Often committed simply to cause offence to, and declare opposition to, Christianity, sometimes in an attempt to harness dark and negative powers, blasphemy is celebrated. Although he was not strictly speaking a Satanist, perhaps the most notable figure in this regard was the influential occultist Aleister Crowley (1875–1947), who, after beginning life in the Brethren, became heavily involved in several occult groups and eventually began referring to himself as 'the Great Beast 666'.

BIBLIOGRAPHY

M. M. Ahsan and A. R. Kidwai (eds.), *Sacrilege Versus Civility: Muslim Perspectives on 'The Satanic Verses Affair'* (Leicester, 1991); L. W. Levy, 'Blasphemy', in *ER* 2, pp. 238–245; R. Simpson, *Blasphemy and the Law in a Plural Society*, GES 90 (Nottingham, 1993); R. A. Webster, *A Brief History of Blasphemy – Liberalism, Censorship and the Satanic Verses* (Southwold, 1990).

B. J. Nicholls

CHRISTIAN ATTITUDES TO NON-CHRISTIAN RELIGIONS

In one sense followers of Jesus Christ have always had to come to terms with those who embrace different religious beliefs and practices. Christianity emerged as an alternative movement within first-century Judaism, and as the Christian community scattered throughout the Mediterranean world the early Christians encountered not only the formidable intellectual currents of Greece and Rome but also the many popular religious movements of the day. Significantly, it was within this context that the apostles proclaimed Jesus Christ as the one Lord and Saviour, in whose name alone there is salvation (Acts 2:36, 38–39; 4:12; 16:31).

However, contemporary questions about other religions, which became so prominent in the late twentieth century, are significantly different from those the church encountered previously. A cluster of complex and controversial issues have emerged in the West concerning how we are to live in modern democratic societies committed to egalitarian principles and characterized by increasing ethnic, cultural and religious diversity. For Christians, the questions focus upon the implications of basic Christian commitments for how we are to think about non-Christian beliefs and practices and how we should relate to adherents of other traditions. In particular, it is the Christian insistence that God has revealed himself in a unique and definitive manner in the incarnation in Jesus of Nazareth and in the Bible, that Jesus is the only Lord and Saviour for all humankind in all cultures, and that all people – including pious and sincere followers of other religions – are to respond in faith to Jesus Christ as Lord, that is so controversial today. This perspective is increasingly dismissed as not only intellectually untenable but also intolerant and thus morally questionable. The pressures upon Christians to modify or abandon entirely these core Christian commitments have been enormous.

SHIFTING PERSPECTIVES ON OTHER RELIGIONS

It is customary in the literature to distinguish three broad paradigms for understanding Christian faith and other religions: exclusivism, inclusivism and pluralism. Properly qualified, this taxonomy can be helpful, although it is also somewhat misleading. It is best not to think of these categories as mutually exclusive so much as three points on a broader continuum of perspectives, with both continuities and discontinuities on various issues across the paradigms, depending upon the question under consideration.

In very broad terms, until the mid-twentieth century the traditional perspective, both Roman Catholic and Protestant, has been what is often called 'exclusivism'. Given the highly negative connotations of the term, however, many evangelicals now use 'particularism' to refer to this position. *Particularism* can be defined in terms of three principles: first, the Bible is God's unique revelation written, true and fully authoritative, and thus where the claims of Scripture are incompatible with those of other faiths, the latter are to be rejected; secondly, Jesus Christ is the unique incarnation of God, fully God and fully human, and only through the person and work of Jesus is there the possibility of salvation; and thirdly, God's saving grace is not mediated through the teachings, practices or institutions of other religions.

There is no reason to suppose that particularists cannot be culturally sensitive or appropriately tolerant of people from other religious traditions. Furthermore, particularism does not imply that all beliefs of non-Christian religions are false or that there is nothing of value in other religions. Finally, particularism should be distinguished from what is sometimes called restrictivism, the view that only those who hear the gospel of Jesus Christ and respond explicitly in faith to Christ in this life can be saved. The question of the fate of those who never hear the gospel has always been controversial and troubling to sensitive Christians, with various answers proposed by those within the particularist paradigm. Particularism is the dominant perspective among evangelicals and is reflected in such documents as the Lausanne Covenant (1974), the Manila Manifesto (1989) and the World Evangelical Fellowship Manila Declaration (1992).

The European 'discoveries' of non-Western cultures in the fifteenth to nineteenth centuries profoundly affected Western perceptions of 'religious others'. Even as the modern missionary movement was carrying the gospel worldwide, rethinking of the traditional Christian perspective was under way. Interestingly, many of the questions debated today were already the subject of intense discussion by Protestant missionaries in the late nineteenth and early twentieth centuries. The first half of the twentieth century saw mainline Protestant and Roman Catholic theologians, especially after Vatican II (1962–5), adopt much more positive, inclusivistic views of other religions.

Inclusivism can be defined in terms of the following rather ambiguous principles: (1) there is a sense in which Jesus Christ is unique, normative or superior to other religious figures, and in some sense it is through Jesus Christ that salvation is made available; (2) God's grace and salvation, which are somehow based upon Jesus Christ, are also available through the other religions; and thus (3) other religions are generally to be regarded positively, as part of God's purposes for humankind. There is enormous variety among inclusivists on many issues, including just how it is that Jesus is 'normative', or precisely what is meant by 'salvation' and its relation to the person and work of Jesus. Nevertheless, the distinctive feature of inclusivism is the desire to maintain in some sense the uniqueness of Christ while also admitting that God's grace and salvation are present and effective in other religions as well.

But by the 1970s and 1980s a growing number of leading Western theologians were calling for rejection of a basic assumption common to both particularism and inclusivism – that there is something significantly superior or normative about Jesus Christ and Christianity – and were thereby embracing a genuine pluralism. As used here, 'pluralism' goes beyond simple recognition of the fact of religious diversity to advocacy of an egalitarian and democratized perspective which maintains a rough parity among religions concerning truth and soteriological effectiveness. *Pluralism* holds that all religions are in their own way complex historically and culturally conditioned human responses to the one divine reality, and that salvation (or enlightenment or liberation) is present in its own way in each religion. For pluralists, although Christians can hold that Jesus is unique and normative for them, they cannot claim that Jesus is unique or normative in an objective or universal sense. No-one has done more to champion the cause of pluralism in the West than John Hick, who has advanced a sophisticated model which regards the various major religions as roughly equally viable alternative ways, shaped by history and culture, in which humankind responds to the one ultimate reality, 'the Real'.

FACTORS UNDERLYING CONTEMPORARY RELIGIOUS PLURALISM

The current attraction of pluralism must be understood in light of intellectual, social and cultural patterns at work in the West for several centuries. Of particular significance is the widespread scepticism today about traditional Christian truth claims. The intellectual legacies of Hume, Kant, Durkheim, Marx, Freud, Wittgenstein and Rorty; the subtly relativizing effects of disciplines such as comparative religion, cultural anthropology and sociology of religion; the enormous influence of higher criticism upon both academic and popular views of the Bible: all this has contributed to the undermining of confidence in traditional Christian beliefs.

Scepticism about orthodox claims does not necessarily result in the abandoning of religion entirely; paradoxically, it often goes along with a remarkable openness to alternative religious traditions. The eclecticism and consumerism of modern life, combined with scepticism, produces an approach which does not look to religion for 'objectively true' answers to basic questions about the cosmos and human destiny but rather is concerned with the present experiential benefits provided by a given tradition. Religions are thus assessed pragmatically on the basis of how well they meet the felt needs of their adherents.

Furthermore, it is no accident that more open perspectives on other religions emerged as the West became increasingly aware of the cultural and religious diversity in the world. Exposure to such diversity has accelerated dramatically since the 1950s. Immigration has brought different cultures and religions into our neighbourhoods, so that we now work alongside Sikhs and Buddhists and our children are at school with Hindus and Muslims. Pluralization and the growing exposure to religious diversity have subtle but powerful relativizing effects upon orthodox religious commitments.

There is also in the West a deep sense of 'post-colonialist guilt' over the injustice and cultural insensitivity of colonialism. It is often felt that one way to atone for the past sins of colonialism is to embrace enthusiastically and uncritically the cultures of the non-Western world, and for many today genuinely accepting other cultures entails not making negative judgments about other religious beliefs and practices.

EVANGELICALS AND OTHER RELIGIONS

An adequate response to the question of 'religious others' must combine faithfulness to Scripture with an accurate understanding of contemporary realities. A basic issue concerns theological method: do we have access to truth about God which comes to us from outside our particular socio-cultural contexts, or is theology to be done by deriving generalizations from the collective religious experiences of humankind, in all their multifarious diversity? While recognizing the importance of drawing upon ancillary disciplines for understanding our world, Christians hold that the source for our theological reflection about other religions is God's revelation to us, recorded in the Scriptures. Thus ultimately it must be the teachings of Scripture which shape our beliefs and attitudes toward other religions.

There is a great need for evangelicals to develop a theology of religions which not only is faithful to Scripture but also accurately reflects the phenomena of the various religious traditions. Non-Christian religions can be seen as products of at least three factors. First, other religions can be expressions of a genuine, although somewhat misguided, search and longing for God, a longing rooted in a rudimentary awareness of God's reality in all people (Calvin's *sensus divinitatis*), however distorted or incomplete this may be. But religion is also an expression of sinful human beings' suppression of the truth of God and of rebellion against God. We must not forget that, whatever noble qualities are observable in other religions, the fact of religious diversity itself is a product of human sin. Apart from the fall, religious diversity as we know it would not exist. And third, a genuinely biblical perspective on other religions should also recognize that much religious activity and belief is influenced by the Adversary. It would be simplistic to hold that all non-Christian religious phenomena are Satanic, but it would be equally naïve to suggest that none of them is.

Any biblically acceptable view of other religions must reflect the strong sense of urgency for proclaiming the gospel which undergirds both the teaching of the New Testament and the example of the apostles. Although the gospel was no more palatable in the first century than it is today, the apostle Paul's passion for evangelism rested upon his conviction that the gospel 'is the power of God for the salvation of everyone who believes' (Rom. 1:16). Furthermore, the mandate from our Lord is clear: we are to 'make disciples of all nations' (Matt. 28:19), and this includes sincere followers of other traditions.

The engine driving the juggernaut of pluralism today is concern about how to deal with increasing ethnic, cultural and religious diversity. The strong push for an undisciplined tolerance which refuses to make negative judgments about other traditions is undoubtedly excessive, but at its heart is a legitimate concern about the implications of radical religious diversity for society. It is in this context that the Christian church should lead the way, demonstrating how to be both deeply committed to one's own beliefs and also appropriately tolerant and accepting of diversity. Christians must demonstrate that we do accept ethnic and cultural diversity and that we will support the rights of other religious communities. But we cannot abandon our commitment to Jesus Christ as the one Lord and Saviour for all humankind, and thus even as we accept Hindus and Buddhists as friends and fellow citizens we must urge them to be reconciled to God through Jesus Christ.

BIBLIOGRAPHY

D. A. Carson, *The Gagging of God: Christianity Confronts Pluralism* (Leicester and Grand Rapids, 1996); A. D. Clarke and B. Winter (eds.), *One God, One Lord: Christianity in a World of Religious Pluralism* (Cambridge and Grand Rapids, [2]1992); J. Dupuis, *Toward a Christian Theology of Religious Pluralism* (Maryknoll, 1997); J. Hick, *An Interpretation of Religion* (Basingstoke and New Haven, 1989); H. Netland, *Dissonant Voices: Religious Pluralism and the Question of Truth* (Leicester and Grand Rapids, 1991); D. Okholm and T. Phillips (eds.), *Four Views on Salvation in a Pluralistic World* (Grand Rapids, 1996).

H. A. Netland

CONTEMPORARY CHRISTIAN MISSION AND EVANGELISM

The terms 'mission' and 'evangelism' have been variously defined, but they have frequently been used to signify the types of Christian witness appropriate in different geographical locations. Such usage can be traced back to the so-called father of modern missions, William Carey, who in the eighteenth century demanded that Protestant Christians recognize that the binding character of the 'Great Commission' placed them under an obligation to ensure that the message of Christ was taken to 'the heathen'. Mission was thus perceived as a movement *from* the Christian West *to* those vast areas of the world where Christ had never been named, regions brought to the attention of Europeans in the 'Age of Discovery'. Consequently, the missionary societies which came into existence at this time were designed to facilitate the spread of the Christian faith *beyond Christendom*. In contrast, the revival movement which swept through Britain and North America was described as the 'Great Awakening', terminology which implies the renewal and recovery of something previously known and experienced.

Throughout the nineteenth century the growth of the Evangelical movement, particularly in Britain and North America, and the expansion of Western economic and political power across the world had the effect of hardening the distinction between 'evangelism', as an activity designed to make nominal Western Christians into real believers, and 'mission', as the form of witness required overseas among primitive peoples lacking the blessings of a Christian civilization.

One of the assumptions underlying this distinction – namely, that Western nations were essentially Christian – was challenged by a number of dissenters. Most notably, toward the end of his life Søren Kierkegaard launched a blistering attack on Christendom, exposing the hypocrisy of Protestant culture-religion and insisting that what went on in the Danish state church was a travesty of the gospel of Christ. In England at exactly the same time, another 'prophet without honour', Edward Miall, had the temerity to suggest that, at the very floodtide of their nineteenth-century influence, the British churches had lost contact with the teaching of the gospel and had capitulated to a human-centred religion devoid of genuine spiritual power.

The significance of these voices, which were almost completely ignored at the time, is that they anticipated by more than a century perceptions that have only recently become commonplace concerning the demise of the sacral society denoted by the phrase 'the *Corpus Christianum*'. The decline of institutional Christianity in Europe, the privatization and commodification of religion in America, and the growth of religious pluralism, due in part to the movement of large numbers of people of different faiths around the globe, have combined to challenge the fiction of a Christian culture in the Western world. Consequently, when Lesslie Newbigin issued a clarion call in 1987 in the form of the question, 'Can the West be Converted?', this no longer provoked the hostile response experienced by earlier prophets, but was welcomed in a context in which growing numbers of Christians recognized that inherited patterns of evangelism and mission had become largely irrelevant in relation to contemporary social realities.

Meanwhile, major changes have occurred elsewhere in the world in those very regions long designated as the 'mission fields'. The task of communicating the gospel in the non-Western world has been done with astonishing success and resulted in a situation in which Christianity, for centuries assimilated to European culture, has become a truly global faith. As Andrew Walls observes, the indications of Christianity's decline in Europe became evident 'just as it was expanding everywhere else'. Thus, at the dawn of the third millennium well over half of the world's Christian population is to be found in the southern hemisphere, an epochal shift in the centre of gravity of the world Christian movement which is of incalculable significance.

For evangelicals the event that brought these changes into prominence was the Lausanne Congress on World Evangelization in 1974. Western Christian leaders who approached this assembly still thinking of mission in terms of the 'one-way model' (*from* the West, *to* the rest of the world) were surprised to discover that theologians from the young churches in the southern hemisphere rejected this traditional structure and demanded a fundamental rethink of the basis and nature of the Christian mission. The voices raised at Lausanne from the growing churches in the Third World sparked vigorous and extended debates among evangelicals in which the following questions were prominent: How is the gospel related to human cultures? What is the relationship between evangelism and social justice? And does not the secularized culture of the Western world constitute one of the supreme *missionary* challenges confronting the churches today?

However, what may be called the 'modernist paradigm' of mission, which had shaped evangelical thinking and practice for at least two hundred years, remains deeply entrenched in certain quarters, and the notion of the West as a Christianized region of the world, in which *evangelism* and *revival* are the appropriate modes of witness, continues to influence popular thinking. Thus, in a volume purporting to suggest 'Structures and Strategies for the Church in the 21st Century' we read: 'The tide of the gospel has risen and flowed over two-thirds of the earth, and is lapping at the one third where the final bastions and citadels of Satan's kingdom have yet to be broken down' (i.e. the so-called 10/40 window). Whatever else might be said about such an analysis, it is difficult to see how the nineteenth-century assumption underlying it (that the West is an area *immersed* in the gospel tide) connects with the real world we see around us at the beginning of the third millennium.

The contrasting responses of evangelicals in the West to the massive cultural changes that have occurred in the second half of the twentieth century can be explained in terms of the difficulties and deep uncertainties which always accompany periods of transition and radical change. There is security in what is familiar, tried and tested, especially when (as now) the precise shape of a new, still emerging paradigm remains unclear. In such a situation entirely plausible fears begin to surface that the loss of the received conceptions of mission and evangelism may lead, not to renewed faithfulness to Christ, but to the *abandonment* of mission altogether. Where the perception of mission has been shaped by the belief that the nations of the West enjoyed the blessings of a Christian civilization, so that the spread of Western economic and political power around the world could be viewed as an aspect of the global influence of a fundamentally Christian culture, the mental adjustment required to come to terms with a postmodernity that treats metanarratives with suspicion amounts to a revolutionary change.

Nevertheless, just such a transformation is required, since attempts to confess the faith which involve the denial of the new realities of a postmodern world, including the changed status of the churches, cannot succeed. Indeed, it is precisely the emergence of what has been called a 'disciple community', aware of its changed relation to political power, which offers real hope in mission today. Relocated at the margins of a culture gripped by idolatry and driven by the love of money, such a church may be able to 'exercise a prophetic vigilance for God's beloved world that, as part of the world's power elite, it never did and never could achieve' (Douglas John Hall).

What then are the contours of the emerging paradigm of mission and evangelism in the third millennium? Clearly, the traditional manner of defining these terms in relation to the geographical location in which Christian witness occurs must be abandoned. Rather, they must now be understood biblically and theologically as denoting *different aspects of the calling of the whole people of God wherever they may be in the world.* The Peruvian theologian Samuel Escobar has suggested that Jesus' words in John 20:21 ('As the Father sent me, I am sending you') provide us with a basis for mission in a new world order because they contain not only a mandate for mission, 'but also a model of mission'. To take this Johannine model seriously, he says, will require 'the abandonment of the imperial mentality in mission' and its replacement with a praxis reflecting the humility and love of the suffering 'Servant of the Lord'. Within this new missionary paradigm, evangelism will not be jettisoned (as tended to happen with the liberal accommodation to modern culture), nor will it be defined as the primary task of the church (which was the view advocated by fundamentalists in reaction to the 'social gospel'); rather, it will be seen as a crucial component of faithful mission. When thus integrally related to other aspects of biblical mission, such as service, worship, friendship and identification with people, evangelism will be enhanced and given new credibility.

Finally, we may identify five characteristics which are likely to shape the practice of mission and evangelism in the third millennium.

First, mission will increasingly be 'from everywhere to everywhere' and we can confidently expect that new insights and initiatives of major significance will emerge from the churches of the non-Western world. This implies a far more complex picture than the 'one-way' model to which we have been used but, kaleidoscopic as this new pattern may be, it is pregnant with wonderful possibilities for the advance of the kingdom of God, and if we are able to hear what the Spirit is saying to the churches today, the future is one filled with hope.

Second, mission will demand of us a serious engagement with other religious traditions, involving genuine dialogue and profound biblical reflection. In the past the non-Christian religions were encountered only at a considerable distance and by proxy as missionaries reported to the 'homeland' on their contacts with Muslims, Buddhists or Hindus. As a result, the churches of the West are ill-equipped theologically to engage in mission in a multi-religious situation. It is often wrongly assumed that an evangelism based on the assumptions described in this article is appropriate for people living in a 'Christian country', even though their skins may be black or brown and their accents rather strange! There are significant implications here for theological educators, as well as for pastors and evangelists. The time is past when we could afford the luxury of an academic theology unrelated to the urgent missiological needs of the churches, and the production of a credible biblical theology of religions must be granted a high priority on the agenda of evangelical theology today.

Third, mission in the twenty-first century will have to face the immense challenge of a materialistic and technological culture which appears capable of providing the peoples of the world with the 'good life' and remains confident of its ability to solve the problems which threaten humankind, without reference to any transcendent source of values or meaning. Lesslie Newbigin, aware of the urgency of this issue, asked: why is there a plethora of studies on the contextualization of the gospel in cultures from China to Peru, 'but nothing comparable directed to that culture which we call "the modern world"?' Newbigin himself pointed the way forward to a missionary engagement with this culture, but there is much work still to be done on this unfinished agenda. We should neither be daunted by this task, because the inadequacies of a secular worldview are increasingly obvious, nor underestimate the challenge of it, since what is required is nothing less than *the evangelizing of the culture of modernity.*

Fourth, mission in the third millennium will be effective only in so far as believers are able both to speak the word of Christ faithfully and live the life of Christ consistently, modelling both personally and socially the transforming power of the gospel. If, as some commentators believe, we are now entering a new era of barbarism, then the quality of discipleship and the consistency with which Christians bear witness to the justice and love revealed in Christ will be crucial to the long-term impact of the churches' mission.

Fifth, mission will be ecumenical in the sense that it demands the unity of the people of God in love, holiness and truth. While the ecumenical movement which had its origin in the great missionary conference in Edinburgh in 1910 seemed to have run out of steam at the end of the twentieth century, the urgent missiological issues now confronting every Christian tradition make possible a new form of unity shaped by the imperatives of mission in the new world order. Of course, it is possible to engineer forms of church growth which bypass this issue completely. But churches which expand merely by employing the marketing techniques of a consumerist society, so turning the gospel into a product designed to satisfy superficial needs, are not contributing to the growth of Christ's kingdom but merely adding to the range of options available in an already overcrowded religious supermarket. Against this, the prayer of Jesus stands as a searching challenge to all believers at the dawn of the third millennium: 'May they be brought to complete unity to let the world know that you sent me and have loved them even as you have loved me' (John 17:23).

BIBLIOGRAPHY

H. Carrier, *Evangelizing the Culture of Modernity* (New York, 1993); S. Escobar, 'Mission in the New World Order: A Call to Renewal and Change', in *Prism*, December/January 1994, pp. 16–21; D. J. Hall, *The End of Christendom and the Future of Christianity* (Leominster, 1997); J. C. Hoekendijk, *The Church Inside Out* (London, 1967); L. Newbigin, 'Can the West be Converted?', *IBMR*, 1/1, January 1987, pp. 2–7; A. Walls, 'Christian Expansion and the Condition of Western Culture' (the 1985 EMA 'Henry Martyn Lecture'), in *Changing The World* (Bromley and London, n.d.), pp. 14–25.

D. W. Smith

FUNDAMENTALISMS

The original fundamentalists were North American Protestants (revivalist and millennialist evangelicals and traditional Presbyterians and Baptists) who opposed the theological modernism of the early twentieth century. The term 'fundamentalist' was coined in that context, in 1920, to describe those who would do 'battle royal' for the fundamentals of the faith. In the 1950s and subsequently the term was used by G. Hebert, J. Barr and others to describe mainstream evangelicals in Great Britain, though many evangelicals rejected the label. In 1979 the coup in Iran and the return there of Ayatollah Khomeini from exile coincided with the founding of the Moral Majority in America, a political lobbying group with fundamentalist roots. These two developments revealed a mass following for conservative forms of religion, which could be mobilized politically. The label 'fundamentalism' was extended to the Iranian revolutionaries and its meaning shifted from a defence of fundamental beliefs to religio-political activism. Soon it was applied to numerous religious-resurgent movements, including *Hindutva* ('Hindu-ness') organizations in India and Sinhalese Buddhists in Sri Lanka. Many of these movements were not new but had originated as reactions to Western colonial and missionary activity. Whether they are all rightly called 'fundamentalist' (a label reflecting a Western sense of threat), and whether they share significant features in common, are contentious matters.

The concept of fundamentalism has become so elastic that a core definition is impossible to attain, but there are resemblances between so-called fundamentalist groups. For example, Jewish 'fundamentalists' share Muslim 'fundamentalist' devotion to scriptural law, and some share the desire to build a religious state. Like Hindu and Buddhist fundamentalists, they identify their people by the preservation of religious practices and by religio-historical links to a particular land. None of these groups fully exhibit the Protestant fundamentalist approach to Scripture or the emphasis on right belief, but all have absolutist tendencies.

The Fundamentalism Project (1988–93), funded by the American Academy of the Arts and Sciences, studied hundreds of movements, and identified nine recurring characteristics of fundamentalisms (five ideological and four organizational): reactivity to the marginalization of religion; selectivity; moral dualism; absolutism and inerrancy; millennialism and messianism; elect membership; sharp boundaries; charismatic and authoritarian leadership; and behavioural requirements. It found that the movements most strongly reflecting these characteristics were from the Abrahamic religions (religions 'of the book'), for whom scriptural revelations relating to political, moral and social issues form the corpus of demands. It judged groups who promote cultural and national purity, rather than scriptural and doctrinal purity, to be only 'fundamentalistlike'. Therefore, Hindutva groups who recognize true Hindus by their allegiance to the land of India, or Ulster Protestants, or The Nation of Islam, who promote African-American nationalism and demand a separate black state, are judged not to be fundamentalist because they organize primarily around political rather than doctrinal allegiances. Arguably this distinction between religious and political concerns manifests a Western bias, but it also attempts to put some perimeters around the concept 'fundamentalism'. This article will focus on fundamentalisms in the West, including Israel, noting also the opprobrium with which fundamentalisms around the world view the West.

PRINCIPAL CONTEMPORARY BELIEFS AND PRACTICES

Fundamentalist beliefs and practices vary both across and within faiths, and their diversity cannot be communicated in one article. At the most general level, fundamentalists of all traditions regard their organizing truth-claims (be they claims about the authority of Scripture, the upholding of legal principles, or rightful occupation of a land) as absolute. The particular fundamentals of any one movement reflect not the full breadth of their host religion's orthodoxy, but a selective and innovative use of their religious heritage. Protestant fundamentalists place greater emphasis on the Word written (God's revelation in writing) than on the Word incarnate (God's becoming human in Jesus Christ), developing a distinctive notion of Scripture's authority. Khomeini's revolutionaries follow his innovative Shi'a 'concept of the state *(dawlat)*, as supervised by the *ulama* (clergy) and *fugaha* (religious jurists). Ultra-orthodox *haredi* Jews reflect a particular form of European Judaism before *haskalah* (the modernizing, secularizing process).

PROTESTANTS

Protestant fundamentalists are the 'indigenous' fundamentalists of the West. Their principal guiding belief is in the ultimate authority of Scripture, which is believed to be the Word of God in the sense that the individual words are God's chosen words. They claim to be following the 'plain sense' of Scripture, suspecting that 'interpretations' are unwelcome intrusions into God's immediate revelation. In 1881 the doctrine of 'inerrancy' was classically formulated, according to which the Bible contains no errors of any kind. Fundamentalists came to regard this as their most important doctrine. Their other main doctrinal foci include Christ's substitutionary atonement, according to which Christ took on himself the punishment that is rightfully ours, and Christ's second coming. Most fundamentalists are premillennialists, believing that the world will be in decline until Christ returns for a 1,000-year reign. Hence, despite recent political activity, they work more to prepare souls for Christ's return than to create God's kingdom on earth. They strongly emphasize right belief, but are more active evangelistically than theologically. From the evangelical revivals they have inherited an emphasis on the experience of conversion and of knowing Christ as one's personal saviour.

MUSLIMS AND JEWS

A problem in referring to Muslim and Jewish groups as fundamentalist is that they consciously interpret their sacred writings in the light of particular traditions (in contrast to the Protestant fundamentalist suspicion of interpretation). Hence Khomeini insisted that the Qur'an cannot be understood outside of eleven centuries of Shi'a scholarship. Jewish traditions follow the authority of rabbinic commentary, which diversifies rather than closes down interpretative possibilities. Politically, Muslim and Jewish groups range from quietist to militantly activist, but when activist they are more revolutionary (more opposed to secularism) than their Protestant counterparts.

Some Islamizing groups regard the establishment of Islam as a personal, private matter; others hold that it requires governmental, legal and social reform based on Qur'anic principles. The Muslim Brotherhood, founded in Egypt in 1927 by Hassan al Banna and now influencing much of the Sunni Muslim world, called for the establishment of an Islamic state governed by *Shari'a* (divine law), as distinct from the secular Arab states governed by European laws. They are now criticized by more radical groups, like Jama'a, for operating in mainstream politics. Several off-shoots from the Brotherhood, such as Hamas in Palestine, have become separate entities. Muslim 'fundamentalist' ideology, especially as influenced by the Pakistani revolutionary Abul Ala Maududi, has promoted a pan-Islamic vision, but some groups seek to create individual Muslim nation-states.

Jewish 'fundamentalisms' disagree over the relation between the political state of Israel and the biblical 'Land of Israel' (Eretz Israel). *Haredi*, self-proclaimed 'zealots', such as the Neturei Karta (Guardians of the City, emerging in the 1930s), are anti-Zionist. They believe the Land of Israel will be created by the Messiah, until which time Jews are spiritually exiled from God. In Israel they form enclosed communities, condemn the Zionist compromise with non-Jews and challenge the religious leadership verbally and through the destruction of property. They do not take up arms. Settler groups, notably Kach and Gush Emunim (est. 1974), believe that the Zionist return to Israel will herald the coming of the Messiah. They sometimes violently defend the territories disputed between Israel and Palestine.

ENCOUNTERING MODERN AND POSTMODERN CULTURE

Fundamentalist movements are products of modernity. They emerged in reaction to modern philosophical and political systems, and reflect deeply modernist aspects of thought. This is especially true of Protestant fundamentalism, whose central conviction is that we need a reliable Bible upon which to ground faith. This conviction manifests assumptions that faith must be based on reason or evidence, as opposed to more traditional notions of faith as a gift from God which guides our reason. Protestant fundamentalism is also primitivist and non-traditionalist (as are other fundamentalisms, but to a lesser extent), attempting to be true to a time past – that of the New Testament church – and bypassing elements of tradition which seem to obscure or deviate from that past. It is the flip-side to Protestant liberalism, which sought to strip away cultural accretions in order to find the kernel of the Christian gospel, and reflects a modernist, non-contextual, non-developmental notion of truth. Similar attempts to uncover pure Ancient Wisdom are found in strains of Westernized Hindu and Buddhist thought, going back to the Theosophical Society of the nineteenth century. Philosophically, fundamentalists are anxious about so-called 'postmodern' trends which emphasize the open-endedness of truth and the role of tradition and community in constructing understanding. However, they are sometimes regarded as 'postmodern' sociologically, because they are eclectic and adapt pragmatically and with ease to changing cultural forms in propagating their message and organizing their followers. Protestant fundamentalist churches and evangelistic programmes, for example, strongly reflect the principles of consumer choice.

PROTESTANTS

Politically, Protestant fundamentalists remain modern: pro-democratic, committed to the freedom of the individual and ostensibly supportive of church-state separation, despite supporting US anti-communist foreign policy goals. They object to the encroachment of the federal government on church affairs and defend their right to bear arms in protection against government interference. (The 'far religious right', militia groups such as the white supremacist Christian Identity, store arms in hideaways.) They reflect modern ideas about the privacy of religion and, where politically involved, focus intently on 'private' matters relating to piety and sexuality. They are political pluralists, claiming a right to be heard alongside other interest groups. But they are not religious pluralists: they believe that they rather than others have the truth.

ANTI-WESTERN GROUPS

Other 'fundamentalist' movements perceive Western secularism and capitalist influence as continuing to undermine their cultural and religious identity. In particular, they regard the separation of religion and politics in the West as symptomatic of Western spiritual bankruptcy, and reject suggestions that individuals possess characteristics independently of the community or of God. Muslim, Hindu and Buddhist groups have used strong language and imagery to depict Westerners as heathen and lawless and as peddlers of drink, drugs and sexual promiscuity.

POPULAR TRADITIONS AND RELATED GROUPS

PROTESTANTS

Protestant fundamentalists in the West exist largely in the USA, and in two forms. Old-style fundamentalists reside mainly in the Bible-Belt of the southern-eastern states. They are staunchly separatist and condemn politicized fundamentalists for co-operating with non-believers. The separatist institution Bob Jones University awarded Ian Paisley his honorary doctorate for his anti-liberal, anti-papist sympathies rather than for his Ulster politics. New-style fundamentalists, such as those mobilized by Jerry Falwell and Pat Robertson, are politically active and wield influence globally by financing missionary and political activity. The relationship between fundamentalist and conservative evangelical views of Scripture is still debated, with some scholars arguing that they are essentially the same and most evangelicals continuing to insist that there are important differences. Fundamentalist views of Scripture are also propagated (and sometimes rejected) in Pentecostal or charismatic Christianity, which is the fastest-growing form of religion in the world.

MUSLIMS

Muslim immigrants face difficulties maintaining Islamic values in secular societies, as evidenced by the Rushdie affair and the struggle in Creil, France, to allow Muslim girls to wear headscarves to school. Islamicist organizations in Western countries include Young Muslims, Al Muntada al Islami, Muslim Welfare House, Al-Muhajiroun and Hizb ut Tahrir (Liberation Party). The last is the most militant, and preaches separation from Western society. It is active in student societies and operates independently of mosques. The Tablighi Jama'at (Association for the Propagation of Islam, est. 1926) proselytizes Muslims within both Muslim and Western countries and shuns politics.

JEWS

Besides the Zionist settlers, many of whom are American Jews, and the ultra-orthodox, who emphasize their Central- and Eastern-European heritage, there is a strongly proselytizing, *Chasidic* Jewish group called the Lubavitch. They extend the mission of Rabbi Joseph Isaac Schneerson, who arrived in New York during the Nazi purging of European Jewry, to make America a new 'Torah centre'. They are New York-based with centres around the world. They undertake a 'War against Assimilation' by aiming to revitalize Jewish life and intensify the individual's relationship to God.

BUDDHISTS

The Western Buddhist Order (est. 1968 by Sangharakshita) is purist in accusing other forms of Buddhism of elevating matters of secondary importance over the primary act of 'Going for Refuge'. The Order claims to develop a Buddhism for people living in the modern world and has been described as 'Protestant Buddhist' because it contains some deeply ingrained Western assumptions. It had links, which it severed, with theosophy.

BIBLIOGRAPHY

J. Barr, *Fundamentalism* (London, 1977, 1981); H. A. Harris, *Fundamentalism and Evangelicals* (Oxford, 1998); J. Haynes, *Religion in Global Politics* (London, 1998); G. Kepel, *The Revenge of God: The Resurgence of Islam, Christianity and Judaism in the Modern World* (France 1991; Cambridge, 1994); M. E. Marty and R. Scott Appleby (eds.), *Fundamentalisms Comprehended* (Chicago, 1995); J. I. Packer, *'Fundamentalism' and the Word of God* (London and Grand Rapids, 1958).

H. A. Harris

INTERFAITH DIALOGUE

It must seem odd to amend the text of Mark 16:15 to read: 'Go ye into all the world and discuss the Gospel . . .' Yet, for some in Christianity, that is what interfaith dialogue seems to imply. In the last quarter of the twentieth century dialogue has come to be a vogue word. How does the practice of dialogue relate to mission and how does it cope with traditional faith in the finality of Christ? Asian faiths, Hinduism especially, are ready for religious discourse, unless it conflicts with national loyalties where these demand a near equation between Hinduism and Hindustan.

Semitic faiths, however, have a characteristic sense of their own validity as not open to debate, seeing in 'chosen people', or 'God in Christ', or the holy Qur'an as 'the speech of God', absolutes that do not admit of tribunals of truth other than their own. Theirs is the instinct to fear that, as a witticism has it, comparative religion makes people comparatively religious. Somehow, for them, the core of religious conviction is lost if we reduce it to a private option. There are moods, too, in Asian faiths that share a necessary assertivism. Buddhism, for example, cannot self-consistently tolerate the theisms that affirm a real creation and an authentic selfhood.

Yet, despite this tenacity in faith-orthodoxy and the sundry problems about finality, authority, truth, revelation and meaning itself, which the dialogue theme approaches, not to mention the extent to which it queries the will to mission, dialogue finds increasing advocacy and a growing sense of its legitimacy as, perhaps, even the surest expression of the religious spirit.

The factors tending to this habit of mind need careful reckoning. One is the increasing proximity of faiths to each other. When religions were being shaped, they and their cultures were relatively isolated, although bilateral factors clearly did play some part in their origins. The modern world has brought (in globalism, the interpenetration of peoples and cultures, the media revolution and sundry diasporas) a degree of *de facto* mutuality stimulating interest and perplexity. Generally speaking, religions are no longer isolated, certainly not as isolated as they once were. Hence, a degree of coexistence becomes mandatory; pluralism is a fact of life.

How enterprising can coexistence be? The question has a double edge because (1) faiths have for so long been factors in human conflict and (2) vast human populations and massive social and spiritual needs remain inside the separate purview of many of them. Moreover, all of them are in their own characteristic tension with secularity. These two aspects, which seem to encourage, if not necessitate dialogue, need review.

The chronic and unhappy role religions have historically played in abetting ethnic antagonism and national enmity is tragically evident on all sides. Bigotry, unholy zeal, mutual denigration and absolute sanctioning of pride and fear are aspects of their image and their story. In a world compelled into a quest for world community by science and technology and many factors in politics, have religions no place in that quest or do they only continue to divide?

The profoundly Christian Secretary General of the United Nations Dag Hammarskjöld wrestled long with the role of religions in the quest for peace and devised in its headquarters a place for prayer that might somehow belong to all faiths and none. What he could conceive, however, was only a symbol of the issue.

Clearly no faith is positioned, or conditioned, to take over the destiny of nations, their sharp inequalities of wealth and poverty, the imbalance of trade, the inner tensions, the human rights of men and women, matters of war and peace. The aegis of historically dominant religions inside cultures means that the moral and social tasks of each can only be assisted (not usurped) by other religions, alongside as minorities and neighbours. Must not this mean some degree of mutual exchange, maybe a ministry of ideas? Could this, circumspectly, be a valid form of 'mission'?

Furthermore, in the same context, it is evident that all faiths are now in urgent debate with themselves. There is a sort of laicization of thought, away from punditry and expertise, in view of the plethora of problems. May not this suggest that there is a point in the religions talking with each other? Moreover, it has long been true that issues which exist *between* them (e.g. truth, grace, honesty, liberty) have long been issues *inside* each of them. There are reasons for patient cross-reference.

It is not simply that secularity makes all faiths akin, or that they join forces to meet some common enemy, but rather that responding to religious diversity has become necessarily part of the inner integrity of any single faith-system. Dialogue is hardly an option to reject, but rather a vocation to embrace. The task is to abate polemic and identify what can best promote some mutual answering, analytical and practical, for the vexing communal and social problems between faiths within the nations and between cultures and world community. The recognition and address of minority grievances, the pursuit of racial harmony, the rights and duties of citizenship are all matters of daily life which must presuppose the engagement, in dialogue, of religious minds as to the spiritual resources and doctrinal bearings by which they might be undertaken.

Does making such a case for the concept and for the practice of dialogue mean, after all, that we 'debate the Gospel'? Is traditional 'mission' now to be in limbo?

It will fall to every faith to work out its own rationale around the rejection or the acceptance of dialogue. Most great religions are inherently missionary, although Hinduism may think its logic of tolerance exceptional. They are duly keen to recruit since discipleship is their *raison d'être*, unless they have acceded to the view held in some quarters that any 'conversion' from or to is unnecessary on the ground that faith, as 'a humane science', should never be a plural word; only the forms it has in doctrines and rituals and codes are multiple. Any such view of 'truth' in religions, however, runs the risk of abandoning any critical criteria relating to the contents of dogmas and rituals and their social implications. It can hardly be that facts of belief are 'facts', except in the empirical sense that there are those who hold them. We seem to be thrown back on to necessary converse concerning faith-content, converse alerted to our separate, and mutual, liability for integrity.

But where does any conceding of the onus for dialogue leave the Christian obligation for witness? Is there an irreducible either/or about mission and dialogue? Or is there, rather, a recognizable, positive bearing of either on the other? If the latter, it will need careful scrutiny and exposition.

A right Christianity will surely want to say that mission is mandatory. The church owes to mission the New Testament Scriptures themselves. The New Testament was the consequence of the fact of Christ as taken by mission in expanding place and ongoing time. New disciples in a diaspora needed to learn about their Galilean origins; hence the gospels. As many scattered, they had apostolic letters binding the one Christian community in self-comprehension and moral living. Can any generation of Christians rightly assume a moratorium on the very mission that gave it being? For nowhere outside Jerusalem and Galilee was the gospel not something brought. What became native everywhere was only there its first native self. That 'you also may have fellowship with us' has been the church's true heartbeat ever since. To forgo the sense of mission or tacitly to concede it obsolete is to forfeit Christ; it is to reduce the gospel to a private option. What is not in debt to be shared is not in credit to be received.

The issue about mission, then, becomes not *whether* but *how*. Here, duly disciplined, dialogue comes in, but only in a careful readiness for tension. The tension might be likened to that of the strings of a violin (which if loosened are useless). There is no integrity in dialogue pursued merely as a device for subtler conquest. It will quickly be detected as such and will lose its good faith. There has to be a certain *epoché* (or suspension of bare assertiveness that has not stayed to listen), a readiness to relate in genuine openness as if, for the time being, outside the constraints of dogmatic creed.

Conviction and commitment inwardly are not at stake. They are in a certain abeyance, so that the other party is honestly invited to a similar unclosing of the mind in order to ponder the strange or the inconceivable without immediate censure or denial.

The relation might be seen under the analogy of hospitality, where a considerate courtesy obtains between guest and host and where, as the defining identities are not in doubt, the postures, then or later, could be interchangeable.

There are two main reasons why this shape of dialogue suggests itself as central to communication, where 'vested-interest witness' is not proceeding. The one is negative, the other positive. They often merge. Negatively, there are chronic misconstruings on many counts between religions. History, prejudice and what some have called 'hideboundness' perpetuate them. Many Christians, for example, have reproached Buddhism for proposing our human 'extinction', when, in fact, there is 'no-thing' in Buddhist selfhood to 'extinguish'. *Nirvana* is a much more subtle concept. There is a massive misreading by Muslims of what Christian faith truly means by Jesus' Sonship, by 'original sin' and as to how apostolic letters qualify as 'scripture' when revelation, as understood in the Qur'an, only 'comes down' from God in Heaven. To what extent has Jewry ever measured how and why Christians see 'Messiahship' achieved in one crucified?

Occasions of such incomprehension are legion and work all ways. To remove such misunderstanding would seem imperative if meaning is ever to carry. There needs to be an instinct to feel the possibility that our own assumptions are distorting what we judge. Has there not been too easy a notion concerning 'we whose souls are lighted' and 'the heathen in his blindness ...'? There is, indeed, a blindness, but it needs a right exploring.

Positively, this is why (as with Philip and the Ethiopian) parties must be open to offering and receiving an exposition that commends what is authentic but also reckons with what, unless obviated, will obstruct all recognition. Perhaps the teaching method of Jesus in the parables is the model of how dialogue moves. In asking 'What man of you ...?' he is searching for what is not in question, what is generally accepted. For example, most people know well enough about usurping tenants and wayward adolescents. Again, the way the father behaves in the parable of the prodigal son is a paradigm of the divine nature. The truly revolutionary ideas come in the context of a realized province of meaning already recognized. 'Come now, let us reason together ...' is not alien to prophetic and missionary tasks.

Such dialogue need not be anxious about its own orthodoxy. Doctrine is never more alert than when it wills to interpret. The gospel has always been intended for the outsider ('the church exists for those who do not belong to it'); the outsider then must always be squarely in its ministering perspective.

Have we then come back round to preaching, to sheer proclamation? Hardly. For we are realizing that our very trust with the faith has to deserve a hearing. Its truth is never coercive – as *some* shapes of preaching are. For it has to do with one who 'stands at the door and knocks'. The knocking is infinitely courteous and presupposes that there is an autonomous mind and will within the door. Dialogue renews that posture of attentiveness in hope.

BIBLIOGRAPHY

J. B. Carman, *Majesty and Meekness: A Comparative Study of Contrast and Harmony in the Concept of God* (Grand Rapids, 1994); K. Cracknell, *Justice, Courtesy and Love: Theologians and Missionaries Encountering World Religions 1846–1914* (London, 1995); W. G. Oxtoby, *The Meaning of Other Faiths* (Philadelphia, 1983); World Council of Churches, *Faith in the Midst of Faiths* (Geneva, 1977); World Council of Churches, *Guidelines for Dialogue with People of Other Faiths and Ideologies* (Geneva, 1979).

K. Cragg

MILLENNIALISM AND APOCALYPTICISM

Millennialism (or millenarianism) and apocalypticism overlap, but they are not the same. 'Millennialism', derived from the Latin word for 'a thousand', refers to a belief in a lengthy period of blessedness, often a literal thousand years ('Chiliasm', drawn from the Greek, has the same meaning). Christian millennialism is based on a literal interpretation of Revelation 20: 1–10. Many apocalyptists are millenarians, believing that cataclysmic events will either precede or follow a millennium. There are, however, apocalyptists who do not speak of a millennium and millennialists who do not believe that the world will experience a catastrophic end.

The word 'apocalypse' means 'revelation', the uncovering or unveiling of a divine secret. Apocalyptic is eschatological in nature, that is, it is concerned with final things: the end of the present age, the judgment day and the age to come. Apocalyptic thinking has several characteristics. First, it is dualistic, viewing human history as a cosmic struggle between absolute good and evil. Secondly, it is catastrophic, in that it holds that this historical conflict will be settled by battles and disasters in which evil will be defeated. Although 'apocalypse' is currently used as a synonym for 'disaster', this identification is only a half-truth. Apocalypse concerns both cataclysm and millennium, tribulation and triumph. Thirdly, generally speaking, apocalyptic thinking is deterministic, assuming that the sequence of events in the final conflict is predetermined.

In Western culture, Christian millennialism falls into three main groups: pre-, post- and amillennialism. These positions differ as to when Christ will return; but their differences go well beyond the timing of Christ's return. They touch upon attitudes towards life, the way in which Scripture is interpreted, the number of resurrections, and the nature of the millennium itself.

Pre-, post- and amillennialism are relatively modern terms. Nevertheless, many of the millennial positions expressed through the course of Western history roughly approximate to the outlines of pre-, post- and amillennialism.

Premillennialists believe that Christ will return before the millennium. They tend to be apocalyptists, believing that a new age will be inaugurated in a cataclysmic and supernatural manner. They also interpret Scripture literally and adopt a somewhat pessimistic attitude towards history. Premillennialism has been the dominant position both during the first few centuries of the Christian era and among evangelicals during the twentieth century.

Conversely, postmillennialists say that Christ will not come until the end of a golden age. Many of them are not apocalyptists; they insist that the millennium will come in a gradual, less violent way. Moreover, they tend to interpret Scripture spiritually and to view history optimistically, believing that human efforts will help inaugurate the millennium. Post-millennialism achieved a dominant position during the eighteenth and nineteenth centuries.

From the fourth to the seventeenth century, amillennialism was the predominant view. Amillennialists do not interpret Revelation 20 literally. In their opinion, it symbolizes present realities. Thus they do not believe that Christ will establish a literal earthly rule before the judgment. Rather, the glorious new heaven and earth will immediately follow the present dispensation of the kingdom of God.

Apocalyptic and millennial thinking has not been confined to the Christian tradition. Such beliefs can be found in non-Christian and non-Western religions. Apocalypticism and millennialism can also be found in secular thought; in fact, Nazism and communism include such strands.

Apocalyptic speculation goes back thousands of years. But our concern must be with the modern Western world, a time and place where apocalypticism abounds. In the late twentieth century, end-time ideas spring primarily from three sources: Christianity, fringe religions and secular movements. Many Christian fundamentalists insist that the second coming of Christ is imminent. They claim to hear louder than ever the Four Horsemen of the Apocalypse (War, Plague, Famine and Death) galloping toward Armageddon. Occultists tell of great calamities to come at the end of the second millennium. Even down-to-earth scientists have joined in warning of impending human-caused disasters.

Of all the groups that have been influenced by this apocalyptic mood, the Christian dispensational premillennialists have operated at the highest pitch. They point to a series of events as confirmation of biblical prophecy. The return of the Jews to Israel in 1948 began the countdown to Armageddon. Following on its heels came other developments: the threat of nuclear destruction, the European Common Market, Israel's seizure of Jerusalem in 1967, the perception of the Soviet Union as the great northern power, the Persian Gulf War and Y2K, the computer bug scare.

Resting on a literal interpretation of the prophetic passages, dispensational eschatology is overwhelmingly premillennial and pretribulational. By means of a secret rapture, millions of Christians suddenly vanish. Snatched up to heaven to meet Christ in the clouds, they do not have to face the trials that are to come upon the earth. This disappearing act ushers in the seven-year tribulation. For the first three and a half years, human conditions gradually deteriorate. Meanwhile, political and military power shifts to a European confederacy led by the Antichrist. At a point of crisis he orchestrates a seven-year peace treaty in the Middle East. However, the Antichrist, who bears Satan's mark (666), then demonstrates his true nature. About midway through the tribulation he and his assistant, the false prophet, terrorize the world and compel everyone to bear the mark 666 on their hands or forehead. At this point the Antichrist moves from Rome, where he has been ruling, to Jerusalem. In the rebuilt temple of Jerusalem he blasphemes God, breaks the peace pact and persecutes Israel. Chaos breaks out: looting, arson, famines, pollution, plagues, drug abuse, occultism, demon possession, economic dislocations and lawlessness are rampant. Natural disasters abound: earthquakes destroy the land, the weather becomes bizarre and stars fall from the sky.

Then, as history draws to a close, a great battle takes place. Armies from the North, the Far East and the Arab nations meet on the mountain of Megiddo in Israel. The bloody battle of Armageddon rages for about a year, killing millions of people. Jesus Christ now appears, destroying what is left of the armies and throwing the Antichrist and the false prophet into the lake of fire. The long-awaited millennium (the thousand-year utopia) begins. From Jerusalem Jesus and his saints rule the world.

But this is not the end. After the thousand years of peace, Satan is released from the bottomless pit. Organizing an army for the final battle, he challenges God for one last time. Fire comes down from heaven, destroying these satanic forces, and the devil is cast into the lake of fire. The dead are now resurrected for the last judgment. The individuals whose names are not found in the book of life are cast into hell for ever. God now creates a new heaven and a new earth. Peace and joy reign for ever.

But these Christians, many of whom are fundamentalists, are not the only ones preoccupied with end-time notions. The same apocalyptic impulse has driven a number of individuals and groups on the fringes of American religion. Some of them have also made apocalyptic pronouncements. In general, such alternative religions can be divided into two categories: pseudo-Christian and occult/mystical/New Age groups. However, unlike most dispensationalists, they do not share common themes.

A number of pseudo-Christian groups have experienced end-time anxieties. During the lifetime of its founder, Herbert Armstrong, the Worldwide Church of God believed that the tribulation would begin in the 1970s. Not to be outdone, the Jehovah's Witnesses have made numerous end-of-the-world predictions, the last ones pointing to 1975 and 1984. The Children of God (now called the Love Family), a radical millennial group, had an end-time countdown culminating in the rapture in the early 1990s.

The tragedy of the People's Temple at Jonestown, Guyana (founded in 1978 by the Marxist minister of the Church of Christ, Jim Jones) also had apocalyptic implications. Jones' prophetic views set before him two choices: either fighting the beast (the American social and economic system) or collective flight from the impending disaster to set up a kingdom of the elect. He turned to the latter possibility and eventually to mass suicide. Before their fiery end at Waco, the Branch Davidians evinced an intense apocalyptic outlook. They believed that humanity had already entered the tribulation prophesied in Revelation. Christian Identity (an extreme racist movement) embraces an apocalyptic worldview. They see humanity on the verge of a race war in which the white Aryans will triumph and rule with Christ through the millennium.

The New Age movement can be viewed as a millennial movement. It regards humanity as standing between two ages in human history, the Age of Pisces and the Age of Aquarius. The heart of the New Age vision is the spiritual and psychological transformation of individual people; but this is only the first step. As the name indicates, the New Age envisages a new world, a new era in human history. When enough individuals experience transformation, the New Age will begin. While most New Agers view the future through rose-coloured spectacles, some foresee future disasters. For example, Elizabeth Clare, Prophet of the Church, Universal and Triumphant, declares that an 'Ascended Master' communicated to her that a nuclear catastrophe would befall the world in the 1990s.

Several famous prophets have had 'bad vibrations' about the next few years. Nostradamus, the sixteenth-century French seer, foresaw the years 1999–2000 as a time of wars, tremendous upheavals, and possible global destruction. The American psychic and founder of the Association for Research and Enlightenment Edgar Cayce (the 'sleeping prophet') also saw catastrophic events coming in the 1990s. Psychic Jeane Dixon (made famous by her claimed prediction of the assassination of President Kennedy) believed that the Antichrist is now on earth and will assume great power before 2000. Again, psychic Ruth Montgomery predicts a cosmic disaster in which the North and South Poles suddenly reverse their positions, thus wreaking incredible havoc.

Throughout history, most end-time scenarios have had a religious base. But in recent years apocalyptic thought has undergone at least a partial secularization. It extends beyond religious lines and often reaches the public not in the language of divine revelation, but in the secular dress of science, history and journalism. In fact, the most significant outbreaks of millenarianism in our time may be secular.

Most secular millenarian views are catastrophic. But one exception is the Third Wave, popularized by futurologist Alvin Toffler. He breaks history down into three waves. The Third Wave will bring about a totally new wave of existence, a utopian society in which the present problems will recede. Indeed, the prospects of human civilization are bright.

Nevertheless, the catastrophic theories drown out such optimistic views. For much of human history, the end of the world could have come only at the hands of God or through a natural calamity. But now humankind can accomplish it without God's help. We have developed the means to destroy ourselves. For many people today nuclear annihilation is a very real threat. As a result, in recent decades millions of people have experienced anxiety attacks about a nuclear apocalypse.

That said, because in 1991 the Soviet Union unravelled and the Cold War ended, nuclear apocalypticism has receded. This vacuum, however, is sufficiently filled by the 'ecocatastrophists'. They tell of disasters to be caused by overpopulation, global warming, ozone depletion, chemical weapons, world hunger, a collision with another celestial body, AIDS and other diseases.

Clearly, religion no longer has a corner on the apocalypse. While new to the game, science has exerted a considerable impact on end-time thinking. It has given us a depersonalized end: there will be no redemption, no survivors and no paradise. Scientists warn us that forces are at work in the universe that can literally blow us out of existence.

Predictions regarding the end of the world have persisted for centuries. Why? end-time thinking has been incredibly elastic. It has been moulded and shaped to the events of at least two thousand years of Western history. Prophets and soothsayers have predicted the end countless times. Fortunately their batting average has been a perfect zero. But apocalyptic thinking has withstood many disconfirmations and is still going strong.

BIBLIOGRAPHY

R. Abanes, *End Time Visions: The Road to Armageddon?* (London, New York and Nashville, 1998, 1999); P. Boyer, *When Time Shall Be No More* (Cambridge, 1992); R. Clouse (ed.), *The Meaning of the Millennium* (Downers Grove, 1977); R. Clouse, R. Hosack and R. Pierard, *The New Millennium Manual* (Grand Rapids, 1999); R. Kyle, *The Last Days Are Here Again* (Leicester and Grand Rapids, 1998); B. McGinn, *Antichrist* (San Francisco, 1994); T. Weber, *Living in the Shadow of the Second Coming* (Chicago, 1987).

R. Kyle

MODERN AND POSTMODERN CULTURE

Only since the 1960s has the question of religion and modernity been raised. It has often taken the form of a challenge like this: modern outlooks and lifestyles are now taken so much for granted that many religious people do not even realize that they are influenced by or colluding with a system that may in some important ways be inimical to their faith commitments. Perhaps they depend too heavily on science and technology, trust in the capacities of autonomous humanity, see work as the centre of life, or believe in progress. Faith and modernity are in tension.

But just as Westerners were getting used to that uncomfortable thought, they found themselves confronted with the idea of postmodernity, which for many is perplexing on a number of counts. Is this yet another epochal change, to which our sensing equipment needs to be recalibrated? Is postmodernity an intellectual arena (for instance, where relativism rules) or a set of social conditions (that fragment the family, for example) or both? And what has happened to modernity, that once seemed so solid and so secure? Has it been abandoned, eclipsed, or sidelined? And for all that modernity had its faults, did it not also have some strong affinities with religious, and particularly Christian, worldviews?

The very idea of modernity could really take hold only when certain conditions, such as factory-based industrial production, liberal democracy and rapid growth of cities, became visible in a number of countries around the world, but especially in the North Atlantic region. These were dependent upon the cultural visions of the European Renaissance and Enlightenment as well as on Reformational Christianity, all of which were expressed in the major economic and political systems of capitalism, science and technology, and liberal democracy. Paradoxically, while a Christian ethos lent aspects of these their initial dynamic, their momentum was then maintained without the benefit of that original thrust. But if the idea of the modern represents a growing cultural self-awareness, this is even more true of the postmodern. Indeed, from one angle the postmodern seems like an intensification of clear-eyed awareness. For example, those almost unchallenged assumptions of the modern age, especially the notion that progress could be guaranteed by further applications of technology or by a more democratic process, are now exposed to question. Can this increasingly polluted and war-torn world really be described as progressive? Curiously enough, that postmodern critique does not often stretch to questioning whether the modern dismissal of religion in the name of progress was warranted.

At this point it is worth making a distinction between modernism/modernity and postmodernism/postmodernity. All too often, it is assumed that the modern and the postmodern refer to some intellectual or aesthetic domain, where French philosophers or mixed-style architecture are the key features. But these two concepts represent much more than some elite argument about ideas, crucially important though those ideas may be; they refer rather to the earthy realities of everyday life, to what people actually do at home, at work, at play. So a rough distinction may be drawn that stresses at one end of the spectrum modernism and postmodernism, as the cultural, aesthetic and intellectual dimensions, and at the other modernity and postmodernity, as the social, political and economic ones. They work together and inform each other.

Focusing on the postmodern, we could say that here certain elements of the modern are inflated so as to make the older forms scarcely recognizable as such. In particular, the effects of electronic communication and information technologies (CITs) (the social dimension) help to alter our sense of what is authoritative, from printed word to electronic text and image (the cultural dimension). Likewise, the capitalist system has tilted increasingly towards consumption (the social-economic dimension), so that more and more people seek their identity as consumers rather than as workers (the cultural dimension). From this, we can see that postmodernity relates to material alterations in our social environments as well as to cultural reorientations which both are formed by and inform them. But the changes over time are also connected with changes over space. Modernity is not the singular item that modernization theorists once thought it was. The latter, however well-intentioned, prescribed to non-modern societies how they could achieve the conditions for 'take-off' into the modern world; but in fact the routes into the modern have been varied. Not only did European modernity depend upon colonialism, whereas North American variants relied on subjugating indigenous peoples; Pacific modernities have taken yet other paths. The latter are well-known for their tendency to depend on strong state direction, particularly in economic matters, and simultaneously to invoke Confucian, Islamic or other non-Western values as their guide. The postmodern refers in part to this acknowledgment of plural modernities.

The questions of modernity and postmodernity are important in religious settings because they focus attention on the social and cultural contexts of faith. But in those religious settings where texts are crucially significant, faithful living involves a double reading, of text and context, where the former is normative. Paul, in the early Christian church, argues that believers should never allow themselves merely to be shaped by cultural context, but rather to be transformed by a renewal of worldview (which is where Scripture and Spirit come in) so that situations, experiences and events can be evaluated in relation to the divine will. This is an ongoing, intentional, communal, active process which results in the development of the capacity to 'test all things, and hold fast to the good'. Nothing, then, apart from clearly prohibited or proscribed behaviour or custom, is judged in advance. Christian living is a dynamic journey of discovery in which discernment is critical.

For all that religious life contributed to early modernity, in particular the Christian impetus given to the development of science and technology, to democratic polity and to what Max Weber called the 'spirit of capitalism', much economic, scientific and political momentum is maintained today largely independently of Christianity. And in some respects, each of these has generated elements that are inimical to Christian belief and practice. For instance, much scientific and technological activity occurs in a self-augmenting manner, without reference to broader commitments to justice or community life, and supposedly democratic decisions may be made as to who may practise what religious faith, thus limiting the freedoms once guaranteed by democracy. As for capitalism, at the start of the twenty-first century the biggest pressures worldwide are towards minimal regulation of economic life in the mistaken and discredited belief that this will somehow provide for growth that will benefit all.

Philosophically, modernism tended to totalize: that is, to assume that all human life could be subsumed under one grand plan of progress, in which modes of classifying and ordering would eliminate all irrational and disorderly aspects of life. Such outlooks produced prejudicial policies and practices that led politically to twentieth-century horrors such as the South African apartheid system or the Holocaust in Europe. That which could be defined as different or particular could also be marginalized and excluded from the mainstream of modern life. Modernist utilitarian philosophy, for example, claimed only to seek the greatest happiness of the greatest number. This, applied politically, militates directly against the deepest strands of Jewish and Christian teaching, which stress that the success of any government is judged in light of its care for the most vulnerable members of society.

At the everyday life level, modernity's challenge is seen clearly in McDonaldization. It is not merely that McDonald's is a global corporation with franchises everywhere, but that these restaurants display certain principles that are applied elsewhere. McDonaldization is much bigger than McDonalds. McDonaldization means that the principles of the fast-food restaurant (efficiency, calculability, predictability and control) are coming to dominate more and more sectors of American society as well as the world. Drive-through outlets make fast food faster (and keep the mess in the car!) and more efficient. Data about customers makes consumption calculable, so that future trends can be predicted, and everything from ingredient delivery to the smile on the waiter's face, or to the way the customer approaches the food bar, can be controlled with great accuracy. And of course, food is fast; eating is refuelling, which can be done, as it were, in mid-air, in transit, without really stopping. Slow food, such as a relaxed family mealtime, is disadvantaged in such a world. One might imagine, following this, that movements critical of modernity would be welcomed within religious communities, especially Christian ones that could with some justification see twentieth-century modernity as a betrayal of some of Christianity's founding features. But while it is true that some Christian groups have struggled for modes of development other than unfettered capitalism for disadvantaged countries, or have persisted in the attempt to shape technological activity in ways that do not simply induce dependency and increase risk, many Christians have placed themselves on the defensive when it comes to critiques of the modern. There are two main reasons for this. One is that it has become increasingly difficult to exert influence within the globalized system of capitalism, technology and governance, and counter-cultural activities seem feeble. The other is that the postmodern first exhibited itself publicly as a cultural tendency to fragment and to disintegrate, which is viewed negatively by those who see order and cohesion as godly traits.

In certain respects, of course, postmodernity does raise some acute challenges for Christian commitment. Take the issue of CITs. Again, it is not just that global satellite television is available everywhere, that people have access to the means to receive signals, that American programming dominates, or that the content of some shows is morally dubious. Rather, the important point is that the very mode of communication is changing: print media are giving way to electronic, and electronic media are diverse and interchangeable. Certain kinds of information are privileged by CITs, leading to a downgrading of others. The brevity and ephemerality of many messages, for instance, favours forgetting. The past is reduced to nostalgia and the future is seen as the outcome of new technological development. This is problematic for religious life, which at its best relies upon what Danièle Hervieu-Léger calls communities of memory. Equally, the multiplication of messages means that a cacophony of competing voices drowns out the authoritative speech that starts with 'thus says the Lord'. The dilemma is that if Christian people are to communicate at all, the styles and idioms of the new mode of information are almost unavoidable; yet if they are used, the message is merely one among many, with no more rights to a hearing than the next.

If one considers contemporary consumerism, something similar must be said. It is not merely that consumption is more prominent through television advertising or the ubiquitous tee-shirt. Rather, consumption is a cultural phenomenon that is eclipsing other sources of identity and meaning (such as the significance of work) that once were much more central to modernity. In the West, and increasingly elsewhere, consuming has become the way in which one responds to life, whether encountered in school, the hospital, local government or even the church. The student or citizen now consumes knowledge or government services, and the church member, too, may view what religious organizations offer as something to choose and to consume. As the experience of employment slips from its modern pedestal of full-time, long-term commitment to a company to a downsized, short-contract, flexible event of great unpredictablity, stable identities are sought elsewhere (especially through consuming, which is where the distinctive tee-shirt or the customized kitchen comes in).

All this goes beyond McDonaldization, with its familiar face of modern bureaucratic organization and Ford factory-style production and management. Postmodern situations evidence more Disneyfication, even though these may operate alongside McDonald's influences. Disney principles involve things like the theme park, merchandise, emotional labour (the waiter's photo-ready smile) and the breakdown of the boundaries between different kinds of consumption (not to mention between consumption and everything else). If full Disneyfication takes over, then in the theme park history is downsized to nostalgia, and the sign (Mickey Mouse) sums up the story. As with the Disney movies, the pervasiveness of selfishness and of conflict and the messiness of real life are sanitized and sidelined. So, while laudable elements such as the pleasurable enjoyment of life, or the idea that there still is a story that can hold life together, may be seen in shadow at Disneyland, in other ways Disneyfication distracts from the realities and the responsibilities of life.

The problem, with the postmodern as with the modern, is how to live in this world. Clearly, the response that sees either the modern or the postmodern as 'bad' and the other as 'good' is inappropriate. For Christians, Jesus' prayer at the end of his earthly life remains very relevant, when he asked that his followers might not be taken out of the world, but that in the world they would be protected from evil. This has often been reduced to the highly appropriate but also risk-ridden slogan, 'in but not of the world'. Dangers abound with Christian over-identification with either the modern or the postmodern. A critical distance, as well as inevitable immersion, is required in relation to each. Christians will wish to affirm aspects of both, while also retaining a healthy scepticism, and sometimes a radical resistance, toward them.

For example, the tendency was mentioned above for modernity to eliminate ambivalence and the 'other' that did not fit. In a quest for universals modernity tried to squeeze out the particular, meaning that the poor, ethnic minorities and people with disabilities were disadvantaged in specific ways. Many Christian social efforts in modern times have been directed towards redressing this injustice and speaking for the 'other'. But postmodernity tends to the other extreme, where the particular is vital and difference is welcome. In such contexts the very idea of universals falls on hard times. It thus becomes more and more difficult to uphold the virtues of items such as heterosexual monogamous marriage, or the commonality of interests within a multicultural society. Identity politics and sectional rights are raised to a high profile, challenging older notions of justice or of community. Christian contributions to such situations are distinctive, emphasizing neither universals or particulars but rather both together, each in ways that do not compromise or demean the other. Thus texts and contexts interact in the process of finding faithful modes of living, as Christian people seek to express their commitment to Jesus of Nazareth as the one who brings good news for all.

BIBLIOGRAPHY

C. Gunton, *The One, the Three and the Many* (Cambridge, 1993); R. Lundin, *The Culture of Interpretation* (Grand Rapids, 1993); D. Lyon, *Postmodernity* (Buckingham, 1999); P. Sampson, V. Samuel and C. Sugden (eds.), *Faith and Modernity* (Oxford, 1995); B. Walsh and R. Middleton, *The Truth is stranger than it used to be* (London and Downers Grove, 1995).

D. Lyon

MYSTICISM

'Mysticism' is neither a clearly defined term nor an unambiguous concept. Since to define is to limit, and no single definition will cover all aspects of mysticism, the term can be used only descriptively or discursively. Yet it reflects the richness and complexity of human experience and our fascination with the frontiers of human consciousness. Beyond sense knowledge and knowledge by inference, mystics claim a third kind of knowledge: an intuition or spiritual sense of things transcending the temporal categories of the understanding. The mystical claim to have direct experience, contact or communion with the supernatural is commonly used to confirm the validity of religions and their practices. It is inferred that there is a non-physical element in human nature, such as 'spirit' or 'soul', which is in tune – or even in union – with the spiritual realm, transcending the human plane of existence. Thus mysticism has been described as 'the science of the hidden life', as 'enlightenment', transcendent 'illumination', 'naked encounter with the divine', the 'immediacy of divine union' and much else.

HISTORY OF THE TERM 'MYSTICISM'

The term 'mysticism', understood to refer to the study of the opinions and thoughts of mystics, is relatively recent in the West. According to Michel de Certau, the term was used in France in the seventeenth century, then in England in 1736. Nevertheless, the first edition of the *Encyclopaedia Britannica* in 1771 did not include it. It became a focus for academic inquiry in the English-speaking world only after the end of the nineteenth century, when comparative religious, psychological, philosophical and theological studies all began to develop an interest in it. In more recent years mysticism has again become a subject of growing interest.

Very different is the ancient usage of the term 'mysticism', as in the Greek term 'mysteries', used to refer to 'closing the eyes' (from *myein,* meaning 'to close'). In contrast to contemporary curiosity to explore the significance of mystical experience, this word implied secretiveness concerning initiation and other religious rites. There was a mystical element in most schools of Greek philosophy, such as the Orphic theory of the divinity of the soul, or the Pythagorean theory of transmigration of souls. The understanding of mysticism in esoteric religions like freemasonry, theosophy, Rosicrucianism and 'New Age' religion still has elements of this focus upon secretive 'mysteries'.

Following Plato, Plotinus provided a Neoplatonic framework for mysticism. This was utilized in Western Christian thought, which, in turn, sought to explore the mystical way in the three stages of purgation, illumination and union. The complex changes (reform, renewal, renaissance and revolt) of the high and late Middle Ages brought into new prominence the mystical life of women, in association with the rise of lay movements, the use of vernacular language and new forms of consciousness. But as Grace Jantzen has argued, feminine mystical experiences were closely scrutinized by a male-dominated *ecclesia*. After the Reformation, Catholic Neoplatonic spirituality was also strongly challenged by Protestant theologians. Both as an Enlightenment philosopher and as a nominal Lutheran, Immanuel Kant (1724–1804) demonstrated the futility of relating to God by rational means, while in reaction Friedrich Schleiermacher (1768–1834) gave a significant role to 'mystical piety'. In a further reaction, Albrecht Ritschl (1822–89) denounced mysticism as 'the practice of Neoplatonic metaphysics', arguing that 'the Universal Being as God into which the mystic wishes to be mingled is a cheat'. Adolf von Harnack (1851–1930), although slightly more sympathetic, concludes that 'a mystic that does not become a Catholic is a dilettante!' In contrast, Ernst Troeltsch (1865–1923) argued that an adequate study of religion must leave scope for mystical experiences and perceptively saw why mystics can live within church structures in ways sectarians cannot.

William James (1842–1910), the American pragmatist philosopher and psychologist, in his *The Varieties of Religious Experience* (1902) set the stage for both philosophical and psychological studies of mysticism, claiming that 'personal religion has its root and centre in mystical states of consciousness'. But he left a legacy of doubt as to how mysticism could be both cognitive and non-cognitive at the same time. Nor did Baron Friedrich von Hügel (1852–1925) and his pupil Evelyn Underhill (1875–1941), who interpreted mysticism as an 'innate human tendency', avoid interpreting mysticism as a tendency towards pantheism. Von Hügel called it 'panentheism' and Underhill described it as 'harmony with the Universal order'.

Since the middle of the twentieth century, attitudes towards mysticism have been further modified by an awareness of subliminal consciousness, extrasensory perception, the challenge of psychoanalysis, mystical postulates for evolutionary perspectives, the study of comparative religion, the appeal of religious pluralism and the influence of Eastern mysticism upon Western religious thought. Thus, as the definition of mysticism is developed in different ways, according to the many divergent and expanding investigations into states of human consciousness, it is becoming ever more elusive. Indeed, mysticism in the West has always tended to be a counterpoise to changes in human consciousness, such as occurred in late medieval scholasticism, the Enlightenment, the modern therapeutic culture and now in postmodernism.

MYSTICISM IN WORLD RELIGIONS

The somewhat marginal interest in mysticism in the West is in sharp contrast to that in the East, where mysticism occupies a central and even dominant position in religious thought. Rudolf Otto (1869–1937), in his classic study *Mysticism East and West* (1932), started a fashion among scholars of religion of noting basic similarities between Eastern and Western mysticism. In particular, he compared the Christian mysticism of Meister Eckhart (c.1260–c.1327) with the

Hindu mysticism of Shankara (AD c.750). Many notable scholars of religion have produced similar studies. For example, Edvard Lehmann (1862–1930), Nathan Söderblom (1866–1931) and, more recently, Robert C. Zaehner (1913–74) have all provided comparative treatments of Eastern and Western mysticism. Unfortunately these studies betray a tendency to impose a Western mindset upon the study of Eastern religious phenomena.

Others, like Carl Jung (1875–1961) and the evolutionist Christian thinker Teilhard de Chardin (1881–1955), argued for the existence of an expanding world mysticism encompassing and unifying all world religions. Similarly, contemporary pluralists like John Hick, arguing for a universal sense of a single divine reality, have often turned to mysticism to explain and support their theories.

In India today, as a result of political pressure to create more religious uniformity within Hinduism, mysticism has become a popular but ambiguous term, serving diverse purposes. According to Surendranath Dasgupta, there are five major stages and varieties of Hindu mysticism. First, Ancient Vedic ritual texts (1500–1000 BC) indicate a belief in the ability to control magically both the forces of nature and the gods. Secondly, the *Upanishads* (1000–500 BC) speculate about humanity's relationship with the universe. Thirdly, the *Yoga Sutra* (composed by Patanjali some time between 200 BC and AD 500) assumes that humans can realize union with the divine by means of physical and mental control. Fourthly, the Buddhistic Eightfold Path seeks to realize the extinction of desire. Lastly, *Bhakti* devotion has, since the medieval period, explored the relationship between dualistic and monistic understandings of divine–human relations. Though this is understood in various ways, generally speaking the goal is to realize the identity of oneself with *Brahman*, or ultimate reality. Such realization is in essence a release which might be termed 'salvation' (*moksha*). The control of mind and body is often understood to be the means of realizing this goal. (Tantrism – in which the body is understood to be a microcosm of the whole cosmos, including the divine – is also a feature of the mystical quest for divine union.) Ancient and modern forms of Hindu mysticism mingle to produce increasingly complex forms which are indifferent to dogma.

While, generally speaking, Hindu mysticism seeks an existential realization of the self with ultimate reality or the divine, the aim of Buddhist mysticism is *nirvana*. *Nirvana* means 'extinction': the release from the painful world of continual rebirth powered by passion, hatred and ignorance. Because meditation is presented as the only successful means to attain *nirvana*, Buddhism has developed many meditation techniques. However, in basic Buddhist meditation there are two fundamental elements: *samatha* (meaning 'calm' or 'tranquility') and *vipassana* (meaning 'insight'). In *samatha*, the meditator seeks to concentrate (*samadhi*) on a particular neutral and unexciting object, or indeed upon his or her own breathing, alone (i.e. to the exclusion of all else). As one's discipline develops and as one's concentration increases, so the mind becomes more tranquil. *Samatha* is sometimes practised as preparation for *vipassana*. *Vipassana*, it is claimed, is a meditative state in which the mind is opened and the awareness of reality significantly increased. As the meditator allows fears and repressions to surface, recognizing them and yet remaining neutral towards them, so they eventually disappear. When the mind settles, the meditator enters into what might be described as a mystical state in which there is an awareness of the true nature of existence, including one's own existence.

In the later Mahayana forms of Buddhism there were various developments. New styles of meditation emerged, such as that of Japanese Zen. In Zen the quest is an immediate experience in which the innate 'Buddha-nature' is realized. This comes through the practice of meditation and the use of *koan* (a statement that challenges the normal thought process). In Tibetan Buddhism use is also made of visualizations, repetition of sacred sounds (*mantras*) and sacred designs (*mandalas*). The central quest in the Mahayana tradition is emptiness (*Shunyata*), in contrast with that of mysticism in the monotheistic religions.

Although Islam is no stranger to mysticism, as was evident from an early stage in its development, mysticism has always produced tensions within the faith and has even been rejected as a valid form of Islamic belief and practice. The mystic within Islam is known as a Sufi (from *suf*, meaning 'coarse wool', out of which an ascetic's garments were made). Devotees are taught to pursue a life of love and pure devotion to God, and to aspire to a state in which they will no longer be aware of the self–God and self–world dualisms. Indeed, Sufis will speak not simply of union with God, but of merging and even becoming God. For example, perhaps the most famous Sufi teacher, al-Hallaj (d. 922), an ardent admirer of Jesus, not only spoke of God's love for humanity but is also said to have claimed 'I am the Real – *al Haqq*'. It is claims and ideas such as these that have led to tensions within a faith which traditionally places great stress on the distinction between God and humanity. Hence statements such as those of al-Hallaj are often understood by Muslims to be simply blasphemous. Indeed, al-Hallaj was crucified as a blasphemer. Later in its history, Sufism found a powerful defender in the Islamic philosopher al-Ghazali (1058–1111).

Popularized by thinkers such as Idries Shah (b. 1924), Sufism has attracted great interest and many devotees in the contemporary Western world. The emphases on divine and human love, mystical union with God, and dance and poetry, are very attractive to the Western spiritual seeker.

Judaism has always sought the face of God, to live in his Presence (*shekhinah*). 'Mysticism', however, is not a traditional Jewish category. Perhaps because of the eclectic effects of diaspora in Jewish history and culture, Judaism has sought instead to maintain an ethical monotheism in the *halakhah*, or 'Way of Israel', as well as in the unifying use of the Hebrew language. Having said that, R. Brasch comments that 'an understanding of Judaism is incomplete without a knowledge of its great mystical force. This left its early traces in the Bible, the Apocrypha and the Talmud, but it also created its own invaluable writings. Far from being a mere literary movement, mysticism moulded the lives of millions of Jews in eastern Europe.' Yet prophecy, apocalypse, asceticism and Platonism have fostered the development of mystical schools such as the Hekhalot and Merkavah. The word *merkavah* ('chariot') refers to the chariot in which Elijah ascended to heaven. This picture is understood by Merkavah mystics to symbolize the soul's ascent to higher levels of experience, to an increased sense of union with God. As Jewish mystical thought spread into medieval Europe, so other forms of mysticism developed. Of particular note is the Kabbalah or Qabbalah (meaning 'tradition'), which, drawing on Platonic thought, sought to establish a relationship between mystical experience and the religion of Israel. Emerging in Europe in the twelfth and thirteenth centuries, the Kabbalah is principally expressed in the thirteenth-century Spanish text the *Zohar* (written as a commentary on the Pentateuch). Like other mystics, Kabbalists emphasized interior experience and contemplation. They also spoke of absorption into God, whom they understood as the *Ein Sof* (the 'Endless/Infinite One'), and developed techniques to aid meditation and the experience of ecstasy.

The Kabbalah has attracted a great deal of attention, particularly from those interested in modern Western esoteric spirituality. This is principally because of the strange and complex esoteric symbolism developed by Kabbalists to explain the relations between God, humanity and the cosmos. Hence, whether for contemporary

Jewish mystics, or for occult groups such as the Hermetic Order of the Golden Dawn, or for contemporary Pagans and New Agers, Jewish mysticism and the Kabbalah have remained important.

MYSTICISM IN CHRISTIAN NEOPLATONISM

During the rationalist years of the eighteenth century, interest in the medieval Christian mystics waned. However, they have begun again to be studied seriously in the twentieth century. The heritage of classical scholarship, together with the Augustinian tradition of the Western church, has long identified Christian mysticism with Neoplatonism. Such mysticism has been understood as a way of life, rather than simply a theoretical exercise. It was a quest for peace of mind (*atarexia*), inner freedom (*autarkeia*) and a cosmic consciousness. It sought to overcome all dualities and complications in a soul at home in the spiritual cosmos of being and thought. Platonism taught that the soul belongs to a higher, truer, eternal and immutable world. To regain a relationship with that world, a person's soul must be purified from the body; the appetites of the body must not be allowed to impair the contemplation of the soul. This contemplation was *theoria*, the Good, the Beautiful, the Truth, resulting in ecstasy.

Plotinus (AD c.205–270), the founder of Neoplatonism, borrowed much from Plato (427–347 BC) in describing the contemplative life. The Christian Neoplatonists, such as Clement of Alexandria (d. c.215), Origen (c.185–c.254), Evagrius (346–399), Augustine (354–430), Gregory of Nyssa (c.335–c.395) and Denys the Areopagite (sixth century), adopted elements of this mindset: the soul's journey inward and upward; the discovery of one's true nature; and the threefold way of purgation, vision and union. A.-J. Festugiere thus observed: 'when the Fathers [of the Church] "think" their mysticism, they platonize'. But to the Christian Fathers 'God' was no metaphysical construct, as he was for Plato. He was the personal God of Abraham, Isaac and Jacob, not the 'god of the philosophers'. So, for example, Gregory of Nyssa's contemplation on Moses' ascent up Mount Sinai is a polemic against Plato's allegory of the cave. Clement of Alexandria and, even more, Origen base their mysticism upon the interpretation of Christ in all the Scriptures. Athanasius further emphasizes the profound distinction between the Creator and the creature by observing that God's creation is *creatio ex nihilo*. Instead of seeking the divine in mystical contemplation, Augustine experienced a personal God finding him. Further, instead of the classical self-knowledge, Augustine discovered the Christian 'double-knowledge', of oneself before God, and of the need to know both God and self (rather than simply being a solitary knowing self). The theological issues of the triune God of grace, his self-revelatory nature and his manifestation in Jesus Christ likewise lie wholly outside the scope of Neoplatonic mysticism. However, since Neoplatonism is an extremely complex metaphysical system, and since the Christian Fathers responded to it in a variety of ways, it is impossible in an article of this length even to outline the principal points of debate.

PSYCHOLOGICAL AND PHILOSOPHICAL EVALUATIONS OF MYSTICISM

At the beginning of the twentieth century, psychological investigations (among others, those of George Albert Coe and Robert H. Thouless) into abnormal states of consciousness, which Roman Catholic theologians too often associated with mysticism, treated them as examples of 'hysteria'. James H. Leuba (1868–1946), a critic of religion, saw in them a sexual component. Sigmund Freud (1856–1939) tended to interpret all religion as regressive. For example, in *The Future of an*

Illusion (1927) he argues that 'the terrifying impression of helplessness in childhood aroused the need for protection – for protection through love – which was provided by the father; and the recognition that this helplessness lasts throughout life made it necessary to cling to the existence of a father, but this time a more powerful one.' For Freud, any mystical experience needs to be understood primarily in this context.

The Jesuit Joseph Maréchal (1878–1944) did not question the legitimacy of psychological empirical enquiry into mysticism, but challenged the tendency of scientists to distort or disregard evidence in their explanatory theories. For him, mystical experience is the form of intuition that senses the presence of God as direct and unmediated in transcendent dynamism. It is a drive towards the 'Transcendental Object' – that is, God – who is not subject to psychological investigation. That said, the preparatory states of consciousness (e.g. meditation, dreams, autosuggestion, monoideism, breath control, fasting) can be analysed empirically. For Maréchal, mysticism involves a combination of religious doctrine, certain unusual psychological facts, and a synthesis of the two. Incomplete as his explanations were, he led the way to the present prevailing interpretation that contextualizes mystical experiences within particular religious frameworks.

Steven Katz has argued against unmediated mystical experiences, arguing that 'all experience is processed through, organized by, and makes itself available to us in extremely complex epistemological ways'. Thus a Buddhist will have Buddhistic experiences, a Jew will have Jewish experiences, and a Christian will have experiences of Christ. Subsequently, other scholars (such as James R. Price, Antony M. Perovich and Wayne Proudfoot) have focused attention on the cognitive criteria by which mystical data can be understood and interpreted.

Roman Catholic philosophers of religion are increasingly preoccupied with mysticism. Louis Dupré has explored the experience of the self in theistic mysticism. He argues that it is more than a mere self, being both transcendent and immanent; a deep sense of self-awareness leads the soul to recognize its identity with God. Ewert Cousins, exploring Franciscan mysticism, has argued that by the empathetic reading of the texts of Christian mystics, we can explore the structures of consciousness they entered. Bernard McGinn, now engaged in writing a five-volume history of Western Christian mysticism, explores the texts and thoughts of Christian mystics and summarizes what they may mean for contemporary reflection.

MYSTICISM AS THE ORDINARY CHRISTIAN LIFE

The apostle Paul writes frequently of *mysterion*, not as a secretive nor as an esoteric expression of mysticism, but as the mystery of the gospel publicly revealed, of God manifest in the humanity of Christ and of the Christian's life of community in Christ. But scholasticism, ancient and modern, has divorced the science of revelation from the mystical experience of revelation. Hans Urs von Balthasar (1905–88) has voiced the need to reintegrate a lived theology in the contemplation of the mystery of the Trinity. This was an issue faced by Adolf Schlatter (1852–1938) at Tübingen, against the academic view that theology must be taught 'atheistically' (i.e. 'non-mystically') to be 'scientific'. Likewise Louis Bouyer has emphasized 'the mystery of Christ in us', and of our intimacy with God as 'Father', as the heart of Christian spirituality, made possible only by the Holy Spirit. This is manifest in baptism and the eucharist, and in the exercise of Christian love one to another. Christians must live the dogma, itself an unfathomable mystery, personally to experience an inner transformation of the human spirit that is truly mystical.

BIBLIOGRAPHY

A. H. Armstrong (ed.), *Classical Mediterranean Spirituality* (London and New York, 1986); L. Bouyer, *The Christian Mystery: from pagan myth to Christian mysticism* (ET I. Trethowan, Edinburgh, 1990); O. Clement, *The Roots of Christian Mysticism* (London, Dublin and Edinburgh, 1993); E. Cousins (ed.), *Classics of Western Spirituality* (London and New York, 1985–); L. Dupré and J. A. Wiseman (eds.), *Light from Light* (New York, 1988); P. Hadot, *Philosophy as a way of life* (Oxford and Cambridge, MA, 1995); J. M. Houston, 'Reflections on Mysticism: How Valid is Evangelical Anti-Mysticism?', in M. Bockmuehl and H. Burkhardt (eds.), *Loving God and Keeping his Commandments* (Basel, 1991), pp. 163–181; Baron F. von Hügel, *The Mystical Element of Religion*, 2 vols. (Edinburgh, 1961); W. R. Inge, *Mysticism in Religion* (London and Chicago, 1948, 1977); W. James, *The Varieties of Religious Experience* (London and New York, 1963, 1983); G. H. Jantzen, *Power, Gender and Christian Mysticism* (Cambridge, 1995); W. Johnston, *The Inner Eye of Love: Mysticism and Religion* (New York, 1978); S. Kakar, *The Inner World* (Delhi, 1980); S. Katz, *Mysticism and Philosophical Analysis* (Oxford and New York, 1978); S. Katz, *Mysticism and Religious Traditions* (New York, 1983); R. Kieckhefer, *Unquiet Souls: fourteenth century saints and their religious milieu* (Chicago, 1984); J. H. Leuba, *The Psychology of Religious Mysticism* (London, 1972); A. Louth, *The Origins of the Christian Mystical Tradition from Plato to Denys* (Oxford, 1981); B. McGinn, *The Presence of God, A History of Western Christian Mysticism*, 3 vols. (New York, 1991, 1994, 1998; London, 1995); M. A. McIntosh, *Mystical Theology: The Integrity of Spirituality and Theology* (Oxford and Malden, MA, 1998); R. Otto, *The Idea of the Holy* (Oxford and New York, 1950); R. Otto, *Mysticism East and West* (New York, 1932); D. Turner, *The Darkness of God: Negativity in Christian Mysticism* (Cambridge, 1995); E. Underhill, *Mysticism* (Oxford and New York, 1974, 1993); A. Wikenhauser, *Pauline Mysticism: Christ in the mystical teaching of Paul* (New York, 1960); R. Woods, *Understanding Mysticism* (London and Garden City, 1980, 1981); R. C. Zaehner, *Mysticism Sacred and Profane* (London and New York, 1975).

J. M. Houston

NOMINALISM

Nominalism is widespread in the Western world today. The phenomenon is not unique to Christianity; all religions today have nominal adherents. Some perceive the word 'nominalism' as pejorative, meaning that those who are 'nominal' are second-class followers, with 'problems' which need to be solved.

In some parts of the world second, third and fourth generations of religious people have become less committed to their faith, entertain views contrary to the basic teachings of their religion and have a lifestyle inconsistent with those teachings. Whilst some are content with the status quo, others wish to bring about change and to see a deeper, more committed faith.

WHAT IS NOMINALISM?

The Oxford English Dictionary defines nominalism as 'existing in name only, not real or actual'. This definition, however, suggests a static mode without any likelihood of change and apparently posits no relationship between belief and behaviour. In the 1990s research has shown that Christian nominalism is often less a permanent 'state' and more a temporary position held for a period of time, sometimes many years.

Are nominal Christians in the process of becoming real or actual Christians? In other words, are they moving towards a more substantial belief? Or are nominal Christians those who are moving away from substantial belief? Or are nominal Christians those who have accepted an inadequate or misrepresented form of belief and have no opportunity to move towards substantial belief (and are therefore static)? Christian nominalism seems more related to behaviour than belief, even if the behaviour is defined only negatively ('not a regular attender'). The parable of the sower defines different groups in behavioural terms, not faith terms. What nominal Christians might or might not believe is only one issue of several.

DEFINING RELIGIOUS INVOLVEMENT

There are three broad categories available to describe religious people: 'community', 'member' and 'attender'. The Christian community can be seen as being made up of all those who would positively identify with a church, even if they attend only irregularly, or were just baptized as a child; their religious allegiance or preference is Christian. Some call the constituents of the community 'adherents'. The Christian community is made up of members, attenders and nominal Christians. In 2000 the estimated world Christian community was 28% of the population; in the UK it was 64% (all other religions 7%), and in the USA 69%.

Membership naturally means those who belong. However, Christian denominations define membership differently, and therefore, though widely registered, it generates only a collection of disparate numbers given the same appellation. The value of membership figures is that they may be available over many decades, even centuries, and that because they have usually been registered using the same definition within a particular denomination, the trends in the figures may be judged accurate. In 2000 church membership was 16% of the world's population; in the UK it was 12% of the population (all other religions 5%); in the USA it was 46%.

Attendance is conceptually easier: either people are in a church or temple or mosque or synagogue, or they are not. Counting the number of people present on a particular day therefore gives a uniformity to the numbers. However, attendance figures are not universally collected and, even when regularly gathered, are counted on different Sundays by different Christian denominations. The process is actually more complicated than this practice suggests, because not everyone who attends church attends every Sunday, and not all who worship necessarily attend a *Sunday* worship service (midweek services are becoming increasingly popular). In 1998 an estimated 10% of the English population attended a Christian worship service at least once a month; in 1994 in the USA the figure was 42%. It should be noted not only that membership and attendance are not the same, but that they are not necessarily even causally linked.

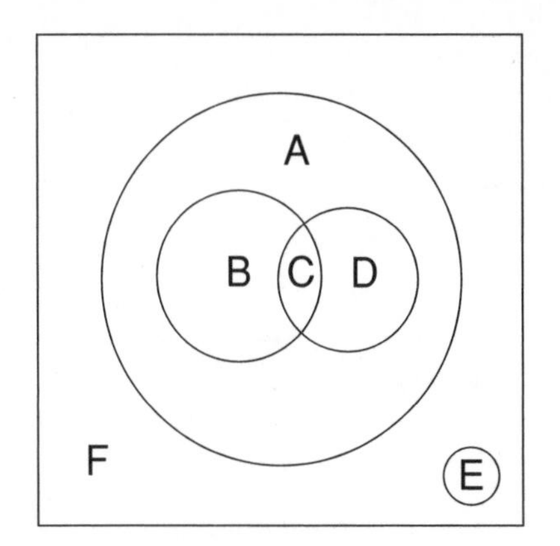

Figure 1: Membership, attendance and nominal adherence.

Figure 1, where the outer square represents the whole population, illustrates the interrelationship of the three categories. *Area A* represents those who call themselves Christian, but are not members or regular attenders of any church (e.g. they may go only at Christmas or Easter). Those in *area B* are regular church attenders but not, or not yet, members. *Area C* comprises both regular attenders who are also members of their church, and *area D* members who are not regular attenders. *Area E* shows members of other faith communities and *area F* the non-religious, who are not in any faith community.

People in category D, as well as those in category A, are often called 'nominal Christians'. To distinguish between these two categories some prefer to call those in category A '*notional* Christians' instead.

At the International Lausanne Consultation on Nominality in 1998, twelve types were identified. The religious commitment of those with *ethnic-religious identity* is closely tied to their ethnic or national identity, while *second generation* adherents are those who have distanced themselves from the faith of their parents or of their parents' church. *Ritualistic* worshippers are those whose outward acts of devotion are not accompanied by an inner reality of faith; *syncretistic* are those who retain some dimensions of one religion but have embraced aspects of spirituality and moral values from other religions or worldviews.

For the *disillusioned*, religion has not worked; while the *burned-out* – professional or lay – have given all they could to their faith community to their own personal detriment; they have either opted out altogether or remained in as a duty.

The *bifurcated* live dual, compartmentalized lives, so that their faith is not integrated into everyday life. The *compromised* have a primary commitment to a spiritual, intellectual or organizational system of values which takes priority over their religion. The *disobedient* have left their faith community because they are not prepared to live up to the moral standards of their particular religious tradition. The *secularized* uphold religious values and principles without embracing religious beliefs.

The *socially distanced* have never attended a place of worship regularly but want it to be there when they need it. The *alienated* feel that they do not fit culturally or socially within their religion.

BIBLIOGRAPHY

P. W. Brierley, *Future Church* (Crowborough, 1998); P. W. Brierley, *Steps to the Future* (Milton Keynes, 2000); E. Gibbs, *Winning Them Back* (Crowborough, 1993); H. Wraight (ed.), *They Call Themselves Christian*, papers presented to the 1998 Lausanne Consultation (London, 1999).

P. W. Brierley

NON-CHRISTIAN ATTITUDES TO CHRISTIANITY

In one sense the religious and spiritual plurality of the contemporary Western world is a result of centuries of trade, inter-cultural contact and empire. In another, and important, sense, however, it is also an ideological construct based, on the one hand, on Enlightenment values of freedom of thought and belief and, on the other hand, on the restriction of religious beliefs to the private sphere of life. This denial of a public space for religious discourse encourages a proliferation of beliefs and practices which can become more and more idiosyncratic. Here, as elsewhere, the modern has given birth to the postmodern.

Any comments, then, on non-Christian attitudes to Christianity have to be divided between those associated with recognized world religions present in the Western world and those connected to new or old indigenous systems of belief. An added difficulty here is the eclectic nature of much postmodern believing: beliefs and values which have their origins in one system are detached and used in another.

JUDAISM

As far as the world religions are concerned, Judaism, naturally, has a special place. This is for two main reasons. The first is that Judaism has been present in Western contexts, at least intermittently, for longer than any other world religion. The other is that an understanding of Judaism is necessary for a proper study of Christian origins and development.

Although Jewish Christians survived in the Fertile Crescent of the Near East for several centuries and it was possible to belong to both synagogue and church, the early history of Jewish–Christian relationships is, unfortunately, one of vigorous polemic and of mutual anathematization. The medieval 'teaching of contempt', the so-called 'blood-libel' and widespread anti-Semitism in the West all generated negative views of Christianity among Jews. Towards the end of the nineteenth century, however, as Jews became more enfranchised in Western countries, a new attitude began to emerge. Scholars such as Israel Abrahams and C. G. Montefiore began to relate Christian origins to their Rabbinic background and to re-evaluate the place of Jesus in first-century Judaism. This work has been given added impetus by the discovery of the Dead Sea Scrolls and by the work of Christian and Jewish scholars such as Geza Vermes, E. P. Sanders and N. T. Wright. In the middle years of the twentieth century it was, however, dealt a severe blow with the rise of fascism in Western Europe.

Although Jews are aware that the anti-Semitic roots of Nazism lie in a theory of race which is far removed from Christianity, many claim, nevertheless, that Nazi policies were able to flourish because of the history of anti-Jewish bias in the churches.

The emergence of Councils of Christians and Jews after the terrible events of the *Shoah* or Holocaust has helped, however, to increase mutual understanding. While the dialogue has often been about social and political issues, there are signs that serious theological engagement is also taking place. Jews are particularly concerned that Christians should see them as representatives of a truly living faith and not as 'museum-pieces'. They are concerned also about the 'ambivalent' Christian attitude to the State of Israel. Theological issues such as the nature of covenant, the Messiah and the eschatology and universalism of the Hebrew and Christian Bibles remain on the agenda. Many Jews continue to be concerned about 'proselytism' by Christian missionaries, particularly when this is seen as 'targeting' vulnerable groups such as children, or young people. Jews tend, however, to acknowledge the legitimate role of religion in the public sphere, even when this religion is Christianity. They often cooperate with Christians on issues of public policy such as racism or the fair treatment of refugees. They are increasingly recognizing the Jewishness of Jesus, but feel also that Gentile Christianity's divinizing of Jesus and doctrine of the Trinity has compromised the essential monotheism of the Hebrew Bible.

ISLAM

Even though there have been large populations of Muslims in Europe for many centuries, the *present* Muslim population in Western Europe, North America and Australasia is largely of comparatively recent origin. It is made up of communities of immigrants and their descendants who have arrived from the former colonial territories of their hosts. It is very much a case of 'the Empire striking back'.

Islam is a monotheistic faith with an explicit claim to continuity with the Judeo-Christian tradition (Qur'an 2:136). Many biblical characters and events are mentioned in the Qur'an. Jesus himself is mentioned 25 times and is called 'the Messiah', an 'apostle' and a 'prophet of God'. Indeed, along with Noah, Moses, Abraham and Muhammad, Jesus is one of the five principal prophets in Islam. His virgin birth, his miracles and his teaching are all mentioned, as are his death, resurrection and ascension. That said, Muslims do deny that he was crucified. It is claimed that he was rescued by God from his enemies and raised to God's presence (Q 4:158, cf. 3:55). He is called 'God's word' and is understood to be a spirit from God. In Sufism (Islamic mysticism) Jesus is often portrayed as an example for those who would deny the pleasures of this world so that they may achieve nearness to God. Finally, many Muslims expect his return as the just judge.

Such a background naturally affects how Muslims in the West see Jesus today. On the whole, their attitude is much more reverent than that of many secularized Westerners. This attitude is clearly evident in their strong opposition to films, plays or books which they believe to denigrate Jesus (e.g. by portraying him as a homosexual). Muslims are sometimes quite open to learning from the teachings and life of Jesus. The place of Jesus in the spiritual experiences of Muslims is also quite well documented.

Like the Jewish people, however, Muslims believe that the doctrines of Jesus' divinity and the Trinity are Christian corruptions of the pure monotheism of God's original revelation. Although Jesus is a prophet and apostle of God, he is human and not divine. Prince Hassan of Jordan is the latest in a long line of Muslim commentators to assert that the original message of Jesus was later corrupted by Paul, who is supposed to have created the doctrine of the Trinity and to have divinized Jesus as a way of universalizing an essentially Jewish message. Such commentators, naturally, find support for their views in the works of certain Jewish and even Christian writers.

Although Muslim–Christian relations throughout the course of history have often been characterized by conflict, there has also been significant cooperation. In the Middle East and in Spain, Jews and Christians made a notable contribution to the emergence of 'Islamic' civilization. There was also a certain amount of inter-religious encounter and discussion. Inevitably some of this was polemical, but there was much that was eirenical and constructive as well. Relations between Muslims, on the one hand, and the West and Byzantium on the other, were often much worse than those between Muslims and the oriental Christians of the Islamic world. Here there was, at times, a great deal of mutual respect and tolerance. Muslims often see contemporary Western hostility to Islam as rooted in the polemic of those early days.

The constant pressure on Constantinople and the blockade of Western pilgrims to the Holy Land were among the immediate causes of the Crusades. The Crusades were not, of course, directed only against Muslims. Jews, oriental Christians and 'heretics' in the West were also targets. The unprincipled brutality, thuggery and opportunism of the Crusaders has, nevertheless, left a very bitter taste in most Muslim mouths. Even today, Muslims living in the West will often refer to the Crusades as an example of gratuitous cruelty and destruction, forgetting the actions of their own armies in changing the shape of the world and in occupying large parts of the globe, sometimes for centuries. More importantly, perhaps, Muslims sometimes see the Crusades as precursors of later colonialism and, therefore, of present-day predatory attitudes in the West. This, of course, has implications for Christian missionary thinking. For example, evangelistic campaigns styled 'crusades' are seen by Muslims (and others) as the spiritual aspect of a colonial and aggressive mentality.

Because Muslims have a strong view of the inerrancy of their own scripture, the Qur'an, they tend to see the work of biblical criticism as destructive of Christian orthodoxy and as confirming their claim that the Jewish and Christian Scriptures are not as they were originally given but have been altered as a result of a long process of doctrinal development and theological redaction. It is important not to underestimate the knowledge many Muslims have of historical and literary criticism of the Bible. At the same time, it has to be admitted, they often view the complex nature and history of the Bible in terms of their own, rather direct, theories of revelation, which tend not to allow an adequate place for human agency, language and culture.

HINDUISM

There have been Christian communities in India from the early years of the Christian era and, as might be expected, they have interacted socially with Hindus for many centuries. It is, however, true to say that interfaith encounter and theological dialogue did not really begin until the advent of Western mission in the sixteenth century. The Jesuits, for example, had to undertake a study of Brahmanical Hinduism so that they could contextualize their living, preaching and worshipping in the Indian context. Anglican and Protestant missionaries not only studied the written and oral tradition but also mounted a vigorous attack on socio-religious customs such as caste, widow-burning (*satì*) and other practices. Some of these had, of course, already been challenged by Buddhism, Islam and Sikhism.

What is important, from the point of view of this article, is that this criticism was noticed and that from the eighteenth century onwards Hindu reformers like Ram Mohan Roy, the Brahmo Samaj, Rabindranath Tagore and, of course, Mahatma Gandhi all incorporated this missionary agenda (especially modern education, including female education, and reform of marriage practices) into their social and political programmes. Alongside this recognition of the validity of the Christian critique (continued by distinguished Indian Christian individuals and organizations) there was also an acknowledgment of the person and teachings of Jesus Christ, even if the cross was often seen only as an example of supreme self-sacrifice in the cause of a profoundly humanist agenda. This acknowledgment has been well documented by the eminent Indian scholar the late M. M. Thomas, of the Mar Thoma Syrian Church.

The place of Jesus Christ in Hindu devotion is extremely complex. Many would be willing, indeed eager, to see him as an *avatara* (a descent or incarnation of God). However, to understand him as an *avatara* is to understand him as one in a long line of *avataras* and therefore not unique. Whilst many Hindus give Jesus a place in their pantheon of gods, goddesses and *avataras*, some are devotees only of Jesus, without necessarily denying the existence of other gods. There are also groups and individuals who believe in Jesus as Saviour and Lord, in a fully Christian way, but remain culturally and socially within a Hindu milieu.

The comparatively recent resurgence of Hindu nationalism can, in fact, be traced back to nineteenth-century Hindu revivalist movements like the *Arya Samaj*, which fiercely attacked Christianity as a threat to Hinduism. Indeed, the historical and contemporary reactions have targeted not only Christianity but Islam, Buddhism and Sikhism as well. There is a strong contemporary impulse to reject any external influence on Indian life, even though Hinduism is extensively interpreted in the light of the encounter with Islam, Christianity and modern Western knowledge generally.

The whole range of Hindu responses to Christianity is represented in the West. In addition, many Hindus are aware of the significant influence of the Vedantic, Yogic and Tantric aspects of Hinduism on the popular imagination in the West since the 1960s. These have made a notable contribution to the climate of spiritual, moral and cultural relativism so prevalent in the Western world today. It can almost be said that there has been a paradigm shift from a 'semitic' emphasis on the distinctiveness of revelation to an 'indic' view of inclusiveness and indifferentism. While many people in the West are influenced by Hindu themes through the media, some have actually become adherents of one kind of Hinduism or another. The *Hare Krishna* movement (ISKCON) is one Hindu group with a substantial Western following. Hindus see such interest in their spirituality as a sign of barrenness in traditional Christianity, which is failing to assuage the spiritual hunger of large numbers of people.

Many Hindus have for long been puzzled about the exclusive claims to faith and salvation made by Christianity. They often see the different faiths as culturally and historically determined paths leading to the same experience of liberation and salvation. There can be particular resentment, therefore, at attempts by Christians to detach Hindus from their historic *dharma* or spiritual way of life. Moreover, the Hindu worldview is often viewed by Westerners as a model for a philosophy of religious plurality.

Support from wealthy Hindus and from local authorities has encouraged the emergence of temples and other places of meeting which are also community centres. They cater not only for the spiritual needs of Hindus but also for their social and educational needs. Some are now deliberately opening their doors to the wider community and becoming centres for lifelong learning, recreation and support for those in need. This is a new departure, as Hindu temples have not, generally, functioned in this way. It may be that in this area there has been some learning, conscious or unconscious, from the churches.

SIKHISM

Sikhism, by contrast, remains a largely communal faith. It has strong traditions of egalitarianism, hospitality and social service. Although these have made some impact on the wider scene, their effects are most clearly seen within the Sikh community itself. In the West, Sikhs tend to emphasize the monotheistic nature of their beliefs and the original purpose of Sikhism as seeking unity between the different faiths. There is a Sikh Missionary Society and, although there are some Western converts, its main work is educational. It seeks to keep Sikhs faithful to their ancestral beliefs and to explain these beliefs and Sikh practices to others. Generally speaking, Sikhs are friendly towards Christians and will even attend church services and other Christian gatherings. Tensions can, however, arise if they perceive that evangelism is targeted at their community.

BUDDHISM

Interest in Buddhism began in the West in the nineteenth century with the visits of leading Buddhist figures and the influence of movements like the Theosophical Society. In the middle years of the twentieth century this interest was extended to the Zen and other traditions within Buddhism. The escape of the Dalai Lama from Tibet into India resulted in the growth of Tibetan Buddhist Centres all over the world, including the West. The Dalai Lama continues to wield enormous influence in the West, out of all proportion to the number of his followers.

Buddhism has continued to attract, in addition to adherents from Asia, sizeable numbers of Western followers. They gravitate towards it because of its alleged practical bent and its non-theistic nature (at least in its *Theravada* forms). Buddhists point, sometimes, to certain similarities between their faith and Christianity. The Eightfold Path of right understanding and thought, right speech and action, right effort and devotion, and so on, is often compared to the Sermon on the Mount. The notion of the Buddha-nature, particularly as it developed in *Mahayana* Buddhism, is sometimes thought of as fulfilling the same function in Buddhism as the *imago dei* (or image of God) does in the Judeo-Christian tradition. *Mahayana* also developed the idea of the *Bodhisattva*, a personal saviour figure who postpones entering into *nirvana* because of compassion for fellow human beings. The similarities with Christian thought are obvious. Some scholars believe that aspects of *Mahayana* developed because of contact with Christianity. Nor was this a one-way activity, as the romance of *Barlaam and Joasaph* demonstrates.

Some Buddhists criticize Christianity as too world-affirming and not taking seriously enough the impermanence of all existence. The Christian view of the soul is also criticized as a sign of continuing 'attachment' to what is passing.

Because of Christianity's missionary nature, there can be some tension between Christians and Buddhists. In the West, Buddhists often emphasize the bloody history of Western Christianity and portray Buddhism as a way of non-violence. They can also resent what they see as the privileged position of the Christian churches in many Western societies. At the same time, there are well-established traditions of dialogue, spiritual learning from one another and common cause in the struggle for justice, freedom and democracy (e.g., in different ways, for Tibet, Myanmar and the *Dalits* of India).

THE NEW AGE

The renewal of interest in the West's pre-Christian roots is another characteristic of our age. People are discovering and sometimes even inventing a pre-Christian golden age where men and women were well integrated into their environment and had a close relationship with the land. They see Christianity as a 'foreign' influence which has alienated people from their ancestral habitat. Such a mythological framework tends not to acknowledge the many migrations of Europe's pre-Christian past. In an age of intense interest in our relationship to the environment, however, it can be quite an effective anti-Christian apologetic.

New Age spiritualities are, perhaps, more widespread than Neo-Paganism itself. They tend to be eclectic, drawing on Pagan beliefs, non-Christian religions and even elements of Christianity. The emphasis is on a manipulation of the self and the environment so that people may experience self-fulfilment. Christianity is seen as too cerebral and rationalistic. Credulity is encouraged regarding the mysterious nature of the universe. There is much interest in the supernatural and the extent to which it can be manipulated for our own ends. The closing years of the millennium are seen as the ending of the Age of Pisces, which gave rise to Christianity. We are about to enter a 'new age', the Age of Aquarius, which will bring tolerance and harmony to the earth for the next two thousand years. Many New Agers see themselves as harbingers of such an age. In this age 'poor talkative Christianity' will simply fade away as people rely more and more on instinct, intuition and mystical experience of one kind or another.

CONCLUSION

In a brief article of this kind it is not possible, of course, to indicate all of the different attitudes there are towards Christianity. Even less is it possible to develop any kind of adequate Christian response to these attitudes. It is to be hoped, however, that the main attitudes have been outlined and that the reader will be able to follow up the issues with the help of the short bibliography provided for this purpose.

BIBLIOGRAPHY

A. S. Ahmed, *Living Islam: From Samarkand to Stornaway* (London, 1993); O. Chadwick, *The Secularisation of the European Mind in the Nineteenth Century* (Cambridge, 1992); H. Croner (ed.), *Stepping Stones to Further Jewish-Christian Relations*, Vols. I and II (London, 1977); P. Griffiths (ed.), *Christianity Through Non-Christian Eyes* (New York, 1989); El Hassan bin Talal, *Christianity in the Arab World* (Amman, Jordan, 1994); Mission Theological Advisory Group, *The Search for Faith and the Witness of the Church* (London, 1996); L. Newbigin, *The Gospel in a Pluralist Society* (London, 1989); A. Pieris, *Love Meets Wisdom: A Christian Experience of Buddhism* (New York, 1988); C. Strohmer, *Wise as a Serpent, Harmless as a Dove: Understanding and Communication in the New Age World* (Milton Keynes, 1994); M. M. Thomas, *The Acknowledged Christ of the Indian Renaissance* (London, 1969); A. Wessels, *Europe: Was it Ever Really Christian?* (London, 1994).

M. Nazir-Ali

PASTORAL CARE IN MULTI-FAITH AREAS

The church has traditionally believed that it must care for the community in which it lives. Loving one's neighbour is an inescapable part of the gospel. But it is not so simple as it used to be, for one's neighbour may belong to any of the world's religions and come from any continent. Certainly in many cities of the Western world there are large immigrant communities from Asia, the Middle East and Africa, whose members may be, for example, Muslim, Hindu, Buddhist or Sikh. Pastoral care in such areas requires particular knowledge and skills. (It is of course important to understand that the word 'immigrant' is very often used inaccurately with reference to the members of these communities. A great and increasing number of such persons are not immigrants; they were born in the West.)

The biblical imperative to be concerned for one's neighbours, whoever they may be, implies that care must be the responsibility of the whole church, not simply of the minister, the missionary or the trained lay worker. Church members, as carers, need to be equipped to be good neighbours in the multi-faith environment in which they live.

COMMON PASTORAL ISSUES

FAMILY ISSUES

In Asian and African culture a person is not an autonomous individual responsible in the last analysis to herself or himself, but rather a member of a family with a particular role and responsibility. Husband and wife, parents and children, old and young all have their own particular place within the family. Given this scenario, it is hardly surprising that the clash between immigrant communities and Western society irrupts within the family group. It is within the family that non-Westerners feel the impact of Western culture most acutely. For example, the Western practice of divorce and choice of partners creates severe problems. For a woman to make use of the Western legal system to divorce her husband is often perceived as an affront to the family. Again, mixed-faith (as distinct from mixed-race) marriages can pose problems. For example, one of the partners, usually the bride, may experience some pressure to convert.

Other areas which need to be understood by those working in multi-faith communities, particularly because they involve a clash with Western values, are: gender roles; relations between parents and children; the place of the aged and the young; the authority of the family; the care of the elderly; the practice of hospitality; and the treatment of converts. Whether one thinks of, for example, violence to women or the lack of understanding between first and subsequent immigrant generations, there is need for a broad grasp of the issues, the causes and the impact upon families and communities.

COMMUNITY ISSUES

Because Asian immigrant communities are often well-organized, they are able both to cope with their internal needs and to voice their concerns in the societies where they live. Various concerns emerge simply as a result of living in Western culture and society. For example, some have taken action to rid their streets of prostitutes and drug dealers. For various reasons, others have been accused of harbouring drug dealers. These sorts of activities and accusations have sometimes led to strained relations with the police. As a result, the church may sometimes be called upon to represent minority faith groups. A specific instance of such representation is the protection of asylum seekers, in that often Christians have felt bound to take up the cause of those who, they believe, are being unjustly treated by a Western government.

Issues of a political nature affecting non-Christian religious communities often involve events in other countries. For example, the Gulf War, the conflict in the Balkans and events in the Indian subcontinent (such as the destruction of the mosque at Ayodhya) have all caused tensions between Muslim and Hindu communities in the West. On a local level, political issues may arise when, for instance, Muslims want to purchase land to build a mosque, or Hindus want to build or enlarge a temple, or Buddhists buy a country estate in order to establish a monastery. In all such cases, Asian-language papers are quick to focus on such political issues and to draw attention to racial prejudice. Likewise racially motivated attacks are widely reported and the political implications drawn out.

There are also issues of a specifically Christian nature. For example, Christians will become concerned when the authoritarian structures of other faith communities are used to bring pressure on the marginalized or to threaten Asians who wish to follow Christ. The pressures put on new disciples of Christ by families and communities create further challenges for the caring church. A specific case in point is the care of Asian Christians from other faith backgrounds. It is important for Christians to understand that such persons have not become Western simply because they have joined a church. Hence, in dealing with their pastoral needs Christians must not treat them as Westerners with Western worldviews, but must rather seek to understand their cultural inheritance and their particular problems and expectations from their perspective. For instance, a common expectation which needs to be borne in mind is that the church should be an alternative community, not just a building for services and meetings.

SICKNESS AND DEATH

Response to sickness and ill health will be conditioned to a large extent by people's religious background, as well as by their cultural expectations. The fact that, despite the impact of Western medicine, those of other faiths will often rely on alternative therapies, spiritual healers, charms and mantras shows that their faith in the supernatural is strong. Therefore people of other faiths will often feel comfortable with, and sometimes welcome, prayers for healing by Christians. That said, here as elsewhere one's approach needs to be sensitive.

Hospitals are nowadays increasingly aware of the needs of patients from a variety of faith backgrounds; they are reshaping their procedures more and more to take account of the multi-faith environment in which they operate. Matters of concern include not only diet, fasting, privacy, modesty, organ transplants and care of the dying, but also space for prayer and scripture readings.

Funerals in a mixed society become increasingly complex, especially when more than one faith community is involved in the ceremony. Ministers need to be able to adapt sensitively to unforeseen demands and situations without causing offence. Similarly, the care of the bereaved and bereavement counselling may no longer be controlled or carried out according to the traditions of one religious community. They may sometimes need to be shaped by the multi-faith context in which the minister works.

Also worth mentioning under the heading of 'sickness and health' are requests for exorcisms and deliverance ministry, since these too represent an aspect of health care. Widespread belief in the occult and the supernatural, in demonic and divine forces, leads to a demand for religious specialists who can deal with manifestations of evil. Hence, although this is an area that requires great sensitivity, it is also an area in which a Christian specialist might usefully minister.

Related to the foregoing are psychiatric problems and the common, although decreasing, reluctance to resort to Western psychiatry. This might be another area in which the Christian minister might help to ease worry, to inform and perhaps to pave the way for patients to visit psychiatrists.

EDUCATION

Whether we think of parents or children, schools are the most important meeting ground in multi-faith areas. Christian teachers have pastoral concerns not only for children at school but also for parents at home. Indeed, it is very important that ministers and indeed the church as a whole support teachers in dealing with the complex world of differing cultures.

In further and higher education, apart from the obvious and massive impact of Western culture upon students, there are many issues demanding attention: for instance, the search of those from other faith communities for personal identity, and the Islamic radicalizing of religion on some university campuses.

APPROACH TO PASTORAL CARE

Life in multi-faith areas presents a variety of challenges. Some may say that, whatever the faith of a person in need, the practice of pastoral care should be the same. Others take the view that the differences between faiths are so great that Christians are not in a position to counsel people of other faiths. The truth is more complex than either view suggests.

As long ago as 1948, Kluckhohn and Murray suggested that 'Every person is in certain respects (a) like all others (universal), (b) like some others (cultural), (c) like no other (unique).' These three dimensions overlap like interlocking circles. It is, perhaps surprisingly, a common mistake to think of all Muslims or all Hindus as essentially the same. In actual fact, no two are the same. People are unique, each with his or her own views.

Alternatively, the carer and client may be seen as two overlapping circles: they have some things in common but are distinct in other ways. For example, it is generally true to say that immigrants from Asia or Africa have little in common with local Westerners. However, their children and grandchildren, the second and third generations, have an increasingly large area of shared experience with Westerners.

Whatever the extent of the experience that Christians share with others, they have to begin with that shared experience. Moreover, it is also important to realize that what people do not understand about each other is just as important as what they do understand. If carers are to be effective then they must begin to explore what is different in other people, appreciating their culture and loving the whole person, not just the Westernized part and the common humanity. It follows therefore that Christians, whether church members or ministers, must aim to put themselves in the shoes of others; they must seek to understand life from the others' point of view.

Multi-faith areas are places of adventure, where those who enjoy exploration and the unknown can feel at home. However, the adventurous spirit that is required is not that of the tourist, nor that of the scholar armed with books about the religions of the world, but rather the spirit of those who are excited by the discovery of a different culture. Effective carers in multi-faith areas will enjoy meeting those from other cultures and will give themselves in service to those people. The need is for caring people who are comfortable with difference and variety. Such people will also know the value of discovering one's own assumptions, values and biases. One needs to understand how these differ from those of the people one is getting to know.

If we return to the fundamental importance of the family and the community in Asian religion and culture, it needs to be understood that, whereas the individual is the primary unit in Western society, the family, caste and community are primary in Asian culture. The individual does not exist in isolation; one's identity and role in life is determined by one's position in the family and community. This of course has many consequences. For example, an Asian friend may agree to meet you at a certain time and place, but may fail to turn up simply because a family visitor has arrived unexpectedly. Family comes first!

Again, it is not difficult for Europeans to think that their Hindu friends are completely Westernized. After all, they speak the same language, they receive the same education, they live in similar houses, they work in the same business or profession and they play and support the same sports. However, see the same Hindu friend at a family wedding or funeral with five hundred relatives belonging to the same caste and the realization dawns that, while Western in some respects, they are also the products of another faith background with centuries of tradition behind them. This is the other half, the side that the Westerner often does not see, especially in the second and third generation after immigration. It is this side that the carer needs to know and respect and enjoy. According to Augsburger, seeing the individual-in-community as the basic unit of humanness is the key to understanding.

Bearing this in mind, it is clearly of immense importance that the carer is cognizant of the spiritual dimension. Whereas Westerners regard religion as of marginal significance, for Hindus, Muslims, Buddhists, Sikhs and other faith communities the spiritual is part of everyday life. The spiritual world, however they view it, is as real as the material world. Spiritual forces both good and evil are a normal part of life for them. Unlike many Westerners, and possibly many Christians, they are convinced that prayer has power. As mentioned above, they may therefore appreciate Christians praying for them during periods of illness or depression. There is always a need for the Christian carer, when approaching such circumstances, to be sensitive and to rely on the guidance of the Holy Spirit.

SKILLS NEEDED

In some unpublished notes on cross-cultural counselling, B. J. Prasantham makes the point that, whilst the concepts and skills needed 'can be learnt in a brief time, [they] take a life time to master ... However by practising some of them reasonably, one could have greater effectiveness.' Some of these skills are outlined below.

Attentive listening and observing. Whilst this is always important, it is doubly so when the persons cared for are from a different culture informed by a different worldview. The other half of their person, which is culturally unknown to the Westerner, needs to be discovered and appreciated. For this the carer must be willing to observe patiently and learn accurately to interpret non-verbal communication, which may very well not be the same as Western forms of non-verbal expression.

Patience and use of time. Listening and learning take time. This is true of all care and counselling. Carers need to be patient with themselves and their limitations. Indeed, patience is a prime virtue in Asian cultures and, it is worth noting, anger is regarded as a cardinal sin in a religious person. The Asian and African view of time is not governed by the clock. All the more reason then to be unhurried and to avoid hasty judgments.

Sensitivity to gender roles and core values. Normally, carers should care for people of their own sex. Likewise, sensitivity is important regarding actions and words which may cause offence (e.g. taboos concerning dress and physical contact).

Accurate sending and receiving of verbal and non-verbal messages. As understanding grows this will become possible, and the carer should consciously aim to achieve it.

Checking conclusions. It is easy to misunderstand. Carers should check wherever possible that their understanding is correct. Check with the person concerned and, where relevant, with others who know them, that the situation has been understood correctly.

Offering constructive non-judgmental feedback. Since persons understand their own cultures better than outsiders do, the Christian carer should seek to assist those persons in receiving the help they need from God, rather than being dogmatically prescriptive.

CONCLUSION

In the global village where people of different faith communities rub shoulders, the peace of the world depends on human beings learning to communicate across religious and cultural divides. Christians, who belong to a worldwide family of immense cultural diversity, should be leaders in this field and communicators of the love revealed in Jesus Christ.

BIBLIOGRAPHY

B. T. Adeney, *Strange Virtues – Ethics in a Multicultural World* (Leicester and Downers Grover, 1995); D. W. Augsburger, *Pastoral Counselling Across Cultures* (Philadelphia, PA, 1986); R. Hooker and C. Lamb, *Love the Stranger – Ministry in Multi-Faith Areas* (London, [2]1993); C. Kluckhohn and H. Murray, *Personality in Nature, Society and Culture* (New York, 1948); E. Y. Lartey, *In Living Colour – An Intercultural Approach to Pastoral Care and Counselling* (London, 1997); B. J. Prasantham, *Indian Case Studies in Therapeutic Counselling* (Vellore, India, 1988).

B. J. M. Scott

PILGRIMAGE

Most people understand pilgrimage to be a journey to a holy place or shrine, either in the pilgrim's home country or overseas. In many cases both the journey – which may involve sacrifices in terms of money, time away from work, home and family – and the destination are important. Definitions of pilgrimage usually include the sacredness attached to the journey as a crucial factor. Key ingredients in a pilgrimage are obviously travel, rituals and objects of veneration. Some forms of tourism come close to being a pilgrimage if they involve a journey to a distant place which has religious significance. In such instances part of a holiday may become a 'holy day'. The journey in itself may be considered as meritorious. In pre-industrial times journeys were most often made on foot and were hazardous and dangerous. In modern times, however, pilgrims make use of air travel, trains and automobiles. The company and the common bond with other pilgrims are also significant aspects for many pilgrims. In all world religions, apart from Islam, pilgrimage is not seen as an essential duty.

One of the most notable pilgrimages in the modern world is 'the Great Pilgrimage' or *Hajj* to the *Ka'ba* and other sacred places and monuments in and around Mecca. The *Hajj* is a once-in-a-lifetime requirement for all adults, resources permitting. Indeed, it is one of the five pillars of the faith. The Qur'an states: 'Make the pilgrimage and visit the Sacred House for Allah's sake ... in the appointed month. He that intends to perform it in those months must abstain from sexual intercourse, obscene language, and acrimonious disputes while on the pilgrimage. Allah is aware of whatever good you do. Provide yourselves well: the best provision is piety' (Sura 2:196–197).

The *Hajj* is carried out on specified days in the last month of the Muslim year. Each participant begins by putting on a special garment or *ihram*. For a man this is two pieces of unsewn cloth. For a woman, who must be accompanied by her husband or a male relative, it is a single piece of white cloth which covers the head and arms and reaches down to the ankles. Men often shave their heads before the *Hajj* but women only have a few hairs clipped. For footwear pilgrims are required to wear backless sandals. Once they are correctly clothed they make their way to the *Ka'ba* or Black Stone, which is actually a cube-shaped shrine 48 feet long, 32 feet wide and 45 feet high. It is covered with black cloth embroidered with the work of the Qur'an. The Black Stone, an oval 5 inches in diameter set in the southeast corner, is said to have been received by Abraham's son Ishmael from the angel Gabriel. The pilgrims circle the *Ka'ba* seven times in an anti-clockwise direction. If they are close to the sacred stone they touch or kiss it. If they are too far away waving will suffice. After they have encircled the *Ka'ba* the pilgrims make their way to al'Safa and al'Marwa, two small hillocks in the centre of Mecca which are associated with Abraham and his son Ishmael. It was here, while Hagar searched desperately for water, that her baby son released a spring as he lay kicking in the sand. The pilgrims imitate her search by going backwards and forwards along the path between the two hills seven times. On the tenth and final day pilgrims go to Mina and sheep are sacrificed, commemorating Abraham's sacrifice of the sheep which God gave him in place of his son Ishmael. There is a well on this site known as *Zamzam*, which Muslims believe was created by the angel Gabriel. Muslims bring home from this place small bottles of water, which they later share with family members. The *Hajj* represents the solidarity and fellowship of the Islamic *Umma*, or global community. Muslims also state that the journey represents the spiritual journey of a life spent seeking God. Towards the close of the *Hajj* pilgrims assemble at Mount Arafat, where they meditate from noon to sunset. This activity represents standing before God for judgment.

In order to ensure that Mecca will be able to cope with the influx of pilgrims, each country is issued with an annual quota of numbers. In Britain, because the Muslim population is relatively small, there is no limit on those who wish to make the journey.

THE PURPOSE OF PILGRIMAGE

Clearly there are a variety of purposes and motivations which underlie a pilgrimage. These vary according to the nature of the religion and the intentions of the individuals concerned. In the case of Islam, the *Hajj* is a requirement and therefore the fulfilment of a solemn duty by which it is anticipated that merit will be obtained. At the very least, all pilgrims anticipate that both physical and spiritual blessings will result from their journey. At the most basic level these might be simply a break from a busy schedule and the benefit gained from walking in the fresh air and eating little.

All pilgrims hope that their pilgrimage will bring them into close contact with the god or gods they serve. Some religious traditions teach their adherents that they will achieve spiritual merit as a result of their journey. Hindu pilgrims who journey to and bathe in the waters of the Ganges will feel a sense of accomplishment and believe that they have built up 'good *karma*': that is, good deeds which will counterbalance the wrongs they have committed. The degree of merit which is achieved is largely dependent on the distance being travelled and the type of transport which is utilized. To walk on foot from Delhi to Dwarka, where Krishna was said to have left the world, is obviously more meritorious than to use public transport from a nearby town or village. For the Buddhist, the greater the demands of a pilgrimage, the greater the blessing. A Buddhist adherent who visits the *Bodh-Gaya* earns merit towards a better rebirth and brings special blessing to his or her current life. In medieval times Christian pilgrimages to great shrines such as Hailes Abbey or Canterbury were a means of obtaining merit. For certain journeys made to Hailes, for example, special indulgences were granted by the papacy.

Numerous pilgrims anticipate that their journey will culminate in healing. This is very much the case with Christians who journey to Knock in Southern Ireland and more particularly to Lourdes in France. Many who make their way to this town in the foothills of the Pyrenees are seriously ill or severely handicapped. Despite the fact that only a very small percentage testify to any lasting physical healing, there is a huge influx of visitors every year between Easter and December. Others embark on a sacred journey in order to find renewed hope after a bereavement, a failed relationship or a broken marriage.

Many pilgrims make their way to sacred shrines in order to pray for loved ones and close family members who are sick, suffering or in need of guidance and help. Hindus, for example, will make their way to one of the holy places on the Ganges river, where they will scatter the ashes of their departed relatives in the hope that they will be spared from rebirth. Hindu pilgrims often return with bottles of Ganges water, which they may keep in their homes. The majority of Hindus in Western nations have the bodies of their relatives cremated or buried. A small number, however, do retain the ashes in a casket in the hope that they may be able to visit India on some future occasion.

Clearly, in all pilgrimages, it is the state of the travellers' hearts and their secret intentions which are the crucial factors. At worst, pilgrimage can degenerate to the kind of revelry and camaraderie portrayed by Geoffrey Chaucer in his *Canterbury Tales*. At best, it can be perceived as a deepening of the worshipper's communion with God and a transforming experience which refocuses the individual's experience, purpose and quality of life. Pilgrimages are also a means of expressing religious solidarity. Muslims who journey to Mecca or Christians who travel to Jerusalem are expressing their solidarity with fellow believers from other parts of the world and from differing social backgrounds.

Martin Luther's superior, John Staupitz, sent him on his famous journey to Rome in 1510 in order to give him time for theological reflection and spiritual refreshment. Pilgrimage was attacked by the Protestant clergy and theologians at the time of the Reformation as part of what they regarded as a system of salvation by works. For this reason, religious pilgrimage has not been a major feature within Protestant Christianity. That said, however, during the reign of Elizabeth I (1558–1603) the idea of a 'Grand Tour' of the continent started to gain in popularity as a substitute for medieval pilgrimage. No longer were excursions undertaken to places where the efficacy of what Protestants regarded as 'superstitious relics' could be invoked; instead, journeys were made for the purposes of education and pleasure. Travellers kept diaries and journals and noted details of ancient sites, paintings and other artefacts. Some also returned with mementoes and souvenirs. In more recent times, Thomas Cook, a Baptist preacher, set up a travel company which sought to provide 'wholesome' holidays away from the temptations of drink. For increasing numbers these kinds of journey became a kind of pilgrimage.

Significantly, the late twentieth century has witnessed an increase in the numbers of Protestant Christians visiting the Holy Land, with Christian tour operators providing all-inclusive package trips. Also, between 1994 and 1995 more than half a million Protestant Christians journeyed to Toronto seeking 'the Toronto Blessing', a charismatic experience marked by phenomena including falling to the ground and 'holy laughter'. The late twentieth and early twenty-first century have witnessed the growth of 'secularized' forms of pilgrimage. This can be seen, for example, in the numbers of individuals who visit the grave of Elvis Presley at Graceland in Memphis. The site is regularly covered with flowers and prayers written on small pieces of paper. Equally, the burial place of Diana, Princess of Wales, at Althorp House in Northamptonshire has become a significant shrine, attracting 147,000 visitors in 1999.

PLACES OF PILGRIMAGE

The shrines and places of pilgrimage in the major world religions are numerous. Some authorities suggest that there are fifty-eight significant sites to which Hindus make pilgrimages. In addition, there are hundreds of smaller places which also have significance. These include rivers, riverbanks, hills and mountains. Generally speaking places of pilgrimage can be classified in the following ways.

PLACES OF HISTORICAL SIGNIFICANCE

First and most obvious are historical sites connected with the gods and founders of the world's faiths. For the Hindu, the most important sacred city and centre of pilgrimage is Banaras (also Kosi or Vārāṇasī), which stands on the banks of the Ganges. The town is regarded as sacred because of its close links with Shiva, 'the Lord of Banaras'. Vrindaban, which is regarded as the place of Krishna's birth, is also a major centre of Hindu pilgrimage, particularly for worshippers of Vishnu, of whom Krishna is an incarnation (*avatara*). Prior to his death Gautama, the Buddha, informed his followers that four places which had featured significantly in his life could be visited with spiritual profit. These sites fell into disuse after the twelfth century but were revived in the nineteenth. They are the Lumbini Grove, close to Nepal, where the Buddha was born; Bodh-Gaya, the place of his enlightenment; the Deer Park at Sarnath, where the Buddha preached his first sermon; and Kusinara, the site of the Buddha's death.

Within the Christian tradition a number of key sites have become major places of pilgrimage. Helena, the mother of the Emperor Constantine the Great, transformed the idea of Christians journeying to the Holy Land by building churches at or near to the major sites of Jesus' life and ministry. The most obvious is Jerusalem, near which is the place of Jesus' death and resurrection. At Eastertide every year many thousands of pilgrims come to walk the *via dolorosa* and celebrate Jesus' resurrection at the Church of the Holy Sepulchre and the Garden Tomb. Other obvious historical sites of pilgrimage within the Christian tradition are the Church of the Nativity in Bethlehem, and the city of Rome, where the great apostles Peter and Paul were martyred. Another historical shrine which enjoyed great popularity during the Middle Ages was Santiago de Compostela in Spain, where the remains of the apostle James the Great are believed to rest. Many Christians also journey to the sixth-century monastery of St Catherine at Mount Sinai; it is claimed that the site marks the spot where the law was given to Moses.

In Islam there are three centres of pilgrimage, each of which has historical importance. Mecca is the city where all Muslims believe Abraham and Ishmael, in obedience to God, built the first temple. It was later rebuilt by Mohammed. Hajj Karbala in Iraq has the tomb of the first Shi'a martyr, Hussayn, the grandson of the prophet, and is a place of pilgrimage for Shi'a Muslims. Medina, the first Islamic city, the city of the prophet, is also a noted centre of Muslim pilgrimage.

Pilgrimage is not a requirement in Judaism, but there are historical holy places to which Jews travel. Since the formation of Israel as an independent nation in 1948, increasing numbers of Jews journey to Jerusalem for the Passover festival. In the city itself the Western Wall, which is all that remains of Herod's temple, is an important place of prayer. Many also visit Yad Vashem, which is a great memorial to the Jews who died in the Holocaust.

Early Sikhs reacted against what they perceived as the superstition attached to Indian shrines to which pilgrims journeyed. Guru Nanak declared, 'God's name is the real pilgrimage place which consists of contemplation of the word of God, and the cultivation of inner knowledge.' With the passing of time, however, Amritsar became the headquarters of Sikhism. Here the famous Golden Temple was built beside a huge pool. Many Sikhs now travel to the city; for some the journey has become a kind of pilgrimage, while for others it is little more than a sightseeing tour to a historical site.

PLACES OF SUPERNATURAL APPEARANCES

Places become centres of pilgrimage not only because of their historical significance (their links with the founder or a deity etc.), but also because they are places where miracles or supernatural appearances are said to have been experienced. At Knock in the Irish Republic several individuals claimed to have witnessed an appearance of the Virgin Mary, and at Lourdes in Southern France a young girl, Bernadette Soubirous, also encountered the Virgin. In such places pilgrims often clamour to touch holy relics or to pray in particularly sacred spots because they believe that by doing so they will connect with the healing powers of the holy person who sanctified the shrine.

PLACES OF RETREAT AND REFRESHMENT

The late twentieth and early twenty-first century have been marked by an increasing pace of life associated for many with growing pressures in their workplaces. In consequence, significant numbers of people have suffered stress and chronic fatigue. This has led to a form of pilgrimage in which individuals have sought out places of retreat and quiet away from the bustle of their daily routine. Within the Christian tradition in the UK sacred places associated with early Celtic Christianity have proved to be increasingly popular venues. Notable among them are St David's, Lindisfarne and Iona, all of which are close to the sea and offer the tranquillity and peace of beautiful surrounding countryside. In such locations pilgrims are able to rest, be still and reflect, as well as to rekindle their spiritual resources.

CONCLUSION

Pilgrimage is a journey made with a spiritual purpose: crucial is the inner intention of the pilgrims. Although not mandatory in all the world's religions, pilgrimage nevertheless plays a significant part in their life and worship. In some traditions, most notably Hinduism and Islam, pilgrimage is seen as a means of achieving divine merit. In others, it is a source of challenge, of spiritual refreshment and of drawing closer to God.

BIBLIOGRAPHY

I. Bradley, *The Celtic Way* (London, 1993); S. Coleman and J. Elsner, *Pilgrimage Past and Present: Sacred Travel and Sacred Space in the World's Religions* (London, 1995); J. G. Davies, *Pilgrimage Yesterday and Today: Why? Where? How?* (London, 1988); J. R. Hinnells, *A New Handbook of Living Religions* (Oxford, 1997); N. Smart, *The World's Religions* (Cambridge, 1998); J. Sumption, *Pilgrimage: An Image of Medieval Religion* (1975).

N. A. D. Scotland

RELIGION (DEFINITIONS)

The word 'religion' is derived from the Latin term *religio*, which Cicero (106–43 BC) traced back to *relegere*, meaning to 'reread'. He thus claimed that *religio* should be understood in terms of 'tradition', that which is handed down (reread) from generation to generation. On the other hand, Lactantius (c.240–320) traced the word back to *religare*, meaning 'to bind fast'. Hence, for Lactantius, *religio* is that which binds communities of people to each other and to their gods. Although it is not now possible to know which interpretation is correct, both understandings of *religio* are still evident in contemporary definitions of 'religion'.

The academic study of religions has always been concerned with the task of definition. Before one begins studying religion, one needs to have some idea of what should be included in the scope of the study. In other words, the process of defining is essentially a process of circumscription: the scholar circumscribes or marks out the limits of what is to be studied. The problem is that, when it comes to concepts like 'religion', 'culture' or 'art', there is often a lack of consensus as to what these limits should be. Indeed, if there is a great deal of debate over what is and what is not 'art', there is even more over what is and what is not 'religion'.

It should also be recognized that the very term 'religion' is itself problematic, in that it is a peculiarly Western term, originating in late antiquity and developed within the context of Christian thought. Many non-Western vocabularies simply do not contain the word. There are terms and concepts which might be translated as, for example, 'law', 'duty', 'worldview', 'custom', or 'way', but not 'religion'. There is thus a question as to how helpful 'religion' is when it comes to describing certain non-Western traditions and 'worldviews'.

WORKING AND TACTICAL DEFINITIONS

A useful starting point for understanding definitions of religion is Eric Sharpe's distinction between 'working definitions' and 'tactical definitions'. 'Working definitions' are essentially descriptions of religion which are, as far as possible, determined by the object of study, rather than by any particular theories the scholar might have. 'Tactical definitions', on the other hand, are usually short, polemical statements formulated in accordance with a particular theory. As such they often tell us more about the author of the definition than they do about the object defined. For example, Karl Marx's (1818–1883) famous definition of religion as 'the opium of the people' does not accurately describe religion as such, but rather makes a polemical point informed by certain philosophical presuppositions. His argument is that religion consoles the oppressed, maintains the capitalist status quo and thereby serves the oppressors. Although there may be some truth in Marx's definition, he is clearly not a scholar interested in an objective understanding of religion for its own sake, but rather a social and economic theorist seeking to *explain* the function religion performs in the light of what he calls 'the materialist conception of history'.

In the final analysis, tactical definitions are principally polemical. 'They may be clever, barbed, witty; but they do not describe. They merely epitomise.

Descriptive or working definitions, on the other hand, seldom emerge easily or spontaneously, and where religion is concerned, their subject-matter is so complex that they can seldom be terse, pithy or succinct' (Sharpe).

DEFINITIONS AND PRESUPPOSITIONS

While Sharpe's distinction between tactical and working definitions is helpful, even working definitions of religion, the aim of which is to be descriptive, will often betray the presuppositions of their definers. All definitions are, to some extent, determined by some preconceived general theory about what religion is and what function it performs. As William Arnal notes, 'In the case of religious studies, the issue of definition overlaps so extensively with the issue of general theories that, in some instances, the two appear almost entirely coextensive.' That is to say, definitions will to some extent explain religion's function and origin, but in doing so they betray the definer's general theory of religion. All definitions of religion have their roots in some general theory.

Although religion has both an 'inside' (experience, convictions etc.) and an 'outside' (institutions, practices etc.), theorists will often focus on one to the detriment of the other. Whereas, for example, the definitions of psychologists or theologians might focus, as in the case of William James (1842–1910), on religious experience and beliefs (the inside), the sociologist or anthropologist might overemphasize, as in the case of Émile Durkheim (1858–1917), the institutional or organizational (the outside).

It is often argued that theological and philosophical definitions suffer from an overemphasis on a particular concept or theme which is taken to be the interpretative key to religion. For example, Friedrich Schleiermacher (1768–1834) identified 'the feeling of absolute dependence' as the key element in the religious response to the world; Rudolf Otto (1869–1937) famously coined the term 'numinous' to describe the key constituent of religion; and the theologian H. H. Farmer (1892–1981) thought of 'religion' in terms of a divine–human personal encounter. Informed by particular theories of religion, such thinkers explicitly formulate their definitions by separating out certain elements which they identify as being foundational; this leads to a narrowness of definition (which usually excludes certain religions) and also to a failure to account for all the facets of religion.

THREE CATEGORIES OF DEFINITION

While there are several ways that one might categorize definitions of religion, perhaps the most helpful and straightforward is that used by John Hick in *An Interpretation of Religion* and the late James Thrower in *Religion: The Classical Theories*. Hick and Thrower simply divide the various theories and definitions into two broad categories: those posited by religious believers and those 'naturalistic' definitions or explanations (many of which are hostile to religion) posited by anthropologists, sociologists and psychologists. One might also label the categories 'definitions from the inside' and 'definitions from the outside', or, using Paul Ricoeur's distinction, understand them in terms of 'a hermeneutics of recollection' (which is sympathetic to religious claims that there is something transcendent to be reflected upon or 'recollected') and 'a hermeneutics of suspicion' (which, suspicious of religious accounts, seeks to uncover hidden, naturalistic explanations).

However, useful though this twofold division is, it tends to give the impression that scholars offer *either* religious *or* naturalistic definitions. In fact, sometimes a combination of both categories is offered; or, indeed, a definition which simply defies easy classification. In particular, some definitions offered from within the discipline of religious studies seek to avoid religious or naturalistic commitment, being the product of methodological agnosticism (i.e. adopting non-judgmental agnosticism to aid objective research). Although there is a question as to how far methodological agnosticism or neutrality is possible (see 'The Study of Religion'), I have added the further category of 'agnostic definitions' to those of Hick and Thrower.

RELIGIOUS DEFINITIONS

Religious definitions 'accept that religion is in touch with something objective, real and ultimately other than the consciousness of the individual religious believer' (Thrower). In thus presupposing the reality of the object of religious thought and experience, religious definitions imply that, in the final analysis, religion cannot be reduced to a naturalistic interpretation.

Religious definitions are of course the most ancient, in that believers have always provided tradition-specific interpretations of their own thoughts and practices. Such theological reflection has often produced definitions which understand religion in terms of a particular way of life or system of doctrine 'revealed' by a supernatural source. Because such definitions are determined by a particular religious tradition, they tend to be fairly narrow. For example, as in the Christian theologies of Karl Barth (1886–1968) and Hendrik Kraemer (1888–1966), a distinction might be made between 'true' and 'false' religion. Only that belief and practice which is the direct and obedient product of a particular revelation can be considered 'true' religion. Indeed, although Barth makes a distinction between true and false religion, his primary distinction is between 'religion' and 'revelation', religion being defined as 'unbelief', the manifestation of sinful error, blindness and ignorance of God.

Other religious definitions have been much broader. Rather than arguing that 'true religion' is limited to one religious tradition, or that 'religion *per se*', in contrast with revelation, is the product of human sin and ignorance, some have developed 'essentialist' definitions. Religion is defined in terms of a primordial 'essence': the religions of the world are manifestations of a single religious essence, and it is this essence which is truly 'religion'. Of course, the manifestations of this essence (the historical religions) are often graded according to the extent to which they are believed to be accurate manifestations. For instance, in his 1951 Gifford lectures, *Revelation and Religion* (published in 1954), Farmer argues that the essence of religion (which he terms 'living religion') is a divine–human personal encounter. The personal God revealed in Jesus Christ is actively and constantly revealing himself to the souls of men and women, the result of which is the rise of the historical religions. Needless to say, the Christian faith, when it is true to the biblical witness, is the most perfect manifestation of this 'living religion'. So the closer a non-Christian religious understanding is to the Christian understanding, the more that religion can be considered a manifestation of 'living religion'.

Another essentialist definition is that provided by Otto in his influential work *The Idea of the Holy* (1917). At the core of all *truly* 'religious' experience is a basic response to the sacred which is neither moral nor rational (morality and rationality come later). He thus abandoned the word 'holy' (because of its moral overtones) and coined the term 'numinous' (from the Latin *numen*, meaning 'sacred'). However, being non-rational, this essential element of religion is not something which can be conceptualized and described; it can only be evoked and experienced. He thus writes, rather intriguingly, 'It will be our endeavour to suggest this unnamed Something to the reader as far as we may, so that he may himself feel it.' He describes this subjective apprehension of the numinous as an experience of a *mysterium tremendum et fascinans*, a phrase which refers to the feelings aroused in people when they encounter the numinous: strangeness, awfulness, dread, fear, the uncanny, majesty, power, urgency, energy and a sense of mystery which arouses amazement and fascination. It is this numinous experience which, argues Otto, lies at the heart of all religions and constitutes the essence of 'religion'.

Similar essentialist definitions of religion are also found in Eastern religious thought. For example, the Indian philosopher Sarvepalli Radhakrishnan (1888–1975) defined religion as an unchanging essence which is mystically experienced and intuitively apprehended. The religions of the world are simply historical manifestations of this essence.

NATURALISTIC DEFINITIONS

Naturalistic definitions are reductionist in that they describe religion as a purely human phenomenon. For instance, the anthropologist James Frazer (1854–1941) provides this definition: 'a propitiation or conciliation of powers superior to man which are believed to direct or control the course of nature and human life'. Firstly, it is worth noting that such definitions are sometimes referred to as 'intellectualist' definitions because of their emphasis on beliefs and the intellect: a person is religious because that person holds certain *beliefs* and *thinks* in a particular way. Secondly, it is a naturalistic definition because Frazer does not believe that such beliefs have any basis in fact. Indeed, his definition is part of a larger theory which explicitly contrasts religion with science. Frazer argues that human cultural and intellectual evolution can be separated into three eras: the Age of Magic, the Age of Religion and the Age of Science. Just as the religious worldview had replaced the magical worldview, so the dawning of the Age of Science has heralded the slow but inevitable decline of religion. Religion is not rational or scientific and is thus destined to become obsolete. Hence religion is not a response to a transcendent reality; it is rather an immature stage in human cultural and intellectual evolution.

Many naturalistic definitions can also be described as 'functionalist', in that they focus on the role or function of religion. 'Functionalists prefer to define "religion" not in terms of *what* is believed by the religious, but in terms of *how* they believe it (that is in terms of the role belief plays in people's lives). Certain individual or social needs are specified and religion is identified as any system whose beliefs, practices or symbols serve to meet those needs' (Clarke and Byrne).

Such definitions present religion as nothing more ultimate than the interplay of psychological, sociological and biological factors. For example, Durkheim offers the definition: 'a religion is a unified system of beliefs and practices relative to sacred things, that is to say, things set apart and forbidden – beliefs and practices which unite into one single moral community called Church, all who adhere to them'. Convinced that believers do not understand *why* they believe in supernatural realities, he sought to uncover the true nature of religion, the origins of which he believed to be essentially social. Basically, the function of religion is to pass on social ideals from one generation to the next. It also, by means of symbols and rituals, binds the members of a society together into a community. As such, the integrity of a society is protected and sustained by religion. Religion thus has a key social function.

More recently, the anthropologist Clifford Geertz has produced the following influential 'symbolist' definition which focuses on the way symbols and rituals function as metaphors for the life of the community: 'Religion is (1) a system of symbols which acts to (2) establish powerful, pervasive, and long-lasting moods and motivations in men by (3) formulating conceptions of a general order of existence and (4) clothing these conceptions with such an aura of factuality that (5) the moods and motivations seem uniquely realistic.'

AGNOSTIC DEFINITIONS

While there is some debate as to how far agnosticism or neutrality is possible, agnostic definitions are those 'working' or 'descriptive' definitions which are supposed to record the facts of religion, without importing any particular psychological, sociological, anthropological or theological theories.

Perhaps the most influential contemporary definition of this type is that provided by the phenomenologist, Ninian Smart (1927–2001). His 'dimensional definition' identifies seven basic dimensions of religion: the ritual or practical; the doctrinal or philosophical; the mythic or narrative; the experiential or emotional; the ethical or legal; the organizational or social; and the material or artistic. To these seven he adds, in his book *Dimensions of the Sacred* (1996), two further dimensions: the political and the economic. The advantage of Smart's dimensional definition of religion is that it is more likely to produce a rounded analysis. In other words, it functions (as Smart intends) as a sort of checklist that helps to steer scholars of religion away from lopsided and simplistic interpretations.

THE PROBLEM OF BREADTH

A generally recognized problem with definitions of religion – particularly those which focus on a single idea, theme or dimension – is that they not only fail fully to account for all the facets of a religion, but also tend to be rather narrow and thus fail to make sense of the whole range of the world's religious traditions. For example, it is very difficult, using a definition such as Farmer's, to account for traditions such as atheistic Buddhism. Indeed, Farmer refuses to accept that some forms of Buddhism can be termed 'religious'. Similarly, if one were to ask Christians to define 'religion', many would probably begin with 'belief in God' as a key element. This, likewise, rules out traditions which would normally be termed 'religious', but which are actually atheistic, such as Jainism, Confucianism and some forms of Buddhism.

Clearly, from the perspective of religious studies certain definitions do seem to be too narrow. However, when one considers broader definitions other problems start to emerge. It is, for example, difficult to find a definition of 'religion' which is broad enough legitimately to include everything from Christianity to obscure tribal and folk religions, from Judaism to Buddhism, and from Islam to 'implicit religion', without at the same time being so broad and amorphous that it becomes practically meaningless. Certainly, some definitions could, without much difficulty, be applied to secular political ideologies or even hobbies, most of which common sense would regard as not 'religious'.

RELIGION AS A FAMILY RESEMBLANCE CONCEPT

Unconvinced by general definitions of religion which seek to embrace all religious worldviews, and in attempting to alleviate the above problem, some have turned to the philosopher Ludwig Wittgenstein (1889–1951) for help. Wittgenstein was likewise unconvinced by such general definitions. There are, he argued, some clusters of activities or ideas which have no common essence, but do have 'family resemblances'. For example, it would be extremely difficult to come up with a definition which accurately describes all games: not all games are competitive; not all are social; not all are played with balls; not all are structured. In Wittgenstein's words: 'if you look at them you will not see something that is common to *all*, but similarities, relationships, and a whole series of them at that . . . [We] see a complicated network of similarities overlapping and criss-crossing: sometimes overall similarities, sometimes similarities of detail. I can think of no better expression to characterise these similarities than "family resemblances"; for the various resemblances between members of a family: build, features, colour of eyes, gait, temperament, etc. etc. overlap and criss-cross in the same way – And I shall say: "games" form a family.'

The point is that the word 'religion' can be substituted for the word 'game'. Religions share a number of common 'religious' characteristics (family resemblances), without any of these characteristics being essential to their being defined as 'religious'. In other words, bearing Smart's dimensional definition in mind, a way of life might be defined as 'religious' although it contains only a few of the dimensions listed, just as another way of life containing different dimensions might also be termed 'religious'. Religions are not religious because they share a single set of characteristics, but because they are part of a network of relationships with similarities and overlapping characteristics.

CONCLUSION

Whilst 'religion' is very difficult, if not impossible, to define in any definitive sense, there is always the need to circumscribe the area of study. There are four points to bear in mind. (1) A definition should do the job we want it to do; it should be neither too narrow nor too broad and nebulous. (2) Wittgenstein's family resemblance thesis reminds us that no single set of characteristics should be sought in every example of religion. (3) The family resemblance model also reminds us that religions do have some things in common: they do belong to 'a family'. (4) In a sense, defining religion is far less important than 'the ability to recognise it when we come across it' (Sharpe).

That said, if we are to recognize it when we come across it, some criterion of recognition is needed. While Smart's dimensional approach is certainly helpful, the following working definition by Gavin Flood is a good concise alternative: 'value-laden narratives and behaviours that bind people to their objectives, to each other, and to non-empirical claims and beings.' Although 'symbols' should be added to 'narratives and behaviours', this definition makes reference to narratives, to behaviour or practice and to the communal and the 'binding' (*religare*) nature of religion. Unlike many purely functionalist definitions, it takes us to the heart of religion, namely the non-empirical, the supernatural, the transcendent. This last point should be fundamental to any definition of religion because, to quote Sharpe: 'dismiss the supernatural order from the picture altogether, and you are left with sacred symbols which refer to nothing in particular. What you are left with may be moral, inspiring, intellectually or aesthetically satisfying ... but it will not be religion, and some other word ought to be found to describe it.'

Whilst there is a need to formulate a working definition for the study of religions, and whilst, from the perspective of religious studies, certain definitions do seem to be too narrow, it is important to understand that definitions such as Farmer's are explicitly and unashamedly theological, certainly do not claim neutrality, and provide persuasive arguments for their particular interpretations. As long as presuppositions are acknowledged and critiqued, and as long as scholars seek to avoid the misinterpretation of others' beliefs and practices, there is no reason why such definitions should not be formulated. In particular, Christian scholars, who are bound to reflect theologically upon their study of religions, should seek to provide, along with a working definition of religion, a specifically Christian theological definition as their contribution to the task of constructing a Christian worldview.

BIBLIOGRAPHY

W. E. Arnal, 'Definition', in W. Braun and R. T. McCutcheon (eds.), *Guide to the Study of Religion* (London, 2000), pp. 21–34; P. B. Clarke and P. Byrne, *Religion Defined and Explained* (London, 1993); G. Flood, *Beyond Phenomenology: Rethinking the Study of Religion* (London, 1999); J. Hick, *An Interpretation of Religion: Human Responses to the Transcendent* (London, 1989); D. A. Hughes, *Has God Many Names: An Introduction to Religious Studies* (Leicester, 1996); C. H. Partridge, *H. H. Farmer's Theological Interpretation of Religion* (New York, 1998); E. J. Sharpe, *Understanding Religion* (London, 1983); J. Thrower, *Religion: The Classical Theories* (Edinburgh, 1999).

C. H. Partridge

RELIGION AND THE ARTS

The relationship of religions to the arts must be described as ambiguous at best. This remains the case whether a narrow or broad definition of 'the arts' is adopted. Taking a broad definition – including, for example, visual or fine art (pictorial, symbolic or abstract), calligraphy, drama and theatre, music, poetry, prose, rhetoric, architecture, sculpture, film – it is clear that religions make quite explicit use of the arts. Christian services of worship, for example, are likely to use prose, poetry and music. Some Christian traditions make more of their architectural settings, of the visual arts and of the drama of worship itself, than others. But hardly any Christian worship avoids the use of the arts altogether. From the fourth to the nineteenth century, the history of the visual arts in Western culture comprised in large part an engagement with Christian themes. Beyond Christianity, the accounts of Guru Nanak's life (the *janamsakhis*) invite pictorial portrayal, thus providing Sikhism with a rich culture of popular art, used by Sikhs for devotional purposes. In Islam, architecture and calligraphy are the main avenues through which the arts find religious expression. Daoism's concern for nature has had a profound effect on Chinese art, in which human beings are often lost or hidden within the natural world. Judaism's primary artistic expression is found through music. Most religions have left striking visible evidence of their existence, and of the way in which they draw their adherents together, through buildings constructed, often on an enormous scale, out of respect for ultimate reality, or to the glory of the deity.

Alongside these basic examples of how religions and the arts interweave positively and creatively, there are, however, plenty of examples of reserve, even hostility, amongst the religions of the world towards the arts. It is sometimes said that the three great monotheistic religions of the world, Judaism, Christianity and Islam, share a resistance to the potential power of the arts (visual art in particular), born of the fear of idolatry. This is in part true, though it needs careful nuancing. All three traditions oppose the shaping or portraying of any image of Yahweh, God or Allah. Of the three, however, Christianity is weakest in its opposition. God (as Father) has been painted (even if not sculpted). God has also been painted, sculpted, dramatized and filmed in countless versions in the form of Jesus Christ. Adherence to a particular doctrine of incarnation has, then, qualified the opposition to portrayals of the deity. Within Christianity, there have been major disputes concerning portrayals used for supposedly idolatrous purposes (for instance in the eighth-century iconoclastic controversies, and at the time of the Reformation). From outside, it can appear that Christianity has simply broken a basic rule of monotheism.

Judaism and Islam have more rigorously retained the ban on portrayals of the deity. In the case of Islam, the opposition to visual images in particular is extended in two ways: first, portrayals of the Prophet Muhammad are very rare indeed; second, the opposition is not confined simply to human forms, for no living forms at all are to be portrayed. Though often wrongly assumed to be a Qur'anic law, the ban in fact derives from the *Traditions of the Prophet*. Even if it was not as rigorously followed in the earliest history of Islam (and became more prominent as a result of Jewish influence), it is now widely, even if not universally, observed in the Islamic world. Judaism has until recently rarely portrayed human beings in visual art, and the portrayal of animals was often symbolic. It is, however, accurate to speak of a 'Jewish art', examples of which abounded in the twentieth century, which portrays the Jewish people, in the process providing a record of religion and culture in the closest proximity.

The fear of idolatry is not the only cause of religious hostility towards the arts. Human creativity, as expressed through any art-form, can itself function as a Promethean challenge to God's own creativity. In other words, when artists assert their artistic skills in such a way that they fail to respect those skills as gifts, then, according to many religious traditions, they are prone to turn themselves into gods. For artistic activity can imply the worship of the humanity the artists represent, and at worst the worship of the artists themselves.

Despite these profound hesitations about the arts, all religious traditions not merely practise the arts, but also enable them to flourish, neither simply in ways directly connected with worship, nor only when religiously sanctioned. Divine creativity is seen to overrule and break through the human reticence usually deemed appropriate in religion. Religious scriptures, for example, contain work of great literary merit and impact. The Bibles of Judaism and Christianity include Psalms in Hebrew, the literary value of which is recognized in addition to their religious function. Even translations of scriptures become significant in their own right, the King James Version of the Christian Bible being a clear example. By providing a central narrative core for different forms of Hindusim, the epic poems (the *Mahabharata* and the *Ramayana*) reveal how the literary arts function within religions. The literature of religion operates at many different pitches of language (e.g. as literary art, in liturgical forms, in theological concepts or as common speech). This fact highlights the way in which religions' use of the arts interweaves with their being made up of people from many social and educational backgrounds. Discussion of 'religion and the arts' can thus too easily focus on high art alone, overlooking the important overlap between religion and (e.g.) media, kitsch and popular devotional aids.

Much religious architecture has a *de facto* wide public function. It is 'religious art' by being functionally religious, yet it provides national landmarks, tourist destinations and sacred space for those who do not necessarily deem themselves religious. The Vatican, York Minster, the Golden Temple at Amritsar, the lotus-flower-shaped Baha'i house of worship in New Delhi and Stonehenge all function in this way. Sculptures as diverse as the vast golden Buddhas throughout South-East Asia or the Christ-figure overlooking Rio de Janeiro fulfil similar public functions, as focal points for observers who may or may not share the religious tradition of the sculpture itself.

Moreover, some art may be in no way 'religious', when viewed from the perspective of its fashioner or subject matter, yet may nevertheless be deemed religious in so far as it may seem, to a religious observer, to address questions about the ultimacy or purpose of humanity, or of the created order as a whole.

What do examples of religions' engagement with the arts teach the student of religion? First, they suggest that all human creativity is derivative. The creator remains the source of creativity. The notion of human beings as 'co-creators' with God, however, opens up the possibility that 'originality' in the arts may provide an example of God's own self being open to a novelty prompted from within the created order.

Second, faith needs to be expressed. There are undoubted problems associated with seeing artistic self-expression in theological terms. (When does expression of self cease and divine self-expression begin? Why are the arts not simply a form of fideism, expressing an artist's/writer's/sculptor's faith regardless of whether that faith has any real content to it?) But the arts are a prime location of the inevitable meeting point between the deity's creative presence within the world and the apparent incipient religiosity of the human being.

Third, the arts serve as a potent reminder of the limits of seeing religious truth in primarily propositional terms (i.e., as a collection of theological statements). Though some of the arts are to do with words, even rhetoric, novels and poetry do much more than offer statements about God, human beings or the world. More clearly still through other art-forms, the arts reveal the extent to which the desire to express the inexpressible takes the theological interpreter of life to the limits of words and beyond. In this way they offer a salutary warning about the limits of theology itself.

Fourth, at a time of so-called 'secular culture' in the West, the arts suggest themselves as an alternative 'religion' or as an alternative to religion. Despite the persistence of religions themselves, the sheer plurality of religions within a plurality of worldviews provides for the contemporary Western citizen a complex set of influences within which the arts (arguably now subsumed within contemporary forms of media) play a crucial role. The apparent return to the primacy of the visual in Western culture, and the lack of unity of worldview across an irreducibly plural world, suggest a powerful meaning-making role for the arts.

Fifth, the current prominent public role of the arts in the West invites religions in turn to reconsider their own relationship to the arts. In addition to being media through which religions do their work, the arts create a space and form within which the boundaries of religion can themselves be stretched. Artists of all kinds often challenge religious traditions from within.

Religions cannot, however, overlook aesthetic theory. In the modern and postmodern periods, the reluctance to entertain, or the desire actively to exclude, metaphysical concerns throughout the humanities have profoundly challenged theology and religion. In the analysis of texts, for example, the modern period can be said to be characterized by a concern for authorial intention, and the postmodern period by the relationship between the text and the reader. These concerns are reflected throughout the arts. Common to both periods is reserve about the reference of a text *beyond* itself. When reflected across the arts, preoccupation with an author's (painter's, musician's, dramatist's, sculptor's, architect's) intention runs the risk of reducing works of art to their historical circumstances, whether understood in social, political, psychological or economic terms. Attention to what occurs between a work of art and an interpreter often leads (as in some viewer- and reader-response theories) to the manipulation of the work by the receiver. It is difficult, on this axis of interpretation, to allow works of art to maintain their own integrity. Their function and use then become paramount.

Religions are, however, unlikely to be wholly persuaded by either of these tendencies, despite noting the importance of their emphases. At issue, then, is how religions relate to the arts in a way which enables the arts really to refer (ultimately, to God), without simply sidestepping the challenges of post-Enlightenment Western thought and culture.

The relationship between religion and the arts can thus helpfully be read through the framework of 'sign', 'symbol' and 'means'. Do works of art of any kind actually refer to any reality beyond themselves other than the receiver (viewer, reader, hearer, watcher)? If so, then they may be able to fulfil a symbolic function, participating in some way in the reality to which they refer (ultimately, the truth of God), however distant their own symbolic approximation to that truth may be. But are works of art capable of more than this? Are they a crucial means by which God becomes present to the recipient? In Christian terms, can works of art be sacramental? Most exploration in the field of religion and the arts undoubtedly affirms that they can. But this insight issues in a number of challenges: to define in metaphysical terms an ontology of the arts which does justice to their sacramental function; to clarify the way in which an ontology of art relates to the existence of a diversity of religions; and to identify the theological assumptions which lie implicit within one's understanding of that relationship.

The danger of taking up this series of necessary challenges in contemporary discussion is that of losing sight of the intrinsic value of works of art. Recognizing the value, and the irreducible quality, of a work of art is not the same as supporting 'art for art's sake'. Attention to a work of art's subject matter, and to the relationship between the work of art and the recipient/believer, can, however, easily lead to the neglect of a work's apparent purpose. On the other hand, attention to what lies beyond or behind a work can too easily lead to dispensing with the symbol, in favour of that which is symbolized.

Religions hold their own in a so-called secular age precisely because human beings recognize that in talking about (and writing about, making music about, and painting) themselves, they do well to do more than this, and talk about God or gods or ultimate reality too. The arts therefore serve religion even when they are not explicitly (or institutionally) religious. But it is too early to predict the form the future relationship will take in a religiously plural world beyond its so-called 'secular' phase.

BIBLIOGRAPHY

J. Begbie, *Voicing Creation's Praise: Towards a Theology of the Arts* (Edinburgh, 1991); J. Dillenberger, *A Theology of Artistic Sensibilities: The Visual Arts and the Church* (New York, 1986; London, 1987); C. Marsh and G. Ortiz (eds.), *Explorations in Theology and Film* (Oxford, 1997; Cambridge, MA, 1998); G. Pattison, *Art, Modernity and Faith* (London, [2]1998); G. Steiner, *Real Presences* (London and Boston, 1989); N. Wolterstorff, *Art in Action: Towards a Christian Aesthetic* (Grand Rapids, 1980; Carlisle 1997); T. R. Wright, *Theology and Literature* (Oxford, 1988).

C. Marsh

RELIGION IN EDUCATION

Religion characteristically educates. The survival of religion depends upon its transmission from one generation to the next. Christianity has shaped the Western world over the last millennium and a half. Symbolic of Christianity's formative power was the educational network connected with the monasteries and cathedrals of the Middle Ages, a network that covered an area roughly coterminous with the Roman Empire. Subsequently, the Reformation stimulated schooling, particularly after Luther's call to establish schools in which the biblical languages might be learnt. Even the foundation of modern science in the sixteenth century was conceptually, if not institutionally, linked with Christian thought. The exploration of the cosmos made sense if the natural world was the product of God's rational and orderly power. Religion, then, was implicated in education with regard to both its content – what was taught – and its infrastructure – the institutions in which it took place.

The relationship between religion and education that eventually emerged in the Western world in the twentieth century varied from country to country; the factors that determined this relationship often depended on the accommodation reached by church and state in the post-Reformation period. Three basic models emerged. The first depended upon the complete separation of church and state (e.g. in the USA). The second depended upon an accommodation between church and state (e.g. in the UK). The third presumed that the secular state would take over any functions the church might once have had (e.g. in the USSR). There were variations upon these models because, although church and state might be separated, the relationship between them might be either of mutual support or of mutual antagonism. Similarly, where church and state were in partnership, the church itself might be fragmented, so that this partnership became a multiple one with various church groups. As a result the state could either foment religious rivalry or find itself under pressure when religious groups combined against it. Even the third model underwent subtle change as the state softened or hardened its attitude to the church depending upon external pressures and national needs.

By contrast, a completely separate line of development derived from Islam is to be found in other countries that could also be defined as Western in terms of their orientation and degree of economic and scientific sophistication. From the establishment of Muslim dominance of the city of Medina in the seventh century, Islamic theology took its religious community to be congruent with society. Religious law is also community law and ideally should be derived not from democratic processes but from Qur'anic revelation. Consequently, resurgent Islam in the late twentieth century has contained reforming parties whose aim is to bring states that have hitherto followed religious arrangements parallel to those flowing from Christian theology back to the original Islamic model. This is the Islamicization project to be found in Pakistan, Iran and, perhaps, Malaysia. It usually has unwelcome implications for Christian minorities and their schools.

Primary sources defining the formal relationship between religion and the structure and functioning of the education system include the legal enactments of each individual nation, official guidelines, local or state laws and case law. Where the teaching of religion in schools is vested in religious professionals or specially trained teachers, primary sources also include legal and other documentation covering training and certification. In addition to these sources, statistics and regulations revealing the expenditure of public money are also important. In most nations the support or otherwise for religion in education can be gauged from the size of the financial backing that comes from the public purse. Beyond these direct sources, academic debate helps more obliquely to shape the content of religious material at all educational levels; in most countries, it is possible to point to key publications that influenced the intellectual climate in which law was made, training took place and expenditure was fixed.

SEPARATION OF CHURCH AND STATE

A separation of church and state is to be found in France, Canada and the United States. In *France* the revolution of 1789 and the subsequent Napoleonic era centralized control of education. Constitutional changes, balancing left and right wing elements, resulted in the 1959 Fifth Republic in a secular system, but one that allowed state support for Roman Catholic schools under a system of contracts not unlike the 1944 settlement in England and Wales (see below). Teaching about religion in the state schools occurs haphazardly in relation to literature, history or philosophy and without the support of the teaching unions.

Private schools in France, of which the majority are Roman Catholic, may also receive government funding, in which case two contractual possibilities are offered. In one, the state takes over financial responsibility and the school adopts the methods and curricula of the standard state schools but has the right to retain its religious ethos and, jointly with the state, appoints teachers of religion. In the other, the state provides each school with the finance for salaries and its staff are not bound to the national curriculum or to the state. This arrangement allows appointments to be made without state interference.

Canada, which devolves regulation of schooling to its provinces, allows religious minorities to apply for public funding to run public, religious schools using tax money from their own religious constituencies. In Quebec the minority is Protestant and in Ontario it is Catholic. At the level of higher education, students studying religion can receive financial help from public funds in the form of repayable loans. Seminaries can receive public funding. All the issues related to the public support of religion and religious institutions are affected by the shifting base of electoral power in the provinces and (indirectly) by educational discussion in the United States. For instance, Charter schools (see below) are under discussion.

In the *United States* in 1787 the First Amendment to the Constitution forbade the Congress from making any law 'respecting the establishment of religion, or prohibiting the free exercise thereof'. Yet, because the term 'establishment' is not unambiguous, between 1800 and 1947 the Supreme Court settled the constitutional right of the government to provide financial assistance to religion. Free transport of pupils to religious schools could be offered, for example. Even in the public (state) schools, prayer at the start of the day and the teaching of biblical materials were permissible. In the 1960s the Supreme Court made a series of judgments that had the effect of banning religion, including public prayers and confessional religious courses from schools. Towards the end of the twentieth century, however, the secularization of the public school system, the appearance of independent Christian schools, the willingness of the Roman Catholic Church to provide schooling for the urban poor and the continued strength of the Judeo-Christian tradition has led to a series of challenges to the status quo. The teaching of religious dogma continues to be prohibited, but teaching *about* religion in history and literature courses is possible, and attempts to broaden the appeal of Charter Schools (which are set up by parents) continued into the 1990s. Pupils (though not staff) seem to be permitted to pray publicly at school events.

At college level students at religiously founded institutions, and ministerial students, can receive all the financial resources more generally available.

ACCOMMODATION BETWEEN RELIGION AND STATE

Historically in *England* and *Wales*, accommodation between the state and the education system grew because the church, Protestant and Catholic, was almost entirely responsible for the education of the nation's children in the first half of the nineteenth century. The churches built the schools (helped after the 1830s by small grants from the state) and paid the teachers. After the Educational Acts of 1902 and 1944 church schools were incorporated in what became known as the 'dual system', a system that contains church schools and schools built out of public funds and now provides education for about 94% of the nation's children. The remaining children are educated privately from parental fees in schools that receive no public funding. The dual system has succeeded in integrating the schools within its confines by the use of a national curriculum, inspection, common certification of teachers and similar administrative patterns of religious education. Schools which were originally church foundations (which amount to roughly 25% of all primary schools) may maintain their linkage with the church by becoming 'voluntary aided' schools. If they choose this categorization, they are able to offer denominational worship and religious instruction and to command a majority of seats on the governing body that is responsible for most aspects of school life. As a result of earlier legislation, the religious bodies behind voluntary aided schools must still provide a percentage of the finance necessary for the upkeep of school premises. This financial arrangement and its associated governance and religious provisions also include small numbers of Muslim, Jewish, Sikh and ecumenical schools.

Community schools meanwhile still offer religious education according to 'agreed syllabuses' that may not include the teaching of denominational doctrines. They may, however, include the teaching of world faiths other than Christianity. As a result of academic debate (rather than public debate) dating from the 1970s onwards, religious education within schools has become non-confessional and descriptive rather than confessional and moral. Christianity is expected to occupy about half the time available to religious education, though, where syllabuses are thematic in nature, this is difficult to verify.

Collective worship during the course of the school day is also theoretically part of the religious education offered to pupils (as the legislative stipulations from 1944 onwards make clear). In practice, collective worship is usually not seen in this way. Where a substantial proportion of pupils belong to a faith community that is not Christian, application may be made at local level for non-Christian worship. But in any event, religious provision is covered by a conscience clause allowing parents to withdraw children from any part of it. To this extent, and to the extent that agreed syllabuses are drawn up by local religious representatives, the provision of religious teaching and experience within maintained schools is varied, voluntary and flexible.

Within an almost entirely government-sponsored higher education system students who wish to study theology may obtain low cost student loans in the normal way. In the old universities (e.g. Oxford, Cambridge, Durham) theology continues to be taught as an academic subject covering the biblical text in the original languages as well as church historical and patristic concerns. In the new universities, which are more self-consciously secular and postmodern, the tendency is for 'study of religion' or 'religious studies' to be offered. A selection of world religions is studied. The methods of study often make use of social science perspectives for investigating religious communities and contemporary issues. One way of understanding the position of religion at all levels in British education is to see it as a shifting balance between the pluralistic and secular nature of modern British society and a monocultural, self-confident and imperial Christian past.

Variations on these themes may be found in other parts of Europe. *Germany* allows private religious schools to receive government support. In the state sector religious education is required, though students frequently choose between courses with a religious or even confessional content and those whose focus is purely on ethics. Syllabuses suited to Islamic teaching have been constructed in Westphalia. A Roman Catholic university exists in Bavaria. *Austria* has accepted such arrangements since 1980. In *Belgium* a concordat has allowed Catholic and secular state schools each to receive full support. In *Sweden* since 1992 the government has supported private schools; a number of these are Muslim, though the majority are Christian. *Finland* is due to adopt this policy. In *Spain*, after many years of Roman Catholic domination, the education system is now under secular control, though the church retains influence in the private sphere that, subject to academic conditions, receives government aid on a differential basis similar to that found in the UK and France. In the *Republic of Ireland* a similar 'aided' system operates: the state provides funding to assist other agencies at primary, secondary and tertiary levels. In *Scotland* the administration of (Protestant) education was transferred from the churches to the state in 1872 on the condition that 'instruction in religious subjects' according to 'use and wont' should continue, subject to a conscience clause. This is still the legal position. The Roman Catholic Church transferred its schools to secular administration in 1918 but on the condition that the Church has the right to approve teachers appointed to these schools as regards religious belief and character. A similar arrangement exists with respect to Jewish schools. This is still the legal position.

Denmark (whose state schools offer compulsory RE, safeguarded by a conscience clause) and the *Netherlands* (which does not offer RE in state schools) implement what are effectively the most flexible and liberal of religio-educational policies: they allow parents to set up religious schools at government expense by letting the money designated for the education of each child follow the child to whatever school the parents choose. This policy has produced various kinds of Christian and Muslim schools. Such policies are in accordance with the European Community's concern for minorities and may, as the Community expands, find favour among new members. Because of its strong Catholic community, religious schools in *Poland* survived the incursions of first Nazi and then Soviet hegemony. After 1990 all pupils in Polish state schools were allowed RE based on their own confession, which allows the 9% of the population who are not Roman Catholic an acceptable choice. In *Hungary* the state is religiously neutral and upholds the free choice of citizens in matters of religious education by offering time and classroom space if required. The state also financially supports the educational activities of Catholic, Calvinist, Jewish and Pentecostal groups, for example in the running of Sunday schools or residential schools. In the *Czech Republic* there is relative religious freedom. Church schools exist and attract the funding that would have been spent on their pupils had they gone to a state school. Religious education in state schools is also permissible, though it takes place after normal lessons and must be organized by the person wanting to run it. The arrangements then put in place must be approved by the school's director.

Similar accommodations occur in countries where education, because of colonial or imperial histories, was linked with the European patterns. *Australia* and *New Zealand* have substantial networks of church schools supported by public funds though, as in the United States, home schooling and new independent church schools have also come into vigorous existence. *Israel* offers a complicated system of state education as well as subsystems of private education; these allow varieties of state-funded religious education conditional only upon the teachers' recognized academic qualifications.

Church schools are allowed in *Romania* as long as they are funded by the religious community, and pupils may be taught their distinctive religious doctrines in addition to the normal secular subjects stipulated by the state. In state schools religious education is allowed and RE teachers favour Orthodox expressions of Christianity. Where pupils belonging to other Christian denominations (such as Baptist or Pentecostal) are present, their spiritual leader will be contacted and allowed to lead the religion class. At university level, theology can be studied, and theology graduates usually choose to become priests or RE teachers.

SECULAR STATES AND RELIGION

China is a secular state and controls religion by registering congregations and regulating any religious education taking place outside the school system. In *Russia*, still freeing itself from the atheistic communist legacy, a law passed by the Duma in 1997 permitted religious freedom to religions established in the country for more than fifteen years. Religious education in secondary schools has been mooted, though it is likely to be non-confessional and supportive of Russian Orthodoxy, especially in the Russian heartlands. Its provision is, in any event, very uneven. Clergy training, both Christian and Muslim, takes place and public money has been spent on the renovation of architecturally important religious buildings, some of which are seminaries. In *Macedonia* religious education in schools is forbidden.

BIBLIOGRAPHY

J. Astley, L. J. Francis and C. Crowder (eds.), *Theological Perspectives on Christian Formation: a reader on theology and Christian education* (Leominster, UK, 1996); D. Coulby, R. Cowen and C. Jones, *World Yearbook of Education 2000* (London, 2000); L. J. Francis and D. W. Lankshear (eds.), *Christian Perspectives on Church Schools* (Leominster, UK, 1993); F. Heyting, J. Koppen, D. Lenzen, F. Thiel and P. Mortimore (eds.), *Educational Studies in Europe* (London, 1997); T. McLaughlin, J. O'Keefe and B. O'Keeffe, *The Contemporary Catholic School: context, identity and diversity* (London, 1996); P. Schreiner (ed.), *Religious Education in Europe* (Munster, 2000); W. Tulasiewicz and C. Brock, *Christianity and Educational Provision* (London, 1998); D. Westerlund and I. Svanberg (eds.), *Islam Outside the Arab World* (London, 1999).

W. K. Kay

RELIGION AND THE ENVIRONMENT

The recent devastation of our natural environment has come to be known as the 'ecological crisis'. While it is clear that human activity has contributed to environmental damage throughout history, the scope, extent and scale of this crisis are new. The causes of the damage are complex and related to political, economic and technological developments. For religious traditions, however, the crisis extends not just to the physical analysis of the events themselves, but to a crisis in civilization. In particular, rejection of religious traditions and the loss of the sense of the earth as sacred seem to allow a destructive approach to the natural world to emerge. Hans Küng has called for a new global ethic where different religions of the world come together to search for shared solutions to common problems facing humanity, including that of the environment. Whether such a solution is feasible remains to be seen, given the diversity of approaches to the environment amongst different religious groups. This article attempts to delineate something of this diversity, as well as shared religious insights. Given the limited scope, it will be possible to discuss only major religious traditions.

The Abrahamic faiths – Judaism, Islam and Christianity – all share a belief in God as Creator of the earth. They all affirm the goodness of creation and humanity as its ultimate expression. All stress human responsibility to care for the earth. They all, in their various ways, recognize the freedom given to humanity with the real possibility of what Christians call 'sin'. However, each possesses some distinctive features. Judaism has a particular concern for the interrelationships between the people and the land, affirming that they depend on each other in a way that is prototypical for all peoples everywhere. The prosperity of the land depends on social justice and moral integrity, formalized in the idea of the sabbath year of rest every seventh year and the Jubilee at the fiftieth anniversary. The Jubilee release of prisoners and the cancellation of debt help to prevent exploitation of those who are without means. Devastation of the land is associated with the judgment of God following human disobedience. The contemporary realization of a much closer relationship between human development and ecology is epitomized in the Jewish understanding of the relationship between people and land.

One of the key relevant aspects of Islamic faith is the idea of stewardship. Humans are considered to be viceregents who are responsible for the care of the earth. For many Muslims, the buried tradition of Islamic science is significant as well, since it is based on a different philosophy from that of Western scientific traditions. The latter seem to foster alienation from nature, rather than an acknowledgment that the natural world is in some sense sacred. Islamic science, on the other hand, retained its sense of the religious significance of the natural world. A recovery from the ecological crisis will include a reformulation of science and technology along lines that are more in tune with ancient religious cosmologies.

Christianity has a somewhat chequered history in its approach to ecology. An understanding of the earth as created by God permitted experimental science and technology to flourish. Those who give credit to Christian faith for the rise of modern science have to face the charge that it is in some way indirectly responsible for the ecological crisis. The possible direct contribution of Christianity to environmental destruction through an interpretation of the Genesis concept of dominion as domination has been the subject of intense scholarly debate. Most argue that blaming Christianity for the ecological crisis is naïve and inappropriate. Other strands in the Christian tradition stress responsible stewardship, in common with Islam. The Christian understanding of Christ as divine undoubtedly affirms humanity as made in the 'image of God'. Christian tradition has viewed human beings as the culmination of God's creative activity, or the 'crown of creation'. Yet many Christians regard the incarnation of God in the created order as also an affirmation of the goodness of the created order as such. Moreover, if we consider Christ as the model for human action, we find one who is humble in his approach to others and the natural world. St Francis of Assisi, along with many saints in the Celtic Christian tradition, welcomed all life forms as fellow companions in the praise of God. While there is a tendency today to have an overly romantic view of the environmental practice of these saints, they do at least indicate that the concept of domination is far removed from any idea of Christian sainthood.

Chinese religious traditions are very different from the above in that they have no concepts of a creator god or goddess or story of creation. The three major forms of Chinese religion expressed as Daoism, Confucianism and Buddhism, are all influenced by the idea of the *Dao*, as that which is the inexpressible source of all life. According to this philosophy all things have an innate nature and any violation of this transgresses *Dao*, the Principle that underlies and guides the natural processes. Also central to much Chinese philosophy is the *yin–yang* polarity. *Yin* and *yang* symbolize the cosmic struggle whereby energy emerges, though neither is, strictly, considered good or evil in itself, or even divine. In humanity we find both *yin* and *yang*, which the wise seek to harmonize. In the more activist Confucian form there is a hierarchical view of nature, a distrust of spontaneity and a strong desire to pursue the good. Humans act against this natural hierarchy at their peril. The more passive Daoism, on the other hand, is less concerned with order and allows for a greater degree of spontaneity, resisting any attempt by humanity to control the natural world. For Daoists the environmental crisis is an outcome of the imbalance in harmony of *yin* and *yang*. The response should be one of constraint, letting nature be itself without human interference. The hallmark of the Buddhist Chinese tradition, like Buddhism generally, is compassion for nature.

The Indian religious traditions are, to a large extent, based on the teaching of the *Vedas*, which were written after a long oral tradition. As in the Chinese religions, humanity achieves its proper place only by giving equal value to the whole natural environment. The harmony of the cosmic sphere comes to find expression in the social and moral sphere as well, so that not only is everything connected to everything else, but also everything has moral worth. The authors of the *Vedas* were aware of the need for biodiversity, though the ritual use of animals led to some exploitation. As Hinduism evolved, the early Vedic understanding of natural law or *rita* was replaced to some extent with the moral concept of *dharma*. This is a more systematic and prescriptive understanding of moral order in the universe. However, the rule of *karma* (action and consequence), makes no distinction between humanity and other life forms, implying a duty not to injure any form of life. The Buddhist and Jainist traditions grew from a reaction against strict forms of ritualism and have a tendency to be more esoteric. A core belief is that of overcoming attachment of all kinds, especially to material aspects of the world. However, alongside this there is recognition that consciousness is not just confined to humanity, but includes all life. This leads to a considerable sympathy for all life forms in a way that embraces the Hindu tradition of non-injury (*ahimsa*). While the aim of the individual is the transcendence of the self, this is achieved through accumulation of positive *karma*. Any injury to life leads to negative *karma* and thus is self-destructive. Buddhism advocates the minimizing of any suffering or pain of any living creature.

In the contemporary West, Eastern religious traditions have been commended and adapted particularly by New Age advocates and Neo-Pagans as environmentally friendly philosophies. Traditional Christianity, on the other hand, has more often than not been rejected by these groups as environmentally harmful. However, in addition to the classical religious traditions, there are more general contemporary religious approaches to the environment, including creation spirituality and ecofeminism. Some adherents of these approaches still consider themselves Christians, though of a radicalized kind. Creation spirituality has grown from a reaction to the largely historical transcendent emphasis in Christianity. Those influenced by it argue that the linear account of history in Christianity described as creation, fall and redemption needs to be replaced by a more cyclical vision of all nature, including humanity, in cycles of birth and death and re-birth. The original story of creation is significant not so much as the story of the curse of humanity, but rather as that of its original blessing and of blessing for the whole creation. The idea of the earth as a biotic community replaces any notion of anthropocentrism and reflects the perspective of Indian or Chinese religions. This kind of spirituality, which is focused on creation, is also characteristic of what has come to be known as deep ecology. None the less, deep ecology has a particular green political agenda to pursue that is largely lacking in creation spirituality. Many ecofeminists will endorse creation spirituality, with its stress on the immanence of God in the created order, while appealing at the same time to feminist politics. While this spirituality is sometimes regarded as pantheism, it bears little resemblance to the pantheism of philosophers such as Spinoza, where the all is in the One and one in the All. Instead, all of creation has intrinsic worth because it shares in the divinity. Many ecofeminists point to the interconnections between the human devastation of the earth and the patriarchal oppression of women. Both women and nature suffer through men's exploitation. The identification of women and nature may be taken up and celebrated as a way of affirming women. Ancient traditions of the earth goddesses, including *Gaia* and *Isis*, become symbols of this form of spirituality. On the other hand, such close identification of women with the earth is acutely problematic for other ecofeminists, since it seems to reinforce the very structures set in place by oppressive forms of dualism: for example, between women and men, body and mind, emotions and spirit, or earth and heaven.

The practical relationship between different religious traditions and the environment is worth pondering before coming to too hasty a conclusion about which religion may or may not offer an adequate response to the crisis. The historical record of the treatment of the natural world does not always follow from the particular religious teachings. Many will lament the fact that the Indian religious traditions with their emphasis on interconnectedness have not been able to withstand the pressure towards industrialization and consumerism. The story of the Chinese invasion of Tibet around 1950 has been a sad one, of the replacement of a balance between humanity and nature with massive deforestation, land erosion, pollution of rivers and general destruction of the environment. Christianity, too, while it may escape from being blamed for the ecological crisis, has not led the way forward in tackling environmental issues.

Yet in spite of these reservations, all religious traditions do have something to offer in terms of spiritual resources. While not all may advocate equality of status between humanity and the earth, all seek to behave responsibly out of a heart of love for all creatures. There are signs too that this attitude leads to practical action. The World Council of Churches has consistently campaigned for better treatment of both the poorer nations of the world and the environment. At the Rio Earth Summit in 1991 a start, at least, was made in bringing together environmental political and economic concern and religious understanding. Small-scale activities throughout the world are beginning to have an impact. The Chipko movement in India is a good example, where ordinary Indians hugged trees in order to prevent deforestation. Activities such as these give reason to hope that religious traditions have a contribution to make, not just in the reawakening of a deeper intimacy with the natural world, but in practice as well. Christianity, in particular, needs to instil a deeper sense of responsibility to work for a greater respect for the natural world, a respect inherent in the Christian tradition. There are positive signs that Christians are moving beyond a narrow concept of their mission as defined in terms of salvation of souls. A deeper appreciation of the importance of understanding ourselves as interdependent on the natural world is surely necessary not only for the survival of Christianity and all religious traditions, but also for the survival of our planet.

BIBLIOGRAPHY

M. Batchelor and K. Brown (eds.), *Buddhism and Ecology* (London and New York, 1992); D. E. Cooper and J. A. Palmer, *Spirit of the Environment: Religion, Value and Environmental Concern* (London and New York, 1998); R. S. Gottlieb, *This Sacred Earth: Religion, Nature, Environment* (London and New York, 1996); D. Kinsley, *Ecology and Religion: Ecological Spirituality in Cross-Cultural Perspective* (Englewood Cliffs, NJ, 1995); H. Küng, *Yes to a Global Ethic* (London, 1996); N. McCagney, *Religion and Ecology* (Oxford, 1999); S. H. Nasr, *Religion and the Order of Nature* (New York, 1996); R. Prime, *Hinduism and Ecology: Seeds of Truth* (London and New York, 1992); A. Rose (ed.), *Judaism and Ecology* (London and New York, 1992); M. E. Tucker and J. A. Grim (eds.), *Worldviews and Ecology: Religion, Philosophy and the Environment* (Maryknoll, NY, 1994).

C. E. Deane-Drummond

RELIGION AND ETHICS

It is perfectly possible for people to hold ethical views and behave morally without being religious. But it is clear that each and every religion embodies and propounds some kind of ethic, fundamental values, frameworks for moral decision making, expectations of and recommendations for appropriate behaviour and some notion of sanctions for failing to act morally.

In a pluralist, postmodern and increasingly secularized world, there are many competing philosophies, worldviews and religions. In assessing these different perspectives, it is important to explore the similarities, differences and common ground between the specific ethical teaching of religions and moral philosophies.

ETHICS AND MORAL PHILOSOPHY

Ethical teaching and decision making in philosophy have tended to concentrate on principles (deontology), consequences (teleology) or virtues and character as the basis of morality. There are usually four main foci in ethical reflection – in deciding what is right, wrong, good or bad: (1) the *agent* (the one who acts or fails to act); (2) the *motives* (aims, purposes and intentions); (3) the *nature* of the action itself; and (4) the principles at stake and the likely *results* and consequences.

Deontology is based on some form of law, principle or categorical imperative: act so that you treat others as ends in themselves rather than as means to some other end. Teleology stresses the results of actions: for example, aim for the greatest happiness of the greatest number. Virtue or character ethics emphasizes that the good person exhibits positive virtues and will nearly always behave appropriately.

Every moral philosophy offers a description and prescription of how we ought to live and why. Underlying such ethical approaches are beliefs about the nature of human being and what leads to human flourishing, what are good and worthy goals and purposes, and some account of human motivation and the place of rules and guidelines in human behaviour.

All of us seem fascinated by moral issues. Matters of life and death, justice, sexual expression, relationships, work, the environment, social and political organization and responsibilities are heated topics in debate. Such questions affect us individually and collectively. They are not only theoretical questions; they are an integral part of how we live together and how we order our social life. Morality matters. Moral philosophy and ethics can play a key role in clarifying and directing our thought and action.

RELIGION AND ETHICS

The major world religions offer accounts of the nature of the world, divine being, immanence and transcendence. They also describe the nature of humanity, how women and men ought to live, as well as the basis and rationale for ethical behaviour. It is important to explore briefly some of the main ethical teachings of the major world religions and to assess the degree of common ground and fundamental difference.

JUDAISM

Ethics and religion cannot be separated in historic Judaism. Judaism is a religion with a very practical emphasis. Jews are meant to live so as to fulfil the command of being holy by walking in God's ways. Whether Reformed, Liberal or Orthodox, there is a concrete, applied way of life, which does not separate the religious from the criminal, civil and moral law. There is no separate ethic. To be a good Jew is to follow the Jewish law (*Halakhah*). This is Torah-based and finds expression in the Ten Commandments and the summary of the law in Leviticus 19:18 and Deuteronomy 6:5: to love the Lord your God with all your heart and with all your soul and with all your strength and to love your neighbour as yourself.

Obviously how the law is to be applied has been codified by the rabbis of the *Mishnah* and *Talmud*. This application is a dynamic process as society's questions change and develop. However, at the heart of such application of the law are the command to be holy as God is holy and a respect for others founded on our having been created in the image of God. While the Bible and *Talmud* contain much ethical teaching, there is no worked-out moral system. Hillel summed up the importance of respect for others and the practical application of Judaism in his famous dictum, 'What you dislike don't do to others; that is the whole Torah' (B. T. Shabbat 31a).

CHRISTIANITY

In common with Judaism, Christianity bases morality on the nature of God and the nature of human beings, made in God's image. God not only created humanity, but also entered into a series of covenant relationships with human beings. In these covenants, God commanded certain moral behaviour and condemned the breaking of his law and commands. The Old Testament contains much specific moral teaching and warns of the consequences of failing to obey that teaching.

Christians claim that in the incarnation of Jesus Christ God incarnated how humans should live in harmony and obedience with God and with each other. The positive expression of Hillel's Golden Rule, the Sermon on the Mount in Matthew 5 and the great commandment (to love one another as Christ loved) are the heart of the specific moral teaching of Jesus. However, the New Testament is concerned to encourage Christians to be imitators of Christ and to incarnate the values of Jesus. More specifically, the saving work of Christ is understood to provide both the motivation and that which is necessary to enable a person to incarnate these values. The crucifixion and resurrection of Christ are, therefore, central to Christian ethical reflection, in that the resulting reconciliation of humans to God has immediate and far-reaching ethical implications. Not only are those within the redeemed community (the kingdom of God) stimulated to imitate God (Matt. 5:48) and bear witness to their new relationships, but, by virtue of their reconciled status, they now have access to supernatural assistance (the power of the Holy Spirit) in their struggle to overcome sin and live the moral life.

Different expressions of Christianity have framed different emphases in ethical teaching, stressing not only the Bible, but also natural law, common grace, tradition and the role of the church and the guidance and direction of the Holy Spirit. Christians are to live as salt and light in the world.

ISLAM

The ultimate sources of Islamic ethics lie in the Qur'an and in the life and teaching of the Prophet, Muhammad, collectively called the *Sunnah*. Where it deals with what we ought to do, the focus is on the moral authority and will of Allah. The moral code is grounded on the divine will, so is open to rational understanding. There is a moral grounding to human action and an ethical conscience making humanity aware of responsibilities to God and society.

The Muslim community is the context through which the Qur'anic ideals and values are translated to the social level. In the Muslim polity, all of life is to be regulated and in conformity with the will of Allah. This requires regular prayer, fasting, pilgrimage and charitable giving. Economic, scientific, marriage and family, legal, social and political relationships and structures are integrated with the ritual practice of Islamic faith. There is no separation of ethics and religion. Interpreting and applying the tradition and scriptures is the role of the Imam (priest), especially among the Shiʿa.

There are different traditions within Islam, including Sufism with its greater emphasis on personal, mystical union with God. However, there is a consistent moral framework and set of values at the heart of the Muslim faith.

BUDDHISM

The meditative practices of Buddhists are means of reaching tranquillity and insight. Different countries have adopted different emphases within Buddhism, but all are concerned with impermanence, suffering and the death of the ego or self.

At the heart of the ethical perspectives lie the Four Noble Truths and the Noble Eightfold Path. The Noble Truths deal with truth, origin, cessation and how to end suffering through the Noble Eightfold Path. This deals with right understanding, thinking, speech, bodily action, livelihood, effort, mindfulness and concentration. This is a combination of wisdom, ethical conduct and mental training. Thus the Buddhist seeks to practise virtue, avoid vice, practise meditation and develop wisdom.

Essentially consequentialist, Buddhism embodies the ideal of the ultimate happiness of the individual with a social ethic for the spiritual and material well-being of humankind. Duties and obligations are fundamental, but failure is more a lack of wisdom than a matter of sin or guilt. Buddhism is essentially humanistic, with a strong sense of reverence for all of life. Morality is simply a means to *nirvana*, which is the end of desire. To that end the abstention from killing, harming living creatures, stealing, wrongful sensual pleasures, lying and intoxicants are basic requirements for living a good life and establishing a good community.

HINDUISM

Within Hinduism, the social and moral order is part of the natural order. The highest good is identified with the total harmony of the cosmic or natural order. The practice of religious rites and observances is convergent with the ethical life. Together these help fulfil the natural order of harmony. The ultimate Hindu authority rests in the *Vedas*, the canonical collection of sacred texts. These recount principles which are embodied in the gods. They are the models for human conduct and behaviour.

Society is divided into different classes, each of which fulfils specific roles in religion and instruction, defence, agriculture and economic life and menial labour. Many Vedic hymns express the ethical values and moral ideals required of human beings. Hindus believe that life is a progression through stages, each requiring a particular code of conduct. These culminate in renunciation, final liberation and the shedding of egoistic and altruistic tendencies. Duty (*dharma*) maintains and gives order to reality, nature, society and the individual. Often this is expressed in laws, social and moral regulations for each group. *Karma* refers to action and effects, which culminate in rebirth.

Different emphases within Hinduism embody ascetic, mystical and ritual practices, yet retain some central notions of self-restraint, self-sacrifice and compassion. Hindu ethics are holistic, naturalistic and self-denying.

CONFUCIANISM

Confucianism is more an outlook and embodiment of patterns of living than a religion with specific rites and rituals. For Confucians, humanity is social. 'The Way' is a blend of public, objective guidance and the physical realization of that as part of the human system. The ideas of ritual and humanity are closely aligned and cover etiquette, manners, propriety and human conventions. There is little sense of moral prescription in Confucianism; rather people are to engage in proper action to fulfil their social roles. There are Five Relationships: Lord and retainer; father and son; older and younger brother; husband and wife; and friend and friend. These relationships provide a sequence for the moral priorities of life, requiring respect and obedience. Morality is a social rather than an individual matter and it is more a question of how we fulfil our social roles and relationships than a propounding of a set of rules or principles.

Different Asian nations have adapted and applied the teaching of Confucius in different ways, blending cultural and traditional perspectives to give unique emphasis to particular relationships.

RELIGION AND SECULARIZATION

Part of what is called postmodernism is a shift away from religion as the base and ultimate reference point for ethics towards a more relativistic, humanistic and individualistic moral perspective. Postmodernists are sceptical of overarching explanations (metanarratives) and celebrate difference in outlooks, histories and moralities. This attitude leaves individuals and societies without much help in coping with conflicts between moral perspectives. A plea for tolerance does not really help in the framing of laws, practices and social norms in relation to disputed moral areas.

This has led religions to a twofold approach. Each religion seeks to practise and teach its particular perspective, thus enabling its followers to live out their religion and its ethical way of life. This may act as a challenge and attract others to emulate and participate in it. Part of such an expression of a particular religious life is often a proclamation of what is important in what humans believe and how they live. Such a prophetic challenge offers a critique of secular and alternative moral systems and practices as well as an alternative ethical outlook.

At the same time, many religions believe that they have a responsibility to work with those of other or no faiths to maximize human flourishing and limit human harm. The restraint of evil and the reinforcement of good are regarded as a vital part of the practice of many religions, either as a good thing in itself or as a means of moving towards a more religiously based society.

Such strategies require some account of common ground, especially in understandings of what it means to be human, human harm and flourishing and the good life.

RELIGION AND ETHICS IN THE MODERN WORLD

At the heart of the debate over religion and ethics are questions of objectivity, law, human nature, nature itself and the common good. Religion and ethical systems argue over whether ethics is grounded on some objective source or divine command and will which is beyond the purely and exclusively human, or whether morality is purely a human construct. The answer given makes a fundamental difference to ethics, especially to our approach to moral conflict and disagreement.

Law and morality are not the same, if only because we can always ask whether or not a particular law is ethical. However, morality is expressed to some degree in law and the important question of how far we can legislate for morality is important. Is it appropriate for a religion or state to require certain moral practices and to enforce that requirement through law?

All religions and philosophies are based on some kind of account of what it means to be human. In moral terms, this deals with human happiness, flourishing, harm and destiny. Discussions about the anthropology and expressions of human nature clarify areas of agreement and difference and point to ways to deal with fundamental divergence.

Human relationship with and responsibility for nature and the cosmos as a whole is an important part of ethical and religious life and perspectives. Common concerns and strategies may well emerge and enable plural ethical views and religions to live and work harmoniously together.

Living in a pluralist world, facing the extraordinary global ethical issues of justice, peace, environment, social and family ordering and issues of technology, medical science and the host of moral questions raised by humans relating to each other and to their environment, requires that we develop a strategy for coping with moral disagreement. One way to aid discussion is to contemplate the common ground between religions and between religion and ethical philosophies. Values of respect, dignity, truth, the sanctity of life, property and belonging, human flourishing and human harm offer some hope that we can at least agree on a framework of moral values by which to address moral problems.

While religion and ethics are not entirely synonymous, they are closely and intimately related.

BIBLIOGRAPHY

D. Brown, *All Their Splendour: World Faiths the Way to Community* (London, 1982); D. Z. Phillips (ed.), *Religion and Morality* (London, 1996); J. Runzo (ed.), *Ethics Religion and the Good Society: New Directions in a Pluralistic World* (Louisville, 1992); P. Singer (ed.), *A Companion to Ethics* (Oxford, 1993); N. Smart, *The World's Religions* (Cambridge, [2]1998).

E. D. Cook

RELIGION AND FEMINISM

Three identifiable tendencies govern contemporary feminist discourse on religion. Within each of these exists a multiplicity of approaches and positions. The first tendency is exemplified in the reformist stance of those who continue the work of first-wave liberal feminism by focusing on issues of equality and exposing the sexism of their respective traditions. These feminists are critically affirmative of the central doctrines and/or teachings of their respective faiths and have made it their task to fight for reform within their traditions by concentrating on issues such as inclusive language and concepts, women's ordination and so on. The second tendency reflects the more complex and varied nature of second-wave feminism. During the 1970s, change occurred in one important aspect of feminist analysis and this was highlighted in a number of significant publications that focused on the sex-equality/sex-difference issue. Thus second-wave feminism began to grapple with the differences of opinion within the movement regarding the issue of sex-equality/difference/sameness, and many began to postulate a feminist perspective derived from women's varied experiences of subordination and, for some, biology. The third tendency emerged out of second-wave feminism and is associated with radical feminism. Radical feminism (e.g. Charlene Spretnak) celebrates gender difference and emphasizes the need to construct a post-patriarchal feminist spirituality.

As feminists from the Judeo-Christian tradition sought to develop a clearer understanding of the formation of male/female identity and relationships and to interpret Scripture and tradition in the light of women's experience, the need for a distinctive feminist perspective in theology was highlighted. It is argued that a feminist perspective or a woman's viewpoint will enable us to see what is wrong with male-defined notions of God, the self and creation and to correct them. For example, it is claimed that the historical roots of sexism, environmental exploitation and somatophobia (denigration of the body) in the Western tradition can be traced to both Hebraic and Hellenistic philosophic thought forms and a dualistic worldview that is based upon an essentially male perception of reality. Thus the biblical stress on divine sovereignty and transcendence is seen to place God beyond and above the world in a way that neglects the intrinsic interdependence and interrelatedness of God, humanity and the rest of creation. Similarly, the radical separation of the mind from the body in Platonic thought is viewed as having culminated in the somatophobic and world-denying spirituality of patriarchal religion.

Contemporary feminism, whether first, second or third wave, is overwhelmingly influenced by insights drawn from the ecological feminist analysis of the theological and philosophical constructs that contribute to the oppression of both women and nature. Since the 1970s, the relationship between the structures of social domination and the domination of nature has come to be a central theme in much contemporary feminist discourse. Thus the feminist concern for gender has come to be successfully interwoven with the more widespread concern for the environment, as exemplified in the emergence of the ecofeminist movement. Under the umbrella of ecofeminism, again, there are many varied approaches and positions.

However, underpinning much contemporary feminist analysis of religion is a systematic critique of dualism. Historically, it is claimed, patriarchal religions have deemed superior that which is associated with the mind as against the body. In Christian thought, for example, Augustine identified the image of God (*imago dei*) with the mind rather than the body; the mind in turn was held to be more manifest in men than in women. Influenced by this critique, feminists from other traditions, such as Islam (e.g. F. Berktay), point to the way in which the subjugation of females by males is justified on the grounds that reason, order or the godly principle is represented by the male element while the female element represents desire, chaos and the devil – that is, all that needs to be controlled. Hence, within the thought forms of both Western and Eastern religions there is seen to be a tendency towards placing greater value upon that which is associated more strongly with the mind. In so doing, those religions have subsequently placed spirit, reason and culture over against that which is traditionally construed as their opposite (matter, emotion and nature) thus creating a subject–object, value-hierarchical dualism within male–female, culture–nature and God–world relationships.

During the 1990s, the impact of the postmodernist deconstruction of 'modernist totalizing and foundationalist discourse' on feminist thought was reflected in the innovative ways in which theologians such as Rosemary Radford Ruether and Sallie McFague have attempted a radical reconstruction of Christian theology. This task has been undertaken with a view to developing alternative holistic theocosmologies that, it is argued, will help to bring about necessary change in the behaviour of human beings towards both particular others and the ecosystem as a whole. Under the umbrella of the ecological feminist movement, the ideas of these feminists have been brought together over the last two decades in a number of significant publications, such as *Ecofeminism and the Sacred*, edited by C. J. Adams, and *Reweaving the World*, edited by I. Diamond and G. F. Orenstein. In these works it is claimed that an adequate feminist position cannot be achieved without its being informed by ecological insights, specifically women–nature insights. It is argued that these are attained by focusing attention on the connections between the twin oppressions of women and nature. Similarly, an adequate environmental philosophy needs to be informed by ecofeminist insights because these show the way in which the domination of nature by humanity is rooted in the patriarchal worldview, a worldview justifying the domination of women. The broad appeal of this approach lies also in the multicultural stance of its analysis of these women–nature connections, in that it incorporates the inextricable interconnections between all systems of social domination, such as racism, classism, imperialism, sexism and ageism. Hence, under the umbrella of ecofeminism exist a plurality of positions which are united by a commitment, on the one hand, to exposing and eliminating male-gender bias wherever it occurs and, on the other, to underscoring the importance of recognizing the offending dualisms of patriarchal religion.

The task of contemporary feminist theology is twofold: to sacralize the cosmos and to reimage the divine. In so doing, some of these feminist spiritualities look to alternative voices within their own traditions; others look to long-lost pre-patriarchal sacred traditions and/or earth-based spiritualities, developing alternatives to the dominant theologies, such as the fast-growing new religious movement known as the Wicca and/or the goddess spirituality movement. These alternative spiritualities seek to rehabilitate the concept of the goddess in an attempt to 'rebalance or redefine the relationship between male/female aspects of the deity'. According to the Wicca feminists, institutional religions with their overwhelming focus on patriarchal male deities are responsible for perpetuating the repression of the feminine aspect of divine reality. For example, they point to the way in which pre-Christian spiritualities were eventually repressed and successfully demonized. Likewise, it is argued, the spiritualities of indigenous or primal cultures sharing the same earth-based focus and basic metaphysical assumptions met the same fate. For this reason, it is claimed, the feminine cannot be found in the dominant monotheistic religions but has to be sought outside this context or in a culture that historically precedes its emergence.

The force of this conceptual analysis of the dualisms that underpin the dominant Western perception of reality is reflected in the way that 'dualism' has become the term used in contemporary thought to criticize patriarchy, environmental complacency and antipathy towards physical existence.

With regard to the analysis of the 'oppressive conceptual framework' that governs what may be characterized as the Western *patriarchal spiritual dynamic*, feminists tend towards *essentialist* and/or *conceptualist* strategies. Essentialists argue that women's socialization and/or reproductive cycle make it easier for them to feel a connection with nature and, as a result, women are better suited to lead the ecological movement. Many feminists, however, find the essentialist strategy to be both damaging and dangerous to women and adhere strictly to a conceptual analysis of the overlapping oppressions of women and nature. In their works, the solution to sexism, environmental crises, racism and so on is thought to lie instead in a total change in the way in which we think about the self, divine reality and the ecosystem.

Nevertheless, all spiritual feminisms have in common the twofold aim of (1) seeking a unitary view of the divine, the self and creation and (2) highlighting the importance of a sacramental and unitary view of the cosmos with respect to environmental ethics. Hence the very nature of the methodology employed by feminism means that it is essentially *holistic* in intention.

These varied feminist perspectives have been further influenced by insights drawn from postmodern science, which has provided contemporary feminist analysis with an alternative lens through which to view the nature of reality. Emerging from postmodern science is a holistic view of the universe, in which matter is seen to be a form of energy capable of modification and transformation. Hence, contrary to the mechanistic view of the world, individual objects, such as stars or stones, are all bundles of energy that, contrary to earlier theory, are not inert, lifeless pieces of matter but living energies. Therefore, it is argued, it makes sense to perceive the material world as a living universe wherein everything, including God, is interconnected, interrelated and in a continual process of becoming. According to feminist analysis, postmodern science offers a view of reality that is compatible with a core element of both women's and indigenous or primal cultures' experience: that is, an intuitive grasp of the underlying unity, diversity and harmony of reality. The universe is thus construed in terms of an organic whole, in which everything is seen to be of equal worth in the sense of having an intrinsic value of its own. Enriched with this new perceptual lens, contemporary feminism offers a new theological paradigm from which to challenge and critique traditional religious concepts.

With regard to the dual task of sacralizing the cosmos and reimaging the divine, each of these feminist spiritualities suggests that it is necessary to abandon classical notions of divine transcendence that depict God as a reality standing over and against creation. Rather, God/Goddess or divine creativity in or with the creation is perceived to be inherently immanent; hence divine reality is not seen to be concentrated in 'some distant seat of power, or transcendent sky God'. From this perspective, divine transcendence is perceived in terms of the *sacred whole*, which in turn expresses ongoing regeneration within the cycles of nature and contains the mystery of diversity within unity.

Coupled with this tendency towards pantheism or panentheism in configuring the God–world relationship is the rise of a reductive materialism with regard to the concept of the self. Thus these contemporary theologies seek to overcome both the God–world dualism of traditional religions and what they consider to be the world denying tendencies that are believed to stem from the traditional body–soul dualism and from notions of life after death.

BIBLIOGRAPHY

C. A. Adams (ed.), *Ecofeminism and the Sacred* (New York, [2]1994); F. Berktay, *Women and Religion* (London, Montreal and New York, 1998); I. Diamond and G. F. Orenstein, *Reweaving the World* (San Francisco, 1990); A. Loades (ed.), *Feminist Theology: A Reader* (London and Louisville, KY, 1990); G. McCulloch, *The Deconstruction of Dualism in Theology: With Special Reference to Ecofeminist Theology and New Age Spirituality* (Carlisle, 2001); C. Spretnak (ed.), *The Politics of Women's Spirituality* (New York, 1982).

G. McCulloch

RELIGION AND GLOBALIZATION

If the 'global village' has become a cliché it is because Marshall McLuhan was right, at least in this respect: the world is indeed increasingly becoming a single place. Those electronic technologies of communication and information of which he wrote are now found everywhere, and they enable almost instantaneous contact over vast distances. Indeed, the new technologies have expanded far beyond McLuhan's dreams, to include cyberspace, virtual reality and electronic commerce. On the other hand, while they do permit rapid communication, there is a growing gap between those who can benefit from access and those who are effectively switched off. The global village is not utopia.

Globalization refers most commonly to an economic process in which the global system has become the reference point for transactions. In this and several other respects categories such as nation, state and region have become less significant by comparison. Those who enthuse about globalization tend to see it as the motor of economic growth for the twenty-first century. But it also draws people into new kinds of relationships, not only in new trading areas, but within transnational political and cultural arrangements as well. Indeed, the culture of globalization is very much a consumer culture, fostered by mass-media advertising and transnational electronic commerce. Coca-Colonization, Disneyization, McDonalds and the Nike swoosh are powerful symbols of such global consumerism.

Whatever the direct cause, then, people once separate and isolated from each other are drawn together into frequent and almost necessary contact. It is hard not to know about Mickey Mouse or Big Macs. On the one hand, this provides new opportunities for mutual understanding and cooperation, a common transnational context for activity. It may mean, for instance, that peoples across the world may be more united against a common foe, such as industrial pollution and environmental degradation. Roland Robertson argues that this positive side of globalization includes the possibility of shared global themes such as 'person-planet', which puts the mutually dependent health of each person on an almost sacred plane. But on the other hand, fresh fuel for conflict may be furnished by unfamiliar contacts. Cultures may clash, as in the celebrated case of the Islamic *fatwa* that threatened the life of Indian-British novelist Salman Rushdie in the 1990s. Some differences are deepened in globalizing situations, as basic disagreements divide.

Ben Barber's striking thesis is that globalization spells 'Jihad vs McWorld': the rise of both consumerist economic imperialism that brings greater homogeneity in its wake, and cultural heterogeneity that stresses distinctive identities and particularities. Similarly, Samuel Huntington warns that globalization involves an inevitable 'clash of civilizations' in which increased culture contact sparks conflict between incommensurate belief systems and practices. But Barber misses the point that a religious – particularly Christian – impetus is already involved in globalization, and thus the dichotomy is less stark than he suggests. And Huntington, in his effort to warn of the dangers of what is essentially Islamic fundamentalism, fails to note the hazards attending some Christian fundamentalisms in the West. The clashes, however, are real enough. The problem is partly one of meaning: being confronted with another way of doing things or of seeing the world is disturbing if you previously thought of yours as the right or only way. But it is also an issue of power, as Peter Beyer shows.

While cultural identities may seem to be threatened by globalization, asserting exclusive and particularistic identity may also be the means of striving for or asserting power. To pronounce a *fatwa* is to show muscle in a globalizing world, not to attack globalization itself. Neither does *Gush Emunim*, the Jewish 'faithful bloc', attack globalization itself when it appeals to a sacred right to 'all' of Israel. But globalization is part of the perceived threat. In some countries, such as Palestine or the former Yugoslavia, large-scale bloodshed has marked the expression of neo-tribal rivalries. In others, such as Singapore or Canada, the violent assertion of particularistic identities has largely been held in check by historical circumstances and multiculturalist policies. These factors may still create difficulties for some religious minorities, however. Multiculturalism may be erected not on a basis of justice, but in relation to linguistic or ethnic groups, so that true tolerance of all is not in fact permitted.

Religion thus enters the debates over globalization, most often through discussions of fundamentalisms, but also through optimistic notions of harmonious ecumenism. Either way, much scope for misunderstanding exists, particularly as all too often those engaging in the debate either know little about religion, or come to its study with misleading or inadequate assumptions, or both. So, while it may be gratifying to those who recognize religion's importance to see attention being paid to it, the study of religion and globalization calls for some fresh and creative approaches. Such approaches nevertheless have to be keyed into existing analyses, of which three are especially significant. One asks what is revealed by global fundamentalist and evangelical movements; a second explores the religious-historical background to globalization; and a third inquires about the interaction between religion and consumer cultures.

The case of Salman Rushdie is a significant one, not least because it points up ways in which representatives of organized religion, in this case Islam, experience what they feel as abrasive culture contact with the West, particularly from someone they see as an apostate from their midst. The resulting *fatwa*, with its roots in a perspective that does not distinguish, as Westerners usually do, between 'religious' and 'state' activity, has consequences in distant parts of the world, and not only for Rushdie himself. These Muslims understandably object that the price demanded for inclusion in the global system is too high. Why should they deny who they are and what they believe in face of globalizing pressure? Events like this serve to accentuate difference, both in the aggressive assertion of Muslim cultural identities and in the reinforcement of stereotypical views of 'Islamic terrorists', which are then also gratuitously transferred by association to Muslim minorities in Europe and North America.

One additional lesson from this is that 'Islam' is far from monolithic, and that each particular Muslim group is located in a different way in globalizing situations. Certain Iranian Shi'ite Muslims may be fundamentalists but many other followers of Islam are not. To take a parallel example, many Christian groups would be justifiably dismayed to be associated with violence and murder at anti-abortion clinics. But other issues lie beyond these. Not only is the particular religious identity of Muslims (or Sikhs, or Hindus, or Jews, or Christians) potentially relativized by globalization; religious language itself is marginalized. It becomes harder to communicate using religious terms. To try to appeal to arguments deriving from a specific religious position is difficult in a world where tolerance is increasingly understood as a presumption of worth in any and all views different from one's own. The fact that such a view of tolerance is ultimately untenable, logically speaking, does not preclude it having powerful social effects where it is popularly held. These constraints on religious communication arise, paradoxically, from a sense of too much openness, from the feeling that there may be more than one permissible or possible religious way. When Gilles Kepel suggests that fundamentalisms 'have a singular capacity to reveal the ills of society', Zygmunt Bauman takes this to mean that society's sense of dis-ease arises from having too many choices. Relativism and uncertainty are counteracted with absolutism and certitude. These responses, claims Bauman, characterize those 'on the receiving end of globalization'.

Not surprisingly, then, it seems to be those religious groups that are most 'conservative' which experience growth despite – and sometimes perhaps because of – globalization. This growth can be related to the hegemony of once-'Christian' countries which – apart from Japan – own or control most productive and resource wealth in the world. Pat Robertson's American religious broadcasting network and Paul Yonggi Cho's Korean megachurch would be obvious examples. But other much more marginalized groups may wield power resulting from growth, as witness the capacity of African Anglican churches to push back the liberalizing agendas originating in the USA at the 1998 Lambeth conference in England. They may also have an influence that is hidden from globally dominant anglophones, as in the palpable 'globalization from below' (the term is Richard Falk's) evidenced in the burgeoning hispanic and Portuguese-speaking Pentecostal churches of Latin America. In both cases, distant connections with the Western world exist (with the UK and the USA respectively), but also, in both cases, the churches are independent and in most meaningful senses indigenous. The language barrier may limit the influence outside Latin America of its exuberant evangelicals, but the same cannot be said for the Africans, whose more traditional views are clearly irritants to their co-religionists from much wealthier countries.

All this connects with the second issue, the historical backgrounds to globalization. World religions have global aspects almost by definition. Islam and Christianity in particular contain within themselves expansionist imperatives, which have sometimes also been intertwined with territorial claims. Even where there is no territorial agenda, Christians are constrained by Jesus' call to 'go into all the world to preach the gospel', and by his reminder that it was because 'God loved the world so much' that he himself had been sent. If the rise of capitalism can be related in part to certain Protestant emphases on thrift and hard work within callings, perhaps some openness to the world (a willingness to travel and to be exposed to other cultures for the sake of the gospel), now expressed as globalization, could also be traced to similar sources. Such ideas find concrete expression in the experience of global Christian missions that began in the seventeenth century with Spanish, French and Portuguese Catholics, and reached their anglophone Protestant peak in the late nineteenth and early twentieth centuries, first under British and then under Canadian and American leadership. In the later twentieth century the flows began to reverse, as Africans, East Asians and Latin Americans brought the same gospel to an increasingly 'decadent West'. The nineteenth-century connections of missions with colonialism are complex, but it has to be said that much marxist invective against flag-waving imperialism or 'cross-and-capital' exploitation is far off the mark. Evidence abounds of the rapid indigenization of Christianity in 'foreign fields' and of mission-based opposition to economic adventuring, military appropriation of native lands and the abuse or enslavement of native peoples. Globalization by these means does not have to be read negatively.

If care must be taken in considering the historical background to religion and globalization, the same surely holds for the present as well. Capitalist expansionism is as unavoidable an aspect of the world in the age of Disney and McDonalds as in the age of Darwin and Marx. Capitalism did contribute to the globalizing of Christianity, though not necessarily from economic motives. Western ways of life did often pass as 'Christian' ones, but they were as frequently dropped by missionaries, or replaced by local substitutes. Today, as globalization intensifies, attention to such issues also raises acute questions. The interaction of religious believers and organizations with consumer cultures is the third key area of consideration.

The option of ignoring consumer cultures is available only in very remote and inaccessible areas and thus for most purposes can be discounted. Consumerism is being globalized, using communications media, as the vital lubricant to the whole global system. It supports some forms of fundamentalist Christianity, especially via pernicious 'prosperity doctrines' (which also reveal their proponents as being far from economic underdogs, an impression given by Kepel). Neither the transnational practices of corporations nor those of political power blocs could last for long without the constant stimulation of insatiable demand for products and services. Consumerism attempts to encourage induced wants, which it does very successfully, but by varying means, in both richer and poorer parts of the world. By definition, however, those needs can never be satisified. The obvious downside in the overdeveloped world – which also inevitably spreads elsewhere – is in growing risks to the environment and indeed to the sustainability of the planet. In the under-developed world, as Elizabeth Cardova puts it, 'Cultural dependency means that people in our country have to brush their teeth three times a day even if they don't have anything to eat.'

All religious traditions encounter consumer cultures, but with varying degrees of conflict and struggle. Some Muslim groups react negatively to the spread of mass-media allurements to lifestyles that could corrode conventional customs and beliefs, while simultaneously some Christian agencies produce their own TV and music shows that closely resemble the ones proscribed by Islam. As consumer cultures become more entrenched and universal, so they increasingly compete with explicitly religious orientations to life. For while most religions have some concern with materiality and bodily existence, they, like consumerism, also exhibit preoccupations with felt desires beyond the satisfaction of mere biological needs. In the case of Christian commitments, these include strong teachings both about how all should have 'enough' to lead fulfilling lives and how those with 'enough' should be content. The basic contradiction with consumerism is palpable. In a globalizing world the cross may turn out to have more in common with the crescent than with the swoosh or the golden arches.

BIBLIOGRAPHY

B. Barber, *Jihad vs McWorld* (New York, 1996); Z. Bauman, *Globalization: The Human Consequences* (Cambridge and New York, 1998); P. Beyer, *Religion and Globalization* (London, 1994); R. Falk, *On Humane Governance: Towards a New Global Politics* (Philadelphia, PA, 1995); S. Huntington, *The Clash of Civilizations* (New York, 1996); O. Kalu and M. Hutchinson (eds.), *Global Faith: Essays on Evangelicalism and Globalization* (Sydney, NSW, 1998); G. Kepel, *The Revenge of God* (Cambridge, 1994).

D. Lyon

RELIGION AND HUMAN RIGHTS

A human right is an entitlement that a person has simply by virtue of being human. The term is a twentieth-century one which has acquired a particular status in international law since 1945. However, the idea has many connections with the older concept of natural rights, fashionable in the seventeenth and eighteenth centuries and derived from natural law.

John Locke in particular used the idea of theologically derived natural rights of life, liberty and property to explain the limits to the powers of the sovereign and to develop a concept of trusteeship which both justified revolution and laid the foundations for modern democratic governance (*Two Treatises on Government*, 1690). Such ideas in turn inspired claims of inalienable rights in the great constitutional documents of the period, like the Virginia Declaration of Rights (1776), the French revolutionary Declaration of the Rights of Man and of the Citizen (1789) and the United States Bill of Rights (1791).

Positivist critics argued that rights are descriptive, not prescriptive, and pointed to the absence of a lawmaker (a sovereign) as a source for natural rights. Bentham wrote: 'from real laws come real rights; but from imaginary laws, from laws of nature, come imaginary rights ... Natural Rights is simple nonsense, natural and imprescriptible rights, rhetorical nonsense, nonsense on stilts.' From the late eighteenth century onwards the sovereignty of states came to be seen as the dominant source of law, rather than natural law. Human rights would only re-emerge in the twentieth century as a by-product of international concern to limit the disastrous consequences of state sovereignty during two world wars. The positivist objections about the source of rights have been largely bypassed by the modern human rights movement through the recognition of human rights in multilateral treaties, which give a distinct *legal* basis for the rights claimed through the consent of the signatory states.

The United Nations has been concerned with human rights since its formation: the Preamble to the UN Charter (1945) reaffirmed faith in fundamental human rights and the Universal Declaration of Human Rights was adopted by the General Assembly in 1948. Strictly the Declaration is not legally enforceable, although some scholars assert that it has become part of customary international law and so is binding on new states created since 1948, irrespective of their consent. More specific binding multilateral treaties have been drawn up by the UN, notably the International Covenant on Civil and Political Rights and the International Covenant on Economic, Social and Cultural Rights, both of which came into force in 1976.

The earliest recognition of human rights in international law came in treaties protecting minorities from religious persecution, such as the Treaty of Westphalia, 1648. Although international law was traditionally concerned with the rights and duties of states, growing recognition of duties owed by states towards individuals came with a series of treaties confirming the abolition of slavery in the nineteenth and early twentieth centuries. It was, however, a conceptual leap from such agreements to establishing the international legal machinery by which an individual could bring a human rights complaint against a state. This was first achieved with the right of individual petition under the European Convention on Human Rights and Fundamental Freedoms (1950). The system was at first voluntary, but since 1998 (the coming into force of the Eleventh Protocol to the Convention) is now binding on all member states. The reformed Convention system allows more than 300 million inhabitants of some forty states across virtually the entire continent of Europe to petition the court at Strasbourg. (A Commission which previously existed to sift complaints was fused with the Court under the 1998 reforms.) The European Convention has been followed by other continental systems of Human Rights protection: the African Charter on Human and People's Rights and the American Convention on Human Rights.

Many countries recognize the European Convention as a source of law superior to domestic law and enforceable through their domestic courts also. Until recently the position in Britain reflected the tradition of parliamentary supremacy, which subordinated the courts to Parliament. This was held by some commentators to imply that meaningful human rights protection could never be adopted without more fundamental constitutional change limiting the power of the legislature. The courts in turn gave the European Convention only a limited role, in developing United Kingdom law where legislation was unclear or ambiguous and, more recently, in reforming the common law. Nevertheless, since the mid-1970s there has been a substantial debate about the merits of incorporating the European Convention into British law. The Blair administration, in its 1997 White Paper *Rights Brought Home*, overcame the historic distrust of many in the Labour Party towards the judiciary by proposing a novel form of incorporation which seeks to preserve parliamentary supremacy. The Human Rights Act 1998 (which came into force in October 2000) will require the courts wherever possible to give a Convention-friendly reading to legislation and to refer to the Strasbourg case-law on the meaning of Convention rights. This 'interpretative' approach (modelled on the New Zealand Bill of Rights Act 1990) allows freedom to Parliament to legislate contrary to the Convention when it chooses to do so. Other provisions require ministers introducing legislation to vet it for compliance with the Convention and to make an accompanying statement. Where legislation conflicts with the Convention and cannot be interpreted to comply, the higher courts can make a 'declaration of incompatibility' which, although it does not directly assist the litigant concerned, may allow for speedy reform of the law. A final feature of note is that all public authorities (such as the police, government departments and councils) will be under a duty not to act in contravention of a person's Convention rights. The Act is primarily intended as a protection for individuals against state institutions, and considerable uncertainty surrounds the question of whether the courts could use it to adjudicate between private individuals or against non-state bodies (i.e. with reference to 'horizontal' rights).

SOME OBJECTIONS

The abandonment of natural rights in the Enlightenment era has left a theoretical deficit, with modern writers struggling to explain why human rights should be treated as more fundamental than any other aspect of law. The common assertion that human rights are derived from the common equality of all people faces the difficulty that both the diversity of human societies and the oppression of some groups (for example, women) is so widespread as to appear natural. The latter point can be overcome if it is accepted that it is human dignity and potential, not factual equality, which ground the entitlement to human rights. One of the more celebrated contemporary attempts to provide a theoretical basis is Alan Gewirth's derivation of human rights from inherent human dignity, using the 'Principle of Generic Consistency' to show that purposive human agents must logically accept that everyone has the same rights as themselves to freedom and well-being (A. Gewirth, 'The Epistemology of Human Rights', *SPP* 1, 1984, pp. 1–24).

Many commentators point to the increasingly ambitious claims made for human rights. From the 'first generation' civil and political rights (such as freedom of speech, freedom from arbitrary arrest, freedom of religion), protection has now moved on to social and economic rights (e.g. housing, education and employment) and third-generation rights (e.g. a right to a clean environment). International protection of these rights also varies considerably in substance and detail, particularly in the scope of the exceptions permitted under various treaties. These differences tend to undercut idealistic claims about the universal nature of human rights.

Diversity is often also cited by critics of the 'universalism' of human rights who point to the variable and contingent scope of the rights protected, both over time and in substance. At the extreme, such criticisms may treat human rights as a Western product of the Judeo-Christian tradition which has little relevance to the East (there is as yet no regional system of human rights protection in Asia). Alternatively, human rights are dismissed by some leftist writers (especially Marxists and members of the Critical Legal Studies movement) as a bourgeois liberal construct which, wittingly or not, distracts attention from economic and social inequalities.

A further line of criticism concerns clashing rights. Exponents commonly claim protection for human rights in absolute or at least strong terms: protection of free speech should take priority over the sensitivities of people who may encounter ideas they find offensive, for example. However, many rights conflict when pursued to their full potential: free speech and privacy in the case of investigative journalism; free speech and freedom of religion in the case of blasphemy; equality rights with freedom of religion (ordination of women); bodily autonomy with rights of the unborn (abortion); property and personal freedom (slavery); and so on. Moreover, the exercise of some rights may contain an internal inconsistency: should a political party which intends to abolish elections once in office and to restrict the free speech of its opponents be able to shelter behind rights which it does not believe in to seek election? Should terrorists be allowed free speech? All of these issues are routinely handled at the legal level by delineating the extent of the right and giving priority in effect to one right over another, depending on the historical, cultural and social context. Pragmatic solutions of this type, however, suggest that human rights are contingent, not universal, absolute and unchanging.

FREEDOM OF RELIGION

The religious conflict of the sixteenth and seventeenth centuries led to the first attempts to protect religious liberty. The Treaty of Westphalia of 1648, which brought to an end the Thirty Years War, gave protections to Protestant and Catholic minorities in different parts of Germany. In 1689 John Locke published his *Letter Concerning Toleration* to argue both the wrongness and the ineffectiveness of state religious persecution. In Britain legislation prohibiting Catholics, Jews and Nonconformists from worshipping and from participating in various aspects of public life was progressively relaxed from the Glorious Revolution (1689) into the nineteenth century.

Freedom of religion is one of the 'first generation' civil and political rights invariably recognized in domestic Bills of Rights (including, famously, the First Amendment to the US Constitution) and international agreements. It is included in the Universal Declaration and the International Covenant on Civil and Political Rights. There is also a specific UN Declaration on the Elimination of All Forms of Intolerance of Discrimination Based on Religion or Belief (1981). Article 9 of the European Convention on Human Rights 1950 recognizes freedom of religion, thought and conscience, and to change one's religion. It also protects manifestation of one's religion, both individually and collectively, subject to limitations which the state may impose by law in the interests of democratic society, to protect interests such as public safety, public order, health or morals or the rights and freedoms of others. This provision had attracted relatively few legal challenges until a series of cases brought by Jehovah's Witnesses against Greece in the 1990s. In Britain concern about the potential for equality rights being used to override freedom of religion led Christian organizations to seek additional protection in the Human Rights Act 1998, which instructs the courts to have 'particular regard' to the importance of the latter right.

International protection of religious liberty is perhaps most obviously necessary for minorities in states where there is an official state religion. Such countries vary from those where the established church merely has certain privileges which other denominations or religions do not enjoy (as, for example, in the case of the Church of England) to those where the constitution grants a protected status to a particular religion and is grounded on its teachings (as with the Roman Catholic Church under the constitution of Eire). The practice of some Islamic countries goes a stage further in that non-Muslims or converts from Islam may face active state discrimination and persecution, be denied benefits available to the majority of the population and be subject to legal sanctions for apostasy.

However, protection may be necessary in other contexts too. Other countries (e.g. the United States, France and Australia) maintain a strict divide between the state and religion, treating belief as a private matter on which the state should remain neutral and disengaged. Although this may accord equal treatment to all religions, such purported state neutrality is not of itself a guarantee of religious liberty and can be a bar to the manifestation of religious belief. In recent decades there have been clashes, for example, over whether pupils should be permitted to pray in public schools in the United States or to wear the *hijab* in French schools. It is harder still for the state to remain 'neutral' where religious controversy arises between two private litigants: for instance, concerning religious upbringing in a child custody dispute between parents. A third model is adopted by countries which give constitutional recognition or protection to several religions (e.g. Belgium and India). While this may be a way of reconciling the differing religious and cultural communities in a new state, it does not accord protection to newly arrived religions or equality to small religious minorities.

CONCLUSION

Where freedom of religion is recognized, domestically or internationally, it is rarely if ever an absolute or unqualified right. States do not generally accord their citizens liberty to disregard laws which they may claim it would be against their conscience to keep, or to give effect to their beliefs to another person's detriment. All of this exposes an underlying tension between the philosophical basis of human rights (including freedom of religion) and the practices and beliefs of several major religions. While Liberation theologians have embraced human rights as a protection against repressive regimes, more conservative religious groups within both Christianity and Islam are troubled by the individualism and the elevation of personal autonomy implicit in much modern human rights thinking. Wherever religious belief refuses to be confined to the 'private' sphere of life and demands public action or proclamation as truth, rather than private belief, there are bound to be clashes with the state, even if it is one that grants a degree of religious toleration. Ultimately, human rights based on a public–private divide and on 'neutrality' between religions are inconsistent with the claims of those liberals often labelled as 'fundamentalists'. On the other hand, the accommodation of religion poses the greatest challenge to the contemporary human rights movement, since it presents a series of claims which cannot be captured solely within a liberal worldview.

BIBLIOGRAPHY

P. Beaumont (ed.), *Christian Perspectives on Human Rights and Legal Philosophy* (Carlisle, 1998); A. Bradney, *Religions, Rights and Laws* (Leicester, 1993); C. Evans, *Freedom of Religion under the European Convention on Human Rights* (Oxford, 2001); M. Evans, *Religious Liberty and International Law in Europe* (Cambridge, 1997); C. Hamilton, *Family, Law and Religion* (London, 1995); D. Harris, M. O'Boyle and C. Warbrick, *The Law of the European Convention on Human Rights* (London, 1985); J. Horton and S. Mendus (eds.), *John Locke: A Letter Concerning Toleration in Focus* (London, 1991); P. Marshall, *Their Blood Cries Out* (Texas, 1997); A. H. Robertson and J. G. Merrills, *Human Rights in the World* (Manchester, [3]1996); W. Sadurski, 'On Legal Definitions of "Religion"' (1989), 63 *ALJ* 834; P. Sieghart, *The Lawful Rights of Mankind* (Oxford, 1986); H. J. Steiner and P. Alston, *International Human Rights in Context: Law, Politics and Morals* (Oxford, 1996).

I. Leigh

RELIGION AND MEDIA

Religions have always been concerned with 'media': that is, the means by which truths are communicated. On one level, the theologies of word and sacrament, worship practices, the use of art and techniques of proclamation and meditation are all issues of 'media'. Communications media (not only the printing press but also television and the Internet) are central to the essence of the contemporary 'Information Age'.

Though religions played a formative role in the development of contemporary media, today religions and media are often hostile to each other. And yet, as the media become more and more diverse and decentralized, religions are finding that new ways are opening up to communicate their message.

THE PRESS

The first mass medium, revolutionary in its effect, was the printing press. With this technological innovation, books (not to mention pamphlets, broadsides and eventually newspapers and every other kind of information) could be mass-produced and put in the hands of everyone.

The printing press was invented in China, but in Western Europe it was turned into a communication technology for the masses because of religion. The Protestant Reformation, as Luther and other Reformers admitted, was made possible by the printing press. Both Luther's Ninety-Five Theses and his translation of the Bible could now be mass-produced.

Bible reading became the central religious act of the Reformation and eventually led to an explosion of education among all social classes. Not only men, but also women; not only the wealthy and middle classes, but also the peasants and the servants – everyone needed to be able to read the Bible. And once they could read the Bible, they could read anything. Literacy led to unprecedented social mobility and eventually to political change, as an educated citizenry came to feel more and more qualified to govern themselves. And for all of this, they needed the information that came from the media.

The early products of the printing press, which included not only books but also pamphlets and broadsides, were overwhelmingly religious, from serious works of theology and devotion to scurrilous religious satires and politically tinged religious agit-prop. In England, the early newspapers of the eighteenth century from Addison, Steele and Dr Johnson dealt with religious and moral topics, though presented with a neoclassical style and sophistication. In the United States, as Marvin Olasky has shown, the printing press, the freedom of which was insisted upon in the American Constitution, produced numerous political discussions. That being said, it is important to note that most of the American newspapers had a strong Christian component. Even the early periodicals devoted to a special topic, such as the influential art journal *The Crayon*, had a strongly theological bent. 'Of all the reading of the people three-fourths is religious,' observed Howard Kenberry as late as 1920. In his study of American journalism to that date, he concluded that 'of all the issues of the press three-fourths are theological, ethical and devotional'.

Certainly, though, the intellectual and cultural climate was changing, as the educated elite began rejecting supernatural explanations in favour of scientific materialism. The journalistic turning point was no doubt the coverage of the Scopes Trial in Dayton, Tennessee, in July 1925. This judicial hearing on a schoolteacher's right to teach Darwin's theory of evolution turned into the century's first major media event. Hundreds of 'big-city' reporters converged on the small Southern town and, using another media innovation, 'wired' their stories to their editors, stories which were printed nationwide. These stories tended to follow a common theme: modern, progressive science versus ignorant, 'backwoods' fundamentalism.

This was hardly fair; after all, the citizens of Dayton who believed in a literal creation according to Genesis were holding on to a belief that had been universal only a few years earlier. But the issue was framed by the devastating pen of the great American journalist H. L. Mencken: 'On the one side was bigotry, ignorance, hatred, superstition, every sort of blackness that the human mind is capable of. On the other side was sense.' To many religious believers, this has been the attitude of mainstream journalists ever since.

Whereas the old journalism freely blended facts and moralizing, reporting and ideology, the ideal for twentieth-century journalists was total objectivity. In line with the canons of modernism, the only truth was what could be empirically verified. As a result, reporters were trained to give just the facts, to leave out their own biases and to stick to what could be observed. This training ruled out, as a matter of principle, any references to transcendent moral principles or supernatural realities. The only things that counted as news would be observable events, economic facts and material, describable objects. Moral discourse and references to God disappeared from the newspapers.

Of course, this ideal of modernist objectivity is an illusion. The reporter chooses from a large number of possible stories and selects which facts to present, in what order and to what purpose. Even many of the early twentieth-century journalists admitted the role of their own perceptions and beliefs in shaping their stories. Still, efforts were made to compensate for the inevitable bias by, for example, writing with 'balance'; that is, quoting advocates on both sides of a controversial issue. Religious people, however, objected that their concerns were often excluded from the process, and when they were included they were often presented in a negative light.

Postmodernist journalism, coming into vogue in the 1960s, took a different stance: since bias could not be eliminated, journalists should feel free to express their biases. Since truth-claims are essentially constructions, not objective discoveries, journalism is not just about reporting; it is also about constructing. Politically engaged journalists should use their craft in a liberating way, to deconstruct existing power structures and to uphold the cause of the oppressed.

As the 'culture wars' heated up in the late

twentieth century, followers of traditional religions were thrown into conflict with the nation's cultural elite over issues such as abortion, feminism, sexual permissiveness, homosexual rights and related causes. Most members of the media, as demonstrated by a number of studies, tended to be more liberal on such issues than most others. And the graduates of postmodern journalism schools felt increasingly justified in using their power as cultural gatekeepers to shape public attitudes. Religion was again excluded, but for different reasons.

Often the bias was blatant. When hundreds of thousands of anti-abortion demonstrators marched on Washington, many newspapers showed on their front page a picture not of the marchers, but of the handful of counter-protesters holding pro-abortion signs.

Sometimes, though, the lack of attention to religion was a matter of sheer ignorance. The reporters were not religious, so they simply did not understand religion when it was presented to them. When President Nixon, at the height of the Watergate scandal, went to church in Key Biscayne, Florida, the reporters, who were stalking his every move, did so too. The pastor preached a sermon, as was his wont, on human sin and the need for forgiveness in Christ. Afterwards, the reporters mobbed the pastor, asking him if he was preaching at the president. The pastor tried to explain that the message was what he always preached and that he was not thinking of Watergate in particular; his message applied to everyone in the congregation. The next day the headlines were all about how Nixon was denounced from the pulpit for his sins.

As American journalism was growing more secular, in other parts of the world newspapers remained an important religious voice. Certainly European journalism retained part of the older tradition of 'advocacy journalism', and in the century's ideological conflicts that broke out in world wars, Holocaust and the Gulags, religious journalism often raised its voice.

To the extent that they were marginalized by the mainstream (or forcibly oppressed, in totalitarian countries) religious newspapers or crudely copied underground typescripts became a way of holding together and mobilizing particular communities of faith. For example, Zionist publications kept alive, and made possible, the hope of a Jewish state. The Islamic revolution in Iran and the Muslim revival throughout the Middle East were promoted by Islamic newspapers and underground publications. In some African states (e.g. Nigeria) Christian media vie with Muslim media.

If postmodernism accepts the reality of bias, it also opens the door for a diversity of opinions. Religious people who feel shut out of the mainstream are currently starting their own publications (much cheaper and more feasible with the advances in publishing technology), using the press once again as a medium not only to express their faith but also to engage their cultures.

ELECTRONIC MEDIA

A new phase of media opened up when a devout Christian artist with a head for science had the idea of communicating by means of electronics. Samuel Morse, a deeply religious portrait painter, invented the telegraph, a way of using electricity, wires and magnetism to transmit coded messages. On 24 May 1844, on 37 miles of line he had strung between Baltimore and Washington, he transmitted the first message by means of electronic media. Appropriately, the first words sent over the wires were taken from the Bible: 'What hath God wrought' (Num. 23:23, AV).

Before long the telegraph gave way to the telephone, and the electronic media mutated still further into radio, film, television and the Internet.

Radio was a medium made for Protestant Christianity. With radio, a purely aural medium, the word could be broadcast like seed in the field. For evangelicalism, a tradition that had pared away ritual and liturgy in favour of preaching, radio was a vehicle for direct proclamation of the word. Preachers began delivering sermons and Bible studies over the air. Before long, specialized 'radio ministries' grew up. At first, religious shows were part of radio stations' mix of programmes; later, entire radio stations devoted themselves to religion.

Radio was especially prized as an evangelism tool. Radios became so cheap that even people of poor nations could afford them, so missionaries used the medium to reach people in the remotest areas with the gospel. In the developed countries too, radio was an ideal medium for religious discourse, not just for evangelical preachers. Bishop Fulton Sheen became one of the most influential spokesmen for Catholicism, making the Catholic church palatable to a mass American audience in a country that had historically been suspicious of Rome, through his radio show in the 1930s. Another immigrant church gained a hearing in the United States with 'The Lutheran Hour', one of the earliest religious programmes, featuring the learned sermons of Walter Maier. In the UK during the Second World War the Oxford don C. S. Lewis recorded for the BBC a series of broadcasts which were later published as *Mere Christianity*, perhaps the century's single most popular and effective work of Christian apologetics.

Christianity did not do quite as well, though, with television. Certainly Bishop Sheen made the transition from radio and became a major television personality in the 1950s, and Billy Graham's evangelistic crusades became a fixture of American television. Still, the video screen worked best as a medium of entertainment rather than as a medium of devotion. Television, with some notable exceptions, was better fitted for the formation of a pop culture. Religious people again felt under siege, as the entertainment mindset put a premium on titillating viewers with images of sex, lawlessness and violence, thereby undermining traditional morality.

As the entertainment industry became the United States' biggest export, Hollywood began to have a global reach. Judging from America's television and movies, it would appear that America had no religion. To devotees of traditional religions in developing nations, American pop culture was eroding their family values and their traditional beliefs. Muslims, appalled at the pornography and moral nihilism they saw in Hollywood artefacts, began calling America 'the Great Satan'.

Some Christians tried to develop an alternative and attempted to exploit television as they had the other media. But their efforts tended to imitate the secular players. In the United States the Pentecostal evangelist Pat Robertson turned his '700 Club', a Christian talk show with news breaks, into a small media empire. Through his cable network, the Family Channel showed mostly old westerns and mysteries, with few explicitly religious shows. (The venture was eventually sold to the global media magnate Rupert Murdoch.) The fate of another talk show, 'The PTL Club', hosted by Jim Bakker, another Pentecostal preacher, brought all television evangelists into disrepute when its host was caught in a sex and financial scandal that sent him to prison.

The problem went deeper. The gospel according to television tended to become celebrity-driven and focused on what is tangible. The TV preachers' message promised health and wealth to those who believed. Their programmes were heavily political, obsessed with this world rather than the next. Their theology was experiential and emotional, minimizing doctrine and ideas. Their preaching consisted not so much of exploration of Scripture as of vividly dramatic personal testimonies of miraculous healings, spectacular conversions and spiritual battles.

With Bakker's public fall (and there were similar scandals with other video preachers at around the same time) his theology was laid bare as shallow, fraudulent and manipulative. Despite some noble efforts, the medium proved unsuitable for more substantive theology. Real Christianity requires participation in a community, not the isolating, private experience of watching television.

Media theorist Marshall McLuhan discusses how the medium tends to become the message. Communications scholar Neil Postman has argued that Judaism, Christianity and Islam are inherently religions of the word, as opposed to the image. The problem with religious television, he says, is that it opens up an image-driven frame of mind, which favours religious expressions that are immediate, sensate and as one-dimensional as icons lighting up on a screen. The word, on the other hand, promotes inwardness, depth, personal reflection and communal relationships.

Whether Postman's analysis is correct or not, it is certainly true that Hinduism, in which devotion has traditionally centred around images, has been far more successful than Christianity in the use of visual media. India has managed to develop an extensive film industry of its own, and its citizens are some of the world's most devoted filmgoers. The production of films and television series based on Hindu epics is reportedly a major factor in the current revival of Hindu nationalism.

RELIGION IN CYBERSPACE

The new media of computers and the Internet create their own challenges and opportunities for religion. Some see in the new technology a harbinger of a new religious consciousness, as individuals withdraw into a private world, where identity and reality itself become lost in cyberspace. Some observers speak of 'cybergnosticism', a new rejection of the material creation in favour of a mentally created realm existing without location in the virtual reality constructed by a network of computers. Thus Timothy Leary, dying of cancer, had the dream of downloading his consciousness into the Internet, where he would enjoy eternal life in the World Wide Web.

On the other hand, the Internet is a realm of language. People are e-mailing each other, discussing ideas via list-serves and forming friendships from around the world, and in so doing are cultivating human relationships. They may be virtual communities, but they are communities none the less.

The Internet is allowing religious people to pray with each other, discuss their faith and evangelize in a personal way with people they would never have been able to meet. At a time when religion is marginalized in the academic and secular establishment, the Internet obliterates the gatekeepers (the publishing companies, the journal editors, the cultural elite) who often determined which voices would be allowed to be heard. The Internet offers a forum in which religious ideas, like others, can gain a hearing and find an audience in a vast intellectual free market.

Cyberspace is a realm that makes equal room for both pornography and faith, bogus identities and authentic communication, entertainment and ideas. It consists of both words and images, with everything that accompanies them both.

Though the media will indeed massage the message, as Marshall McLuhan has shown, religion has come through every media revolution more or less intact. As information technology continues to develop, we can expect religion, as it always has, to find ways of conveying its message by every means at hand.

BIBLIOGRAPHY

S. Hoover, *Religion in the News: Faith and Journalism in American Public Discourse* (Thousand Oaks, CA, 1998); M. McLuhan, *Understanding Media: The Extensions Of Man* (New York, 1964); M. Olasky, *The Prodigal Press: The Anti-Christian Bias Of The American News*

Media (Wheaton, IL, 1988); N. Postman, *Amusing Ourselves to Death: Public Discourse in the Age of Show Business* (New York, 1985); N. Postman, *Technopoly: The Surrender of Culture to Technology* (New York, 1993); W. A. Stahl, *God and the Chip: Religion and the Culture of Technology* (Waterloo, Ontario, 1999).

G. E. Veith

RELIGION AND PHILOSOPHY

Surveying contemporary religion is initially daunting because of its variety and complexity, but from a philosophical point of view it may be said to represent many if not all the recurrent types of relation between faith and reason that have characterized Western thought from the Greeks onwards. This is so whether the contemporary religion in question takes its relations with philosophy from pre-Enlightenment norms, from the Enlightenment itself, or from so-called post-Enlightenment culture.

THREE APPROACHES TO RELIGION

This point can be illustrated and made plausible by first considering three different yet overlapping types of polarization in philosophical thought about the basic questions of religion: religion as cognitive or non-cognitive; religion as the product of projective mechanisms or as non-projective; and religion as objectively or subjectively true or false.

THE COGNITIVITY ISSUE

The idea that religious language is not fact-stating but non-cognitive in character is one characteristically modern strand in thinking about religion, but it may be said to go back to views of the Greek myths, the language of which was held to perform functions other than that of stating truths about the gods. Non-cognitivism in its modern form appears to have two main sources.

The first is the idea that only science is cognitive and, as religion is not a form of science, even of primitive science, the language of religion must be non-cognitive. To put the point rather differently, in the face of the dominance of science many religious thinkers have exulted in what they have seen as the long-overdue emancipation of religious language from the epistemological constraint of having to provide evidence and give grounds for their beliefs. Such language is treated as expressive and evocative rather than fact-stating. Its claims are neither verifiable nor falsifiable. Some have even likened this emancipation to Martin Luther's realization that righteousness is attained by faith, not by works. Others, more cynically, have seen such a development as freeing religion from the need to observe critical standards and as one form of the privatization of religion, its removal from the 'public square' of discourse.

The other contemporary development

has been the renewed attention paid to religious language, particularly to the contrast between the surface grammar of an expression and its real meaning. (However, the impression must not be given that before the twentieth century approaches to religious language lacked nuance. One needs only to think of the attention given to analogy and metaphor, to the idea of divine accommodation and to anthropomorphism, or to negative theology, to be reminded of the rich tradition of thinking in this area.)

Chief among the components of the meaning of religious language given contemporary prominence are its expressive, emotive and performative aspects. If religious language is not fact-stating, then perhaps it is an expression of human emotion, or a fictional depiction of human needs and aspirations, or the enactment, the performance of certain acts. The application of such ideas to the analysis of liturgical and sacramental language ('This is my body'; 'I pronounce you man and wife') is obvious enough. Of course the idea that religious language may perform many functions is not the exclusive property of religious non-cognitivists, but they alone must deny that one of its functions is to state facts.

PROJECTIONIST AND NON-PROJECTIONIST VIEWS

In the third place, cutting across this divide between cognitivist and non-cognitivist views of human language, is the debate between those who think of the phenomenon of religion (however its utterances are to be understood) as the product of certain mechanisms, and those who place emphasis upon reasons and grounds that make religious belief reasonable. Immanuel Kant argued that it was necessary to postulate the existence of God as the *summum bonum* in order to undergird rational morality. From his idea of *postulation* it is a short step to the idea of God and the associated doctrines and practices of a religion as *projections*, which compensate for certain conscious or unconscious human needs or deficiencies. Ludwig Feuerbach, Karl Marx and Sigmund Freud each provides a variant of this, and the idea has remained popular and influential, providing the theoretical basis of much modern sociology of religion. More recently the idea of beliefs as the product of causal mechanisms, rather than of reasons or grounds, has found favour with those holding an orthodox Christian view. A contrast is drawn between well-functioning and malfunctioning belief-producing mechanisms, and it is argued that Feuerbach, Marx and Freud are examples of those who assume without argument that mechanisms producing belief in God are malfunctioning. Why, if men and women are created by God, may they not have been designed so as instinctively to believe in him; and why may not unbelief be the outcome of the malfunctioning of such cognitive mechanisms?

RELIGION AND TRUTH

If religious language is non-cognitive then the issue of the truth or falsity of religion is settled. But if not, then the question arises of the sense in which religious claims may be true. Here two types of response may be discerned. The first may be called, broadly, anti-realist in its conception of the reality of God. The claim that God is real, or that it is true that God exists, is relative to the beliefs of some human group. The strongest forms of such anti-realism are those which stress the idea that the human mind constructs reality, including religious reality, by categories bestowed on it by culture, or by one or other of various language-games, or by some other aspect of human finitude. Weaker forms define truth in one of a variety of epistemic terms: as 'that which satisfies the intellect' (F. H. Bradley); or as 'that opinion which is fated to be ultimately agreed to by all who investigate' (C. S. Peirce); or as an idealization of rational acceptability (Hilary Putnam). Contemporary non-realists in the philosophy of religion include Don Cupitt and D. Z. Phillips.

By contrast, metaphysical realists with respect to God understand his reality as existing independently of and apart from human efforts to categorize or cognize his reality. The facts which make the existence of God real hold – or fail to hold – independently of human cognition. It is true that God exists if and only if God exists, and that he would exist whether or not a world of cognizers existed, and irrespective of how successful human cognitive endeavour was. A theist might think of truth as what God believes: what God believes is true whether or not anyone else believes it. Truth would then be an epistemic concept, and so to this extent such a view would be sympathetic to certain forms of anti-realism; nevertheless truth is not here defined in terms of any human epistemic states. The current renaissance of the philosophy of religion among Christians, energized by the work of such as Alvin Plantinga and Richard Swinburne, takes a broadly realist approach to metaphysical issues.

Metaphysical anti-realism usually emphasizes the plurality of religious positions, and the validity of each insofar as each is faithful to its own criteria of intelligibility and belief. The idea of objective truth, and the possibility of reaching, through reason or revelation, knowledge of this truth, is dismissed. Religion becomes a form of cultural relativism hospitable to one or another version of scepticism. Various 'post-modern' attitudes to religion depend upon an appeal to cultural relativism together with an appeal to unargued-for normative connections between knowledge and power. Insofar as such attitudes are supportive of religion they may be seen as one or another species of fideism.

KNOWLEDGE AND BELIEF

By contrast, metaphysical realism about the existence and nature of God is committed to the objectivity of truth, and, in the contemporary era, is typically coupled with a fallibilist epistemology. This is in sharp contrast to both traditional Roman Catholic and Protestant epistemologies, each of which, in its classic expression, claims to have infallible access to infallible sources of religious truth. It also contrasts with the Enlightenment idea of a body of human knowledge resting upon foundations whose truth is self-evident to any rational human being. This is now widely seen to be unworkable, for such an idea is not itself self-evident; there seems to be no epistemic obligation to accept it. And in any case, paradoxically, such foundationalism, even if viable, does not seem readily to account for much of our knowledge. So the contemporary era seems set to be characterized by efforts to provide accounts of belief, as opposed to knowledge, and to become hospitable to a plurality of epistemic positions, some of which remain foundationalist in structure. Even the tradition of natural theology, which continues to have vigorous representatives, nowadays sets its sights not on proving the existence of God but on the more modest project of making belief in God reasonable, or rebutting objections to the charge that such belief is unreasonable, or showing that God's existence is the best explanation of the unity and diversity of the natural order.

Contemporary thought has also been enlivened by the interaction between philosophy and speculative science, and there is likely to be much further discussion of the relations between cosmology and the idea of creation; of the anthropic principle and the idea of the divine design of the universe, and of artificial intelligence and the nature of the mind. Lying behind all these debates is the most basic controversy, between rival presentations of naturalist metaphysics and its various alternatives.

PLURALISM

Considerable attention has recently been paid to elucidating and critically examining the phenomenon of religious pluralism: the fact of the coexistence of many religions making incompatible claims. Versions of religious exclusivism have been defended on philosophical grounds, and theories of religion have been devised to lend plausibility to the claim that the 'great religions' are alternative and equally viable avenues to the truth (John Hick being the leading exponent of this 'pluralist' hypothesis). Such theories have been accused of falsifying the character of the religions they theorize about and in effect of setting up a novel exclusivism of their own.

FIDEISM

The various positive relations between religion and philosophy which have been described should not obscure the fact that many contemporary religions see themselves as having no positive relationship with philosophy. This is either because they are avowedly fideistic, holding that human reason is incapable of providing any helpful commentary upon or grounding for religion; or because they incorporate a mystical strain according to which the heart of religion is ineffable; or, in a more ethical vein, because they regard the practice of philosophy as 'worldly' and so as spiritually corrupting.

APOLOGETICS

Philosophical interest in religion has often been motivated by the need to develop an 'apologetic', a reasoned defence of the tenets of religion against its detractors. Such an interest in apologetics has continued unabated in the contemporary world, particularly among conservative Christian groups. A distinction may be drawn between negative apologetics, the provision of defences to philosophical objections brought against religion, and positive apologetics, the attempt to develop philosophical prolegomena to religion. Each of these projects continues vigorously in the contemporary world.

Besides considering the grounds of religion, both metaphysical and epistemological, philosophy has fulfilled – at least since the time of Augustine of Hippo – the function of helping faith to gain 'understanding'. From a theoretical point of view, many of the first-order statements of religion are opaque and underdeveloped. They raise questions of a philosophical nature, about God, creation, evil, prayer, life after death, and so on. These topics continue to be intensively discussed: indeed the contemporary world has probably seen a greater number of thorough philosophical treatments of these and other issues than any period since the Middle Ages.

BIBLIOGRAPHY

P. Helm (ed.), *Faith and Reason* (Oxford, 1998); P. L. Quinn and C. Taliaferro (eds.), *A Companion to the Philosophy of Religion* (Oxford, 1997); C. Taliaferro, *Contemporary Philosophy of Religion* (Oxford, 1998).

P. Helm

RELIGION AND POLITICS

The Western world, with headquarters in Europe and North America, yet stretching throughout Latin America, much of Africa and into parts of Asia, was shaped for the most part by Greco-Roman, Judeo-Christian (mostly Catholic and Protestant) and modern European Enlightenment traditions. Though the contemporary West is now the meeting place of most of the world's religions, Western politics shows few signs of being transformed or seriously influenced by non-Western religious traditions. Most contemporary political activity in the West continues to manifest an inner tension between the classical and Christian traditions, on the one hand, and modernism, on the other, and increasingly shows evidence of the impact of postmodernism.

From a religious point of view, the deepest level of tension in Western politics arises from degrees of incompatibility between Christianity and democratic systems of government, which are now accepted and interpreted by most citizens as secular and non-religious. Enlightenment and post-Enlightenment political convictions gained institutional dominance in the West from the middle of the nineteenth to the middle of the twentieth century, mostly by way of the triumph of liberalism, Marxism and national socialism. Most Western countries instituted religious toleration or disestablished the church and moved increasingly to confine religious expression to private life. Public life came to be governed in accord with a secular or non-sectarian rationality purportedly common to everyone.

Today, the modern, private–sacred/public–secular dualism is being challenged from several sides, especially outside Western Europe. Many Christian, Jewish, and Muslim citizens now question whether any political order can stand on its own (on foundations of human autonomy and self-affirmation alone) without religious glue. This is particularly true among those who believe that modern political ideologies have functioned as religions. The more secularized some societies become, the more important the earlier social capital of traditional morality and religion appears to have been. The more that societies become intellectually, culturally, ideologically and religiously diverse, the more problematic 'pluralism' becomes, because little is left to unite citizens of a country at a deeper level. Political scientists today speak of there being a 'thin' rather than a 'thick' bond of citizenship in most Western countries. Many religious people want to hold on to and strengthen democracy and other fruits of modernity, but they believe this can be done only by recovering society-wide adherence to the traditional religious morality that undergirded the modern 'advance'. Other religious adherents, particularly in many Muslim countries, see Western secular culture as the problem and resist it in favour of a traditional religious way of life. Most modernists and postmodernists in the West continue to see religions as outdated or as merely part of the multicultural relativity of the contemporary world.

The greatest impact of postmodernism comes from its exposure of Enlightenment modernism as itself historically relative and parochial. Modern, secular rationalism, it says, is not actually uniting all citizens by drawing them out of traditional religions into universal truth, but, instead, is showing itself to be simply another philosophy, myth or pseudo-religion. Modern democracies, therefore, may have as their foundations and glue nothing more than the power of temporary coalitions of interests that impose their will on society as a whole. Power politics is all there is.

This concept of radical relativism is driving many religious believers, especially in North America, to question their earlier accommodation to secular modernism. Pope John Paul II is advancing this criticism among Roman Catholics, calling for the deepening of Christian humanism and social solidarity over against the secularism and relativism that fuel other evils of our age. Religious revivals in Latin America and Africa, many of them Christian-Pentecostal in character, may initially appear to carry no political aims or philosophy. But many of those touched by these movements are now entering politics for the first time and are raising the question in a new way: what does a Christian way of life have to do with democratic politics?

In the United States, few Christians question the constitutional system of government, but many are engaged in culture wars over public policies that control family life, sexual expression, schooling, the arts and the media. Since the 1960s, and especially after the Supreme Court's approval of abortion in its 1973 *Roe v. Wade* decision, many Catholics and Protestants have been challenging secular humanist dominance in politics and public culture. American religious communities are widely divided, however. Many in the more conservative streams increasingly oppose government itself, contending that Christian politics demand less government, greater individual freedom and traditional morality in public life. Those in more liberal streams criticize economic inequality, human rights violations, the lack of racial and gender equality and environmental degradation as the signs of unjust governance, which the Bible would condemn.

In many respects, however, culture wars in the United States may reveal more about the crisis internal to an American civil religion than about a genuine revival of Christian religious influence in politics. In this respect the contemporary political struggle over religion and public morality in the United States may be more like the nationalist and other culture struggles among religious groups in other parts of the world. It may show the continuing vitality of citizens with religious affiliations, but the political battles are shaped more by modern ideological divides and policy differences than by a distinguishable, coherent and consistent Christianity doing battle with pure secularism.

Another way to make this point is to say that Western Christians have not yet, for the most part, articulated a Christian view of representative government and of the complex, differentiated societies which those governments must govern. The use by Christians of terms such as 'freedom', 'equality', 'fairness', 'responsibility' and 'justice' to justify their political behaviour and their support of the political system in which they live may not be markedly different from the ways that others use the terms.

EXCEPTIONALISM, UNIVERSALISM AND ANTITHESIS

To grasp the wide range of relationships between religion and politics in the Western world today, there are three rubrics that may prove helpful.

The first is *exceptionalism*. Many Christians, Jews and Muslims believe that because their religion is uniquely true, it should have an exceptional political position or be given exceptional recognition. The combination of Jewish uniqueness and the Holocaust combined to establish the conditions and the claim for a modern state of Israel. Many Muslims reject the secular idea of the state and believe that since God is all-powerful, Islam ought to govern all of life, including politics. At best, other religions can be tolerated only on the margin. Few Christians today call for an established or legally privileged church, though the Roman Catholic Church did not give up this position until Vatican II in the 1960s, and established churches remain in religiously tolerant states such as England. However, many Christians in both the North and the South believe that Christians ought to be assured of positions of political leadership because Christianity is the true religion. 'Christian' countries ought to lead the world, and some countries, such as the United Kingdom and the United States, have been exceptionally established or guided by God to do so.

The postmodernist today would deconstruct this belief as a moral justification proffered by those who want to hold on to power. When Constantine took control of the Roman imperium a few centuries after Christ, he established Christianity as the privileged religion. Some such arrangements have existed ever since. By contrast, the earliest Christians, and those who live in countries where they are a small minority (often a persecuted minority) do not necessarily think of themselves or of Christianity in this way.

A second rubric under which we can consider religion and politics today is that of *universalism*. Many Christians and Jews believe that their religions provide the basis for universal human rights, for valuing all persons equally, for non-discriminatory legal treatment and for governmental protection and enhancement of life, including the environment and non-human creatures. Roman Catholic social teaching today typically builds on the 'dignity of the human person'. The special value of each person, created in the image of God, calls for universal human rights protections, including the right to life of the unborn. Liberal Protestants, Catholics and Jews who would approve of abortion typically do so on grounds that the unborn are not yet full persons and that the freedom of choice of all women, universally, should be respected. Many Protestants, particularly in the United States, emphasize the right of each individual to be free and thus the necessity of a constitutionally limited government.

Movements in the world today for environmental protection, for legal protection of the unborn (or of a woman's right to choose), for racial equality and non-discriminatory treatment of different ethnic groups, and for international human rights protections often reveal a religious origin and support. The religious motivation, in these cases, is not to seek political privilege for one religion over others or for people of one religion to have control over others, but for universal implementation of that which the believers are convinced is politically just for all people. Often, however, the 'universalist' argument shows religious adherents at their most secular and secularists at their most religious. The line between secular religion and religious secularity becomes blurred.

Finally, the power of religion can be discerned under the rubric of *antithesis*: the stark opposition between one way of life and another. Many religious pacifists, for example, believe that their obedience to God calls them to stand over against all military actions and designs. For some, this means no more than refusing to serve in the military even if that leads to imprisonment. Partly because of this stance, some Western countries have established policies that give pacifists an alternative to military service. For other pacifists, their antithetical stance leads them to active resistance to arms spending and military engagement by means of lobbying, protesting and refusing to pay taxes.

Many believers decide either to oppose or advance certain government policies or to withdraw from politics altogether out of the sense that their faith calls them to a distinctive political approach that is different from the ways of life others lead. Even though the actions of government for which they call may at times be the same as those demanded by the exceptionalists and the universalists, their motivation is different. Christians who believe that justice is antithetical to racism or abortion may do more than simply vote according to their conscience while living like everyone else. They may change their residences in order to help form a multiracial community, or change vocations so they can help unmarried mothers keep their babies. In some cases, they may refuse to participate in ordinary politics: refuse to vote, or pay taxes, or obey the laws. Others may create Christian or Jewish or Muslim political organizations (think-tanks, civic-education associations and even political parties) not in order to seek a privileged position for themselves, but to work out a way of doing politics consistent with their religion. Black Muslim or New Jewish schools in American cities, Quaker (Society of Friends) relief efforts to people in 'enemy' countries and Protestant or Catholic political parties in Eastern Europe may all be expressions of the conviction that a religious antithesis exists between the religious way of life and the ways of life that other religious communities – or secularized people – follow.

BIBLIOGRAPHY

P. Berger (ed.), *The Desecularization of the World: Resurgent Religion and World Politics* (Grand Rapids, MI, 1999); H. J. Berman, *Law and Revolution: The Formation of the Western Legal Tradition* (Cambridge, MA, 1983); M. P. Fogarty, *Christian Democracy in Western Europe: 1820–1953* (London, 1957); P. Freston, *Evangelicals and Politics in Asia, Africa and Latin America* (Cambridge, 2001); S. P. Huntington, *The Clash of Civilizations and the Remaking of World Order* (New York, 1996); J. W. Skillen, *The Scattered Voice: Christians at Odds in the Public Square* (Grand Rapids, MI, 1990); J. W. Skillen and R. M. McCarthy (eds.), *Political Order and the Plural Structure of Society* (Atlanta, GA, 1991); B. H. Smith, *Religious Politics in Latin America: Pentecostal vs. Catholic* (Notre Dame, IN, 1998); M. L. Stackhouse, *Creeds, Society and Human Rights: A Study in Three Cultures* (Grand Rapids, MI, 1984); J. Witte, Jr (ed.), *Christianity and Democracy in Global Context* (Oxford and Boulder, CO, 1993).

J. W. Skillen

RELIGION, POVERTY AND OPPRESSION

RELIGIOUS TEACHING ON POVERTY AND OPPRESSION

Within the last thirty years, there has been fresh thinking among religious groups in the West about poverty and oppression. The main catalyst has been the impact of liberation theologies from the late 1960s onwards. Although religions have always taught that people of faith have a particular responsibility towards vulnerable and excluded people, the rise of a different approach to theological reflection outside the West has posed new questions.

Thinking, among Christians at least, has undergone a major shift that can best be described as a move from notions of charity to those of justice. In place of an emphasis on the duty of the rich to be generous and compassionate in giving to the poor, the stress now is on the rightful demands of the poor to be included in the benefits of wealth-creation, presently enjoyed only by the rich nations. Part of the reason for the shift has been the influence of the Marxist belief that wealth is created by working people through a process in which some of their labour-time is expropriated (taken from them). On a world scale, this means that the rich nations to a large extent owe their wealth-creation to the exploitation of the resources of the poor nations and the economic and technological advantages that they have always possessed. In part, the shift has been due to a rediscovery of what has been termed 'God's preferential option for the poor'.

From the Hebrew Scriptures of the Old Testament, liberation theology has emphasized the vision of God as one who protects and delivers the poor and oppressed (Pss. 103:6; 146:7–9; Is. 29:19–21). The story of the Hebrew people being rescued from slave labour in Egypt and brought into a land they can call their own has been used to show that God is opposed to those who exploit other human beings for their own ends (Exod. 2:23–25; 6:2–8; Deut. 4: 34–39).

The memory of the exodus is at the heart of the faith of Israel. The laws of the covenant are often prefaced by a reminder that the people may not do violence to their neighbours, because they themselves once suffered violence (Exod. 22:21; Lev. 19:33–36; Deut. 5:6ff.; 24:17–18). Rather, they are to be just, generous and merciful (Lev. 25:35–43; Deut. 14:28–29). Thus, the laws have a number of regulations designed to ensure that each member of society has access to resources needed to satisfy basic needs (Lev. 19:9–10; 23:22; Deut. 24: 19–22). The prophets spoke out clearly and forcefully against the rich and powerful within Israel (and the surrounding nations) who dared to use their position to take property illegally, depress wages and neglect the poor, whilst living in luxury (Amos 1 – 2; 4:1ff.; 5:11–12; Is. 1:23; Mic. 2:1–2; 2:8–9; Jer. 22:17). They frequently called the leaders of the nations to basic principles of human care and the people of Israel to the terms of the covenant instituted by God (Ezek. 28:16–18; Hab. 2:6–17; Mal. 2: 1–10).

In the Christian Scriptures of the New Testament, although perhaps in a less direct way, the prophetic tradition is maintained. Jesus' teaching on the possession and use of wealth is given against the background of a situation in Palestine where some were becoming enormously wealthy on the back of exploited labour. His vision of the kingdom suggests that those who hold on to wealth without regard to the disadvantaged in society will find the challenge to enter into the kingdom too hard to accept (Matt. 6:19–24; Mark 10:17–31; Luke 6:24–25; 12:13–21, 33–34; 16:10–14). However, Jesus does not equate riches as such with a life of injustice (Luke 16:1 with 16:19; 19:7–8; Matt. 21:33; 25:14ff.). He does, however, teach that all are to give an account to God for the use they make of their possessions, for ultimately all of creation belongs to God and is given to humans to use unselfishly on trust (Luke 12:20–21; 16:25, cf. also 1 Tim. 6:6–10, 17–19).

In many ways the social message of the apostolic church in the Acts and epistles takes up the theme of Deuteronomy 15: 'there should be no poor among you'. Thus the picture of the early Jerusalem church is of a group of disciples openly sharing their possessions (Acts 2:44–45; 4:32–37). At a later stage, this was done between Christians in Antioch and those living in need in Judea (Acts 11:29–30). Later still, it was the churches of Macedonia and Achaia that were encouraged to respond to the needs of the poor in Jerusalem (2 Cor. 8 – 9; Acts 24:17).

At the same time, a realistic view of poverty (also echoing Deut. 15:11) is taken: 'The poor you will always have with you' (John 12:8; Matt. 26:11; Mark 14:7). But this statement is not understood as a message of resignation, even less a human historical necessity. Rather it is the context for the exercise of both justice and generosity – 'do not ... view your needy neighbour with hostility and give nothing . . . Open your hand to the poor and needy neighbour in your land' (Deut. 15:9,11, NRSV). James clearly links poverty with the exploitation of paying unjust wages (Jas. 5:1–5) and the author of Revelation sees the destruction of incredible opulence to be the result of an oppressive regime which, among other things, traded in 'slaves and human lives' (Rev. 18:13, NRSV).

Although the passages to which liberation theologians have appealed have always been in the Scriptures, they brought a fresh impetus to their study by relating closely the situation of Israel to that of their own context. They were able to demonstrate how the situation of poverty and oppression lived by the majority of the people of the Third World illuminated the text and gave to its message a new urgency. For this reason, some have asserted that the excluded poor know the Scriptures better than the rich and powerful: they are able to feel more comfortable with a message that proclaims that the social consequences of sin will be reversed.

The other major world religions have their own traditions regarding poverty and oppression. Islam teaches the dignity and importance of every kind of work and the need for people to support themselves. It denounces exploitation in the terms of trade and all dishonesty in business practices. One of the sayings of the prophet Muhammad is: 'On the Day of Resurrection Allah will look not at . . . the person who swears to the truth while lying about his merchandise.' When disasters or times of great need occur, it is the responsibility of others to help the needy. Giving a percentage of one's income to the poor is a religious duty called *zakah*. Spontaneous acts of charity (*sadaqah*) are also encouraged. The principle of giving is designed to help the disadvantaged stand again on their own feet. In the case of loans, the earning of interest is forbidden (Surah 2:278–9; 3:130; 30:39 of the Qur'an), for two reasons: it forces the borrower into debt and dependency and it treats money as a commodity rather than a facility.

Buddhism and Hinduism tend to treat poverty in this life as the result of the bad *karma* people have created in a past life. Such a belief has been given as the reason why these religions sometimes appear to be indifferent towards those suffering poverty. However, by the same token, good *karma* can be created by renouncing the desire to enjoy much material wealth and by generous giving.

Buddhism believes that a craving for an unfulfillable satisfaction through the acquisition of wealth and goods is one of the key causes of suffering (*duhkha*) from which people need deliverance. Part of the Eightfold Path of right living is to treat everyone equally and as equals, not causing suffering by the way one earns a living, nor causing others offence or harm. There is a balance in Buddhism between non-attachment to money and property and the rejection of poverty as detrimental to the well-being of society, producing greed and social instability.

For Hinduism the enjoyment of moderate wealth gained honestly and lawfully (*artha*) is allowed. At the same time, following the rules of *dharma* (religious and social duty) requires compassion towards the needs of others and generosity. *Artha* and *dharma* depend on one another. Hinduism is also governed by the practice of *ahimsa* (non-violence), which enjoins the renunciation of the entire range of thoughts, words and deeds capable of causing harm to others.

Sikhism is well known for teaching the complete equality of all people and opposing all forms of discrimination based on race, gender or religion. The original founder of the Sikh religion, Guru Nanak (1469–1539), taught his followers ('Sikh' means 'learner' or 'disciple') to reject the idea of *karma*, by which suffering in this life might be taken as just punishment for past evils committed. Rather, they were to take every opportunity to serve the needs of the poor and vulnerable. The whole responsibility of Sikhs is summed up in the Punjabi saying 'Meditate on God's name, work honestly, give to those in need.' This is made concrete in the obligation of *seva* (community service). There is no task too menial for Sikhs to perform on behalf of others. The Sikh *gurdwara* is a place of hospitality to anyone who visits. It often acts as a kind of day-care centre for the elderly and unemployed.

RELIGIOUS ACTION ON POVERTY AND OPPRESSION

Religious people have been widely involved with both alleviating poverty and seeking to address its root causes. Here, we can only indicate some of the contemporary work being done. Three specific programmes of the World Council of Churches can be highlighted to indicate the scope of concern. The Programme to Combat Racism, although mainly focused on ending the apartheid regime of South Africa, also engaged the churches with monitoring all forms of individual and social exclusion on the basis of ethnic or racial difference and all kinds of racial stereotyping and abuse. The conciliar process Justice, Peace and the Integrity of Creation has been an invitation to Christians to confess Christ as the life of the world and resist all the powers of death. These latter are identified principally as an unjust world economic order, militarism (the destruction of democratic processes by the armed forces) and the deterioration of the world's environment. The Decade of Solidarity with Women identified women (adults and children) as the most vulnerable among the poor. It called upon all churches to adopt measures both to empower women by including them fully in leadership roles and decision-making processes and to join in the elimination of discriminatory practices and cultural myths about women.

People of different faiths have supported a number of initiatives that are designed to combat the many aspects of poverty and oppression both in their own country and overseas. In the area of development policies, the World Development Movement has campaigned vigorously for just international relations in aid and trade. Similarly, the Jubilee 2000 Coalition has become a powerful voice before the rich nations and international economic institutions of the opinion of millions of people that the debt burden of the poorest nations should be cancelled. There has been wide involvement in action on behalf of homelessness by organizations like Shelter and Child Action on Poverty, on behalf of human rights by Amnesty International and on environmental issues by Greenpeace, Friends of the Earth, The World Wide Fund for Nature and other important agencies. Institutions, like the Life and Peace Institute (Uppsala), are at the cutting edge of both research and the running of practical workshops for the transformation of conflict in troubled areas of the globe.

Development agencies, like CAFOD, Christian Aid, Tear Fund and World Vision have pioneered countless numbers of projects in deprived areas of the world, whose long-term goal has been the establishment of economic self-sufficiency among deprived communities, through the transference of skills, low-interest loans for small-scale enterprises and the use of appropriate technology. Although the idea is more controversial, some agencies believe that the long-term problems of endemic poverty are matters that can be addressed only in the wider arena of national and international political life. As a result, alongside aid and development work, they have also entered the political processes of awareness-raising, demonstrations and lobbying.

World religions other than Christianity have tended to create institutions and agencies mainly, but not exclusively, to meet the needs of their own communities. There are a number of Islamic organizations (such as

Muslim Aid, The Red Crescent, Islamic Relief) that offer relief, aid and care for victims of famine, violence and catastrophes. Buddhists in Britain have created Charity Aid for India and The Buddhist Hospice Trust. An international organization based in Britain, the Sikh Forum, raises money to help the victims of disasters worldwide, Sikh and non-Sikh. Jewish Care runs sheltered accommodation and residential homes for elderly and disabled people and health centres for people with mental health problems. In general terms, it has been mainly the Christian faith that has tended to see concern for the poor and oppressed in terms not only of compassionate care but also of political action.

BIBLIOGRAPHY

W. O. Cole, *Moral Issues in Six Religions* (Oxford, 1991); D. Forrester, *Christian Justice and Public Policy* (Cambridge, 1997); J. A. Kirk, *What is Mission? Theological Explorations* (London, 1999), chs. 6, 8, 9, 10; R. F. Sizemore and D. K. Swearer (eds.), *Ethics, Wealth and Salvation: A Study in Buddhist Social Ethics* (Columbia, SC, 1990); R. W. Wolfe and C. E. Gudorf (eds.), *Ethics and World Religions: Cross-Cultural Case Studies* (Maryknoll, NY, 1999); A. Ziauddin, *Islam, Poverty and Income Distribution* (Leicester, 1991).

J. A. Kirk

RELIGION AND PSYCHOLOGY

While 'psychological' thinking about religion has a long history, psychology as a scholarly discipline, separate from philosophy, is only a little over one hundred years old, and it is that 'psychology' to which this discussion is directed. Most general psychology textbooks date modern psychology's beginning as 1875, when Wilhelm Wundt established a psychophysiological laboratory at the University of Leipzig. Wundt called religion a part of the 'apperceptive mass' which persons brought to their understanding of reality. A quarter of a century later William James's student Edwin Starbuck conducted the first psychological survey of religious issues by writing his doctoral dissertation on conversion. His conclusions still hold true: most persons make serious religious decisions during the stress-time of adolescence. It is during this period of life that reflection on the meaning of life, the choice of vocation, the possibilities of procreation and the viability of values assume central importance. Religion unifies these concerns under a central idealistic focus.

PSYCHOLOGY AND RELIGION IN THE TWENTIETH CENTURY

Starbuck's study, coupled with the writing of William James's *The Varieties of Religious Experience*, ushered in a period of intense activity that lasted over a quarter of a century. Many students of psychology turned their attention to religious topics. A number of them entered graduate study at Clark University, where G. Stanley Hall, the first president of the American Psychological Association (APA), was president. Much of their writing was published in *The Journal of Religious Education and Psychology*, the first publication devoted entirely to religion and psychology. 'Religion' became a well-enough accepted topic in general psychology to be included in several of the early editions of the *Annual Review of Psychology.*

Hall himself, a frustrated ministerial student turned psychologist, not only encouraged this work but also wrote a seminal two-volume treatise entitled *Jesus the Christ in the Light of Psychology* (New York, 1917), in which he proposed the thesis that Jesus represented the apex of 'man soul' to be found in all human beings. Hall also offered a psychological theory as to what happened in religious conversion. He contended that persons were created altruistic at birth but by the time of adolescence they were encrusted with selfishness. Conversion, psychologically understood, was like breaking a geode rock apart and returning life to its altruistic centre. Neither logical reasoning nor moral admiration would be convincing enough to accomplish this transforming miracle among adolescents, according to Hall. Only the awesome realization that God loved them enough to die for them was powerful enough to break through human self-centredness and re-establish life around the crystal-like centre of love for others.

Hall's work exemplified much of what was published during this period. It could be depicted as the 'psychologizing of religion'. Religious experience was understood as the result of human motivation, and the substance of religion, such as the deity, was reduced to imagination – this last development being a violation of James's assertion that psychologists could not prove or disprove the object of faith but should limit their study to study of what persons did in relation to 'that which they considered divine'.

Nevertheless, in spite of this vigorous beginning during the first quarter of the twentieth century, the study of religion by academic psychologists declined significantly after 1930 and was brought back into mainline psychology only in the 1950s. Religion, like sex, came to be considered one of psychology's 'taboo topics'. This rejection of religion as a topic of concern has been credited to three significant trends: the rise of behaviourism; Freud's devastating analysis of religious practice; and the practical application of psychology to religious education. Academics were disinclined to be known as supportive of religion. Although willing to study religion in surveys from that day to this, psychologists have been found to be among the most irreligious of all social scientists.

As might be expected, when Harvard psychologist Gordon Allport turned his attention to religion after the Second World War, the scholarly world listened. His *The Individual and His Religion: A Psychological Interpretation* (New York, 1950) reinstated the study of religion into mainline psychology, a movement that has lasted to the present day and that, in the late 1970s, resulted in the inclusion of religion among the APA's Divisions. Allport's volume reaffirmed William James's contention that religion could have a positive influence on personality integration and mental health, a theme that had been forgotten in the onslaught of behaviourism and psychoanalysis. In subsequent studies on religion and prejudice, Allport went beyond a comparison of church attendees with non-attendees and developed a model of religious 'orientation' that has dominated the field ever since. He concluded that those for whom religion was a master motive of life (intrinsic motivation) were less likely to be racially prejudiced than those for whom religion served secondary gains (extrinsic motivation).

Of course Allport's affirmation of the positive value of religion did not silence religious detractors among psychologists. Some behaviourists continue to ascribe religion to fanciful higher mental processes that are reducible to basic need-based associative learning. Some psychoanalysts continue to repeat Freud's contention that God is a projection of the father image and religion is fixation at a childish level of development or regression to an imaginary level of thinking which impedes maturity. In spite of the fact that from the beginning some thinkers pointed out that Freud made a critique of 'bad' religion (cf. the Swiss pastor Oskar Pfister's assertion that love, not fear, is the core of Christianity), Freud's followers have tended to mouth the nineteenth-century dictum that as science comes of age, religion will disappear.

More recently, the cognitive theorist Albert Ellis has become the contemporary spokesman for religion's critics among psychologists by asserting that religious practice violates the characteristics of good mental health. Instead of self-interest and self-direction, religion, according to Ellis, emphasizes God's interest and God's direction. By its affirmation of absolutes, religion cultivates intolerance and inflexibility. Instead of courageous risk-taking, religious persons want security. They cultivate guilt instead of self-esteem and are committed only to getting to heaven, not to making the world better.

While these are still the opinions of some psychologists, the overall approach has tempered, and many psychologists now perceive religion as a positive force for both mental and social health. In fact, religion has been officially included, along with age, gender, ethnicity and cultural background, among the essential aspects of diversity that psychologists are mandated to consider in counselling individuals. The APA has now published four volumes detailing the ways in which religion and psychology can be constructively related (e.g. E. P. Shafranske (ed.), *Religion and the Clinical Practice of Psychology* [Washington, DC, 1966]). However, attention to religion in general psychology textbooks is still the exception to the rule.

PSYCHOLOGY AND PASTORAL CARE

Up to this point, this article has dealt with psychology's treatment of religion. Religion, likewise, has interacted with psychology. As noted above, religious education appropriated many of the early conclusions of developmental psychology in its curriculum planning and instructional recommendations. Religious themes such as appreciation of nature, heroic biblical stories and the love of God were routinely matched to life-stage developmental needs. Certain themes, such as original sin and atonement, were withheld until they could be appropriated into normal cognitive, emotional and social development. In line with the growing understanding of adolescence, peer group relationships and commitment to ideals were emphasized.

Alongside this positive response of religious educators to the conclusions of educational and developmental psychology was the pastoral counselling movements' appreciation of psychological theorizing about personality development and psychodynamics. While pastoral care predated psychology by many centuries, the emergence of counselling psychology after the First World War profoundly influenced modern pastoral counselling. Without question the greatest single impact has come from the theorizing of Carl Rogers, who advocated a non-directive or client-centred approach. This methodology fitted neatly into a growing appreciation among pastoral counsellors for the theological conviction that persons were created in the divine image and needed the chance for religious self-development. This approach was further supported by the psychodynamic thesis that much organized religion impeded self-development and, in fact, functioned in a repressive manner that confirmed many of Freud's contentions.

Reviews of themes in the pastoral care movement from 1925 to 1975 show that the field turned away from its theological roots and depended heavily on secular developmental and personality theorists such as Jung, Maslow and Fromm. One writer has called this period the 'Babylonian Captivity of Pastoral Care'.

More recently, theorists such as theologian Thomas Oden and psychologist Paul Pruyser have attempted to balance pastoral care in a more traditional religious manner. Oden has admonished pastoral counsellors for not relying more on their theological and ecclesiastical traditions, and Pruyser has provided pastoral counsellors with a practical guide for assessing the functional faith of their parishioners as an alternative to evaluating them in purely psychological terms.

THE RELIGION OF PSYCHOLOGY AND THE PSYCHOLOGY OF RELIGION

Currently, the interrelationship of religion and psychology can be understood under two labels: 'the religion of psychology' and 'the psychology of religion'. In regard to the first, Paul Vitz in his book *Psychology as Religion* poignantly asserts the idea that psychology has become a religion for many. Called the 'triumph of the therapeutic' by one writer, the psychological elevation of the 'self' came to function as religion for many persons in the Western world. Relationship with God was replaced by concern for self-development. In fact the Swiss psychiatrist Carl Jung defined religion as the courage to look inside oneself and be loyal to what one discovered. Some, such as Illinois psychologist O. Hobart Mower, pointed out the danger of narcissism in this approach. Instead, Mower advocated a more realistic self-examination which would often result in admission of guilt followed by repentance and recompense, rather than in self-aggrandizement.

A somewhat different aspect of 'the religion of psychology' perspective can be seen in the thinking of the existentialist theologian Paul Tillich, and in his contemporary interpreter James Fowler. Tillich defined 'religion' as the universal search for meaning or being 'ultimately concerned'. Since everyone engages in this search, everyone has a religion, although it may not be expressed in traditional terms. Fowler, appropriating developmental psychology, added to Tillich's thesis by contending that people go through '*stages of faith*' just as they pass through chronological life phases of cognitive, emotional and social development.

Turning lastly to the 'psychology of religion', the precursors and effects of religious experience have been of continuing interest to psychologists (cf. W. H. Clark and H. N. Malony, *Religious Experience: Its Nature and Function in Human Psyche* [New Jersey, 1972]). While theorists from Augustine to contemporary social psychologist Theodore Sarbin have postulated that experience of transcendent reality is common in every culture, religious experience is typically considered a *human capacity* rather than a *human need*; otherwise *every* individual would report its occurrence. The prime motivations underlying religious experience, in addition to cultural conformity, are considered to be anxieties resulting from tragedies (premature loss), circumstance (thwarted life fulfilment) or mysteries (lack of meaning and purpose). These three motives are thought to be sufficient for explaining religious experiences of all types, ranging from those of the apostle Paul to those of Mother Teresa to those of Billy Graham.

Support for James's and Allport's contentions that religious experience can have positive effects on life, has been mixed (cf. C. D. Batson, P. Schoenrade and W. L. Ventis, *Religion and the Individual* [New York, 1993]). While religion seems to have good effects on mental health, it seems to have less effect on morals. Some authors have suggested that the prime result of religious experience is relief from the stress of life and the providing of social identity and self-esteem.

The psychology of religion remains a viable endeavour both among those who seek to apply their conclusions to religious life and among those who seek knowledge for its own sake.

BIBLIOGRAPHY

D. Browning, *Religious Thought and the Modern Psychologies* (Philadelphia, 1987); J. W. Fowler, *Stages of Faith* (San Francisco, 1981); W. James, *The Varieties of Religious Experience* (New York, 1902, 1961); H. N. Malony, *The Psychology of Religion: Personalities, Problems, Possibilities* (Grand Rapids, MI, 1986); O. H. Mowrer, *The Crisis in Psychiatry and Religion* (Princeton, NJ, 1961); P. C. Vitz, *Psychology as Religion: The Cult of Self-Worship* (Grand Rapids, MI, 1977, 1994).

H. N. Maloney

RELIGION AND SCIENCE

Two initial questions are 'what religion?' and 'which science?' The meaning of 'religion' stretches from a vague feeling of the numinous to, say, major world faiths with comprehensively articulated theologies. Some have even taken 'religion' to include 'stances for living' like secular humanism. The contemporary meaning of 'science' is also a matter of philosophical debate. Science encompasses a very wide range of studies which can only partially be summarized under the headings of physical, life, earth and behavioural sciences. So an initial delimitation of the scope of this entry is necessary.

Most issues of religion and science arise because of cognitive claims made by particular religions which have a central belief in 'God'. Consequently a large proportion of matters which fall under the heading of 'religion and science' is encompassed by a general consideration of theistic religions like Christianity, Islam and Judaism. However, it is a matter of history that, in the West, issues of science and religion have primarily occurred within the context of the Christian religion, which therefore merits special attention. For present purposes, 'God' can be taken as the 'God of the philosophers', namely, *transcendent, conscious agency*. Detailed aspects of God's relationships with people fall outside the scope of this entry.

Three questions guide this brief overview of an extensive area of study.

HOW DOES ANY INTERPLAY BETWEEN RELIGION AND SCIENCE ARISE?

It needs to be said at the outset that some take the view that there is no interplay. Both religion and science are seen as existing in their own watertight compartments. More commonly held is the view that there *is* some kind of interplay, which arises in three ways.

THE DATA OF SCIENCE

Certain statements in religious writings like the Jewish Torah and the Qur'an make references to aspects of the physical world which have been seen as interacting with scientific *data* drawn, for example, from cosmology, biology and the earth sciences.

Attempts have been made to read scientific ideas (e.g. the age of the earth, or the origin of life in general and of humankind in particular) out of religious writings. Galileo gave some wise warnings about this practice, from his experience of those who tried to wrest astronomical ideas out of the Bible: 'the primary purpose of the sacred writings', he said, 'is the service of God and the salvation of souls ... I would say here something that was heard from an ecclesiastic of the most eminent degree: "That the intention of the Holy Ghost is to teach us how one goes to heaven, not how heaven goes."' History bears abundant testimony to well-meaning but disastrous attempts to drag current science (which changes) from religious texts. What may start out as *exegesis* frequently ends up as *eisegesis*, reading preconceived ideas into the text.

The matter of hermeneutics needs to be addressed before looking for confirmation or contradiction of contemporary science in ancient religious writings. Key questions are: How is language being used? What are the authors' intentions? What are the thought forms of the day? What are the literary genres employed? In the Bible alone, some thirty-three different literary genres have been identified, including allegory, apocalyptic literature, elevated prose, enigmatic sayings, euphemisms, history, hyperbole, irony, jokes, letters (personal and circular), metaphors, parables, paradoxes, personification, poetry, prayers, prophecies, riddles, similes and songs. To take everything at the bare, literal meaning of the text is to fail to take divine inspiration seriously. In no place is such care more necessary than in the so-called 'creationist' debates, and interesting parallels can be drawn between those within Judeo-Christianity who think their religious texts commit them to a young earth and an anti-evolutionary stance, and their Islamic counterparts who interpret the Qur'an in a similar way (see S. A. Mabud, in *MEQ* 4 (1), pp. 9–56).

THE NATURE OF SCIENCE

Typical issues in this area include miracles, determinism and the nature of explanation.

Miracles and the uniformity of nature. It has been claimed that the idea of the uniformity of nature, assumed by scientists, renders religious belief in miracles untenable. But the uniformity of nature is a methodological principle without which science could not be pursued. It assumes that (apart from minute fractions of a second after the Big Bang) the laws of nature are the same throughout space and time and that, quantum considerations apart, doing the same experiment again will give the same result. It needs to be remembered, however, that there are vast areas of science, in cosmology, geology and biology, where repeatability is not possible.

Miracles are clearly exceptions to the uniformity of nature, but there is no legitimate way of elevating uniformity as a methodological principle to the status of a metaphysical belief that things could never be otherwise, thereby precluding miracles. The behaviour of the natural world would need to have been observed in every detail from the beginning of time to establish whether this were so. One could know that miracles could not occur *iff* (*iff* = 'if and only if') the uniformity of nature were known to be absolute; and one could know this *iff* one knew that no exceptions (such as miracles) to this uniformity had occurred. Arguments against miracles from the uniformity of nature are circular. Theologically, the uniformity of nature reflects the faithfulness of God. God is not capricious, but if he wishes to act in unique ways for particular significant purposes, that is up to him. Scientific laws are human attempts to give concise descriptions of the *normal* behaviour of the natural world. They certainly do not legislate what is bound to happen and they have nothing to say about the possibility or impossibility of miracles, other than what was known from antiquity: that they are not what is normally to be expected.

Determinism and freewill. Do deterministic beliefs in the potential predictability of the future render religious belief in freewill and accountability to God no longer viable? The French astronomer and mathematician Pierre Laplace (1749–1827), confident in Newtonian theory, postulated a superbeing who, knowing the positions and forces acting on each particle in the universe, would have no uncertainties, 'and the future, as the past, would be present to its eyes'. What place, then, for freewill? But the twentieth century has generally been seen as presenting us with a much more open-ended view of the universe. Werner Heisenberg (1901–76), in his *principle of indeterminacy* in 1927, showed that the act of accurately measuring the position of a particle destroys the possibility of measuring the momentum of that particle to any degree of precision desired. This quantum mechanical limitation on accuracy, and therefore on prediction of the future positions and speeds of particles, is most significant at subatomic levels.

The more recent *chaos theory*, though deterministic, has indicated that many systems in nature are so exquisitely sensitive to the initial conditions that prediction of anything other than very short-term outcomes is computationally impossible. For example, to predict the position of a billiard ball accurately after fifty collisions, the gravitational force due to a single electron at the far edge of the universe would need to be taken into account!

A contemporary issue which is allied to determinism is the question of how, within a chain-mesh of cause and effect, God freely acts in the world: for example, in answer to prayers.

Explanations. One of the ubiquitous mistakes in popular literature which refers to religion and science is to think there is only one type of explanation: scientific explanations. It has led to the philosophical muddle of the 'God-of-the-gaps', in which explanations in terms of divine activity are viewed as limited to the parts of nature for which there are as yet no scientific explanations. This caused anxiety among some believers, who saw God's place as author and sustainer of the world as being usurped. It also caused renewed zeal for science by some atheists, who sought thereby to remove any possible place for God. But both the anxiety and the zeal rest on insecure foundations, since scientific explanations about mechanisms and development are logically compatible with religious explanations about divine purpose and agency. Even at a human level it would be odd to deny the purpose and activity of the creator of a novel device on the grounds that the mechanisms of that device, or how it was produced, were understood. Imagine denying the purposes, or even the existence, of Alexander Graham Bell because the mechanisms and the origin of the telephone were understood!

THE APPLICATIONS OF SCIENCE

Much is now technically possible: for example in medicine, in 'defence' and in food science. This raises issues of whether one *ought* to do such things. An ever-growing range of issues is involved in this 'moral maze', including genetic engineering, xenotransplantation, IVF, genetic screening and abortion, care of the elderly and those in a persistent vegetative state, cloning, GM foods and costly 'smart' weapons versus cheaper, less discriminate ones. Although *ought* implies *can*, *can* does not imply *ought*. Religious beliefs have much to say in informing ethical decisions, even though some ethical systems are not based on religious beliefs. So if these are some of the ways in which the interplay between science and religion has arisen, the second guiding question is as follows:

HOW HAS SUCH INTERPLAY BEEN SEEN?

CONFLICT

The *conflict thesis*, known also as the *warfare model* and the *military metaphor*, is largely a product of the nineteenth century; for some decades now, leading academics in the history of science have indicated its inadequacy. It fails to do justice to the complexity of historical interactions between the two disciplines, not least to the important contribution which religious, and in particular Christian, beliefs have made to the development of science in the West. But the idea of conflict is deeply entrenched in popular folklore and is commonly promoted by the media, with their thirst for confrontation. The origins of the conflict thesis lie in nineteenth-century struggles to wrest cultural supremacy from the established church and to transfer it to a developing professional scientific community. The evolution debates, for example, were manipulated by some to promote a conflict view of religion and science. The conflict view was reinforced by the polemical writings of J. W. Draper (1875) and A. D. White (1895), as well as the early twentieth-century philosophical movement *logical positivism*, which sought to make science the final arbiter of what it made sense to talk about and hence of truth. Although this philosophical position, like the conflict thesis, has been academically discredited, it proves very difficult to lay its ghost. This apparition is evident in odd demands like 'prove to me scientifically that God exists', as though science, the study of the natural world, was appropriate for answering questions about whether there is anything (God?) *other* than nature to which nature owes its existence.

PEACEFUL COEXISTENCE

The *peaceful coexistence* view was one which characterized the first 300 years of the development of science in the West, with well-known perturbations like the Galileo affair. This particular historical episode repays careful study if one is to understand events which are much more interesting than the popular, and erroneous, belief in a scientist standing out against the obscurantist forces of organized religion (see Brooke and Cantor, *Reconstructing Nature*, pp. 106–138).

From the time of Francis Bacon (1561–1626), and earlier, it was common to hear reference to the 'Two Books' metaphor. In it God was seen as the author of two great 'books'. One was the Book of Scripture, the Bible, the 'Book of God's Words'; the other was the 'Book of Nature', the 'Book of God's Works'. Those who believed, to use Galileo's words, that 'the holy Bible and the phenomena of nature proceed alike from the divine Word' did not expect that, when properly understood, they would be at variance. There is still mileage in this metaphor, provided it is remembered there is a hermeneutical circle involved in the 'reading' of each 'book'. We come to the 'texts' with preconceived ideas of our own which colour our understanding. In science, this circle can be expressed in the form 'theory precedes experiment'. Both the words of the scriptures and the data of the world play back upon our preconceptions and modify them, so that the next time we 'read' we start with a modified set of preconceptions, and so the circular process goes on.

DYNAMIC INTERCHANGE

Perhaps the most fruitful way of regarding the interplay between science and religion is one of *dynamic interchange*, in which each discipline stimulates and informs the other. Examples follow.

Science raises *questions which science itself cannot answer*. 'Why is there something rather than nothing?' is an early example. The outstanding contemporary one is the *anthropic principle*, in which the apparent 'fine-tuning' of the fundamental constants of nature is 'just right' for human life to exist. Dubbed the 'Goldilocks effect', the precision of the balance is such that changes, in some cases no larger that one part in 10^{60}, would mean that we would not be here. While not being a 'knock-down' argument for God, it is entirely consistent with views of the significance of humankind held by major world religions. Arguments for an intelligent design have persuasive force for the believer, but do not coerce the unbeliever into a logical corner from which there is no escape.

Recent claims have been made that certain biological structures could not possibly have developed by evolutionary processes. They are declared to exhibit 'irreducible complexity' that can be due only to intelligent design by God. Caution is needed here, however; a better understanding of biology has shown the subject of many such 'God-of-the-gaps' assertions to be explicable without reference to unusual activity by God. It is important to remember that the whole natural order exhibits God's handiwork, not just the bits that currently puzzle us. It is unbiblical to see the parts understood by science as 'naturalistic' and only the puzzles as 'God's design'. Science adopts the methodological convention of not referring to First Causes, thereby enabling atheists, agnostics and those of different faiths to work together on a common enterprise. But although individual scientists may take a naturalistic view of science, the scientific enterprise entails no such denial of divine agency. Hence I have avoided the misleading, but increasingly common, phrase 'methodological naturalism' as a label for this pragmatic position. 'Naturalism' is usually understood to mean that 'ultimately nothing resists explanation by the methods characteristic of the natural sciences', and *that* denial goes far beyond being a methodological principle. The arguments and counter-arguments for the position which has been termed 'the intelligent design movement' can be consulted in P. E. Johnson, D. O. Lamoureux et al., *Darwinism Defeated?*, and D. L. Ratzch, *Science and its Limits*.

Science studies can *steer exegetes away from inappropriate interpretations* of sacred writings, like those made in Galileo's time, when the poetry of Psalm 19:1–2 was used to defend a stationary Earth and a moving Sun.

There are interesting *parallels* to be drawn *between religion and science* as each grapples with the new, the invisible and the conceptually difficult in their use of metaphors and models. The 'plain, straightforward language of science', which the religiously unsympathetic sometimes extol, turns out to be far from plain or straightforward, as an increasingly counter-intuitive science explores fresh ways to be articulate.

Science can *contribute to religious studies* in fruitful ways, as can be seen in the scientific detective work of Humphreys and Waddington in dating the crucifixion and birth of Jesus, using well-attested astronomical events from those times (C. J. Humphreys and W. G. Waddington, in *Nature* 306, pp. 743–746; C. J. Humphreys, in *SCB* 5, pp. 83–101).

The third of the guiding questions is:

CAN THESE PERCEPTIONS BE JUSTIFIED?

It is one thing to say how people have perceived and do perceive the interactions between religion and science; these are historical and sociological questions. It is quite another to examine whether there are sound arguments for retaining such perceptions. This raises philosophical questions, and issues of justification have been implicit in some matters already discussed. So the above heading could indicate the strategy for a *magnum opus* on a wide range of issues of religion and science, marking out, as it does, the need for justification of positions taken. But in a dictionary such as this the question posed in the heading must serve both to mark the conclusion of this item and to point towards the further study of issues of religion and science by reference to literature such as that cited below and further sources cited therein.

BIBLIOGRAPHY

I. G. Barbour, *Religion and Science: Historical and Contemporary Issues* (London, 1998); J. H. Brooke, *Science and Religion: Some Historical Perspectives* (Cambridge, 1991); J. H. Brooke and G. Cantor, *Reconstructing Nature: The Engagement of Science and Religion* (Edinburgh, 1998); R. Hooykaas, *Religion and the Rise of Modern Science* (Edinburgh, 1972); C. J. Humphreys, 'The Star of Bethlehem', in *SCB* 5, 1993, pp. 83–101; C. J. Humphreys and W. G. Waddington, 'Dating the Crucifixion', *Nature* 306, 1983, pp. 743–746; P. E. Johnson, D. O. Lamoureux et al., *Darwinism Defeated? The Johnson–Lamoureux Debate on Biological Origins* (Vancouver, 1999); S. A. Mabud, 'Theory of Evolution: An Assessment from the Islamic Point of View', *MEQ* 4(1), 1986, pp. 9–56; J. Polkinghorne, *Science & Theology: An Introduction* (London, 1998); M. W. Poole, *Beliefs and Values in Science Education* (Buckingham, 1995); M. W. Poole, *A Guide to Science and Belief* (Oxford, [2]1997); D. L. Ratzch, *Science and its Limits: The Natural Sciences in Christian Perspective* (Downers Grove and Leicester, [2]2000); C. A. Russell, *Cross-currents: Interactions between Science and Faith* (London, 1995, reissue of Leicester, 1985).

M. W. Poole

RELIGION AND SEXUALITY

At the dawn of the third millennium, the relationship of Western humanity to questions of sexual behaviour is fraught with difficulty and much contested. The difficulties are not only theological, and the debate must be located within profound changes in Western culture. In terms of its influence and the debate it produced, the single most important Christian document addressing sexual ethics in the twentieth century was *Humanae Vitae*, the encyclical issued by Pope Paul VI on 25 July 1968. Although often cited out of context (and demonized) for its condemnation of artificial contraception, the encyclical recognized and attempted to hold together the unitive and procreative uses of sex while offering an eloquent defence of the ideals of Christian marriage and the dignity of women.

In the late 1980s and 1990s a number of British and American churches produced significant reports reassessing their teaching on sexual matters and setting the agenda for subsequent debate. These include, from the Church of England: *Homosexual Relationships: A Con-tribution to Discussion* (1979) and *Issues in Human Sexuality: A Statement by the House of Bishops* (1991); from the Methodist Conference in the UK: *Report of the Commission on Human Sexuality* (1990); from the United Reformed Church (UK): *Homosexuality: A Christian View* (1991); from the United States Catholic Conference: *Human Sexuality: A Catholic*

Perspective for Education and Lifelong Learning (1991); and from the Church of Scotland: *Report on the Theology of Marriage* (1994).

PRINCIPAL CONTEMPORARY BELIEFS AND PRACTICES

Since the Second World War, individuals in the West have increasingly accepted a separation of the unitive from the procreative use of sex. This has been enabled by the advent of a variety of effective and convenient means of contraception. Inevitably this has had a vast social effect, as it has enabled women to exercise and maintain an indisputable right to control their own fertility. Sexual behaviour has come to be understood as a largely private matter. Sex outside marriage, provided it is neither exploitative nor promiscuous, is no longer a cause for social disapproval and often is not seen as incompatible with Christian belief. A homosexual orientation is widely accepted as a given condition. Homosexual practice is increasingly, though still often uneasily, accepted. Incest, paedophilia and rape are universally condemned. It is increasingly accepted that marriage does not confer unqualified sexual access, and that a married woman may legitimately accuse her husband of rape.

THE MODERN/POSTMODERN CULTURAL CONTEXT

Contemporary Western culture has had immense and complicated effects. Increased secularization has distanced secular legislation from its earlier relation to canon law and has eroded and isolated distinctively Christian speech, virtues and distinctions. Awareness of the social location of text has opened a gulf between the world of the Bible and contemporary society. An understanding of practices as social constructs has led to acceptance of a greater variety of lifestyles. The increasing authority of international over local legislation on individual rights and non-discrimination has fostered individualism. Imbalance and misuse of power has been unmasked, by feminism especially, and there is a much increased awareness of the potential for abuse in sexual relationships. Increased attention has been given to the notion of 'person', sometimes separated from a notion of 'responsibility'. There is new awareness and sensitivity to gender differences and roles. Empiricism in philosophy has concentrated on the consequences of acts, rather than the worth or merit of the acts themselves. There is vastly increased commercialization of allure and exploitation of desire through television, advertising and style gurus. This has produced a totalizing rhetoric of its own promoting the icons of thinness, beauty, availability and youth, exacerbated by a compulsion for instant gratification fostered by the speed of contemporary transactions and communication. Increasingly strident, liberal Western society appears to lack toleration: trends and lifestyles are either condemned or accepted. When combined with a concern to avoid discrimination, this attitude has led to increased claims for the 'moral equivalence' of alternative lifestyles.

ENCOUNTERING MODERN/POSTMODERN CULTURE

Christianity, still the major religion in the West but now much more pluralist, has responded with bewildering inconsistency.

The *Roman Catholic Church*, through the Second Vatican Council, Pope Paul VI and Pope John Paul II, has, along with other modern institutions, come much more fully to understand the role of sexuality in human personhood and interpersonal relating. This is called the *unitive* aspect of sex, and it is increasingly uncommon for it to be argued that the *primary* purpose of human sexuality is procreative. The problem for official Roman Catholic statements is to explain the relation between the unitive and the procreative aspects. Responsible human sexual activity is understood as an act of self-giving. It is argued that for the mutual, total giving of oneself to another (which is marriage) the gift of one's fertility must be included. That gift is considered authentic only if given to and received by someone capable of receiving it (a member of the opposite sex). Thus, it is argued that artificial contraception and homosexual activity involve a partial withholding of the total gift of oneself. It follows that, despite a much more positive understanding of the unitive aspect of sex, the Roman Catholic Church, in its official teaching, maintains the immorality of homosexual acts and considers the homosexual orientation not as sinful (because not chosen), but as ontically disordered.

In a society where procreation is controlled through contraceptives, the *Protestant churches* have recently tended to tie together the unitive and procreative aspects of sex much less closely, and thus have been obliged more starkly to ask how they are to evaluate sex which has no procreative intent, sex outside marriage and homosexual acts. Some answers, though prophetic in that they have genuinely believed themselves to be extending a biblical message of liberation to minorities and the oppressed, have not met with wholesale support. Characteristic statements are that 'love, trust, forgiveness and faithfulness are the most significant criteria by which all relationships are to be assessed' and that 'congregations should not discriminate against any person on grounds of marital status or sexual orientation' (Church of Scotland, 1994, p. 257). The Church of England, though acknowledging that sexuality is a very important element in our human makeup, maintained that it is only one aspect of it. Significantly and controversially, it stated that the 'homophile orientation and its expression do not constitute a parallel and alternative form of human sexuality as complete within the terms of the created order as the heterosexual' (*Issues in Human Sexuality*, 1991, p. 40). Equally, it maintained that 'homosexual people are in every way as valuable to and as valued by God as heterosexual people'. The church, it maintained, does 'not reject those who sincerely believe it is God's call to them' (*Issues*, p. 41).

Such reports have provoked passionate debate, in which it is maintained that the very identity of Christianity is at stake. The cry of the modern world is for relevance: that Christianity adapt to changed social circumstances, allowing for critical study of its scriptures, new scientific claims and newer sensitivities. Christianity has responded with an internal debate on how literally to read its scriptures. One approach has been to hold to a core or central strand of Scripture, perhaps the rule of love. Another view is that this constitutes a new abstraction and a diversion from what Christianity is all about; the task of the church is not to try to fit God into our histories, but to understand the good news that God has made us part of God's history. Consequently, what is required is not a refined biblicism which might be no less legalistic than the old, but the elaboration of an anthropology which takes account of the biblical teaching that God is creator, reconciler and redeemer.

Inevitably, further questions arise from such replies. It has been objected that they are too tidy and too totalizing. Even today, about so significant a fact as human sexual orientation, we know depressingly little. There has been pervasive *human* difficulty in appropriating this aspect of self-awareness (which is also acknowledged by the non-Christian religions), and the Christian church, in its various branches, may not yet adequately have drawn on its own distinctive glimpse of new possibilities of living.

The contemporary debate about the evaluation and propriety of sexual acts is inseparable from fundamental questioning in European culture concerning its *understanding of sexual identity and equality*. Sexual identity is to do with how, within a culture, biological differences are used as the basis for differing social expectations.

Christianity (along with liberty and equality) has been a dominant Western metanarrative and has both contributed to and inhibited the shaping of sexual equality. Areas in which this influence is evident include: equality of access to educational resources; images of men's and women's spiritual potential; access to specialist religious roles, especially ordination and the episcopate; status and authority within the family; equality of legal status in divorce, divorce settlements and inheritance; opportunity for political power (cf. Harvey, *An Introduction to Buddhist Ethics*, p. 353). Sex may, of its nature, be a pleasurable and uninhibited act, but it may equally be disturbing and speak to some of humanity's deepest anxieties. Christianity has tended to try to contain such disturbance by insisting that sex should be contained within marriage. Clearly this insistence has contributed unintentionally to the construction of gender roles for men and especially women. In postmodernity, gender stereotyping is becoming fractured, along with the religious metanarratives which underpinned it. Along with this, it is questioned whether responsible sex *must* be tied to childbearing and may take place only within marriage. Widespread contraception and temporary or permanent sterilization have eroded the credibility of an intrinsic link between the unitive and the procreative use of sex. This fracture is underlined by the more frequent occurrence of *in vitro* fertilization, which further distances childbearing from physical intercourse. A reassessment of homosexual sex naturally follows, especially when an attempt is made to think of it in its own, different terms, rather than through heterosexual spectacles. Moreover, third-millennium homosexuality, the overt endorsement of an orientation, may be something new (cf. G. Herdt) which eschews easy categorization from historical dual-sex traditions.

Whether and how any Western religion aids or impedes navigation of this human vulnerability is what is at issue; whether a religion *inevitably* wraps sex into particular gender constructions and family structures. It is appropriate to explore whether Christianity, for instance, has a sexual ethic, or only, in fact, a marital ethic. If a religion considers sex only as bundled with a metanarrative of identity and family, this view should not necessarily be taken as a flaw. It constitutes the very serious claim that this is where transformation may be found. Inevitably, the religions present in the West navigate this passage differently. What is important is whether, at a time of great change, they facilitate or blight serious discussion of what is different.

Sex in *Judaism* has never been furtive or taboo, though Judaism maintains that promiscuity cheapens sex and erodes self-respect. Adultery was condemned in the Ten Commandments and remains prohibited. Marriage is for companionship as much as children; the wife is not subservient to the husband. In relation to homosexuality, it is the activity, not the person, which is condemned (Lev. 18:22; 20:13).

Muslims, on the basis of their understanding of God, strive to meet their commitments. They seek to remove hypocrisy, greed, selfishness and envy from their lives. They are concerned to live in cooperation, not competition, with others. Sexual intercourse is understood as an act of worship (*'ibada*). It fulfils human emotional and procreative needs, but also contributes to the continuation of God's creation. Islam prohibits sex outside marriage, so as to preserve its seriousness. Homosexuality is explicitly forbidden in the Qur'an (26:165–166).

Traditionally, *Hinduism* lays stress on duties rather than on individual rights. Classic virtues include non-violence, truthfulness, purity, control of one's organs. It is recognized that the motivating force of human life is desire, but the ideal is to maintain a balance between the four aims of life, one of which is sensual pleasure (*kama*). Premarital chastity is highly valued, but sex is given its place in married life. Homosexuality is a taboo subject and Hindu literary sources are silent on it. There are evolving attitudes, but they tend to be controlled, even in the West, by a persistent metanarrative of 'Indian' culture and morality.

At the heart of *Buddhism* is transcendence of the self, so anything exploitative will be avoided. Sexuality is not seen as part of personal identity. Traditionally Buddhism saw two types of sexuality: celibacy and that of those who were married. Any uncontrolled desire would be seen as potentially destructive, unwise and possibly a misuse of the senses.

BIBLIOGRAPHY

M. Banner, *Christian Ethics and Contemporary Moral Problems* (Cambridge, 1999); P. Harvey, *An Introduction to Buddhist Ethics* (Cambridge, 2000); G. Herdt, 'Homosexuality', in *ER* 6, pp. 445–453; M. Lamm, *The Jewish Way in Love and Marriage* (San Francisco, 1982); P. Morgan and C. Lawton (eds.), *Ethical Issues in Six Religious Traditions* (Edinburgh, 1996).

I. R. Torrance

RELIGION AND SOCIOLOGY

Sociology and religion have always had an ambivalent relationship. Sociologists cannot expect their analyses of religion to be uncontested, any more than can people wishing to demonstrate the relevance of explicit religious commitments to sociology. The terms of the debate are altering in the early twenty-first century, however, as both sociologists and persons of specific faith rethink their relationship with modernity. In what follows I shall address these issues mainly from the point of view of Christian commitments, even though some of what I say may be generalized to other perspectives.

A dismissive attitude towards religion characterized much social science during the twentieth century, and in some quarters it still does. This may be traced largely to the animosity of some early sociologists to what they saw, variously, as the human origins and social oppressiveness of religion. It is a short step from reducing religion to a social product to seeing it as epiphen-o-menal, anachronistic, and a diversion from progressive 'real life'. Karl Marx denounced religion by depicting it as an upside-down worldview, as a camera obscura might show it, although even he could not help also acknowledging its positive side as the 'heart of a heartless world'.

Max Weber, Émile Durkheim, and Georg Simmel were more careful and more kind to religion, even though their work gave rise to a certain pessimism about the prospects for institutional Christianity and even for religion-in-general. Weber gave the sociology of religion some of its key concepts, including the famous idea of the Protestant ethic, which, he argued, lay behind the development of aspects of Western capitalism. A line of thought may be traced from

Weber through Ernst Troeltsch, H. R. Niebuhr and Bryan Wilson, analysing the development of church, sect, denomination and cult, which many see as an almost inexorable process of secularization.

In the early nineteenth century Auguste Comte asserted that sociology was replacing theological interpretations of the world and this idea remained implicit in much subsequent sociological theory. Add to this the fact that religion tended to be seen merely as an institution and not as possessing integrity, adaptability or a real link with a world beyond empirical reality, narrowly conceived, and it is unsurprising that religion was seldom seen as a dialogue partner with sociology. Even more unfortunately, theology's response frequently was a retreat into safety zones of protected parkland in which, as it were, industry, commerce and urban development were denied access.

Thus the idea of a generalized secularization accompanying the growth of modernity became in part a self-fulfilling prophecy. Conventional religiosity not only conformed to the institutional patterns prevailing in joint-stock companies and bureaucratic modes of organization, but also suffered from nerve failure when it realized that it could scarcely compete on their terms with those models. Sociology sounded confident and self-assured as the rapid shrinkage of church membership and the Christian evacuation of the public sphere in many Western countries after the Second World War seemed to confirm its most dogmatic predictions of religious decline.

Towards the end of the twentieth century, however, confidence about the future of modernity began to falter on many fronts, giving rise to a debate about late or even postmodernity. Old authorities, whether religious or scientific, were challenged by cultural contacts enabled by the proliferation of new technologies and by travel. Uncertainty seemed to characterize most social, cultural, economic and political experiences. Spiritualities and cultic activities began to flourish more visibly. And religion reappeared in new locations, in different parts of the world, in political guise in both right and left formations, and as a vital component of globalization in, for example, the *jihad* of Islam. Erstwhile leading commentators, such as Peter L. Berger, declared that substantial analyses of secularization were mistaken. Sociologists such as James Beckford and Daniele Hervieu-Leger argued that religion is a cultural resource drawn upon in varying but still possibly influential ways.

None of this makes the possibility of conversation between sociology and religion any easier although the doors for such dialogue appear more open now. Indeed, recent articles in both sociological and religion journals suggest that at least peace talks are possible. But the context cannot be ignored. There are two key axes framing the context in which any dialogue between religion and sociology must be understood: the fragmentation of cultural identities, along with the elevation of market choice to the level of an ultimate value, hints at one axis of the frame, while the realization that risks chronically attend every new development and intervention, with potentially global and transgenerational consequences, provides the other. These circumstances have encouraged a new quest for ethics within sociology, a quest that may provide a bridge for two-way traffic.

What does Christian thought offer? In the early twentieth century a so-called social gospel encouraged a break with pietism and individualism and an engagement with the realities of urban industrial life under capitalism. Its roots are intertwined with the founding of American sociology. In Europe at the same time attempts to rehabilitate Catholic social teachings were also influential, for instance in the writing of R. H. Tawney, and in the Christendom Group. Later in the century an interchange between Christianity and Marxism produced varieties of liberation theology. At its best this drew upon both biblical and sociological resources to understand the world of capitalism and colonialism, and also influenced discussions of ecology, of race and ethnicity, and of gender relations.

Two other models also suggest themselves: the erudite *Theology and Social Theory* of British ethicist John Milbank and the lifelong analyses of modernity of French sociologist Jacques Ellul. *The first* mounts a devastating critique of sociology and social theory as a denial of the transcendent and pleads for a fresh social theology planted in the soil of an 'ontology of peace'. *The second* uses sociological tools to present a fearful story of society in the thrall of technology, but parallels this with a theology of ambivalence, seen for example in *The Meaning of the City*. The first is a stimulating reminder that Christian thought speaks to sociology but leaves little room for dialogue. The second implicitly fosters dialogue between disciplines, but only in service of culturally relevant discipleship.

While all these resources may critically be drawn upon in the attempt to produce Christianly nuanced sociological imaginations, they are also products of modernity and as such may have less to say about postmodern conditions. While retrieval and the revival of Christian memory is vital to the task, a future orientation (equally threatened by aspects of the postmodern) calls for openness to new modes of analysis. Social life under the sign of mobility, for example, may not satisfactorily be comprehended using tools from more static and seemingly more stable times. Equally, whilst clearly debatable, some might argue that Christian thought is able to cheerfully jettison concepts such as 'society' or 'the individual' as having no necessary referent in biblical thought or Christian tradition.

What if Christian social thought could see its role as making a constructive if critical contribution to contemporary sociological analysis and theory? The transcendent critique that is unafraid to name idolatry and to unmask injustice may also suggest new concepts and theoretical resources for grasping the realities of social relationship in electronically mediated conditions, or the intrinsic connections between the worlds of 'nature' and 'culture' that modernity mistakenly split asunder. The sociality and materiality, as well as the spirituality, of the human body is another domain calling for Christian comment today.

In this sense there is no going back to situations where Christian 'authority' could be assumed. As in other life spheres, pluralism is the order of the day, which calls for both respect for the Other and clarity about difference. Christians may embrace post-empiricism, which acknowledges that theory is undetermined by facts and that all so-called facts are theory-laden. The concepts that we ineluctably use in theory-making draw upon metaphors that reveal their closeness to or their distance from Christian thought. To recognize that all concepts are contestable goes along with a commitment to speak to contemporary sociology even though Christian contributions may meet with hostility or rejection. This is where the demands of discipleship outweigh the desire for dialogue.

BIBLIOGRAPHY

J. Ellul, *The Meaning of the City* (Grand Rapids, 1970); D. Lyon, *Jesus in Disneyland: Religion in Postmodern Times* (Oxford, 2000); D. Lyon, *Sociology and the Human Image* (Downers Grove, 1983); J. Milbank, *Theology and Social Theory* (Oxford, 1990); E. Storkey, *The Origins of Difference: The Gender Debate Revisited* (Grand Rapids, 2001).

D. Lyon

RELIGION AND TECHNOLOGY

All the major world religions began and were propagated before the advent of modern technology. The sacred writings of Judaism, Christianity and Islam, the religions that have made the greatest impact in the Western world, lack any direct reference to contemporary technologies. Even the Baha'i faith, which began in the mid-nineteenth century in Persia, arose before the technological inventions that contemporary Westerners take for granted (although one of its stated goals is the unity of science and religion). Nevertheless, religious adherents of all kinds in the industrialized world face the influence of these technologies daily.

Technologies are artefacts that result from the intersection of nature and uniquely human ingenuity. For example, at a very basic level, nature provides a tree and humans shape it to construct a bow and arrow in accordance with their aims. As Marshall McLuhan (1911–80) emphasized, technologies are typically created in order to extend human powers: the telephone extends the reach of the human voice; the bulldozer extends human strength; the computer extends computation speed; and so on. However, technologies also amputate. The telephone and radio project the human voice beyond its natural capacities, but eliminate physical presence. Technologies are more than isolated and multifaceted artefacts. Many technologies, particularly electronic media (such as radio, television and the Internet), form involved systems that are distributed over vast areas and transform cultures in profound and unexpected ways.

All tools may be considered as technologies, but technologies vary in scope, significance and sophistication. Most advanced technologies require scientific knowledge and much scientific knowledge requires technology (advanced astronomy requires telescopes; advanced chemistry requires microscopes; etc.), but technology and science are not identical. Rather, some rudimentary technologies such as chariots are hardly scientific at all, since they require little knowledge of scientific laws. More developed technologies are cases of applied science, wherein scientific knowledge of nature is used to create an artefact not found in nature itself, such as an automotive or jet engine.

In *Technopoly*, social critic Neil Postman argues that cultures move through three fundamental historical stages. The first is the 'tool-using culture', in which simple technologies have little systemic effect on the culture at large. Religion and social mores are not significantly affected by these technologies. The next stage, beginning at about the time of the Industrial Revolution in the West, is what Postman calls a 'technocracy', in which technologies gain an increasing role in nearly every aspect of culture and thus begin to challenge established religious perspectives. For instance, the value of efficiency, so vital to mechanical production, challenges the traditional emphasis on contemplation and reflection. The industrial revolution disrupted traditional patterns of family life and religion as men who worked in the cities were separated from their families for longer periods of time.

The last stage is what Postman dubs a 'technopoly', in which a web of technologies shapes culture in every dimension. Postman argues that the USA was the first technopoly, but (as of 1992) several other nations were near to attaining this status. In a technopoly, technologies are not mere adjuncts or rivals to received culture; they monopolize the culture itself and tend to overwhelm or reconstitute religious values. For example, as the ethos of television shapes people's sensibilities, religious activities tend to take on the form of television: quick, smart, light and (above all) entertaining. Whether or not one accepts Postman's provocative and plausible thesis *in toto*, he rightly highlights the challenges that technologies bring to religious practices and worldviews.

Although there is much discussion and debate concerning the defining features of postmodernity (as opposed to modernity), increasing technological saturation seems to be one of these differentiating aspects. The postmodern sense of reality, identity and even the sacred is highly mediated by communications technologies, particularly video and computer media. David Lyon argues that sacred symbols, once largely controlled or authorized by religious institutions, have become overproduced, free-floating and detached from their original referents. This process tends to destabilize and redefine the idea of the sacred, even subjecting it to the demands associated with commodities. Many denizens of post-modernity eclectically appropriate religious symbols and ideas as though they were consumer items, that are easily available through technologies such as web pages, films, television programmes and even video games, rather than as markers of transcendent meaning rooted in a particular historical tradition.

The cultures of the Bible were tool-using cultures. The Hebrew Scriptures speak of technologies such as chariots used in warfare, the architectural and agricultural exploits of the author of Ecclesiastes, and the construction of the temple and tabernacle. Such references address rudimentary technologies, but nothing beyond what was powered by animals, humans or natural forces such as wind, fire and water. Nevertheless, several texts warn the faithful against trusting in mechanical, human or animal strength instead of the covenant Lord of Israel (Ps. 20:7–8). The Genesis account of the tower of Babel portrays God as judging the efforts of fallen humans, who, after the flood, said 'Come, let us build ourselves a city, with a tower that reaches to the heavens, so that we may make a name for ourselves and not be scattered over the face of the whole earth' (Gen. 11:4). Their grandiose architectural ambitions manifested a rebellious desire to establish a proud culture apart from the directives of God. The Hebrew Scriptures also condemn as pointless and blasphemous any mechanical means used to produce idols, since these finite objects can neither represent God nor bestow blessings (Exod. 32; Is. 40:18–20; 44:9–11).

Although advanced technologies were far in the future for the biblical writers, some premillennial dispensationalists, such as Hal Lindsey and his many imitators, have variously interpreted some of the apocalyptic symbolism of the book of Revelation and selected Old Testament passages as predictions of modern technologies of warfare, such as tanks and nuclear weaponry. However, these interpretations are highly speculative and seem to violate the symbolism of the genres themselves. One may grant that at least some of these passages are yet to be wholly fulfilled without assuming that they make specific references to modern technologies.

The Christian orientation towards technology has, of course, been varied, and no simple summary is possible. However, the biblical doctrine of a good creation presided over by its Creator who calls humans to develop that creation for God's glory and human flourishing (see Gen. 1:26–28) helped historically to establish a worldview favourable to 'the mechanical arts'. The historian David F. Noble notes that in the early Middle Ages 'technology came to be identified more closely with both lost perfection and the possibility of renewed perfection, and the advance of the arts took on new significance, not only as evidence of grace, but as a means or preparation for, and a true sign of, imminent salvation' (*Religion of Technology*). Advances in agriculture during this time, especially the introduction of the heavy plough, along with a strong emphasis on manual labour as spiritual service in Christian monasteries further increased the perceived value of technological pursuits.

The Reformation's emphasis on the priesthood of all believers and the doctrine of calling as applicable to Christians in all walks of life served to reinforce the dignity of labour, advance material betterment and encourage technological innovation wherever it took root in Europe and later in America through the Puritans. The Reformers also celebrated the printing press of Gutenberg as a providentially provided technological means of mass producing both the Scriptures in the vernacular and the teachings of Martin Luther and others.

A key Western Protestant philosopher who developed a messianic vision for technology was Francis Bacon (1561–1626). Although Bacon made no significant scientific or technological discoveries, he heralded the advance of an inductive and experimental scientific method over the pronouncements of the received Aristotelian tradition, which Bacon took to be overly deductive and stultifying to scientific and technological progress. He viewed technologies as tools of human progress that could ameliorate the physical effects of the fall and restore humanity to an Edenic state. He says in *Novum Organum*, 'Man by the Fall fell at the same time from his state of innocence and from his dominion over creation. Both of these losses can even in this life be in some parts repaired; the former by religion and faith, the latter by the arts and sciences.' Less modestly, in *The New Atlantis*, Bacon's unfinished utopian novel, an exemplary character exclaims, 'the End of our Foundation is the knowledge of Causes, and the secret motions of things; and the enlarging of the bounds of Human Empire, to the effecting of all things possible'. In *Valerius Terminus* he boldly states that humans through the restoration of creation by means of technology may become 'not animals on their hind legs, but moral gods'.

The Roman Catholic philosopher, mathematician and scientist Blaise Pascal (1623–62), who far exceeded Bacon in scientific knowledge and technological inventiveness, took a more cautious view concerning human mastery of nature. Although he invented and marketed the first calculating machine and had other prodigious scientific achievements, Pascal mused at length in *Pensées* on the limits of human knowing in a vast and still mysterious cosmos, where humans are strangely situated between 'nothingness and infinity' and thus limited in both their knowledge and their power. He saw human beings as 'deposed royalty': great by virtue of their divine origin and fatally flawed because of sin. He famously remarked, 'What sort of a freak is man! How novel, how monstrous, how chaotic, how paradoxical, how prodigious! Judge of all things, feeble earthworm, repository of truth, sink of doubt and error, glory and refuse of the universe.' Although Pascal affirmed that these paradoxical creatures could find redemption through Christ, the Mediator, his understanding of the human situation east of Eden never allowed him to be tempted by the technological utopianism of Bacon. Nor did he affirm Bacon's vision of the restoration of Adam's pre-fall powers through scientific discovery and the control of nature. His understanding of original sin precluded any such this-worldly millenarianism.

The innovations of the scientific revolution (led by Pascal, Galileo, Faraday, Newton and others) were well rooted in theism, as was Bacon's more programmatic and utopian vision. Nevertheless, the dream of harnessing nature for human betterment was secularized by later Enlightenment and post-Enlightenment thinkers such as the French philosopher Auguste Comte (1798–1857). Comte was one of the founders of sociology, and deemed science and technology as the real liberators of a humanity that must outgrow religious authority and metaphysical speculations in order to embrace an entirely empirical or 'positive' philosophy (positivism). He founded the Religion of Humanity to further this noble goal and hailed the rise of scientific engineers who would bring structure and purpose to the new order of mature humanity.

Contemporary secular humanists and sceptics (as represented in the USA by *The Humanist* and *Skeptic* periodicals) typically hail 'the scientific method' or scientific rationality as human thought at its best. Many have high hopes that technology, which employs the scientific method for pragmatic results, will ensure a more humane human future, provided that 'superstitious' (i.e. religious) sensibilities succumb to more rational ones.

Contemporary religious thinkers have assessed technologies in terms of their theologies of culture. Not surprisingly, a variety of approaches has resulted. At the extremes are those who embrace technologies uncritically and enthusiastically as God-given means to further religious ends, and those who reject most technologies as engines of secularization and dehumanization. Those who adopt what H. Richard Niebuhr called the 'Christ Transformer of Culture' model may embrace technologies as forces for redemptive social change. However, some in the transformationist tradition deem aspects of modern technology as intrinsically unworthy of Christian ends. (See Groothuis, *The Soul in Cyberspace*.) Those holding to the opposite model of 'Christ against culture' assess technologies with suspicion, as they do most aspects of culture. (Nevertheless, members of the Protestant Bruderhof communities, who live communally and reject much of contemporary culture as violent, materialistic and individualistic, operate a web page connected to their publishing house, Plough Publishers.) At the far end of the spectrum we find the Amish, who refuse to have cars and most (but not all) other modern technologies in their separatist communities.

Jacques Ellul (1912–94), the French Protestant activist, sociologist and theologian, was a distinguished and influential critic of modern technology. He argued in several books that what he called 'the technological society' displaced traditional forms and ideas of work, family, politics and religion in favour of a social system in which *technique* (rational, reproducible and efficient means to predetermined results) overrides and subjugates all other values. In his theologically oriented books Ellul summoned Christians to discern, expose and resist the impersonal and dehumanizing domination of technique in favour of authentic Christian freedom. In *The Humiliation of the Word* he warns that with the advent of photography, cinema and television technological societies have marginalized the written and spoken word in favour of mass-produced images, which are quite limited in their ability to communicate truth and which easily serve the purposes of propaganda. Christians who succumb to technologies that exalt the image over the word fail to realize that not all media suit the nature of the Christian message itself. He counsels, 'It is vital that we ask ourselves whether the means we use are able to convey the truth of Jesus Christ.'

The Western counter-cultural movement of the 1960s, intellectually led by social critics such as Theodore Roszak and William Irwin Thompson, challenged received assumptions about Western religion and culture, including much of modern technology. This ostensibly 'back to nature' movement, rooted largely in Eastern and occult mystical notions and experimental drug usage, questioned much of modern technology (stereo hi-fi systems excepted), especially in so far as it contributed to ecological pollution and warfare. The movement served as the forerunner of later New Age spiritualities, which developed in the 1980s and still have a wide influence through various therapies, seminars and charismatic figures (all with their own web pages).

The rapid and extensive computerization of American culture in the 1990s, along with the influence of New Age spiritualities, occasioned a hybrid spirituality sometimes called 'techno-shamanism' or 'techno-animism'. This perspective combines a pantheistic or animistic worldview inherited from the counter-culture with an obsession with computer-mediated communication (or cyberspace) technologies, which are interpreted as sacramental (or even divine) zones for magic and spiritual transformation. An ageing Timothy Leary led the way for techno-shamanism in the last few years before his death in 1996, hailing cyberspace as a better trip than LSD. Whether techno-shamanism is a mere fad or a culturally significant religious approach to cyberspace technologies remains to be seen, but it is certain that the interaction of religion and technology will continue to be a matter for intellectual discussion and daily engagement in the contemporary world.

BIBLIOGRAPHY

J. Ellul, *The Humiliation of the Word* (Grand Rapids, MI, 1985); J. Ellul, *The Technological Society* (New York, 1964); D. Groothuis, 'Bacon and Pascal on Mastery Over Nature', *RPT* 14, 1994, pp. 191–203; D. Groothuis, *The Soul in Cyberspace* (Eugene, OR, 1999); D. Lyon, *Jesus in Disneyland: Religion in Postmodern Times* (Malden, MA, 2000); D. F. Noble, *The Religion of Technology: The Divinity of Man and The Spirit of Technology* (New York, 1997); N. Postman, *Technopoly: The Surrender of Culture to Technology* (New York, 1992).

D. Groothuis

RELIGION AND YOUTH CULTURE

INTRODUCTION AND HISTORICAL OVERVIEW

The development of youth as a particular subculture within society is a relatively recent phenomenon. By the middle of the nineteenth century changing family, work and cultural patterns and the development of public education meant that the gradual awareness of 'youth' as a defined and separate group had begun. Specific 'clubs' for young people had been established and youth organizations began to spring up. Towards the end of the nineteenth century denominational churches began to establish specific programmes for young people. As the age at which the majority of young people left formal education rose through the twentieth century and the age of the onset of puberty lowered, so the identity of young people as a specific and unique group was established.

It was in the United States of America during the post-war period that advertisers began to target young people and to use the term 'teenager'. With the rise of a consumer market directed at the young and their release from the responsibilities of work, there came a freedom to allow the full complexity of the physical, social, emotional and spiritual changes associated with adolescence to become expressed in a defined and definite youth culture.

Youth can thus be seen as 'the transition between the dependence of childhood and the independence of adulthood' (A. Lee & Associates, *Our Target* [Singapore, 1985], p. 2). In the Western world, those who choose to work with young people recognize the need to support them in the change from the dependence of childhood, through the independence of youth, to the interdependence of full citizenship and adulthood.

In terms of age the United Nations defines 'youth' as the period between 15 and 24 years, whilst the majority of countries in the Western world generally regard the age of 21 as the point at which someone is no longer technically a 'young person'. Society, however, now glorifies and almost deifies 'youth' to the point where there is an earnest desire on the part of many to stay 'forever young'. As a result the concept of a youth culture is difficult to define in terms of age.

If by 'youth culture' we mean a single set of beliefs, behaviour and structures which are identifiable, then some would argue that we need to talk in terms of cultures in the plural, or of subcultures, in order to explain the many and divergent lifestyles of young people. Whilst that may be true at the micro level, at the macro level there are sufficient similarities for us to be able to make generalizations about the relationship between religion and youth culture.

PRINCIPAL CONTEMPORARY BELIEFS AND PRACTICES

THE PRESENT CONTEXT

The attitude of many young people in the Western world to religion was summed up in the words of a Spice Girl, Mel C, when she said to a reporter from the *Big Issue* (London, 1999): 'I'm a Christian but I'm more spiritual now. I do a lot of yoga. I believe in a God but I think it's more within. Our generation can't see any good in religion when it causes such destruction and war.' Whilst Mel C comes from within Generation X, her ideas are echoed by many young people.

The tidal flow of youth culture away from organized religion has to be held up against the fact that young people still search for meaning beyond themselves (spirituality). Leslie Francis, Professor of Practical Theology at the University of Wales, Bangor, has undertaken extensive research in the area of young people and religion. In one survey 13,000 young people were asked if they believed in God. Two out of every five were theists (39%), slightly fewer agnostics (35%) and the rest (26%) were atheists. In *Teenage Religion and Values* Leslie J. Francis and William K. Kay note that 'even in the materialistic and largely secular society of modern Britain, theism is significantly more acceptable than atheism and, though these figures show a more sceptical population than would be the case if the previous generation were surveyed, it is clear that both the churches and religious educators ought to be able to gain a hearing from the young' (p. 147).

In an as yet unpublished paper on 'Religion and Modernity: The Social Significance of Religious Affiliation among Adolescents in England and Wales', Leslie Francis has researched the attitudes of almost 30,000 young people aged 13–15 years. When asked about religious affiliation, 46% checked 'none' and 53% identified with a faith group. Young people appear to regard themselves as belonging to a particular group even though they do not attend worship (belong) nor accept the tenets of the faith group (believe). The survey did show that, in general, they choose to behave according to the principles of the faith grouping to which they belong.

If an organized religion can be understood in terms of the triumvirate of believing, behaving and belonging, then young people in the Western world are happy to dislocate each from the others and to choose what they want and what meets their gently hedonistic criteria. They are happy to select some beliefs but fail to see that certain behaviour should result. They are sometimes happy to belong because a faith community can be just that – a community of people in relationship together – whilst questioning some of the community's beliefs and behaving in one way with the faithful and in another way during the rest of the week. And as Leslie Francis' research has shown, many young people align themselves with a faith, and behave accordingly, without either necessarily accepting the tenets of that group or active involvement in that community.

THE ROOTS OF THE PRESENT CONTEXT

Youth culture has been affected by various changes in society, most especially the rise of individualism and the ability to be a consumer, not just in the actual market in town, but also in the market of ideas, beliefs, behaviour and the group to which one wishes to belong. As a result it can appear that for this generation, religion has been 'deconstructed' into constituent parts to enable a 'pick 'n' mix' approach. Young people choose in which God to believe, which beliefs to accept, which forms of behaviour to adopt and to which groups of people to belong. Or, to express the point in another way, they presume that it is their right to create their own religion as it were out of toy bricks, bringing together the parts that they wish to use from whichever source seems appropriate.

The roots of this approach to religion lie in a number of changes. In education across the Western world there has been a shift from the didactic to the critical and analytical approaches to learning, resulting in a positive questioning and a negative cynicism. Everything can be questioned and no 'truth' is beyond critical examination. At the family level, breakdown of formerly secure relationships and the resultant loss of appropriate adults have forced young people to survive on their own and question the value of marriage.

The nature of the community to which young people relate has changed from the local to the plural: they travel to virtual communities at school, at work, at the leisure centre, at the shops and possibly at the worship centre. For today's young people 'there is no such thing as society' (Margaret Thatcher interviewed on *Today*, BBC Radio 4, 1987).

At the same time the expectation of a certain level of enjoyment and activity has raised the boredom threshold for young people. As a result they are less satisfied and more restless, forever seeking the next experience, the failure to achieve such experiences being measured by the rising suicide statistics among young people in the West. Hedonism has become a way of life. The value of the 'now' over and above the past means that wisdom is rejected in favour of knowledge and history is seen as well and truly past.

The rise of the importance of the external image above internal integrity means that for young people how one looks is infinitely more important than the sort of person one is. To a great extent this view has been fuelled by the media and advertising because of the spending power of the younger generation. The Western world has bought in totally to the free market, and as a number of commentators have so eloquently expressed it, 'Tesco ergo sum', or 'I shop, therefore I am'.

Further weight has been gained by the 'pick 'n' mix' theory from research undertaken in Europe. Some Muslim young people in Europe use those parts of their religion which suit the aim of establishing themselves within the community. 'Muslim European Youth have inherited a sharp sense of organized action and often find adherence to Islam attractive as a self-conscious expression of identity and as a form of resistance to Western and white imperialism' (Vertovec and Rogers [eds.], *Muslim European Youth*). More generally across Europe, as a result of uncertainty and dislocation young people are seeking spiritual or metaphysical phenomena to give meaning to their lives.

ENCOUNTERING MODERN AND POSTMODERN CULTURE

Needless to say, attendance by young people at places of worship has declined rapidly in the last hundred years across most of the Western world. Many of the reasons have already been stated, but the additional impact of postmodernism, with its 'incredulity towards meta-narratives' (Lyotard) and its absolute insistence that there are no absolutes, and thereby no ultimate 'truths', has also had its impact on the thought patterns of young people.

The 'pick 'n' mix' approach is itself symptomatic of postmodernism, as is the move from verbal to visual communication. In general, the main religions of the Western world have not been able to make the same transitions in the style of their presentation.

The result of postmodernism is that there are four key foci around which young people construct their worldview and from which they then approach religion: their response to themselves; their response to their friends; their response to their world; and their response to that which is beyond all of these, the divine.

Young people live in a culture which lays great value on *self*. Fulfilment of personal desires is seen as a primary motive for all action. Sometimes those desires are altruistic, sometimes selfish. This motivation has affected young people's social patterns, their approach to sexuality, their drive to consume and their fear of death, at one and the same time both the ultimate non-self and the ultimate experience.

Young people also live in a culture where relationships are a key focus. They are committed to their *peers*. It is with those of similar age and interest that they seek acceptance. Image thus becomes part of the process of seeking acceptance, alongside professed sexual activity and their support of appropriate football teams and musical styles. Nick Pollard argues that this is actually their replacement for a lost sense of community: 'Many of today's teenagers who have lived their formative years during this time of upheaval, are in consequence desperately looking for some kind of community to which they can belong' (*Why Do They Do That?*, p. 47).

Young people are concerned about the *world* in which they live. They believe in equality; they are concerned for human rights, animal rights and ecological 'rights'. Generally this concern is driven by the concern for self: 'I should be able to have what everyone else has.' Occasionally it is driven by a God-given sense of justice: 'Everyone should be able to have what I have.' Pressure groups and the music industry have encouraged young people to be concerned for their world, as witness Bandaid, Comic Relief, Greenpeace and others. Some of these groups have been composed of young people.

The fourth, and perhaps least, of the four foci is a commitment to that which is *beyond*. Whilst the trend over the years has been to denigrate belief in God, Leslie Francis' research has shown a slight upturn since the beginning of the 1990s. Young people are aware that they no longer live in a closed physical universe, and many are seeking answers to life beyond themselves and the world as they know it. Some are looking into premodern culture; hence the rise in interest in shamanism, ancient cultures and Celtic Christianity, again evidence of a 'pick 'n' mix' approach.

Whilst postmodernism has brought into question the metanarrative, it has recognized the value of story. Religions where the 'story' is an integral part have found a new means by which to engage young people. The other important value which postmodernism has sought to establish is the principle of 'tolerance': you can have your view; I can have my view. However, this is being challenged by the rise of neo-nationalism and of a form of neo-religionism in which the faith community becomes a means of identity formation and a means of establishing who one is over against others.

POPULAR TRADITIONS AND RELATED GROUPS

Within the Christian tradition in the Western world there have been a number of attempts to address the problem of the decline in church attendance (belonging) demonstrated by young people. Some approaches have been along the lines of entertainment: to attract young people who live in an entertainment culture, we must seek to provide the same style, if a different content. The risk has been that of following the culture, elevating style over content and providing yet another 'experience' for young people.

Most developments show awareness of the risk of becoming a subculture, in which the values of the prevailing culture have not been sufficiently questioned. Graham Cray argues that 'A counter-culture offers a different view of the overarching story and may offer an alternative pattern of overall belief. This is the primary purpose of the church's work with young people' (*Postmodern Culture and Youth Discipleship*, pp. 21–22).

Other approaches have sought to hold the balance of style and content. There has been a rise in the number of youth 'congregrations', where young people can meet and belong together, learn together and begin to be a community on a pilgrimage of faith. Attempts at forming distinct faith communities made up solely of young people have not, on the whole, been successful.

The challenge for all those involved in seeking to enable young people to encounter and become part of a religion is to hold that balance of style and content.

BIBLIOGRAPHY

G. Cray, *Postmodern Culture and Youth Discipleship* (Cambridge, 1998); L. J. Francis and W. K. Kay, *Teenage Religion and Values* (Leominster, 1995); L. J. Francis, W. K. Kay, A. Kerbey and O. Fogwill, *Fast Moving Currents in Youth Culture* (Oxford, 1995); General Synod Board of Education, *Youth A Part* (London, 1996); N. Pollard, *Why Do They Do That?* (Oxford, 1998); S. Vertovec and A. Rogers (eds.), *Muslim European Youth* (Aldershot, 1998); P. Ward, *Youthwork and the Mission of God* (London, 1997).

D. Howell

RELIGIOUS EXPERIENCE

Religious experience has been an integral part of Christianity from its origins to the present. Most of the main actors in the New Testament would have testified to powerful religious experiences during which they felt themselves to be in direct communication with God, and these eperiences, or similar ones, have often occurred during Christian revivals and in the lives of individuals in church history.

Within religions other than Christianity religious experience can have analogous functions. Adherents may see their beliefs or practices as a necessary precondition for a sought-after experience of the divine. But they may also be less specific and find religious experience difficult to separate from religious rituals, ceremonies and communal activities.

Academic enquiry into religious experience has been initiated mainly through three disciplines: philosophy, psychology and theology. Some enquiries have used an interdisciplinary approach but, for purposes of analysis, it is simpler to discuss each discipline separately.

Disciplines may be defined in a variety of ways. Here they will be regarded as characterized by their distinctive concepts and methods. Mathematics could not function without the concept of numbers, and though numbers may be used in other disciplines, their natural home is in the discipline of mathematics. Moreover, the methods associated with particular disciplines very often employ their characteristic concepts in rule-based ways.

Philosophy has a long history, and its characteristic concepts are matters of debate and disagreement. Yet it is reasonable to assert that in the English-speaking world in the twentieth century philosophy has been characterized by the method of analysis and the concepts which make this possible, particularly those found in language and logic. In this respect philosophy is a second-order activity, an activity which depends on others.

When philosophy considers religious experience it asks what religion is, what experience is, and how the two may be connected. It may begin by asking how it is possible for human beings to claim to have experience, and what the necessary conditions are for this to take place. When examining the subject in this way, it claims to clarify common-sense assumptions. For example, it will disclose the essential *dualism* that lies behind the claims that there are both experiences and those who experience, minds and an external world to which minds relate. The notion of dualism, which presumes that each of us is an 'I' with a centre of consciousness, is the common-sense one. Our language presumes that this is how the world is. But philosophical analysis also entertains the possibility that there is no division between the individual consciousness and the external world, that dualism is a fiction, that ultimately there is only one kind of 'stuff' in the universe, and that this is material, not spiritual or immaterial.

Most philosophical positions, however, do not deny the existence of the external world and so concentrate on the relationship between that world and the mind. How are concepts formed? Why is it that we all seem to share some concepts (for instance, those of space and cause) while disagreeing over others? To what extent are the conclusions of mathematics, for instance, more or less certain than those of our immediate sense perceptions: for example, that here is a cup of tea and over there is a tree? The philosophical position that emphasizes the role of logic and reason is called *rationalism*. It asserts that there are certain 'necessary truths' that are quite independent of the external world: for example, that 2 + 2 = 4 in whatever kind of world we might happen to live. The philosophical position that emphasizes the importance of sense experience is called *empiricism*. It asserts that the truths of reason are true only because they conform to the way the external world is. Sense experience is a reliable guide to the products of the mind, and observation and measurement are the way to knowledge. From empiricism comes much modern scientific method.

Attempts to investigate religious experience using philosophy generally represent one or other of these major schools of thought. Some philosophers argue that experience cannot be equated with mental events and that dualism is fundamentally flawed; religious experience cannot therefore provide evidence for the existence of a transcendent supernatural being. Religious experiences are just perceptions of the material world. Others argue that religious experience should be judged by reason, but they have difficulty in deciding what exactly might be called 'reasonable' and often suggest that every claim to a genuine religious experience should be assessed against a set of (sometimes arbitrary) criteria.

More radical, though less specific, is the work of Ludwig Wittgenstein in *Tractatus Logico-Philosophicus*, 6.51. He considered that religion and ethics lie beyond the limits of language, and that scepticism is nonsensical because it raises doubts where no questions can be asked. Indeed, Wittgenstein viewed religion as he viewed music and asserted that he would reject explanations of religion just as he would reject explanations of music, precisely because they were explanations.

Psychological studies may be traced back to roots similar to those that inspired philosophy. The beginnings of modern psychology may be dated to the middle of the nineteenth century with the work of the German Wilhelm Wundt, whose voluminous but unsystematic writings make three proposals: that there is a parallel between the electrochemical discharges of the brain and human consciousness; that psychology should be seen as a science requiring experimentation; and that conscious mental processes are composed of a combination of immediate sensations and the functions of association, creativity, judgment and memory. In other words, mental life follows its own laws, which are separate from the laws that govern the physical world.

Modern psychological investigations of religious experience go back to William James, whose psychology, though it made use of experiments occasionally, was largely based on his own introspection. It is no surprise, given his interest in his own mental processes, that the accounts of other people concerning their religious experiences also appealed to him. His *The Varieties of Religious Experience* attributes such experience to two essentially different kinds of people, one optimistic and outgoing and the other morbid and fearful. He linked these two sorts of people in his discussion of conversion, which he saw primarily as the means by which the divided self is united and its conflicts resolved.

Francis Galton, whose wide-ranging work was driven by mathematical precision, pioneered another psychological approach, which gave less prominence to consciousness. Galton worked out how correlations might be calculated and laid the foundations of a series of psychological methods that utilized countable entities. This approach later involved the use of surveys and the interpretation of their results in terms of departure from chance associations. From the 1920s till about the 1960s, psychology largely avoided the study of introspection and consciousness and concentrated instead upon what could be clearly observed and measured: behaviour.

More recently the two streams within psychology have converged. Consciousness is not ruled out as an object of enquiry, but statistical methods are applied to its investigation. Recent publications (e.g. by Beit-hallahmi and Argyle (1997) and by Hood, Spilka, Hunsberger and Gorsuch ([2]1996) have summarized extensive work on a range of religious experiences, including mystical experience, speaking in tongues and near-death experiences. This work has utilized survey reports, interviews, observations, laboratory experiments, correlations between their findings and background information about respondents and correlations between sets of variables. In relation to religious experience four main conclusions may be drawn.

Firstly, the incidence of reported religious experience varies from culture to culture, but is certainly higher than would be expected if the western world were really post-Christian and entirely secular. Surveys by Gallup, for instance, show that 15% of Americans claim to have had near-death experiences and that about a third of respondents in wide-ranging studies answered 'yes' to the question 'Have you felt as though you were close to a powerful spiritual force that seemed to lift you out of yourself?' These findings were replicated in the United Kingdom and Australia. The surveys also show that reports of religious experience increase with age and socio-economic status.

Secondly, women in various cultures consistently report religious experiences more frequently than men do. Thirdly, for both genders, experiences of a kind compatible with the main features of Christian doctrine are mostly associated with an increased sense of well-being and purpose in life. Fourthly, speaking with tongues (one of the most common religious experiences) is not associated with neuroticism or mental impairment.

The issues raised by reports of religious experiences of a general kind raise a subset of questions that cross disciplinary boundaries. For example, do religious experiences have a common core or are they essentially diverse? Do religious experiences validate religious doctrines?

In answer to the first question psychologists have identified two basic kinds of religious experience. An experience of the numinous is an experience of a power or presence that produces fear and awe and a sense of the holy. A mystical experience, in contrast, is an experience of unity: either a unity of oneself with the world, with nature, with all living things, or a unity that is more inwardly directed and imageless, without any sense of time or space and incommunicable in words.

Whether religious experiences validate religious doctrines is not fundamentally a psychological question. On the one hand, irreligious thinkers have proposed that religious experience is an evolved form of consciousness that helps to provide coping mechanisms in human crises. On the other hand, religious thinkers have argued that religious experiences are the best evidence for the reality of a God who cannot be enclosed in the concepts and categories of the human intellect.

Theological exploration of religious experiences must utilize the characteristic methods and resources of theology. These include (for Christians) Scripture-based enquiries, the records of church history, and systematics, which form doctrines into a logically coherent structure. Theology itself very frequently develops into theolog*ies* (evangelical, Catholic, Latin American and so on), suggesting that theology is an intellectual struggle for coherence and clarification within particular traditions. This struggle is complicated by the need to address three audiences: the academic world, the churches and society as a whole. In all three of these arenas theology is bound to engage with concerns and discourses that are not its own. In respect of the social sciences (including psychology) theology may draw on the categories of other disciplines, reinterpret them, repudiate them or try to absorb them.

A slightly different view, found in the writings of Kierkegaard, Luther and C. S. Lewis, is that theology should interpret experience. On this view the experiences of life may be interpreted religiously: for example, a longing for joy and peace points towards the means by which they may be obtained – that is, Christ. An analogy may be drawn with our need for food: it would be absurd to feel hunger in a foodless world.

The position most acceptable to most Christians is that doctrine, text and experience must co-relate in a way that gives ultimate authority to the canonical text but that allows experience an opportunity to be heard. This is a theological position that allows psychology to ask questions but not to dictate interpretations. If theology fails to utilize all its resources, it degenerates into a dilute form of psychology and soon dates as theology. An examination of commentaries on the visions of Ezekiel that invoke the categories of 1940s psychology demonstrates this point clearly.

Crucially for the issues raised by philosophy and psychology, biblical theology is almost certainly bound to rule in favour of dualism, to support empiricism (1 Thess.

5:21) but also to accept a limited form of rationalism (because the 'image of God' implies rationality: Gen. 1:27). Moreover, an examination of the many accounts of religious experience in the canon of Scripture suggests that the meaning of a religious experience is almost always implicit within the experience itself (*e.g.* Exod. 34:5–8; Acts 2:4, 16).

BIBLIOGRAPHY

B. Beit-hallahmi and M. Argyle, *The Psychology of Religious Behaviour, Belief and Experience* (London, 1997); R. W. Hood, Jr, B. Spilka, B. Hunsberger and R. Gorsuch, *The Psychology of Religion: An Empirical Approach* (London, [2]1996); W. James, *The Varieties of Religious Experience* (The Gifford Lectures, given in Edinburgh 1901–2; subsequently published variously); W. K. Kay and L. J. Francis, *Drift from the Churches* (Cardiff, 1996); D. Middlemiss, *Interpreting Charismatic Experience* (London, 1996); L. Wittgenstein, *Tractatus Logico-Philosophicus* (London, 1922).

W. K. Kay

THE STUDY OF RELIGION

Whilst there is a long history of curiosity and scholarship regarding the religions of other people, the study of religions is a relative newcomer to the halls of academia. Greatly indebted to the impressive work and influence of Friedrich Max Müller (1823–1900), the first university professorships were established in the final quarter of the nineteenth century. By the second half of the twentieth century the study of religion had emerged as a prominent and important field of academic enquiry. In a period of history in which the scientism and rationalism of the earlier part of the century has seen a decline and in which there has been a rise of interest particularly in non-Christian spirituality, since 1945 there has been a growth in academic institutions offering courses and modules in the study of religion. Moreover, work done in the social sciences has increasingly converged with the work done by students of religion. These factors, amongst others, have made it possible for the study of religion in universities and colleges gradually to pull away from its traditional asymmetrical place alongside the study of Christian theology in order to establish itself as an independent field of enquiry. That is to say, whereas earlier in the century the study of non-Christian faiths was undertaken in faculties of Christian theology and studied as part of a theology degree, there was a move, particularly in the late 1960s and the 1970s when the term 'religious studies' became common currency, to establish separate departments of religious studies.

PHENOMENOLOGY IN RELIGIOUS STUDIES

The term *Religionsphänomenologie* was first used by the Dutch scholar Pierre Daniel

Chantepie de la Saussaye (1848–1920) in his work *Lehrbuch der Religionsgeschichte* (1887), which simply documented religious phenomena. This documentation might be described as 'descriptive' phenomenology, the aim being simply to gather information about the various religions and, as botanists might classify plants, identify varieties of particular religious phenomena. This classification of types of religious phenomena is one of the hallmarks of the phenomenological method and can be seen in the works of contemporary scholars such as Ninian Smart (1927–2001) and even Mircea Eliade (1907–86). Such typologies (certainly in earlier works) tend to lead to an account of religious phenomena which, to continue with the analogy, reads much the same as a botanical handbook. Various species are identified (higher religion, lower religion, prophetic religion, mystical religion and so on) and particular religious beliefs and practices are then categorized and discussed.

As the study of religion progressed 'phenomenology' came to refer to a method which was more complex and claimed rather more for itself than did Chantepie's mere cataloguing of facts. This later development in the discipline (which was due, in part, to the inspiration of the philosophy of Edmund Husserl (1859–1938) was a recognition of how easy it is for prior beliefs and interpretations unconsciously to influence one's thinking. Hence, scholars such as Gerardus van der Leeuw (1890–1950) stressed the need for phenomenological *epoché* (the 'bracketing' or suspension of one's presuppositions, beliefs and values). Also central to phenomenology is the need for empathy (*Einfühlung*), which helps towards an understanding of the religion *from within*. Phenomenologists spoke further of 'eidetic vision', the capacity of the observer to see beyond the particularities of a religion and to grasp its essence and meaning. Whilst we often see only what we want or expect to see, eidetic vision is the ability to see a phenomenon without such distortions and limitations. Hence, later phenomenologists did not merely catalogue the facts of religious history but, by means of *epoché*, *Einfühlung* and eidetic vision, sought to understand (*verstehen*) their meaning for the believer. Whilst phenomenologists are very aware that there will always be some distance between the believer's understandings of religious facts and those of the scholar, the aim of phenomenology is, as far as possible, to testify only to what has been observed. Phenomenology aims to strip away all that would stand in the way of a neutral, judgment-free presentation of the facts.

Although many phenomenologists argued for a simple presentation of the facts and against drawing any wider conclusions about, for example, the veracity of claimed religious experiences or the existence of a universal essence of religion underlying all the various historical religions of the world, there were phenomenologists who wanted to take this further step. A classic example of such a thesis is Rudolf Otto's (1869–1937) *Idea of the Holy* (1917), which, on the basis of the study of religions and his own particular theology, claims that central to all religious expression is an *a priori* sense of 'the numinous' or 'the holy'. The point is that this goes beyond a simple presentation of the facts of religious history to the development of a particular philosophical interpretation of those facts. Not only does this demonstrate the breadth of approaches covered by the umbrella term 'phenomenology', but it also highlights a key issue in religious studies, namely the problem of neutrality.

NEUTRALITY?

Whilst Otto's type of phenomenology clearly displays a fundamental lack of objectivity, it is now generally recognized that this is a problem for the study of religions as such. Whilst many contemporary religious studies scholars would want to defend the notion of *epoché* as an ideal to which one should aspire, there is a question as to whether this ideal entails a certain hermeneutical *naïveté*. For example, the very process of selection and the production of typologies assumes an interpretative framework. To select certain facts rather than others and to present them, with other facts, as the description of a particular type of religion presupposes an interpretative framework in the mind of the scholar. Indeed, even were a scholar able to attain a state of pure, unadulterated objectivity, the very belief that this is a desirable state for which to strive is a value judgment arising out of a particular Western worldview. Hence, the belief in detached objectivity and the claim to be purely 'descriptive' are now considered to be hermeneutically naïve.

That this is so has been persuasively argued by Gavin Flood in *Beyond Phenomenology*. Making use of theories developed within the social sciences and humanities, and clearly influenced by the shift in contemporary theoretical discourse from a philosophy of consciousness to a philosophy of the sign, which recognizes that all knowledge is tradition-specific and embodied within particular cultural narratives, Flood argues first that religions should not be abstracted and studied apart from their historical, political, cultural, linguistic and social contexts, and secondly that scholars (who are likewise shaped by their own particular contexts) always bring conceptual baggage to the study of religion. Hence, whether we think of, for example, the effect research has on the community being studied, or the scholar's own prejudices, preconceptions, instincts, emotions and personal characteristics which significantly influence that research, we realize that the academic study of religion can never be neutral and purely objective. Flood thus argues for 'a rigorous metatheoretical discourse' in religious studies. 'Metatheory' is the critical analysis of theory and practice, the aim of which is to 'unravel the underlying assumptions inherent in any research programme and to critically comment on them'. Metatheory is thus important because it 'questions the contexts of inquiry, the nature of inquiry, and the kinds of interests represented in inquiry'. In so doing, it questions the idea of detached objectivity in the study of religion and the notion that one can be a disinterested observer who is able to produce neutral descriptions of religious phenomena free of evaluative judgments.

INSIDERS AND OUTSIDERS

The above is closely related to another important issue in contemporary religious studies, namely the 'insider–outsider' problem. To what extent can a person who is not a believer ('an outsider') understand a faith in the way a believer ('an insider') understands that faith? Firstly, it is argued that outsiders, simply because they are outsiders, will never be able fully to grasp the insider's experience. Even people who experience the same event at the same time will (because of their contexts and personal histories) interpret it in different ways. Secondly, some scholars have insisted that there is a definite advantage to being an outsider. Since members of a religion tend to be conditioned by and often pressurized into accepting a particular and usually narrow understanding of their faith, the outsider is in the important scholarly position of not being influenced by such forces and conditions. Impartiality and disinterest allow greater objectivity. However, whilst there is undoubtedly a value to scholarly detachment and whilst the scholar may have a greater knowledge of the history, texts, philosophy, structure and social implications of a particular faith than the average believer, not to have experienced and grasped that faith from the inside is surely to have a rather large hole in the centre of his or her understanding. Indeed, many insiders will insist that such scholarly 'head-knowledge' is, in the final analysis, peripheral to the 'meaning' of their faith.

Hence, bearing these issues in mind, *empathy* and *imagination* would appear to be important scholarly attributes which make possible some grasp of other people's worldviews. Indeed, concerning empathy, Joachim Wach (1898–1955), the German-American historian and sociologist of religions, himself a Christian, insisted on the value of a scholar's own personal religious experience. Dry, academic objectivity can never adequately empathize with religious feelings.

ANTHROPOLOGY AND THE STUDY OF RELIGION

It is, of course, hard to underestimate the significance of the evolutionary thesis set forth in Charles Darwin's (1809–82) *The Origin of the Species* (1859) and *The Descent of Man* (1871). The influence of evolutionism, particularly as it was developed by theorists such as Herbert Spencer (1820–1903), is clearly evident in the emergence of modern anthropology. Beginning life as a quest for human origins, much late nineteenth-century anthropology was determined by the idea of evolution. Just as biological life had evolved from simple beginnings to more complex 'higher' forms, so it was believed that human culture and religion had similarly progressed. This led to the construction of grand evolutionary theories of intellectual progress. One of the earliest and most important works of evolutionary anthropology was Edward Burnett Tylor's (1832–1917) *Primitive Culture* (1871), which argued that by studying contemporary 'primitive' societies one could determine the nature of prehistoric religion and culture. This was, argued Tylor, made possible because of 'survivals', by which he meant certain elements of contemporary primal cultures which had 'survived' the process of evolution in much the same form as they were believed and practised in prehistory. Hence, convinced that they were able to access 'primitive culture', anthropologists sought to demonstrate their various evolutionary theses by working their way through history and up their scales of religious belief and practice to Western civilization and Christianity, which, of course, they believed to be the pinnacle of evolutionary progress.

Perhaps the best, most influential and certainly largest example of early evolutionary anthropology was James George Frazer's (1854–1941) twelve-volume masterpiece, *The Golden Bough* (1890–1915, published in abridged form in 1922). Influenced by Tylor, Frazer sought to provide 'an epic of humanity' which would map human cultural and religious evolution. The work sets forth the thesis that human cultural and intellectual evolution can be separated into three eras: the Age of Magic, the Age of Religion and the Age of Science. Just as the religious worldview had replaced the magical worldview, so the dawning of the Age of Science heralded the slow but inevitable decline of religion. Moreover, convinced of the sovereignty of evolution, he points out near the end of *The Golden Bough* that 'the history of thought should warn us against concluding that because the scientific theory of the world is the best that has yet been formulated, it is necessarily complete and final ... [As] science has supplanted its predecessors, so it may hereafter be itself superseded by some more perfect hypothesis, perhaps by some totally different way of looking at the phenomena ... of which this generation can form no idea'. Whilst the abridged version of *The Golden Bough* is still in print, still has some interesting points to make and is still used (by, for example, some contemporary Pagan writers), and whilst at a popular level many people still find this type of evolutionary thesis convincing, in scholarly circles the three-stage idea has been abandoned, as have many of Frazer's 'facts', definitions and conclusions.

There are several problems with the early evolutionary approach to the study of religion and culture. For example: first, the *evolutionary thesis* on which the work was based is problematic. For instance, it is now known that religion was not preceded by an 'Age of Magic', that religion and magic often develop together, and that primal religions do not lack sophistication and development. Secondly, partly because the early anthropologists were, generally speaking, 'armchair' scholars, relying on the reports and observations of others, they tended to *prioritize the formulation* of their grand evolutionary theories. That is to say, they formulated their theories first, then looked around for beliefs that would support those theories. This of course led to a 'pick and mix' attitude to religious facts from around the world, to a Procrustean treatment of those facts and, in the final analysis, to a distorted and contrived grand theory. Thirdly, *religious beliefs* and practices were often *misunderstood*, because they were interpreted without regard to the contexts from which they were plucked.

As anthropology developed and the grand evolutionary theories of an earlier generation were increasingly found wanting, the emphasis moved to understanding religions and cultures by means of detailed field studies. Because, as is now generally recognized, all symbols, including words, derive their meanings from their total context, it was argued that beliefs, practices, texts and indeed all aspects of culture should be studied together as they are lived out. Hence anthropologists began to stress the importance of 'participant observation'. This method, pioneered by the important Polish-born, English anthropologist Bronislaw Malinowski (1884–1942), requires living with the community being studied, learning its language and participating in its life without seeking to alter it; as a participant, the scholar simply observes and tries to get as close as possible to seeing a religion from the 'inside'. This approach represents a move away, not only from early evolutionary anthropology, but also from the phenomenological theories of such as van der Leeuw who tended simply to gather facts, often historical facts.

Another anthropologist, Clifford Geertz (b. 1923), has developed what he calls 'interpretative anthropology' which aims to interpret events and the like as 'insiders' do. This, he argues, is possible only if the scholar is a participant observer. Geertz, however, moves beyond Malinowski in distinguishing between 'thick' and 'thin' descriptions. 'Thick' descriptions describe, for example, not merely what a person is doing, but also, as far as is possible, what the person *thinks* s/he is doing. A 'thin' description is simply a description of a practice with no indication of how the practice is understood from the inside. In other words, Geertz is rightly concerned with *meaning*. For example, during worship Christians regularly eat bread and drink red wine. Simply to provide a 'thin' description of this practice could easily lead to a misunderstanding of a central Christian rite. For a person unfamiliar with Christianity adequately to grasp what is taking place, there needs to be some 'thick' description, some understanding of what the practice *means* to the worshippers.

LISTENING AND DIALOGUE

In recent years a move towards the study of contemporary religions and towards participant observation has led to a consideration of what has been called the 'response threshold' in religious studies. The crossing of the response threshold happens when insiders question the scholar's interpretations. An insider's interpretation, which may conflict with scholarly interpretations, is felt to carry equal if not more weight. Indeed, Wilfred Cantwell Smith (b. 1916) has argued that no understanding of a faith is valid until it has been acknowledged by an insider. Religious studies is thus carried out in the context of a dialogue which takes seriously the views of the insider. Although dialogue can have several purposes, this form of dialogue is not a common search for an ultimate religious truth or some other questionable enterprise; it is rather about seeking a deeper understanding of the insider's worldview, and may eventually develop into introducing one's dialogue partner to a greater understanding of one's own worldview.

CHRISTIAN THEOLOGY AND RELIGIOUS STUDIES

If theology is essentially *fides quaerens intellectum* ('faith seeking understanding'), then it is clearly much narrower in its remit than we have seen religious studies to be. Moreover, religious studies is distinct from theology in that, in a sense, it stands outside a particular faith. Whether one approaches it from a phenomenological, anthropological, sociological or psychological angle, the aim (which can never be fully realized) is generally understood to be descriptive and objective. When the study of religion moves beyond this, becoming explicitly faith thinking about religions, it becomes a theology of religions or a theological or philosophical interpretation of religion, rather than religious studies.

However, we have seen that even the above distinction is perhaps too simplistic, in that even religious studies research cannot avoid being interpretative; neutrality is not an option. Nevertheless, there is a need for what might be called 'qualified *epoché*'; *epoché* informed by metatheoretical analysis. With constant critical reflection upon the research undertaken, the scholar should engage in a sensitive study, the aim of which is, as far as possible, empathetically and imaginatively to understand a faith from the 'inside', to see as the believer sees, to feel as the believer feels, 'to walk a mile in another's moccasins'. Certainly, from the perspective of Christian scholarship, just as Christians would prefer or expect others to spend time seeking to understand the Christian faith from the inside in order to avoid caricatures and misunderstanding, so they should do no less when seeking to understand non-Christian religions and when formulating theologies concerning those religions: 'in everything, do to others what you would have them do to you' (Matt. 7:12). It is the Christian's duty to make sure that his or her theological interpretation of religion is based on the most accurate understanding possible; Christians need to work at securing an accurate and informed understanding of the world in which they live.

Moreover, to follow this line of thought a little further, because books and second-hand reports are not enough to give scholars a firm grasp of the particular religions they study, some degree of participant observation is required. Hence, dialogue *within the context of friendship* is important in that it allows greater access to the 'inside' of personal faith. This is important because it is persons and personal faith with which we are dealing, not abstract religious systems. The point is that we cannot simply rely on religious data to provide us with understanding, because faith is a quality of the personal life. It is therefore distorted when it is abstracted from its personal context. Simply to know the facts about a person's religious tradition is *not* to know the individual personal faith-response which that tradition evokes. Friendship, dialogue, an understanding of cultural and linguistic contexts, qualified *epoché*, empathy and imagination will allow one to gain a deeper, more rounded understanding of personal faith.

In recent years there has been some debate as to the relationship between theology and religious studies. On the one hand, some argue that essentially theology and religious studies are methodologically indistinct and both able to tackle issues of truth and value. On the other hand, it is argued that religious studies deals with religion as a human phenomenon, whilst theology addresses issues of truth and value. Although this latter position would seem to be the correct one, for Christians the two are naturally closer together than they would be for non-Christian scholars. Christians are bound to reflect theologically on their religious studies. In this sense, Christian theology and the study of religion should not be separated.

Furthermore, whilst in order to forward knowledge in their particular research areas (Islamic studies, Indology, Buddhist studies etc.) Christian students of religion will produce work which is not explicitly theological (just as Christian archaeologists, physicists, botanists and philosophers do in their particular areas), if they are to be distinctively Christian there will always be the need for explicit theological engagement. Christians will need to speak to their friends in other faiths as Christians and address the specific concerns and needs of the Christian community (e.g. provide reliable information for churches, theologians, pastors and missionaries). As such, the study of religion is part of the larger task of constructing a Christian worldview and responding to Jesus' Great Commission (Matt. 28:16–20).

BIBLIOGRAPHY

F. Bowie, *The Anthropology of Religion: An Introduction* (Oxford, 1999); W. Braun and R. McCutcheon (eds.), *Guide to the Study of Religion* (London, 2000); P. Connolly (ed.), *Approaches to the Study of Religion* (London, 1999); G. Flood, *Beyond Phenomenology: Rethinking the Study of Religion* (London, 1999); C. Geertz, *The Interpretation of Cultures* (New York, 1973); D. Hughes, *Has God Many Names? An Introduction to Religious Studies* (Leicester, 1996); U. King (ed.), *Turning Points in Religious Studies: Essays in Honour of Geoffrey Parrinder* (Edinburgh, 1990); R. McCutcheon (ed.), *The Insider/Outsider Problem in the Study of Religion* (London, 1998); E. Sharpe, *Comparative Religion: A History* (London, 1975); G. van der Leeuw, *Religion in Essence and Manifestation* (Princeton, NJ, 1986).

C. H. Partridge

RITES OF PASSAGE

THE THREE STAGES OF A RITE OF PASSAGE

'The life of an individual in any society is a series of passages from one age to another' (van Gennep, *Rites of Passage*, pp. 2–3).

Rites of passage is the term used to describe rituals which mark the transition from one stage of life to another. These rituals may be 'life cycle' rituals associated mainly with birth, initiation, marriage, childbirth and death, or they may mark out calendric transitions such as the passage from winter to spring. Traditionally they were communal affairs in which the extended family or the village would participate. Rituals marking periods of transition are more than mere celebrations of the passing of time. There is a difference, for example, between the annual celebration of a person's birthday and rituals marking the transition from boyhood to manhood in, say, the Jewish *bar mitzvah*.

Rituals are different from theatre. They are believed to bring about what they signify. Spiritual powers, God, gods, spirits or ancestors are called to assist in the transition process. Rituals, however, are distinct from magic, which implies the manipulation of forces and powers by certain techniques. In ritual, the priests or similar figures in the community appeal to spiritual powers through prayer or sacrifice, without claiming to control them.

The Belgian anthropologist Arnold van Gennep drew attention to the threefold pattern common to all rites of passage. He had analysed reports on rituals in many different societies, and noted that the common features of all such rituals were firstly rites of separation, then a period of transition and finally rites of incorporation. From the Latin word *limen* ('threshold') he classified these stages as pre-liminal, liminal and post-liminal. In many cases the separation from one state is marked by cutting, such as the cutting of the foreskin in circumcision or the cutting of hair for those entering the priesthood or the monkhood. The transition or liminal stage is sometimes marked by a physical separation from the village or community. There may be a literal crossing of a threshold to indicate that the period of transition has ended and a new status has been attained. In some African societies, for example, teenage boys were taken away into seclusion for a period of time, during which they underwent circumcision and returned to their village with the new status of adults. Similarly, girls experiencing their first menstruation would often be separated from the rest of the community, remaining in a hut until the end of their period. Then, crossing the threshold of the hut, they would emerge and be incorporated back into the village as mature women.

Much of van Gennep's work was based on research among tribal or pre-literate societies. This fact has led to some questioning of the validity of applying this threefold pattern of rites of passage to more complex societies. Nevertheless, it does provide a framework for understanding many rites within more complex societies and religious traditions. For example, the transition from the single state to the state of being married in almost all cultures is marked byan engagement ceremony (pre-liminal), a period of betrothal (liminal) and then a wedding ceremony (post-liminal). Similarly, the traditional pattern of entry into the Christian church was marked by rites of separation from the old life, such as confession of sin or exorcism; a period of transition, marked by instruction in the faith; and incorporation, marked by baptism and being welcomed into the church. A strongly sacramental view of baptism, which is held in some Christian traditions (e.g. Roman Catholic, Orthodox and High Anglican), is closely related to the understanding of rites of passage as in some way efficacious.

Van Gennep noted that the emphasis placed on each of the three stages will vary depending on the nature of the passage. For example, rites associated with new birth focus on incorporation into the community, as in Jewish circumcision or naming ceremonies in various traditions. On the other hand, rites associated with death may well focus on the aspect of separation, including ways of helping people grieve. Sometimes the liminal period can also be seen as a way of helping deal with grief. In Greek Orthodoxy, for example, bones are interred in the family grave for up to five years before being transferred to the village ossuary. During this period, the bereaved will visit the grave and continue a kind of relationship with the deceased person. More than other rites of passage, those associated with death will reflect the religious understanding of the society. Those religions, such as Protestant Christianity, which have a strong sense of assurance that the new status of the dead person is in the hands of a loving God will differ from those, such as Japanese or Chinese Buddhism, where there is a strong sense that the state of the dead person is dependent on the actions of those who survive. Japanese and Chinese ancestor worship is often motivated at least in part by a desire to placate the spirits of the ancestors, who will bring harm to their surviving relatives if these relatives do not demonstrate sufficient care and respect for them.

VICTOR TURNER AND *COMMUNITAS*

The Scottish anthropologist Victor Turner explored the transitional, or liminal, stage, particularly in rites experienced by a group of people together, or in which the liminal period may be quite lengthy. This stage has some distinct characteristics which contrast markedly with both the pre-liminal and post-liminal stages. It is, he argued, a stage of anti-structure. The shared experience of transition, and the rituals accompanying that, bind people from different levels in society together in a way which they do not normally experience. This period is 'a cultural realm that has few or none of the attributes of the past or coming state' (Turner, *The Ritual Process*, p. 94). It is characterized by a sense of equality among the initiands, despite their previous or future social status. There are no distinctions of wealth or rank. There is also a sense of humility, sometimes even of abasement, and passivity, in which the initiands obey totally those initiating them. This is particularly the case in rites which are initiatory into a new status of authority within a village, tribe or community, where the initiand is often treated as a kind of *tabula rasa*, a blank slate onto which new knowledge appropriate to his or her new status is inscribed.

To describe this period Turner used the Latin word *communitas*, preferring this to the English 'community', which has a much wider connotation. He noted that the distinguishing features of this liminal period of *communitas* – including equality, humility, passivity, a continued dependence on spiritual powers and an acceptance of pain and suffering – are those which often characterize religious life, notably monastic or millenarian movements. Turner pointed to the Rule of St Benedict as one example of this, and also to religious movements which, in expectation of some apocalyptic event, abandoned the normal structures of society and adopted egalitarian patterns of living. Writing in the 1960s, Turner also saw a manifestation of this *communitas* in the hippie counter-culture. Turner distinguished between different types of *communitas*, which he identified as spontaneous, normative and ideological. Spontaneous *communitas* is that shared experience which is unplanned, yet undoubtedly real; the shared national mourning in the United Kingdom in 1997 after the death of Diana, Princess of Wales, could be seen as an example. Normative *communitas* is a conscious levelling, in order to achieve a particular goal. The shared experience of religious pilgrimage, notably the Muslim *Hajj*, is one of the best instances of this kind of *communitas*. Equality among all the pilgrims, regardless of racial background or social status, is signified in the simple white clothes which both male and female pilgrims adopt upon arrival at Mecca. Ideological *communitas* refers to the kind of lifestyle and values often adopted by religious groups which are aiming to create some kind of utopian existence of perfect equality and harmony.

Turner noted that the experience of *communitas* was not one that could be sustained indefinitely. Anti-structure needs structure in order for it to exist. If there is no return to the structured distinctions of life after the liminal period, then structure will evolve within the group striving to maintain *communitas*. Many monastic groups, for example, despite their ideals of equality, developed hierarchical structures. Many utopian religious cults come to focus on a strong leader figure. If such structure does not develop the movement is likely to disintegrate, which explains the failure of many such millenarian and utopian movements.

Recent writings have highlighted the fact that women's rites of initiation are somewhat different in pattern and often include violence inflicted upon the woman being initiated. Female circumcision, or genital mutilation as it is becoming known, is the most obvious example of this.

RITES OF PASSAGE IN THE CONTEMPORARY WESTERN WORLD

The significant question is how rites of passage will be expressed in a society which is becoming increasingly secular. The phrase 'rites of passage' has entered the public consciousness, but often already carries a secular meaning, as in, for example, William Golding's novel entitled *Rites of Passage* or the designation of films which deal with the transition from childhood to adulthood as 'rites of passage films'.

Among the non-Christian religious traditions represented in the West, rites of passage, particularly those which deal with initiation and incorporation into the religious community, such as the Sikh ceremony of *Amrit* in which Sikhs are admitted into the *Khalsa*, take on greater significance as ways of affirming a community's identity. Rites of passage have played a part in the maintaining of Jewish identity for many centuries.

But will rites of passage which have their origin in Christianity disappear outside of the community of practising Christians, and at the same time become ways of more clearly maintaining Christian identity? For many centuries, baptism of infants, wedding ceremonies in churches and Christian funerals were part of Western culture as much as of Christian belief. Among many churches now, however, there is unease that the secularization of society has led to the frequent practice of these rites without any commitment to the religious beliefs inherent in the practice, especially to the baptism of children of parents with no apparent Christian faith and to wedding ceremonies in churches in which those involved are not practising Christians. The view of marriage in secular society is changing, with many more couples now living together and opting for a formal marriage ceremony after a number of years, sometimes to accompany the birth of children. It remains a widespread assumption that a Christian funeral will be conducted for those who have died.

Numbers of parents bringing their children for baptism and numbers getting married in church are both in decline, suggesting that both these rites may return to being associated specifically with Christian faith rather than being a cultural pattern. However, writers such as John Drane have pointed out that the decline in organized religious practice within the West, a trend more marked in Europe than in the United States (but observable there also), does not equate to a decline in spiritual awareness. This fact suggests that new and more varied expressions of life-cycle rites may emerge. Some of these will still have links with the Christian tradition; some will reflect the growing influence of non-traditional forms of spirituality; and some will simply be secular equivalents. On this last point, however, it may be that, since rites of passage generally have religious or spiritual aspects to them, even people who claim no particular religious faith may still feel the need to mark these transitional phases in a spiritual way, as well as by a secular celebration. An appropriate response from the church in the West to this desire may offer significant opportunities for mission in a secular society.

BIBLIOGRAPHY

F. Bowie, *The Anthropology of Religion* (Oxford, 2000); J. Drane, *Faith in a Changing Culture* (London, 1997); R. Girard, *Violence and the Sacred* (Baltimore, 1992); J. Holm and J. Bowker (eds.), *Rites of Passage* (London, 1994); B. Lincoln, *Emerging from the Chrysalis: Rituals of Women's Initiation* (Oxford, 2000); V. Turner, *The Ritual Process: Structure and Anti-Structure* (Chicago, 1969); A. van Gennep, *The Rites of Passage* (London, 1960).

I. D. Miller

SECULARIZATION

The word 'secular' comes to us from the Latin *saeculum*, meaning 'period' or 'age', which, in turn, translated the Greek *aion*, which was often used to denote temporality as over and against the eternal or, in Christian terms, '*this* world' as over and against 'the world to come'. The term 'secularization' was first used in Europe during the seventeenth century in negotiating the Peace of Westphalia, to denote the transfer of properties from ecclesiastical to 'secular' political authorities; the word has subsequently been used in Roman Catholic canon law to describe the return to 'the world' of a person formerly under monastic or clerical orders. More significantly, the notion of 'secularization' has been employed by social theorists to denote the process by which religion, at least as it has traditionally been understood, has seemed to forfeit its place in the modern context. Secularization theory describes the process in which religious ideas, values and institutions lose their public status and influence, and eventually even their plausibility, in modern industrial societies.

Although the decline of traditional religious observance in modern societies is largely indisputable, secularization theory has generated a vast literature characterized by considerable disagreement. In the first instance, the notion of secularization begs the definition of 'religion', and whether religion ought to be defined *functionally*, in terms of how religious beliefs operate socially and/or psychologically, or *substantively*, in terms of religious beliefs *per se*. One's initial definition of 'religion' tends to delimit the possibilities of secularization. While it would not be difficult to show, for example, that certain religious beliefs (say, the traditional Christian belief in 'eternal life') have largely dropped out of contemporary public discourse, it is difficult to envisage any society that does not exhibit something like the functional equivalent of religious worship: beliefs and rituals that bind people together in their quest for meaning. Hence, from a 'functionalist' point of view, total secularization becomes impossible *by definition*. What may appear to be the decline of religious belief in modern society is more accurately described as the transposition of allegiance from traditional dogma either to certain aspects of modern secular life (i.e. to the 'gods' of scientific and technological 'progress', to economic 'growth', to 'family values', 'well-being', expressive individuality etc.) or to exotic beliefs such as those commonly discussed under the heading of the 'New Age'.

Objections have also been raised to secularization theory's tendency to contrast contemporary secularity with the alleged religiosity of former periods. In short, it has turned out to be rather difficult to say whether the average person-on-the-street in, say, the twelfth century was really any more or less 'religious' than he or she is now.

A number of divergent explanations of secularization have been advanced over the past several centuries. It has been suggested, for example, that secularization is the inevitable result of the maturing of the human race (Comte) and/or a reflection of the progressive evolution of human consciousness of freedom (Hegel, Feuerbach, Durkheim). More specifically, it has been contended that secularization simply describes the evaporation of religious 'illusion' under the intense illumination of enlightened scientific scrutiny (Marx,

Nietzsche, Freud). On the other hand, it has been suggested that secularization is only a kind of accidental by-product of the progressive differentiation of social institutions in modern societies: that religious interpretations have simply not managed to keep pace with modernity's rapidly changing social conditions and so have become increasingly irrelevant and implausible to modern urban dwellers (Weber). But virtually all of these 'explanations' of secularization continue to be debated, and hence it is not surprising that Canadian political philosopher Charles Taylor claims that secularization is more 'a locus of questions than a source of explanations'. Yet in spite of his reservations, Taylor goes on to suggest the following 'undeniable' features of modern life: '[T]he regression of belief in God, and even more, the decline in the practice of religion, to the point where from being central to the whole life of Western societies, public and private, this has become sub-cultural, one of many private forms of involvement which some people indulge in' (*Sources of the Self*, p. 309).

Taylor's observations accurately reflect the state of the ongoing debate over the problem of secularization, for the decline of traditional religious observance in modern societies is at once undeniable and yet very difficult to explain. The 'classical' explanation of secularization, developed perhaps most insightfully by Max Weber, is that in modern society religion, and Christianity in particular, has suffered under the twin processes of 'disenchantment' and 'rationalization'.

Disenchantment refers to the criticism, emerging initially out of the Protestant Reformation, of magic and of the belief that the world is somehow infused with supernatural forces and spirits. Originally theologically motivated, such criticism was subsequently developed and disseminated within modern society and culture by science and technology. Many people today no longer believe the world to be animated and 'enchanted' by spiritual forces. Rather, ordinarily, the world is viewed naturalistically as a closed, interlocking system of natural and material causes and effects. That such a view is largely taken for granted in modern society and culture, Weber contended, is the result of the process of disenchantment.

Rationalization refers to the process in which social actions have come to depend increasingly upon purely calculable and controllable (i.e. 'rational') criteria. Steven Seidman helpfully summarizes Weber's argument as follows: 'As the secular-scientific ethos permeates the culture and psychology of modernity, religion is pushed into the realm of the irrational. Religion is viewed as an emotive and expressive act of the private individual ... Weber contends, moreover, that the irreligious nature of the scientific and intellectualized culture of modernity compels religious belief and practice to empty itself of worldly content. Religion in the modern world assumes an other-worldly and mystical form. [This] mystical turn of religion further sustains its status as irrational and a private concern of the individual. Furthermore, even mystical striving and the creation of intimate religious circles is unable to withstand the overwhelming power of secular culture ...' ('Modernity', p. 269).

Peter L. Berger has been perhaps the chief theoretical exponent of the Weberian interpretation of secularization since the middle of the twentieth century. In his most important work on the subject of secularization, *The Sacred Canopy*, Berger defines secularization as a 'process by which sectors of society and culture are removed from the domination of religious institutions and symbols'. Of the sectors from which religion has been removed, Berger (like Weber) understands the economic to have been the first and most important, but he suggests that any number of other areas, such as modern science and technology, modern political life, mass media and modern educational institutions, have been equally subject to the process of secularization. One after another, the central institutional aspects of modern social life have, for a variety of reasons, ceased to appeal to religion for either direction or legitimacy.

The evacuation of religion from the institutional centre of modern societies, Berger contends, led to the secularization and 'pluralization' of modern consciousness. Whereas religious understanding once provided an overarching interpretation, or 'sacred canopy', over the entire social order, modern society has become so institutionally diverse and complicated that individuals are now left largely to their own devices in choosing whichever explanation and interpretation of the social order makes the most sense of their own individual circumstances and experience. Religion has thus been forced to forfeit its role as interpreter of the social order and has instead become simply a matter of personal preference.

The remarkable irony in this process, Berger contends (again following Weber), is that Christianity, and in particular Protestant Christianity, appears to have set the historical stage for it. In criticizing Roman Catholicism's extravagant emphases upon mystery, miracle and magic, the Protestant Reformers effectively narrowed the possibilities of relating to God to that of the single channel of God's sovereign and gracious call to the individual and the individual's response in faith. 'It needed only the cutting of this one narrow channel of mediation, though, to open the floodgates of secularization ... A sky empty of angels becomes open to the intervention of the astronomer and, eventually, of the astronaut. It may be maintained, then, that Protestantism served as a historically decisive prelude to secularization, whatever may have been the importance of other factors' (*Sacred Canopy*, pp. 112–113).

Yet Berger's (and Weber's) interpretation of modern secularity perhaps understates the dialectic at the heart of the process of secularization: that the modern orientation toward the secular has not simply 'happened', but has been and continues to be *chosen*. Indeed, modernity may be said to have been inaugurated in the kind of impatient repudiation of the traditional philosophical and theological conviction that we must somehow penetrate behind that which is more-or-less obviously given in human experience to the true meaning of things. This repudiation was based upon the conviction that human beings could construct a much more peaceful and prosperous social and political order more reliably and more quickly if left to pursue scientific and technological progress unencumbered by arcane philosophical disputation about 'the Good' and invidious theological wrangling about such things as 'the Kingdom of God'. The various thinkers who launched the modern project (Machiavelli, Descartes, Bacon, Hobbes, Locke, Rousseau etc.) recognized that this entailed a certain 'lowering of our sights', as it were, but it was hoped that the material pay-off that would accrue to us from opting for the secular would more than adequately compensate us for the loss of religion's 'sacred canopy' of meaning. After all, the moderns and now the 'postmoderns' have replied in effect, 'Meaning is in the eye of the beholder. It lies only in what we choose to make meaningful.' Putting this point in Christian perspective, we might say that the modern project is founded upon a kind of impatient rejoinder to Jesus' assertion that one does not live by bread alone. 'On the contrary,' modern thinkers retort, 'one lives quite well by bread alone so long as one's attention can be redirected away, by means of such things as entertainment and therapy, from interpreting "this world" (the *saeculum*) in terms of some putative "world to come".' Modernity's impatient repudiation of religious and theological reasoning has since been built into many of the central institutional features of modern society and culture, a fact that goes some distance towards interpreting the phenomenon of secularization.

Yet the stubborn persistence of so-called religious 'fundamentalism', even in the most apparently 'advanced' modern or postmodern contexts, would seem to indicate that the advocates of secularism, as correct as they have perhaps been about the divisive and retrogressive possibilities latent in traditional religions, remain essentially mistaken about basic human aspirations. Secularization is not likely ever to be the last word with respect to modern and postmodern societies. Given the social fact of institutional secularization, however, and given that secularized institutions underwrite the ongoing plausibility of secularism, it is equally unlikely that Western societies will ever again be sheltered beneath a single 'sacred canopy' of religious meaning.

BIBLIOGRAPHY

P. L. Berger, *The Sacred Canopy: Elements of a Sociological Theory of Religion* (Garden City, NY, 1967); S. Bruce (ed.), *Religion and Modernization: Sociologists and Historians Debate the Secularization Thesis* (Oxford, 1992); C. M. Gay, *The Way of the (Modern) World: Or Why It's Tempting to Live as if God Doesn't Exist* (Grand Rapids, MI, 1998); T. Luckmann, *The Invisible Religion: The Transformation of Symbols in Industrial Society* (New York, 1967); D. Lyon, *The Steeple's Shadow: On the Myths and Realities of Secularization* (Grand Rapids, MI, 1985); S. Seidman, 'Modernity, Meaning and Cultural Pessimism in Max Weber', *SA* 44.4, 1983, pp. 267–278; C. Taylor, *Sources of the Self: The Making of the Modern Identity* (Cambridge, MA, 1989); M. Weber, *The Protestant Ethic and the Spirit of Capitalism* (ET T. Parsons, New York, 1958); M. Weber, *The Sociology of Religion* (ET and ed. E. Fischoff, Boston, 1963); B. Wilson, *Religion in Sociological Perspective* (Oxford, 1982).

C. M. Gay

PART 2

ABORIGINAL RELIGION IN AUSTRALIA AND NEW ZEALAND

Aboriginal peoples occupied the continent of Australia over 60,000 years ago (one of humanity's oldest tools was found near Sydney) and, unless autochthonous, they were the first humans to discover a habitable continent by crossing the ocean. At the time of their discovery in modern times, the so-called brown-skinned Australoid populations made up around 500 discrete cultures and half as many languages. The effects of European occupation drastically reduced their numbers from over a million in 1770 to 300,000 today. Of the self-designating Aborigines today, many share non-indigenous ancestries. Government and mission pressure to encourage settlement have all but destroyed their typically nomadic (hunting and gathering) ways of life, although traditional modes continue in the Western Desert and Arnhem Land.

Australia's borders now include the Torres Strait Islands, inhabited by Melanesian groups, who practised horticulture and lived in hamlets. They influenced the mainlanders of Cape York in religious matters, but not in modes of production. A few Melanesian enclaves on the Queensland coast have been detected, one of which practised cannibalism. The people of these enclaves should be distinguished from the Queensland Melanesians called Kanakas, who are descended from imported plantation labourers of the 1870s and 1880s. The appearance and surviving ritual chants of the traditional Tasmanians to the south suggest that they too were Melanesian. Yet if this is so, they were unusual in not being sedentary peoples. (Even in Victoria stone villages were built by mainland Aborigines.)

Although lexical equivalents to the word 'religion' are rarely found, mainland Aboriginal traditions do reveal characteristic preoccupations with the sacredness of land(s). Land was not owned by descent (as in Melanesia), but was given spiritually through 'abiding events' told in myth. The relational connection between land and peoples was not something laid down only in the past, in the so-called 'Dream Time' (when it is believed that primordial spirit beings emerged and made the landscape what it is, in what could be superficially interpreted as creation events). Rather the relationship forms part of the 'Dream*ing*', which is ever-existing and spatial more than temporal. Each grouping (cluster of bands, not 'tribes') moved across and managed their traditional territories, or better, followed their 'mythic maps', with the intercrossing of tracks and shared sites of significance allowing for trading, marriage and ceremonial interconnections.

The Dreaming is especially marked by groups stopping at special places to sing their stories and to acknowledge how these places bring about relatedness between people. The landscapes criss-crossed by Aboriginal tracks varied in size according to population density, the amount of game and produce, and thus the degree of collective mobility: areas on the east coast of Australia, for example, were often fairly small (and vulnerable to damage by colonization, as with those of Yuin groups near Sydney), whereas the land of 'outback' Aborigines (such as the desert Walpiri) was enormous. In every instance, however, the scope of group movements and the places of profound meaning (mountains, bluffs, rocks etc.) were read as a conceptually integrated, sacred cosmos, requiring ritual response.

The 'core ritual' of Aboriginal religion is the initiation of young adolescents, and again spatial elements are central. Initiatory rites literally widen a boy's world, opening up new tracks for him to explore and sometimes involving a solitary journey of endurance. The rituals themselves usually entail ordeals: circumcision and scarification are common among the desert Aranda.

Birth and death are linked to place. One's identity derives from the significant spot(s) where conception occurs, more than from parents. Typically, one returns to the same spirit place at death, or to the place where ancestral 'collective power' brings about human generation. 'Totems' also contribute to identity, in that one is forbidden to eat a living thing (wallaby, snake etc.) which is a totem of one's group. This is because people share the space of their coming-into-being with other existents which also derive from there. As one consequence, one may work to increase the population of one's totem, as in the Aranda *Intichiuma* increase (or fertility) rites, but the rituals performed will be on behalf of other totemic groups, and so contribute to collective survival. Here we see how spatial orientation expresses in Aboriginal life a sacral ecology. Debate continues, however, as to whether Australians traditionally thought in terms of 'Mother Earth'. Phrases such as 'father's land' are common (denoting where one's fathers walked, rather than the territory they possessed), while maternal associations with the land have apparently been conveyed more subtly and require further examination.

Argument has persisted since the 1880s over whether Aborigines believed in a supreme being or high god. In that decade cults of the All-Mothers and All-Fathers (in the north and southeast respectively) were documented, and each seemed to be directed toward one Great Spirit. Recent denials that these cults were traditional have been based on the view that only attention to ancestors could maintain the spatio-local emphasis of the old traditions. The cults were thus 'post-contact' adaptations in response to the new 'whiteman's talk' about God. A universal being, on this argument, would supposedly subvert the old claims of land, yet belief in such a being was threatened when land was rapidly lost. On the other hand, the higher beings in these cults were not necessarily as 'universal' as some maintain, and worship of one of these deities, Biami, among the Yuin long predates other documented All-Father/Mother movements.

Much in Aboriginal ritual life has been kept secret because of the desire to survive culturally against the great colonial incursion. Moreover, Aboriginal mythologies are the world's most complex, and their subtleties require in-house decipherment. Various payback methods, such as sorcery-like 'singing' and 'pointing the bone', need better analysis, as do revenge warfare patterns, although the open regimen of strict punishment for taboo and rule breakages has been well described. Moral sanctioning is often called 'the Law'; significantly, this is integrally related to upholding the land.

Until the early 1980s mission work to the Aboriginal peoples suffered from the effects of paternalism, dependency and misguided government policies. Aboriginal Christian initiatives are now blossoming, however, there being proportionately more black 'working theologians' in Australia than expatriates. Most famous are Djinniyini Gondarra, George Rosendale and Anne Pattel-Gray. While Christianity has been strengthened by indigenous Australians, there are many worship forms that may look too 'introduced' and artificial to outsiders: for example, charismatic enthusiasms. But this almost global form of religious expression is probably a halfway house to more specifically and authentically Aboriginal Christian worship. A question still exists, however, as to how much traditional spirituality can be maintained in the transition to Christianity. Certainly some indigenously run church groups want to expunge it as devilish.

One must remember the impact of other traditions (Islam and, to a very limited extent, Indian traditions) and also that of secular influences. Also the massive effect of utter dislocation should not be ignored. When people are taken out of the sacred spaces so existentially crucial for them, 'behavioural problems' will be noticeable in their interactions with the wider, modern society: alcoholism, aggressiveness, suicide, malaise.

Across the Tasman Sea, the Maori live under the modern political order of New Zealand, which, like Australia, experienced European colonial settlement (from 1839). Now numbering around 360,000, the Maori belong to the culturo-anthropological complex called Polynesia, covering the stratified societies of light-brown-skinned indigenes within a huge triangle in Oceania, from Hawai'i to the north, Easter Island in the east, to New Zealand (Aotearoa) in the southwest. The Maori trace their major occupancy of Aotearoa's huge islands to a Great Fleet which, on genealogical reckoning, arrived in the Middle Ages. They share with other Polynesians the ramage system, a social organization in which high chiefs claim seniority according to whoever first led a great canoe to a chosen territory.

Maori religion has typically Polynesian features. A range of gods (*atua*) is worshipped, ancestors honoured and precautionary measures taken against problematic spirits. Most present-day Maori, though, claim that their forebears believed in a Supreme Being called Io who, unusually for the region, dwelt in the highest heaven far above the deities with whom they mainly dealt. Debate about Io continues, particularly among Europeans, some alleging that Theosophists invented a neo-Gnostic myth which Maori could use as a foil against plainer Christian teachings. Examination of the relevant Maori manuscripts, only now being published, may settle matters. Certainly one line of oral tradition has Io on a level comparable with that of well-known gods, but others present interesting conundra.

Of the departmental deities drawing forth ritual response, the strongest was Tanemahuta, god of forests, who separated the sky (*Rangi*) and earth (*Papa*) from their embrace in the state of precosmic matter (*po*). The story of the lifting of the heavens gives the cosmos a vertical dimension which complements the social hierarchy (of chiefs, priests and commoners). A hero god, Maui, has to confront the Underworld. In the in-between world fierce battles were won and lost over blood and territorial control, and the war god (Tu) was frequently invoked ceremonially. Various ritual practices accompanied Maori 'warriorhood religion': male tattooing, the warcry (*haka*), 'spying' kites, headhunting and head-shrinking, cannibalism and others. Concern for the ancestors and the upholding of their honour in bravery and festal exchanges were crucial aspects of religious life, and Maori architecture symbolically reflects the people's attention to deities and the dead.

Like the Australian Aborigines, the Maori upheld strict rules and precautionary procedures. We owe the term 'taboo' above all to the Maori *tapu*, but in their social hierarchy they attached much more importance to the inherited lordship (*mana*) of chiefs over commoners, whereas Australian systems were 'gerontocratic' (elders eventually becoming 'men of high degree'). Among the Maori, then, power, was passed down from the top; the chiefs' last testaments and funerals were great religious occasions, in preparation for their special future state as stars in the sky.

Christianity has deeply affected the Maori as it has other Polynesian peoples. During and after the Maori Wars (1860–72), transitions to Christianity were affected by indigenous prophets (such as Ratana), and today Maori theologians and Christian leaders (Hone Ka'a etc.) play a forceful and enriching role in New Zealand affairs.

BIBLIOGRAPHY

M. Engelhart, *Extending the Tracks: A Cross-Reductionistic Approach to Australian Aboriginal Male Initiation Rites*

(Stockholm Studies in Comparative Religion 34) (Stockholm, 1998); J. Irwin, *An Introduction to Maori Religion* (Special Studies in Religion 4) (Adelaide, 1984); A. Pattel-Gray (ed.), *Aboriginal Spirituality: Past, Present, Future* (Sydney, 1996); T. Swain, *A Place for Strangers: Towards a History of Australian Aboriginal Being* (Cambridge, 1993); T. Swain and G. W. Trompf, *Religions of Oceania* (Library of Religious Beliefs and Practices) (London, 1995).

G. W. Trompf

AFRICAN TRADITIONAL RELIGIONS

The African religions classified as 'traditional' share common characteristics with premodern religions found among tribal peoples throughout the world. Historians of religion, social anthropologists and missionaries have all in the past designated such religions by terms which contained negative value-judgments. These are clear in the phrase 'savage religion' (terminology which remained common well into the second half of the twentieth century; witness Claude Lévi-Strauss's *The Savage Mind* of 1962), but are present also in descriptive terms such as 'primitive' and 'animist'. Such language reflects the influence of a now discredited evolutionary theory of the history of religions which consigned the spiritual experience and wisdom of Africa to an earlier, childish phase in the development of humankind. It is ironic that many missionaries who are inveterate opponents of evolutionary theory in other contexts continue to describe African religions as 'animist', apparently unaware of the extent to which such language is freighted with Darwinian assumptions.

While a number of alternative definitions unencumbered by the presuppositions described above have been proposed, the term which has gained broad scholarly consensus is 'primal religions'. This has the advantage of underlining the historical importance of such religions while, at the same time, indicating what has been called their 'elemental status' in human experience. The study of African traditional religion thus focuses upon the particular forms which the universal phenomenon of primal religion has taken among sub-Saharan peoples on the African continent.

When viewed through the lenses provided by modern, Western culture the potential for misunderstanding the primal traditions of Africa is considerable. For example, in traditional societies religion was never regarded as something distinct and isolated from the rest of life, nor could it be an option chosen by certain individuals within the group. On the contrary, African Traditional Religions existed within sociocultural contexts in which ethics, art, politics and religion were unified and everywhere intertwined. Thus the assumptions about life and religion which have come to be taken for granted in the highly differentiated cultures of the West appear both strange and profoundly disturbing in tribal settings. In such small-scale societies the identity and experience of individuals is inseparable from their relationships within the community. Against Descartes, traditional Africa would declare, 'We are, therefore I am.'

This sense of the holistic nature of life points towards a fundamental aspect of African traditional religions. Individuals exist within communities which extend outwards through the web of kinship relationships and backwards to the ancestors, who have been described as 'the living dead'. Human beings are thus embedded within a social structure which provides them with a sense of identity and meaning, but they also form part of a long stream of life that has always flowed through their community. Cultures of this kind give birth to values that contrast with those prized in the West: individuality is not encouraged, indeed it threatens life itself; childlessness is an unbearable tragedy and there are social mechanisms to mitigate it; death is not repressed since it is but one of a series of rites of passage by which people move from one status to another.

Early studies of African religions assumed the absence of belief in God and stressed the bewildering multiplicity of spiritual powers inhabiting the primitive cosmos. The anthropologist Lewis Henry Morgan declared all African religions to be 'grotesque and to some extent unintelligible'. It was noticed that in many parts of the continent there was no trace of a cult devoted to God, prayer was rarely directed to him, and often no name could be discovered in vernacular tongues to describe the Creator. However, this apparent absence of divine names often reflected the existence of taboos on uttering of the name of God, a practice that stemmed not from a desire to suppress the knowledge of the Creator, but rather from a heightened awareness of his supreme majesty and power. One missionary reported the surprised reaction of a student to his enquiry concerning the meaning of the Herero name for God, 'Njabi': 'I was brought up in the Christian faith,' he said, 'yet this name for God was so holy to us that we never used it ... And now I find myself sitting next to a white man and he uses this old Herero name for God as if it were of no significance!' As to the absence of specific acts of worship, the response of an Anlo elder in Ghana to the identification of the God of the Bible with Mawu, the Anlo Supreme God, is eloquent: 'My son! *Mawu* is too big to be put in a small room and worshipped only in that place. In all Anloland, it is only the Christians who do this. How can we put into a room a Being we can never see and who is like the wind blowing everywhere?'

The encounter between African traditional religions and the invasive culture of the modern West has been experienced by many tribal peoples as a profound crisis in which, to use the title of Chinua Achebe's great novel, *Things Fall Apart*. Initial resistance to the Christian mission did not necessarily imply the rejection of Christ but stemmed from the perception that the new faith was part of a larger package, acceptance of which would involve the abandonment of the traditions which had always provided people with their identity and meaning. Despite this, the cultural clash was one in which the enormous technological power of the West was bound to eclipse traditional religions, and in this situation Christian missions reaped an unprecedented harvest among the primal peoples of Africa. However, a religious heritage as venerable and as deeply embedded within cultures as were the traditional beliefs of the peoples of Africa could not simply be replaced by a new religion which, when presented in highly individualized and secularized forms, was bound to remain alien at the deepest levels of people's affections and needs. Thus traditional religious beliefs did not disappear; rather they took new forms in response to the impact of modernity, and they continue to exert considerable influence on the lives of millions of people on the African continent today.

The sheer vastness of Africa and the remoteness of many of its ethnic groups provide an environment in which considerable numbers of people have been able to mount successful resistance to the incursions of the modern world. For example, while 80% of the population of Kenya and Uganda profess to be Christian, significant groups in both countries have resisted the seemingly unstoppable tides of evangelization and development and retain their traditional religions relatively intact. The Karamojong of Uganda and (to a lesser extent) the Turkana of northern Kenya are examples. Elsewhere on the continent, traditional beliefs have been fused with selected elements of the invasive culture and given expression in new religious movements which can be described as neo-primal. The Bwiti religion among the Fang people of Gabon, for example, represents an attempt to deal with the malaise which threatened the destruction of the culture. Such movements (often initiated by prophetic leaders) seek to restore the broken unity of the world and to reconcile past and present.

At the opposite end of the spectrum of the thousands of new religious movements to have emerged in Africa in the twentieth century, there are many which intend to be Christian and identify themselves as churches. Although frequently viewed with considerable suspicion by missionaries and by African leaders in the mission-founded churches, movements of this kind have played a crucial role in the spread of Christianity in modern Africa and have contributed significantly to the emergence of an African theology. According to Lamin Sanneh, these African Independent (or Initiated) Churches (AIC) have combined the two fundamental elements of Christianity and African culture in a way that 'advertises their Christian intentions without undervaluing their African credentials' (*West African Christianity – The Religious Impact* [New York, 1983]). In recent years the growing recognition of the need for theology to be contextualized within the mission-founded churches has led to increasing convergence between them and the AIC and may have set the scene for the emergence of a genuinely African expression of Christianity in the twenty-first century. This is the view of Kwame Bediako, who suggests that African Christians need to be open to a profound engagement with their own cultures 'through the medium of the Word of God heard, read and interpreted in the categories of African thought'.

The relevance of this discussion to the contemporary religious situation in the West can be seen in the light of four factors which have led to the increasing salience of African religious traditions in postmodern Europe and America. First, anthropological studies, using the media of literature, film and exhibitions, have raised the profile of traditional Africa and alerted many people to those aspects of its cultures that are clearly beautiful and good. While such studies have sometimes been highly selective and have suppressed negative cultural elements, they have nonetheless compelled Western people to enquire whether the loss of such cultures would not only impoverish Africa but leave the whole of humankind much the poorer.

Second, the emergence of New Age religion in the West, prompted by the quest for a spirituality that might give birth to new ways of looking at the natural world, has added further impetus to the interest in African traditions. In particular, the holism of African religions and their ability to discern the sacred everywhere in the world has seemed to offer an escape from the aridity and destructiveness of Enlightenment rationalism. Mention should be made here of the powerful medium of the cinema, since many recent films have contained messages encouraging the re-evaluation of primal traditions. An example is Steven Spielberg's film *Amistad*, which not only depicted the horrors of the Atlantic slave trade in graphic detail, but also suggested that people in the West have much to learn from African worldviews.

Third, the extraordinary flowering of African literary talent, seen in the publication of dozens of post-colonial African novels, has created yet another channel through which information concerning both the impact of the West on African religion and culture and the distinctive insights of African religions has been widely disseminated. It is particularly interesting that in the final pages of Chinua Achebe's last novel, *Anthills of the Savannah* (nominated for the 1987 Booker Prize), we hear an old man reflecting in prayer on what he regards as the poverty of Christian theology when compared to the traditional view of God: 'Owner of the world! Man of countless names! The church people call you three-in-one. It is a good name. But it carries miserly and insufficient praise. Four-hundred-in-one would be more fitting in our eyes.' Clearly such a perspective contrasts radically with the first Western perceptions of African religion!

Fourth, and by no means least, there is now a substantial African diaspora scattered throughout the Western world, and within the African communities in (for example) Birmingham, Liverpool, Amsterdam and Berlin distinctively African approaches to religion are retained and nurtured. For example, Jerisdan H. Jehu-Appiah, pastor of the Ghana-originated Musama Disco Christo Church in London (an AIC now operating, like many others, in the West), writes in a British journal about 'Spirituality and Black Culture' and informs his readers that in the African churches 'spirituality is primarily a corporate affair' (*The Bible in Transmission*, summer 1999, pp. 8–9).

At this point we have come full circle. We began with the classical Western assessment of African traditions, according to which they were viewed as so permeated by superstition as to scarcely deserve the name 'religion'. It then seemed self-evident that African religions would disappear, vanishing like mist before the rising of the sun as the blessings of civilization spread around the globe. Now, however, in the chastened atmosphere of a postmodern culture, that smug confidence has been eroded and in the context of a growing existential crisis perhaps people in the West may be able to listen to, and learn from, sisters and brothers in Africa. What the consequences of such a dialogue might be it is impossible to predict, but perhaps the third millennium will witness the great continent of Africa bringing its own treasures to the store of human knowledge and experience and increasing the church's perception of the immensity of the grace of God in Jesus Christ. In the wise words of John V. Taylor, 'No man, least of all Christian man, can live fully in that protracted paranoia which exalts and idealises his cerebral life and demotes his instinctual being ... We never leave primitive [*sic!*] man behind but must learn to travel with him in the company.'

BIBLIOGRAPHY

K. Bediako, *Christianity in Africa, The Renewal of a Non-Western Religion* (Oxford, 1994); D. Forde (ed.), *African Worlds: Studies in the Cosmological Ideas and Social Values of African Peoples* (Oxford, 1954); G. ter Haar, *Halfway To Paradise: African Christians in Europe* (Cardiff, 1998); T. Sundermeier, *The Individual and Community in African Traditional Religion* (Hamburg, 1998); J. V. Taylor, *The Primal Vision* (London, 1965); A. Walls, 'Primal Religious Traditions in Today's World', in F. Whaling (ed.), *Religion in Today's World* (Edinburgh, 1987), pp. 250–278.

D. W. Smith

ASTROLOGY AND HOROSCOPES

Astrology is variously regarded as a science, pseudoscience or occult practice. It is based on esoteric influences (alleged, not proved) of the sun, moon, planets and stars in human affairs and the ability of astrologers to interpret how those influences affect a person. The theoretical basis for its assumptions lies chiefly in Hellenistic philosophy (c.300 BC–c.AD 300). Astrology is also used to predict trends and events, not only for individuals but also for corporate entities such as businesses and nations. Throughout its long and varied history (in antiquity it was everywhere linked to astronomy and religion), astrology has had both powerful detractors and benefactors. Despite its lack of overt ritual, it has the potential to influence every aspect of a person's life, and its worldview is as comprehensive as that of a world religion.

THE HOROSCOPE CHART

A horoscope chart is a map, or snapshot, of the planets, the sun and the moon as they were located in the twelve constellations at the time, place and date of a person's birth. Often called a birth chart, natal chart or nativity, the horoscope is constructed using an ephemeris and is fundamental to the practice of astrology. On paper, this circular map is divided into twelve roughly 30-degree sections called signs of the zodiac, or sun signs: Aries, Taurus, Gemini, Cancer, Leo, Virgo, Libra, Scorpio, Sagittarius, Capricorn, Aquarius, Pisces. Each sign represents the constellation location of the sun in relation to the earth, in one month of the year. Still used in the West today, this division of the heavens is a completely arbitrary invention of the ancient Babylonians and is derived from their mythology. Other cultures had their own mythological bases: the Egyptians divided the sun's path into thirty-six divisions; a Chinese tradition used twenty-eight signs.

The sun sign – the constellation location of the sun at one's birth – is believed by most astrologers to be the most important influence in a horoscope. Each sign is said to represent characteristics of human life and potential: Gemini symbolizes mentality and communication; Leo, power and ambition; Scorpio, passion and will-power.

There are also twelve 'houses' to a horoscope. The houses are an imaginary circle divided into twelve 30-degree sections overlaid on the twelve signs to represent different aspects of life. The first house indicates self-expression, character, abilities and appearance. The second house controls matters relating to finances and possessions. The seventh house represents spouse, partners and social life. Characteristics of both signs and houses figure prominently in horoscope interpretation.

In a horoscope chart, the planets are located in the signs and houses by the time, place and date for which the chart is constructed. A planet's influence is said to be strengthened or weakened according to its placement by sign and house, and a planet's characteristics must be synthesized with those of its particular sign, house and any relevant planets to determine its range of influence. Because the planets orbit the sun at different speeds, they form different angular configurations, called aspects, with each other and with Earth. These planetary aspects (trine, square, opposition etc.) are essential to chart interpretation, each aspect having different meanings: difficult, adverse or favourable. There are also major and minor aspects. Two other significant astrological influences are the moon sign and the ascendant, the latter also known as the rising sign. Once an astrologer has determined the chief influences of a particular horoscope, the lengthy synthesis of chart interpretation may begin.

THE MODERN EVOLUTION OF ASTROLOGY

The literature of astrology has gone through a significant evolution since the nineteenth century, when the practice was mostly regarded by its practitioners as an occult science: that is, a description of the hidden and spiritual (esoteric) forces of the universe. 'As a science, it was as new and modern as the latest scientific journal, aligned to the wave of the future. As an occult body of thought, it was allowed to make "religious" affirmations about the place of individuals . . . Minimally, these affirmations might be little more than reflections about the nature of life, but astrology, taken to its natural conclusion, led directly to the religion of the stars. Astrologers, even the most secular, were aware that they were offering a religious alternative to Christianity' (Dr J. G. Melton, in Lewi, *Astrology for the Millions*, p. xxx).

Publicly, astrology shed its occult coat as a result of widespread changes in the Western worldview, both academic and populist, in the late nineteenth and early twentieth centuries. A vast number of scientific facts and technological feats, and a number of stunning scientific arguments, struck fatal blows against the claims of astrology to be regarded as science (Strohmer, *America's Fascination with Astrology*, ch. 6). These culminated in 1975, when 186 leading scientists, including 18 Nobel laureates, signed a widely publicized formal statement, 'Objections to Astrology', stressing its unscientific nature. This rationalistic scientific statement, which appeared in the September–October 1975 issue of *The Humanist* magazine, concluded by saying that those 'who have faith in astrology do so in spite of the fact that there is no verified scientific basis for their beliefs, and indeed that there is strong evidence to the contrary'.

More recently, influenced by New Age and postmodern categories, astrological literature has virtually abandoned causal scientific language for an acausal legitimation. The stars and planets are no longer said to determine human conditions; instead, the heavenly bodies and their aspects merely *coincide meaningfully* with human affairs and terrestrial events. The meanings of such coincidences are explained to a client during a horoscope reading. Astrologically, the meanings derive from 'the principle of symbolic correspondences', which is a metaphysical shorthand for the vast mythological symbolism (see below) of the astrological heavens as it relates to people and events. A typical symbolic correspondence (reading, meaning) would be: 'Venus represents artistic ability' + 'Venus is prominent in a horoscope' = 'the person has artistic ability.' This is an *acausal* linkage, because there is no known cause and effect between the planet Venus and the person's artistic abilities. Often called transformational, or archetypal, astrology, this 'new' astrology relies heavily on mishandled ideas from quantum theory (Culver and Ianna, *Astrology: True or False?*, p. 37) and on archetypal psychological theory (Marks, *The Astrology of Self-Discovery*; Guttman and Johnson, *Mythic Astrology*), especially Carl Jung's psychologized occult cosmology.

THE MYTHOLOGY OF ASTROLOGY

Both traditional and modern astrology rely solely on a vast body of ancient mythological knowledge as the basis for horoscope readings. This is true across the whole spectrum, from the advice found in daily sun sign newspaper columns to expensive professional readings. Astrologers do not interpret physical influences from the planets or the stars; they use modern psychological language and categories to interpret the characteristics and attributes of ancient gods and goddesses, the myths which in antiquity were overlaid upon the planets and the stars. 'The name of each planet gives us a clue to its nature, for each is called after the gods and goddesses of mythology' (Davison, *Astrology*, p. 27). 'Myth has always been closely linked with astrology; all our planets are names for the Graeco-Roman deities and derive their interpretive meanings from them' (Guttman and Johnson, *Mythic Astrology*, back cover). Mercury, as messenger of the gods, represents movement, travel and the reasoning mind. Jupiter's nature is said to be expansive, good-willed and representing success in finances. Saturn is constricting, binding and difficult.

Mythology also surrounds the signs. Sagittarians are said to be freedom loving and optimistic; they like travelling, horses, books and giving advice; they have interests in philosophy and religion, are at home with abstract ideas and are powerfully idealistic. These characteristics are derived from the symbolism of the Sagittarius myth, in which the horse represents the intuitive mind, and the arrow, being propelled, represents aspirations that direct the mind's creative energies toward philosophy and religion.

ASTROLOGY AND MAGIC

Magic is based on the assumption that a ritual power exists between certain objects (amulet; rabbit's foot), symbols (five-pointed star; upside-down cross) or words (incantations) and common experiences in the real world, such as death, childbirth, good health, the growth of crops, failure in love and protection from evil. Since there is no physical or scientific evidence for such linkages, *symbolic correspondences* are made within the mind of people who want to believe in them. The system of symbolic correspondences influences and controls according to the strength of will by which someone makes the magic link between object (e.g. rabbit's foot) and event (e.g. warding off disaster).

This principle is also a basic law of astrology. Mars is said to influence blood, war, iron and muscular energy, but there is no physical evidence for this. It is merely an astrological correspondence, the linkage being found only within the mind of the one who believes it. Mars, therefore, is *magically* related to blood, war, iron and muscular energy. So, too, with the other astrological influences. There is no physical evidence that the second house relates to finances or that Sagittarius relates to philosophy and religion. There is no scientific evidence that Aries relates to fire and to the human head and brain or that Virgo relates to one's hands, abdomen and intestines. These are merely astrological correspondences. The worldview in which magic makes sense is therefore one in which astrology makes sense (L. E. Jerome, 'Astrology: Magic or Science?', *The Humanist*, Sept.–Oct. 1975).

When magical thinking is applied to astrology, the practice guides, governs or rules people according to the strength of will by which they believe in the acausal correspondences between the mythological symbolism of their horoscopes and the events, characteristics and conditions the symbolism is said to represent in their lives. A famous example was the 'Nancy Reagan Astrology in the White House' story, which broke in the media during the spring of 1988. Magical thinking can lead an Aries (the Ram) person to feel justified about being headstrong, or a Taurus (the Bull) person in being stubborn. Someone may decide to leave a good job because of 'inauspicious planetary indications'. The willingness of a person to believe that he or she is 'incompatible' with a spouse may sap the moral and emotional strength needed to save the marriage when trouble arises.

Ultimately, astrology places its believers in the hands of a peculiar polytheistic religion. It is not the planets but the gods after which they are named that are being interpreted. The antithetical contrast with Christian monotheism helps to explain why the practice of astrology is so strongly condemned in injunctions such as Deuteronomy 18:10–13 and Isaiah 47:8–15. The modernist rationalistic scientific criticism of astrology is reductionist: it precludes a religious or theological analysis and therefore cannot account for what astrologers argue is the real power base of the practice: its supernatural, or spiritual, dimension. A Christian vision will include theological criticism (Strohmer, *America's Fascination with Astrology*, chs. 7–10) while affirming the scientific rebuttal.

BIBLIOGRAPHY

R. B. Culver and P. A. Ianna, *Astrology: True or False? A Scientific Evaluation* (Buffalo, NY, 1988); R. C. Davison, *Astrology: The Classic Guide to Understanding Your Horoscope* (Sebastopol, CA, 1987); A. Guttman and K. Johnson, *Mythic Astrology: Archetypal Powers in the Horoscope* (St Paul, MN, 1996); G. Lewi, *Astrology for the Millions* (St Paul, MN, 1993); T. Marks, *The Astrology of Self-Discovery* (Sebastopol, CA, 1985); C. R. Strohmer, *What Your Horoscope Doesn't Tell You* (Milton Keynes, 1991); C. R. Strohmer, *America's Fascination with Astrology: Is It Healthy?* (Greenville, SC, 1998).

C. R. Strohmer

ATHEISM

Atheism is best understood in terms of what it denies: the existence of a god or gods, including, for example, the divine Creator worshipped by the major Western religions and the gods of the Greeks and Hindus. Atheism's contemporary corollaries (humanism, materialism and naturalism) are based on the atheistic assumption: there is no god. The naturalist claims that there is nothing beyond nature, no supernatural beings or powers. The materialist believes that there is nothing but matter and energy in their various manifestations. And humanism, according to Jean-Paul Sartre (1905–80), begins with a sense of abandonment: it is committed to the belief that God does not exist and follows out the consequences of living in a world devoid of God.

Naturalism, materialism and humanism are not primarily negative philosophies. Their adherents develop their views about the ultimate nature of reality into a complete philosophical system. How should we understand the nature of the cosmos in general and humans in particular if the universe is not created by God? The metaphysical naturalist believes that everything that exists is in space and time and is, therefore, knowable, if it can be known, through scientific methods. The naturalist views the world as a series of processes governed by cause and effect and therefore closed off to miracles or perhaps to free will. Materialism, a form of naturalism, seeks to provide an account of human persons in terms of matter without reference to an immaterial mind or soul. Humanism denies transcendent realities and develops a human-oriented view of the world concerned primarily with moral and social issues.

Although contemporary atheists seem almost uniform in their rejection of religious beiefs, atheism is not necessarily opposed to religion. Some religions are decidedly anti-theistic. Some versions of Hinduism and Buddhism, even the Buddha himself, are atheistic.

ATHEISM OR AGNOSTICISM?

How can the atheist really know that a god, somewhere and somehow, does not exist? Some contend that since it is difficult to prove the non-existence of anything, even God, the atheist cannot rule out the possibility that God exists. This simple, logical point may make agnosticism more intellectually respectable but keeps the unbeliever a safe distance from theism. The issue here may prove pragmatically otiose since, for all practical purposes, the atheist and the agnostic are likely to live similar lives and develop similar worldviews based on their common rejection of belief in God.

RATIONAL OBJECTIONS TO THEISM

Why are people atheists? This question is a puzzle for some devout believers who find profound intellectual and spiritual sustenance in their theistic beliefs. But the Bible itself bears witness to the deepest problem for belief (Job 23; Pss. 13, 83, 88). As the philosopher Blaise Pascal (1623–62) writes: 'Truly Thou art a hidden god.' Divine hiddenness is taken by the atheist as evidence of God's non-existence. God's apparent absence is perhaps the most compelling reason for atheism. The hiddenness of God has elicited a demand for evidence for rational belief in God. Bertrand Russell (1872 – 1970) was once asked, if he were to come before God in the next life, what he would say to God if asked why he had not believed in God. Russell, acceding to his need for evidence, replied: 'Not enough evidence, God, not enough evidence.' Some atheists claim that the burden of proof is on the one who affirms, namely the theist, and that if the burden of proof is not satisfied, the theist believes on pain of irrationality.

At this point theists often hastily retort that, although there may not be conclusive evidence for God's existence, it is impossible to disprove God's existence. The impossibility of disproving God's existence is then asserted as a reason to believe in God's existence. However, it is surely not a principle of reason to believe in the existence of things whose existence has not been disproved. Theists themselves typically do not believe in the existence of Zeus, fairies and phlogiston and do not feel any compulsion to believe in them simply on the grounds that no one has disproved their existence. Without experience of fairies, for example, it is difficult for most of us to drum up belief in them. So too, many atheists, lacking experience or evidence of God, find it difficult to drum up belief in God or gods.

Perhaps the second biggest reason people offer for their atheism is the problem of human suffering. This often finds expression in a deductive disproof of God's existence, typically called 'the problem of evil'. Very briefly stated, the argument goes as follows: If there were a God who is omnipotent, omniscient and perfectly good (as theism maintains), he could and would want to create a world without evil and consequent suffering. But there is evil, so God does not exist. This argument has been shown to be problematic because, for all we know, an omnipotent, omniscient, wholly good being might have a good reason for allowing evil. However, new versions of the argument have been developed which claim that there is simply too much evil to justify theistic belief and that it is highly improbable that such a God exists.

MORAL OBJECTIONS TO THEISM

Not all defences of atheism are evidential. Some are more practical or moral. Sigmund Freud (1856–1939), Karl Marx (1818–83) and Friedrich Nietzsche (1844–1900) assume God's non-existence and proceed to employ the hermeneutics of suspicion in order to unmask the supposedly ignoble motives of religious believers and demonstrate that they are often motivated to believe or act in ways contrary to their religious beliefs. Nietzsche shows how meekness, for example, can mask the lust for power as Christians secretly revel in God's eternal revenge on those who harm them. Marx challenges bourgeois Christian belief that God has blessed their privileged economic status and the oppressive system that supports it. Religion is the 'opiate of the people' because it dulls the pain of injustice and oppression and thereby maintains the status quo. Underneath the veneer of gratitude and humility lie greed and self-satisfaction. Beneath religious belief Freud finds the need for consolation. By creating a God in our own image we make the otherwise hostile world manageable. Christians scapegoat others (unbelievers), Freud contends, to feel better about themselves: righteous indignation hides their incessantly demanding egos. Although many Christians reject the theories of Freud, Nietzsche and Marx, and although there are serious problems with some of their ideas, their hermeneutics of suspicion can be used for legitimate self-criticism. (See Westphal, *Suspicion and Faith*.)

ATHEISM AND MORALITY

A common theistic response to atheism is that it cannot provide any foundations for morality. If there is a god who created human beings, then morality probably bears a significant relation to that being's will, to his purposes for his creatures or to their created nature. Morality is determined by God prior to human existence and the moral project is to act in accordance with divinely given human nature or divinely ordained morality. The roots of western morality are, of course, theistic. If those roots are killed, morality dies. On this point Fyodor Dostoevsky (1821–81) is often quoted: 'If God does not exist, everything is permitted.' This is often taken to mean that if God does not exist, morality is no longer possible.

While theists seem to assume that if they were to give up their religious beliefs, they would lose all sense of morality, atheists nonetheless have developed distinctively non-theistic foundations of morality. For example, social contract theorists, who find their inspiration in the work of Thomas Hobbes (1588–1679), argue that right and wrong are nothing more than the agreement among rationally self-interested individuals to give up the unhindered pursuit of their own desires and interests for the security of living in peace with one another. In order to secure this peace, one willingly forgoes the liberty of total self-determination and takes on the constraints of morality. It is in my best interest, so the argument goes, to have my desires constrained by entering into a society where the desires of everyone are constrained by an agreed power.

The social contract theory has some promise as a foundation of morality, but has problems adequately addressing the question 'Why should I be moral?' If rationality is understood in terms of maximizing self-interest, then it will occasionally be rational (if it maximizes one's self-interest) to be immoral. As long as one's actions do not undermine the social contract and one gets away with wrongdoing, then it is reasonable, for example, not to pay all of one's taxes or to lie to protect one's interests. In such instances, one may reasonably judge that immorality is rational (because it enhances one's self-interest), as long, again, as one gets away with it.

THE MEANING OF LIFE

Theists often claim that life is meaningful because God has given it a purpose and because our strifes and strivings in this life are not in vain as they make us fit for eternity. The atheist typically denies both an overall purpose for life and the consolations of eternity. Are atheists doomed to a meaningless existence? Atheists divide on this issue into the absurdists and the temporalists. Absurdists, such as Albert Camus and Jean-Paul Sartre, contend that human beings are ill-suited for the cosmos since the cosmos seems indifferent and even hostile to the satisfaction of human desires. The temporalists simply reduce the demand for human satisfaction: if eternal rewards exceed human reach, people can find satisfaction and meaning with the pleasures granted in their brief earthly sojourn.

CONCLUSION

Atheism is a powerful intellectual option that is gaining adherents both in the decreasingly religious West and in the atheistic Communisms of the East. Like any other worldview it must, for the philosophically aware, answer the fundamental human questions: Who or what am I? What ought I do? What is my goal or purpose? It must also respond to intellectual challenges such as the scientific evidence of the universe's beginning in time or the apparent defects in the atheistic grounding of morality and the meaning of life. Whether or not it is up to these challenges remains to be seen.

BIBLIOGRAPHY

M. Buckley, *At the Origins of Modern Atheism* (New Haven, CT, 1990); A. Flew, *God and Philosophy* (New York, 1966); S. Freud, *The Future of an Illusion* (New York, 1961); M. Martin, *Atheism: A Philosophical Justification* (Philadelphia, 1990); F. Nietzsche, *The Genealogy of Morals* (New York, 1989); M. Westphal, *Suspicion and Faith: The Religious Uses of Modern Atheism* (New York, 1998).

K. J. Clark

BAHA'I FAITH, THE

HISTORY

The Baha'i faith (or Baha'ism) has its origin in mid-nineteenth century Persia (Iran). Although once considered a sect of Islam, the Baha'i faith is treated by contemporary scholars as an independent world religion. Just as Christianity is no longer considered a sect of Judaism, Baha'ism is no longer considered a sect of Islam.

In 1844, a Shi'ite Muslim named Mirza Ali Muhammad (1819–50) took on the name 'Bab', which literally means 'gate'. He claimed to be the rightful successor of the prophet Muhammad's son-in-law, 'Ali. 'Ali had led the Shi'ite sect after Muhammad's death. (The larger group of Muslims, the Sunnis, recognize no successor for Muhammad.) According to the Shi'ites, there were twelve descendants of Muhammad (beginning with 'Ali), known as Imams (lit. 'leaders'). In 873 the twelfth and final Imam, Mahdi, who was only a child at the time, disappeared. Following his disappearance the Shi'ites claimed that he would return again at the end of time in order to vanquish the infidels and usher in a time of blessedness. The Bab, who is one of the manifestations of God in Baha'i theology, claimed to be this returned twelfth Imam, thus provoking the wrath of the Shi'ites.

The Babi movement had a short lifespan. After years of persecution, of both the Bab and his followers, he was executed publicly in 1850. The Baha'i faith teaches that prior to his death the Bab said that he had prepared the way for one whom he predicted would soon arrive and form a universal religion.

Mirza Husayn Ali (1817–92) was a follower of the Bab and claimed in 1863 to be the one whom the Bab predicted would succeed him. Changing his name to Baha' Allah or Baha'u'llah (lit. 'the glory of God'), Mirza Husayn Ali declared himself to be a manifestation of God. Those Babis who believed his declaration and obeyed his commands were known as Baha'is.

After Baha'u'llah's death in 1892, the religion's leadership was passed on to his son, Abbas Effendi (1844–1921), who later became known as Abd al-Baha or 'Abdu'l-Baha'. However, unlike his father and the Bab, 'Abdu'l-Baha' never claimed to be a manifestation of God. He was, however, instrumental in bringing Baha'ism to Europe and North America. His many travels included a coast to coast visit to the United States in 1912 which brought him into contact with many different American religious groups as well as students and faculty on university campuses. After his death in 1921, Baha'i leadership was placed in the hands of 'Abdu'l-Baha's grandson, Shoghi Effendi (1897–1957), who led the Baha'i World Faith until his death in 1957. Since the time of Shoghi Effendi's death the Baha'i faith has not been led by a descendent of Baha'u'llah, but by an elected body of Baha'is representing all portions of the globe, the Universal House of Justice (UHJ), founded in 1963. However, this transition of leadership did not go unchallenged within the Baha'i community. Arising out of the controversy was the Orthodox Baha'i faith. Organized by excommunicated Mason Remey (1874–1974), this group differs little from the Baha'i World Faith in its doctrines. Its chief dispute with the main body concerns the line of leadership. Orthodox Baha'is claim that Remey, not the UHJ, is Shoghi Effendi's proper successor.

The Baha'i World Faith has its international headquarters (the Baha'i World Centre) in Haifa, Israel. Its headquarters in the United States, located in Wilmette, Illinois, is well known for its opulent nine-sided temple, which represents the nine great religious leaders of the world whom Baha'is believe to be manifestations of the one God (see the list below).

In 2000 there were over six million Baha'is worldwide, with an impressive geographic spread in comparison to other religions. The Baha'i faith is second only to Christianity in the number of countries in which it has significant communities.

BELIEFS

The Baha'i faith derives its doctrines from the writings and talks of the Bab and Baha'u'llah, with the latter taking precedence over the former. Baha'u'llah dictated over one hundred books and tablets, the 'most weighted and sacred' work being the *Kitab-i-Aqdas* ('Most Holy Book'). Baha'i beliefs are also derived from the interpretations of Baha'u'llah's works by

'Abdu'l'-Baha', Shoghi Effendi and the UHJ. Although Baha'is believe that the scriptures of other religions, such as the Qur'an and the Bible, are valuable, they doubt their authenticity. In addition, the Baha'i faith maintains that these scriptures should be interpreted in light of the teachings of the most recent manifestation of God, Baha'u'llah.

Many people today are attracted to the Baha'i faith because of its social and political ideals. Baha'is call for a one-world government to institute the following precepts and general policies: the unfettered search for truth; the oneness of humankind; the reconciliation of science and religion; universal peace; an international language (Esperanto); education for all; equal opportunity for both genders; work for all; the elimination of extremes of wealth and poverty; equal freedom for all; and unity among religions, nations and races.

Although the Baha'i faith is popularly known for these high ideals, it also has a distinct set of beliefs about God, revelation and humanity that clearly distinguish it from other world religions but also serve as the philosophical foundation for its high ideals. Its primary and basic belief is that the major world religions derive from the same source. This is based on the doctrine that the great religious figures (see list below) in human history were manifestations of the same God, an invisible and unknowable essence. Baha'ism teaches that these manifestations reflect, though they do not directly reveal, the glorious attributes of God. The manifestations are to God just as the sun's rays and reflection are to the sun. Baha'ism also teaches that knowledge of God may be acquired through general revelation: that one may recognize God's handiwork by observing and reflecting on both human nature and the natural world.

It is difficult to find in Baha'i literature a definitive list of manifestations. One list that is generally accepted by contemporary Baha'is contains Adam, Abraham, Buddha, Krishna, Moses, Jesus, Muhammad, the Bab and Baha'u'llah. However, Baha'i leaders (including the Bab, Baha'u'llah, 'Abdu'l-Baha' and Shoghi Effendi) have presented differing lists of manifestations over the years. Some of these lists have included Noah, Zoroaster and Confucius and the Arabian prophets Hud and Salih. Other lists have left out Buddha and Krishna.

According to Baha'i doctrine, each manifestation brings to his era new laws and revelations that would have been too difficult for and not applicable to the people of previous dispensations. Thus in Baha'ism special revelation is progressive, and the revelation binding for previous eras cannot be rightly applied to present or future ones unless it is included in the revelation of the current manifestation. The teachings that are subject to change are those that the Baha'i faith maintains to be non-essential to knowing the truth about God. These include moral, ceremonial, dietary and doctrinal teachings. The truths not subject to change are ones that Baha'ism teaches as fundamental to true religion: the oneness of God; the brotherhood of humanity; and the doctrine of progressive revelation through God's manifestations. This is why the apparent inconsistencies between the teachings of the religious systems founded by the manifestations are generally not considered problematic for Baha'is.

Unlike the orthodox versions of Islam, Judaism and Christianity, which teach creation of the universe by a personal God out of nothing, Baha'ism teaches a form of pantheism known as emanationism: the view that the universe is without beginning and is a perpetual emanation from God. Yet there is much in Baha'i literature that speaks of God in terms that seem consistent with classical monotheism. Concerning the afterlife, the Baha'i faith teaches that the depictions of heaven and hell in other religions ought to be read symbolically. It does, however, teach that there is disembodied conscious existence in the afterlife. Those who cared for their souls in this mortal realm will be able to enjoy the next world and continue to make progress. Those who neglected their souls will for ever be in an unhappy state.

BIBLIOGRAPHY

'Abdu'l-Baha', *Some Answered Questions* (1930); Baha'u'llah and 'Abdu'l-Baha', *Baha'i World Faith: Selected Writings of Baha'u'llah and 'Abdu'l-Baha'* (1943); F. J. Beckwith, *Baha'i* (1985); J. E. Esslemont, *Baha'u'llah and the New Era* ([3]1970); William S. Hatcher and J. Douglas Martin, *The Baha'i Faith: The Emerging Global Religion* (1984); W. M. Miller, *The Baha'i Faith: Its History and Teachings* (1984).

F. J. Beckwith

BUDDHISM (MAHAYANA)

Soon after the death (*parinirvana*) of the Buddha various schools emerged within the new religion. These essentially divided into two groupings: those who held strictly to the traditions and those who were willing to accept innovations. Of the first category only the *Theravada* tradition remains today and this is discussed in a separate article. The innovative schools were known as *Mahayana* meaning 'great vehicle [to enlightenment]' as opposed to *Hinayana* ('lesser vehicle'). Mahayana emerged in northern India sometime in the first century before Christ. Various theories have been proposed for the emergence of Mahayana, but the issue is still unresolved. It was probably a popular movement of those disillusioned with the indifference of the higher monks and seeking a ritual expression of their devotion to the Buddha.

The Buddha is claimed to have said that to the monks he gave the *Dharma* (teaching) and to the laity his relics. The Buddha's body was cremated, the remains were divided into a number of portions, and a *stupa* (domed edifice built to house Buddhist or Jain relics) was constructed over them, as was the practice for royalty of the period. These *stupas* became the centre for pilgrimages for lay Buddhists possibly performing functions similar to those of the sacred sites of the Hindus.

MULTIPLE BUDDHAS AND *BODHISATTVAS*

In early Buddhism, as in Theravada, it was assumed that there was only one enlightened being in any world cycle – the Buddha. Later, the belief developed that there were many Buddhas and enlightened beings at any one time. In order to account for the various ways in which buddhahood could be experienced Mahayana developed a doctrine of the 'three bodies' (*trikaya*) of the Buddha. The earthly manifestation body of a Buddha is called the 'transformation body' (*nirmanakaya*) as was Sakyamuni himself, the Buddha of our age. The 'enjoyment body' (*sambhogakaya*) of a Buddha is one of magical transformation that the Buddha 'enjoys' as the fruit of the merit generated through vast periods of religious practice. In this form a Buddha may preside over a particular Buddha-realm or 'Pure Land'. The ultimate form is the Dharma body (*dharmakaya*), which is the absolute essence of the universe. By making a connection between the earthly Buddha and the *Dharma* body, Mahayana moved Buddhist teaching in the direction of theism in contrast to early Buddhism, and provided an alternative soteriological path centred on the figure of the *bodhisattva*.

The word *bodhisattva* means 'a being (*sattva*) who seeks enlightenment (*bodhi*)'. It is believed that out of compassion for the needy a potential *bodhisattva* makes a vow not to enter *Nirvana* until all beings are delivered from their sufferings. Their objective is therefore not merely personal liberation, but a cosmic process. Mahayana teaches that all living beings have the potential to achieve Buddhahood and this is what the *bodhisattva* seeks to realize. The career of the *bodhisattva* is held to begin when the devotee first aspires for enlightenment, which requires a distinct act of the will. It is like a seed that is considered will eventually become an enlightened mind. Mahayana Buddhism also recognized a new class of heavenly *bodhisattvas* in their pantheon. There were four that are of great importance: Amitabha, Manjusri, Maitreya, and Avalokitesvara.

Amitabha figures in many Mahayana scriptures as the lord of a heavenly realm, and becomes the focus of devotion in many of the Pure Land sects that will be discussed later. 'Manjusri' means 'gentle or sweet glory', and is regarded as the embodiment of wisdom. He is the crown prince of *Dharma*, because like other great *bodhisattvas*, he will become a future Buddha. Manjusri usually appears to human beings in dreams. It is said that whoever worships him is born time and again into a Buddhist family, and is protected by Manjusri's power. Maitreya is the *bodhisattva* mentioned in the earliest texts, and is considered as one who in the distant future will arise in the world with thousands of disciples. Maitreya, unlike the Buddhas before him, is now alive, so he can respond to the prayers of his worshippers. The Sanskrit root of his name means 'benevolent', and likewise he is willing to help those who call to him. The origin of Avalokitesvara is obscure, but his name comes from the Sanskrit roots *avalokita* ('looking down') and *isvara* ('Lord'). He is thus seen as the one who looks down upon the world and responds in compassion to the suffering he sees. In Chinese texts this *bodhisattva* is venerated in the feminine form under the name Kuan-yin ('sound-regarder'). This gender shift is considered to be an example of his power to change shape to benefit the believers.

MAHAYANA LITERATURE

The Theravada canon was closed within two or three centuries of the Buddha's *parinirvana*. This fixed the oral tradition and set an authentic canon known as *Tipitaka* written in Pali, which all Buddhists accept. The earliest Mahayana scriptures deal with *prajnaparmita* ('perfection of wisdom'). They consist of thirty-eight different books, composed in India between 100 BC and AD 600, which is the high point of Mahayana scholarship. The wisdom spoken of in these *sutras* goes beyond that of everyday life, and is often expressed in terms of praise:

> 'Homage to Thee, Perfect Wisdom,
> Boundless, and transcending thought!
> All Thy limbs are without blemish,
> Faultless those who Thee discern'
> (*Rahulabhadra*, *Prajnaparamitasutra*, v. 1.)

The most renowned of the Wisdom texts are the *Diamond Sutra* and the *Heart Sutra*, both originating from the fourth century. Another important Mahayana scripture is the *Lotus of the Wonderful Law*, which Parrinder refers to as the 'Gospel of half Asia'. Little is known of where and when the *Lotus Sutra* was composed, or in what language, but a Chinese translation is known to have existed as early as AD 255. It depicts events that take place in a vast cosmic universe reflecting contemporary Indian cosmology. Outside the present world exist countless others spreading in all directions each presided over by different Buddhas. All these worlds, like our own, are caught up in a never-ending cycle of formation, continuance, decline and disintegration over vast periods of time.

PHILOSOPHICAL SCHOOLS

Mahayana gave rise to complex theological discussions, which led to the emergence of two important schools. The origins of the *Madhyamika* school are obscure, but the key philosophical assertion was the concept of 'emptiness' (*sunyata*). The great exponent was the philosopher Nagarjuna who did not seek to establish a new dogma, but to prove the fallacies of others using the argument of *reductio ad absurdum*. *Sunyata* is, according to Nagarjuna, the middle way between affirmations of being and non-being. The teaching therefore steers a middle path between the extremes of nihilism and eternalism.

The adoption of this approach led to the theory that there are two kinds of truth, *samurt-satya* and *paramartha-satya*. The first is our everyday, mundane, linguistically constructed truth, and the latter is the ultimate, inexpressible truth. However, the two truths depend upon each other, for any distinction between mundane and ultimate is itself empty of reality. Worldly truth is not without its uses, because higher truth can be reached only by going through it.

The second school was *Yogacara* which accepted the ideas of Nagarjuna, but assumed that although the cosmos does not exist, the mind does exist. The central doctrine was therefore *citta-matra* ('mind only', or 'nothing but consciousness'), and the school is often known in the West as the 'Mind Only' school. It taught that the objects of the world do not exist *per se*, but all phenomena are merely manifestations of 'seeds' (*bija*) deposited by past actions. These seeds are held in a 'receptacle', and under the appropriate conditions these seeds manifest themselves as our psychological selves and as the contents of our everyday consciousness. Thus, no object exists apart from the function of cognition by the subject. The founder of the school is considered to be Maitreya sometimes identified with the *bodhisattva* of the same name.

MAHAYANA SCHOOLS

Mahayana spread from India to Central Asia, Mongolia, Tibet, China, Japan, and other countries of East Asia. Mahayana expressed itself in various ways. A popular form was 'Pure Land', a devotional form of Buddhism usually based upon the *Lotus Sutra* that describes the realm of the *bodhisattva* Amitabha. To have faith in Amitabha means that one is reborn into his heavenly realm, where it is easy to practise Buddhism and gain enlightenment. Pure Land Buddhism is popular amongst Chinese around the world.

A second form of Mahayana is Ch'en, or Zen, that developed in China, Korea and Japan. It emphasizes a direct transmission of the teaching from the teacher to the pupil rather than through a written text. Meditation is the central practice and may enable a person to achieve immediate enlightenment. Enlightenment may therefore be achieved in one lifetime, and not thousands as presented in Theravada. Zen had a great influence in both Chinese and Japanese culture, as can be seen in their painting, poetry, gardens and even martial arts.

Third was Nichiren named after a thirteenth-century Buddhist teacher who felt that the Buddhism of his day was corrupt, and who called the Japanese people back to the teaching of the *sutra* of the *Lotus of the Wonderful Law*. The central practice of Nichiren Buddhism is the recitation of the mantra *namo myoho renge kyo*. Sōka Gakkai is a remarkable lay organization that advocates the chanting of this mantra, and has now become a worldwide movement.

BIBLIOGRAPHY

E. Conze, *Buddhist Thought in India: Three Phases of Buddhist Philosophy* (London, 1962); E. Conze, *Buddhist Wisdom Literature* (London, 1958); I. C. Harris, *The Continuity of Madhyamika and Yogacara in Indian Mahayana Buddhism* (Leiden, 1991); P. William, *Mahayana Buddhism: The Doctrinal Foundations* (London, 1989).

D. G. Burnett

BUDDHISM (NICHIREN)

The Nichiren tradition within Japanese Buddhism began as one of several new Buddhist movements during the Kamakura period (c.1185–1333). Recently Nichiren and Nichirenism have attracted international attention due in large part to the prominence of Nichiren Shō-shu (Nichiren Orthodox Sect) and the lay movement Sōka Gakkai ('Value-Creation Society').

NICHIREN – A BUDDHIST PROPHET IN JAPAN

HIS LIFE

The son of a fisherman, Nichiren was born in what is now Chiba Prefecture in 1222. At the age of twelve he was given into the care of a local Tendai temple, where he studied for four years. The next ten years were devoted to studies in Pure Land, Zen and Shingon as well as further studies in Tendai. Ultimately he concluded that Saichō (Dengyō Daishi), the Chinese monk who introduced Tendai to Japan in the eighth century, was correct in holding to the superiority of the *Lotus Sutra* over all other *sutras*.

Most Nichiren sects date their founding to 1253, when the prophet gave his first sermon and assumed the name 'Nichiren' ('Sun-lotus', symbolizing the Shinto ideal of the light and life of the sun and the Buddhist ideal of the purity and perfection of the lotus). His times were some of the most troubled in Japanese history: emperors and feudal lords fought for political ascendancy; Shinto and Buddhism vied for popular support; and, within Buddhism, a variety of sects competed for the allegiance of the ruling elite and the common people. All the while the nation was plagued by devastating earthquakes, ferocious storms, widespread famine, the appearance of comets and the persistent threat of a Mongol invasion. Nichiren took all of these as signs of the advent of *Mappo* (Age of Deterioration of the Law).

Nichiren took it upon himself to denounce other Buddhist sects and issue warnings of disaster that would ensue if Japan's rulers did not renounce false faiths and embrace the teaching of the *Lotus Sutra*. For his efforts he was banished on two occasions and sentenced to be executed on another. But he survived to bequeath to Japan and the world hundreds of writings, a worship object, a place of worship and a missionizing faith. He succumbed to illness in 1282.

HIS TEACHINGS

Nichiren pressed Tendai teachings into the moulds of pragmatism, exclusivism and iconoclasm. The *Ichinen Sanzen* (Three Thousand Realms in One Thought Moment) doctrine that all the *Dharma* (Truth, Law) worlds of Buddhism exist simultaneously in an instantaneous act of meditation meant that everyone had the potential of achieving enlightenment in the present moment. The *Lotus Sutra* was not only a superior, but the only, means of salvation and the only *sutra* relevant to this present age of *Mappo*.

Central to Nichiren's teaching was the *San Daihihō* (Three Great Secret Laws), which turn out to be as much method as doctrine. The first was veneration of a *mandala*, which included symbols of the *Trikaya* (Three Bodies of the Buddha), the Buddhas and the *bodhisattvas*, and exemplified the Buddha-nature in all creatures. The second was constant repetition of the *Daimoku* or Sacred Title *Namu myōhō renge kyō* (Adoration to the law of perfect truth), as inscribed on the *Gohonzon* (Grand Worship Object). To utter it was to recognize the *Lotus Sutra* as the embodiment of truth and to realize the enlightenment of Buddhahood and identification with the cosmic soul. The third was the establishment of a *Kaidan* (Ordination Platform), a sacred place dedicated to the training of believers.

Nichiren identified himself as the 'Pillar' (i.e. supporter or lord), 'Eyes' (i.e. teacher, revealer of truth) and 'Great Vessel' (i.e. life source, saviour or father) of Japan. He prophesied that 'Vulture Peak,' the mythical mountain where Sakyamuni supposedly delivered the *Lotus Sutra*, would eventually have its earthly manifestation in Japan. And he identified an area at the foot of Mount Fuji as its location.

HIS WRITINGS

Nichiren's extant corpus contains some 498 writings, 66 charts, outlines and extracts, and several hundred holographic fragments. The authorship of many of these is problematic, but 115 of them survive in his own handwriting. Some of the most important are *Rishō Ankoku-ron* (On the Establishment of True Teaching for the Security of the Country), *Kaimokushō* (Opening of the Eyes) and *Honzonshō* (Contemplation of the True Object of Worship). The *Gosho* (Holy Writings), containing various of Nichiren's writings, serves as the bible of Nichirenism.

NICHIRENISM IN TODAY'S WORLD

Currently almost forty traditional Buddhist sects and new religious movements lay claim to the legacy of Nichiren. Most of them have only limited significance outside Japan. Three exceptions are Nichiren-shu (Nichiren Sect) and, especially, Nichiren Shō-shu (Nichiren Orthodox Sect), and the lay organization Sōka Gakkai (Value-Creation Society).

NICHIREN-SHU AND NICHIREN SHŌ-SHU

Nichiren-shu holds that Nichiren selected six disciples who were to share responsibility for disseminating the faith, caring for his grave and serving as custodians of a temple he established at Mount Minobu. Nichiren Shō-shu, however, claims to have documents proving that Nichiren transmitted the secrets of his 'true Buddhism' to Nikkō, his finest disciple. Since the feudal lord of Minobu refused to submit to his religious authority, Nikkō packed up the *Gohonzon* and other sacred relics and went to Mount Fuji, where he established Taisekiji, a rival temple. Accordingly, priestly succession is held to have passed from the temple at Mount Minobu to the one at Mount Fuji, and that temple now qualifies as the *Kaidan* of the world.

Doctrinally, Nichiren-shu holds that the Buddha is Sakyamuni, the *Dharma* is the *Daimoku*, which is the literal meaning of the *Lotus Sutra*, and the priest is Nichiren. Nichiren Shō-shu believes that the Buddha is Nichiren, the *Dharma* is the summation of the Three Great Secret Laws found in the *Daimoku*, and the priest is Nikkō

NICHIREN SHŌ-SHU AND SŌKA GAKKAI

The Sōka Gakkai (Value-Creation Society) began in 1937 as a pedagogical society (Sōka Kyōiku Gakkai or Value-Creation Study Society) under the leadership of Tsunesaburō Makiguchi and his protégé, Jōsei Toda. It was initiated as a protest against the authoritarian approach of the Ministry of Education. Converted to Nichiren Shō-shu, its members accepted the *Lotus Sutra* as truth, chanted the *Daimoku* and worshipped the *Gohonzon*. Thereafter the word *kyōiku* was dropped from the name and the Society became concerned both with propagation of the 'true Buddhism' and with the creation of *ri* ('value, benefit, profit'). The former was to be accomplished by means of *shakubuku* (lit. 'break and subdue'), the coercive conversion methods deemed necessary in this age by many followers of Nichiren. The latter was to be accomplished by 'scientifically' controlling relationships between the external world and the individual in society in such a way as to benefit all. In effect, the key word was 'happiness' and, according to the propaganda, the *Gohonzon* was a 'happiness machine'.

Along with twenty-one adherents, in 1943 Makiguchi and Toda were accused of disloyalty to the government and incarcerated. Makiguchi died in prison but the younger Toda was released in 1945 and immediately set out to reorganize and reinvigorate the Society. Two years after his death in 1958, one of his lieutenants, Daisaku Ikeda, became president. Under Ikeda's leadership the organization undertook a mission to the entire world. It pursued a programme of building and beautification at Taisekiji that culminated in the dedication in 1972 of the *Shohondo* (Grand Worship Hall), deemed to be the centre of the world faith of the future. In 1964 it launched the *Komeito* (Clean Government Party; subsequently reorganized as the New *Komeito*), which has had the support of almost eight million Japanese voters and recently gained representation in the Japanese cabinet. In 1975 Ikeda took the lead in forming Sōka Gakkai International, an organization that now boasts seventy-six constituent organizations, members in 120 countries and territories and various institutions in some of them. (Perhaps most notable is its growth to a membership of 300,000 in the USA, mostly in California, where it is also founding a new university.) Statistics vary, but quite possibly world membership approaches the 15,000,000 mark. And all the while Ikeda has made himself conspicuous on the world scene, lecturing in leading universities, speaking in international forums and consorting with leaders of many religions and nations.

In 1979 Daisaku Ikeda was succeeded by the current president of Sōka Gakkai, Einosuke Akiya. However, he remained as honorary president and a dominant influence. So if Ikeda is to be credited with successes, he must also share blame for antagonisms and schisms. There has been continuing friction between the Society and the New *Komeito* over the years. But the ultimate schism occurred in 1991 when the Nichiren Shō-shu High Priest, Nikken Abe, excommunicated Ikeda and all his followers and closed the *Shohondo* (Worship Hall) at Taisekiji. Although he was opposed by leading architects, educational institutions and Sōka Gakkai leaders, Abe demolished Taisekiji in the summer of 1999 at a cost of $35,000,000 (it cost $100,000,000 to build in the early 1970s). Since 1991 the Society has been a lay movement without a priest. Nevertheless, it continues, at times referring to itself as the 'first Protestant movement in Buddhism' and always promoting itself as a liberation movement and upholder of human rights. Therefore, though currently at daggers drawn, both groups find it justifiable to lay claim to the mantle of Nichiren.

BIBLIOGRAPHY

M. Anesaki, *Nichiren the Buddhist Prophet* (Cambridge, MA, 1916); N. S. Brannen, *Sōka Gakkai, Japan's Militant Buddhists* (Richmond, VA, 1968); R. L. F. Habito and J. I. Stone, 'Revisiting Nichiren', *JJRS* 26/3–4 (1999), pp. 223–238.

D. J. Hesselgrave

BUDDHISM (THERAVADA)

Early in Indian Buddhism eighteen divisions developed; one called itself the 'Way of the Elders', which in Pali is *Theravada*. Theravada was conservative in outlook, as its name suggested, and consciously sought to preserve the original teaching of the Buddha. It refused to deify the Buddha, as occurred in the later Mahayana ('Great Vehicle') tradition. They were sometimes called, in somewhat derogatory fashion, Hinayana, meaning 'Lesser Vehicle'.

Little is known of the early history of Theravada, but it appears widespread in northern India at the time of King Asoka. He sent missionaries to various countries including his own son Mahinda to Sri Lanka, in the third century BC. The account is told in the *Great Chronicle* of the island (*Mahavamsa*). Mahinda led a company of monks who travelled through the air using psychic powers, and arrived at a large hill near the capital, Anuradhapura, where the king was hunting. The king and his party met the monks and were converted as a result of their preaching. Within days most of the capital was converted to Buddhism.

TIPITAKA CANON

While in north India Theravada existed as one school among many, in Sri Lanka it was the only tradition and became firmly established. It was here that the Pali texts were compiled and preserved by the Sinhala monks. According to the *Mahavamsa*, between 29 and 17 BC the island was threatened with invasion, and the Theravada monks feared the loss of the oral tradition. They therefore gathered together and committed to writing the *Tipitaka*, which in the Pali language means 'three baskets'.

The first basket (*pitaka*) is the *Vinaya*, which introduces the rules concerning the conduct of monks and nuns for the proper functioning of a monastery. The second *pitaka* is the *Sutta*, which contains the sermons and sayings attributed to the Buddha. Most of this material is accepted by all traditions of Buddhism. The third *pitaka*, the *Abhidhamma* or 'higher teaching' is different. It contains seven compositions that summarize the Buddhist teaching in a systematic form which characterizes the Theravada tradition.

TEACHING

The Theravada tradition held to the early teaching of the Buddha summarized as the Four Noble Truths.

According to *The Truth of Suffering* (*Dukkha*), all living beings are subject to suffering and change. By this the Buddha did not mean that there was no happiness in life, but that like everything else it is transitory. All things are in a continual state of flux. All beings are caught up in the endless cycle of birth–death–reincarnation.

The Truth of the Cause of Suffering (*Tanha*) teaches that the cause of suffering is the desire for selfish gratification and possessions. It is spiritual ignorance that results in this craving, which in turn results in the endless cycle of rebirths. This spiritual ignorance is eliminated at the 'Enlightenment'.

By *The Truth of the End of Suffering* (*Nibbana*), suffering therefore ceases when desire ceases. When the desire for life is renounced, then the state of genuine peace can be found in this life. Ultimately the cessation of craving means that there are no more rebirths, so that the individual ends as a separate existence.

The Truth of the Path Leading to the End of Suffering (*Magga*) – describes the way that avoids the two extremes of indulgence in sensual pleasure on one hand, and extreme asceticism on the other. It is therefore often called the 'Middle Way'. It is also known as the 'Eightfold Path', because of the eight categories through which insight and peace can be achieved.

Other significant teachings include the doctrine of *anatta* ('non-self'), which has often been misunderstood as meaning that a human being does not have a soul. The Hindu Brahmins viewed the soul (*atman*) as immutable. The Buddha contradicted this view by teaching that an individual is made up of five constituents (body, feelings, perception, volitions and consciousness), each of which is not self, but together they give an impression of the reality of soul.

The second distinctive is the doctrine and role of the *arahant* (Sanskrit *arhats*), monks who are considered to have reached a state of perfection through enlightenment. Like the Buddha before them, they have gained realization and will not be reborn after death, but will achieve *Nibbana*.

MORAL DISCIPLINE: THE PRECEPTS

Moral discipline is essential to progress on the path, and is taught in the *Vinaya* as an aid in the quest for enlightenment. The precepts are considered not as commands as from a god or the Buddha, but as a discipline that one should set oneself. There are five precepts accepted by most Buddhists: 'I undertake to observe the precepts of abstaining: from destroying life of living creatures; from taking things not given; from sexual misconduct; from false speech; and from liquor that causes intoxication. On holy days (new moon days), pious Buddhists may undertake to observe three more precepts of abstaining: from eating after noon; from dancing, singing and making a public show; and from using high and luxurious seats.'

Although lay people follow these precepts, the monks (and nuns, in Western Theravada monasteries) follow a total of 227, of which these eight are the first. In the case of monks the third precept is followed as total celibacy. Within the Theravada tradition there is a clear demarcation between ordained and laity to such a degree that it is almost like two distinct religions. The lay are more concerned with coping with the problems of this life, and the monks with the quest for *Nirvana* through meditation and following the discipline of the 227 precepts. The monks usually live in a monastery as a religious community (*sangha*).

THERAVADA RITUALS

Although Buddhism has rituals, the Buddha was quite critical of the rituals conducted by the Brahmins of his day. He endorsed only those rituals that were helpful in promoting the *Dharma*, and all Theravada rituals are therefore seen as opportunities for making merit. The term 'merit' means good *karma*. Any action in thought, word or deed can be good, bad or neutral. Good actions produce good *karma*: that is, merit. Three of the most important Theravada merit-making rituals are those of alms-giving, *dana*, and the Buddha day festival.

Traditionally, monks leave their monasteries in the early morning and walk in single file through the streets for their daily food. They move slowly, with their eyes on the ground, and do not speak to anyone. The lay people come out of their houses and put cooked food into the bowls carried by the monks. They then bow low to give respect to the *sangha*. In many Buddhist countries this ritual is now less common.

Dana is the practice of giving food and other necessities to the monks. The family will invite a certain number of the *sangha* to conduct the ritual in their homes on some special occasion such as a birthday or wedding anniversary. Upon entering the home the monks pay respect to the Buddha altar, and seat themselves on the floor. They then conduct a service honouring the Buddha. After the chanting, the monks conduct a merit-transferring ritual, in which the merit made by all present through their participation is transferred to all living beings.

Buddha day festivals vary from country to country. Most are held on the day of the full moon around early May known as *Wesak*, the day traditionally considered to be the anniversary of the Buddha's birth, enlightenment and death.

HISTORICAL EXPANSION

One of the greatest Buddhist scholars of Sri Lanka was the fifth-century translator Buddhaghosa, whose role has been equated to that of St Thomas Aquinas in Roman Catholicism. According to tradition he was born a Brahmin in India and converted to Theravada Buddhism. His first work was the *Visuddimagga* (*The Path to Purity*), which is a compendium of Theravada doctrine arranged in three parts according to the old hierarchy of morality, concentration and wisdom.

From Sri Lanka, Theravada spread to Burma, Thailand and many other regions of Southeast Asia. Because of its concern to hold to the traditions, Theravada exported its teaching with the *Tipitaka* and the Pali language. The common language allowed monks from different regions to communicate with one another. When Theravada declined in one area it was often revived by monks coming from another.

When Europeans first came into contact with Buddhism in the beginning of the nineteenth century, it was the Theravada form that attracted their attention. It was regarded as the purer form of Buddhism in contrast to Mahayana with its many Buddhas and later scriptures. In 1880 Madam Blavatsky and Colonel Olcott became the first Westerners to accept the five precepts, in a temple near Colombo, and effectively became the first European and American to convert to Buddhism. It was Theravada Buddhism that was first brought to Britain and was promoted by the Buddhist Society of Great Britain.

BIBLIOGRAPHY

R. Gombrich, *Theravada Buddhism* (London, 1988); R. Gombrich and G.

Obeyesekere, *Buddhism Transformed: Religious Change in Sri Lanka* (Princeton, NJ, 1988); P. Harvey, *An Introduction to Buddhism* (Cambridge, 1992); M. Penechio, *Guide to the Tipitaka: Introduction to the Buddhism Canon* (Bangkok, 1993).

D. G. Burnett

BUDDHISM (TIBETAN)

Tibetan Buddhism is a complex phenomenon based upon the teaching of Mahayana Buddhism. Its advocates refer to it as the 'Third Turning of the Wheel of *Dharma*'. The first turning of the Wheel of *Dharma* commenced with the Buddha's sermon in Deer Park when he spoke to the five sages, and is generally seen as being currently demonstrated by the Theravada tradition. The Mahayana tradition is regarded as the second turning of the Wheel of *Dharma*. Traditionally the explanation given for the origin of the third turning of the Wheel is the esoteric teaching of the Buddha himself. It is given various names, and because of the use of *mantras* it is sometimes known as *Mantrayana* ('Vehicle of the Mantra'). It has also been called *Vajrayana* ('Diamond Vehicle') after the hourglass-like wand used by these Buddhists. Another designation used in English is 'Tantric' Buddhism, after the Indian literature known as *tantras*.

INDIAN ORIGIN

Within Hinduism there were varieties of Tantric cults based around the great deity Shiva and his consort Shakti. The couple are often depicted in sexual union, and sexual symbolism is an important part of Tantra. Many suggest that Buddhist Tantra may have been a minority religion, essentially being an esoteric cult of which the Buddhist establishment of the time disapproved. It eventually gained momentum and became a significant force of innovation and a vehicle for the expression of dissatisfaction with existing religious organization. Some asserted that the new path was superior to that of Mahayana in that it led to spontaneous realization of Buddhahood in this life.

Although Tantra arose as an esoteric, intensely private, visionary and iconoclastic movement, it eventually became an institutionalized literary tradition in India. With this transformation, the magical origins of Tantra were partly disguised by the high Tantra liturgy, but elements remain, as with the use of the secret hand gestures of the Buddhas (*mudra*) and sacred diagrams (*mandalas*). Buddhist Tantra flourished for only a few centuries before Buddhism was extinguished in India. The main line of the Tantric tradition spread into Central Asia as far as Mongolia and Siberia and finally into Tibet, from where we have the most information about the Tantric tradition.

Many great masters took the Buddha's

teaching from India to Tibet during the eighth century, largely through the endeavours of King Khrisong Detsen (AD 704–97). Amongst these teachers was the great Indian scholar Padmasambhava. Buddhism initially flourished and assimilated much of the indigenous Bon religion. In the mid-ninth century King Langdarma launched an anti-Buddhist campaign, which resulted in a decline in its practice until a renaissance in the eleventh century. This renewal was mainly through the work of the great teacher Atisha. In about 1206 Tibet had contact with the Mongolian emperor Genghis Khan; then in 1253 it came totally under Mongolian rule. The great emperor, Khubila Khan, adopted Tibetan Buddhism and promoted the building of monasteries in Mongolia and China. With the exile of the Dalai Lama in 1959 Tibetan Buddhism was brought to the West.

FOUR SCHOOLS

Within the Tibetan tradition there are four main schools, incorporating various subdivisions, and they all share a basic Mahayana Buddhist philosophy. The oldest school is the Nyingma, whose origins can be traced back to the first introduction of Buddhism in Tibet at the end of the sixth century with the scholar Padmasambhava. In the West, the best known exponent of Nyingma is Sogyal Rinpoche, who is based in London but has centres around the world.

The second school is the Sakya whose religious ascendancy occurred during the period of Mongolian influence. It looks back to another translator, Drokmi Shakya Yeshe, who studied in India. Sakya Trizin, who was born in Tibet in 1945, is currently the forty-first spiritual head of the Sakya tradition and is recognized as an emanation of Manjushri, the enlightened principle of wisdom. In Britain there is a group of Sakya centres that operate under the guidance of Ngakpa Jampa Yhaye, a British teacher of this tradition.

The third school is Kagyu, which means 'transmission of the living tradition'. This is so called because it claims its teachings are the deepest of all Buddha's instructions, which have been kept pure by the lineage. Marpa was instrumental in bringing the Kagyu teaching to Tibet, and his disciple was Milarepa. Milarepa is said to have committed murder in his youth and practised black magic, but even so he achieved Buddhahood in one lifetime (an achievement usually considered to require aeons of practice) through his diligent meditation practice in the caves of Tibet. This resulted in a succession of incarnate lamas called the Karmapas. The lineage continued through successive Karmapas and is now held by His Holiness the Seventeenth Gyalwa Karmapa, whose seat is the great monastery of Tsurphu in Tibet. He has been formally recognized by the Chinese government as High Lama and was enthroned in Tibet on 28 September 1992.

Founded in 1967, the Kagyu Samye Ling was the first Tibetan Buddhist centre in the West and was of the Kagyu school. In Tibetan *Samye Ling* means 'place beyond concept', or 'the inconceivable place', which was the name of the very first Buddhist centre founded in Tibet, in the eighth century. Two refugee Tibetan abbots, Chogyam Trungpa Rinpoche and Dr Akong Tulku Rinpoche, founded Samye Ling in a modest country house near the tiny village of Eskdalemuir in Dumfriesshire, Scotland.

The fourth school is that of Geluk, who inherited their tradition from Atisha and Je Tsongkhapa. The teaching of the Dalai Lama is mainly Gelukpa, but another noted teacher of this school in the West was Lama Thubten Yeshe, who died in 1984. He is supposed to have reincarnated as a Spanish boy, who is now named Lama Osel and is the first lama believed to have reincarnated as a Westerner. An offshoot of the Gelukpa schools that is growing in the West is known as the New Kadampa Tradition (NKT), following the Tibetan lama Geshe Kelsang Gyatso.

TEACHING

Within the Tibetan tradition the role of the lama is so significant that followers take refuge in the lama as well as in the normal three refuges (the Buddha, *Dharma* and *Sangha*). The word *blama* is the Tibetan equivalent of the Sanskrit *guru* and refers to a teacher. Within the Tibetan tradition the lama is an important guide through the esoteric teachings of the tradition.

It was the Mongols who ruled China from 1222 to 1368 who appointed the head of the Sakya monastery as their viceroy for Tibet. He then became both the temporal and spiritual head of the nation and was known as the Dalai Lama ('Ocean of Wisdom'). The Dalai Lama is considered to be a reincarnation of a *bodhisattva*, and each Dalai Lama is said to be the reincarnation of the previous Dalai Lama. Other orders make similar claims for their high lamas. When the Dalai Lama dies, a long and complicated search is undertaken to find a young boy who shows the qualities of the Dalai Lama.

A lama will initiate candidates into a tradition by giving them a suitable *mantra* as part of their empowerment. The practice of Tantric visualization is an essential part of ritual. The meditator first goes through a gradual process of purification before visualizing the *mandala* as the illusory universe. The practitioner must thereafter repeat a series of chants, make offerings, repeat the relevant *mantra* and make appropriate gestures (*mudra*) at intervals. Eventually the visualization should become a colourful world filled with Buddhas and heavenly beings. However, even skilled practitioners speak of the complexity of the task. It is an art form whose materials are imagination, thought, feeling and intuition.

To achieve the higher levels of visualization there is a need for special empowerments that are usually provided at retreats when a noted visiting lama is giving instruction. Only after receiving the needed empowerment are people encouraged to go on with the higher levels of visualizations. The practical outworking requires the help of skilled and experienced masters. For this reason centres in the West offer a wide variety of courses and retreats.

The so-called *Tibetan Book of the Dead* has captured the imagination of many Westerners since it was first published in English in 1927. It was used by Tibetan lamas as a book of daily recitation, and was read or recited on the occasion of death. Originally it served as a guide not only for the dying and dead, but also for the living.

The Chinese invasion of Tibet in 1959 has had a dramatic effect on Tibetan Buddhism. The Chinese Communists have destroyed many of the ancient monasteries, and many monks have had to flee. Little now remains of the ancient culture of Tibet within the country. However, with the flight of the Dalai Lama many Tibetan refugees live along the borders of their homeland. Tibetan Buddhism has also spread to many parts of the West and by the end of the twentieth century was showing significant growth. One can only speculate as to the future of Tibetan Buddhism in the world.

BIBLIOGRAPHY

S. Beyer, *The Cult of Tara* (Berkeley, CA, 1978); K. Dowman, *The Sacred Life of Tibet* (London,1997); G. Samuel, *Civilized Shamans* (Washington, DC, 1993); D. Snellgrove, *Indo-Tibetan Buddhism* (London, 1987).

D. G. Burnett

BUDDHISM (ZEN)

The word 'Zen' means 'meditation' and is a translation of the Chinese term Ch'an. Ch'an is a product of the fusion of Indian Buddhism with Chinese culture and is an expression of the broader Mahayana tradition. Bodhidharma is the legendary founder of Ch'an, but much of his life is veiled in obscurity. He is supposed to have been the son of a Brahmin who came from India during the reign of emperor Wu-ti (AD 502–50). A central part of the story is that whilst staying at a monastery in northern China he spent nine years facing a blank wall as an illustration of his teaching.

The essence of Ch'an is contained in a four-line stanza attributed to Bodhidharma and paraphrased by D. T. Suzuki:

> A special tradition outside the scriptures;
> No dependence upon words and letters;
> Direct pointing at the human heart;
> Seeing into one's own nature and the
> attainment of Buddhahood.

The formula expresses the difference between the outer and inner ways. Ch'an does not recognize any scriptural authority, but depends upon a special quality of experience that suddenly breaks into one's inner being. For Ch'an, the Buddha-nature, or potential to achieve enlightenment, is inherent in everyone but lies dormant because of ignorance. It is awakened not by study of scriptures or practice of ceremonies, but by breaking through the boundaries of common thought.

In the tenth century, Ch'an eventually developed into five main 'houses', or schools: Kuei-yang (Japanese Igyo), Lin-chi (Japanese Rinzai), Ts'ao-tung (Japanese Soto), Yun-men (Japanese Ummon) and Fa-yen (Japanese Hogen). The houses of Lin-chi and Ts'ao-tung grew into the most influential schools during the Sung period (960–1279) and had a significant influence upon Chinese society. It was during this period that these schools introduced the practice of *kung-an*, the use of anecdotes and paradoxical sayings known in Japanese as *koan*. One aim of these sayings was to challenge the disciple and bring him or her to the limits of intellectual thinking. As doubt takes hold, the disciple finally breaks through rational consciousness in experience. An example is the famous story of the Japanese teacher Joshu, who, when asked by a monk, 'What is the ultimate principle of Buddhism?' replied, 'The cypress tree in the courtyard.' The statement challenges rational logic.

Ch'an was one of the later schools of Chinese Buddhism to arrive in Japan. Myoan Eisai (1141–1215) is generally regarded as the exponent who brought it to his country. He was a member of the Tendai school in Japan and had opportunity in 1168 to travel to China and study Ch'an. Like many of his contemporaries, Eisai felt the need for a fundamental renewal of Japanese Buddhism and returned to China for a second period (1187–91). He had hoped to journey to India, but was denied permission and had to content himself with staying in China. He entered a Ch'an monastery, where he practised *tso-ch'an* (Japanese *zazen*) and *kung-an* (Japanese *koan*). He finally achieved enlightenment and was presented with the insignia of succession in the Huang-lung line of the Lin-chi school.

On his return to Japan, Eisai began to teach the way of Zen on the southern island of Kyushu in 1194. His teaching stirred up the resentment of the Tendai monks, who succeeded in having the imperial palace prohibit the new sect of Buddhism. Eisai compromised and eventually he founded a monastery at Hakata, which has become known as the first Japanese Zen temple. The more esoteric rites of Tendai were practised alongside Zen meditation. In his book of 1198, *Treatise on the Spread of Zen for the Protection of the Country*, meditation is set alongside perfect doctrine, secret rites and commandments as one of the four essential elements of Tendai. Rinzai slowly gained a following among the ruling elite and especially the Samurai warriors.

Ts'ao-tung (Japanese Soto) was brought to Japan by the Japanese monk Dogen Kigen (1200–53). Like Eisai he went to China to seek a renewal of Japanese Buddhism, and he became a disciple of Ju-ching (1163–1268). When a disciple sitting next to him in Ju-ching's Ch'an hall kept dozing, he was struck by the master, who shouted the phrase 'Body and mind are cast off', meaning that the state in which body and mind have been cast off is the most exact characteristic of the enlightened mind. Upon hearing these words, Dogen is said to have awoken to the great enlightenment, and throughout his life he continued to make use of the phrase 'casting off of body and mind'.

On his return to Japan he introduced the practice of sitting in meditation (*zazen*), for which he gives precise instructions. One should sit on two cushions placed one on top of the other, in a quiet room, in the full or half lotus position, the left hand placed on the right. All one's effort should be directed to overcoming inner unrest and gaining the serene reflection. Dogen was one of the most original thinkers of Japanese Zen. In his study of Buddha-nature he teaches that all living creatures have the Buddha-nature in themselves like a seed. For Dogen the Buddha-nature is not an essence 'hidden' in things, but the world of phenomena quite literally is the Buddha-nature. Beings are already Buddhas. For this reason, when the obscurities have been overcome they attain Buddhahood and the sudden realization is known as *kensho*.

It was through the influence of Eisai and Dogen that Zen became recognized as an established Buddhist tradition in its own right. Both Rinzai and Soto have continued to flourish until modern times, although they have been subject to various schisms throughout the centuries. During the seventeenth-century period of political unrest in Japan the Zen priests had a major influence in Japanese life and culture. It was under the inspiration of Zen that art, literature, the tea ceremony and the famous Noh theatre developed and prospered. Soto had a major renaissance in the seventeeth century and spread throughout Japan to become the second largest school of Buddhism, the largest being Nichiren Shō-shu.

In 1686 in a small rural village, Hakuin, who was to become the most important figure in Rinzai Zen, was born. From his youth he sought spiritual enlightenment, until eventually he became overwhelmed by what he described as 'the Great Doubt'. This was an attitude of radical perplexity that finally smashed so that all former uncertainties dissolved. He wrote poetry and produced many remarkable paintings. He also devised the *koan* which he felt particularly appropriate for his time:

> If someone claps his hands, one hears a
> sound at once.
> Listen now to the sound of a single hand!

Another Zen school that owed its existence to the missionary activities of Chinese monks during the Tokugawa Shogunate (1603–1867) was Obaku. This school employs the methods of Rinzai and also practises *nembutsu*, the continual invocation of the Buddha Amitabha. It has remained reasonably small. Ch'an in China began to decline; by the Ming period (1368–1644) the Lin-chi House had absorbed all the other schools. A popular form of Buddhism came into being with the veneration of Kuan-yin. However, Zen continued in Japan and in recent years considerable interest in Zen has developed in the

West in response to the opening of Japan to the outside world.

The prolific writings of D. T. Suzuki (1870–1966) stimulated an interest in Zen among Western readers during the 1930s and 1940s. The most obvious characteristic of Suzuki's early Zen interpretations was their predominantly psychological bent. Christmas Humphreys of the Buddhist Society in London also published a number of books on Zen that gained a wide readership. In the 1950s and 1960s Zen became an important element of the counter-culture movement, and meditation offered a radically new way of life. Beatnik culture of the period resulted in books such as *Zen and the Art of Motorcycle Maintenance*. However, Zen has since tended to become less significant in the West with the growth of interest in Tibetan Buddhism.

The number of Zen practitioners in the West is relatively small, with few monasteries. One notable expression is Serene Reflection Meditation, which was taken to the USA by Revd Master Jiyu-Kennett. This British-born woman was initiated into Soto Zen in Japan in 1965. She established Shastra Abbey in northern California in 1970, and two years later founded Throssel Hole Priory in the north of England. The Order continues to emphasize meditation, mindfulness in daily life and adherence to the Buddhist precepts. However, the influence of Japanese culture has continued to have a wider influence in Western society, ranging from the distinctive design of Japanese gardens to the skills of martial arts.

BIBLIOGRAPHY

W. L. King, *Zen and the Way of the Sword* (Oxford, 1993); T. J. Kodera, *Dogen's Formative Years in China* (London, 1980); D. T. Suzuki, *An Introduction to Zen Buddhism* (London, 1988); D. T. Suzuki, *The Training of the Zen Buddhist Monk* (New York, 1934).

D. G. Burnett

CELEBRITY-CENTRIC RELIGION

HEROES

The worship or reverencing of celebrities is not a recent phenomenon. Ancient Greek religion may have been focused on the twelve major deities who resided on Mount Olympus, but alongside them a special place was reserved for the 'heroes'. These could include nationally significant figures like those who feature in the epics of Homer (Agamemnon, Achilles, Odysseus and others), but more often they were local heroes who had achieved prominence during their lifetime and who were in some way reverenced after death. There were thousands of such figures, each of them achieving hero status because of some special accomplishment, generally as warriors, athletes or politicians. Their attraction was located in the fact that, unlike the gods, who were of non-human origin, these people began as ordinary members of local communities or particular ethnic groups, which made it easy for others to relate to them. But because of their great achievements, they could be perceived as closer to the gods, providing a bridge between ordinary mortals and some other world.

SAINTS

In the emerging Christian tradition, the saints came to occupy a similar position, as also did the Virgin Mary. To be a saint an individual needed to have led a life of particular devotion to God, which was the basis on which their followers assumed they would have special abilities after death, such as performing miracles of healing, or appearing in visions to provide inspiration and courage in times of special need. Those who had suffered martyrdom, or otherwise died in unusual circumstances, were assumed to have even greater powers, modelled on the example of Christ himself (Rom. 8:34), and to be able to intercede with God on behalf of their devotees. This expectation had already been foreshadowed in some Jewish circles, exemplified by Judas Maccabee's conviction that the dead Onias had special powers to invoke divine aid on behalf of those who were living (2 Macc. 15:12). By the Middle Ages, the tombs of martyrs, and their relics, were regular objects of pilgrimage, as also were sites where the Virgin Mary was believed to have appeared. Those who achieved such status typically did so through a pattern of separation followed by consecration: separation from their humdrum origins during life, and subsequent consecration to God through death. During their lifetime, they were ordinary people who had already broken free from the constraints of their social circumstances, usually through great sanctity or devotion. On the one hand they were people with whom others could easily identify, yet on the other hand their achievements marked them out as special and distinctive. They held up a mirror through which others could glimpse their own potential for bettering themselves. Though they might be admired in life, they truly achieved celebrity status only in death or, in the case of the Virgin Mary, by supposedly transcending death altogether.

CELEBRITIES

In more recent history, Queen Victoria's husband and consort Prince Albert (1819–61) became a saintlike icon after his sudden death and was commemorated and venerated by the construction of the Albert Memorial in Kensington Gardens, London. William Ewart Gladstone likewise evoked considerable public adulation following his death in 1898. The second half of the twentieth century, however, saw a significant growth in the emergence of overt forms of spiritual and religious devotion focused on celebrities. Several figures repeatedly appear as the equivalents of the saints of traditional Christian devotion, foremost among them being Elvis Presley (1935–77) and Diana, Princess of Wales (1961–97), though they include Rudolph Valentino (1895–1926), James Dean (1931–55), Marilyn Monroe (1926–62), John F. Kennedy (1917–63), John Lennon (1940–80) and others. At the same time, the rate at which new Roman Christian saints have been recognized has accelerated, and Pope John Paul II has created more than all his twentieth-century predecessors put together.

In the context of rapid cultural change, late twentieth-century people clearly needed new role models to provide hope and inspiration. In every case of celebrity-centred religion, the new icons of sainthood achieved their status through what was essentially the same route as the medieval saints. They were all individuals with whom others could identify, either because they rose from lowly social origins to accomplish great things (as with Elvis, Marilyn Monroe and John Lennon), or because people were able to identify with their experiences. People felt a kinship with

Prince Albert because, like many more ordinary folk, he died of an untreatable disease (in his case typhoid), while in the case of Diana many women in particular saw their own unhappy experiences mirrored in what they knew of her marriage into the British royal family. Both Elvis and Diana were spiritual role models while they were alive, their combination of vulnerability and success providing an inspirational model for their followers.

In every case, however, those celebrities who have featured in popular adulation achieved their greatest fame only through death and, as with the martyrs, the unusual or tragic nature of their deaths merely served to enhance their appeal as objects of devotion. This point clearly relates to one of the most traditional roles of religious heroes, as sacrificial figures onto whom people can project their own sins, and who in turn bear a representative cross in public. Diana as *mater dolorosa* was the perfect image for the late twentieth century. Furthermore, like traditional saints, such celebrities have their shrines and relics, most notably at Gracel and (Elvis) and Althorp (Diana), though the Beatles Museum in Liverpool serves a similar purpose for some Lennon devotees. Many of them also have their own 'communion of saints' in the form of worldwide fan clubs which preserve their memory.

In early Christian tradition, a major function of the saints was to direct worship to God, and this is also an element in the veneration of modern celebrities. The pilgrim to Graceland, Elvis's home and shrine in Memphis, cannot escape significant encounters with Christian symbolism, not only in relation to the star's early life (at one stage he intended to become an Assemblies of God pastor), but also in connection with his present status. Many of those who visit his grave site wear overtly Christian symbols and clearly think of Elvis as a mediating figure in heaven. They pray both to him and for him and regard him as a spiritual guide through whose intercession it might be possible for them to encounter some higher truth. In effect, he has become a modern member of the pantheon of saints, pointing to Christ and to God rather than being in competition with them.

It is harder to say whether the same thing is true of Diana, partly because her death and subsequent veneration is more recent. The mourning for her and the shrine at Althorp have aspects which suggest a trend towards regarding her as more than a saint, maybe even as some kind of Christ-figure. The lyrics of Elton John's funeral song, 'Candle in the Wind', suggested as much, as also does the inscription opposite her grave site: 'Whenever you call to me, I will come to your aid'.

As theistic belief has been eroded in Western culture, people increasingly look to celebrities just as their forebears looked to God. Some have made transcendent claims during their own lifetimes: for example, John Lennon's comment that the Beatles were 'bigger than Jesus', or Diana's claim to have been a nun in a previous existence. The singer Madonna continues to evoke similar images for herself. The Arthur Dooley statue of the Beatles (1974) portrayed them as cherubs made from plastic dolls, and when one disappeared a notice proclaimed 'Paul [McCartney] has taken wings and flown'. Following Lennon's death a figure with a halo was added, inscribed 'Lennon lives'. Many claim to have seen Elvis alive, while in Diana's case even more overtly religious claims have been made, especially on the World Wide Web, which is a natural place of pilgrimage for younger people. Here, channellers claim to pass on messages from the risen and ascended Diana, including a complete 'Bible', and there is a 'Church of Diana' through which her ministrations can supposedly be dispensed to the faithful.

The collapse of Christianity in the West, with the consequent creation of a religious vacuum in the culture, is undoubtedly a key reason for the rise in celebrity-based spirituality. But the increasing influence of the media has also facilitated it to an extent previously unattainable. For whereas in earlier centuries dead heroes would have existed beyond their own times only as a legendary rumour, today they can be not only remembered, but also experienced. Through the medium of movies, records and news archives they can be made to live for ever and become as real to later generations as they were to those who knew them.

BIBLIOGRAPHY

R. S. Denisoff and G. Plasketes, *True Disbelievers: The Elvis Contagion* (New Brunswick, 1995); C. King, 'His Truth Goes Marching On: Elvis Presley and the Pilgrimage to Graceland', in I. Reader and T. Walter (eds.), *Pilgrimage in Popular Culture* (London, 1993), pp. 92–104; C. Sugden (ed.), *Death of a Princess* (London, 1998).

J. W. Drane

CELTIC SPIRITUALITY

'Celtic spirituality' must be approached cautiously because of the all-encompassing nature of the concept. Potentially it can embrace a very wide range of beliefs, from Pagan or primal to Christian, and commonly includes amalgams of both, all of which are held together by the adjective 'Celtic'. The word 'Celtic' creates a positive image in the contemporary mind, since it represents ways of life, work and worship which, in the eyes of the beholders, are refreshingly different from mainstream practices.

The term 'Celtic' is essentially an ethnic descriptor, derived from *Celtoi* or *Celtae*, 'Celts', applied by the classical writers to groups of tribes occupying parts of Asia Minor and much of Europe, including the British Isles, during the first millennium BC. They spoke non-classical, 'barbarian' languages. From the early eighteenth century AD, the adjective 'Celtic' came to be used by scholars of the family of languages spoken by the Celts on the continent until the early centuries AD, and subsequently in Britain and Ireland. The main continental Celtic languages were Gaulish (in France and Belgium), Celtiberian (in Spain), Lepontic (in the north of Italy and the south-west of Switzerland) and Galatian (in Asia Minor). In Britain and Ireland, two groups of languages survive: Brythonic (Welsh and Cornish, with an offshoot of Cornish, namely Breton, being spoken in Brittany) and Goidelic (Scottish Gaelic, Irish and Manx). Welsh is the strongest of the existing insular Celtic languages; Cornish all but died out in the later eighteenth century, but has been revived in the twentieth century. Scottish Gaelic and Irish are still spoken extensively in Scotland and Ireland respectively, while Manx, having lost its last native speaker in 1974, is being reintroduced to the Isle of Man.

Since Celts still exist as a recognizable linguistic family, and have a long history which reaches back into the first millennium BC, 'Celtic spirituality' can be used to describe their religious practices at any stage from their earliest recorded appearance to the present day. It is thus an extremely elusive term and, to be meaningful, requires to be qualified carefully. It might be argued that the term 'Celtic' in this, or any other, context cannot be applied with any precision beyond the terminal point of a Common Celtic culture in Europe. Even if a generally consistent culture of this kind, with a distinctive spirituality, once existed, the evidence points to many local variations, including numerous local gods and goddesses. We do not have an internal Celtic view of such religions as there were. What we do know of Celtic religious practices in the last 500 years BC is recorded primarily by classical authors who have interpreted these practices through the lenses of their own religions. The Celtic pantheon of Pagan gods is defined by Roman writers through what is commonly called the *interpretatio Romana*, in which the functions of these gods are compared directly with those of the gods in the Roman pantheon. The Druids, popularly associated with ceremonies and sacrifices in oak groves, are prominent in the general perception of pre-Christian religion in the Celtic areas of Europe, but they too are portrayed chiefly in Greek and Roman accounts. Christianity later added another distorting lens for viewing the Pagan past, which is represented in poems and tales produced in a Christian milieu.

In present-day popular usage, the term 'Celtic spirituality' is much more commonly applied to Celtic religion within the Christian era, primarily within Britain and Ireland. Most users of the term assume that whatever form of 'spirituality' they perceive to be 'Celtic' is to be defined, not in terms of a specific time or place, but in terms of the qualities which it contains. To their devotees, these qualities represent a continuum, in which they themselves supposedly share. Modern belief in a continuous and distinctive Celtic spirituality is, however, heavily indebted to the Romantic movement of the eighteenth and nineteenth centuries, which encouraged the reinvention of earlier Celtic features, including Druids. This creative approach to the past was greatly stimulated by James Macpherson (1736–96), the 'discoverer' (or in the opinion of some the 'forger') of the epic poems of Ossian, a legendary blind poet who celebrated the deeds of noble Gaelic heroes located in Scotland in the third century AD. Macpherson interacted with William Stukeley (1687–1765), an Anglican clergyman and antiquarian who claimed that the henges at Stonehenge and Avebury had Druidic associations. Macpherson's work influenced Ernest Renan (1823–92), a native of Brittany and one of the greatest Orientalist scholars of his time. Renan, who rejected Roman Catholic orthodoxy, was the first to perceive a distinctive form of Christianity within the Celtic areas as a whole; Renan emphasized the indigenous purity of Christianity in these areas, stressing that they had received 'Celtic Christianity' (as he called it) independently of Rome and arguing that this form of Christianity had been much kinder to Paganism than western Roman Christianity. Renan's views were absorbed by Matthew Arnold (1822–88), who contended that a Celtic element was to be found in the spiritual make-up of the English people, and that it was this which differentiated them from the wider body of Germanic culture. Renan and Arnold shaped the perspectives through which scholars and collectors of folklore in the Celtic countries (such as Alexander Carmichael, collector of the Hebridean hymns and prayers called *Carmina Gadelica*, published from 1900) interpreted their material in the late nineteenth and early twentieth centuries. The Celtic culture of the west in the period up to c.1100 AD was believed by many respectable turn-of-the-century scholars to have maintained a sturdy independence and to have nourished a type of Christian civilization at once primitive, pure and Pagan-friendly, unspoilt by Rome or by the arrival and growing supremacy of the Anglo-Saxons.

This perception of Christianity formed a quiet substream in the twentieth century, breaking the surface in the works of occasional romantic writers, but after 1960, and most noticeably in the 1980s and 1990s, 'Celtic Christianity' became a very popular alternative form of belief. Its emergence coincided with the growth from c.1980 of a Pagan brand of 'Celtic spirituality' drawing some of its power from the regular commemoration of Celtic festivals at such 'Druidic' locations as Stonehenge. Its appearance reflected not only widespread disillusionment with existing churches and expressions of the faith, but also the influence of theosophy, religious pluralism (with a bias towards Zen Buddhism), postcolonial guilt complexes and New Age interest in the environment, the Jungian subconscious and 'lost' civilizations. All this encouraged the rediscovery and uncritical study of the works of nineteenth-century romantic ideologists, editors and writers. The result was the invention of a postmodern religious primitivism, extolling the faith of the Celtic Fringe of Europe as a spiritual panacea, capable of providing answers to most, if not all, contemporary dilemmas. Pilgrimages to sacred sites associated with Celtic saints, such as Iona and Lindisfarne, on the western and eastern edges of Britain respectively, strengthened interest and devotion.

'Celtic Christianity', as popularly promoted since Renan's time, is highly adaptable. Since 1980 it has been reconstructed as a contemporary spirituality which compensates for the perceived failures of orthodox Christianity. It is environmentally friendly, bridging the Cartesian 'split' between spirit and matter; it is sympathetic to non-Christian culture and can, in some forms, accommodate Pagan or primal practices (for example, in the view that Celtic saints absorbed Druidic teaching); it is also non-aggressive in evangelistic strategy, ecumenical in ecclesiology, eclectic and syncretic in its theology and open to the guidance of visions and spiritual 'impressions'. Both Catholic and Protestant versions have emerged, but Protestant promoters (mainly Anglican and charismatic) have been in the forefront. Alongside popular writers like David Adam, Vicar of Lindisfarne, it has more academic advocates, such as Esther de Waal and Arthur MacDonald Allchin, who reject excessive romantic claims and argue their case from a closer interaction with early Gaelic and Welsh literature.

Though 'Celtic Christianity' draws on material from earlier than 1100, present-day Celtic scholars would dispute most of its underlying presuppositions. They stress the critically important role of Roman civilization in providing the infrastructures whereby the spread of Christianity was facilitated in Europe. Christianity was probably transmitted initially to Britain through the Roman occupation and is first attested in Roman contexts in the south of present-day England and in south-east Wales. The faith is likely to have reached Ireland from Britain, and also from Gaul (by trade routes), as well as by the missions of Palladius (431 AD) and Patrick, the Apostle of Ireland. Once implanted in the Celtic areas, Christianity struck deep roots and was contextualized in terms of existing social conventions. Monasteries in Ireland, for instance, took their physical shape from that of aristocratic ring-forts, were patronized by powerful local kin-groups who provided endowments and leaders (abbots), and became patrons of artistic skills which were put to use in the creation of illuminated gospel books (such as the Book of Kells) and high crosses. However, Christianity also deeply influenced social conventions: law tracts were re-written to accommodate the principles of the Mosaic law, and biblical practice interacted with native custom at various levels. The Druid was gradually dislodged from a position of prominence, and clergy were forbidden by canon law to associate too closely with Druidism. Far from being 'soft', Christianity in the Celtic areas had a strongly ascetic element, derived from the Egyptian desert saints, and severe penance was prescribed for sin. The

Christian institutions and personnel of the period until about 1100 (who included national saints such as David of Wales and Patrick of Ireland, as well as Columba of Iona) are commonly associated with the so-called 'Celtic Church', but this label can be no more than a term of convenience, since a single institution of this kind never existed, although the faith in all Celtic countries had some common contextual features. The older Celtic monasteries and institutions were gradually phased out, absorbed or reformed, as the continental orders (Benedictines, Cistercians, Augustinians and others) entered the Celtic areas after 1100, but memory of the earlier saints and their churches was preserved in archaeological remains, place-names, history and legend.

An interest in the 'Celtic Church' has emerged strongly at different periods since the Middle Ages, usually to bolster arguments about church practices and polity. After the Reformation, for instance, Protestant apologists in Scotland, Wales and Ireland tried to lay claim to it as their ancestral church, arguing that the pure form of apostolic Christianity which had once been present in that church had been corrupted by the later intervention of Rome. Attempts to repossess the 'Celtic Church' as a lineal ancestor continue to be made by different bodies, and some modern so-called Celtic Churches (rooted mainly in Roman Catholicism or Eastern Orthodoxy) have emerged in the USA and Canada, with offshoots in Britain and Ireland.

BIBLIOGRAPHY

M. Bowman, 'Reinventing the Celts', *Religion*, 23 (1993), pp. 147–56; I. Bradley, *Celtic Christianity: Making Myths and Chasing Dreams* (Edinburgh, 1999); D. G. Burnett, *Dawning of the Pagan Moon: An Investigation into the Rise of Western Paganism* (Eastbourne, 1991); B. Maier, *Dictionary of Celtic Religion and Culture* (Woodbridge, 1997); D. E. Meek, *The Quest for Celtic Christianity* (Edinburgh, 2000); S. Piggott, *The Druids* (London, 1975).

D. E. Meek

CHRISTIANITY (EASTERN ORTHODOX)

INTRODUCTION

The growth of Orthodoxy is a fascinating and yet neglected element in the story of modern Western Christianity. Facing major difficulties in adapting to a different model of the relationship between church, state and culture, Orthodox spirituality and thought is nevertheless widely perceived as an invigorating influence.

PRIMARY SOURCES

Scripture, the determinations of the seven Ecumenical Councils and the writings of the Fathers constitute the primary sources for Orthodox faith and thought. They are not viewed as existing apart from the church, but as Tradition, 'the life of the Spirit within the church'. Respect for this unchanging Tradition is coupled with the conviction that each generation experiences afresh the Spirit's working in the church.

HISTORICAL OVERVIEW

Eastern and Western Christianity gradually separated during the medieval period, the division hardening as a result of the Crusades. For centuries most of Eastern Christianity has faced the challenge of maintaining the faith in difficult circumstances under Islamic or Communist rule.

Orthodoxy today is a fellowship of churches sharing a common faith, order and liturgy, each exercising jurisdiction in an area which is usually coterminous with ethnic or national boundaries. A fully fledged Orthodox jurisdiction is accorded autocephalous (self-governing) status, the Patriarchate of Constantinople (the Ecumenical Patriarchate) retaining a primacy of honour. Migration to the West has led to the presence there of overlapping jurisdictions, each with responsibility for a particular ethnic group. In the United States attempts have been made to overcome this, but there is no immediate likelihood of union in one self-governing community. In most other Western countries Orthodox communities do not have the resources to become self-governing and remain under Eastern jurisdictions.

CONTEMPORARY ORTHODOX BELIEF AND PRACTICE

THE UNCHANGING NATURE OF ORTHODOX BELIEF

Orthodox theology emphasizes faithful exposition of the Tradition in each generation and is more closely tied into church life and worship than is much Western Christianity. There has thus been no real parallel to the widespread shift in Western Christian thinking from spiritual to social concerns, nor has theological liberalism been a significant problem. Indeed, since the collapse of communism, a strongly traditionalist 'Orthodox fundamentalism' has come into the open.

ORTHODOXY AND OTHER CHRISTIAN TRADITIONS

In spite of increasing contact, relationships with other Christian communions are often delicate. Whereas many Western churches see ecumenism as a matter of churches working together as far as possible, Orthodox, with their different attitude towards religious pluralism, have often suspected the ecumenical movement of covert protestantizing tendencies.

Orthodox have long been involved in the ecumenical movement, sometimes because the church's interests coincided with those of the Communist state. In recent years, however, they have become increasingly critical of theological liberalism in the World Council of Churches (WCC). Eastern Europe has seen a swing away from ecumenism towards renewed confessionalism, which is causing difficulties for ecumenical relationships. Ecumenism has been seen as a dirty word because of the way in which ecumenical contacts were used to further government interests, while distress has been caused by the alleged proselytizing activities of WCC partner churches.

Bilateral dialogues have been conducted between Orthodoxy and other communions (Anglican, Roman Catholic, Lutheran, Methodist and Reformed) and between Orthodox and evangelicals involved in the WCC. However, many Orthodox have concerns about such activity: does dialogue imply acceptance of the other side as an equal partner? Is it merely an exercise in papering over the differences which exist? Is it a manifestation of Western relativism, an implicit denial of the existence of absolute truth? Does participation betray the conviction that the fullness of the church can be found only in Orthodoxy? If ecumenism involves repentance for past sectarianism and distortion of the truth, Orthodox would assert, in all humility, that they see no reason to repent for their role as custodians of an unchanging and Spirit-given Tradition.

ORTHODOXY AND WESTERN CULTURE

SECULARIZATION

Modernity has eroded the allegiance to the church of many in the younger generation. Only a small proportion of Orthodox attend church regularly, the majority being nominal in their allegiance. Reasons for this include the language barrier, as well as the attraction for many in former Communist states of Western secularized culture and lifestyle. In spite of the traditional Orthodox assertion that the vernacular should be used for worship, many oppose the use of contemporary language, fearing that this would hasten absorption by godless Western culture.

MISSION

Orthodoxy has had to come to terms with the existence of the religious marketplace and the need for active mission, notably to its own nominal adherents. This has been conceived in eucharist-centred terms as 'the liturgy after the liturgy': the faithful gather for the liturgy and are built up to be sent out to engage with the world. In the West, Orthodoxy has had to adjust its approach to take account of the prevailing atmosphere of pluralism and secularism, yet without adopting a relativist approach which would run counter to its self-understanding as the most authentic form of Christianity.

The biggest challenge facing Orthodox in the West is the tendency of many to seek security in their ethnic parishes rather than reaching out to the culture around them. Such an attitude perpetuates the perception of Orthodoxy as an ethnic form of Christianity with nothing to offer those brought up in or influenced by the West; frustrated members may move to non-Orthodox churches or give up any active profession of Christianity.

THE PROBLEM OF PROSELYTISM

Disapproval of the activities of many Western churches and missionary groups in Eastern Europe is not merely a defensive or protective reaction to the prospect of losing members, but is founded on an approach to mission which differs radically from Western notions of 'free market' religious pluralism. Orthodox jurisdictions have tended to follow the principle that each works within its own area of responsibility, or 'canonical territory', in which the people are united in adherence to the particular form of Orthodoxy which has shaped their culture. In traditionally Orthodox countries, Western Christianity is seen by evangelicals as well as Orthodox as moulded by Western culture, and its introduction as thus being culturally inappropriate. Western churches are condemned for encroaching onto Orthodox territory and attempts to make converts of Orthodox people are construed as proselytism. Some agencies have therefore sought to encourage internal renewal within Orthodoxy instead of making converts from it. Such an approach has resulted in the increasing readiness of some Orthodox to work with other churches and agencies in areas such as relief, publishing, religious broadcasting and even theological education.

NATIONALISM

The relationship between gospel and culture is a recurrent problem for Orthodoxy. Many have imbibed their Christianity along with their sense of ethnic identity, through the medium of a culture decisively shaped by religion. There is thus a risk of phyletism, an Orthodox term for excessive identification of Christianity with a nation's culture and self-awareness. Phyletism has been condemned as heresy, but it is an element in the desire of churches in newly independent states to secure autonomy and autocephaly, and in tensions between different jurisdictions as they shake off Russian religious as well as political control. Nationalism was a factor which churches appealed to in their struggle to survive under communism, while nationalist feeling and the ideal of 'Holy Russia' have influenced the attempt to restore Orthodoxy's traditional privileged position in post-Communist Russian reconstruction.

ECOLOGY

Ecology is an area where Orthodoxy has shown itself well placed to contribute constructively to Western debate. Orthodox ecology must be differentiated from any suggestion of New Age pantheism. Its approach has been described as panentheistic, recognizing God's presence in his creation and its consequent goodness but balancing this recognition with a powerful stress on his utter transcendence. The doctrine of the incarnation entails the belief that redemption involves the whole material order, not just humanity, though humanity is given a unique role as priest of creation.

THE IMPACT OF ORTHODOX SPIRITUALITY IN THE WEST

The Russian spiritual tradition has been flourishing in exile since 1917; widespread interest in Orthodox spirituality has been evident and spokesmen such as Metropolitan Anthony (Bloom) have won respect as interpreters of a deeply rooted Christian spirituality to the modern world. Spiritual writings such as the *Philokalia* have influenced many people, while icons now feature in the devotion of many non-Orthodox (though often divorced from their context in the church's prayer). Orthodox spirituality appears on the surface to possess certain features also evident in some New Age spiritualities (e.g. its emphasis on the material, and on discipline in cultivating spirituality), but the underlying reality is radically different, resting on the concept of spirituality as communion with a personal and transcendent (yet incarnate) God.

BIBLIOGRAPHY

I. Bria, *The Liturgy after the Liturgy* (Geneva, 1996); G. Limouris (ed.), *Orthodox Visions of Ecumenism* (Geneva, 1994); P. Ramet (ed.), *Eastern Christianity and Politics in the Twentieth Century* (Durham, NC, 1988); A. Walker and C. Carras (eds.), *Living Orthodoxy in the Modern World* (London, 1996); K. Ware, *The Orthodox Church* (Harmondsworth, rev. edn., 1993); J. Witte, Jr and M. Bourdeaux (eds.), *Proselytism and Orthodoxy in Russia* (Maryknoll, NY, 1999).

T. G. Grass

CHRISTIANITY (EVANGELICAL)

Evangelicalism is a form of Christianity that has been particularly marked by respect for the Bible, a stress on the atonement, an expectation of conversions and vigorous activity. Evangelicals habitually appeal to the Bible as their authority and turn to the same book for their devotions. Sections of the movement, which is not confined to particular denominations, have also valued, though in a subordinate place, the writings of the Protestant Reformers, notably John Calvin, or of the heroes of the Evangelical Revival of the eighteenth century, particularly John Wesley. Although the word 'evangelical' has consistently been used in Germany as a synonym for 'Protestant', the term has normally been applied in the English-speaking world to those stirred by the revival beginning almost simultaneously in the 1730s in America, Wales, England and Scotland and to their descendants in the faith. The movement grew to dominate the culture of nineteenth-century America and Britain, sending missionaries to spread the gospel in most parts of the globe. Although its influence on Western nations declined in the twentieth century, it became once again a powerful force in English-speaking Protestantism before the century's end.

BELIEFS AND PRACTICES

The defining characteristics mould the movement. Its biblicism leads to personal and group Bible study and to preaching that expounds the Scriptures, of which the best contemporary example is that of John Stott, a leading English evangelical Anglican. Although the movement adheres to the historic Trinitarian faith, its special emphasis is on the atoning death of Christ on the cross. The crucifixion of Christ, rather than his incarnation or example, has been its central doctrine, encouraging concern for salvation from sin through his blood. The way to salvation is through conversion, entailing repentance of sins and faith in Christ. Although sudden crises are not required in most branches of evangelicalism, a definite experience of having turned from a non-Christian life to allegiance to Christ is universally expected. The securing of fresh conversions is the grand aim of most evangelical activities, of which the archetype is the large-scale mission with a figure such as the American Southern Baptist Billy Graham as the preacher.

Worship varies widely among evangelicals. They readily use the liturgy in traditions such as Anglicanism with set forms of service, and sometimes, as in the Free Church of Scotland, they follow patterns inherited from the past entailing the singing of psalms rather than hymns and the rejection of musical accompaniment. More common, however, is the adoption of free worship, though in practice this has often meant a pattern alternating hymns with other features such as prayers and preaching. The contemporary trend is towards the singing of modern compositions, especially by Graham Kendrick, from words projected on screens that allow congregations to dispense with hymn books. Preaching, which is often between twenty and thirty minutes in length, is normally of great importance in acts of worship.

The leadership of congregations in most denominations is entrusted to an individual, often called a minister but never a priest, or else to a group, commonly called elders. The tendency, already general in the

United States, is towards having a team ministry in which individuals specialize in preaching, pastoral, youth or music ministries. Whether women are eligible for congregational leadership is a moot question among evangelicals, some insisting that the Bible forbids the practice and others seeing no barrier to the equality of the sexes in ministry. On another issue that divides the churches, the attitude to homosexuality, evangelicals normally condemn homosexual behaviour on biblical grounds. They tend to be stringent on moral questions, though they generally emphasize the ability of wrongdoers to repent.

The trend among most evangelicals since the 1960s has been to abandon an older otherworldliness in favour of a stance that wishes to engage with social and often political issues. This leads many of them, especially in America, to identify with campaigns such as the Christian Coalition that advocate causes such as the prohibition of abortion. Social concern, which was once regarded as a diversion from the gospel, is generally, though by no means universally, applauded and often organized through evangelical agencies. The tendency over time has also been towards greater ecumenical involvement, though many more conservative sections of opinion would reject such a policy as a threat to the purity of the gospel. There has been a gradual fading of anti-Catholicism, together with a willingness to experiment with the observance of the church year and a growing interest in the spirituality of Catholic and Orthodox traditions in the church.

ENCOUNTERING CULTURE

Because the Evangelical Revival coincided with the Enlightenment, the early leaders of the movement left to their successors a legacy of alignment with modernity. The characteristic Enlightenment preference for practical efficiency over inherited traditions, for instance, continues to express itself in a pragmatic willingness to prefer para-church organizations to ecclesiastical bodies as agencies for achieving missionary goals. Evangelicalism, however, was deeply modified in its ethos by the Romantic temper of the nineteenth century, and so there are also symptoms in the contemporary movement that reflect that phase. The strength of prophetic teaching in America and places influenced by America is a major instance. The predominant type of doctrine, which goes back in its present form only to the early nineteenth century, is premillennialism, the belief that the second coming of Christ is to be expected before the millennium predicted in the Bible and so imminent. The Romantic tendency also gave rise to theological liberalism, against which, in the inter-war period, Fundamentalism arose. The Fundamentalists should be seen as the conservative wing of evangelicalism, dismayed at the displacement of the Bible from a central place in society and insistent that its teaching must be reinstated. Fundamentalism became a large and militant sector of American evangelicalism, though in Britain the label was usually repudiated and rarely claimed.

The cultural developments of the twentieth century have exercised a major influence over evangelicalism. The *avant-garde* modernism of its early years filtered down to impinge on a mass audience for the first time in the 1960s, assisted by the emergence in that decade of a youth culture. The evangelical equivalent was the charismatic renewal movement, which carried the marks of spontaneity and informality of the times and so appealed to the young, especially if they were educated and affluent. Originally the movement was most noted for its stress on the work of the Holy Spirit and its advocacy of speaking in tongues, but from the beginning its ethos was distinctive in many other ways. Its most striking features are self-expression, especially in worship, where charismatics commonly raise their hands in praise; a sympathy for depth psychology, with ministries of healing for personal hurts; a stress on personal relations, leading to teaching on the organic nature of the Christian community; a dismissal of traditional inhibitions about such practices as sabbath-breaking; an elevation of experience over doctrine; an aversion to institutional barriers to mission; and a tendency to authoritarianism as a means of preventing spontaneity from lapsing into chaos. The influence of renewal has flowed out to affect many churches that would not claim to be charismatic, for instance through the display of banners in places of worship.

TRADITIONS AND GROUPS

The Christian traditions most hospitable to evangelicalism vary from place to place, but often include Anglicanism. The Sydney diocese, for example, is strongly evangelical. Presbyterians outside church union schemes tend to be overwhelmingly evangelical, and often emphatically Calvinist. Baptists, though internally fragmented in many countries, are predominantly evangelical nearly everywhere. Methodism includes many evangelicals, especially where it has gone back to its Wesleyan roots. The Holiness tradition that sprang from Wesleyan teaching about the possibility of entire sanctification is uniformly evangelical, as are the strong Pentecostalist denominations that emphasize the gifts of the Holy Spirit. Most black-led churches in America and elsewhere belong to evangelical traditions, often Baptist or Pentecostalist. The Brethren have exercised an influence disproportionate to their relatively small numbers, and the Salvation Army, with its military command structure, has specialized in social ministries when other evangelicals ab-stained. Lutherans and Mennonites have been increasingly affected by the evangelical ethos of North America. The charismatic movement has led to the creation of fresh bodies sometimes described collectively as 'New Churches', including the Vineyard Fellowships pioneered by John Wimber. In addition a plethora of mission halls, independent fellowships and obscure sects such as the snake-handlers of the Appalachian Mountains are to be found under the broad umbrella of evangelicalism.

BIBLIOGRAPHY

D. W. Bebbington, *Evangelicalism in Modern Britain* (London, 1989); D. W. Dayton and R. K. Johnston, *The Variety of American Evangelicalism* (Knoxville, TN, 1991); G. M. Marsden, *Understanding Fundamentalism and Evangelicalism* (Grand Rapids, MI, 1991); G. A. Rawlyk, *Is Jesus your Personal Saviour? In Search of Canadian Evangelicalism in the 1990s* (Montreal and Kingston, 1996); C. Smith, *American Evangelicalism: Embattled and Thriving* (Chicago, 1998); D. J. Tidball, *Who are the Evangelicals?* (London, 1994).

D. W. Bebbington

CHRISTIANITY (PENTECOSTAL AND CHARISMATIC)

Classical Pentecostalism is, by and large, a twentieth-century phenomenon. It traces its roots back to the Azusa Street (Los Angeles) revival (1906) associated with a black leader named William Joseph Seymour. This, however, was predated by the ministry of a Bible teacher of the Holiness tradition, Charles Fox Parham, who in 1901, at Topeka, Kansas, identified speaking in tongues with the baptism of the Holy Spirit, the phenomenon of speaking in tongues having occurred decades earlier amongst primitive Shakers, Mormons and, most importantly, in the ministry of Edward Irving, a Scottish Presbyterian minister based in London. Pentecostalism, however, claims a direct line theologically back to the early church, particularly in its emphasis on the role of the Spirit and the miraculous. Its most astounding growth in recent years has taken place in South America.

Charismatic Christianity (Neo-Pentecostalism, charismatic renewal) is a more recent phenomenon (1960s) and is associated with renewal movements within mainstream Protestantism (and Catholicism from the late 1960s), associated with an increased emphasis on and expectation of the work of the Spirit. A 'third wave' of Pentecostalism has also developed, identified by Peter Wagner and best represented by John Wimber. In this the Pauline writings concerning the Spirit are more emphasized. Estimates of the worldwide number of Pentecostal (and charismatic and 'third wave') Christians indicate that there are approximately 500 million, though in disparate groups, the common feature being a commitment to supernatural Christianity resulting from the role of the Spirit in the church.

Pentecostalism is less distinctive in its emphases than it was prior to the growth of the charismatic renewal movements, though it still maintains the belief in a 'baptism in the Holy Spirit', experienced as a secondary event after conversion. Associated with this experience is the expectation of a supernatural power, granted in order to be more effective as a believer; some Pentecostals identify the phenomenon of speaking in tongues as evidence of the baptism in the Holy Spirit having occurred. Charismatic Christianity prefers to concentrate on the necessity of a reliance on the work of the Spirit in the lives of believers, with attendant experiential consequences, rather than to isolate a secondary experience as being of fundamental importance, though many within this tradition also claim to have received such an experience. Both assume that Christians may function with the same power available to the early Christians as a result of the resources of the Holy Spirit being made available to them. Thus spiritual gifts, including healing and prophecy, are major emphases among Pentecostals, though different beliefs and practices exist, which sometimes generate tensions. The two groups have similar beliefs on other major theological issues and both would identify themselves with evangelical Christianity. Pentecostalism has benefited from lessons learnt and battles fought by previous generations of Christians. It has always been ready to borrow from others that which it favours and make such elements its own. Thus with respect to the ordinances it is fundamentally baptistic, whilst its emphasis on the seeking for conscious religious experiences was previously encouraged by the Holiness movement.

A major difference from the Holiness tradition relates to the expectation of an experiential and dynamic Christianity that is focused in power for evangelism and the supernatural, especially manifested in the gift of tongues. Evangelism has been a major *raison d'être* of classical Pentecostalism (as has a firm belief in the second coming of Jesus, itself a further motivation for worldwide evangelization). Crisis (mountain-top) experiences are anticipated in which the human is impacted by the divine, often resulting in phenomenologically observable consequences. Emotion and transparent vulnerability are key features. Such characteristics resonate with much of the lifestyle of Western civilization, with its emphasis on individualism, liberty and freedom to explore, developing recognition of spiritualities, and hedonism. Increasing interest expressed by the media in non-traditional forms of worship has resulted in many aspects associated with Pentecostal or charismatic Christianity being propelled into the homes of non-churchgoers and churchgoers alike. Such exposure, though accommodating extremes, has resulted in a form of worship appropriate to a consumer society that looks to get something out of life, including its religion and particularly its God. At the same time, an increasing recognition of the fragility of life and the uncertainty of the near future has resulted in many being attracted to a religious tradition that stresses the immediacy of a God who likes people and who wishes to impart divine resources that provide support for many whose trust in the economic and social systems is being eroded. At the same time, it provides culturally diverse and fragmented people with a social support network in the relaxed comfort zones found in Pentecostal churches, where the corporate body is fundamental to worship and fellowship. For those in the churches, however, a more rigid framework exists, to enable adherents to grow spiritually.

For most of its history, Pentecostalism has sought to remain as untouched as possible by the world in which it exists. Relationships with unbelievers were not encouraged; they were to be evangelized but not necessarily befriended. Pentecostalism sought to be separate from the world. Cooperation with believers of other denominations was also minimal; this was partly due to the isolation felt by Pentecostals resulting from the attitudes of others who were suspicious of Pentecostalism's enthusiasm and supernatural tendencies. The Holiness movement, which unwittingly spawned the Pentecostal movement, in the main rejected it for many years, as did most other denominations. It was as a result of the pioneering work of David Du Plessis (1905–87) that barriers began to be broken down among the leaders of Pentecostal and traditional denominations, though this process did not gain any real momentum until after the Second World War and became rapid only in the last two decades of the century.

Pentecostalism's unease with its traditional isolation has resulted also from its growing readiness to enter dialogue with others about its own traditions and emphases whilst at the same time exploring and analysing some of its central distinctives. Initially identified as theologically fundamentalist, it has in recent years grown away from fundamentalism and some of its emphases, including dispensationalism, a lack of interest in social problems and anti-intellectualism. Instead, Pentecostalism has moved in the direction of conservative evangelicalism, though retaining its emphasis on the Holy Spirit and the harnessing of his resources. Pentecostal colleges have, since about 1980, developed graduate and postgraduate courses, sympathetic to their fundamental beliefs, that have increasingly provided opportunities for seminal enquiry. This maturing process is allowing the emphases and strengths of Pentecostalism to be considered more positively by others, and the charge that Pentecostalism is biblically naïve and spiritually superficial is made less often. Pragmatism and anti-intellectualism, watchwords in classical Pentecostalism, are slowly being discarded.

Pentecostalism has learnt from experience and reflection. Initially triumphalistic and exclusive with regard to mission activity, it has grappled with cross-cultural issues, though it has remained defensive of the exclusivity of Christianity and is antagonistic towards the claims of other religions. In other areas, there has been a greater readiness to accommodate sociological changes, including an acceptance by many of women in leadership, a greater democratization of congregations, a more professional, educated and trained leadership, a greater social awareness, a readiness to question and analyse, a willingness to offer an attractive product, in terms of both the gospel and church life, and a determination to be inclusive, with an emphasis on the maxim that 'big is best' as far as congregations are concerned. Simultaneously, societal changes of a more clearly negative nature, including issues as diverse as breakdown in marriage, and unemployment, have made their impact on Pentecostalism as on other denominations. Pentecostals have had to learn that they are not immune from the effect of the world in which they live.

Ethical and social issues have rarely been addressed by mainstream Pentecostalism, though recently there have been attempts to take them seriously. Pentecostalism has tended to develop along racial lines with attendant cultural mores. (The fundamentally black Church of God in Christ exemplifies this development.) It has traditionally attracted adherents from the working classes (though it is increasingly becoming middle class) and minority groups, who have been attracted by the vibrant worship and the promises of health and happiness. Its ecclesiastical structures are varied, including presbyterian, congregational and episcopal frameworks. Such inbred variety has led to an increase in sectarianism that shows no sign of diminishing. There also exist major doctrinal differences relating to the Trinity (Oneness Pentecostals) and the sacraments (Church of God, Cleveland); these and many minor differences demonstrate that maintaining the unity of the Spirit is more difficult than receiving the Spirit. The unity promised in the Spirit finds less expression in the denominations that value the Spirit most than one would expect.

Charismatic Christianity, centralized in a more middle-class and professional environment, has been more *avant-garde*. This characteristic has resulted in Pentecostalism being challenged and even threatened by its new sibling. Although the latter often acknowledged its debt to Pentecostalism, it began to provide models of worship, lifestyle and evangelism once thought to be the property of Pentecostalism, though without some of the excesses. Others from outside the Pentecostal fold began to engage in miraculous activity, to create new forms of vital worship and to initiate an expectancy of and a commitment to the work of the Spirit. Perhaps as a consequence of this, a more radical Pentecostalism is emerging that seeks to rediscover the earlier historical emphases of classical Pentecostalism.

Because of Pentecostalism's emphasis on the Spirit, it has shown a greater readiness, especially in the latter decades of the twentieth century, to identify with and cooperate with other evangelical denominations and like-minded believers who are linked with other denominations. Similarly, the Roman Catholic charismatic renewal has resulted in a growing fellowship between believers once far removed from one another.

BIBLIOGRAPHY

S. M. Burgess, E. M. van der Maas, E. van der Maas (eds.), *The New International Dictionary of Pentecostal and Charismatic Movements* (Grand Rapids, MI, 2001); P. Hocken, *Streams of Renewal* (Carlisle, 1977); W. J. Hollenweger, *Pentecostalism: Origins and Developments Worldwide* (Peabody, 1997); K. Warrington (ed.), *Pentecostal Perspectives* (Carlisle, 1998).

K. Warrington

CHRISTIANITY (PROTESTANT)

Protestant Christianity traces its historical origins in the Reformation of the sixteenth century and the theological work of individuals such as Martin Luther (1483–1546) and John Calvin (1509–64). As such, it has traditionally defined itself over against Roman Catholicism through – among other things – its rejection of papal authority, its emphasis upon Scripture alone as the normative foundation for theology and its commitment to justification by grace through faith (defined as trust in God's promise in Christ rather than simple assent to dogma). Central to this latter commitment was a firm belief that every individual believer could expect to be assured of salvation, a view which constituted a significant break with the overall tenor of medieval Catholicism and which implicitly undermined the strongly hierarchical and institutional-sacramental structure of the medieval church.

At the time of the Reformation, Protestantism itself broke into two basic parties, the Lutheran and the Reformed, which were defined according to differing views of the sacraments and the person of Christ. Specifically, Lutherans argued for the physical presence of Christ's humanity in the sacrament, while the Reformed argued for a spiritual presence only, a difference from which derived a number of fundamental theological differences.

A third wing of the Reformation, that of the Radicals and the Anabaptists, was also 'Protestant' in its rejection of the papacy. However, it is more often regarded as the precursor of other modern non-Roman Catholic groups, such as radical Pentecostals and charismatics, than as forebear of more traditional mainstream church groups.

MODERN DENOMINATIONAL FORMS

The principle modern Protestant denominational groups are Anglicans, Lutherans, Presbyterians, Methodists, Free Churches, and Baptists. Protestantism is, however, so diverse and includes so many categories, such as evangelicalism or liberalism, which transcend denominational boundaries that it defies reduction to any simple scheme. Indeed, the rise of the modern missionary movement, increasing engagement with social and political issues and, more recently, the impact of secularization and declining church attendance have, in the West at least, fuelled the growth and enhanced the significance of transdenominational parachurch movements for Protestantism as a whole.

BELIEFS AND PRACTICES

Protestantism takes as its sacred text the sixty-six books of the Old and New Testaments, specifically excluding the Old Testament Apocrypha, a key point of difference with Roman Catholicism. A central element of the Reformers' initial protest was the argument that all believers should be allowed to possess and read the Scriptures for themselves. This was not an attempt to generate a radically individualist form of Christianity but, on the contrary, a means of emphasizing the corporate responsibility of biblical interpretation and Christian faith against the strongly hierarchical and traditionalist approach of Roman Catholicism. In addition to the Bible, different denominations and groups have tended to look to specific confessional documents and individuals for defining their own specific identity within the Protestant spectrum: thus, for example, Lutherans look to the Book of Concord, Presbyterians to the Westminster Confession of Faith and Anglicans to the Thirty-Nine Articles.

In practice, Protestantism as a theological movement has now become so diverse that even the claims that Scripture alone is theologically normative and that justification is by grace through faith now mean different things to different Protestant theologians. As a result, the term Protestantism has come to embrace a vast array of theological viewpoints, from the fundamentalist to the radically liberal, with little to unite them other than membership of denominations which have historically defined themselves as Protestant because of their traditional status in relation to Roman Catholicism. Even this, however, is problematic, as different Protestant groups have adopted a variety of different attitudes to the ecumenical movement, from positive participation to outright opposition. In addition, the term Protestant is used in certain parts of the world, for example, Ulster, more as an ethnic or cultural term than as a description of theological or ecclesiastical commitment.

Protestant worship, taking as its point of departure the Reformer's emphasis upon preaching, has traditionally placed the pulpit at the centre of its life. The move away from an elaborate sacramental piety focused on the sacrifice of the Mass was symbolized at the Reformation and in its aftermath by the increasing physical prominence or centrality of the pulpit and the increasing simplicity of church architecture, particular in the Reformed denominations. This traditional centrality of preaching has not, however, gone unchallenged in recent times. The nineteenth-century Tractarian movement in the Church of England has left a legacy of a more sacrament-oriented form of worship, particularly though not exclusively in episcopalian denominations, which is more akin aesthetically to traditional Roman Catholicism. Furthermore, Pentecostal and charismatic forms of worship, with their greater emphasis upon corporate participation and what might be characterized as non-cognitive forms of religious experience and piety, have made significant impact on Protestant groups, which has led to changing emphases in church life and worship. In such contexts, more emphasis is placed upon corporate participation than upon the pulpit ministry of the individual leader. The move to an emphasis upon experientialism has also led to the weakening of traditional denominational dividing lines, with common ground now being found between, for example, conservative and liberal Protestants, and even between Protestants and Roman Catholics, on the basis not of doctrinal consensus but of shared spiritual experience.

MODERNITY, POSTMODERNITY AND GLOBALIZATION

The impact of modern and postmodern culture on Protestantism has been extensive. The shift away from pulpit-centred worship, with its emphasis upon words, written and spoken, to more corporate and experiential emphases can itself be seen as part of the more general shift away from a verbal–literary to a visual orientation in contemporary Western culture. As Protestantism was born amidst the cultural revolution fuelled by the printing press and the consequent increase in literacy and the rise to prominence of the printed page, it was from its very inception a word-centred movement, and its theology and practice reflected that basic cultural distinctive; although movements regarded in their day as on the fringe of Protestantism (the Anabaptists, radicals and spiritualists) placed less emphasis upon words and more upon experience than their mainstream counterparts. With the end of the word-based cultural revolution, heralded by the rise of the televisual media, serious challenges are being raised for Protestant movements as a whole, and obvious questions are now asked about whether a Protestantism that is not word-centred can retain anything of its original identity or stand in any meaningful and positive continuity with its past. Given this cultural change, it is perhaps not surprising that recent years have witnessed increasing interest among Protestants in the more radical movements of the Reformation and in more aesthetic forms of piety, such as Celtic spirituality.

The change in the emphasis upon the word in Protestantism has also affected the position of the Bible itself. From the Enlightenment onwards, serious challenges to the verbal authority of the Bible as understood by precritical Protestantism had been raised both within and without the Protestant tradition on epistemological, moral and text-critical grounds. With the rise of post-Marxist deconstructive literary criticism in recent times and the crisis in confidence in the ability of literary texts in general to carry in themselves any stable meaning, the Protestant principle of 'Scripture alone' has come to appear to many to be meaningless outside of the limits of particular 'reading communities'. This, of course, raises serious theological questions, particularly for traditions of conservative Protestantism who have argued that the Bible is in itself the words of the living God spoken to his people, in relation to the nature of the truth-claims which such groups traditionally make for their doctrinal positions.

Another aspect of contemporary culture, globalization, raises serious questions for Protestantism as a missionary movement. From its inception, Protestantism was a proselytizing movement and, with the rise of modern missions in the late eighteenth and early nineteenth centuries, this aspect became more prominent, particularly, though not exclusively, in the various evangelical wings. With the collapse of Enlightenment epistemology, the growth of multiculturalism and the awareness of how missionary movements were often, wittingly or unwittingly, the agents of Western imperialism, significant revision of the missionary enterprise is now under way. On one level, Western Protestants face critical questions about how much of their traditional doctrinal formulations and church practice are culturally conditioned to an extent that they cannot be simply transplanted into non-Western cultures. This issue becomes more pressing every year, as the balance of power within Protestant circles shifts from the West to Africa, Asia and countries in the southern hemisphere as churches in these areas grow and those in the West decline. At another, deeper level, globalization, and the relativism that often follows in its wake, raises in an acute form the age-old problems about the exclusivity of Christianity's claims and the fate of those who die without explicit faith in Christ. Of course, these problems are not new: the exclusivity problem has been debated in the church since New Testament times, and the modern missionary movement grew up in the context of precisely such questions. The difference today would appear to be that issues such as the fate of those without faith in Christ have become problems of theodicy rather than straightforward motives for mission, as they had traditionally been. Indeed, the future shape of the various movements which constitute Protestantism will be determined by their response to the issues raised by postmodernity and globalization.

BIBLIOGRAPHY

Protestant Christianity is such a diverse movement that no single book covers all the ground. The following, however, give a general picture.

J. T. McNeill, *The History and Character of Calvinism* (New York, 1954); M. E. Marty, *Protestantism* (London, 1972); M. Pearse, *The Great Restoration* (Carlisle, 1998); J. S. Whale, *The Protestant Tradition* (Cambridge, 1955).

C. Trueman

CHRISTIANITY (ROMAN CATHOLIC)

The Roman Catholic Church embarks on the third millennium facing severe internal and external challenges but with solid grounds for encouragement.

The *aggiornamento* (Italian, 'bringing up to date') set in motion by the Second Vatican Council (1962–5) has had far-reaching effects. Without departing from the substance of its defined faith, including the dogma that the fullness of the church of Christ is to be found only in communion with the bishop of Rome as the successor of Peter, Vatican II developed it, expressed it in fresh, ecumenically friendly terms and spelt out its implications for living in the contemporary world. The most visible change was the replacement of Latin with vernacular languages in the liturgy, which by itself has made Catholic worship much more like the Protestant experience. Only a tiny minority, led by Archbishop Marcel Lefèbvre (who died in 1991), has sought to maintain the Latin rite, but a major debate continues within the Roman communion about the interpretation and implementation of the Council's decrees.

The massive documentation of Vatican II (from before, during and after) has furnished abundant ground for controversy between maximalist and minimalist readings of its intentions and significance: for example, on the church's relationship to non-Christian religions. The pontificate of John Paul II (1978–) and the Congregation for the Doctrine of the Faith under Cardinal Joseph Ratzinger are widely regarded in liberal Catholic circles as betraying, if not the letter, at least the spirit of Vatican II. Rome-based authorities have undoubtedly reined in some of the excesses that rode on the band-wagon of post-Vatican II euphoria. Yet the avoidance of the secession of any major section of the church has been no mean achievement of John Paul II's robust papacy. Nevertheless, the genie is out of the bottle and the stopper thrown away. Vatican II and its aftermath have exposed the scarcely tolerable tensions between 'Roman' and 'Catholic'.

The move to vernacular worship was not the Council's only encouragement of centrifugal change, which shifted the balance away from Rome (Latin was the city's own, ancient language) to national and regional churches. The boost the Council gave to more cordial ecumenical engagement (Pope John XXIII had set up the Secretariat for Promoting Christian Unity in 1960) issued not only in bilateral dialogues at world level (e.g. the Anglican–Roman Catholic International Commission (ARCIC), from 1970), which were easily monitored, but also to a myriad local contacts, which were not. Vatican II's approach to mission fostered contextualization and inculturation, which likewise promoted pluralism in the Catholic communion. Its concern for justice and peace issues similarly turned the focus on particular situations of oppression, need or conflict. Vatican II also paved the way for an episcopal synod to meet in Rome every two or three years, but how would this function: as an occasion for collegial decision-making, as a purely consultative or advisory body or as a papal teach-in inculcating the Roman line? Not surprisingly, in the context of such shifts towards a more truly multicultural, multilingual, multiracial Catholicism, the authoritarian papacy of John Paul II has built up enormous frustration.

At times it has seemed that he has had more admirers outside the Catholic Church than within it. Evangelicals, particularly in mixed mainline denominations, have often envied the doctrinal discipline Rome has been able to exercise over radical theologians like Hans Küng, Leonardo Boff and others (but not liberals such as Karl Rahner). They have appreciated Rome's firm orthodox stance on a range of ethical issues, especially on the family, human sexuality, abortion, euthanasia and biomedical technologies. For although Roman Catholicism, with its ban on unnatural birth control (*Humanae Vitae*, 1968), its celibate, all-male priesthood and its dogmatic irreformability, is readily assumed to be a bastion of conservatism, in reality in the West it has proved almost as vulnerable to secularism, sceptical liberalism and the sexual revolution as have major areas of Protestantism.

A church whose officers are vowed to sexual abstinence has suffered enormous public loss of face by exposés of breaches of its moral standards and, more seriously, attempts at cover-up and neglect of remedial action. In the Republic of Ireland, for example, the ability of the Roman Church to influence public mores has been gravely undermined. Sex and marriage have enticed huge numbers of monks, nuns and priests to depart from their vows, particularly in the Western world, with consequent closures of religious houses and crises in recruitment for the priesthood. The clamour for priests to be allowed to marry is widely based, citing the anomaly of married priests welcomed from other churches (e.g. in England, of Anglican clergy conscientiously opposed to the ordination of women). This change could be effected relatively easily, for priestly celibacy is not part of defined Catholic dogma. Even a cautious prophet might expect it early in the third millennium.

The ordination of women to the Roman priesthood (and higher orders) is an altogether more difficult issue, which John Paul II has declared not even open to discussion. Change in the foreseeable future is highly unlikely, not least in the interests of cordial relationships with the Orthodox churches. Vatican II's decree on ecumenism (*Unitatis Redintegratio*) spoke of 'The Special Position of the Eastern Churches'. In 1965 Pope Paul VI and the Ecumenical Patriarch Athenagoras formally revoked the reciprocal anathemas between the two communions in force since 1054. John Paul II has made closer relations with the Orthodox world a major objective (e.g. in his encyclical *Ut Unum Sint*, 1995), but disputes over jurisdiction and ownership of church buildings in parts of the former Soviet empire have intruded and hindered rapprochement.

The indefatigable travels of John Paul II have made him one of the best-known figures of his day. (Mother Teresa was not far behind.) Not least significant have been the visits of this Polish pope to his homeland. His opposition to communism there and throughout Eastern Europe greatly enhanced respect for the Catholic leadership when the demolition of the Berlin Wall in 1989 initiated the collapse of Communist regimes throughout the Russian-dominated world. The firmness of the papacy's stance contrasted sharply with the pusillanimity of the World Council of Churches, which, latterly with reinforcement from its Orthodox membership, often failed to criticize left-wing injustice as it did right-wing. Since, most recently, Orthodox hierarchies appear to be conniving at a fresh wave of religious discrimination by post-Communist governments, with all non-Orthodox having to justify their presence, how Catholic–Orthodox ecumenism will be affected remains to be seen.

The last decades of the twentieth century have witnessed a spate of bilateral dialogues between official representatives of the Roman Church and Anglicans, Reformed Presbyterians, Lutherans, Baptists, Methodists, Pentecostals, Mennonites and no doubt others also. Some of these have been national or regional (continental), others international. The most remarkable agreements have emerged from the Lutheran–Catholic talks, especially the *Joint Declaration on the Doctrine of*

Justification (Grand Rapids, MI, 2000). (The Anglican conversations in ARCIC have tended to confirm the doctrinal flaccidity of much Anglicanism. While it no doubt views its accommodation of Rome's non-negotiables as an extension of its comprehensiveness, this must look rather different from Rome.) Agreed statements on even justification by faith have not, however, led towards shared communion, to the puzzlement of some observers. It seems as though theological consensus and the experience of ecclesial reconciliation do not progress *pari passu*. Meanwhile, the Catholic refusal to contemplate intercommunion except within a united church taxes the patience of even the most sympathetic ecumenical churchpeople.

A remarkable development of recent years has been the formation of groups which describe themselves as evangelical Catholics (e.g. in Ireland). The impetus has often been the impact of the charismatic movement, which has been widely felt, resulting often in an impressive commitment to biblical truth and to prayer. Such groups are symptomatic of a new sense of kinship felt between conservative Catholics and evangelicals amid the broader churches' supposed abandonment of the apostolic faith. The most remarkable development has come in the USA, under the banner of 'Evangelicals and Catholics Together'. Catholics such as Richard John Neuhaus and Avery Dulles with evangelicals including Charles Colson and James Packer have in the 1990s issued two agreed statements, on 'The Christian Mission in the Third Millennium' and 'The Gift of Salvation'. One Catholic concern in such engagements has been evangelical 'proselytism' of Catholics, especially in Latin America, where the Roman Church has suffered huge losses, chiefly to Pentecostal-type Protestantism.

Such developments have not commended themselves to those evangelicals for whom Rome is incurably unchanging: *semper eadem*. They point to John Paul II's zealous devotion to Mary and the unchecked growth of the cult of Mary, including new shrines such as Medjugorje in former Yugoslavia. The pope has also declared a millennial 'indulgence'. The *Catechism of the Catholic Church* (1992), long enough to serve as a *summa* of modern Catholic doctrinal understanding, is conservative, to be sure, but a remarkable achievement which one can envisage no other church matching. In many respects it is a far cry from the *Roman Catechism* (1566) produced after the Council of Trent. It goes along with the *Rite of Christian Initiation of Adults* (1972), which fulfilled Vatican II's order for the restoration of the catechumenate for adults and has occasioned some reconsideration of baptism also.

The world stature of John Paul II (by contrast Bartholomew I, the senior Orthodox patriarch, is little known) can easily obscure the difficulties the Catholic Church faces at the grass roots. His appointments of cardinals and bishops (he has taken an active hand in episcopal nominations worldwide) will probably ensure that the papacy and the hierarchy remain strongly conservative, although note must be taken of the radical critique of capitalism and materialism in recent papal encyclicals (e.g. *Centesimus Annus*, 1991). Whether, and for how long, significant change can be resisted, especially on qualifications for the priesthood but also on important aspects of the daily life of the faithful, is unpredictable. The very prominence and dominance of John Paul II shows how much depends on who is pope. But evangelicals have no interest in the radical liberalization of Roman Catholicism, only in its continuing biblical reform.

BIBLIOGRAPHY

G. Alberigo and J.-P. Jossua (eds.), *The Reception of Vatican II* (Washington, DC, 1987); J. Armstrong (ed.), *Roman Catholicism: Evangelical Protestants Analyse What Divides and Unites Us* (Chicago, 1994); C. Colson and R. Neuhaus (eds.),

Evangelicals and Catholics Together (Dallas, TX, 1995); A. Flannery (ed.), *Vatican Council II*, 2 vols. (Collegeville, MN, 1975–82) – including post-conciliar documents; T. M. Gannon (ed.), *World Catholicism in Transition* (New York, 1988); A. Hastings (ed.), *Modern Catholicism: Vatican II and After* (London, 1991); K. Lehmann and W. Pannenberg (eds.), *The Condemnations of the Reformation Era: Do They Still Divide?* (Minneapolis, 1990); J. Luxmoore and J. Babiuch, *The Vatican and the Red Flag: The Struggle for the Soul of Eastern Europe* (London, 1999); J. Ratzinger, *Introduction to the Catechism of the Catholic Church* (San Francisco, 1994); J. Ratzinger, *Salt of the Earth: The Church at the End of the Century* (Fort Collins, CO, 1997); A. Stacpoole (ed.), *Vatican II by Those Who Were There* (London, 1986); M. Walsh, *John Paul II: A Biography* (London, 1994); G. Weigel, *Witness to Hope: the Biography of Pope John Paul II* (London, 1999).

D. F. Wright

CHURCH OF CHRIST, SCIENTIST, THE (CHRISTIAN SCIENCE)

The Church of Christ, Scientist (Christian Science) is a 'mind over matter' movement that emphasizes the importance of mental power in the healing of physical ailments. Its founder was Mary Baker Eddy (1821–1910), a New Englander with a Congregational background. The ideas of the movement have their roots in a metaphysical family of religions that make their impact in the nineteenth-century Western world, religions in which the divine is seen as perfect Mind and humans as eternal manifestations of that Mind. The teachings of Emanuel Swedenborg (1688–1772), who posited a connection between all existence, and Franz Anton Mesmer (1734–1815), for whom the connecting principle was 'animal magnetism', had a profound effect. Both stressed the need for cosmic relationships effected by attuning oneself with emanations from Mind or Spirit, the highest realm, and both appeared to give scientific validity to religion. But the main influence on Eddy was Phineas Quimby (1802–1866), a New England mesmerist and healer who went beyond Mesmer in saying that healing was not a physical process but involved 'mind over matter'. Quimby said that God was 'Divine Mind' and that Christ was the spirit of God in all humans. By connecting to spiritual thought, humans could achieve wealth, health and happiness. Quimby's ideas and those of Swedenborg became the foundation of the New Thought movement (which included the Unity School of Christianity) that later emerged as a more secular mind-healing movement, initially indistinguishable from Christian Science.

In October 1862 Quimby treated Mary Baker Eddy, who had up to that time suffered many personal tragedies and afflictions. She became a student of Quimby until his death four years later. Soon after this, she had a fall on ice. She believed that as a result of the revelation of Christian Science, she was miraculously healed by the Divine Mind, which alone had the power to heal. She was convinced that her life-calling was to teach this revelation to the world. She gave Quimby's ideas a more specifically religious dimension, in what she called 'the divine Principle of scientific mental healing' (*Science and Health,* p. 107). In 1875 she established the first 'Christian Scientists' Home' in Lynn, Massachusetts, and published her textbook, *Science and Health.* Catching the mood of her time, she declared, 'To those leaning on the sustaining infinite, to-day is big with blessings' (p. vii). She founded the First Church of Christ, Scientist in Boston (1879), followed by the Massachusetts Metaphysical College (1881) and the National Christian Science Association (Christian Science) (1886).

Eddy increased her hold on the burgeoning movement and reorganized it in 1892, disbanding the Christian Science and making all Christian Science groups 'branch churches' of the 'Mother Church' in Boston. Christian Science has no ordained clergy; Eddy declared that the Bible and *Science and Health* were the 'pastor' of the church. Services in all branch churches were henceforth conducted by 'readers' who read lessons set by the Mother Church from the Bible and *Science and Health.* Since church structures and regulations governing liturgy could not be changed without Eddy's permission, today these are still patterned on *The Manual of the Mother Church*, last revised in 1910 before her death. They have tended to lock Christian Science services in a time warp, but seem to have prevented any significant schisms in the movement. Since Eddy's death, the Mother Church has been led by a five-member Board of Directors.

PRINCIPAL BELIEFS AND PRACTICES

The sacred scriptures of Christian Science are the Bible and *Science and Health with Key to the Scriptures.* The latter volume states (p. 497) that the Bible is the 'inspired Word' that is 'our sufficient guide to eternal Life'. *Science and Health* is regarded by Christian Science as the indispensable key for understanding the Bible and is read at every service. Christian Science clearly differs substantially from mainstream Christianity, although, like the leaders of other new movements at the time, Eddy taught that hers was the restoration of 'true Christianity'.

The fundamental premise of Christian Science is metaphysical: that matter (and therefore sickness, suffering and death) is an illusion, and that everything is Mind, or God. Sickness cannot be healed effectively by material medicines, but only through the power of the mind. Humans are a perfect manifestation of Divine Mind. In the words of Eddy (p. 468), 'Spirit is God, and man is His image and likeness. Therefore man is not material; he is spiritual'. Humans have an indestructible relationship with Divine Mind, and all they need do is realize this. It follows that humanity can be as perfect as God. Perfection is achieved through coming to know the truth of being by departing from the 'errant thinking' of the mortal mind that accepts separate existence from God.

Christian Science focuses on the healing of both sin and sickness through this change in thinking. Evil is a definite and dangerous presence in 'mortal mind', the collective consciousness of all who have not come to the knowledge of Christian Science. Jesus is not God, but he was the ultimate Christian Scientist who overcame sin, sickness and death through his superior understanding of Divine Mind and the nothingness of matter. Jesus is not 'the Christ' but the 'way-shower' to the Christ, a separate entity and 'eternal spiritual selfhood' (*Science and Health*, pp. 29–30). Christ's advent constitutes the decisive spiritual event that makes possible the salvation of humanity from the material flesh. The Holy Spirit is redefined as 'Divine Science', the method by which a person can be healed. Healing comes with a realization of one's nature as a reflection of God, the Divine Mind. Christian Science has full-time 'practitioners' trained to clear the minds of 'patients' in order to facilitate healing. Through the healing, the patient comes to a new spiritual awakening.

ENCOUNTERING CONTEMPORARY CULTURE

Christian Science has been unable to keep pace with changing Western culture. It was clearly a nineteenth-century modernist religious reaction that utilized the uncertainty of the time and the breakdown of the traditional Christian cosmology that separated the natural from the supernatural. It was a distinct religious alternative that was limited neither by traditional creeds nor by the new empirical science of modernity. Its form of alternative healing has resulted in opposition and court cases against Christian Scientists up to the present time, especially over the issue of refusing medical intervention. There were signs that Eddy herself in her later years was bowing to the pressures of the dominant culture, to avoid further confrontation. In 1901 she allowed Christian Scientist parents to have their children vaccinated, and conceded the practices of medical bone setting and the use of painkillers for acute pain.

The movement has been in decline since the 1930s, a fact acknowledged by Christian Science itself, which now has less than half its 1930 membership of some 300,000. Hundreds of Christian Science churches and reading rooms have closed in the past decades. Rodney Stark's recent article 'The Rise and Fall of Christian Science' gives several reasons for its 'fall' and concludes that Christian Science has 'relied too much on an empirically vulnerable therapy and never found the means to truly activate its members'. Christian Science has been in serious financial crisis as a result of this decline in membership, coupled with the rapidly declining readership of its renowned flagship daily newspaper, *The Christian Science Monitor* (founded by Eddy in 1908), and the need to pay large amounts of compensation in lost legal suits.

These pressures have continued to increase, and in 1992 the chairman of the Mother Church resigned following allegations of financial mismanagement. At the same time, many Christian Science media services were sharply curtailed in order to offset the spiralling debt of the organization. Different reasons are given to explain the decline. One explanation, published by the Christian Science Publishing Society, suggests that it might lie in 'the increasing secularization of Western society' and 'an increasingly medically oriented society' (*Christian Science: A Sourcebook*, p. 12).

Whilst this may be true, in recent years many 'mind over matter' ideas have in fact become an integral part of popular Western culture, particularly in the quasi-Protestant Norman Vincent Peale's 'positive thinking', Robert Shuller's 'possibility thinking' and the 'prosperity gospel' of some leading charismatic evangelists, ideas that resonate with the success ethic of Western capitalism. Although it would not be fair to equate these ideas with Christian Science, they seem to some extent to have replaced it as a solution to the Western craving for health and wealth. Again, there are themes within Christian Science and the earlier New Thought philosophy that can be found in the eclectic spirituality of the New Age movement.

Christian Science no longer seems to offer an attractive religious option to secular society, bombarded as it is with sights and sounds resonating with Mary Baker Eddy's thought. As John Simmons observes, Eddy's 'own intuitive insight into the American religious imagination was simply ahead of its time!' ('Christian Science and American Culture', p. 67).

BIBLIOGRAPHY

Christian Science Publishing Society, *Christian Science: A Sourcebook of Contemporary Materials* (Boston, 1990); M. Baker Eddy, *Science and Health with Key to the Scriptures* (Boston, 1895, 1994); S. Gottschalk, 'Christian Science', in *ER* 3; S. Gottschalk, *The Emergence of Christian Science in American Religious Life* (Berkeley, CA, 1973); J. K. Simmons, 'Christian Science and American Culture', in T. Miller (ed.), *America's Alternative Religions* (Albany, NY, 1995), pp. 61–68; R. Stark, 'The Rise and Fall of Christian Science', *JCR* 13:2, 1998, pp. 189–214.

A. H. Anderson

CHURCH OF JESUS CHRIST OF LATTER DAY SAINTS, THE (MORMONS)

There were almost ten million Mormons in 1997 (half of them in the USA), making Mormonism the largest new religious movement from the West outside mainstream Christianity and the first major 'home-grown' North American religion. Some have suggested that Mormonism has become the fourth monotheistic world religion. It continues to multiply because of a zealous missionary programme by which young, well-trained Mormons (mostly North Americans) are sent out across the globe for a period of eighteen months to two years at their own expense. In fact, Mormonism has at least fifty theologically diverse denominations, but by far the largest and best known is the Church of Jesus Christ of Latter Day Saints. The beliefs of present-day Mormons are intimately tied to their unique history.

In 1820, in Palmyra, New York, fourteen-year-old Joseph Smith (1805–44) described a vision in which (he claimed) God the Father and God the Son had appeared to tell him that he was called to be the prophet who would bring the true gospel to the world and restore the original church organized by God. This was the first of many 'revelations'. According to Smith, in 1823 a 'personage' named Moroni appeared to him and told him of golden plates buried under a hill near Palmyra. These were revealed in 1827, when Smith was provided with two reading crystals to translate their mysterious writing, said to be written in ancient hieroglyphics. In 1830 he published this as *The Book of Mormon*, which Mormons believe to contain the story of the lost Israelites, who migrated to America in the sixth century BC but were killed in battle in AD 428. Before their destruction, the angel Mormon (compiler of *The Book of Mormon*) and his son Moroni took the golden plates and buried them; they lay hidden until revealed to Joseph Smith. Smith later claimed to have received another revelation from John the Baptist giving him the 'Aaronic priesthood', and he founded the 'Church of Christ' in 1830; the name was changed in 1838 to 'The Church of Jesus

Christ of Latter Day Saints'. Smith received further 'revelations' telling him to move from New York to Ohio and then to Missouri, but the growing group of Mormons were persecuted for their beliefs. Smith and his followers eventually settled in Illinois, where they built a town named Nauvoo. There Smith instituted polygyny, and when he and his brother were arrested in 1844, a mob stormed the jail and killed them both. After Smith's death there was a schism with those who said that Smith's son should be leader. This group, known as the 'Josephites', became the Reorganized Church of Jesus Christ of Latter Day Saints, with headquarters in Mis-souri; the schism was the first of many. Most Mormons, however, followed Brigham Young as the 'First President' and prophet of the church. In 1847 Young took thousands of followers to the Salt Lake Valley of Utah where they settled permanently and built Salt Lake City, the international centre for Mormonism today. Young remained President until his death in 1877. He encouraged polygyny and had twenty-five wives (Smith had seventeen). In 1857 Young ordered Bishop John Lee to kill 150 non-Mormon immigrants, who were apparently on their way westwards. Mormon leaders resisted any attempt to prohibit polygyny until, in 1890, they were pressurized into doing so by the federal government as a condition of Utah's becoming a state of the USA (1896). Polygyny persists in splinter Mormon groups.

PRINCIPAL BELIEFS AND PRACTICES

The sacred scriptures of Mormonism are the Bible, *The Book of Mormon* (which has equal authority to that of the Bible), *Doctrines and Covenants*, and *The Pearl of Great Price*, the latter two written by Joseph Smith. The *Book of Mormon* purports to be an account of ancient civilizations in America between 2000 BC and AD 400, and of Christ's ministry in America after his resurrection. *Doctrines and Covenants* contains revelations and writings dating from after the 'restoration' of the church, and *The Pearl of Great Price* is a collection of writings by Smith on the faith of the church. In 1982 *The Book of Mormon*'s title was expanded to *The Book of Mormon: Another Testament of Jesus Christ*, to emphasize, said a spokesperson, that the Mormons were a Christian church. But Mormon beliefs are different in several respects from those of mainstream Christianity. Mormons hold that the original church of Jesus Christ abandoned the true faith through apostasy in the early Christian era, and that the Church of Jesus Christ of Latter Day Saints is the restoration of that church, besides which there is no true church. All non-Mormons are 'gentiles'.

Mormons believe in three separate personages: in 'God, the eternal Father, and in His Son, Jesus Christ, and in the Holy Ghost'. These three are one in purpose, but separate in being. The Mormon concept of salvation is linked with the idea of the pre-existence of human beings. God is a God-man, Adam, above other gods. The gods produced spirit children, who waited for human bodies in which to dwell. Christ was one of the spirit children, the offspring of Mary and Adam-God, the God of our world, the one who came into the Garden of Eden with one of his celestial wives, Eve. Christ had three wives (Mary Magdalene, Mary and Martha) and produced children. All people have lived as spirit children with God in a premortal life, in which they were taught God's plans and purposes and God's plan of salvation.

This plan, according to *The Pearl of Great Price*, is for people to experience a physical existence and after death return as gods to God's presence for eternity. At death, the spiritual body separates from the physical one and returns to the spirit world. After people become gods, they rule their own planet with their family and have children there. Life on earth is a test to determine whether people are worthy to return to live with God. God gave several commandments so that people on earth could grow in knowledge, develop their talents, fulfil their callings, exercise free agency without the memories of their premortal life, and establish the foundations for eternal family relationships.

People are placed into one of three 'degrees of glory' in the afterlife, according to the laws people have obeyed on earth: the telestial, terrestial and celestial kingdoms, corresponding to Paul's 'three heavens' in 2 Corinthians 12. The telestial kingdom is the lowest degree, reserved for those who have wilfully disobeyed the gospel of Jesus Christ and have committed serious sins from which they have not repented. They are unable to receive either Jesus Christ or God the Father. The terrestial kingdom is for those who 'have lived honorable lives' but were prevented from being 'valiant in the testimony of Jesus'. These people receive the 'presence of the Son' but not the 'fulness of the Father'. The highest degree of glory, the celestial kingdom, is the one for which all Mormons strive. It is reserved for Latter Day Saints who have been baptized by immersion and have had a temple marriage and sealing. It involves eternal life in the presence of God and becoming 'a God with all the power and glory that God the Father possesses'.

Marriages must be sealed in Mormon temples in order for them to endure for ever in heaven. A man can seal several wives for himself in heaven by this 'celestial marriage', a practice which has now taken the place of polygyny. Women must participate in 'celestial marriage' in order to reach the celestial kingdom. Mormons also practise baptism for the dead, so that dead ancestors (some of whose names are discovered by means of extensive genealogical research) may be saved; these baptisms must be performed in Mormon temples. All Mormon males over twelve are members of the restored priesthood of Aaron; at sixteen they become priests, and about two years later they can receive the Melchizedek priesthood.

ENCOUNTERING CONTEMPORARY CULTURE

The Mormon priesthood excluded blacks until 1978, when a new 'revelation' allowed them to be admitted. Whether social pressure, rather than 'revelation', was the principal factor in the making of this decision is a matter of debate. However, the movement continues to have an uneasy relationship with multi-ethnicity. Recent reports of the disbanding of non-Anglo congregations in the Los Angeles area did not help ease the suspicion of Mormonism among civil rights groups.

Mormons are required to tithe their income and to abstain from illegal drugs, alcohol, tobacco, gambling, extramarital sex, coffee and tea. They have a reputation for morality, community orientation and family values. In the West they tend to be middle class and conservative and to have extensive business and financial interests. They exercise a significant influence on American politics, and several Mormons have held high-profile government positions, mostly as Republicans. They control the state of Utah, forming 70% of its population. Indeed, Mormons believe that their church will grow to become the world power that controls the course of history. Mormonism is nevertheless an example of a marginal religious group that has flourished as it has adapted to a dominant modern culture. It was one of the first religions to respond in creative ways to modernity's philosophy of evolutionary progress, particularly in its idea of eternal progression.

BIBLIOGRAPHY

M. Cornwall (ed.), *Contemporary Mormonism: Social Science Perspectives*

(Urbana, IL, 1994); D. H. Ludlow, *Encyclopedia of Mormonism* (New York, 1992); B. R. McConkie, *Mormon Doctrine* (Salt Lake City, 1966); S. L. Shields, 'The Latter Day Saint Churches', in T. Miller (ed.), *America's Alternative Religions* (Albany, NY, 1995), pp. 47–59; J. Shipps, *Mormonism: The Story of a New Religious Tradition* (Urbana, IL, 1985).

A. H. Anderson

CHURCH OF SCIENTOLOGY INTERNATIONAL, THE

Lafayette Ron Hubbard (1911–86) was born in Nebraska, served in the US Navy during the Second World War and, having been wounded in action, was discharged in 1942 on medical grounds. Reflecting on why some people improved when treated with testosterone whilst others did not, he concluded that the reason was the power of some individuals' minds. It is this understanding of the power of the mind that is the key to grasping the essential ideas of Dianetics and Scientology. In 1949 he attributed the subsequent improvement in his health to his discovery of 'Dianetics', publishing the authoritative textbook of Scientology, *Dianetics: The Modern Science of Mental Health*, an immediate sales success, in 1950. This book, together with Hubbard's many other writings (which include 500 novels and short stories) and over 3,000 recorded lectures, form what can be understood as the sacred scriptures of the Church of Scientology International. Hubbard established Dianetics centres in various cities across the USA. In 1954 the First Church of Scientology was opened in Los Angeles, and in 1955 the Founding Church of Scientology in Washington, DC. Today, Scientology's Religious Technology Centre in California, probably the most powerful section of the organization, guards access to 'upper-level' scriptures, also called 'Operating Thetan' or 'OT' materials, accessible only to those who have completed years of coursework. Whilst actual membership figures are hard to estimate, officially Scientology claims eight million members. Membership occurs at many different levels, from those who have attended courses to the few thousand elite who pledge eternal service to the church.

IS SCIENTOLOGY A RELIGION?

Whilst there has been some debate in recent years about whether or not Scientology can be considered 'a religion', it is now generally agreed that it is (and, therefore, merits charitable status and tax exemption). Indeed, arguably, criticisms of Scientology's status as a religion stem from preconceived ideas about what a religion should be. For example, some have claimed that Scientology cannot be considered a religion because it does not require adherents to relinquish previous religious affiliation.

That is to say, one can be a Scientologist and a practising Buddhist, Hindu or Christian. 'The Wisdom of Scientology can be used by followers of any faith to achieve the goals man has cherished for so long' (Church of Scientology International (CSI), *A Description*, 1994). As George Chryssides comments (*Exploring New Religions*, 1999), 'I have personally known Scientologists who remain members of the Church of England.' However, that this position seems untenable from the perspective of a missionary faith such as Christianity does not, for that reason, disqualify Scientology's claim to be a religion.

Similarly, the fact that Scientology utilizes a set of psychological techniques (termed 'Dianetics') in order to maximize human potential does not mean that it is nothing other than that, with little if any spiritual content. The goal of Dianetics is to enable the 'thetan' (the spiritual self) to achieve 'total freedom' or salvation. 'Scientology is concerned with the salvation of the thetan, its liberation from the encumbrance of matter, energy, space and time, and, in the proximate instance, with its capacity to overcome bodily disabilities and the vicissitudes of daily life' (Wilson, 'Scientology: An Analysis and Comparison'). Indeed, liberation is understood in terms of consciousness of 'ultimate reality', which is sometimes understood in terms of 'the Supreme Being'. The central nature of such beliefs make it difficult to avoid the conclusion that Scientology is essentially a *religious* organization. As the religious studies scholar Darrol Bryant comments, 'In the Church of Scientology, do we encounter a distinctive set of religious beliefs concerning the meaning and ultimate end of human life? Even the most cursory familiarity with the Scientology community and its literature leads one to answer in the affirmative' (*Scientology*). And as Wilson discovered, 'Many Scientologists have a strong sense of their own religious commitment. They perceive their beliefs and practices as a religion ...'

PRINCIPAL BELIEFS AND PRACTICES

Scientology refers to its belief system as 'an applied religious philosophy' whose goal is 'to bring an individual to an understanding of himself and his life as a spiritual being and in relationship to the universe as a whole' (CSI, p. 2). Like other worldviews, Scientology has developeda unique vocabulary. Hubbard's writings assure followers that his techniques will not only make their mental capacities improve through 'dianetic therapy', but ultimately lead them to become perfect thinking beings.

Central to Hubbard's and Scientology's philosophy is a particular tripartite anthropology: the body, the mind, and the most important part, 'the thetan'. 'Man consists of three parts: the body, little more than a machine; the mind, divided into the analytical and reactive, which computes and contains little more than a collection of pictures; and the thetan, life itself, the spirit which animates the body and uses the mind' (CSI). This last comment about the thetan's relationship to the body and the mind is important, for, according to Scientology, it is the thetan that is the real self, not the mind or the body, which are understood in terms of a tool and a vehicle utilized by the thetan. The thetan is an immortal 'individual unit' of 'theta', the life force: 'the term *theta* describes the life force which animates all living things. The life force is separate from, but acts upon, the physical universe, which consists of matter, energy, space and time (called "MEST" in Scientology)' (CSI). For Scientology, this relationship between thetan, theta and MEST is significant, because it is argued not only that the theta(n) is responsible for the creation of MEST/the physical universe, but also that the latter is dependent on the former and has no independent existence. Indeed, the thetan, not MEST, is true reality. Scientology aims to help people to understand this and live accordingly. Humans are fundamentally spiritual beings with the ability to control MEST, rather than being determined by and entrapped within it. Indeed, Scientologists oppose all forms of medicine and therapy that ignore the spiritual side of humanity and treat individuals as little more than matter requiring chemical and surgical intervention.

Within Scientology's tripartite anthropology the mind is further divided into two parts, the 'analytical mind' and the 'reactive mind'. The analytical mind 'is the rational, conscious and aware mind which thinks, observes data, remembers it and resolves problems' (CSI). The mind also stores painful moments and traumatic images of unpleasant events in an individual's personal history. Such experiences contain, it is claimed, harmful energy or 'charge' that has a deleterious effect on an individual's mental and physical well-being. The part of the mind that contains this negative mental energy is the 'reactive mind'. Furthermore, this part of the mind contains what Scientologists call 'engrams', which are, again, memories of past traumatic events which may even have been acquired whilst the individual was unconscious (the mind is always absorbing information).

What is to be done about the above? Scientology's answer is a specific and rather prescriptive type of counselling called 'auditing', which aims to enable individuals to empty the reactive mind of engrams and thereby to make the transition from 'pre-clear' to 'clear'. Indeed, by 'discharging' engrams, one removes the reactive mind altogether, leaving the individual with only the positive analytical mind. The trained Dianetics auditor follows prescribed procedures as s/he encourages the pre-clear to confront negative memories. This is often done using an E-meter (electropsychometer), which consists of two metal cylinders held by the pre-clear and a dial observed by the auditor. The dial monitors electrical currents passed through the body and, it is claimed, indicates engrams which interfere with the current. The purpose is to assist a pre-clear in working through negative images, rather than, as in psychoanalysis, interpreting what emerges. Furthermore, becoming 'a Clear' can be inhibited by the presence of toxins in the body. Hence, many Scientologists will be clean-living and even avoid unnecessary use of medication.

'Beyond Clear, one attains higher states of awareness called Operating Thetan [OT]. In this spiritual state it is possible for the thetan to possess complete spiritual ability, freedom, independence and serenity, to be freed from the endless cycle of birth and death, and to have full awareness and ability independent of the body' (CSI).

In this quotation, mention is made of reincarnation, 'the endless cycle of birth and death'. Thetans are thought to have occupied many bodies prior to the current one. The goal for the Scientologist is, whether in this lifetime or in a future one, to progress from entanglement in MEST through the eight ascending levels or 'dynamics', the eighth being 'infinity', or 'the God dynamic', and ultimately to 'freedom'. In Scientology a cosmic drama unfolds, in which an OT discovers his or her identity as a spirit in existence for billions of years, and attains freedom from multiple lifetimes. The OT category creates the possibility of further statuses for followers of the courses. The levels of OT continue to increase, each new level being associated with new power.

The movement also utilizes a 'Table of Conditions' to regulate the ethics of its members and the use of its technology.

A CONTROVERSIAL RELIGION

Scientology is a modern religion that entered the world in the second half of the twentieth century, and which has in recent years attracted several public figures, including Tom Cruise, Priscilla Presley and John Travolta. After five decades it has moderated its technological claims and has become an international organization, continuing to expand after the death of its founder. It is, however, one of the most controversial religious movements in the West, having been investigated at various times by several governments, including the US Internal Revenue Service, Food and Drug Administration and Federal Bureau of Investigation. In 1966 the US courts took away Scientology's charitable status, ruling that it was neither a religious nor a non-profitable organization. This decision was overturned on appeal, and Scientology now has religious status in the USA; it has had tax exemption since 1 October 1993. Investigated in other parts of the world, its activities have been restricted and banned by some governments. However, many of these decisions have been overturned in recent years, and Scientology has been judged to be a religion and a tax-exempt organization. Hubbard imbued his followers with the need to counter opposition to Scientology's principles, including that from former members. The organization is willing to use litigation against critics.

BIBLIOGRAPHY

M. F. Bednarowski, 'The Church of Scientology: Lightning Rod for Cultural Boundary Conflicts', in T. Miller (ed.), *America's Alternative Religions* (Albany, NY, 1995), pp. 385–392; D. G. Bromley and A. D. Shupe, *Strange Gods: The Great American Cult Scare* (Boston, 1981); M. D. Bryant, *Scientology: A New Religion* (Los Angeles, 1994); G. D. Chryssides, *Exploring New Religions* (London, 1999); The Church of Scientology International, *A Description of the Scientology Religion* (Los Angeles, 1994); L. R. Hubbard, *Dianetics, The Modern Science of Mental Health: A Handbook of Dianetics Procedure* (Los Angeles, 1950, 1987); R. Wallis, *The Road to Total Freedom: A Sociological Analysis of Scientology* (London, 1976); B. R. Wilson, 'Scientology: An Analysis and Comparison of its Religious Systems and Doctrines', in The Church of Scientology International, *Scientology: Theology and Practice of a Contemporary Religion* (Los Angeles, 1998), pp. 111–145.

A. H. Anderson
C. H. Partridge

COMMUNISM AND MARXISM

Communism and Marxism are political and economic theories derived from the thinking of the German political philosopher Karl Marx (1818–83). Though he was born into a Jewish family, Marx's worldview was atheistic, and communism has usually been associated with religious persecution. Even so, because for much of the twentieth century between one-third and one-half of the world's population have had their value systems and lifestyles shaped by Marxism, it has had something of the character of a faith, if not the form of a religion.

Whilst Karl Marx is the iconic figure at the centre of Marxism, other thinkers such as Friedrich Engels (1820–95), Georgi Plekhanov (1856–1918) and Karl Kautsky

(1854–1938) also made important contributions, whilst Lenin masterminded its application in Russia following the October 1917 revolution. Subsequently, Mao Zedong (China), Fidel Castro (Cuba) and others have adapted the core theory in different ways to their own historical and cultural situations.

KEY MARXIST IDEAS

The classic statements of Marxism are the Communist Manifesto (1848) and the three volumes of *Capital* (1867–94, ET 1907), volumes 2 and 3 completed from Marx's manuscript after his death. At the heart of Marxism is the assumption that everything can be reduced to matter. Nothing exists outside nature and humanity. There is no spirit world and no God. Human beings are part of the natural world and must exercise power over it in order to survive.

From a Marxist perspective, everything we are and do is the result of our economic situation. Because we must eat to live, we must produce. Hence, the production of goods and services is basic to everything else. Production is essentially a collective activity and the role we play in production determines our feelings and self-perceptions, our social status and relationships, and our personal development and lifestyle.

The way that the key means of production (land, labour and capital) are brought together determines the economic structure of society, which, in turn, brings into being political and legal institutions designed to underpin the power of those owning the dominant means of production. These institutions shape our social consciousness, and every idea we have, including our religious beliefs, is the product of our economic and social situation.

It follows that there is no place for individualism in Marx's thinking. Survival means interdependence. The notion that individuals can be free to pursue their self-interest is an illusion nurtured by capitalism. If any are denied freedom to experience their full humanity, no-one is free.

A second core element of Marx's thinking concerns the nature of change. He borrowed from the philosopher G. W. F. Hegel (1770–1831) a three-step (or 'dialectical') model of change. At any time, the status quo ('thesis') may be challenged by its opposite ('antithesis'). Out of this conflict will eventually emerge a third position ('synthesis') which incorporates what is true in the thesis and the antithesis. Marx saw this as a continual process. All reality is matter and matter is in a continual state of dialectical change. He interpreted human history in terms of the operation of this model.

We have already noted the primacy of economics in Marx's thinking. He analysed history in five stages, differentiated by the dominant mode of production. The earliest, *primitive* community had no private property. Hunting was the mode of production and people subsisted hand to mouth. The *slave* state depended on a large proportion of the population being owned by the free. Land was the key means of production in the *feudal* society and the ruling elite were the owners of it.

When feudalism gave way to *capitalism*, capital became the most powerful means of production, exploiting wage labourers to maximize profits. In time Marx expected labour to overturn this situation to create the *socialist* society, in which the means of production would be owned collectively. In each stage, apart from the first, the institutions of law and government serve the interests of the ruling class. As conflicts of interest disappear, the socialist society will evolve into the *communist* utopia, in which everyone works for the good of all and each receives according to his or her needs. The coercive institutions of the state will no longer serve any purpose and will wither away.

In this view of history religion is seen as just another tool of the ruling class, an opiate with which to distract the masses from awareness of being exploited. It cannot be denied that organized religion has often been on the side of the rich and powerful and pursued its own interests at the expense of others. But there have also been times when the Christian churches have championed the poor and the cause of social reform. The evangelical revival in eighteenth-century Britain may have been one reason why the revolutions that swept across Europe in the nineteenth century did not cross the English Channel, but the social activism of the Clapham Sect, Shaftesbury and others is another.

For Marx revolution was inevitable. The working people sell their labour in return for a wage. To maximize profits, capitalists keep wages as low as possible. Any surplus, after all the costs of production have been met, goes to the entrepreneurs who provided the capital. Marx believed that this arrangement alienates the workers from the full fruit of their labour. This alienation continues until the workers acquire the class-consciousness that inspires them to overthrow the economic and political structures that have exploited and alienated them. Revolution is the inevitable consequence of the class struggle. Marx saw this as an iron law of history.

THE RISE AND FALL OF COMMUNISM

Marx was an intellectual, not an active revolutionary. The Bolshevik revolution in 1917 owed much to his thinking, but the real founding father of communism was Vladimir Ilich Ulyanov, better known as Lenin (1870–1924). He concentrated both theoretically and practically on the place of revolution in the overthrow of capitalism. After periods of imprisonment and exile he became the effective leader of the Russian revolution until illness forced his retirement in 1922. His successor was Iosif Vissarionovick Dzhugashvili, or Joseph Stalin (1879–1953), who lacked the intellectual gifts of Marx or Lenin but was a shrewd tactician. For thirty years he ruthlessly shaped the way Russian communism developed, was exported to other countries and withstood the challenges of capitalist encirclement.

Marx believed that capitalism carried within it the seeds of its own destruction. Ironically, communism certainly did. Its ideology, collectivism and authoritarianism made it increasingly unacceptable to a postmodern generation that rejected these characteristics and sought personal freedom and the satisfaction of consumerist goals as its highest priorities.

From the late 1980s, Mikhail Gorbachev in Russia sought to liberalize public expression (*glasnost*) and the economy (*perestroika*). Economic liberalization was also happening in China under the leadership of Deng Xiaoping. By the end of the twentieth century only North Korea maintained an unreconstructed communist society.

A major reason for the rejection of Marxism and the collapse of communist states was the failure of centrally planned economies to satisfy citizens' needs and expectations. The complexity of identifying the demand for particular goods and services led to the over-production of some and shortages of others. The price mechanism of the market economies proved a more effective indicator of demand. Increasing globalization made citizens of communist societies aware of the better lifestyles enjoyed elsewhere and produced pressure for change.

Limitations on personal freedom also bred dissent. Instead of withering away, as Marx had anticipated, communist states remained strong and repressive. Dissidents in Russia, such as the writer Alexander Solzhenitsyn, were sent to labour camps and even deported. Again, increasing access to more liberal Western culture made state censorship unacceptable.

Underlying these problems lay the Marxist view of human nature. Whilst the uniqueness of each person was recognized, the individual was seen as insignificant in isolation from the collective because production is a corporate activity. Marx thought that capitalism gave people a false consciousness and that they needed help to lose this, so that they would work for the good of all rather than pursuing self-interest. It was the role of the Communist Party to make this happen. The aim was social justice, equality and interdependence, but the actual result was a bureaucratic police state.

The way communist societies handled religion illustrates the flaws in Marxist anthropology. Religion was suppressed because it competed with the Party for people's minds and hindered the acquisition of class-consciousness and solidarity. Believers were persecuted and religious institutions either closed or manipulated by the state. This policy drove religion underground. However, when open religious expression once more became possible, it became clear that the faith communities had not died, as Marx expected, but rather, in some cases, had grown.

It would be a mistake, though, to write off Marxism too quickly: first, because 1.3 billion Chinese people still live in a predominantly communist society; and secondly, because the formerly communist societies of Eastern Europe lack some of the cultural characteristics required to make capitalism work. This is the main reason why organized crime controls such a large slice of the Russian economy. The weakening of state power has also allowed old ethnic tensions to resurface and give rise to civil wars. Faced with lawlessness and anarchy, it is not surprising that voters are turning back to former communists, now presenting themselves as democratic socialists.

Marxism also retains some influence amongst Western intellectuals, though more commonly the thinking of the Italian communist Antonio Gramsci (1891–1937) than that of Karl Marx. Post-Marxist radicals differ from their classical forerunners in their expectation that it is cultural change rather than class-based revolution that precedes and makes possible socialism. They no longer focus on 'the working class' but on groups who are marginalized because of, for example, race and gender. Such groups are seen as the victims of bourgeois society. These radicals also demonstrate actively against the International Monetary Fund (IMF), the World Bank and other capitalist institutions.

BIBLIOGRAPHY

T. Bottomore, L. Harris, V. G. Kiernan and R. Milibrand (eds.), *A Dictionary of Marxist Thought* (Oxford, 1983); D. Cook, *Blind Alley Beliefs: A Christian Critique* (Basingstoke, 1979); B. Goodwin, *Using Political Ideas* (Chichester, New York, Brisbane, Toronto and Singapore, [3]1992); D. Lyon, *Karl Marx: A Christian Assessment of His Life and Thought* (Downers Grove, IL, 1979); D. McLellan, *Marx* (Glasgow, 1975); D. McLellan, *The Thought of Karl Marx* (London, [2]1980).

M. A. Eden

CONFUCIANISM

Not so much a religion as a worldview and a code of conduct, Confucianism began with the teachings of Kong-fu-zi (K'ung-fu-tzu) (551–479 BC), an ancient Chinese sage who has become known around the world by the Latin version of his name with which he was endowed by the seventeenth-century missionaries.

Confucius lived during a time of upheaval in China. The first great dynasty of kings, the Shang dynasty, had been succeeded by the first Zhou (Chou) dynasty, which in turn had become corrupt and left China in political, social and religious chaos. During this time various schools of thought addressed the issues of the day with attempted remedies, most notably the quietistic Daoists (Taoists), who thought that harmony with nature as given would result in harmony among human beings. Confucius taught the exact opposite, namely that once harmony among people had been re-established, the natural order would follow suit.

Our knowledge of Confucius is sketchy, partly from the absence of sources and partly because later attempts at honouring him concluded by crediting him with achievements that stretch credibility; for example, he is held to have written virtually every classic Chinese book. We do know that he came from a family of nobility and that he pursued a career in the civil service of a provincial king. When he was fifty years old, he was forced out of his position; he spent most of the rest of his life as an itinerant teacher. It is highly probable that the long-term success of his teaching is based on the fact that Confucius, like no-one else before him, established a large group of devoted disciples around himself. They propagated his teachings after his death and collected his sayings in a book called *Conversations* or *Analects*.

Confucius did not teach any new religious doctrines. He saw himself as divinely appointed by heaven (*Tian*) and counselled his students to fulfil traditional obligations to the spirit world, but he personally professed agnosticism when it came to actual knowledge of the supernatural world. Nor ought one to look for the religious significance of Confucianism in the veneration accorded to him after his death, though this went beyond the recognition usually given to a departed human being in Chinese culture. Under the Han dynasty, from the second century BC, Confucianism became an officially sponsored ideology, and Confucius became the centre of an extensive state cult (possibly because his ideas contributed to the legitimization of the Han regime). Nevertheless, his importance lies in the social system that he provided, which became normative not only for Chinese, but also for Japanese and Korean society.

Confucianism is about people: how they should live and how they should relate to each other. As individuals live according to their place in the social order, all society will be healed of its ills. This idea is based on that of a differentiated society in which the social status of individuals plays an important role. In fact, the leadership in society belongs to the prince, who is thereby entitled to certain privileges, but who also carries the responsibility of setting an example for all other people. When the prince fulfils his duty of living an exemplary life, the common people will emulate him in light of their own place in the kingdom.

There are two important principles at work in Confucian thought. First, there is *ren* (*jen*), the principle of harmony among people, expressed by Confucius' 'silver rule': 'Do not do unto others what you do not want them to do unto you.' This is a rule of courtesy and respect, not a rule of self-giving love. Second is the principle of *li*, the principle of virtue and propriety. *Li* designates specific duties for particular occasions. It is this principle that lays down, in the most meticulous detail, exactly what any one person's duties are.

Confucius believed that *ren* and *li* depend on each other. *Li* without *ren* would be nothing but an empty formalism; *ren* without *li* would be the expression of virtuous intentions, but possibly without a proper form or objective. *Ren* has priority, but it needs *li* just as much as *li* needs *ren*.

When *ren* and *li* are fully implemented, they shape the foundational five relationships. In Confucius' system, there are five relationships which, when implemented correctly, will produce a proper society. Each of these relationships consists of two people in their association with each other, and in each case there is a virtue that the person needs to exhibit within the relationship. The relationships with their attendant virtues are: father (kindness) to son (filial piety); older brother (gentility) to younger brother (humility); husband (righteous behaviour) to wife (obedience); older person (humane consideration) to younger person (deference); ruler (benevolence) to subject (loyalty). Clearly one will be a part of several of these relationships at one time – a husband is also a son and perhaps an older brother – so must integrate one's life into the various relationships as necessary.

Historically by far the most important virtue mentioned above is filial piety (*xian*). It denotes the undivided and unconditional devotion of children to their parents, going beyond either honouring one's parents or obeying them. In the Confucian system, the offspring must comply with the parents' wishes at all times and must do so in such a way that no dishonour is brought to the parents, no matter how unreasonable their demands may appear. A logical extension of this principle is the devotion to one's deceased parents that is obligatory for all people, but particularly binding on the oldest son of a household. Even before Confucianism, China had maintained a robust cult of the dead ('ancestor veneration'), but Confucianism with its codification of traditional values made it a central and permanent feature of Chinese culture. It is no exaggeration to say that the highest value by which a traditional Chinese person can live is that of bringing honour to his or her parents, whether they are still alive or departed.

A second highly important effect of Confucianism on Chinese culture was the stress on learning and education. Under the banner of Confucianism China developed a governmental bureaucracy in which advancement was based ideally on one's scholarly achievement in the Confucian classics. Thus Confucianism facilitated a society which placed a high value on learning, but which thereby also maintained its most conservative elements most efficiently.

The twentieth century has seen the erosion of Confucianism in the more outward areas of Chinese culture. Particularly in the 1930s and beyond, the Chinese Communists stressed that political liberation included the repudiation of Confucian ideas. This de-Confucianization included the abolition of traditional Chinese dress (robe and braid), the bureaucratic ideal and anything else that threatened to inhibit the power of the workers. Nevertheless, paradoxically, many of the traits that distinguished communism under Mao from other forms seem to have Confucian roots: the lives of the leaders as examples; the submerging of one's individuality in society; the revision of language (*Pinyin*); the use of social pressure to conform; and even the study of 'sacred texts', such as *Quotations from Chairman Mao*.

By its very nature, Confucianism has had difficulty in establishing a place for itself in the individualistic West. Chinese immigrants to the United States and Canada brought their Confucian thought patterns with them, but in order to survive

Confucianism is dependent on one crucial element, namely a society which as a whole values Confucian ideas. Theoretically Confucianism cannot be propagated by coercion, but only by a society in which anyone departing from its precepts is 'shamed' into compliance. Thus, despite the phenomenon of Chinese families settling into close-knit urban communities ('Chinatowns'), the larger context has made the propagation of Confucian values quite difficult. This problem is found also in some of those Asian societies that are ethnically Chinese but have come under heavy Western cultural influence, such as those of Singapore and Hong Kong.

The above observation should not be construed as meaning that all Confucian ideas have evaporated among Chinese (and Koreans and Japanese) now living in the Western world; just that they are much harder to maintain. Specifically, the value of filial piety is so ingrained that it still dominates many otherwise Westernized Chinese people; their lifestyles and careers are indistinguishable from those of many other Westerners, yet in a sense they are leading their entire lives ultimately subject to their parents' approval.

The centrality of filial piety is crucial in understanding the relationship between Christianity and Confucian culture. Although Christianity also stresses community and family, it values an individual's decision even higher: 'If any one comes to me and does not hate his father and mother, his wife and children, his brothers and sisters – yes, and even his own life – he cannot be my disciple' (Luke 14:26). To Confucianism, such a statement is sheer perversity as it sets an individual's salvation above allegiance to the individual's social core group.

Consequently, Confucianism has both positive and negative features in relation to Christianity. Positively, it emphasizes an objective code of virtue that has affinities with Christian morality, including the Christian appreciation of family and community. Negatively, however, it places a social (not an intellectual) barrier between many Chinese people and Christianity. Because of the supreme importance of filial piety and the fact that it is used to undergird ancestor veneration (if one's son does not carry out the required rituals, one will have a tortuous afterlife), it is very difficult for many Chinese people to become Christians, even though they may be convinced of the truth of the gospel. Christian workers among Chinese people, and particularly Christians working in evangelism among Chinese students, must always be alert to this fact.

BIBLIOGRAPHY

Confucius, *The Analects* (ET D. C. Lau, New York, 1979); W. Corduan, 'Chinese Popular Religion', ch. 10 of *Neighboring Faiths* (Downers Grove, IL, 1998); D. L. Overmyer, *Religions of China: The World as Living System* (San Francisco, 1986); L. G. Thompson, *Chinese Religion* (Belmont, CA, 1989).

W. Corduan

DAOISM

Daoism, along with Confucianism and Buddhism, is one of the three main Chinese religions and the one with the most obscure origins. Unlike Buddhism, it is a philosophical and religious system indigenous to China and of ancient but elusive beginnings. Daoism developed over many centuries and is a complex amalgam of religious ideals and practices closely related to Chinese folk religion and shaped by other religious movements in China. It is a distinctively Chinese religion widely practised today in China, Taiwan and other places to which Chinese people have emigrated. Various aspects of the religion, as will be shown below, have been adapted by contemporary people in pursuit of the ancient spiritual insight and wisdom claimed for Daoism.

While the roots of Daoism probably extend to the earliest stages of Chinese civilization, there is no clear documentation for its development, thus making it very difficult specifically to trace and define its diverse collection of beliefs and practices. The earliest basic statement of the Daoist tradition occurred in the book known as the *Daode jing* ('Classic of the Way and its Virtue'), which appeared about 300 BC, but was allegedly authored by Laozi (Lao-tzu), who lived in the sixth century BC. While there is some doubt about his existence, he is revered as the Daoists' supreme Immortal. The book, still available in many editions, espouses many of the main Daoist concepts: allowing natural forces to have full sway; allowing the *Dao* (translated as 'way' or 'path') unrestricted freedom in order to achieve an innate, natural harmony and balance; people should not make any impositions upon humans, plants, animals and natural forces; and an emphasis on passivity, naturalness, inner solitude, spontaneity, intuition and meditation. Likewise, sensual involvement, including personal desires and ambitions, upsets the balance of the *Dao* and results in misfortune.

Going beyond the ideas of the *Daode jing*, the poetic *Zuang Zi* (*Chuang-Tzu*), supposedly written by an author of the same name who lived from about 369 BC to about 286 BC, is decidedly anti-rational and describes an immanent *Dao*, a quiet spirit which pervades everything. Each person must cultivate deep serenity, identify with the *Dao* and seek a mystical union with nature. Neither the *Daode jing* nor the *Zuang Zi* is a systematic theological treatise; they describe the *Dao* not as a divinity, but as an eternal force and organic order, beyond the senses and without form, in which all things consist and which underlies and gives structure, rhythm and orderly patterns to the world. It cannot be known, only intimated, and people should not impose their will or intellect on the *Dao*'s effect on human events or nature.

The other source commonly identified with Daoism is the *Yi jing* (*I Ching*) or 'Classic of Changes'. This ancient Chinese manual of divination accumulated layers of explanation over many centuries from the seventh to the first centuries BC. Based on sixty-four sets of six horizontal lines both broken and unbroken, the *Yi jing* serves to this day as a handbook consulted for its wisdom and personal guidance. Both Confucians and Daoists have made extensive use of its supposed fortune-telling capabilities.

Despite the fact that Daoism was probably China's first organized religion with its own distinctive clergy, rituals and sacred texts, there are no records of any organized Daoist community before the early centuries AD, when two politico-religious movements emerged – the Way of Heavenly Masters and the Way of Great Peace – and when Laozi was widely recognized as the supreme god and divine source of Daoist teachings. It was in the latter Han and early T'ang dynasties that Daoism flourished, often under imperial patronage. Temples and monasteries flourished, and during the T'ang the Daoist canon and basic practices were established. Daoism prospered also during the Sung and Yüan periods and many new and substantial sects emerged, many of which emphasized mysticism and asceticism. Having no central authority or ecclesiology, Daoism developed as a diverse conglomeration of beliefs and practices popular among common people and mainly organized locally or regionally around significant temples or monasteries.

In Chinese religion various faiths may be viewed as complementary to one another and their rituals may all be practised by the masses. Nevertheless, historically there were differences and conflicts among the religions. Daoism was perceived by both Buddhists and Confucians as too mystical and intuitive, lacking a clear theology and definitive texts. Frequently all three competed over land and political influence. Daoists criticized the ethical rationalism and strict social ethics and governmental structure of the Confucians and they disliked the introduction into China of the highly organized and foreign Buddhism. However, after Buddhism's introduction into China, especially in the third to sixth centuries AD, Daoism definitely borrowed literature, practices and ideas from the well-developed Buddhist tradition. On the other hand, Daoist mysticism and superstitions were often derided, especially by royalty and scholar-gentry, as contrary to the hierarchical social order of rational Confucianism. However, some scholars have suggested that this tension between Daoist intuition, idealism and spontaneity and Confucian reason, practicality and responsibility has provided a social and intellectual stability for Chinese civilization which allows Daoism, often along with Buddhism, to flourish in times of upheaval as an inward solace, and Confucianism to predominate in periods of peace as an ideology of social and political order.

Daoism is such an amalgam of beliefs and customs that it is difficult to generalize about its characteristics as understood by its practitioners. Yet certain elements seem to be widespread. The search for longevity is one such element, deeply rooted in both Daoist and Chinese custom. People complete their allotted life-span if they live so as to prevent the dissipation of vital spirits from their body. *Qi* (*ch'i*), the breath or vital energy of which all things are composed, must continue to flow through the body. These forces must be balanced between the polarities of the *yin*, the female or passive power in the cosmos, and of the *yang*, the male or active power in the cosmos. Though opposites, the *yin* and *yang* are complementary and thus maintain the equilibrium between the five powers of *qi* (wood, fire, earth, metal and water) of which everything in the universe consists.

Longevity results from the proper balance of forces in the body. To achieve this balance certain practices are encouraged in the Daoist tradition. One such practice is inner contemplation. Daoism teaches many methods of spiritual meditation in order to encourage oneness with the *Dao*. Sometimes this contemplation involves the visualization of divinities identified with various parts of the body or visualization of the light or spiritual power of heavenly bodies directed to one's body. In addition to meditation, breathing techniques, exercises and dietary habits are important practices in the pursuit of longevity and prosperity. These practices help to facilitate the flow of *qi* and clear the body of impurities. Best known of these practices are *qigong* exercises of controlled breathing and disciplined, deliberate exercises which develop coordination and facilitate the proper spiritual and biological functioning of the human body. Daoists have also employed and developed Chinese alchemy techniques to promote physical immortality through fortune-telling, use of talismans and elixirs, prayers and fasts. Alchemists intended to facilitate the rhythms of the natural order for the benefit of the individual. Another practice widely used by Daoists is *feng-shui* (literally 'wind and water'). This is a form of geomancy in which buildings and graves are located in propitious directions in order to benefit from the proper alignment of cosmic forces. To do this is to bring good fortune.

Despite Daoism's concern for spirits and natural forces, it also espouses ethical teachings. These include the Five Precepts (not to kill, drink alcohol, lie, steal or commit adultery), which are similar to those of Buddhism. Daoism also propounds the Ten Virtues: filial piety; loyalty to the emperor; loyalty to one's teacher; kindness to all creatures; patience; criticism of evil deeds; aid to the poor; respect for nature; study of the sacred texts; and offering to the gods. Reminiscent of Confucianism, these virtues demonstrate the eclectic nature of Daoism.

Daoism has had profound effects on Chinese culture. Going beyond its religious texts, architecture and sculpture, the influence of Daoism deeply affects the poetry, painting and calligraphy of China. The Daoist texts were admired by Confucians and Buddhists for their literary quality, stories and imagery. The legends of Daoist deities and immortals provided a rich collection of Chinese lore. Daoist emphasis on natural forces, the cosmic order, the balance of *yin* and *yang* and human collaboration with nature have all made great impact on the Chinese style of landscape painting, which displays the harmony of nature. These same principles are applied to other cultural activities such as landscape gardening and the tea ceremony. Calligraphy, one of China's prized art forms, employs Daoist concepts in seeking to demonstrate cosmic rhythms through the artistic expression of Chinese characters.

The Western scientific outlook that clearly distinguishes the material from the spiritual and the past from the present is very different from the Daoist perspective, which sees things as integrally interconnected. Nevertheless, Daoism has achieved a significant measure of popularity in the West today. One needs only to visit the religion or New Age section of a major bookshop to discover the popularity of Daoist texts such as the *Daode jing, Zuang Zi* and *Yi jing*. These, as well as games promoting meditation, *qigong*, *feng-shui* and various Chinese astrological books inspired at least in part by Daoist principles, are all readily available. The attraction seems to be the Daoist principle of unity between all elements of the cosmos, the linkage of humans with natural and spiritual forces and the encouragement of harmony in the universe. The feeling seems to be that the ancient wisdom of Daoism engages one with the primordial truths of the cosmos and reveals the spiritual insights, naturalness and intuitions of spiritual practices followed for millennia in China. Accordingly, the concept of the *Dao* resonates with many who have environmental concerns today. In view of the popularity in the West of psychics and fortune-tellers, some have commented that there may be more practitioners of the *Yi jing* in the West than in China itself.

Many in the West are particularly attracted to the Daoist emphasis on humanity's interconnectedness with the universe. One is encouraged to develop this relationship through natural health procedures: exercise, dieting and use of natural medicines. Also promoted is a concern for all humans and their relationship to nature. Further, it is claimed that the Daoist practices of meditation raise one's level of consciousness and awareness of body, spirit and nature. Others see in Daoism a means of channelling spiritual power to themselves and others through bodily movements, chants and practices followed for many centuries by Daoists. *Qigong* exercises and acupuncture are thought to aid the flow of *qi* and to result in greater balance and harmony and also healing through natural, non-chemical means.

In its contemporary Western revival Daoism is viewed as having a commonality and validity similar to those of the native religions of North America, the mysticisms of Judaism, Christianity and Islam, Hinduism and the folk religions of Africa and early Mesoamerica. Some have even suggested that Christians can attain spiritual benefit and fulfilment from reading Daoist texts such as the *Daode jing*. In this view, by doing so Christians will encounter common universal spiritual truths also advocated by Christianity: for example, simplicity, love, compassion, happiness, meditation and practical morality. They will thus discover the goodness in themselves, their place in the eternal order of the universe, and the common humanity and spirituality of Daoist and Christian teachings. This view has contributed to a renewed interest in Daoism and has encouraged a syncretistic correlation with Christianity, with which Daoism supposedly shares a universal spiritual reality and ethic.

Daoism today is practised in its traditional forms primarily in Chinese communities living (particularly) in China, Taiwan and Singapore. In China believers were severely persecuted and their sacred sites desecrated during the Cultural Revolution (1966–76). However, since 1976 Daoism has recovered and, especially in the countryside, its practices have once again flourished. It is clear that Daoism is firmly established as a religious faith among traditional Chinese people and its influence on Chinese culture is continuous. The sudden and (to the Chinese government) disturbing emergence of the Fulan Gong sect demonstrates that contemporary movements inspired at least in part by Daoism can still be spiritually as well as politically influential. In addition, Daoism has made inroads into Western thought outside the Chinese community, based upon its universal values, ancient truths and religious practices that supposedly heighten spiritual awareness. Daoism is a religion and philosophy still alive amongst Chinese people, and has established itself in some circles as a viable philosophical, spiritual and practical belief for Westerners.

BIBLIOGRAPHY

F. Baldwin, 'Taoism: An Overview', in *ER* 14, pp. 288–306; H. J. Creel, *What is Taoism? and Other Studies in Chinese Cultural History* (Chicago, 1970); P. J. Maclagan, 'Taoism', in J. Hastings (ed.), *Encyclopaedia of Religion and Ethics*, vol. 12 (New York, 1955), pp. 197–202; D. L. Overmyer, 'Religions of China: The World as a Living System', in H. B. Earhart (ed.), *Religious Traditions of the World* (New York, 1993); N. Smart, *Religions of Asia* (Englewood Cliffs, NJ, 1993); E. Wong, *The Shambhala Guide to Taoism* (London and Boston, 1997).

C. W. Weber

ESOTERIC RELIGION

THE SOURCES OF THE ESOTERIC TRADITION

When the Emperor Constantine made Christianity the official religion of Rome, he may have unwittingly created the Western magical tradition. For it was under Constantine, and the immediately succeeding emperors, that Pagan traditions and superstitions were driven underground, where myths and rumours could gather around them.

Much later, when the West began to discover Arabic learning, many of these old traditions re-emerged to fascinate speculative scholars such as Michael Scot (1170–1232) and Albertus Magnus (1193–1280). Four sources were especially important: the Jewish Kabbala, a magical system based upon numerology; the Corpus Hermeticum, written allegedly by the fabled Hermes Trismegistus, containing the groundwork of alchemy; Neo-Platonist tracts, expounding the idea that all created things are linked through a series of correspondences; and Gnostic scriptures, asserting the darkness of this world and the need for humankind to struggle towards enlightenment and union with God.

These books became the inspirational base of medieval and Renaissance magic and remain central to esoteric religion today. As knowledge of them spread, astrologers and alchemists proliferated all over Europe, and some esoteric societies were formed. In 1614 a mysterious anonymous pamphlet, *The Reformation of the World*, caused an international sensation by claiming to describe a secret magical group (the Order of the Rosy Cross) which worthy men might be invited to join. Two more pamphlets followed, though it is unlikely that they were written by the same author, that the group actually existed, or that the great Christian Rosenkreutz (founder of the order) ever lived. However, the idea of 'Rosicrucianism' became extremely popular, and various groups claiming the same 'tradition' have appeared – culminating today in the California-based Rosicrucian Fellowship (AMORC) and also two smaller groups.

Shortly afterwards, English antiquary Elias Ashmole managed to join the old trade association of stonemasons and began to use this connection discreetly to link together like-minded amateur occultists. The 'Freemasons' grew enormously in the years following the French Revolution, when esoteric groups of all sorts began to flourish.

In the nineteenth century, Madame Helena Blavatsky employed ideas from the esoteric tradition in *Isis Unveiled* and *The Secret Doctrine* and thus founded Theosophy, a popular group which believed that the same core of esoteric wisdom ('theosophia') existed at the heart of all great religions; that adepts could be aided by 'Ascended Masters', powerful former humans who now existed in invisible spirit form; and that a recovery of magical powers was now possible. In the 1890s, another revival of occultism, notably in Paris and London, produced the enormously influential Hermetic Order of the Golden Dawn, whose prominent members included W. B. Yeats, Aleister Crowley and Samuel MacGregor Mathers. The group soon splintered (as esoteric societies tend to do) but Crowley (1875–1947) went on to become notorious as 'the wickedest man in the world', the flamboyant public face of twentieth-century magic. Although he was unpleasant, quarrelsome and deeply Fascist, his writings are still revered by (some) New Age and Pagan practitioners today.

An Oxford scholar, Margaret Murray (1862–1963), studied the records of witch trials in previous centuries and became convinced that 'Wicca' was a powerful, secret religious tradition which had always persisted just beneath the surface of Christian Europe. Her book *The Witch-Cult in Western Europe* (1921) persuaded Gerald Gardner (1884–1964) to begin covens operating on lines she described. This appears to have been the beginning of modern Wicca; there is no real continuity with the practice of previous ages.

Since the repeal of the Witchcraft Act in 1951, covens and other esoteric groups have been more confident; they have spread throughout Britain, and in other Western countries too. Several former occultists have used their training to found their own religious or therapeutic cults.

BELIEFS AND PRACTICES TODAY

The magical quest is partly about gaining power over the world. Magician Gareth Knight asserts that there are three ways in which we try to manipulate nature: prayer, science and magic; and magic is 'the link and reconciler of the other two' (*A History of White Magic*, 1978, p. 105). Magical practice is supposedly neutral in itself; adepts can follow the left-hand or right-hand path.

But for many esotericists, power is not important. Magic is about integration, the uniting of all human powers and impulses to create a perfectly balanced life – and by extension, to bring about order and harmony in the world as well. Magic may achieve physical effects, such as changing base metals into gold (alchemy); but its true purpose is to alter our perceptions of reality.

Because they claim unusual powers, and express tremendous confidence in human potential, esotericists have often been condemned by the Christian church for trying to usurp the place of God. Rosicrucianism, for example, reduces Jesus to a vehicle for the Christ-spirit (not the Christ himself) and proclaims that human destiny is to evolve into divinity. Christians object that Freemasonry talks constantly about righteousness, but completely ignores Christ's power to transform human life; the secrets of freemasonry seem sufficient to bring harmony to the universe. Christ is not mentioned in prayers, and although the Bible is central in ceremonies, more is made of unbiblical traditions (such as the legend of Hiram Abiff, the mythical builder of Solomon's temple). God's secret name is a startling composite of Yahweh, Baal and Osiris.

This kind of syncretism is common in esoteric groups. Theosophy incorporates elements of many sorts of mysticism. But it also insists that 'there is no doctrine, no opinion by whomsoever taught or held that is in any way binding on any member of the society'. Practice and experience are more important than dogmatic ideas.

Theosophy has given birth to two other significant movements. Anthroposophy, founded by Rudolf Steiner (1861–1925), asserts that science and occultism need to work together to further human evolution; the earth's aura contains memories which can be read by trained clairvoyants and can help the study of human potential. The gospels fascinated Steiner, but he regarded them as mystical documents which were only for the initiated.

Steiner broke with theosophy when the movement began promoting a young Indian, Jiddhu Krishnamurti, as the Messiah who would inaugurate a new age of mystical awareness. In 1929 Krishna-murti himself defected, denying that he was the Christ. Theosophists split into two camps, and a large group, still active today, followed the teachings of former evangelical Alice Bailey, who proclaimed that although Krishnamurti was not the Messiah, the 'Maitreya' (a Christ-figure for our age) was due to appear soon. (Bailey's most prominent disciple today is Benjamin Creme, who claims that the Christ is living today and will soon reveal himself to the world.)

Wicca, like theosophy, stresses practice more than dogma, although it has a sketchy theology based on Margaret Murray's concept of the Earth Mother and the Horned God. Some witches are more goddess-oriented, others more god-oriented; some believe there is a further supreme God, and that the deities actually worshipped are merely symbols; most believe that their deities are limited in power, and must be helped by the witches themselves, whose active mental energy will provide power for the gods to use. Reincarnation and *karma* are accepted by most, but not all. Gerald Gardner himself commented, 'Exactly what the present day witch believes I find it hard to say.'

It should be noted that although most Wiccans consider themselves to be nature religionists rather than esotericists, it is nevertheless true that esotericism and nature religion meet in Wicca, as they do in other forms of Paganism. The pentagram, for example, a symbol ubiquitous in modern Paganism, can be traced back through esoteric traditions and even medieval Christian thought.

ESOTERIC RELIGION IN THE MODERN WORLD

The 'psychedelic' period of the 1960s opened many young people's minds to the apparent possibilities of magic as a means of personal transformation, and books such as those of Carlos Castaneda, detailing his encounters with a Yaqui Indian sorcerer, became enormously popular. The rise of 'New Age' thinking, following Marilyn Ferguson's book *The Aquarian Conspiracy* (1980), has led to a revival of interest in ritual occultism, Pagan practices and 'earth magic'. Occultists such as G. I. Gurdjieff (1877–1949) and P. D. Ouspensky (1878–1947) have gained a new vogue. And Jungian psychology, with its belief that archetypes in the mind are mirrored in folklore, mythology and alchemical symbolism, has an attraction of its own.

The postmodern idea that reality is personally defined fits well with the magical principle that subjective and objective reality are two poles of the same thing. The eclecticism of the esoteric groups suits the temper of a world in which the confident 'metanarratives' of the past have lost their hold. Esotericism will probably never be the major religious expression of our society; but the conditions are favourable for its continued growth.

BIBLIOGRAPHY

A. Faivre and J. Needleman (eds.), *Modern Esoteric Spirituality* (London, 1992); D. Fortune, *Sane Occultism* (Wellingborough, 1987); S. Holroyd and N. Powell, *Mysteries of Magic* (London, 1991); K. Seligmann, *Magic, Supernaturalism and Religion* (St Albans, 1975).

J. D. Allan

HINDUISM (TANTRISM)

In a broad philosophical sense, *Tantra* (Sanskrit: 'extension', 'warp on a loom') refers to a system of languages designed to achieve the expansion of knowledge. The system ran parallel and often in opposition to mainstream Brahmanical Hinduism from at least the sixth century AD onwards. The study of Tantrism is essential to the understanding of the historical development of Hindu spirituality, for Tantra, next to the *Vedas*, has arguably influenced all aspects of the religious life of the peoples of the subcontinent. Tantra includes erotic ritual, poetry, speculative texts, painting and sculpture. Its most important feature is the cult of Shakti ('energy'), consort of Shiva. Tantra understands reality as bipolar and aims at the restoration of primordial unity by conjoining opposites (male and female, pure and impure castes, good and evil).

More commonly, *Tantra* refers to Indo-Tibetan texts (also known as *Agamas*) dealing with the esoteric practice of a group of Asian religious movements (Hindu, Buddhist and Jain) which use yogic techniques. This practice (*sadhana*) emphasizes the correspondence between the human body and the universe and uses the equilibrium between male and female energies to reach ultimate reality or liberation (*moksha*).

HISTORICAL OVERVIEW

The origin of Tantrism is obscure. Some have found its roots in pre-Vedic female icons from the third millennium BC recovered in the Indus Valley and in pre-Aryan magical fertility cults that worshipped female creative power. Others point to ideas of the earth as mother in the *Atharva Veda* and to the creative power of speech (*vak*) in the *Rig Veda*, also identified with Bharati or Sarasvati, the goddess of speech.

However, what is today known as Tantra developed in the medieval period (600–1200 AD) in India when temple Hinduism dominated the culture. By 900 AD at least sixty-four texts were circulating and Tantric art was in the ascendancy. Tantra continues in diminished form in India today, but has considerable influence in the West through the New Age and Neo-Pagan networks.

PRIMARY SOURCES

Since Tantric practice disregarded social norms, many texts were written in Bengali and Sanskrit using an esoteric (hidden) code called 'intentional language' (*sandhyabhasa*) which was deliberately unintelligible to outsiders. This evasiveness kept Tantric teaching out of the reach of the uninitiated and ensured that the *guru* (teacher) was essential to the system. Intentional language makes Tantra texts difficult for modern scholars to understand and there is uncertainty as to whether or not contemporary Tantra oral teaching reaches back in an unbroken line to medieval times. Nevertheless, there is a vast body of literature which gives evidence of Tantric theory and practice, as well as of internal debates among its proponents. Different Tantric sects follow different texts, but similar practice (*sadhana*) is found in the main texts such as *Guhyasamaya*, *Nityasoda-sikarnava, Kularnava*, *Yoginihrdaya*, *Malinivijaya* and *Tantraraja Tantra*.

CONTEMPORARY BELIEFS AND PRACTICES

Today the worship of Shakti is seen as a return to the source of life. Since the human body in Tantra is a concentrated microcosm of the universe, sexual union is viewed as a way of re-enacting creation, bringing the practitioners into harmony with the forces of the cosmos and enabling them to transcend all dualities (between clean and unclean, sacred and profane, male and female). By affirming evil as good, the devotee causes evil to lose its power.

The body is also seen as connected to a hidden inner universe (the 'subtle' body). All body parts and processes are linked to cosmic forces in a vast mystical network. By manipulating that part of the network to which one has access (the body), one can interact with the overall network (the universe). An uncontrolled universe leads to suffering, death and endless rebirth. For Tantrics, the human body is a means for attaining the highest levels of reality.

In Tantric yoga, women embody the mystery of the universe and hold the key to liberation. Every woman is an incarnation of Shakti (female power), the manifestation of divine creative energy. Tantrics also practise 'reversal' as a means of regaining what was lost after the creation of a bipolar universe. To realize this reversal, Tantrism developed a series of practices that break the usual taboos of Hinduism by indulgence in the five M's (*pancamakara*). In addition to ritual sexual intercourse (*maithuma*), these are: eating meat (*mamsa*); use of intoxicants (*madya*); eating fish (*matsya*); and eating parched grain (*mudra*). 'Left handed' (*vamacara*) Tantras practise the five M's literally and have therefore brought on themselves the wrath of some orthodox Hindus. In contrast, devotees of traditional Vedanta Hinduism practise 'right handed' (*daksinacara*) Tantra, in which the rituals are purely symbolic.

The Shakti principle is also called Kundalini; the Sanskrit word means 'coiled up'. Kundalini is believed to lie serpent-like at the base of the spine. Tantric practice of Kundalini yoga tries to awaken this cosmic energy and allow it to move along the spinal cord through the *chakras* (energy centres of the 'subtle' body) to be united with Shiva, bringing realization of non-duality and supreme consciousness.

Tantric practices vary. However, most devotees have an initiation (*diksha*) which can be given only by a *guru*, transmitting the esoteric doctrine in a one-to-one process. During the initiation the *guru* gives a particular *mantra* which has two purposes: it enables the disciple to concentrate and to internalize the ritual liturgy. *Nyasa* is the yogic practice which identifies the worshipper's body, part by part, with the deity. Thus the unlimited powers of the *mantra* (the 'seed' of the deity) supposedly enable devotees to appropriate the ontological essence of the deity to themselves in a physical, immediate fashion. Tantric ritual requires a *mandala*. This is a circle enclosing symbolic shapes. The most common of these is the *sri yantra*, a series of nine triangles within a circle, five pointing down symbolizing the female Shakti principle and four pointing up representing the male Shiva principle.

POPULAR TRADITIONS AND RELIGIOUS COMPARISONS

Tantrism has been compared to devotional groups (the movements of Sufi in Islam and Bhakti in Hinduism) who use human romance and sexuality as metaphors for the personal relationship between the worshipper and God. The Song of Solomon (with its celebration of physical love) in the Old Testament and the metaphor of the Christian church as 'the bride of Christ' in the New Testament (e.g. Rev. 19:6–9) use similar imagery for the love relationship between people and their God. However, Tantra views sexual union itself as a way of bringing the practitioner into harmony with the forces of the cosmos.

Like the Judeo-Christian tradition, and

unlike Brahmanical Hinduism and most forms of Buddhism, Tantrism affirms the good of the physical creation and male and female bodies. Tantrism does not scorn the world as illusion (*maya*) or a source of temptation and suffering, but embraces it as the material for enjoyment and enlightenment.

TANTRISM IN THE WEST

Sir John Woodroofe (A. Avalon) was the first non-Asian follower of Tantra to write (in the 1920s) on the subject for Westerners. However, Tantric ideas did not reach the popular imagination in the West until the 1984 film *Indiana Jones and the Temple of Doom*, in which the hero rescues the 'Shankara stone' from a Tantric sect and returns it to its rightful owners.

The most influential exponent in the West of spiritual experience through sex was Bhagwan Shree Rajneesh, who established an *ashram* near Pune, India, and in the 1980s bought a ranch in Oregon, USA. Rajneesh blended sex, mysticism and Jungian psychology into a monistic, anti-intellectual philosophy which disallowed the presence or possibility of evil.

Tantric ideas resonate with contemporary feminists in the New Age network because of the prominent place they give to the goddess Shakti. In much Tantric literature Shakti is supreme: without Shakti, Shiva can do nothing. Because Shakti was seen as the real force of the universe, Tantra subverted Shiva's superior role and located Shakti (also known as Parvati, Durga, Kali and all female divinities) at the top of the divine hierarchy, as the animating energy of all. Feminists have found here a theology for emancipation and empowerment. However, critics point out that the equality of sexes (as of castes) does not always extend beyond ritual practice. Likewise, some scholars point out that sexual love is not celebrated as intrinsically good (as in the Song of Solomon) but as a means towards the goal of enlightenment.

Aleister Crowley, an influential Western esoteric thinker, has been influenced by Tantra. Many contemporary Wiccan rituals parallel those of Tantra: group rituals include a priestess, or goddess incarnate, who initiates males through sexual union on a *mandala*-like circle.

At the most popular level, Tantric ideas are being disseminated throughout society by means of the plethora of self-help therapy literature found on the New Age and Neo-Pagan (or 'Body, Mind and Spirit') shelves of mainstream bookshops in the West. Titles such as *New Chakra Healing: The Revolutionary 32-Center Energy System* by Cyndi Dale (1996) and *Chakra Therapy: For Personal Growth and Healing* by Keith Sherwood (1997) are influencing a new generation of those who seek for spiritual truth, psychological healing, personal fulfilment or self-improvement.

BIBLIOGRAPHY

A. Avalon, *Introduction to Tantra Shastra* (Madras, 1955); D. R. Brooks, *The Secret of the Three Cities: An Introduction to Hindu Sakta Tantrism* (Chicago, 1990); D. G. Burnett, *Spirit of Hinduism* (Tunbridge Wells, 1992); M. Eliade, *Patanjali and Yoga* (New York, 1975); A. Rajneesh, *Neo-Tantra* (London, 1976); K. R. Sundarajan and B. Mukerji (eds.), *Hindu Spirituality: Postclassical and Modern* (London, 1997).

R. A. C. Bradby

HINDUISM (VAISHNAVISM)

Vaishnavism in its simplest form is the worship of the god Vishnu, who is a member of what is often called the Hindu Trinity, namely Brahman the creator, Vishnu the sustainer and Shiva the destroyer. Inasmuch as Vaishnavism reflects the non-exclusive worship of Vishnu in his many forms alongside worship of other deities, it is not possible to think of Vaishnavism as a religion in the same sense that Christianity and Islam are religions, but rather as one branch of a larger entity, Hinduism.

HISTORICAL OVERVIEW

In the oldest of the Hindu sacred writings, the *Rig Veda* (c.1200–900 BC), Vishnu is linked with the sun, which bathes the world literally with light and metaphorically with enlightenment (see *Rig Veda* 3.62.10). Later he is identified with Narayan ('cosmic energy'). He is called Ishwar, the Supreme Being, and is also known as Brahman. He becomes incarnate in nine *avataras* (literally 'descended ones'). A tenth *avatara* is awaited. The most prominent *avataras* of Vishnu are Rama (as he appears in the popular Hindu epic, the *Ramayana*) and Krishna (as seen in the section of the *Mahabharata* known as *Bhagavad Gita*, c.500 BC).

Drawing on ideas from folk culture, Vaishnavism developed into one of the major forms of Hindu devotion (Bhakti). Bhakti departed from the more philosophical Advaita Vedanta religion and culture by stressing the ideas of love and grace as early as the second century BC. Bhakti cults grew significantly from about the eighth century AD and were given systematic formulation by Ramanuja in the twelfth century.

Ramanuja opposed worship of the impersonal Brahman by stresssing the personal inadequacy, even self-abasement, of worshippers before their Lord. Bhakti was significant historically as a means of social fusion, a way of salvation (*moksha*) open to all castes and to women.

The sixteenth century saw the rise of reform and revival movements within Vaishnavism. Chaitanya (1486–1533) preached that the fulfilment of Bhakti was to be found in ecstatic love for God, while Vallabha (1478–1531) introduced the concept of Krishna and his consort Radha as the dual form of God, thus elevating the feminine principle. Both Chaitanya and Vallabha were active in the period after the Portuguese first landed in India (1498) bringing European influences.

PRIMARY SOURCES

The two principal *avataras* of Vishnu each figure prominently in one of the great Hindu epics. Rama is the hero of *Ramayana*, which tells of his love for Sita and his great conflict with Ravana. This story has been told in many forms in different languages, first by Valmiki in Sanskrit around the beginning of the Christian era, then by Kamban (twelfth century) in Tamil, Kritivas (fifteenth century) in Bengali and Tulsidas (sixteenth century) in Hindi. *Ramayana* was given a contemporary formulation in English by the erudite C. Rajagopalachari, the first President of independent India. Rajagopalachari gave a similar treatment to *Mahabharata*, including its best-known and loved section, the

Bhagavad Gita. Krishna here is a transcendent *avatara* of Vishnu, very different from the child Krishna and the lover of the *gopis* (milkmaids) portrayed in the other text greatly revered by Krishna devotees, namely *Bhagavata Purana*. Various versions of the *Bhagavata Purana* appeared in different parts of India from the ninth century onwards, and it exerted a powerful influence on both Chaitanya and Vallabha. Krishna and the *gopis* are portrayed also in the Tamil *Alvars* (sixth to ninth century), while the blind poet Surdas (b. 1478) was famous for his descriptions of the childhood of Krishna. The cult of Krishna has also inspired a large body of devotional poetry, prayers and songs.

CONTEMPORARY BELIEFS AND PRACTICES

One of the most important ideas in Hindu cosmology is that of the cycle of creation (Brahman), preservation (Vishnu) and destruction (Shiva). In this cycle, Brahman is responsible for creation, while Shiva is associated with destruction and all that leads up to it, including death (although the *lingam*, Shiva's most familiar representation, is also a symbol of divine creation). Both Brahman and Shiva hold sway outside the limitations of time and space: thus their personalities are not clearly distinguished in anthropomorphic terms. Vishnu, on the other hand, is more closely concerned with the day-to-day experiences of ordinary people. Vishnu preserves and sustains the world, sending, when needed, one of his *avataras*. These *avataras* save the world and teach the way of salvation (*moksha*): that is, release from the cycle of rebirth (*samsara*) and union with Brahman. Fulfilling one's duties (*dharma*) and right actions (*karma*) can lead to *moksha*.

However, in the broad spectrum of Hinduism, three paths can lead to salvation (*moksha*): the way of *jnana* (wisdom); the way of *karma* (works); and the way of *bhakti* (devotion). Most forms of Vaishnavism have followed the way of *bhakti* and some scholars have seen in *bhakti* a reaction against the inexorable process of cause and effect in *karma* and against the need for a priest as intermediary in Sanskritic Brahmanical traditions.

A key element of ritual worship (*puja*) in Vaishnavism is the representation of a deity. This can be a statue (*murti*) or a picture, or it may be aniconic (non-figurative). An aniconic representation of Vishnu is a *shalgram*, a spiral fossil shell which, it is believed, is sacred to him. Most Vaishnavite homes have a shrine (*mandir*), a simple shelf in a room or an entire room dedicated as a temple. Vaishnavites meet together informally in homes for *satsangs* (literally, 'in the company of truth') where *bhajans* (devotional songs) are sung; devotees are marked on the forehead with the coloured paste (*tilak*) of their sect and given sanctified food (*prasad*). Not all, however, follow the full ritual of their sect (*sampradaya*), preferring to focus on major festivals such as *Janmashtami* (the birth of Krishna) and *Diwali* (the Festival of Lights, celebrating Rama's victory over evil). In some forms of Vaishnavism, individuals become the focus of worship: for example, in the nineteenth century, followers of the Swaminarayan movement began worshipping the sect's founder, Swaminarayan, instead of Krishna or Vishnu as the supreme deity.

While Rama (or Ramachandra) is the most popular *avatara* of Vishnu in India, Krishna is more widely worshipped among business communities in the West. Krishna sects link purity and holiness with personal practice and initiation rites rather than caste and geographic location. Thus merchants and migrants can maintain spiritual purity wherever they are in the world. The acquisition of wealth is legitimated in the Krishna cult if this is done in the spirit of service to god, to whom the wealth is dedicated, and if it leads to service (*seva*) to the community. Vaishnavism is appropriate to the business community, for whom the pursuit of wealth is a caste duty (*dharma*).

RELIGIOUS COMPARISONS

The emphasis in the Bhakti strain of Vaishnavism on the love of the worshipper for God has parallels in Islam (the Sufi movement) and in the Judeo-Christian tradition: for example, the lovers in the Song of Solomon and Paul's image of Christ's love for the church as his bride (Eph. 5:25–27). The personal relationship of love between the devotee and his or her Lord also resembles the individualism of Protestant Christianity, particularly that of pietism. The ecstatic dancing and singing in some Vaishnavite groups also find echoes in the present day practices of some forms of charismatic Christianity.

Some Vaishnavite sources speak of the final *avatara*, which will be revealed at the end of the age, when Vishnu will appear as a man on a white horse with a flaming sword in his hand to judge the wicked and reward the good. There are parallels here with parts of the Christian Revelation of John (e.g. Rev. 19:11–15), and some scholars have speculated that these may be explained by the influence of Christianity in South India, possibly from the first century.

VAISHNAVISM IN THE WEST

Vaishnavism first became known in the West through the Theosophical Society (founded in 1875), which taught a blend of Hinduism, Buddhism and occultism. In 1893, Vivekananda (of the Ramakrishna Mission) visited the Parliament of the World's Religions in Chicago and became the first of many Indian teachers travelling to the West to propagate Hindu (including Vaishnavite) teachings. A third source of Vaishnavism in the West came at the turn of the century from the establishment of Indian communities in British colonies in South Africa, East Africa and the Middle East. From the 1940s to the 1970s large numbers from these groups moved into Europe.

More recently, the International Society for Krishna Consciouness (ISKCON), sometimes known as the Hare Krishna Movement, has won adherents among Westerners as well as from the immigrant communities. Founded by Swami Prabhupada in 1965, ISKCON taught a faithful version of Chaitanya's Vaishnavism: Krishna is worshipped not as warrior but as lover; not simply as an incarnation of Vishnu, but as the lord of the universe. The Swaminarayan movement, another Vaishnavite group, has expanded rapidly in the West, particularly among Gujarati communities.

Vaishnavite themes, blended in an eclectic mix with other spiritualities, are being diffused throughout Western culture through the New Age network. Vaishnavite iconography is well established in the Western media. Thus Vaishnavism has grown to become a powerful influence throughout the world. Even on the World Wide Web Vaishnavism is represented, with most sects and many devotees maintaining their own websites.

BIBLIOGRAPHY

R. Ballard (ed.), *Desh Pardesh: The South Asian Presence in Britain* (London, 1994); D. G. Bowen (ed.), *Hinduism in England* (Bradford, 1981); J. L. Brockington, *The Sacred Thread: Hinduism in its Continuity and Diversity* (Edinburgh, 1981); G. Flood, *An Introduction to Hinduism* (Cambridge, 1996); R. Gidoomal and R. Thomson, *A Way of Life: Introducing Hinduism* (London, 1997); K. Klostermaier, *A Survey of Hinduism* (Albany, 1994).

R. A. C. Bradby
R. Gidoomal

HINDUSIM (YOGA)

Yoga (Sanskrit: *yuj*; 'to yoke, harness, join') at its highest level is meant to lead to the silence of the mind (*citta*), allowing the union of the human and the divine within oneself. Thus it is designed as a way to wholeness, integrating all parts of the person.

More commonly, yoga is a set of theories and techniques in Indian religions which have the purpose of controlling consciousness to achieve liberation (*moksha*). By concentrating the mind, one can eliminate the subjective fluctuations of one's natural state (*prakrita*) to become literally 'well-made' (*samskrita*) and capable of supreme absorbed concentration (*samadhi*). This control of consciousness is taught by a *guru* and, it is claimed, may also result in paranormal powers (*siddhi*). Yoga is one of the six classical schools of Indian philosophy and has had an influence not just on Hindu spirituality, but on all forms of South Asian spirituality: Jain, Buddhist, Sufi (in Islam) and even Indian Christian spirituality.

HISTORICAL OVERVIEW

Scholars point to several possible sources of ancient yogic practice. The techniques of trance in the ecstatic spirituality of Shamanism in Central Asia (3000–800 BC) may have been a context for the development of yoga. The famous 'proto-Siva' seal from the Indus Valley civilization (c.2300–c.1750 BC) showing a figure sitting in a yoga-like posture also suggests a pre-Vedic origin. There are possible elements of yoga in the ancient Hindu text, the *Rig Veda*: the *Kesin* hymn to a long-haired, silent ascetic (*muni*) with paranormal powers (*RV* 10.136), and the reference to *tapas* (internal burning). *Tapas* is the internalization of the Vedic fire sacrifice, a force later linked to yoga as austerity (*RV* 8.59.6). The later *Atharva Veda* describes an ascetic group who practise special breathing exercises in unusual postures (*AV* 15).

The term 'yoga' first appears in the *Upanishads* (speculative Hindu texts expounding philosophical and religious ideas). In the *Katha Upanishad*, for example, yoga is compared to a chariot in which the self (*atman*) sits with reason as the driver of the chariot, the body (3.3–6). The *Svetasvatara Upanishad* emphasizes the link between breathing and thought (2.8–10), and the *Maitri Upanishad* lists the six stages of yoga: breath control (*pranayama*); sense-withdrawal (*pratyahara*); meditation (*dhyana*); concentration (*dharana*); contemplative enquiry (*tarka*); and absorption (*samadhi*). In the great epic the *Mahabharata*, especially the *Bhagavad Gita*, knowledge of yoga is assumed.

PRIMARY SOURCES

Yoga was expounded in its classical form in Patanjali's *Yogasutra*. Little is known about the author, Patanjali. Some have identified him with a second-century BC grammarian of the same name, but many scholars prefer to identify his work with the political stability of the Gupta Dynasty (AD 320–540), when Hindu literature, philosophy and religion were given classical expression in systematically formulated collections of aphorisms or *sutras* (literally 'threads'). These *sutras* in turn gave rise to elaborate published commentaries.

Patanjali himself acknowledged that he was compiling the older yoga traditions into what is now known as the *Yogasutra* (*YS* 1.1). Building on Samkhya ('disciplined knowing') philosophy, he added the theistic belief in Ishwara ('Lord'). This 'Lord', however, is not creative, not involved in the problems of the world and not an object of devotion. He is an aid in meditation much like the sacred syllable *aum*.

Patanjali defined yoga as 'the abolition of states of consciousness' (*YS* 1.2). He divided all consciousness into three classes: illusions and dreams; normal psychological states; and states induced by yoga. The *Yogasutra* consists of four chapters: the first is on the aim of meditation, absorption (*samadhi*); the second on practice (*sadhana*); the third on paranormal powers (*vibhuti*); and the fourth on blissful detachment from matter (*kaivalya*).

Much of the *Yogasutra* describes the eight 'limbs' (*ashtanga*) or disciplines needed to achieve *kaivalya*. The first is self-control (*yama*), defined as non-violence (*ahimsa*), truthfulness, not stealing, chastity and non-acquisitiveness. The second is observance (*niyama*), consisting of purity, contentment, austerity (*tapas*), study of scriptures, and devotion to the lord. The third is posture (*asana*). The fourth is breath control (*pranayama*), bringing breathing under the control of the will. The fifth is withdrawal (*pratyahara*) of the senses from their objects. The sixth is concentration (*dharana*), with normal senses suspended. The seventh stage, meditation (*dhyana*), is reached when the mind is concentrated on one point without distraction. The last stage, ecstasy or absorption (*samadhi*), is reached when one loses consciousness of meditation. It cannot be described in words but is regarded as a state of transcendent bliss, universal self-awareness, arising from total detachment from matter (*kaivalya*).

As the *yogin* works through these disciplines, signs of success (*siddhi*) appear which include, it is claimed, paranormal feats such as levitation. These signs of success are both an encouragement and a temptation to the devotee: they indicate successful practice but can also divert from the goal of the final stage, *samadhi*.

From the seventh to the eleventh centuries, many commentaries on the *Yogasutra* were written. Vyasa's *Yogasutrabhasya* ('Commentary on the Aphorisms of Yoga') and Vacaspatimisra's *Tattvavaisharadi* ('An Unerring Interpretation of the Principles of Yoga') are the most important of these, and with Patanjali's work form the authoritative exposition of yoga.

CONTEMPORARY BELIEFS AND PRACTICES

Patanjali's yoga is known as Raja Yoga. Most other forms of contemporary yoga use Patanjali's eight disciplines. Patanjali viewed the paranormal *siddhi* (signs of success), such as levitation, as distracting temptations. He was more concerned with the mind than with the body. However, from the seventh century, Tantrism (Tantric Yoga) viewed extraordinary physical powers, especially prolonged sexual intercourse (*maithuma*), as a route to enlightenment and oneness with ultimate reality. Tantrism influenced Hinduism, Jainism and Tibetan Buddhism, but also brought reactions from orthodox Hindus; all this may account for the variety of yoga systems which emerged and which are practised today.

Three yoga systems are mentioned in the *Bhagavad Gita*: Jnana Yoga, the discipline of knowledge, involving meditation on the Vedic scriptures and exalting mental effort in contrast to Karma Yoga, the discipline of everyday work and selfless action, and Bhakti Yoga, involving devotion to the Lord Krishna and using visualization and repetition of a word or phrase to concentrate the mind. Repetition of a word is also called Mantra Yoga and is found in other yoga systems. Each *mantra* comes from ancient Sanskrit and is chosen to suit the person. The word has no intrinsic meaning, but is believed to have a force created by the placement together of the syllables. The *yogin*, through repetition of the *mantra*, empties his mind and absorbs the force within himself.

Besides Mantra Yoga, the *Yogatattva Upanishad* refers to three other yoga disciplines which influence yogic practice today. The first, Laya Yoga, is the discipline of dissolution, in the contemplation of Ishwara (the 'Lord': the deity an individual has chosen to follow and worship). The second, Hatha Yoga, the discipline of force involves body exercise, posture and breathing techniques. Hatha Yoga leads to the third (and final) royal Raja Yoga of Patanjali.

YOGA IN THE WEST

Patanjali's work reveals a knowledge of the connection between physical and mental well-being long before this was discovered by twentieth-century Western psychology. Yoga influenced the development of Carl Jung's theories. Vivekananda, a disciple of the Hindu mystic Ramakrishna, was the first Hindu 'missionary' to come to the West when he visited the Parliament of World Religions in Chicago in 1893. He wrote books on Jnana Yoga, Bhakti Yoga, Karma Yoga and Raja Yoga which were popular with Americans and gave the West an accessible introduction to Hindu philosophy and spirituality. Mahatma Gandhi was probably the most famous *yogin* of the twentieth century. He practised Karma Yoga and continues to be a source of inspiration to many in the West, including some Christians.

Since the 1960s, the most influential yoga in the West has been a form of Bhakti Yoga called Transcendental Meditation (TM) founded by Maharishi Mahesh Yogi. The Maharishi came to Great Britain in 1958 and moved to the USA a year later. After the popular music group the Beatles began to practise TM, the number of people following TM increased dramatically. Hundreds of thousands of Westerners trained in TM in the 1970s. Although his teachings came largely from the *Bhagavad Gita*, the Maharishi claimed to teach a philosophy, not a religion.

TM uses the Bhakti Yoga technique of repeating *mantras*. The devotee sits with closed eyes for a period each morning and evening repeating his or her personal *mantra*. The mind becomes passive through this repetition and tension is released. TM has successfully adapted Indian spirituality to Western culture. Large corporations use its techniques to increase productivity of staff, and educators use TM to create a better learning environment. Many in the New Age network practise a form of yoga and it is used by devotees of the new religions: ISKCON (Hare Krishna Movement) practises Bhakti Yoga; the Three H (Happy, Healthy, Holy) Organisation practises Tantric Yoga; the Vedanta Society practises Jnana Yoga. Hatha Yoga is widely taught in most Western countries as a regime for physical and mental well-being.

THE CHRISTIAN AND YOGA

Yoga is a discipline found largely in Hinduism, but it is also present in Jainism, Buddhism and in some forms of Sufism (Islam). It can be argued that all believers in whatever tradition, including Christians, are, in a sense, *bhakti yogis*. However, because the aim of Bhakti Yoga is to realize the true self and escape the cycle of rebirth through devotion to a chosen deity, some Christians have argued that it is incompatible with the aims of Christian devotion: a deeper relationship with the God revealed in Christ and with the community of God's people. Christians also disagree with one another on the usefulness of yoga. Some argue that yoga can be a neutral physical discipline which can complement Christian faith. Others view yoga, particularly those types which involve paranormal and occult phenomena, as dangerous. Lastly, Christians in monastic traditions (the French Benedictine monk Jean-Marie Dechanet, for example) regard 'Christian yoga' as a helpful spiritual discipline.

BIBLIOGRAPHY

D. G. Burnett, *The Spirit of Hinduism: A Christian Perspective on Hindu Thought* (Tunbridge Wells, 1992); J. L. Brockington, *The Sacred Thread: Hinduism in its Continuity and Diversity* (Edinburgh, 1981); P. Y. Deshpande, *The Authentic Yoga: A Fresh Look at Patanjali's Yoga Sutras with a New Translation, Notes and Comments* (London, 1978); M. Eliade, *Patanjali and Yoga* (New York, 1975); G. Feuerstein, *The Philosophy of Classical Yoga* (Folkestone, 1982); S. Nikhilananda (ed.), *Vivekananda: The Yogas and Other Works* (New York, 1953); K. R. Sundarajan and B. Mukerji (eds.), *Hindu Spirituality: Postclassical and Modern* (London, 1997).

R. A. C. Bradby

HUMAN POTENTIAL MOVEMENTS

The idea that human beings are potentially very powerful is not new. The Hebrew Bible opens with the statement that women and men are made 'in the image of God' (Gen. 1:26–27), and one way of understanding the spiritual search of humankind is to see it as an effort to actualize that innate potential.

It is not hard to understand why the search for ultimate meanings that are internal to the human subject should have become especially popular in the course of the twentieth century. The rationalist-materialist philosophy promulgated by the European Enlightenment rendered belief in a transcendent God ever more problematic, while the scientific and technological revolution which it spawned proved incapable of providing a satisfying alternative lifestyle, and instead generated increasingly sophisticated forms of brutality, with even genocide and destruction of the planet becoming industrial processes. As the twentieth century proceeded, the need for a new paradigm became increasingly obvious, and since the traditional sources of wisdom and spiritual guidance appeared either to have failed or to have been discredited, it was inevitable that there would be a reversion to what Aldous Huxley once called 'the perennial philosophy'. Whenever materialist revelation has failed (whether secular or religious) Western culture has always reverted to an idealist, essentialist (and therefore timeless and universalist) way of understanding life. But whereas in the past this would typically have expressed itself as a form of mysticism in which cosmic processes took clear precedence over the needs of individuals, in post-Enlightenment culture this was no longer plausible. While the Cartesian reverence for reason may have been increasingly questioned, the notion that the autonomous rational individual is the key to all wisdom and understanding lost none of its appeal. In a world where people feel increasingly exploited and powerless (whether in their personal lives or in corporate or national terms), it is easy to appreciate the attraction of believing that individuals have within themselves the capacity to change things, if only they can discover the secrets that will enable them to tap into their inner persons and unlock the power that will help them to regain control of their lives.

It is not hard to find evidence of the ongoing search for ways of unleashing such hidden human potential. Many recent movies – not to mention popular children's television cartoon series – document the search for spiritual powers that will endow their heroes with extraordinary abilities, while celebrities talk openly about discovering their inner strength at times of crisis, and training courses for business executives teach managers to tune into the hidden depths of their unconscious minds in order to enhance their promotion prospects and increase the profitability of their corporations. At a time when people increasingly feel disempowered and threatened, anything that offers the possibility of regaining control is bound to be attractive. Therapies that are claimed to enable such self-transformation to take place include subliminal and neuro-linguistic programming, Transcendental Meditation, dreamwork and the use of electrical 'brain machines', along with more esoteric practices such as astral projection, out-of-body experiences and rebirthing. Anything that can induce apparently altered states of consciousness is likely to be deemed beneficial.

The theoretical basis for this search can be traced to Freud's understanding of the unconscious mind as a collection of repressed memories that, unless they are addressed, will prevent an individual from achieving psychological wholeness. When combined with Reichian and Jungian psychoanalytical ideas, including the notion of the collective unconscious understood as an individual's way of gaining access to some universal repository of cosmic wisdom, this has inspired the development of a host of techniques which, it is claimed, can empower people to tap into their unconscious minds and use their power to achieve personal transformation, power that Abraham Maslow and his associates working at the Esalen Institute (California) in the 1960s and 1970s identified as a 'slumbering god'.

It is necessary to differentiate between different manifestations of this concern. For example, the work of Norman Vincent Peale, who popularized the concept of 'the power of positive thinking', developed a system that was effectively a means of self-motivation, and the success of which is represented by an organization like Alcoholics Anonymous. Here, the interplay of mind and body is recognized, and by taking account of that, changes in personal behaviour can be both encouraged and achieved – in much the same way as an athlete might prepare mentally as well as physically for a race, or a student might envisage the final outcome of passing an exam, as a means of engendering application and concentration. Exploiting human potential in this way is religiously neutral, and as such can be judged purely on the basis of its effectiveness or otherwise. Given the sense of low self-esteem that Western culture has often engendered, in women in particular, the rediscovery of personal value through such methods can be applauded by all major religious traditions.

But, increasingly, the practices being promoted as pathways to enhanced performance also carry with them specific theological or spiritual baggage. An obvious example is Transcendental Meditation. More often, a kind of magical worldview underlies such practices, as highlighted in the work of Shakti Gawain, who writes that 'When we create something . . . the idea is like a blueprint: it creates an image of the form, which then magnetizes and guides the physical energy to flow into that form and eventually manifest it on the physical plane . . . If we are basically positive in attitude, expecting and envisioning pleasure, satisfaction and happiness, we will attract and create people, situations, and events which will conform to our positive expectations. So the more positive energy we put into imaging what we want, the more it begins to manifest in our lives' (*Creative Visualization*, pp. 19–20). This view is clearly a version of the classic occult principle, 'as above, so below, though in a different form', and the underlying assumption is that human will-power (in this case expressed through creative visualization) can actually change the nature of reality in some objective sense. In its contemporary manifestation, this emerges as a new 'physics of the mind', claiming that since positive subliminal affirmations can apparently influence an individual's life without much conscious effort ('mind over matter', the Freudian perspective), and since an individual's feeling, thought and intuition are deeply rooted in wider cosmic processes (the Jungian perspective, as developed through Maslow and transpersonal psychology), then an individual's thinking can also bring about alterations in the physical universe, because the interconnection between humans and the cosmos operates in both directions. This in turn means that we create the situations in which we live, and every individual can therefore choose to change them by taking responsibility for their own lives and uncovering the source of transformation through tapping into their deeper, unconscious self, taking appropriate initiatives to identify the methods that will produce the required change.

This notion of 'creating your own reality' is frequently described in terms of taking responsibility for one's own personal growth, and as such can seem morally neutral, or even positively praiseworthy. However, there are obvious ethical questions raised by the notion that individuals are totally responsible for the reality they experience. Taken to its logical conclusion, the idea that we have all chosen to be who we now are means that no-one need have a social conscience. Those who are poor and marginalized must have chosen to be that way, just as the rich and famous have. Moreover (and some human potential advocates do not hesitate to draw this conclusion) people afflicted with undeserved suffering must have brought it on themselves, or have chosen to experience it in order to achieve their own self-determined spiritual purposes. In such a worldview there is no place for the notion of objective evil, or the idea that people can be the victims of undeserved suffering, for if everyone chooses to do what they do, then cruelty, murder and rape are morally neutral actions, for we are all just playing a part in some vast cosmic drama.

BIBLIOGRAPHY

N. Drury, *The Elements of Human Potential* (Shaftesbury, 1989); D. S. Ferguson (ed.), *New Age Spirituality* (Louisville, KY, 1993); S. Gawain, *Creative Visualization: Use the Power of your Imagination to Create Whatever you want in your Life* (San Rafael, CA, 1991); E. Kurtz, *Not God: A History of Alcoholics Anonymous* (Minneapolis, 1991); B. Lancaster, *Mind, Brain and Human Potential* (Shaftesbury, 1991); N. V. Peale, *The Power of Positive Thinking* (London, 1990; originally 1952); J. Silva and P. Miele, *The Silva Mind Control Method* (New York, 1977); P. Telesco, *Wishing Well: Empowering your Hopes and Dreams* (Freedom, CA, 1997); F. A. Wolf, *The Body Quantum: Mind, Consciousness and Quantum Physics* (New York, 1984).

J. W. Drane

IMPLICIT RELIGION

Whereas the underlying concept is not new, the term 'implicit religion' has been popularized by the Revd Canon Professor Dr Edward Bailey, rector of an Anglican church in the parish of Winterbourne, near Bristol. His thinking on the subject was first developed in his 1984 thesis, entitled 'Implicit Religion of an English Parish', the research for which began many years earlier when he worked behind the bar in a public house.

Bailey observed the 'rite of the "entrance"', when 'all eyes turned to see who was coming through the door'; the 'ritual' of 'buying a drink'; the 'regulars', who 'are the pub'; the manager, who is 'the incarnation of it'; and the 'integrating focus', that 'of Being a Man, by dint of Holding your Own. In part this meant being able to master alcohol'. He further noticed, in 400 hours of observation, that 'only one person' simply came in for a drink because he was actually thirsty.

He has since applied similar observations to shopping malls and to the Church of England parish in which he served. He has noted the myths of association ('You get all types in a pub') and the 'sacramental' language ('Well, you see ... I believe in ... Christianity').

In 1978, Bailey began the Network for the Study of Implicit Religion, now a registered charity, which holds day-long seminars and annual conferences (often called the Denton Conferences because of their location in North Yorkshire). In 1997 he became the first Professor of Implicit Religion at the Centre for the Study of Implicit Religion and Contemporary Spirituality at the University of Middlesex. His inaugural lecture was held in the crypt in Lambeth Palace and was attended by the Archbishop of Canterbury. The Centre publishes the journal *Implicit Religion*, as well as promoting normal academic studies on the topic.

WHAT IS IMPLICIT RELIGION?

There is no single or simple definition of 'implicit religion', although Bailey suggests it 'assumes that the religiosity has not been articulated, or, perhaps more cogently, has not been understood (or is not conventionally understood) as religious'. Implicit religion is not implicit *Christianity* (it takes a much wider stance), nor is it *nominal* religion (it has no inherent structure).

Implicit religion is not the same as *civic* religion, although much civic religion has an implicit religiosity. The trappings of the established churches in Britain, such as civic services at high moments of state, the Lords Spiritual in the Upper House and the Parliamentary prayers said every day before proceedings begin, contain an implicit religion; in this case, an implicit Christianity.

Implicit religion is not necessarily the same as the *folk* religion that is seen, for example, in attitudes to, and the use made of, church bells. The fascination many have with these may reflect a religiosity associated with Christianity because most bells happen to be located in churches. When Terry Waite returned from nearly five years in captivity, church bells across the land were rung. Again, hundreds of church towers rang in the millennium; St Paul's bells rang all day. 'The ringing of church bells symbolises and gives a dense experience of the "over and beyond", the transcendent' (Pettersson, 1996), an experience shared by many Swedish people following the *Estonia* disaster.

Implicit religion is reflected in the many churchyards in the country and in municipal cemeteries. Each has its own character. Eric Gill's masonry is deemed 'proper' for a churchyard, with its sacralized religion, but a piece of granite in the form of a valentine card is considered more appropriate in a municipal graveyard. The idea of sleeping is often expressed in a municipal yard, perhaps reflecting a sense of uninterrupted continuation, whereas the future life is often more apparent in a churchyard, reflecting an expectation of coming change. Many who desire to be buried in a churchyard, if not churchgoers, at least went to Sunday school as children.

It has been suggested that our search for health is a form of implicit religion. Attitudes towards hospitals are similar to people's feelings towards God. 'Hospitals [are] indications of a final indomitable goodness.' 'It holds before me life and death and does not allow me to choose.' 'Both the hospital and God are taken on trust ... The fact that I don't understand doesn't worry me – the hospital understands and does so on my behalf.' In other words, attitudes to hospitals are indicative of a 'mystical religion, operating at a pre-cognitive level' (Grainger, 1987).

Implicit religion is sometimes reflected in commercial activities. In the autumn of 1995 Audi ran several advertisements with an implicit religious motif; for example, one had a model car between two lighted torches (as if on an altar) with the words 'worship here' underneath. In Britain, Littlewoods Pools did something similar to try to encourage people back in the face of the challenge from the National Lottery. Neither company would have bothered if there had not been something implicitly religious in those who saw the advertisements, to which they would appeal.

The way the British National Lottery is avidly followed each week and the number of tickets bought have led some to think of it in terms of a religion, an implicit (or invisible) religion. A similar kind of implicit religion may be seen in the following of Elvis Presley (the sacredness of mementoes and the pilgrimages to Graceland), in devotion to football, in the rituals involved in cooking and eating, and even in the pornographic page 3 photographs in the British tabloid newspaper the *Sun* (distinguishing between the sacred and the profane). All these subjects have been discussed at the Denton Conferences.

American sport (and doubtless that of other nationalities also) is considered by some to be folk religion because it consists of a 'distinctive set of myths, values and beliefs'. 'Sport ... projects values on to the culture with a normative certitude.' 'If I believe the myth that "sport builds character" then I will guide my children toward youthful athletic participation.' 'Sport's collective cultic observances [and] historical character function as a common religion' (Mathisen, 1988).

Implicit religion may reflect the impact of religion as seen in our art and music, words and phrases, or the names given to children, but this may not be a conscious reflection. Many may not now be aware of the biblical references in our great literature, such as the plays of Shakespeare, or in commonly accepted sayings such as 'pride goes before a fall'. Also still evident is the legacy of historical reformers such as Shaftesbury, Wilberforce and Elizabeth Fry, who influenced society by acting on their Christian principles. The impact of 48,000 church buildings on the UK landscape – about the same number as that of the 'pubs' – gives something of a religious presence at least. So do the many church schools and the chaplains working in the hospitals, prisons, armed forces, football clubs, city missions, department stores and elsewhere.

But all this is *external*. Implicit religion is *internal*; it is the religion of any person in the world, and what (s)he considers his or her religion to be. It is *emotional* rather than logical, felt rather than reasoned. It is *personal* not impersonal, and thus individualized, consistent with a postmodern world.

Implicit religion is perhaps seen most tangibly in the public responses to tragedies which affect whole communities and even nations. Often many people visit churches, leave flowers at the site of the tragedy, light candles or pay their respects in other ways. Such implicitly religious responses were made to the death of Diana, Princess of Wales, on 31 August 1997.

Implicit religion may not be to do with ‘sacredness’ *per se*, but it is to do with ‘spirituality’. It may not have anything consciously to do with God, though it may be God-given. The topic is gaining interest; it was discussed at the Church of England’s General Synod in 1997 and at the World Congress of Sociology at Montreal in 1998 and appears in syllabi for Religious Education.

BIBLIOGRAPHY

E. Bailey, *Implicit Religion: An Introduction* (London, 1998); R. Grainger, ‘Thoughts on the Search for Health as Implicit Religion’ (unpublished Denton Conference paper, 1987); J. A. Mathisen, ‘American Sport as Folk Religion’ (unpublished Denton Conference paper, 1988); P. Pettersson, ‘Implicit Religion Turned Explicit’ (unpublished Denton Conference paper, 1996).

P. W. Brierley

ISLAM (SHI‘A)

The Shi‘a represent the principal minority grouping within the world of Islam. Shi‘a numbers stood at around 90–100 million in the late 1990s, representing approximately 10% of the world’s Muslims.

The primary sacred sources for Shi’ite Islam are, as for the Sunnis, the Qur’an and the Traditions of the Prophet (*Hadith*). There is general agreement between Shi’ites and Sunnis on the authenticity of the existing form of the Qur’anic text. With regard to the Hadith collections, however, there is greater disagreement between the two groups. Shi’ites deny that the Sunni *Hadith* collections are reliable, claiming that they were based on reports which were produced by supporters of the Umayyad dynasty caliphs (AD 661–750) in order to undermine Shi’ite beliefs regarding leadership of the Muslim community.

Shi’ites have compiled their own commentaries on the Qur’anic text over the centuries. Similarly, Shi’ites have drawn up their own rich collection of literature on legal matters. Many parallels can be found between Shi’ite and Sunni law, despite the fact that Shi’ites draw on their own rather than Sunni *Hadith* collections as one of the principal sources of law. Nevertheless, specific differences exist between the two, such as that concerning temporary (*mut‘a*) marriage, which Sunnis reject, and that concerning the Shi’ite view of community leadership, which gives the Imams a far more integrated temporal and spiritual authority than they have among the Sunnis.

The emergence of the Shi‘a as a distinct group within the Islamic fold can be traced back to the earliest stages of Islamic history. With the death of Muhammad in 632, Muslim tradition relates that a group, known as the Party of 'Ali (*Shi'at 'Ali*), emerged to champion 'Ali's right to succeed as head of the Islamic community. A schism ensued, essentially concerning the question of whether the leader of the *umma* (community) should be elected or drawn from the family of the Prophet.

Over the centuries the Shi'a in turn evolved into three main sub-groups or offshoots. The Imamis, also known as the Ithna 'Asheris ('Twelvers'), are the most numerous by far of the Shi'ite groups. They consider the twelve successive Imams, spiritual leaders of their community and commencing with 'Ali, to be mortal but to be the inheritors of divine inspiration. Today Twelvers include most Iranians, most Iraqi Shi'ites and other groups in Syria and South Asia. They also include the Khoja Ithna 'Asheris, a group which according to its own traditions originated in India and converted from Hinduism in the fourteenth century.

The second group among the Shi'a are the Zaidis, who believe there is a limit of divine/right guidance on the degree to which God manifests himself within the Imams. They are particularly well represented among the Muslim population of Southern Arabia. The third Shi'ite offshoot includes the Isma'ilis, who recognize only seven Imams commencing with 'Ali and who currently regard the Aga Khan as the head of their community.

The martyrdom of the early Shi'ite Imams, and the continuous persecution which Shi'ites experienced at the hands of Sunni authorities over the centuries, led to the emergence of a persecuted minority mentality among the community, as well as a cult of martyrdom. However, rapprochement between Sunnis and Shi'a occurred in the twentieth century, with various pronouncements by Sunni and Shi'ite scholars accepting each other's jurisprudence as a valid alternative. An example can be seen in the *fatwa* issued by the Sunni scholar Mahmud Shaltut, Shaykh of Al-Azhar, on 6 July, 1959, which declared that 'The Ja'fari school of thought, which is also known as "al-Shi'a al-Imamiyyah al-Ithna 'Ashariyyah" [i.e. The Twelver Imami Shi'ites] is a school of thought that is religiously correct to follow in worship ...'

PRINCIPAL CONTEMPORARY BELIEFS AND PRACTICES

The articles of faith of the Shi'a conform essentially to Sunni belief. The Shi'a identify as key doctrines of Islam the oneness of God, belief in angels, prophets and messengers, revealed books, the Last Day and God's decree. However, they also emphasize divine justice as a core doctrine, as well as the *Imamah*, belief that the true leadership of the *umma* rests with the family of the Prophet through 'Ali.

On the issue of ritual, the Shi'a observe the same five pillars as the Sunnis: pronouncement of the creed; compulsory prayer; performance of the fast in *Ramaḏan*; charitable payments; and performing the pilgrimage to the holy sites in Arabia. Shi'ites also add *jihad* in its various forms (both military engagement and personal striving to be more devout) as a key pillar of Islamic practice.

The Shi'a have historically shown a greater willingness than the Sunnis to engage in *ijtihad*, or scrutinizing of the sacred sources to seek fresh answers to new challenges. In other ways also Shi'ite practice is distinctive. For the Shi'a there are supplementary sites for pilgrimage in addition to the holy sites in Arabia. These include the tomb of Husain at Karbala in southern Iraq and the tomb of the eighth Imam in Mashhad, Iran.

In festivals and religious holy days, the Shi'a can also point to distinctives. The festival of '*Ashura* is widely celebrated around the world among the Shi'a, including communities located in the West. This festival commemorates the martyrdom of Husain at Karbala in 681, and is marked typically by young Shi'ite men marching in procession and flagellating themselves as they march. This festival of self-punishment is one aspect of the Shi'ite cult of martyrdom mentioned above.

ENCOUNTERING MODERN AND POSTMODERN CULTURE

The substantial movement of Shi'ite populations into Western countries in the last quarter of the twentieth century has posed a number of challenges for the Shi'ites concerned. While accustomed to being a minority (more so than Sunni immigrants to the West), the Shi'ite newcomers nevertheless found that the majority now surrounding them did not share their belief in the Qur'an or the mission of Muhammad.

This situation has typically produced two responses from Shi'ite minorities in the West. First, some have energetically sought to affirm in an assertive manner their Islamic identity. They have done this by various means, establishing Shi'ite schools, mosques and a whole range of community groups. Many Shi'ites in the West have also committed themselves to *da'wa* (mission) activities, seeing this as a fulfilment of *jihad*, through striving to make their Muslim community more devout, as well as engaging in mission to non-Muslims among the surrounding majority community. Moreover, many have engaged in political activism: a good example of this is the establishment (with considerable support from Iran) of the Muslim Parliament of Great Britain and the Muslim Institute in London in the early 1990s.

The perception of the need for the first response has been fuelled by a second, competing response among Shi'a living in the midst of Western societies. A gradual but perceptible process of secularization has affected many Shi'ites; this is especially evident among the young in the West. It is strongly influenced by increasing secularization among Western youth, leading to a gradual loss of sectarian distinctiveness among the Shi'ite youth affected. Furthermore, intermarriage between young Shi'ites and Westerners is inevitably taking its toll on Shi'ite minority communities in Western countries.

There is marked diversity among Shi'ites in the West. Communities of Shi'ite immigrants have tended to cluster in specific locations in Western societies and have established mosques, schools and community organizations.

Britain is home to Shi'ites of various origin: Iranians, Lebanese, East African Asians and Pakistanis, comprising refugees, immigrants and students. Some have at times been in the forefront of political agitation: the most notable example was the Rushdie crisis, in which 28 Iranians were deported between March 1989 and January 1990. British Shi'ites have been particularly active in developing community structures and institutions. An example is the Shi'i Ithnasheri Community of Middlesex (SICM) centred in North Harrow, with a sizeable contingent of members from among the East African Shi'ite immigrants, which has established a registered charity and organizes weekly meetings and lectures. The community has bought the former North Harrow Assembly Hall and established the permanent SICM Centre. It has also secured a dedicated graveyard in Harefield and is planning to establish a library and information centre for increased *da'wa* activities.

France now hosts a sizeable population of Muslims, with the Shi'ite element comprising Twelver Shi'ites, principally Iranian refugees and immigrants, supplemented by Lebanese; Isma'ilis, whose world headquarters is located in Paris, with a Society for Isma'ili Studies; and small communities of Khojas and Bhoras originating from Mauritius and Madagascar and also based around Paris.

In *Germany* there are several centres of Shi'ite community life and worship. Shi'ites have set up an Islamic Centre in Hamburg, which belongs to the large umbrella body (the Central Council of Muslims in Germany) responsible for promoting Muslim concerns. Hanover hosts a community of around 3,000 Twelver Shi'ites, mostly refugees from Iran and Lebanon, but also including Iraqis, Turks, Azerbaidjanis, Pakistanis and Afghans. The community has established a mosque, which also runs Qur'an classes for children, and which has an Imam who originates from Iran. Both the Imam's stipend and the mosque's construction were funded by the local community. The Hanover community maintains links with the Shi'ite community in Hamburg as well as with another in Hagen.

Other Western European countries include Shi'ite groups among their Muslim minorities. In *Spain* most Shi'ites originate from Iran. They have established Shi'ite Islamic centres in Madrid, Barcelona and Granada. In the *Netherlands*, Turkish and Pakistani Shi'ite immigrants and refugees have established various types of facility, including a Shi'ite mosque in The Hague.

The Shi'ite presence in *North America* is increasing in numbers and improving in organization. One of the largest Shi'ite communities is located in Dearborn, Michigan. Established as the Islamic Center of America (ICA) in 1962, this community initially founded a small mosque and imported its first Imam from Lebanon. The current Imam, Hassan Qazwini, originates from Iraq and studied in the holy city of Qom, Iran, before being recruited by the ICA in 1998. He is overseeing an ambitious programme of expansion, focusing on the construction of a $15,000,000 mosque, with a 1,000-person prayer room and adjoining community centre. The ICA focuses on outreach to both Muslims and non-Muslims and publishes the periodical *Islamic Insights*. The community organizes local celebrations of *'Ashura*, runs public lectures and an Arabic school and maintains a website.

Elsewhere, California is home to over 500,000 Iranians, many of whom fled their country after the Islamic revolution in 1979. Shi'ite communities can also be found in other parts of the USA and typically seek to structure themselves into groups to preserve and pass on their community's social and religious distinctiveness. The Midwest Association of Shia Organized Muslims is centred in Chicago and is active in various sectors: worship; education; social life and events; and interfaith contacts and *da'wa*. The Kufa Center of Islamic Knowledge in Roanoke, Virginia, is registered with the local authorities as an Islamic non-profit organization and issues a monthly newsletter, runs a school and library, offers scholarships, sponsors orphans, maintains various charitable involvements and is active in *da'wa* to Muslims and non-Muslims. Such groups also exist in *Canada*, which also plays host to several communities of Isma'ilis who are active in promoting their brand of Shi'ite Islam through the sponsoring of conferences, the funding of awards and other activities.

CONCLUSION

It would be a mistake to think of Shi'ism in the West only with reference to national boundaries. The sense of worldwide community embedded in the Muslim concept of *umma* is also directly relevant to the Shi'a in the West. In a sense being a British Shi'ite as against a French Shi'ite is of little significance. What counts increasingly for many Shi'ites based in Western countries is their membership of international networks or community organizations. Hence Isma'ilis all around the world, in both the West and Muslim countries, look to their headquarters in Paris, mentioned above. Likewise the World Federation of Khoja Ithna 'Asheri Muslim communities has its secretariat based in Stanmore, London.

The decision of such groups to choose headquarters in the West is significant, for such bases are able to draw on resources from within local Shi'ite communities, as well as move ahead with international projects of expansion. Thus since its establishment in 1976, the World Federation of Khoja Ithna 'Asheri Muslim communities has raised funds, mainly in the West, to enable it to build centres (*jama'ats*) for communities of Twelver Khojas all around the world, including some in Western Europe and North America (e.g. Wessex, Peterborough, Milton Keynes, Stockholm, Washington, Paris, Toronto and Vancouver). This group claims a worldwide membership of only 105,000, which is testimony to the effectiveness of community organization. The World Federation of Khoja Ithna Asheri Muslim communities publishes the periodical *The Shia World*, has a major international conference every three years to plan worldwide activities, and raises funds among its members in the West for development projects among Khoja communities in the Third World.

BIBLIOGRAPHY

S. Z. Abedin and Z. Sardar (eds.), *Muslim Minorities in the West* (London, 1995); *Encyclopaedia of Islam* (Leiden, new edn, 1961–); J. L. Esposito (ed.), *The Oxford Encyclopedia of the Modern Islamic World* (New York and Oxford, 1995); H. A. R. Gibb and J. H. Kramers, *Shorter Encyclopaedia of Islam* (Leiden, 1974); J. Nielsen, *Muslims in Western Europe* (Edinburgh, 1992); G. Nonneman, T. Niblock and B. Szajkowski (eds.), *Muslim Communities in the New Europe* (Reading, 1996); M. S. Raza, *Islam in Britain: Past, Present and the Future* (Leicester, 1991); W. A. R. Shadid and P. S. Van Koningsveld (eds.), *Islam in Dutch Society: Current Developments and Future Prospects* (The Hague, 1992); *A Shi'ite Encyclopedia*, Version 2.0, http://www.al-islam.org/encyclopedia/, September 1999.

P. G. Riddell

ISLAM (SUFISM)

The mystical trend within Islam is known as Sufism. The derivation of the Arabic word *ṣufiyya* or *taṣawwuf* (from which we have 'Sufism') is uncertain. It is likely that it comes from *ṣuf*, 'wool', in reference to the woollen garment worn by the early Muslim mystics.

Sufism is a protest against orthodox Islam, in which people's relationship to God is essentially that of servants willingly submitted to their sovereign Lord, *rabb*. This relationship, based on obeying God's law in all its details and with all its external demands, could hardly quench the spiritual thirst of the human heart. Therefore, from early times, many Muslims have sought a deeper and more personal relationship with the Creator. Thus Sufism represents an alternative to Islam's rationalistic theology and law-centred religious life.

In its historical development Sufism has been influenced by Greek philosophy and Christian spirituality as well as Persian and Indian traditions. However, Sufism's main sources have always been the Qur'an and the *Hadith* or Prophetic Tradition. Muhammad himself had his first revelation when he was living a secluded life in the cave of Hira near Mecca (cf. Bukhari, *Sahih* 'bad' al-wahy' 3; Arab.–Eng. edn [Beirut, 1985] vol. I, p. 2, no. 3). Later, in spite of his busy career, he was often drawn to solitude and fasting.

THE GOD OF THE SUFIS

In reaction to Islamic theology's emphasis on God's transcendence, Sufis focus on the immanent God whom they find depicted in many Qur'anic texts. God is portrayed as 'the First and the Last, the Evident and the Immanent' (57:3; ET Y. Ali). He is nearer to his human creatures than their jugular vein (50:16) and he is with them wherever they go (57:4). Not only is God so close to people (cf. 2:186), but he also loves them and expects them to love him too (2:165; 3:31; 5:54). One of 'God's most beautiful names' is *al-wadud*, which is understood by many Sufis as 'the Loving One'. God is also 'the Merciful One', *al-rahman*, and his mercy is emphatically stated at the beginning of all Qur'anic *suras* (*sura* 9 excepted): 'In the Name of God, the merciful Lord of mercy' (ET K. Cragg, *Readings in the Qur'an*, London, 1988). God's mercy is greater than that of a mother for her children (cf. Bukhari, *Sahih* 'adab' 18; Arab.–Eng. edn, vol. VIII, p. 19, no. 28). The God of the Sufis loves his people so much that he somehow identifies with them. This is how Muslim mystics have understood a famous *hadith qudsi* (i.e. a saying in which Muhammad is acting as God's spokesman) known as *hadith al-nawafil* or 'the *hadith* about supererogatory deeds': 'I will declare war against him who shows hostility to a pious worshipper of Mine. And the most beloved things with which My slave comes nearer to Me is what I have enjoined upon him. And My slave keeps on coming closer to Me through performing *nawafil* till I love him, so I become his sense of sight with which he sees, and his hand with which he grips, and his leg with which he walks; and if he asks Me, I will give him; and if he asks my protection I will protect him; and I do not hesitate to do anything as I hesitate to take the soul of the believer, for he hates death, and I hate to disappoint him (Bukhari, *Sahih* 'riqaq' 38; Arab.–Eng. edn, vol. VIII, p. 336, no. 509).

Thus the loving God is intimately united with his devout servants. This union fulfils God's purpose in creating humankind: 'God created Adam in his own image' (cf. Bukhari, *Sahih* 'isti'dhan' 1; Arab.–Eng. edn, vol. VIII, p. 160, no. 246; Muslim, *Sahih* 'birr' 115; Eng. edn [New Delhi, 1977], vol. IV, p. 1378, no. 6325 and 'janna' 28; vol. IV, p. 1421, no. 6809). The whole approach of the Sufis is characterized by this spiritual and more personal understanding of Islamic teaching. If ordinary *jihad* means fighting against the enemies of Islam, the greater holy war consists in fighting against oneself; as the Prophet said: 'The *mujahid* [or 'fighter'] is he who fights against his own soul' (Tirmidhi, *Sahih* 'fada'il al-jihad' 2).

THE SUFI PATH

For the Sufis God's most cherished name is *al-Haqq* or 'the Truth' (cf. Qur'an 18:44; 22:6, and 62; 24:25; 31:30). The Sufi aim is to know the ultimate Truth not intellectually but existentially. This experiential knowledge is called *ma'rifa*. It is attained through following the way, *tariqa*, that leads to God. The spiritual pilgrimage consists in reaching God, not just going to his house (i.e. the *Ka'aba*). This pilgrimage is made through different stages (*maqam*); at each stage the pilgrim acquires a new spiritual state (*hal*). This is not a solitary journey, for the Sufis live in communities in which the *shaykh* or spiritual leader plays a decisive role.

Traditionally there are seven stages, though some Sufi treatises vary as to the number of the stages and their nature.

However, all Sufis agree that the first stage is *tawba*, a word which literally means 'to turn' or 'to return'. Often in the Qur'an *tawba* refers either to the conversion of non-Muslims to Islam (cf. 5:33–34) or to the renunciation of sin by Muslims (cf. 24:31). The Sufis understand this word in the sense of Muslims converting to God (cf. 66:8). All people, including Muslims, they claim, need to 'turn back' to God in response to the Qur'anic call: 'Believers! Turn to God in sincere repentance. Your Lord may absolve you of your evil doings and bring you into gardens where streams flow' (66:8; ET K. Cragg, p. 244). Indeed, many Sufis (including those who have been practising Muslims) tell how they have been converted to God through a dramatic experience.

When Sufis reach the final stage they gain a double state: extinction of selfhood (*fana'*), and subsistence with God (*baqa'*): 'Passing-away is a state in which all passions pass away, so that the mystic experiences no feelings towards anything whatsoever, and loses all sense of discrimination: he has passed away from all things, and is wholly absorbed with that through which he has passed away' (A. J. Arberry (tr.), *The Doctrine of the Sufis* [Cambridge, 1935, repr. 1977], p. 120). This supreme experience is the privilege of the saints (*awliya'*). Otherwise, people are divided into two main categories: the Common, *al-'awamm* (those who have not started their journey), and the Elect, *al-khawaṣṣ* (those who are on their way to God).

JESUS IN SUFISM

Jesus is highly respected by Sufis, who consider him one of their leaders. Ibn 'Arabi (d. 638 AH/AD 1240) describes Jesus as 'the Seal of the Saints', as distinct from Prophet Muhammad, who is, according to the Qur'an (33:40), 'the Seal of the Prophets'. The Spanish-born mystic speaks of his relationship with Jesus as follows: 'I had many encounters with him in my visions; it is he who converted me and he prayed for me that I may persevere in religion in this world and the next. He called me "the beloved one" and he commanded me to practise asceticism, *zuhd*, and deprivation, *tajrid*' (*al-Futuḫat al-makkiyya* [1911, repr. Beirut, 1980], vol. II, p. 49).

The Jesus of the Sufis, however, remains much closer to the Qur'anic teaching than to that of the gospels. In many ways the Sufi understanding of God is similar to Christian teaching. On the other hand, the fact that the Sufi God is not the Triune God means that very often Sufis do not acknowledge the radical and defining difference between God the Creator and the world he has created. Thus, like that of many others, Ibn 'Arabi's mysticism is rooted in his *waḫdat al-wujud* or monism (i.e. the doctrine that God and the universe partake of the one and same essence). Referring to his perfected union with God, Ḫallaj (d. 309 AH/AD 922) declared *ana l-Ḫaqq*, 'I am the Truth (or God)'. He was subsequently condemned for blasphemy and hung on a gibbet by Muslim authorities. Ḫallaj had yearned for this death, which he considered a sacrificial offering for the sake of his people. 'I am going to die', he had said, 'according to the religion of the Cross' (see L. Massignon, *Hallaj: Mystic and Martyr* [abridged edn, Princeton, NJ, 1994], pp. 64–71, 273–275, 292).

SUFISM TODAY

Sufism's golden age spanned from the third to the seventh century of Islamic history (the ninth to the thirteenth century AD). But Sufism has never ceased to attract a large number of Muslims as well as non-Muslims. In many parts of the world (e.g. Sub-Saharan Africa, Central Asia, Southeast Asia) Sufi brotherhoods played a key role in the spreading of Islam. What is known as 'folk Islam' often originates in a living Sufi tradition which has degenerated over the years.

Today there is a revival of Islamic mysticism in different places, including some parts of Europe. European converts to Islam include the Jewish-born Léopold Weiss, alias Muhammad Asad; the French choreographer Maurice Béjart; the British singer Cat Stevens, alias Yusuf Islam; the German writer Ahmad von Denffer; and the French scholar Michel Chodkiewicz. These people became converts because they were attracted by the spiritual side of Islam, though not all of them were members of a Sufi brotherhood. People come to know spiritual Islam through various channels: Sufi brotherhoods, literature, art or philosophy. Ibn 'Arabi's theosophical mysticism seems to attract a number of intellectuals, although his influence is not confined to the academic elite.

Several factors explain the resurgence of Sufism. People disenchanted with secular culture, and sometimes with Western Christianity, find in Sufism what the church is meant to represent: a spiritual alternative to a materialistic and individualistic society. Western scholarship, together with growing Islamic activity, have contributed to the presentation of Sufism as an attractive option, and it appeals to many in a postmodern society. Sufism is often seen by its adherents not just as the vibrant soul of Islam, but as a universal spirituality; conflicting claims of Christianity and Islam are transcended in God who is said to be beyond theological definitions. Islamic mysticism is also understood as a humanistic spirituality. It is based on people's shared humanity and their common longing for the one who is paradoxically 'closer to them than themselves' (Ibn 'Arabi's commentary on Qur'an 56:85). Sufism's emphasis on experiential knowledge is another reason for its popularity. In an age characterized by a search for strong emotions, Sufism offers everyone the possibility of knowing God deep within one's life.

BIBLIOGRAPHY

A. J. Arberry, *Muslim Saints and Mystics* (London, 1966); M. Chodkiewicz, *The Seal of the Saints: Prophethood and Sainthood in the Doctrine of Ibn 'Arabi* (Cambridge, 1993); M. Lings, *What is Sufism?* (London, 1975); C. E. Padwick, *Muslim Devotions* (Oxford, [2]1996); A. Schimmel, *Mystical Dimensions in Islam* (Chapel Hill, NC, 1975); J. S. Trimingham, *The Sufi Orders in Islam* (Oxford, 1971).

C. G. Moucarry

ISLAM (SUNNI)

ORIGINS

Sunni Muslims represent 90% of the Muslim community, which numbers over one billion people. Thus Sunni Islam is mainstream Islam, and Sunni Muslims consider Shi'a or Khariji Muslims as non-orthodox Muslims.

The historical divide between Sunni and non-Sunni Muslims originates in the disagreement over the succession of Muhammad following his unexpected death.

Those Muslims who acknowledged the legitimacy of the four 'Rightly Guided Caliphs' were later known as Sunnites, whereas Muslims who recognized only the right of the fourth Caliph 'Ali (Muhammad's cousin and son-in-law) to succeed to the Prophet were called the Shi'a (or Shi'is).

The adjective 'sunni' derives from *sunna*, which means 'way', 'practice' or 'tradition'. The Qur'an speaks of God's *sunna* (i.e. the way he deals with people), which is unchangeable (33:62; 35:43; 48:23). Sunnism, however, refers to the Prophet's *sunna*: in other words, to the teaching and the life of Muhammad, who is described in the Qur'an as 'an excellent example' for all Muslims (33:21). The Prophet's way of living as a Muslim is known through the *Hadith* or Prophetic Tradition, which records the sayings and the actions attributed to Muhammad. Therefore Sunni Muslims consider the *Hadith* (of which there are nine 'canonical collections') as a major source for Islamic religion, and its authority is second only to the Qur'an. Shi'a Muslims do not credit the *Hadith* with such authority and they have their own records of the Prophetic Tradition. Insofar as Sunni Islam relies on the *Hadith* it can be characterized as 'traditional Islam', in contrast with Shi'a Islam, in which the Imam (i.e. the leader of the community) is the central figure.

FAITH AND PRACTICE

The faith (*iman*) of all Muslims, Sunni and Shi'a alike, is traditionally summed up in five articles which we find enumerated in the second part of the following Qur'anic verse: 'Believers! Believe in God and in His apostle, and in the Book which He has sent down upon His apostle and in the Book He sent down aforetime. Whoever repudiates faith in God, and His angels, His Books and His messengers, and in the last Day, has indeed gone far into error' (4:136, tr. K. Cragg, *Readings in the Qur'an* [London, 1988], p. 295).

Islam (the word means literally 'submission' or 'surrender', i.e. to God) is based on the following five pillars, *arkan*: confession of faith (*shahada*), which consists in reciting Islam's shortest creed, 'There is no god but God and Muhammad is God's Apostle'; ritual prayer (*ṣalat*), performed five times a day facing Mecca; statutory almsgiving (*zakat*), which is a solidarity tax; fasting (*ṣawm*), in the month of *Ramaḏan*; and pilgrimage (*ḥajj*) to Mecca.

According to the Qur'anic account (2:127), while in Mecca Abraham and his son Ishmael built *al-Ka'ba*, a sanctuary which owes its name to its cubic configuration. Some Muslims consider holy war (*jihad*), as Islam's sixth pillar, just as predestination is sometimes seen as the sixth article of faith (cf. Muslim, *Ṣaḥiḥ* 'iman' 1; Eng. edn [New Delhi, 1977], vol. I, p. 1, no. 1; Abu Dawud, *Sunan* 'sunna' 16; Eng. edn [Lahore, 1984], vol. III, p. 1315, no. 4678). Sunni Muslims have two major festivals (*'id*). The first is the festival of Sacrifice (*'id al-aḏḥa*), in which they commemorate Abraham's sacrifice. Although the Qur'an does not specify the name of Abraham's son, whom God redeemed 'with a great sacrifice', most Muslims believe him to be Ishmael (cf. 37:99–111). The second is the Breakfasting festival (*'id al-fiṯr*), which marks the end of the month of *Ramaḏan*.

Muslim theologians are divided over the respective roles of faith and deeds in defining one's religious identity: is a non-practising Muslim still to be seen as a Muslim? The Kharijites and Mu'tazilites equate believing in God with obeying his law; for them, therefore, a sinful Muslim (*fasiq*) is not a Muslim. Mainline Sunni theologians consider that a disobedient Muslim is still a Muslim. As they define faith basically in terms of trusting God (*al-taṣdiq bi-llah*), they claim that as long as people sincerely adhere to the Islamic doctrine they are Muslims, regardless of their compliance with God's law. This is not just an academic debate. If, rightly or wrongly, some Muslims are no longer seen as Muslims but as unbelievers or (even worse) apostates, then radical Muslims may consider it their duty to oppose them and possibly to wage holy war against them. In recent years the outworking of this view has been seen in the Salman Rushdie affair and, on a much larger and more dramatic scale, in civil wars in Algeria and Afghanistan.

GOD IN ISLAMIC THEOLOGY

The first article of faith and the first pillar of Islam are both about the oneness of Allah, which is the Arabic word for God used by Muslim and Christian Arabs alike. Islam is first and foremost a theocentric religion. The unity of God is emphatically proclaimed in *sura* 112: 'Say: He is God, One, God the ever self-sufficing, unbegetting, unbegotten. None is like to Him' (ET K. Cragg, p. 87). The Qur'an speaks of 'God's most beautiful names' (cf. 7:180; 17:110; 20:7; 59:24). According to Islamic tradition these names are ninety-nine (cf. Bukhari, *Sahih* 'tawhid' 12; Arab.–Eng. edn [Beirut, 1985], vol. IX, p. 363, no. 489).

In Sunni theology, exemplified by the Ash'arite school, which derives its name from al-Ash'ari (d. 320 AH/AD 930), sovereignty is God's paramount attribute. This is in line with many Qur'anic texts (e.g. 21:23: 'He cannot be questioned for His acts, but they will be questioned [for theirs]'; ET Y. Ali). In other words, God has the right to do whatever he wants. The ultimate outcome of such an emphasis on God's arbitrary authority is fatalism, which is rife in many Muslim countries. In contrast, Mu'tazili theologians have stressed that God's justice is his overarching attribute; hence their whole approach seems much more rationalistic. Many modern Muslim writers appear to be more in tune with Mu'tazilite theology than with traditional Islamic teaching.

God's transcendence is another major divine attribute in Islamic theology. Unlike the Bible (cf. Gen. 1:26), the Qur'an does not say that God created humankind in his own image. Islamic scripture claims the opposite: 'There is nothing whatever like unto Him' (42:11; ET Y. Ali). In the *Hadith*, however, there is a narrative parallel to Genesis (cf. Islam [Sufism]), but Muslim theologians have given it a minimalist interpretation. The Islamic understanding of God's transcendence rules out the Christian doctrine of the incarnation. Muslims believe that Jesus is one of God's greatest prophets but he is certainly not the Son of God. Thus the Christian teaching about the divinity of Christ amounts to *shirk*, which in Islam means associating a creature with God. This is the only sin that God will never forgive: 'God forgiveth not that partners should be set up with Him; but He forgiveth anything else, to whom He pleaseth' (4:48; ET Y. Ali).

ISLAMIC JURISPRUDENCE

Islam is a law-based religion. The *Shari'a* plays a key role in regulating the relations of Muslims in society as well as their relationship with God. In addition to the Qur'an and the *Sunna* of the Prophet (as preserved in the *Hadith*), Islamic law has two other sources: the *ijma'*, or consensus of the Muslim community, and the *qiyas*, or analogical reasoning. Sunni Islam recognizes four orthodox schools of jurisprudence. They are named after their founders: the Hanafi school founded by Abu Hanifa (d. 150 AH/AD 766), the Maliki school by Malik ibn Anas (d. 179 AH/AD 795), the Shafi'i school by Shafi'i (d. 204 AH/AD 820) and the Hanbali school by Ahmad ibn Hanbal (d. 239 AH/AD 855). The second and the fourth of these jurists were also 'traditionalists' who each provided a compilation of the Prophetic Tradition. Islamic jurisprudence groups human actions into five categories (*ahkam*), according to the degree of their conformity with the teaching of the law: required, recommended, indifferent, reprehensible, and unlawful. This codification of human life has left a great number of Muslims with deep spiritual frustrations. Many have sought for an alternative, which some have found in Sufism or Islamic mysticism.

ISLAM TODAY

In trying to respond to present-day challenges, Muslims have adopted different approaches. Some have advocated a more rigorous enforcement of Islamic teaching on Muslim societies, so as to resist both secularism and nationalism. Their aim is to vindicate the *Umma*, or the Muslim community worldwide. This option, known as Islamic fundamentalism, feeds on the economic, social and political frustrations felt by many Muslims. Other Muslims (e.g. M. 'Abduh, I. al-Faruqi) have pleaded for major reforms within the Muslim community, so that Islam may offer a credible alternative to both fundamentalism and atheism. Finally, there have been a few Muslims who have called not just for reform but for radical changes and a critical examination of Islamic beliefs. This emerging movement, championed by scholars such as the Algerian-born Parisian Professor Mohammed Arkoun, challenges traditional Islamic teaching in key areas, for instance revelation and scripture, the role of man and woman, and the relationship between Islam and the state.

BIBLIOGRAPHY

A. Ahmed, *Islam Today: A Short Introduction to the Muslim World* (London, 1999); I. al-Faruqi, *Islam and other faiths* (Leicester, 1998); M. Arkoun, *Rethinking Islam: Common Questions, Uncommon Answers* (Boulder, CO, and Oxford, 1994); H. Corbin, *History of Islamic Philosophy* (London, 1993); C. Kurzman (ed.), *Liberal Islam: A Sourcebook* (New York and Oxford, 1998); S. A. A. Mawdudi, *Let us be Muslims* (Leicester, 1985).

C. G. Moucarry

JAINISM

Not only is it one of the oldest religions in the world, dating as far back as the sixth century BC if not earlier, Jainism is also one of the least well known.

BASIC BELIEFS

According to Jain cosmology there is no supreme being or creator God. The occupied universe, consisting of upper, middle and lower worlds, is surrounded by an infinity of empty space. At the apex of the upper world in the supreme heaven are the *siddhas* (perfected beings), who have attained *moksha* (liberation). The universe consists of two eternal realities, which are *jiva* (sentient) and *ajiva* (non-sentient). *Jivas* are embodied souls, which are eternal. The body inhabited by the *jiva* is determined by its *karma* in previous lives. This results in a hierarchy of beings which includes humans, animal and plant life, but ranges far wider to include celestial beings and hellish beings. The ultimate aim of *jivas* is to achieve liberation and attain to the abode of the *siddhas* and *tirthankaras* (lit. 'crossing-makers', teachers and exemplars who help others achieve the same goal). *Ajiva* (non-soul) consists of everything in the universe that is insentient, including all matter and the principles of space, time, motion and rest.

Human beings live in the middle world of the inhabited universe. In the upper world are fourteen heavens graded according to their perfection and in the lower world are seven hells of increasing misery. Only from the middle world of human existence can the *jiva* achieve liberation.

In the present cycle of time Jains believe that there are twenty-four *tirthankaras*, who help *jivas* to cross the ocean of *samsara* (i.e. to escape the cycle of birth and rebirth). The last of these is known as Mahavira ('great hero'), the title given to Vardhamana for achieving enlightenment without assistance from any other being. It is a mistake to think that Jains believe their religion to have been founded by Mahavira. Jainism is said to be eternal and Mahavira (b. c.599 BC) is revered as the last to gain liberation in this era. Mahavira achieved enlightenment, or a state of complete omniscience (*kevalajnana*), after twelve years of intense ascetic practices. He is called a *jina* ('victor'), one who has conquered self. The word 'Jain' comes from the same word *jina*, as does the Jain greeting, *Jai Jinendra*, meaning 'honour to those who have conquered'.

Like his near contemporary Buddha, Mahavira was born a prince of the warrior caste in the part of India we now call Bihar. Like Buddhism, Jainism criticized the ritualism of the priestly caste, and parted from Hinduism in denying the existence of *Brahman* (the Supreme Being). However, unlike Buddhism, it retained belief in *atman*, the eternal soul present in all living beings. Jains believe that the enlightenment achieved by Mahavira was superior to that of Buddha, because it resulted in a state of absolute omniscience, a knowledge of everything in space and time, whereas Buddha taught that all that was necessary was the knowledge of the way to *nirvana*. Jains believe, as do Hindus and Buddhists, in the principles of *karma* and rebirth and in *moksha* as the goal of release from the cycle of birth, death and rebirth (*samsara*). According to Jainism the path to liberation passed on by Mahavira consists in a process of renunciation, involving a rigorous regime of ascetic practices based on *ahimsa*, or non-violence, toward all living things, including plant and insect life, which can be pursued to its final stages only by monks and nuns. For example, monks and nuns brush the path before them as they walk in order not to step on small creatures such as insects.

SCRIPTURES

Jain scriptures contain the teachings of Mahavira and other *tirthankaras*. They were transmitted orally and were not written down for many centuries. In that process some were lost. By the fifth century the Shvetambara Jains had collected forty-five extant texts into a canon, the *Siddhanta*, the oldest and most revered of these texts being the *angas*. The *angas* are mostly early sermons, sayings of Mahavira and accounts of monastic discipline. However, not all Jains recognize the authority of the forty-five texts of the *Siddhanta*. For example, whilst the Digambara Jains accept that these texts convey much that is doctrinally sound, they claim that they lack authenticity. The normative texts of the Digambaras are two ancient Prakrit texts, the *Shatkhandagama* and the *Kashayaprabhrta*.

HISTORY

Mahavira organized the Jain community (*sangha*) into the fourfold order of monks, nuns, laymen and laywomen. Between the third and fifth centuries AD two main traditions arose, the Shvetambara and the Digambara. The majority of Jains are Shvetambara (white-robed). The monks and nuns in this tradition wear three pieces of white clothing and carry a begging bowl and a whisk to avoid harming insects. Included in the Shvetambara are the Sthanakvasis and their sub-group the Terapanthis, both of whom are strictly against image worship and are well known for wearing a piece of cloth over their mouths to avoid breathing in the tiniest insects. Digambara monks have no property and renounce clothes and begging. Because of the restrictions on travel placed upon both them and the Shvetambara monks, neither can travel abroad, so that leadership of the community outside India devolves on lay scholars and teachers.

CURRENT PRACTICES

Ahimsa, or non-violence, is the central ethical teaching of Jainism. This is the first of the five vows to which monks and nuns are expected to adhere; lay people observe this teaching in a modified form. Because there are *jivas* in every living thing, harm to all forms of life must be avoided. This principle affects not only the Jain diet but also the employment that a Jain accepts. Other vows include the following: truthfulness in order not to harm; not taking what belongs to another; avoiding sexual promiscuity; and non-attachment to material things.

Jains do not worship a supreme being, but they do have shrines at home and in temples. They are expected to chant *mantras* three times a day, which include paying homage to the *tirthankaras* and teachers. The temples usually include images of the *tirthankaras*, though Sthanakvasis remove all images and meditate in plain halls.

The most important Jain festival is the eight-day festival of *Paryusana Parva*, which occurs in August or September and is a time for fasting. The Hindu festival of *Diwali* is celebrated, as it marks the anniversary of the liberation of Mahavira. There are also festivals marking the anniversaries of the birth and death of Mahavira.

JAINISM IN THE WEST

The estimated Jain population in the world is five to eight million, of whom the vast majority live in India. Since the last century, Jains have migrated, especially to East Africa. Since the Second World War, Jains have moved to Europe and America. There are about 30,000 Jains in the UK and about 50,000 in North America.

Cut off from the religious leadership of their monks and nuns, who are unable to travel out of India, Jains in the West have had to adapt to new conditions by relying on lay leaders and by unifying their sects. The Jain Centre in Leicester (UK) is one product of this adaptation. The centre is a unique combination of Shvetambara, Digambara and Guru Gautama temples, as well as Sthanakvasi and Shrimad Rajchandra meditation halls.

Marcus Banks identifies two significant trends in belief among Jains in England. He calls these ‘heterodoxy’ and ‘neo-orthodoxy’, as distinct from ‘orthodox’ practice in India. By ‘heterodoxy’ he means the trend toward theism, which involves seeing the *tirthankaras* as manifestations of a supreme deity with the ability to intervene in human life and give devotees their assistance. This leads to *bhakti*-style worship, in which God is the focus of devotion. It is not surprising that Jains who worship in this way are willing to attend Hindu or Sikh temples. Indeed, this theistic trend comes from Hindu influence.

‘Neo-orthodoxy’ refers to those who think of themselves as modern and progressive, in touch with scientific and rational thought and therefore well adapted to the West. According to Natubhai Shah, ‘Jainism has a basis in logic and science which makes it relevant to the modern age’

(*Jainism*, vol. 1, p. 267). Prominent among the key ideas associated with this modernist trend are vegetarianism and the importance of a balanced diet for mental health; non-violence; ecology; animal welfare; meditation as opposed to ritualism; and the downplaying of strict asceticism and sectarian divides. The American-based *guru* Chitrabhanu exemplifies this approach. He was a Shvetambara monk who left his order after many years and married one of his disciples before setting up the International Jain Meditation Centre in New York. His eclectic brand of teaching denies the necessity of strict asceticism and is geared to the achievement of spiritual perfection by individual meditation. The modernists would like to see a modified form of the fourfold order of monks, nuns, laymen and laywomen, and an educated priesthood under less rigorous vows.

So far, few Westerners have become Jains, though there are said to be some German and American Jains. However, Jainism is well placed to influence the West with its well-developed exposition of ecology, animal welfare and non-violence. L. M. Singhvi, formerly Indian High Commissioner in Britain, was influential in drawing up a 'Jain Declaration on Nature', which was presented to the Worldwide Fund for Nature in 1990. In this he wrote, 'All life is bound together by mutual support and interdependence.' Jainism teaches that the major principle of ecology is the mutual interdependence of all living things and the material universe. It opposes the destruction of natural resources and its emphasis on conserving and recycling matter fits well with current concerns. But as yet Jains have not developed an organization to promote their beliefs in the Western world.

BIBLIOGRAPHY

M. Banks, *Organizing Jainism in India and England* (Oxford, 1992); P. Chitrabhanu, *Jain Symbols, Ceremonies and Practices* (New York, 1993); P. Dundas, *The Jains* (London, 1992); K. Oldfield, *Jainism, The Path of Purity and Peace* (Derby, 1989); N. Shah, *Jainism: The World of Conquerors* (Brighton, UK, and Portland, OR, 1998); S. Stevenson, *The Heart of Jainism* (Oxford, 1915).

B. J. M. Scott

JEHOVAH'S WITNESSES

The founder of the Jehovah's Witnesses was Charles Taze Russell (1852–1916), a businessman in Pittsburgh (USA) who began Bible study classes in 1869 in Allegheny, Pennsylvania, under the influence of a Seventh-Day Adventist teacher, Jonas Wendell. Although he later disagreed with the Adventists on some points, particularly their calculation of the date of the second coming of Christ, he maintained his connections with them. He and another disaffected Adventist, N. H. Barbour, edited a periodical called *The Herald of the Morning*, in which they said that Adventists had been incorrect in predicting the physical return of Christ. Christ's 'second presence' was an invisible and spiritual one that had taken place in 1874 and would be consummated in 1914. Russell soon had theological disagreements with Barbour and in 1879 began his own magazine called *Zion's Watch Tower and Herald of Christ's Presence*, the forerunner of the *Watchtower* magazine of today. Within a year, thirty congregations of the new movement had been founded. Russell founded Zion's Watch Tower Tract Society as a religious corporation in 1884, which many regard as the founding date of the movement. He began writing what is now a sacred text of the religion, *Studies in the Scriptures*, in 1886 and renamed the organization 'Watch Tower Bible and Tract Society' in 1896. In 1908 the headquarters moved to Brooklyn, New York, its present location.

In 1917, after Russell's death, a former lawyer, Joseph Franklin Rutherford, a loyal devotee of Russell and legal adviser to the movement, became president until his death in 1942, wielding absolute authority. Russell had not named a successor, and there were many schisms from the movement at this time, the largest being those of the Dawn Bible Students' Association and the Laymen's Home Missionary Movement. In 1931, at an international conference, 'Judge' Rutherford proposed a change of the name of the Watch Tower Bible and Tract Society to 'Jehovah's Witnesses', a name based on Isaiah 43:10. Although some think the change was intended to break the connection with Russell, the movement continues to propagate Russell's doctrines to this day, and the legal name of the corporation remains Watch Tower Bible and Tract Society. Rutherford began to denounce all other religions and Christian churches, and to issue many publications, including the magazine *Golden Age*, later renamed *Consolation* and then *Awake*. In 1942 Nathan Homer Knorr, a gifted administrator, became president, and publications were henceforth anonymous, including the magazines intended for mass circulation, *Awake* and *Watchtower*. The most significant event of Knorr's presidency was the publication in 1960 of *The New World Translation of the Holy Scriptures*, an anonymous translation, which some think subjectively weaves distinctive Jehovah's Witness doctrines into the text. This is now the main sacred text of the movement, together with *Studies in the Scriptures*. During Knorr's leadership, concentrated training of members in various methods of propagating the movement internationally took place, the Watch Tower Bible School of Gilead was opened in New York State for the training of missionaries, and the membership continued to grow. Knorr died in 1977 and was replaced by Frederick W. Franz, who died in 1992. Leadership now resides in a collective 'Governing Body' of eighteen men.

PRINCIPAL BELIEFS AND PRACTICES

Although Jehovah's Witnesses adopt a literal, fundamentalist approach to the Bible, they claim that the Bible can be understood only through the official interpretation of the organization. The interpretations of all other Christian churches are suspect since it is believed that these churches are under the control of the devil. Jehovah's Witnesses deny some of the fundamental teachings of mainstream Christianity, such as the deity of Christ, the Trinity and the incarnation. Jehovah is the all-powerful, all-knowing and everlasting Creator. Jesus Christ is the first created being, pre-existent but not eternal. Before his life on earth as a perfect human, born of a virgin, he was the archangel Michael. After his death, regarded as a 'ransom sacrifice' for Adam's sin, there was no bodily resurrection, but Christ resumed his pre-existent spiritual state. The Holy Spirit is an active, impersonal force that intervenes for Jehovah on the earth. Jehovah's Witnesses teach the personality of Satan, the enemy of God; and the Genesis account of the fall of humanity is taken literally. They believe that the human soul is inseparable from the body and is mortal and ceases to exist when the person dies, unless that person qualifies for resurrection. There is no hell (which is a symbol of annihilation in the grave) or eternal punishment in Jehovah's Witness teaching. Salvation is only through the Jehovah's Witnesses organization, is earned by good works and is not a gift of free grace, as many Christian traditions believe.

Jehovah's Witnesses have emphasized a utopian eschatology, often the subject of discussion in house-to-house visitation and periodicals. The Kingdom of God and the return of Christ to heaven took place in 1914. At that time, Satan and his evil angels were expelled from heaven and sent to the earth, where they are responsible for the increase in suffering, wars, criminal and all non-Jehovah's Witness religious activities, and other evils in the world today, the 'last days'. Heaven is where Christ and other 'true Christians' live since it was 'cleansed' in 1918. The number of true Christians is limited, however; only a sealed group of 144,000 'heavenly' Jehovah's Witnesses will reign with Christ over the Kingdom. These spiritual beings in heaven will rule over the 'Great Crowd' of other Witnesses on the new earth. Most of humanity will be annihilated at the imminent 'Battle of Armageddon', the final war before the new order, the millennium or thousand-year reign of Christ, comes, in which paradise will be restored to the earth. The date of Armageddon has been wrongly predicted five times in official publications, but not since 1941. As the twenty-first century progresses, and if the expected Armageddon does not occur, Jehovah's Witness beliefs may have to be altered significantly.

The extreme sectarianism of Jehovah's Witnesses means that the 'Kingdom of God' is identified exclusively with the movement, and meeting places are called 'Kingdom Halls'. Members, who are either 'Publishers' (part-time missionaries) or 'Pioneers' (full-time missionaries), must meet in the Kingdom Halls five times a week and keep full records of their missionary activities. The main concern of Jehovah's Witnesses is to gain members, and all existing members are obliged to be involved in 'publishing'. For this they are trained in how to approach people, sell literature, teach people by means of 'proof texts' and follow them up. There are few religions in the world where members work so hard and sacrificially at recruitment.

ENCOUNTERING CONTEMPORARY CULTURE

Estimated to have five and a half million committed adult members worldwide in 1997, with an annual growth rate of 5%, Jehovah's Witnesses are one of the fastest-growing religious movements today. This is largely due to highly visible and surprisingly effective door-to-door recruitment techniques and a highly organized structure coordinated from the headquarters in Brooklyn. The movement increased by 64% between 1990 and 1994, but in Latin America by a staggering 239% during the same period. Witnesses are in 232 countries all over the world, with less than 40% of their membership in the West.

Like other forms of religious fundamentalism, Jehovah's Witnesses are a very modern product, a radical world-rejecting movement, well known for its members' refusal to receive blood transfusions, based on a command in Leviticus not to 'eat blood'. Because its members are to be separated from the 'world', they are to reject all forms of military service, higher education, voting and membership of political parties, pledges of allegiance to governments (which are seen as idolatry) and even participation in sports and other social activities. These prohibitions have resulted in imprisonment and legal battles for thousands of Jehovah's Witnesses.

They reject Christian holidays (e.g. Christmas and Easter) and the celebration of birthdays, which are seen as 'pagan' festivals. They publish prolifically against the theory of evolution, and Jehovah's Witnesses are enjoined to read only literature from their organization. Any Jehovah's Witness who breaks any one of these stringent rules is excommunicated and regarded as having died.

Jehovah's Witnesses are one of the most persecuted religious groups in the world today, having been banned and harassed in many countries, especially in Nazi Germany, the Soviet Union and more recently in some Islamic countries. In the USA, more Jehovah's Witnesses have appealed to the Supreme Court on the grounds of the First Amendment on religious freedom than members of any other religious group. They won thirty-six out of forty-five such appeals between 1938 and 1955. Several cases in US divorce courts in the 1990s awarded child custody to the non-Jehovah's Witness father, and focused on the allegedly harmful effects on the child of the Jehovah's Witnesses religion. Jehovah's Witnesses are still the most disliked of any minority, religious or ethnic, in the USA. It remains to be seen whether Jehovah's Witnesses will adapt to a changing postmodern society.

BIBLIOGRAPHY

J. Beckford, *The Trumpet of Prophecy: A Sociological Study of Jehovah's Witnesses* (Oxford, 1975); J. Bergman, 'The Adventist and Jehovah's Witness Branch of Protestantism', in T. Miller (ed.), *America's Alternative Religions* (Albany, NY, 1995), pp. 33–46; J. Penton, *Apocalypse Delayed: The Story of Jehovah's Witnesses* (Buffalo, 1997); A. Rogerson, *Millions Now Living Will Never Die: A Study of Jehovah's Witnesses* (London, 1969); R. Stark and L. Iannaccone, 'Why the Jehovah's Witnesses Grow So Rapidly: A Theoretical Application', *JCR* 12:2, 1997, pp. 133–156.

A. H. Anderson

JUDAISM (HASIDISM)

Hasidism was a religious revival movement with charismatic leadership. It began with a wandering mystic and healer called Baal Shem Tov (or the Besht; d. 1760) from the Ukrainian regions of Podolia and Volhynia, though the impetus for a movement as such was given by his successor, Dov Baer of Mezireth, who sent out missionaries to Jewish communities throughout Eastern Europe. The early stages of Hasidism have given scholars the most difficulty because the Besht did not leave any significant written work. The first biography of him appeared some fifty-five years after his death, when he had already acquired a legendary status.

Since the movement originated in communities where the Sabbatian movement had taken firmest root, scholars have understandably explored the possible religious and social links. Some (like Benzion Dinur) have argued that Hasidism was itself messianic as well as a movement of social protest. Recent scholarship, however, has preferred to see it as a neutralization of the dangers inherent in any movement asserting the imminent appearance of the Messiah, and has attributed its remarkable growth to its popular devotional characteristics. Two features have been highlighted. The first was a change in the old kabbalistic attitude to *devekut* (cleaving to God). Originally this had been an extreme ideal to be reached only by a few at the end of a mystical path. But with Hasidism it became the starting point. Any Jew who took monotheistic faith seriously had in effect attained *devekut*. Earthly pursuits, according to the Besht, were as legitimate a sphere to serve God as more spiritual pursuits. There was no need to engage in the ascetic practices characteristic of Lurianic Kabbalism, which had proved a burden to ordinary people. Instead, stress was laid on a right attitude of heart, which implied in practice an emotional approach. As a result, early Hasidism often used stimuli such as loud chanting, jumping and dancing to attain ecstasy before performing religious rituals.

The prominence given to the *zaddik* (or *rebbe*) was the other novel feature of Hasidism which contributed to its growth as a popular movement. The *zaddik* was a charismatic figure who had great mystical skills but who was prepared to use his religious experience for the benefit of others. Hasidic literature consisted of stories of wonders performed by such figures as well as accounts of their spiritual teaching. But the *zaddikim* were not divorced from the ordinary Jews. Their task was to elevate the souls of the Jewish faithful to the divine light. They both prayed for their people and immersed themselves in their everyday lives in order to instruct them. In effect, the *zaddikim* became the embodiment of the Torah for their followers. It was the immediacy of the *zaddik*, as distinct from the remoteness of the traditional Torah scholar, that attracted many Jews living under oppressive conditions. At the same time, it is a paradox that a movement stressing at one level the value of the devotion of every Jew should not only recognize but require a special group whose mystical attainments were so much higher than those of anyone else.

As Hasidism spread from its heartlands in the Ukraine, it began to encounter opposition, especially from the traditional rabbinic stronghold of Lithuania. For two generations the Hasidic movement was subject to fierce criticism from the Mitnaggedim (opponents) over real or imagined breaches of halachic observance. These concerned changes to the liturgy, to the set times of prayer and to the methods of ritual slaughter. The most significant criticism, however, involved the movement's neglect of Torah study. This range of objections might suggest that Hasidism was a revolutionary or at least an innovative movement. But not all scholars have taken this view. Some (like Isidore Epstein) have denied that Hasidism introduced new doctrine; it simply established new emphases. Certainly at the start of the movement priority was given to ecstatic prayer over Torah study. Eventually, when it became clear to leaders of the Hasidic movement that this priority caused some offence, they rethought the issue and made the study of Torah a major plank in their piety. This development went a long way to securing reconciliation between the Hasidim and their opponents. Moreover, by the 1830s it was recognized by non-Hasidic orthodox that the Jewish *Haskalah* (Enlightenment) posed a much greater threat to Jewish identity than did the Hasidic movement. As a result, the Hasidim and their opponents became allies in the struggle against modernism.

In fact, Hasidic opposition to the secular study associated with the Enlightenment derived not primarily from a fear of assimilation but from Hasidism's kabbalistic worldview. According to this, every secular area of study was to be shunned because it came from the other side (*sitra ahra*), the realm of demonic powers opposed to God. Besides, the Hasidim viewed the growth of capitalism, which went hand in hand with the new scientific knowledge, as a threat to the sort of feudal society in which they had lived for generations. By the mid-nineteenth century the initial creative thrust of Hasidism was lost. For the next century it would remain an essentially conservative and defensive movement within Judaism.

Before 1945 Hasidic communities did not find it difficult to retain their distinctiveness, as they lived in societies in Eastern Europe that were suspicious of Jews and were happy to isolate them. But the end of the Second World War found Hasidism's traditional heartlands virtually denuded of Hasidic leaders and adherents. Surviving Hasidim had to move elsewhere, setting up new centres in the USA, London and Antwerp as well as in Israel. There they had to come to terms with less hostile societies that were correspondingly more open to Jewish assimilation. Hasidic groups responded to this challenge by becoming more consciously introversionist. They make sure that their children are socialized entirely within the community. The values of their schools reinforce those of their homes, and they strictly limit any education designed to equip them with skills to cope in wider society. They use Yiddish as the language of everyday discourse, a practice which sets them apart even from other Jews in the state of Israel because they alone ensure that their children use it as their first language. Parents tend to make the important decisions for their children, including the choice of marriage partner. Marriage is the point at which the children transfer their dependence from their parents to the *zaddik*. Hasidim will also wear traditional dress to mark them out from others in their society.

Presently there are about twelve main groups of Hasidim, of whom the Lubavitch (or Habad) and the Satmar are the most prominent. These groups also display the greatest contrasts and have often been in serious dispute with one another. The Satmar are rigorously isolationist even toward non-Hasidic Jews, but the Lubavitch have adopted a more confident attitude towards their own inheritance. They have, for example, engaged in proselytizing activities from their Brooklyn headquarters to encourage other Jews towards more faithful Torah observance. As a result, the Lubavitch have become a significant international movement. They have also been active in promoting the view among Jewish communities that the messianic age is at hand. Indeed, many thought that their late *zaddik*, Menahem Mendel Schneerson (d. 1994), would turn out to be the Messiah. There are certain conditions, however, that have to be fulfilled before the Messiah can come, notably that the majority of Jews repent and return to Torah observance.

In fact, Hasidism has shown surprising growth in the last thirty years or so. In part this growth may reflect a high birth rate, and in part the Hasidim's clear authority structure, with the *zaddik* commanding absolute respect. The Hasidim have been free of the sort of identity crisis that has afflicted many other sections of the Jewish community. Thus, recent developments reinforce the irony that a movement which was at first suspect because of its novelty and antinomian tendencies should have become one of the leading bastions of Jewish orthodoxy.

The influence of the Hasidic movement is not confined to those who are attached to one of the Hasidic groups. Two outstanding Jewish thinkers of the twentieth century, Martin Buber and Abraham Heschel, had a high regard for eighteenth-century Hasidic leaders, though they did not belong to a Hasidic group. It is also interesting that these two figures should have emphasized different aspects of the Hasidic legacy. Buber stressed the immanence of the divine in the bringing of the sacred into the everyday realities of life, while Heschel highlighted God's transcendence by insisting that distinctive Jewish practices were the means whereby God drew close and enabled his people to rise above the mundane into the sacred.

BIBLIOGRAPHY

M. Buber, *The Origin and Meaning of Hasidism* (ET New York, 1960); M. Buber, *Tales of the Hasidim* (ET New York, 1991); G. D. Hundert (ed.), *Essential Papers on Hasidism – Origins to Present* (London and New York, 1991); M. Idel, *Hasidism: Between Ecstasy and Magic* (Albany, NY, 1995); J. Weiss, *Studies in Eastern European Mysticism* (Oxford, 1985).

G. A. Keith

JUDAISM (KABBALISM)

'Kabbalism' denotes the branch of Jewish mysticism which originated in Spain and Provence in the thirteenth century. From the Middle Ages to the seventeenth century it was a significant component of Jewish piety complementary to the philosophical approaches associated with Maimonides. Its leading text was the *Zohar*, composed by Rabbi Moses de Leon but ascribed to a third-century teacher, Shimon bar Yohai. In fact, the word 'Kabbalah' means 'tradition', and from the start Kabbalism was represented as an oral tradition from the same time as the written Torah.

The Kabbalists accepted Maimonides' idea of God as *Ein Sof* (the Infinite), who was hidden and unknowable. The relationship between God and the finite world was established through ten *Sefirot*, emanations from God that are accessible to humans. This concentration on the *Sefirot* marked out Kabbalists from earlier Jewish mystics. The *Sefirot* may be regarded as various phases in the manifestation of God. In effect, something of God's creative power has broken through the closed shell of his hidden self. The *Sefirot* not only leave their mark on the natural world; they also form an independent world which is both prior to the natural world and represents a higher stage of reality. This was the world to which the Kabbalists sought entry, and for which they looked to the words of the Torah as a sort of route map.

Originally harmony existed between God and the *Sefirot* so that his power surged unhindered through all stages of being, but that harmony has been disrupted through human sinfulness. Humans, who were to exist in pure spiritual form in regular association with the divine, were plunged into an inferior condition. As a result, traces of divine blessing are found only here and there in pious individuals and communities. Humans do, however, have the ability to engage in *tikkun*, the repair of the disharmony in the universe. They can do this because humans are God's image: that is, models of the *Sefirot* and effectively replicas of the cosmos as a whole. There were two main ways in which the Kabbalists set about this repair: by prayer, a means for the soul to ascend into higher spheres, and by meditation on the Torah, particularly the diverse and hidden meanings behind its words.

It would be misleading to speak of a

single thread of kabbalistic doctrine. There were considerable variations among Kabbalists on their central themes of creation, the existence of evil and the possibility of redemption. But Jewish Kabbalists were distinctive in their idea that God not only commanded but also needed human service. All that people did in this world, whether good or evil, left its imprint on the supernal world. The Jewish people, with their possession of the Torah, held a unique position. They had in the Torah the means to grapple with the secrets of the universe and in its commands a practical strategy for the redemption of the world. The mystics were not primarily concerned to achieve bliss as they ascended closer to God. Rather, they desired to assist God in the corporate goal of restoring harmony to the disordered universe. Though the Kabbalists began as an esoteric group, they did not distance themselves from the Jewish community. On the contrary, they saw their regular worship and festivals as a vital means of shaping the world above.

One Kabbalist, Isaac of Luria (1534–72), deserves special mention, because he triggered the last religious movement in Judaism to predominate among all sections of the Jewish people and in every part of the diaspora. In essence he provided a mystical interpretation of the great themes of Jewish history, exile and redemption. Even his doctrine of the creation involved God in a form of exile, since in it creation was accomplished through *zimzum*: that is, the contraction of the Godhead into itself. God had to go into exile from the empty space so that the processes of creation could take place. But God projected his light into the dark vacuum, providing it at the same time with 'vessels' to manifest his attributes in the world. These vessels, however, could not bear the influx of divine light and so they shattered. The result was disharmony in the worlds above and chaos in the world below, an intense struggle between good and evil.

The situation was aggravated by the sin of the first man (Adam), whose original vocation had been to defeat the evil within himself and so to end the domain of evil. That task had now been entrusted to the Jewish people rather than to a single individual. By their prayers and their ethical deeds in obedience to Torah, the Jews would help to repair the broken vessels. Correspondingly, every time a Jew sinned, the process of repair was set back.

Isaac viewed the coming of the Messiah, which he believed to be near, as the end of the struggle for the restoration of harmony both to human souls and to the cosmos as a whole. The Jewish people had the potential to accelerate or to postpone the coming of the Messiah, depending on how seriously they devoted themselves to the commandments. Thus in this system each Jew was a vital protagonist in the battle for cosmic restoration.

As well as explaining the Jewish exile, Isaac suggested a motive for the Jewish diaspora. This was the salvation of all human souls, since the purified souls of Jews would unite with souls of other races and assist in their purification. This explanation of the Jewish diaspora enjoyed considerable popularity until it was challenged by Zionism.

Isaac's teaching also generated messianic expectations, notably those associated with Shabbatai Zevi, that were to have traumatic effects on Jewish communities in the late seventeenth century. Even after these expectations had been shattered for most Jews, Lurianic Kabbalah retained its importance, not least because of its explanation of the Jewish exile and its hope for a better future.

The Kabbalah, especially in its Lurianic form, had a significant effect on the Hasidic movement in the eighteenth century, though by then it had been purged of its more esoteric and ascetic elements. Its influence, however, was on the wane when Jews began to face new challenges as a result of the Enlightenment and their political emancipation. Jewish scholarship in the nineteenth century, as embodied in the *Wissenschaft des Judentums*, ignored the Kabbalah in its concern to emphasize all that was rational in the Jewish religion and that would serve to make Jews respectable in the eyes of Gentile society.

In the twentieth century, renewed interest was shown in the Kabbalah and in Jewish mysticism more generally as a result of the writings of a university professor, Gershom Scholem (1897–1982). He not only made Jewish mysticism a respectable subject for scholarly study, but also used his scholarship to buttress his belief that mysticism provided the key to the continuity of Judaism over many centuries. Thus, Scholem deliberately advocated a different solution to the problems of modernity from those offered by Orthodoxy and by the *Wissenschaft des Judentums*. He believed that a reinforcement of Jewish institutions and practices in the manner of the Orthodox would stifle religious life; he followed the Kabbalistic belief that the Torah did not contain one fixed meaning, but would be a source of multiple meanings for those who were spiritually attuned to it. At the other extreme he considered the *Wissenschaft* too apologetic in tone and too much directed toward the political goal of the successful assimilation of Jews. Just as mystical movements had provided the necessary creative spark to revitalize Jewish life in the past, so Scholem believed that they were needed to combat the challenge of secular modernity, though he himself did not attempt to say how they would do so.

Recently Scholem's views have been challenged on both historical and religious grounds. It has been argued that Jews have made other responses to earlier crises besides resorting to mysticism. Moreover, when mystical tendencies have occupied a central role in Jewish life, as at the time of Shabbatai Zevi, the results have been destructive, not least because they have encouraged the Jewish people to neglect their social and political situation on earth in favour of experiences purportedly at a higher level of reality. These critics believe that the central role in Judaism must be given to the Torah and the various *halakhah* associated with it. Mysticism functions best within Judaism when it occupies a secondary role and is followed by individuals rather than by Jewish society as a whole.

Certainly mysticism does not feature significantly among the main branches of modern Judaism, except possibly in Hasidism. The Orthodox, for example, have little time for either mystical or philosophical reflections. Kabbalism does, however, remain popular with individuals, especially those attracted to New Age ideas or to the occult. In Western society, with its belief that people may pick their spirituality from a range of sources, these individuals are not confined to the Jewish community.

BIBLIOGRAPHY

M. Halamish, *An Introduction to the Kabbalah* (Albany, NY, 1999), pp. 164–184; Z. B. S. Halevi, *The Way of Kabbalah* (Bath, 1991); M. Idel, *Kabbalah – New Perspectives* (London and New Haven, CT, 1988); G. G. Scholem, *Major Trends in Jewish Mysticism* (New York, 1995); E. Schweid, *Judaism and Mysticism According to Gershom Scholem* (ET Atlanta, GA, 1985); H. Sperling and M. Simon (trans.), *The Zohar* (London, 1934).

G. A. Keith

JUDAISM (ORTHODOX)

It was supporters of Reform Judaism in early nineteenth-century Germany who first coined the term 'Orthodox', to refer to those who opposed them. They intended it pejoratively to represent their opponents as shackled by obsolete standards. These opponents responded by saying that historically Judaism had known only one distinction, between Judaism and non-Judaism. It was inappropriate to speak of Orthodox and Liberal Jews or of any other such distinction. They could defend this claim because Judaism of the dual Torah had reigned virtually unchallenged since the early centuries of the Christian era. According to this, the Law, as given through Moses to the Jewish people in both its written and oral forms, was intended by God to stand for all time and for all situations of the Jewish people, the idea expressed in the rabbinic principle 'There is no before or after in Torah.' The Orthodox therefore rejected the idea of progressive revelation that was central to Reform Judaism and that would be taken up by other non-Orthodox groups.

Orthodox Jews, however, were not insensitive to the new pressures on the Jewish community in Germany and other European states where the Jewish people had experienced political emancipation and were expected to play their part as good citizens. Indeed, one leading Orthodox opponent of the Reform movement, Samson Raphael Hirsch (1808–88), was exceptionally confident that traditional Jewish attitudes to the Torah could happily be combined with gentile forms of learning and with public life in European society. It was perfectly possible to be an observant Jew and still participate in modern Gentile society through business, culture and social interaction. This policy was enshrined in the slogan *Torah im derekh eretz* ('Torah and the way of the land'). It was designed in part to assure outsiders that emancipated Jews would make good and productive citizens, but at the same time it did lead to the confining of Jewish practice to the home and the synagogue. In other words, it promoted a distinction between the religious and the secular in the life of many Jews, a distinction foreign to previous generations. Even Hirsch himself argued that where modernity and Jewish observance clashed, the latter should have priority; otherwise Judaism would degenerate into a religion of convenience. He was hopeful that such clashes need not arise very often.

In effect, Hirsch shared the conviction of the Reform movement that it was desirable for Jews to integrate happily into wider European society, but he differed from the Reformers regarding the means necessary to attain this end. Above all, he rejected their claim that it was traditional Judaism that had impoverished the Jewish people and left them an object of contempt in wider society. He was, however, prepared to make adjustments to what he saw as the externals of the Jewish religion. Thus he was happy for Jews to adopt the clothing and language of those countries in which they resided. He made some aesthetic changes to synagogue ritual, though he would not tamper with the traditional liturgy and he insisted on Hebrew as the sole language of prayer. Most important of all, he encouraged Jews to pursue a secular education in addition to their Torah studies. He was careful to justify these modest changes with traditional arguments. But when the Reform movement went on to scrap the dietary laws and to remove the ban on intermarriage, Hirsch thought it impossible to continue in fellowship with them and effectively encouraged a split in the Jewish community.

Hirsch claimed the high ground of Jewish tradition for his stance, but the question does arise as to how far it was an innovation. Even in the nineteenth century his was not the only type of Orthodox opposition to the Reform movement. There were those, like the famous Hungarian talmudic scholar Moses (Hatam) Sofer, who urged Jews to maintain their religious integrity by clinging to a segregationist style of life, in which they were to avoid Gentile dress and first names and use non-Jewish languages only for instrumental purposes. In contrast, Hirsch's approach to Jewish tradition seems selective. Moreover, under Judaism of the dual Torah many had lived as though all that was worth knowing was to be found in the Torah. Hirsch altered that approach by ascribing value to secular learning. Since Hirsch was not altogether representative of the dual Torah ideology, he and his followers have sometimes been described as 'Neo-Orthodox' by contrast to the 'Ultra-Orthodox' like Moses Sofer and his disciples.

The Jewish tradition, however, is not so monolithic as to allow Hirsch to be dismissed as a more conservative innovator than the main German Reformers. There were times, notably in the Arabic-Spanish period, when Jews had participated in wider culture and commerce with no apparent dilution of their distinctive identity. More riskily perhaps, Hirsch took over an idea of Jewish mission to the whole world from his Reform opponents. It is true that his concept of the Jewish mission to the nations, to teach that God is the source of all blessing and so of all true progress, was more diffuse than that of the Reformers. It also depended on careful observance of the *halakhah* and made much of a future restoration of the Jewish people to the land of Israel, where they could more completely follow these ordinances. But again it could be argued that this was a departure from traditional Judaism of the dual Torah, in which emphasis was placed on the distinctiveness of the Jewish people among the nations. Hirsch ambitiously thought that it was possible to combine this distinctiveness with a missionary thrust to Gentile society. No doubt he was influenced by current political expectations of a positive Jewish contribution to European society. Critics, however, could accuse Hirsch of naïvety in pursuit of what over many centuries had been incompatible goals for the Jewish people.

If nineteenth-century Orthodoxy included both isolationist and integrationist responses to the political, social and intellectual changes of that time, the same variety has persisted into the twentieth century. After all, the essential characteristic of Orthodoxy is to endorse the divine and immutable character of the Sinai revelation. In itself, this endorsement does not provide detailed help in dealing with the challenges of modernity, other than a rebuttal of any scholarship ascribing a human rather than a divine origin to the Torah. It leaves open the question of how far Jews should involve themselves in Gentile society. It also provides little guidance on the new phenomenon of a secular Jewish state in Israel. Not surprisingly, there are different Orthodox responses to those unavoidable issues.

Today the integrationist Orthodox Judaism favoured by Hirsch is represented in the state of Israel by Zionist Orthodox Judaism and in the USA by Yeshiva University (New York City) and the Rabbinical Council of America. In Great Britain the equivalent group is called the United Synagogue Orthodox. In contrast, the Haredim, who include the Hasidic groups, represent the segregationist side of Orthodoxy, urging a separate Jewish life within the 'four walls of *halakhah*'. After the emergence of the independent state of Israel an acute political and ideological difference opened up between the Haredim and the Zionist Orthodox. The latter have been prepared to see the establishment of even a secular Jewish state as a first step on the path to messianic redemption. Hence they have been keen to integrate into Israeli society and have seen themselves as a sort of bridge between the secular and religious communities. The Haredim, however, suspecting that Zionism was designed to root out the Jewish religion, have accused the Zionist Orthodox of futile compromise. They have launched a constructive challenge to the very idea of the Jewish state as the defender of Jewish existence and reasserted the older idea that the Torah alone guarantees separate Jewish existence. For them Jewish life in Israel is justified only by the establishment of traditional Torah schools. There is a related theological difference: the Zionist Orthodox believe that human activity can help to pave the way for the coming of the Messiah, but Haredi groups insist that the coming of the Messiah is thoroughly supernatural.

The variety of stances and the liveliness of debate in Orthodox circles may come as a surprise, especially as in the earlier part of the twentieth century the movement was losing adherents *en masse* and seemed to many to be in its death throes. Some contemporary commentators have actually described it as the most nuanced of all the Judaisms currently practised. This subtlety has contributed to its emergence at the end of the twentieth century as one of the liveliest branches of Judaism. A further reason for this unexpected development is the perception that in the Western world assimilation presents the greatest danger to a separate Jewish identity. In its outlook on the Sinai revelation Orthodoxy offers a divine rationale for distinctive Jewish identity, for which other forms of Judaism can give only humanistic and therefore weaker alternatives.

BIBLIOGRAPHY

B. Brown, 'Orthodox Judaism', in J. Neusner and A. J. Avery-Peck (eds.), *The Blackwell Companion to Judaism* (Oxford and Malden, MA, 2000); M. H. Danzger, *Returning to Tradition: The Contemporary Revival of Orthodox Judaism* (New Haven, CT, 1989); S. Heilman, *Defenders of the Faith: Inside Ultra-Orthodox Jewry* (New York, 1992); J. Neusner, *Judaism in Modern Times* (Oxford and Cambridge MA, 1995), pp. 73–98; J. Sacks (ed.), *Orthodoxy confronts Modernity* (London and Hoboken, NJ, 1991).

G. A. Keith

JUDAISM (REFORM)

The Reform movement began in early nineteenth-century Germany with some modest changes to synagogue services and liturgy, largely to bring them into line with prevailing aesthetic standards. The impetus for change did not, however, stop there. It was felt that many of the *halakhah* were now irrelevant, indeed detrimental to the Jewish people in their modern situation. This problem was clear from the numbers of Jews who were so embarrassed by Judaism as to leave it altogether. The

Reformers wanted to preserve Judaism by recasting it in a form that would give it an appeal not only to Jews but also to a wider society that was demanding a more productive and less isolationist role from Jews in response to their new political rights. The Reform movement in Germany struggled, however, to find alternative principles on which it could agree. It was only when the centre of the movement transferred to the United States that such principles were first enunciated in detail, in the Pittsburgh Platform (1885).

The Reformers affirmed that Judaism was simply the highest form of ethical monotheism, and denied that it was intrinsically different from other religions. It was described as 'a progressive religion, ever striving to be in accord with the postulates of reason'. (Indeed, the movement is sometimes termed 'Progressive' or 'Liberal Judaism' as well as 'Reform Judaism'.) Hence there should be no contradiction between essential Judaism and the findings of modern science or scholarship generally. Wherever recent scholarship presented a different picture from that of the Bible, the latter was to be dismissed as an accommodation to the needs of a bygone era. A similar criterion was used to determine which of the *halakhah* should be observed in the modern era. The moral law was emphasized but the place of ritual much reduced, in accordance with this principle: 'we accept as binding only the moral laws and maintain only such ceremonies as elevate and sanctify our lives, but reject all such as are not adapted to the views and habits of modern civilization'.

This position might seem to imply an indiscriminate acceptance of modernity and an almost complete capitulation to the demands of outsiders that Jews no longer form a state within a state. Indeed, the Pittsburgh Platform went on to deny any hope of a future Jewish state; Reform Jews were to be considered a religious community rather than a nation. This was a highly appropriate stance within the USA, with its longstanding tradition of religious freedom for a variety of Christian denominations. Needless to say, Reform Jews were criticized by other Jews for adapting their religion to suit the prevailing political and intellectual climate. But this criticism overlooked the strengths in the position of the Reformers. They were anxious to avoid further defections from Judaism, not to end Jewish distinctiveness. In this they have proved relatively successful, at least in the USA, where Reform Judaism was the largest Jewish group at the end of the twentieth century. Moreover, not only have they avoided the dangers of nationalism, by which Judaism has certainly been threatened throughout its history, but they have also emphasized the Jewish mission to the whole of humanity. This mission is to guide humanity, through ethical monotheism, to the establishment of the kingdom of truth, righteousness and peace among all people, which is Israel's messianic hope. At the time of the Pittsburgh Platform the Reformers were optimistic that this hope was soon to be fulfilled because of 'the modern era of universal culture of heart and intellect'. Thus they were willing to co-operate with people of good will in other religions to bring to fruition the messianic age. Though these optimistic hopes have been dented by the events of the twentieth century, in Jewish Reform circles they have not been entirely extinguished, and Reform Jews remain more open than many others to insights from other cultures and religions.

The Pittsburgh Platform was never intended as a definitive statement for all time for Reform Jews. Such a statement would be foreign to the ethos of a movement which has stressed flexibility in the face of a changing society. Thus Reform Jews have enthusiastically embraced feminist concerns for the equality of women within their synagogues. More recently, and more controversially among their fellow-Jews, they have supported gay rights.

Reform Jews have also proved flexible enough to alter their stance when they feel they have underestimated certain elements in the Jewish tradition or that the needs of the times have radically changed. Their most significant change relates to the Zionist ideal. Initially Reform Jews opposed this because they saw it as a fruit of a misguided nationalism that would detract from the universal mission of the Jews. By the time of the Columbus Platform of 1937, when the Nazi era had begun, their outlook had changed. They welcomed the Zionist goal as not only a haven of security for Jews but also a centre of Jewish culture and spiritual life that in time would benefit all humankind. A more recent Reform Jewish statement (from the San Francisco Platform of 1976) expressed the hope that Jews in Israel and in the diaspora would engage in creative dialogue to avoid the excesses of nationalism as well as to affirm the value of Jewish self-expression. This highlights a major strength of Reform Judaism: its recognition that authentic Judaism must do justice to both the particularistic and the universalistic tendencies within its traditions. It also shows that Reform Jews try to stand within the Jewish tradition; they are not blind followers of modernity.

Another area where Reform Jews have had to modify their views has been that of ritual. They were faced with the fact that when many Jews came to believe that Judaism was just one species of the broader genus of ethical monotheism, they went on to question the logic of Jewish distinctiveness and left Judaism. The Reform response was to stress Jewish rituals and Jewish education within the family and the synagogue as the means to preserve the Jewish allegiance of their young people.

Reform Jews have, however, struggled with the issue of authority. While stressing the importance of personal conscience and individual decision, they have been anxious to ensure that conscience is enlightened by Jewish tradition. This explains why their rabbinate has seen fit on four separate occasions, from the Pittsburgh Platform of 1885 to another gathering in Pittsburgh in 1999, to issue statements of guiding principles for the movement. The last two of these fully recognize and even welcome the diversity of Reform Jewish beliefs and practices. The most recent statement avoids a prescriptive tone and simply invites all Reform Jews to 'engage in a dialogue with the sources of our tradition, responding out of our knowledge, our experience and our faith'. In the last resort, however, it is up to individual Jews to make their own responsible choice of what they find helpful in the tradition. Indeed, the Pittsburgh statement of 1999 emphasizes the existential consideration of what 'gives meaning and purpose to our lives'. It may seem ironic that a movement which has always set great store on the results of critical scholarship should resort to such subjective criteria in determining the worth of Jewish tradition. Yet Reform Jews have been more keenly aware than most of the different interpretations and even inconsistencies within the wider Jewish tradition.

This difficulty with authority is not merely theoretical; it has also been apparent in Reform Jewish handling of practical issues. Though the Central Conference of American Rabbis (a Reform body) in 1990 discouraged rabbinic participation in interfaith marriages, an estimated 40% of rabbis have ignored this ruling and have officiated in such ceremonies.

Perhaps the greatest challenge to the Reform outlook has come from Professor Alvin Reines of Hebrew Union College. He has pointed out the logical corollary of the Reform rejection of verbal revelation. If God was not responsible for either the oral or the written Torah, then they are of human origin, and no human, either from the past or in the present, has the right to impose his or her views on anyone else. Hence Reines affirms what he calls the Freedom Covenant: 'every member of a religious community possesses an ultimate right to religious self-authority'. Therefore participation in traditional aspects of Judaism must be entirely voluntary. Though no religious institutions have been formed along the lines of Reines' principles, his ideas have had a significant impact on a number of Reform rabbis. It seems that if

Reform Judaism is to be maintained as a distinct and recognizably Jewish movement, it will be dependent on the goodwill of its members rather than on some agreed basis of authority.

BIBLIOGRAPHY

E. B. Borowitz, *Reform Judaism Today*, 3 vols. (New York, 1977); D. Cohn-Sherbok, *The Future of Judaism* (Edinburgh, 1994), pp. 91–119; P. Mendes-Flohr and J. Reinharz (eds.), *The Jew in the Modern World* (Oxford and New York, ²1995), pp. 155–206; M. Meyer, *Response to Modernity: A History of the Reform Movement in Judaism* (New York, 1988); J. Neusner, *Judaism in Modern Times* (Oxford and Cambridge, MA, 1995), pp. 52–72.

G. A. Keith

LATIN AMERICAN AND CARIBBEAN SPIRITISM

The dominant religious and cultural influence in the Caribbean and north-eastern Brazil is West African. The new spiritistic religions of the region evolved primarily through oral tradition over five centuries. The integration of the religions of African slaves with the religions of other inhabitants of the Americas created a syncretism between African religion, Native American religion and Catholic Christianity. The spiritistic movements are the result of this distinctive synthesis and are of many varieties, from those with a predominantly Christian element to syncretistic movements that combine Christian, Native American and African elements. A common emphasis is spirit possession by *orishas*, a Yoruba (West African) term for 'spirits'. Devotees undergo a stringent initiation to become spirit mediums, and complex symbolic media identify spirits.

CARIBBEAN MOVEMENTS

Some movements have greater Christian content than others. Spiritual Baptists combine Christian and Yoruba religious practices, and in St Vincent, where they are called 'Shakers', they claim possession by the Holy Spirit similar to that of Pentecostalism. In Trinidad, where they are known as 'Shouters', more ecstatic manifestations occur, including possession by Shango (the Yoruba god of thunder) and other African spirits or *orishas*. This usually takes place during baptism by immersion and in 'mourning' rituals for spiritual development, in which a person is isolated for several days. Pukkumina or Pocomania ('a little madness') is a Jamaican movement. 'Bands' are formed under a leader, whose house is next to a 'tabernacle' (meeting place) containing a ritual bath-house and a holy 'seal' area, where ritual dances around a flagpole are believed to induce possession by angel-spirits and ancestors. Baptism by immersion, holy communion and the Bible are accepted, and ritual baths and herbal medicines are used in healing rituals.

Shango in Trinidad, Santería ('the way of the saints') in Cuba and Voodoo in Haiti are similar movements with a predominant African element. In Shango Saint Barbara is identified with Shango, and saints and biblical figures join other Yoruba divinities. Drumming, dancing and singing in cult centres supposedly induce possession leading to revelation and protection. The leader of each centre is sought for healing through ritual objects such as power-laden stones, herbs used to 'feed' the stones and worshippers and blood from a sacrificed animal presented to the spirits. Santería, a synthesis of African religion and Catholicism, identifies its Supreme Being Oshun, the Yoruba river spirit, with the Virgin Mary. *Orishas*, translated *santos* in Spanish, are identified with Catholic saints who guard the world. Santería is practised in cult houses called *reglas* and has become a movement of cultural and religious resistance.

In Haiti, Voodoo (from the Fon word for 'spirit') is practised by 75% of Haitians, virtually all of whom are also Catholics. It permeates all of life and provided the ideology for the struggle that made Haiti the first black republic in the Caribbean in 1804. Voodoo (Vodou), also known as Vodun, represents an entire system of African beliefs, but has developed to include Catholic elements. The most prominent divinities are hundreds of *loa* or *lwa* ('the invisibles', equivalent to *orishas*), of which most are African divinities, fewer are of Haitian origin and others are Catholic saints. *Loa* are understood as protectors who impose taboos on their followers and require offerings and ceremonies in their honour. If these are performed, the *loa* will be generous, but if they are neglected, sickness, death or other troubles will result. Each *loa*, conceived as a deity with human characteristics identifiable in a person possessed, has a recognizable image, rhythm, favourite food, drink and colour(s), with specific powers and functions. *Loa* are thought sometimes to give songs to people who are possessed or dreaming, which are then sung in Voodoo rituals.

BRAZILIAN MOVEMENTS

The cult centres of northern Brazilian spiritism are given different names such as 'Pagelança' and 'Catimbó'; they combine ancient Native American and African divinities. In north-east Brazil the African influence is stronger and cult centres are known as 'Xangô' ('Shango') or 'Candomblé'. Here too the *orixás* (*orishas*) are honoured by animal sacrifices and prayers, after which they enter mediums, who fall into a trance, dress in the clothing of the divinity and dance to the spirits. Secret societies of priests preside over a cult in which the spirits of the dead are invoked. Both Candomblé and Xangô are divided into different 'nations', with distinctive rituals, music and language. Sometimes *orixás* are identified with Catholic saints. In central and southern Brazil, the influence of African religion is weaker, but remains in syncretistic religions like Batuque and Macumba, which thrive in oppressed urban slums, and where the influence of Catholicism, Native American religion and European spiritualism is stronger. It is from Macumba that the largest of Brazil's new religions, Umbanda, emerged.

Umbanda retains characteristics of the African religions, especially Candomblé and Macumba. In 1965 it had over 100,000 *terreiros* (temples), with some ten million active members, Umbandistas, 60% of Brazil's population, most of whom still considered themselves to be Catholics. It is strongest in the southern industrial cities, where it originated. The movement combines traditional Yoruba religion, Native American Tupi religion, Kardecist spiritualism, popular Catholicism and even a measure of Hinduism. It thus includes the religious beliefs of most Brazilians, and its followers believe it enhances national consciousness. For Umbandistas, being possessed by good spirits increases spiritual perfection. Contact with spirits is established through mediums who take the characteristics of a particular spirit. Umbandistas attain spirit possession after a rigorous training programme and examination. Umbanda uses magic (including potions, charms, sacred rattles, incense, herbs and flowers) to manipulate good spirits and chase away evil ones. *Terreiros* face east and are patterned after Catholic churches. Elaborate rituals on different days of the week differ according to which *orixá* is being honoured. Spirit mediums assume liturgical positions before possession; food is offered to sustain the power of the spirits; and mediums give advice to people coming for healing or other problems. New members are given the sign of the cross seven times on different parts of the body, followed by baptism in the presence of godparents in the name of Olôrun, Oxalá and the seven *orixá*s, and a sevenfold incensing. Thereafter they are trained as mediums.

ENCOUNTERING CONTEMPORARY CULTURE

These movements have adapted to contemporary society and become popular religious options for masses of people. The deliberately syncretistic Umbanda, with millions of devotees, claims to be the Brazilian national religion, and provides its followers with a sense of significance in an impersonal urban society. Santería is Cuba's most popular religion, practised by an estimated 70% or seven million Cubans, with another million devotees in the USA. Haiti's former dictator Duvalier used Voodoo to strengthen his control in local communities, and in 1991 President Aristide rededicated Haiti to Voodoo. Migrations of Caribbeans northwards, especially Haitians and Cubans in the USA, resulted in the transplanting of movements such as Santería and Voodoo. Centres for African spiritism have been established, particularly in Miami and New York, where they have become community centres for immigrants that have also attracted African Americans and a few white Americans. While some centres focus on the revitalization of African religion purged of foreign elements, most centres have become 'Americanized', and written texts for training initiates are replacing oral traditions. New Age and Neo-Pagan retreats now offer workshops in Voodoo and Santería. Tensions have arisen over the practice of animal sacrifice in particular, and Caribbean spiritism struggles to overcome the Western stereotype of 'black magic'.

BIBLIOGRAPHY

R. Bastide, *The African Religions of Brazil: Towards a Sociology of the Interpenetration of Civilizations* (New York, 1978); M. S. Laguerre, *Voodoo Heritage* (London, 1980); J. M. Murphy, *Santería: An African Religion in America* (Boston, 1988); J. M. Murphy, 'Santería and Vodou in the United States', in T. Miller (ed.), *America's Alternative Religions* (Albany, NY, 1995), pp. 291–296; G. E. Simpson, *Black Religions in the New World* (New York, 1978).

A. H. Anderson

MARTIAL ARTS

In popular Western culture, the term 'martial arts' has come to refer to the various forms of Asian 'empty-hand' and specialized weapons combat extolled in hundreds of films, mostly made in Hong Kong and Hollywood. These arts include some associated with China, such as *gung-fu*, *tai-ch'i*, *pa qua* and *jeet kune do*; some associated with Japan, including *karate-do*, *judo*, *aikido*, *jiujitsu*, *kenpo*, *sumo* and *kyudo*; some associated with Korea, like *taekwondo*, *hapkido* and *hwarangdo*; and *muay thai*, or Thai kick-boxing. (This list is not exhaustive.) While it is indisputable that there have been *karate* schools, *judo* clubs and *gung-fu* studios in the West for many years, it was the release of Bruce Lee's film *Enter the Dragon* in 1975 which launched popular interest in Asian martial arts, an interest which continues to this day.

Most martial arts comprise two elements: training in form and timing and training in awareness in combative engagement. The former is often developed through the practice of *kata*, a set series of moves which allow the student to 'shadow fight' without an opponent. The latter, in Japanese known as *kumite*, is a sparring match which takes place either in the controlled environment of the martial arts school or in the competitive world of sport martial arts.

In addition to the physical training, most martial arts include some ritual acknowledgment at the beginning and ending of a class and before and after a bout. This acknowledgment can be as elaborate as the offering of salt to the gods (as in *sumo*) or seated meditation prior to training (as in some schools of *karate* and *gung-fu*), or as simple as a single bow which indicates respect for one's teacher and one's fellow students.

Buddhism and Daoism form the traditional religious underpinnings of many of the Asian martial arts. According to popular convention, Shao-lin *gung-fu* began when the Indian Buddhist monk Bodhidharma (c.470–563) arrived in China in the late fifth century. Settling in the Shao-lin monastery on Sung-shan Mountain, Bodhidharma is said to have developed a series of mind–body exercises designed to improve the general health of the Daoist monks there and to assist them in their meditation. Based on Bodhidharma's observations of different real and mythological animals (e.g. dragon, crane, tiger, snake and panther), these exercises are traditionally thought to have evolved into the style of combat known as Shao-lin *gung-fu*. It is this tradition which was popularized in the television series *Kung Fu* (1972–75) and *Kung Fu: The Legend Continues* (1992–6). Artwork found at the Dunhuang caves in Chinese central Asia depicts the link between Buddhism and the martial arts as far back as the sixth century. However, while many modern schools of *gung-fu* claim to trace their lineage back to these original Shao-lin temple monks, there is little direct evidence to support this claim.

For practitioners of the Asian martial arts, *qi* (Chinese *ch'i*) is the central spiritual component. *Qi* is the life-energy, the 'intrinsic energy' which flows through each individual. By developing and harnessing *qi*, practitioners are able to manifest combative levels far beyond what might be expected. Through the control, direction and release of *qi*, advanced practitioners are said to be able to defeat multiple opponents, to break piles of bricks or stacked boards and to direct arrows to their targets with unerring accuracy. *Qi* is developed through specialized breathing and meditation techniques. In some schools *zazen* (or seated meditation) is an integral part of this training process.

Central to many of the Asian martial arts is the Daoist concept of the *yin* and the *yang*, represented by the symbol ☯. These are the principles of 'gentleness' and 'firmness', principles which are held to exist not in opposition to one another, but in complementarity. Martial arts are thought to be a manifestation of this relationship. A popular conception of the martial arts is that they involve inordinate force; this is incorrect. Such force supposedly manifests only one part of the *yin–yang* structure. In some instances hard contact is made in order to stop or stun an opponent; in others, however, the practitioner yields to the energy of the opponent, accepting it and redirecting it, thereby allowing the opponent to defeat himself or herself. This redirection, it is believed, actually brings one into harmony with one's opponent and can allow for the resolution of combat at the lowest possible level of injury.

The aspect of many martial arts which places them outside the normal pale of Western thinking is the ideal absence of a mind–body split. That is, everything which happens does so in the mind. A strike is only a strike until the mind attaches some particular meaning to it. A simple example is the difference between blocking and striking. In both instances, contact with one's opponent takes place. However, when one has been hit, and acknowledges that hit in the mind, one's reaction is distinctly different from when one interprets the event as a block. For example, I might judge that my opponent did not kick me, but that I blocked the kick with my ribs. My mind thus attaches a more positive meaning to the physical contact, and I am able to remain intentionally combative.

There is much popular advertising of the martial arts that depicts 'death touch' techniques, and there are videotapes which claim to teach one how to 'defeat any opponent, no matter how large' and to reveal 'secret teachings never before revealed'. While 'fraudulent' is perhaps too strong a word, these advertisements and popular videos are definitely misleading. A strike, a block or a kick is nothing more than a component of one's body moving in a certain direction, along a particular 'kinetic path', employing carefully chosen muscle tensions and velocity. The mind chooses what that combination of elements will manifest. At the more advanced levels of martial arts, it is the mind which an opponent must defeat, not the hands and the feet.

Much Christian commentary on the martial arts has inveighed against their connection with Asian religious and philosophical traditions. While there are religious and religio-spiritual aspects to many of the Asian martial arts, in the West few of these arts actually qualify as religious movements. That is, although meditation and the development of *qi* play a large role in some systems, those systems rarely seek to meet all the religious needs of the practitioner and rarely, if ever, require disaffiliation with one's own religious tradition.

BIBLIOGRAPHY

Journal of Asian Martial Arts; W. L. King, *Zen and the Way of the Sword: Arming the Samurai Psyche* (New York, 1993); B. Lee, *The Tao of Gung Fu: A Study in the Way of Chinese Martial Art* (Boston, MA, 1997); M. Maliszewski, *Spiritual Dimensions of the Martial Arts* (Rutland, VT, 1996); S. Shaw, *The Warrior is Silent: Martial Arts and the Spiritual Path* (Rochester, VT, 1998); Y. Tsunetomo, *The Hagakure: A Code to the Way of the Samurai* (ET T. Mukoh, Tokyo, 1980).

D. E. Cowan

NATIVE AMERICAN RELIGIONS

The term 'Native American' is ambivalent as it serves two slightly different functions. It can refer to all the peoples inhabiting the American continent before contact with Europeans, in which case it includes the Inuit, Aleuts and American Indians. Secondly, it is often used as a replacement for 'American Indian', a term sometimes seen as impugning the integrity of Native American people and culture. By and large, however, the term 'American Indian' is still acceptable and is used as an honourable self-designation by many Native Americans. This article will use 'Native American' in its more general sense.

It is difficult to make general statements about the features of Native American religion because of the great diversity from tribe to tribe, some of which is no doubt due to economic differences. For example, the Hopi, an agrarian people, focus on the Kachina spirits, who are believed to ensure the success of their crops by coming to dwell among the people each year. On the other hand, the Plains tribes recognize many Wakan beings (nature spirits) in their environment and seek good relations with them for the sake of successful hunts and battles. The Algonquin tribes of the Northeast revere a supreme god (Kitche Manitou), who supposedly watches over them and expects them to live by his commandments.

Because of the diversity of Native American cultures, it has become common practice to treat them according to geographic distribution. As different groups have come to occupy certain parts of the land, they have adopted similar ways of life and ritual practices. However, neighbouring groups often have radically different ethnic origins, as reflected in their languages, which frequently have nothing in common.

The eight main regions are: the *Arctic*, including Inuit and Aleuts; the *North-west Coast*, including the Tlingit and Haida; the *West Coast*, including the Wintou; the *Central Plateau*, including the Utes and Shoshones; the *Southwest*, including the Hopi and Navajo; the *Great Plains*, including the Sioux and the Blackfoot; the *Northeast* (together with the vast subarctic area), including the Cree and the Algonquin; and the *Southeast*, including the Creek and Cherokee.

There is one trait that is nearly universal among the Native American cultures, and that is the practice of 'shamanism'. It is not dominant among all Native American groups, but even where it is not dominant it still usually appears, whether among American Indians, Inuit or Aleuts (of whose original religion we actually know relatively little). A shaman is a spiritual leader, usually healer and diviner, who practises his art by allowing himself to be possessed by spiritual beings and then letting them speak and heal through him. The word 'shaman' was originally derived from Siberian culture, and the practice of shamanism is heavily ingrained in traditional East Asian cultures (including the Chinese and Japanese), thus lending some credence to the idea that the Native Americans came to the American continent by crossing the Bering Straits from East Asia. In popular descriptions of Native American religion, the shaman has often been called the 'medicine man'. In some societies, for example the Inuit and the Tlingit, shamans carry great power, while in others, such as the Cree and the Algonquin, their role is relatively marginal, providing primarily for the physical health of their people. In general either a man or a woman could be a shaman.

As implied in the practice of shamanism, most Native American religions are 'animistic', recognizing nature spirits of many kinds. With a few exceptions, ancestor spirits are not particularly important. The Algonquin tribes of the Northeast as well as some of the tribes of California hold to a form of monotheism, and many more tribes recognize a creator, sometimes in the form of an animal, and sometimes defamed by a 'trickster', such as the coyote.

Among the four nearly universal rites of passage (birth, puberty, marriage, death) Native Americans tend most to stress the puberty rites. Among some of the tribes of the Great Plains the young man needs to undertake a 'vision quest', in which he must live alone in the wild under difficult conditions until he receives an apparition of his personal medicine (an animal, plant or object). Among the Hopi, puberty is the time when the adolescent is inducted into the Kachina society. Women usually have to undergo ordeals at the time of their first menstruation.

As for the other three rites, birth is sometimes seen as the return of a deceased relative. Among the Inuit, marriage is remarkable in that there is very little ritual associated with it aside from a declaration. With a few exceptions, death rituals do not go much further than the disposal of the corpse; however, burial grounds are frequently considered taboo. Further common practices among Native Americans are the sweat bath, which is seen as a form of spiritual purification, and lengthy dances that combine bringing the community together with renewing its spiritual awareness.

Other than on reservations, Native American religion is not widely practised today. A glorified adaptation of American Indian spirituality, 'love the earth and live in harmony with nature', has become popular today, but it is often neither accurate with regard to actual practice nor appreciated by Native American leaders, who consider it a form of exploitation and trivialization. American Indians attempting to practise their religion have had to resort to legal remedies in order to receive formal recognition for some sacred places and practices.

Native Americans have occasionally attempted to fuse Christianity with indigenous religion. Notable examples of such fusion are the ghost-dancing movement of the 1890s and the Native American Churches, which practise a kind of communion with the hallucinogenic peyote cactus. Some American Indians today consider Christianity the religion of genocide, but others are finding it to be a religion which motivates acts of healing on the reservations.

BIBLIOGRAPHY

J. J. Collins, *Native American Religions: A Geographical Survey* (Lewiston, NY, 1991); W. Corduan, 'Native American Religion', ch. 6 of *Neighboring Faiths* (Downers Grove, IL, 1998); A. Hirschfelder and P. Molin, *The Encyclopedia of Native American Religion* (New York, 1992); W. Krickberg, H. Trimborn, W. Müller and O. Zeries, *Pre-Columbian American Religions* (London, 1968); R. F. Spencer, J. D. Jennings et al., *The Native Americans: Ethnology and Backgrounds of the North American Indians* (New York, 1977); R. M. Underhill, *Red Man's Religion: Beliefs and Practices of the Indians North of Mexico* (Chicago, 1965).

W. Corduan

NEW AGE SPIRITUALITIES

The term 'New Age', as in 'New Age spiritualities' or the 'New Age movement', has a variety of meanings. Christians have sometimes spoken of the new age inaugurated through Christ's life, death and resurrection. In the past few decades, however, 'New Age' has been used to describe a social movement (or network), as well as a family of spiritual approaches to life involving both doctrine and religious activities that are taken by most analysts to lie outside the bounds of orthodox Christianity. The popularity of the term 'New Age' reached its height in the 1980s. Many now opt for 'new/alternative spirituality' or merely 'spirituality'. However, 'New Age' is still used by some scholars, and not merely pejoratively.

New Age ideas and practices came to the fore through the countercultural revolt in Western nations in the 1960s. However their roots go further back to the nineteenth-century movements of Transcendentalism, the Mind Science churches and the Theosophical Society. Those people associated with the New Age often controversially claim to continue an ancient esoteric tradition frequently suppressed by traditional religiosity and secular philosophy.

As a social movement, the New Age has no one leader, organization or official creed, although celebrity enthusiasts abound. In the 1980s, actress Shirley MacLaine chronicled her conversion to New Age thought in several best-selling autobiographies and multiple media appearances, which helped bring the New Age perspective into the limelight. A number of New Age oriented writers, such as Marilyn Ferguson, refer to the New Age as a network of like-minded organizations and individuals who share a concern for human and planetary transformation through spiritual experiences focused on the potential of the untrammelled self. The New Age will dawn when people turn away from both atheism and the restrictive dogmas of traditional Western religions and instead embrace ideas and practices that free the self to realize its divine possibilities. This view is sometimes correlated with the astrological claim that we are moving into the Age of Aquarius. In this sense, New Age spiritualty can be loosely described as millenarian and messianic, though different people express different eschatologies. Although the New Age as a movement is composed of many different groups, New Age partisans congregate at psychic and metaphysical fairs, for special spiritual events (such as the much-hyped Harmonic Convergence of 1987), or at sacred natural sites such as Sedona, Arizona (thought to be a centre of mystical energy vortexes), or Stonehenge in England.

COMMON THEMES

Although New Age spiritualities are eclectic, syncretistic and somewhat flexible with respect to beliefs, some common themes consistently emerge. Paul Heelas rightly claims that 'the most pervasive and significant aspect of the *lingua franca* of the New Age is that the person is, in essence, spiritual.' He goes on to specify what the New Age takes the spiritual self to be. 'To experience the "Self" itself is to experience "God", the "Goddess", the "Source", "Christ Consciousness", the "inner child", the "way of the heart" or most simply and, I think, most frequently, "inner spirituality".' In other words, the self is the spiritual centre of the universe. Ted Peters captures this notion in the title of his critique of the New Age, *The Cosmic Self*. This view of self challenges the claim of monotheism that a transcendent, personal and moral Creator stands above and beyond the created self, which should submit to the Creator's authority.

Like Christianity, the New Age worldview repudiates materialistic secularism, deeming it reductionistic and unfit to accommodate our spiritual natures and possibilities. Unlike Christianity, it deems monotheism to be overly authoritarian, because it shackles the self to the concepts of finitude and sin, and fails to see Christ as uniquely God incarnate. The worldview of recent influential New Age thinkers (they may not accept the designation), such as best-selling author and medical doctor Deepak Chopra and mystic-scholar Ken Wilber, is generally pantheistic and monistic. As such, it is representative of much, though not all, of New Age spirituality. In pantheistic monism, the Deep Self or True Self or Higher Self is one with the divine essence, however infrequently it may be experienced. Chopra, much influenced by the non-dualistic Hinduism of Transcendental Meditation, holds that awareness of this divine oneness is the source of spiritual and physical health. Wilber, influenced by Zen Buddhism, works on a more theoretical level, claiming that he has synthesized both Eastern and Western traditions across a broad range of disciplines. The emphasis on monism leads many New Age teachers to deny any ultimate ontological separation between God and creation or between good and evil. New Age teachers also affirm belief in reincarnation and an openness to paranormal experiences such as past-life regression, extra-sensory perception, telepathy, telekinesis, spirit contact (or channelling), encounters with unidentified flying objects and so on.

However, New Age spiritualities are not uniformly pantheistic and monistic, and even those that are come in different varieties. Some New Age adherents advocate panentheism, a worldview that affirms that while God is in everything and everything is in God, God in some sense transcends the cosmos. This is the view of Matthew Fox, a former Catholic priest who became an Episcopalian. Furthermore, while pantheism classically affirms an impersonal and amoral deity, some New Agers, influenced by the monotheism of Judaism and Christianity, seem to attribute personal qualities (such as love and purpose) to the impersonal/amoral divine force, principle or consciousness. This tendency is found, for example, in the writings of Marianne Williamson, a popular New Age writer and speaker in the USA. Others involved in New Age spirituality are almost polytheistic in their insistence that we 'create our own reality', yet invoke the notion of universal deity and cosmic oneness in other contexts. Some traces of dualism can also be found in New Age thought, especially those schools of thought influenced by Gnosticism, which rejects matter as illusory, evil or less real than spirit.

In New Age spirituality experience is often deemed more important than mere beliefs. This experientialism is found in the use of such consciousness-expanding therapies as yoga, visualization, chanting, meditation and the group experiences offered through seminars such as Werner Erhard's 'est' (later called 'the Forum'). These 'psychotechnologies' claim to empower people to cut through their sense of limitation and finitude in order to reach the 'God within'.

Heelas has noted that New Age practitioners of many stripes employ religious traditions in a 'detraditionalized' way; that is, they select elements from various Eastern mystical and Western occult and pagan traditions that suit their individual, interior needs. The ultimate authority on spiritual matters is the self, not some external source, whether church, society or holy writ. Following the sociologist Roy Wallis, Christopher Partridge refers to this orientation as 'epistemological individualism', which is often (paradoxically, some might say) wedded to a metaphysical monism.

PREMODERN, MODERN, OR POSTMODERN?

In its cobbled-together eclecticism, New Age spirituality is akin to postmodernism, an approach that rejects fixed boundaries, foundations and established definitions in favour of alternative and rather *ad hoc* social and personal arrangements. However, the religious traditions to which the New Age typically appeals, such as Hinduism, Buddhism, Daoism and ancient Paganism, are premodern. To further complicate matters, New Age adherents may be considered modernists in at least three senses.

(1) Despite monistic claims, they retain a focus on the individual and autonomous self's sense of meaning and purpose, thus opposing the postmodernist notion of the decentred self, wherein the self dissolves into contingent social structures.

(2) New Age spiritualities maintain a commitment to the idea of cosmic progress by claiming that we are moving into a superior New Age, which is often understood as the result of 'spiritual evolution'. The idea of social progress is anathema to postmodernist sensibilities, since it smacks of a positive modernist metanarrative or totalizing ideology.

(3) Some New Age theorists, such as physicist Fritjof Capra in *The Tao of Physics* and subsequent writings, claim that the discoveries of modern physics substantiate the metaphysical claims made by ancient Eastern mystics. Whether successfully or not, this strategy seeks rational support for mystical views from modern scientific knowledge, which it takes to be reliable and objective. Therefore it seeks legitimization from a source of knowledge taken to be authoritative by modernist thinking.

CRITICISMS

Many of the first critiques of New Age spirituality came from conservative Protestant writers who saw its perspective as unbiblical and even demonic in some of its aspects. These polemical approaches ranged from sensational and apocalyptic accounts that tied the movement into end-times prophecy to more apologetic and theological evaluations. Similar treatments by conservative Roman Catholics followed, though without the apocalyptic elements. More liberal writers of both traditions often hailed the New Age as reinvigorating spirituality, albeit in heterodox ways. Sceptical, modernist critics condemned the New Age as superstitious and retrograde, since they believe that it dismissed critical rationality and the advances of secular, modernist society. Since the early 1990s, a growing number of non-confessional, scholarly books and journal articles have appeared which describe the phenomenon historically, sociologically and ethnographically.

BIBLIOGRAPHY

R. Basil (ed.), *Not Necessarily the New Age: Critical Essays* (New York, 1988); M. Ferguson, *The Aquarian Conspiracy* (Los Angeles, 1980); D. Groothuis, *Unmasking the New Age: Is There a New Religious Movement Trying to Transform Society?* (Downers Grove, IL, 1986); P. Heelas, *The New Age Movement: The Celebration of the Self and the Sacralization of Modernity* (Cambridge, MA, 1996); C. H. Partridge, 'Truth, Authority and Epistemological Individualism in New Age Thought', *JCR* 14.1, 1999, pp. 77–95; T. Peters, *The Cosmic Self: A Penetrating Look at Today's New Age Movements* (New York, 1991); S. Sutcliffe and M. Bowman (eds.), *Beyond New Age: Exploring Alternative Spirituality* (Edinburgh, 2000); K. Wilber, *A Brief History of Everything* (Boulder, CO, 1996).

D. Groothuis

NEW AGE THERAPIES

The past century has seen unprecedented progress in our understanding of how the human body works and our ability to take meaningful action when it malfunctions. Yet, in the face of the spectacular achievements of Western scientific medicine, a significant number of people in North America, Europe and Australia have embraced some very different approaches to healing, at least for certain types of problems.

In the 1970s many unorthodox therapies gathered behind the banner of 'holistic' medicine, reflecting the conviction of its proponents that they were attending to the 'whole person – body, mind and spirit'. This movement was notable for its orientation towards Eastern metaphysical and New Age spirituality, which to a large degree reflected the roots and practices of many of the therapies that congregated under its sprawling tent. For many years the holistic health movement was to some degree frustrated in its efforts to move from the fringes to the cultural mainstream. But during the 1990s the apparent stagnation came to an end as a large cadre of unconventional practices regrouped under the title of 'alternative' medicine. Some have used the term 'complementary' medicine to suggest that these practices occupy a place alongside conventional therapies, or the more optimistic term 'integrative' medicine to suggest that distinctions between alternative and conventional medicine can and should ultimately be eliminated.

Alternative therapies are now promoted in books, videos and, perhaps most extensively, on the Internet; they are given credence by governmental agencies; and they are widely presented to medical students and practising physicians as viable options, or at least practices worthy of further investigation. Amidst this decisive cultural advance, the spiritual underpinnings of many of the therapies have not been lost. Indeed, some newer faces, such as Deepak Chopra, MD, have widely proclaimed predigested Eastern mysticism as the most direct path to health and wholeness.

Such a wide and bewildering array of alternative therapies have entered the public square that any attempts to describe them in depth in an article of this length would be impossible. Some observers have attempted to bring highly diverse therapies together under broad categories such as 'mind–body' or 'bodywork' practices, but all too often such groupings place approaches that are straightforward and sensible on the same footing with others that are far-fetched or even bizarre. For our purposes, it is far more useful to place alternative therapies into four broad categories based upon their compatibility with well-established principles of biology and physics. It should be noted that, in nearly every case, the more distant a practice drifts from the scientific mainstream, the more likely it is to carry spiritual overtones that are at odds with the fundamental teachings of Scripture.

CATEGORY I: IN LINE WITH SCIENTIFIC PRINCIPLE

The assumptions and practices of these therapies do not require a departure from well-established principles of biology and scientific research.

For these practices, the primary issues are efficacy and safety. For example, many herbal preparations (St John's wort,

Echinacea, *Ginkgo biloba* and goldenseal, to name a few) are now actively marketed to consumers for a variety of ills. (In the United States, however, claims that a given preparation is effective for treating a specific disease may not be made, though more vague 'structure and function' claims are allowed. For example, *Ginkgo biloba* can be marketed as a substance that 'improves mental sharpness' but not as a treatment for Alzheimer's disease.) The evidence supporting the usefulness of these preparations varies considerably from one substance to the next, but the answer to the question 'How might this work?' does not require a departure from basic biochemical principles.

Biofeedback utilizes electronic equipment to help an individual gain some influence over bodily functions that are not normally under conscious control. This has been useful, for example, in helping patients control migraine headaches. In this context biofeedback is not pushing against any scientific or spiritual boundaries. Some researchers, however, have attempted to utilize biofeedback as a sort of 'electronic yoga', combining it with meditative techniques in an effort to generate 'higher states of consciousness'. Such hybrid practices fall into category III or even category IV, to be described below.

CATEGORY II: SCIENTIFIC CONNECTIONS

Therapies in this class keep at least some connection (if only in terminology) with widely accepted principles of biology, but then take a 'flying leap' into uncharted (or self-charted) territory.

Many current alternative therapies, and nostrums from bygone days, fall into this category. These include a number of dietary regimes and nutritional supplements, including megavitamin therapies, which claim to improve practically any chronic symptom. Proponents of 'environmental medicine' claim that a bewildering variety of vaguely defined toxins, food allergies, mercury in dental fillings, radiation from electronic devices and power lines, organisms such as the yeast *Candida albicans* and even the ingredients in clothing are responsible for a host of chronic symptoms, especially fatigue. The diagnostic tests for these disturbances (sometimes called 'multiple chemical sensitivities') usually strain credibility, as do the proposed solutions. Nevertheless, most practitioners attempt to base their deliberations, however convoluted, on the language of contemporary science, even if they stray considerably from its methodologies.

The same could be said of the use of magnets to treat a variety of chronic conditions. Some even suggest that many of us suffer from 'magnetic field deficiency syndrome', arising from changes in the earth's magnetic field and the shielding effects of concrete and steel in cities. There is an abundance of suspiciously grandiose claims about magnets and a scant supply of solid evidence to support them, although further research may in fact confirm that magnets are of some use in the treatment of conditions such as chronic pain.

Hard-core (or 'straight') chiropractic, which claims that most or all disease can be treated using spinal manipulation, also falls into this category. Explanations of how manipulative therapy might help many cases of back and neck pain do not strain credibility. (This application of chiropractic would fit into category I above.) But the claim that dominion may be gained over the entire body via the spinal column and the nerve trunks that exit from it definitely takes some liberties with human anatomy and physiology.

CATEGORY III: RADICAL DEPARTURES FROM SCIENTIFIC PRINCIPLES

These therapies (often comprehensive systems of health care) postulate mechanisms of disease and treatment which are a radical departure from well-established principles of biology. ('If these are true, rewrite the textbooks.') Alternative practices in this category, some of which are hundreds or even thousands of years old, make a decisive break with well-validated science and usually arrive with metaphysical baggage firmly attached.

Traditional Chinese medicine, for example, is a direct outgrowth of Daoism, in which health is defined as a balance of *yin* and *yang*, the two basic forces that are said to generate all transformations in the universe. The ancient Chinese described the flow of an invisible energy, *qi* (or *ch'i*), through twelve pairs of equally invisible channels in the body. Traditional practitioners today continue to describe disease in terms of disturbances in this energy flow, which they diagnose through an elaborate assessment of the appearance of the tongue and the pulses of the wrists. (Categories of disease commonly recognized in the West – pneumonia, for example – are meaningless in this system.) Treatments of imbalances in *qi* may involve dietary changes, herbs, breathing techniques, meditative and physical exercises and direct manipulation via acupuncture needles placed at strategic locations in the skin.

Acupuncture has made a considerable splash in the West, and many researchers have postulated a variety of neurological mechanisms by which it might alter pain and certain other symptoms. Aside from such narrowly defined applications (which represent a drastic departure from the ancient understanding), traditional Chinese medicine is inseparable from its religious roots, both in theory and in practice.

The same could be said for *ayurveda*, the East Indian traditional medicine that has been promulgated in the West with metaphysical flair by Deepak Chopra, MD. In numerous best-sellers such as *Quantum Healing* and *Ageless Body, Timeless Mind*, Dr Chopra has set forth a popularized vision of Eastern mysticism in which transformation of consciousness, and in particular grasping one's divinity or godhood, leads to optimal health, happiness and prosperity.

Practitioners of therapeutic touch, a technique circulated most commonly among nurses, claim that variations in another kind of invisible life energy called *prana* can be detected by passing one's hands a few inches above the body of the patient. Excesses or deficiencies in this energy are said to be improved by sweeping it away with the hands or infusing it where needed, all while in a meditative state. In spite of its overt mysticism, profound subjectivism and general defiance of the laws of physics, it has been taught in dozens of universities around the world and has been the subject of a number of serious research studies.

These practices, along with other category III therapies such as homeopathy, promote an age-old notion called 'vitalism': the idea that an invisible, nonmaterial, unmeasurable 'life energy' flows throughout the universe and in all living things. Over the centuries this energy has been given many names. In Daoism and ancient Chinese medicine it is *qi* (*ch'i, ki*); in Hinduism and *ayurveda*, *prana*; in Polynesian traditions, *mana*. Franz Anton Mesmer and subsequent 'magnetic healers' have referred to 'animal magnetism'; D. D. Palmer and 'straight' chiropractic speak of 'innate intelligence'; Samuel Hahnemann and homeopathy of 'vital energy'; Wilhelm Reich of 'orgone energy'; and contemporary energy therapists of 'subtle energy'.

Both ancient and contemporary proponents of 'life energy' therapies routinely make a number of assumptions (set out below) which have profound implications in the realms of biology, physics and theology.

Life energy is the fabric of the universe. By whatever name it is called, this energy is said to flow throughout the universe and through all living (and in some traditions, non-living) entities. Some enthusiasts have misapplied Einstein's equation $E = mc^2$, which describes the conversion of matter into energy in very specific conditions (such as an atomic reactor), to living organisms as 'proof' that we are all congealed energy. Conventional medicine is thus described as old-fashioned, mechanistic and 'Newtonian' because it deals with the human body in material rather than 'energetic' terms.

Disease arises from an imbalance or blockage of the flow of life energy in the body. In many life energy therapies, specific diagnoses such as diabetes or rheumatoid arthritis are far less meaningful than detecting disturbances in energy flow. Furthermore, each person's energy problem tends to be seen as a 'one of a kind' event, in terms of both underlying problem and treatment. As a result, research which attempts to assess the effects of an energy therapy on a certain condition – and especially to compare one treatment with another, or with no treatment – may be very difficult to design and carry out.

Life energy and its disturbances can be detected in a variety of ways. Although there is no consistent or coherent scientific evidence that *qi*, *prana*, or any of the other invisible energies actually exists, and such existence has never been acknowledged by the scientific establishment, proponents describe a number of techniques which are said to provide information about the status of such energies within the body. Most of these are low-tech (though often complex and esoteric), highly subjective, or even quasi- or overtly psychic in nature. Traditional Chinese practitioners, for example, assess six different positions of each radial (wrist) pulse in order to determine how *qi* is allegedly flowing through each of twelve pairs of invisible channels, called 'meridians'. Some contemporary variations, such as 'applied kinesiology' (not to be confused with kinesiology, the well-recognized study of body movements), test the strength of certain 'indicator' muscles to uncover the same information. Some electronic devices which claim to detect changes in *qi* or the presence of acupuncture points are essentially measuring local variations in skin resistance, which by no means prove the existence of this or any other type of energy flow (let alone the presence of health problems related to it).

Life energy can be adjusted, activated, channelled or otherwise manipulated in order to treat illness or maximize health. Therapists may claim to normalize the flow of energy in any number of ways, including massage, light touch or acupuncture needling at certain points on the skin, hand passes along the body, dietary, herbal or homeopathic remedies, or electronic gadgets of various sorts. Many claim that life energy can be manipulated through meditative techniques in which one visualizes a change in its flow through the body. As with diagnostic techniques, the actual effects of such treatments are unmeasurable, with validation hinging upon subjective changes in symptoms, testimonies concerning the improvement or cure of illness and so forth.

Alterations of life energy are the cause of events that previously have been called 'supernatural' or 'miraculous'. Despite claims that the flow of life energy is as natural as the flow of ultraviolet rays from the sun, its alleged importance in the well-being of living tissue and its purported response to human consciousness make it a prime candidate as the explanation for events which have previously been considered supernatural. However, such dramatic manifestations have appeared only on the silver screen, as, for example, in the depiction of the Force in George Lucas's immensely popular *Star Wars* films. But even without convincing physical demonstrations of its alleged power, life energy comes with a very potent spiritual dimension securely attached (see below).

Life energy is what religions have called 'God'. If life energy, by whatever name it is addressed, fills and flows through the universe and has intelligence and power, it must be God; in using the term 'God', however, we are thinking of a being or entity very different from the personal, loving God of the Bible. In much New Age thought 'God' and 'energy' are simply interchangeable. Furthermore, if our true identity, the stuff of which we are made, is in fact an impersonal energy which fills the universe, than we are in essence God. The idea of a universal life energy is a powerful connecting link between the metaphysical notion of monism (the idea that 'All is One' in the universe) and everyday concerns about health. While not all energy therapists are actively proclaiming themselves (and their patients) to be God (in fact, some would deny any connection between their treatment and Eastern mysticism), this spiritual baggage is pervasive throughout the ancient roots and modern manifestations of these practices.

CATEGORY IV: THE SUPERNATURAL

These therapies explicitly claim to engage with and manipulate supernatural forces and entities.

In pursuit of healing for oneself and others, the individual engaging in these practices intends to interact with supernatural forces and entities in order to control them (or vice versa) and/or to tap into some form of expanded consciousness in which all manner of extraordinary knowledge and power is supposedly available.

Shamans psychic diagnosticians and healers fall into this category, as do psychic surgeons, although the latter have been widely debunked through close observation by professional magicians. The former may refer to themselves as 'medical intuitives' in an effort to add some semantic respectability to their practice, and may claim to visualize the flows of 'life energy' such as *qi* and *prana*, which are invisible to the rest of humanity.

CONCLUSION

This article has raised concerns and warnings about a variety of alternative therapies, but it is worth noting that conventional Western medicine (and its patients) could benefit by paying closer attention to a number of themes that are prominent within the alternative movement. These include: (1) an emphasis on the body's *capacity to heal itself*, given time and reasonable support; (2) the importance of *lifestyle* (especially food choices and exercise patterns) in maintaining health; (3) the role of *belief and expectation* in illness and healing, and thus the importance of a trusting, positive relationship between patient and health-care provider; (4) the importance of a '*support team*' of caring people (family, friends, fellow church members) in health and healing; and (5) the role of a *meaningful faith* in health and recovery from illness.

There is no reason why such themes should remain primarily within the province of practices that wander far from the scientific mainstream or that propagate the false gospel that God is energy and that 'All is One'. It is to be hoped that in the next decade conventional practitioners, especially those who are committed to Christ, will not only resist the advance of mythological and New Age medicine but also take the initiative to address and reframe the important themes of the alternative movement.

BIBLIOGRAPHY

D. O'Mathuna and W. Larimore, *Alternative Medicine: The Christian Handbook* (Grand Rapids, 2001); P. C. Reisser, D. Mabe and R. Velarde, *Examining Alternative Medicine* (Downers Grove, 2001); J. Sire, *The Universe Next Door* (Leicester and Downers Grove, 1997).

P. C. Reisser

NEW RELIGIOUS MOVEMENTS (DEFINITIONS)

'New religious movement' (NRM) is the preferred term used by most sociologists and religious studies scholars to identify a religious group of recent origin that is usually referred to as a 'cult' or a 'sect'. Henry Fielding's comment in his novel *Tom Jones*, 'By religion I mean Christianity; by Christianity I mean Protestantism; by Protestantism I mean the Church of England as established by law', helps us understand the terminological debate surrounding terms like 'cult' and 'NRM'. No doubt, if we substituted 'the Jehovah's Witnesses', or 'the Latter Day Saints', for 'the Church of England', many Jehovah's Witnesses and Mormons could easily adopt Fielding's view as their own. Unfortunately, this sort of definition identifies 'religion', or 'true religion', with one particular tradition to the exclusion and stigmatization of all others. Therefore, many academics, particularly those working in sociology and religious studies, prefer to use the term 'NRMs' to identify religious movements such as the Hare Krishna Movement, the Unification Church, Scientology and a host of similar groups that rose to prominence in Western society in the 1960s and 1970s.

THE TERM 'CULT'

Most theologians, particularly evangelicals, prefer to use the term 'cult' for such groups, which in parts of Europe are also called 'youth religions'. The problem with this usage is that it implies deviation from a particular standard of truth based on a framework of Christian orthodoxy that is rejected by many people in modern society. Many psychologists also prefer to use the term 'cult' for those movements they identify as being psychologically manipulative. However, the problem with such psychological critiques is that they usually apply with equal force to most aspects of Christian experience, particularly conversion. For these and similar reasons many scholars argue that the use of value-free terminology is essential if we are to understand the beliefs and social significance of groups that are all too easily dismissed as cults.

Countering this argument, many theologians and psychologists argue that value-free terminology fails to distinguish between good or bad, true or false religions. Advocates of value-free terminology reply that understanding precedes criticism and that it is impossible to decide whether a religion is good or bad until its beliefs and practices are both understood and seen in a comparative context alongside those of other religious groups. Thus in their article 'The Tnevnoc Cult' David Bromley and Anson Shupe (*Sociological Analysis* 40, 1980, pp. 361–366) describe in great detail an apparently evil cult that takes total control of its members' lives. After building up the reader's expectations, the authors reveal that 'Tnevnoc' is 'convent' spelt backwards and that their description is of a traditional Roman Catholic convent, their aim being to illustrate how easy it is to apply a double standard when discussing religious issues.

ARE ALL RELIGIONS NEW RELIGIOUS MOVEMENTS?

At some point in time all religions were 'new'. Consequently, some people speak about Christianity, Islam and other historic religions in their formative years as 'NRMs'. Although this usage may be helpful in understanding social processes, it runs the risk of making all religions new religions and so diluting the term that it loses all significance. It also fails to recognize certain fundamental ideological differences between historic religions and contemporary NRMs. Therefore, most scholars who use the term 'NRM' restrict its use to groups that have emerged in the last 200 years.

NEW RELIGIOUS MOVEMENTS AND TECHNOLOGY

One reason for choosing the beginning of the nineteenth century as the watershed that divides NRMs from world religions like Christianity and Islam is the impact of technology on human thought. Whilst initially one might get the opposite impression, without exception NRMs are actually claiming to be compatible with science and technology in ways that traditional religions are not. Of course, most scientists reject the claims of NRMs about the relationship of their beliefs to science. Nevertheless, the role of these claims distinguishes NRMs from traditional religions.

During the nineteenth century rapid technological changes created a new outlook on life. Instead of looking to the past for guidance, as they had until that time, people began to look to the future. At the same time the entire basis of daily life was changed as agricultural societies were transformed into urban industrial societies. These changes created equally great and largely unrecognized shifts in attitudes toward religion in general and Christianity in particular. Prior to the nineteenth century, Christians identified with the wisdom of the ages and claimed the heritage of Roman civilization. Consequently, belief in miracles and prophecy and a host of other beliefs that modern people find problematic were not an issue for our ancestors. Indeed, until the mid-nineteenth century, Christian apologists freely appealed to miracles and prophecy as evidence for the truth of Christianity. All of this changed rapidly as technology made science a living reality and the Romans began to appear technologically primitive, superstitious and irrational. Thus the conversion of Roman civilization to Christianity was no longer considered remarkable; it simply confirmed the credulity of ignorant people. Religion came to be regarded, in other words, as old-fashioned, and Christian teachings about miracles and prophecies became embarrassments. It was as if science had declared biblical and other spiritual realities illusions. This displacement of Christianity created a spiritual vacuum, a vacuum that NRMs began to fill.

Recognizing the role of science and technology in shaping the beliefs of NRMs, it is possible to distinguish between NRMs and traditional world religions. Thus while all world religions make some accommodation to science, none incorporates ideas about science in its core beliefs and mythologies. On the other hand, NRMs make their claims about the scientific nature of their worldviews a central part of their apologetic, understanding their beliefs to be philosophically superior to those of traditional world religions, particularly Christianity.

Bernard Grun's study *The Timetables of History* enables a careful comparison of the developments in technology with those in religion and philosophy. It reveals that whilst prior to 1775 technological developments were few and far between, after that date their frequency rapidly increased. When one then examines the types of religion that emerged before and after this watershed date, it becomes apparent that, whilst before 1775 there are continuous religious developments as sects grow out of existing religions, after 1775 a new type of religion emerges. Although, at first, there are a few transitional religions (e.g. Swedenborgianism) which span the two eras, eventually the truly 'modern' religions begin to appear, such as, for example, the

Church of Jesus Christ of Latter Day Saints (the Mormons), Christian Science and, more recently, Scientology and a variety of new religions of Eastern origin. That technological change did have an impact on these groups can be seen in the speeches given by, for example, Swami Vivekananda (1863–1902) and other non-Christian speakers at the World Parliament of Religions in Chicago in 1893, where a sense of modernity pervades the entire proceedings. Again and again speakers emphasize that their religion is 'true' because, unlike Christianity, it is compatible with the modern world.

Hence, whereas initially the claim that, for example, Mormonism is a truly modern religious reaction to technological change may seem absurd to anyone unfamiliar with Mormon theology, a close examination of Mormon scriptures, particularly *Doctrine and Covenants* (1835) and *The Pearl of Great Price* (1851) and the church's earliest systematic theology, Parley P. Pratt's (1805–1859) *The Key To Theology* (1855), will demonstrate that a major feature is speculation about other worlds and the evolutionary development of humankind through what they term 'the law of eternal progression'. These teachings clearly reflect the impact of science and technology and demonstrate their role in reshaping traditional religious themes derived from the Christian tradition. Similarly, an examination of the texts of other new religions, including more traditional groups like the Hare Krishna movement (ISKCON), reveals similar reactions to modernity and attempts to present themselves as truly scientific and at home with technology.

TYPOLOGIES

Because of the vast diversity of NRMs, which number thousands, some very small indeed, scholars have proposed various typological models to aid classification. (1) *Monistic* and *dualistic* groups: monistic groups are characterized by subjectivity and moral relativism; dualistic groups believe in a transcendent reality and moral absolutes. (2) Groups which seek the sacred *inside* or *outside* the human self. (3) Groups that aim to *integrate* or to *transform* the individual and society. (4) Groups may be identified by the extent to which members share *a common life*. (5) Groups can be classified according to their degree of *world affirmation* or *world denial*. (6) Classification might also focus on the *individual's involvement*, as follows: *audience cults* provide people with teachings but little else; *client cults* provide spiritual services to members in return for a low level of involvement; *cult movements* make heavy demands on their members and often require communal living. (7) Some scholars identify *devotee*, *discipleship* and *apprenticeship* groups as the three main social types found among NRMs. (8) Finally, a theological classification might also be attempted. This way of classifying NRMs, which focuses on a group's ideological roots, identifies four major sources that NRMs use to create their own belief systems. The *Abramic*, it is claimed, go back to the patriarch Abraham and involve belief in a creator God; the *yogic* have one of the many forms of yoga at their core; the *primal* draw upon spiritual experiences, such as communication with spirit beings, dreams, etc., common in primal religions; and the *modern* emphasize the use of scientific and pseudo-scientific terminology.

NEW RELIGIOUS MOVEMENTS AS 'DANGEROUS CULTS'

Newspapers, particularly in the 1980s, often published, and still do publish, lurid stories about life in the 'cults'. Although there are some sensational exceptions, most of these stories owe far more to the need to sell newspapers than to anything else. Most NRMs are relatively harmless groups that genuinely seek spiritual solutions to the problems of modern life. The greatest difficulty facing new religions is that, because they are *new*, they often lack the built-in safeguards that established religions have developed over time. When Buddhist, Hindu or Islamic sects are transported to the West they tend to lose contact with the culture that nourished them. Consequently, they can easily go astray and act as though they have no roots. Similarly, Christian Bible study groups which gradually gain their independence from the established church are also prone to develop authoritarian structures, because they too lack the restraints which traditional churches provide.

With NRMs the danger is even greater, because most lack the restraints that even transplanted sects retain. Fortunately, many NRMs adopt from established traditions mechanisms of social control that limit the ability of their members to act in socially destructive ways. For example, religions such as Mormonism, the Zulu religion known as the amaNazaretha and the Unification Church are all firmly rooted in the moral teachings of the world religions. Therefore, there are some things, such as committing suicide, that devoted members will not do because they are against a moral code which is external to the group and its leadership structure.

Here it is important to recognize that when Joseph Smith created the Latter Day Saints in the 1830s he rooted its ethics and social outlook in traditional Christianity. Therefore, in moral terms, the Mormons are Christian. Isaiah Shembe, the founder of the South African NRM the amaNazaretha, welded Christian ethics to traditional Zulu codes of behaviour. Thus he created a clear moral framework for his followers. Similarly, Sun Myung Moon united Christian and Confucian ethics in a creative dialogue that his followers claim has maintained the best of both systems.

Other new religions, unfortunately, are not rooted in established moral systems. Rather, they seek to create their own standard of values that they see as transcending all previous moralities. In many cases these values may be perfectly reasonable. Indeed, they may be admirable. But, cut loose from historical roots, they can easily become bizarre and socially destructive. The best example of this type of NRM can be seen in the proliferation of 'scientific religions' like the Ludendorf Bewegung, which proliferated in Germany between 1919 and 1945. These groups rejected traditional Christian morality because of its link to Judaism and positively valued Hitler and the Nazi movement. Today many similar groups exist, particularly in what is generally known as the New Age movement, movements that in Germany at least, as Peter Kratz has shown, have direct links to the Nazi past.

INTERPRETING NEW RELIGIOUS MOVEMENTS

There are several conflicting interpretations of the significance of NRMs. Some scholars suggest that they are the last fling of a dying religious consciousness in the face of science and secularization, whilst others argue that religions do not die; they simply change. NRMs are therefore a symptom of a massive change in modern society.

All NRMs must be seen in a global context, not simply in a Western context. NRMs, whether in the West or elsewhere, draw inspiration from each other in very complex ways that tap into local and global traditions. Finally, many Christian writers see NRMs as part of a continuing revolt against Christian belief originating in the Enlightenment, or even as the result of demonic activity.

RESEARCH INTO NEW RELIGIOUS MOVEMENTS

Although a vast literature exits dealing with 'cults' and NRMs, a great deal of it is based on secondary sources that discuss the literature and doctrines of NRMs or else it consists of scholarly discussions of other scholars' views, particularly on issues such as conversion and accusations of 'brainwashing'. Surprisingly, there are very few studies of particular NRMs such as the Unification Church, or ritual magic, and not many comparative studies based on field research, primary sources or solid historical research. Nevertheless, NRMs are a fast-growing field in both university teaching and research which promises to attract considerable attention in the future.

BIBLIOGRAPHY

E. Barker, *New Religious Movements: A Practical Introduction* (London, 1989); M. F. Bednarowski, *New Religions and the Theological Imagination in America* (Bloomington, IN, 1989); D. Bromley and A. Shupe, *Strange Gods: The Great American Cult Scare* (Boston, MA, 1981); B. Grun, *The Timetables of History* (New York, 1975); I. Hexham and K. Poewe, *Understanding Cults and New Religions* (Grand Rapids, IL, 1986; reprinted Vancouver, 1998); P. Kratz, *Des Götter des New Age* (Berlin, 1994); R. Stark and W. S. Bainbridge, *The Future of Religion: Secularization, Revival and Cult Formation* (Berkeley, CA, 1985).

I. Hexham

NEW RELIGIONS OF AFRICAN ORIGIN

Professor Walter Hollenweger has repeatedly pointed out that within the black community in the city of Birmingham, England, there exist literally scores of new African religious movements (NARMs) that are virtually ignored by scholars. Similarly, Professor Christoph Bochinger, of the University of Bayreuth, Germany, recently began work on a major study of African religions in Germany after observing that they 'are spreading like wildfire among immigrant communities. Yet nobody knows anything about them.' Actually there are a few books dealing with this increasingly important area (see Bibliography), but unfortunately, such studies are few and far between and a lot of work remains to be done.

A HISTORY OF NEW AFRICAN RELIGIOUS MOVEMENTS

To understand NARMs it is necessary to consider the history of so-called African Independent, or Indigenous, Churches (AICs) and European reactions to them. The first recorded genuine AIC was founded by the Methodist preacher Nehemiah Tile in South Africa. He dissented from the racist policies of his white supervisors in 1883 and founded his own church in 1884. An essentially Thembu movement, Tile's movement combined Christian teachings with Thembu nationalism. Unfortunately this brave experiment soon disintegrated after Tile's death in 1891. From the 1880s onwards many AICs developed throughout Africa. But most of these were small affairs that attracted few followers and soon failed. It was not until the turn of the century that large-scale AICs finally took root among black Africans. Today there are literally thousands of AICs in South Africa alone and many more throughout the continent. The majority of these movements are very small affairs with their own prophet and a handful of members organized as house churches. Several, however, are very large, well-organized movements with a membership in the millions, and have stood the test of time.

The oldest continuously existing major AIC is the Nazareth Baptist Church of the amaNazarites, founded in 1912 by the Zulu prophet Isaiah Shembe (1867–1935) and having about one million members. Today the largest Southern African AIC is the Zion Christian Church, which was founded in 1924 by Ignatius Lekganyane (1885–1948) and has around five million members. In Central Africa, the Church of Jesus Christ on Earth through the Prophet Simon Kimbangu (d. 1951) is equally large, while in West Africa the Aladura movement probably has the most members. No one East African church seems to dominate the scene, although the Jamaa movement and churches such as the African Israel Church Nineveh and the African Brotherhood Church have a significant presence.

Taken together, however, AIC membership throughout Africa involves millions of people and far outstrips the membership of established mission churches or denominations. In South Africa alone, for example, David Chidester estimates that in 1990 'over 30% of the Black population of South Africa' actively belonged to AICs. This figure represents a doubling of Independent Church membership in Southern Africa during the thirty years since 1960. Equally significant is the fact that over the last twenty-five years increasing numbers of African immigrants have brought their religions to Europe and North America, where they thrive within immigrant communities.

WESTERN SCHOLARSHIP AND NEW AFRICAN RELIGIOUS MOVEMENTS

The earliest European interpreters of NARMs understood them to be either a return to paganism and/or a direct political challenge to Western imperialism. This attitude is reflected in John Buchan's best-selling novel *Prester John* (1910): the highly offensive language shocks the contemporary reader into recognizing the depth of prejudice against African religious leaders and AICs. Although Buchan is an extreme case, similar attitudes were widespread until quite recently. Known until the 1930s as 'the Separatist Church Movement' or 'Ethiopianism', AICs were viewed by colonial administrators as attempts by Africans to organize politically under the guise of religion.

Many missionaries acknowledged that some Africans genuinely created new churches, but generally attributed this to a desire 'to be freed from European control', 'personal ambition', a lack of church discipline, and a return to 'tribal customs', along with an urge 'to administer church property and money'. Thus, established mission church leaders tended to agree with their colonial counterparts about the political nature of Ethiopianism but added a religious twist. The phenomenal growth of African Independent Churches, they argued, was the direct result of 'sheep stealing'; that is, these churches gained converts by stealing them from established mission churches. Unlike 'true Christians', AICs did not convert the heathens, but rather returned new converts to Christianized forms of 'paganism'.

Behind the negative reaction of white observers lies the deeply ingrained belief that black Africans are unspiritual beings incapable of genuine religious activity. The idea that Africans could sincerely disagree with white interpretations of theology and develop their own indigenous theologies was unthinkable. (The irony in such an attitude can be seen when it is realized that many British missionaries to Africa were Scots whose theology drew upon the work of that greatest of African theologians, Augustine.) The legacy of such prejudicial scholarship can be seen as late as 1990, when the award-winning journalist Allister Sparks dismissed AICs as 'deeply conservative' movements that, he falsely claimed, attract the less-educated.

Against these negative evaluations of African spirituality, some missionaries, such as the Anglican Henry Callaway (1817–90), recognized the importance of understanding African religious beliefs and appreciating African spirituality. But, on the whole, Callaway's approach was ignored by most English-speaking missionaries. On the other hand, under the influence of Romanticism and the writings of the church historian August Neander (1789–1850), who emphasized the importance of personal biography in his histories of the early church, German missions took a more positive attitude to African spirituality by, for example, encouraging their converts to record their dreams and other spiritual experiences. Nevertheless, it is true to say that German missionaries were as shocked as their English counterparts when Africans actually founded their own churches.

The first positive evaluation of AICs came with the publication of Lindsay Roberts' 1934 MA thesis. In this pioneering work Roberts argued that whatever one might say about 'other Separatist Movements', Shembe's church was a genuine missionary movement that made real converts from paganism. In the same year, John Dube, a famous African leader and writer, agreed with Roberts' viewpoint in a book he published in Zulu. Twelve years later Bishop Bengt Sundkler, a Swedish Lutheran missionary, published his groundbreaking *Bantu Prophets in South Africa* (1948), which was the first widely circulated academic work to take AICs seriously. A year later Katesa Schlosser published the first book to survey the rise of AICs in Africa south of the Sahara. Unfortunately, it was published in German and was never translated into English. Therefore, it was not until the appearance of Fred Welbourn's *East African Rebels* (1961), followed by the studies of H. W. Turner, David Barrett and J. D. Y. Peel in the late 1960s, that AICs received serious attention in the English-speaking world. The work of Marie-Louise Martin on the Kimbanguists in the late 1960s also needs to be noted, although, initially published in German, it was not translated into English until the early 1970s.

'NEW AFRICAN RELIGIOUS MOVEMENTS' OR 'AFRICAN INDEPENDENT CHURCHES'?

As a result of their neglect and the clearly racist attacks upon AICs, there is a tendency today among Christians and academics to see all AICs as Africanized forms of Christianity, Christianity in an African cultural garb. Yet this evaluation is not necessarily correct and is rejected by some African leaders. Londa Shembe (1944–89), the grandson of Isaiah Shembe and leader of one branch of the amaNazarites with 75,000 followers, persuasively argued that 'in the past Europeans used a stick in their attempt to destroy us by claiming that NARMs resulted from a mindless return to traditional paganism. Today, they use the carrot and attempt to convince us that we are really all Christians with a few minor cultural adaptations. Neither viewpoint is correct.'

According to Londa Shembe, the amaNazarites are a NARM with roots in both Judaism and the Hindu tradition that was brought to Natal by Indian migrants in the 1880s. Recent research by Andreas Hauser has shown that Londa Shembe's suggestion that his grandfather Isaiah Shembe had close contact with the Indian community is correct, although it has still to be established that this contact decisively affected his theology. Nevertheless, the idea that Hinduism may have influenced the amaNazarites raises serious objections against identifying all NARMs as AICs.

Many may well be distinct NARMs, as Londa Shembe claimed. This interpretation is supported by the fact that in the 1920s the South African theosophical healer Johanna Brant (1876–1964) had several of her mystical writings translated into the major African languages and freely distributed among black Africans. At the same time, Swedenborgian and other esoteric missions were active in South Africa and, according to Rosalind Hackett, among blacks in Nigeria.

All of this suggests that we are wrong to see NARMs as simply 'African forms of Christianity', when many may actually be genuinely *new* religions outside the Christian tradition. Yet even here we must be careful. Some leaders, like Isaiah Shembe, left behind a complex and often divided heritage. Londa Shembe's uncle and rival, Amos Shembe (1907–96), was the leader of the largest branch of the movement with around 750,000 members. There is no doubt that he saw himself as an African Christian and his movement as an African form of Christianity. Nor is there any doubt that both the Bible and Jesus Christ play a major role in the worship and theology of this branch of the amaNazarites. In the final analysis, far more research needs to be done on all AICs and NARMs before we can reach any firm conclusions about their true nature.

DISTINCTIVES OF 'AFRICAN INDEPENDENT CHURCHES' AND 'NEW AFRICAN RELIGIOUS MOVEMENTS'

Bengt Sundkler popularized a basic distinction between what he called 'Zionist' and 'Ethiopian' type churches in Africa. Essentially, Sundkler argued that Zionist churches are churches that consciously identify themselves with Zion and use terms like 'Zion', 'Apostolic', 'Jerusalem', etc. in their names. These churches, he argued, can be traced to the work of John Alexander Dowie, who in 1896 founded the Christian Catholic Apostolic Church in Zion City, Illinois. The other main type he designated 'Ethiopian'; in his view these are (a) churches that 'seceded from White Mission Churches chiefly on racial grounds, or (b) other Bantu Churches seceding from the Bantu leaders classified under (a)' (B. Sundkler, *Bantu Prophets in South Africa*, pp. 53–54). These basic polar distinctions have bedevilled the study of AICs until today because, although they were ignored by Welbourn, they were quickly adopted by popular writers and some scholars.

More recently, however, the distinction has clearly broken down; most people working in the field tend to argue that a large number of different types of religious movement can be found among AICs along a spectrum that moves from churches which are virtually indistinguishable from mission churches, such as the Namibian Herero Oruuano Church, to 'pagan' revivalist movements like the one led by the Zulu prophet Laduma Madela. Between these two extremes are many variations and shades of cultural accommodation, all creating movements that provide Africans with 'a place to feel at home' (Welbourn) in a world of rapid social change.

Nevertheless, most AICs and NARMs seem to centre on a founder who may or may not claim prophetic and healing gifts, but who is certainly supported in his or her work by prophets and healers. The Bible usually figures prominently in the theology of AICs and even in some NARMs. Thus aspects of biblical teaching often ignored by European Christians, such as footwashing, baptism for ritual purposes such as exorcism, and the spiritual power of running water or the sea, are often emphasized. Furthermore, while most AICs and NARMs form local congregations that meet as house churches or worship groups, the majority of them, including the Christian AICs, proclaim the sacred nature of particular mountains, streams, springs or holy cities, and almost all of these groups practise pilgrimage to sacred sites associated with their founder's vision and use icons of the founder and other religious leaders.

CONCLUSION

NARMs are a growing and little-studied aspect of NRMs generally. Although they usually attract African migrants in Europe and North America, a few members of other ethnic groups are attracted to them and some even become initiates. Having said that, to date no NARM has enjoyed the success of similar movements of Asian origin in the West. However, given the contemporary popularity of African art and music in the West, it is probably only a matter of time before one of these groups breaks out of its immigrant ghetto.

BIBLIOGRAPHY

E. O. A. Adejobi, *A Brief History of the Pioneering of the Church of the Lord (Aladura) South London* (Birmingham, 1979); S. Barnes, *Africa's Ogun* (Chicago, 1989); T. T. Booth, *We True Christians* (Birmingham, 1984); G. ter Harr, *Halfway to Paradise: African Christians in Europe* (Cardiff, 1998); C. S. Hill, *Black Churches: West Indian and African Sects in Britain* (London, 1971); G. E. Simpson, *Black Religions in the New World* (New York, 1978); B. Sundkler, *Bantu Prophets in South Africa* (London, 21961); F. Welbourn, *East African Rebels* (London, 1961).

I. Hexham

NEW RELIGIOUS MOVEMENTS IN BUDDHISM

It is 2,500 years since the time of the Buddha, and during that period many great traditions have emerged in Buddhism and some have died away. Designation of religious movements as *new* has to be qualified in at least two ways. First, movements are new in the sense that they have emerged in the West during the twentieth century. Second, movements are new in that they have only recently emerged as a distinct tradition within Buddhism as a whole. This article is particularly concerned with Buddhist movements that have won adherents among Western people.

The first European to be ordained as a Buddhist monk was Gordon Douglas, who was ordained as Asoka at a temple near Colombo in 1899, but he died shortly afterwards. Alan Bennett McGregor (1872–1923) entered a Burmese monastery in 1901; he returned to Britain in 1907 to form a small Buddhist society supported by the Theosophical Society and including the influential Christmas Humphreys. A year later a small group of Buddhist missionaries came from Sri Lanka and settled in Britain. In 1924 Humphreys, with others, formed the Buddhist Lodge of the Theosophical Society, which continued until 1943, when the name was changed to the Buddhist Society of Great Britain.

These early Western Buddhists were interested in Theravada and particularly stressed the advantages of Buddhism over Christianity. They argued that Buddhism was a religion of reason that rested on insight and knowledge alone. Buddhism was presented as the oldest and wisest religion, that would enable European culture to step out of the gloom into a new and glorious century. In reality, most of these early Buddhists approached the subject as a philosophy rather than as practitioners. However, in the 1960s and 1970s the use of meditation stimulated an interest in Buddhism and many young people began to practise.

THERAVADA FOREST TRADITION

Theravada meditation gained popularity in Britain through the Thai master Ajahn Chah (1918–92), who founded the Chithurst Forest Monastery in West Sussex in 1978. This was the first successful Theravada *sangha* comprising Western members. Under its British abbot Ajahn Sumedho (formerly Robert Jackman) other centres were established in Britain, Germany, Italy and Switzerland.

The Forest tradition seeks to follow the early teachings of the Buddha as set out in the *Tipitaka*. The practice requires a monk to accept the 227 rules presented in the first section of the *Tipitaka*. This acceptance results in conventions of behaviour within the monastery known as 'form'. It is bad form, for example, for adults to run, shout or argue. It is good form to be respectful to monks and to act quietly and kindly towards others. These conventions are often expressed as the Eight Precepts: Harmlessness, Trustworthiness, Chastity, Right Speech, Sobriety, Renunciation, Restraint and Alertness. Insight Meditation is an important practice of the Forest tradition. This practice seeks to calm the mind through sustained attention usually accomplished whilst sitting or walking.

SERENE REFLECTION MEDITATION

Peggy Kennett was born in England in 1924. She studied medicine before winning a scholarship to Trinity College of Music in London. From her youth she had an interest in Theravada Buddhism and was actively involved with the Buddhist Society in London, and it was there she met D. T. Suzuki, who inspired her interest in Zen. It was Koho Keido Zenji, the chief abbot of Sojiji, who invited her to come to Japan as his disciple. She arrived in Yokohama on 13 April 1962, was admitted into Sojiji, and was known as 'Jiyu'. A year later she was formerly confirmed into the Soto Zen lineage. Koho Zenji also appointed her Soto Zen Bishop to London, but Christmas Humphreys did not approve of this initiative.

Jiyu therefore went to California, where the Zen Mission Society was founded in 1970 with its headquarters at Mount Shasta. In 1972 a small group of British disciples established a small monastery at Throssel Hole Priory near Hexham in Northumberland. In 1978 the name 'Zen Mission Society' was changed to 'The Order of Buddhist Contemplatives'. The Order believes that meditation is the means through which one can discover one's own inner Buddha-nature. All beings are Buddhas, although they may not realize it. Nothing is considered to be apart from the Buddha-nature. Serene reflection meditation consists of sitting in a meditation position, with eyes open, in a place without distractions. Thoughts are gently allowed to arise. They are not grasped and considered, but are allowed to slip away. The movement has only a small following.

SŌKA GAKKAI

Sōka Gakkai is an example of a new movement that commenced in the twentieth century and has spread to many parts of the world. It sees its tradition as from Nichiren (1222–82), who was one of the most significant Japanese Buddhists. He proclaimed that an invocation of the title of the *Lotus Sutra* was the actual source of enlightenment. He therefore encouraged people to chant *Nam myoho renge kyo*. After his death, some thirty-one divisions emerged claiming to follow his teaching, of which Nichiren Shō-shu was one of the smaller. In the 1920s, Tsunesaburo Makiguchi became the leader of the lay association and implemented changes that resulted in its growth. He died in 1944, and Toda took over as the leader of the movement, which became known as Sōka Gakkai ('Value Creation Society'). In 1958 Daisaku Ikeda became the third president, and Sōka Gakkai showed accelerated growth, gaining many millions of followers in Japan. It even developed its own political party. Ikeda first visited Britain in 1961 after establishing a US branch the previous year. In Britain, the movement began with a handful of Japanese business people and their families who were on temporary placement in Britain. The influence of Japanese members diminished as more British people joined, so that by 1990 only 6% were Japanese.

The main teaching of the movement focuses upon chanting towards a scroll containing portions of the *Lotus Sutra* inscribed in ancient Chinese and Sanskrit characters and known as the *Gohonzon*. Down the centre of the *Gohonzon*, in larger and bolder characters than the rest of the text, is written '*Nam myoho renge kyo* Nichiren'. The *Gohonzon* is seen as an object that draws forth from the worshipper qualities of his or her own Buddha-nature, like a mirror reflecting the buddhahood within. The basic practice of Nichiren Shō-shu therefore consists of chanting the *Nam myoho renge kyo* to the *Gohonzon*. It is claimed that this practice not only brings out the Buddha-nature, but also provides answers to current practical needs.

TIBETAN TRADITIONS

Following the flight of the Dalai Lama from Tibet in 1959 when the Chinese invaded his country, many Tibetans settled in northern India and Nepal. It was here that the distinctive teaching of Tibetan Buddhism attracted Westerners who were part of the 1960s hippie movement. When they returned to their home countries some of these young people were anxious not only to help the Tibetan refugees, but also to introduce Buddhism to their homelands. Various leading lamas were therefore invited to teach in the West.

There are four main schools within the Tibetan tradition. The oldest school is Nyingma; its best-known exponent in the West is Sogyal Rinpoche, who is based in London, but it has centres around the world. The second school is Sakya, which was dominant during the period of Mongolian influence. In Britain there is a group of Sakya centres that operate under the guidance of Ngakpa Jampa Yhaye, a British teacher of this tradition. The third school is Kagyu, which means 'transmission of the living tradition'. In 1967 it founded the *Kagyu Samye Ling*, which was the first Tibetan Buddhist centre in the West. Two Tibetan abbots, Chogyam Trungpa Rinpoche and Dr Akong Tulku Rinpoche, founded it in a modest country house near the tiny village of Eskdalemuir, Scotland. The fourth school is Geluk; its best known exponent is the Dalai Lama.

In 1991 a division arose in the Geluk school that resulted in the formation of the New Kadampa Tradition (NKT) following the teaching of Lama Geshe Kelsang (b. 1931). The first centre was established in 1976 at Conishead Priory near Ulverston, Cumbria, and Geshe Kelsang arrived in Britain in the following year. Unlike other Tibetan schools, where participants chant in Tibetan, Geshe Kelsang has translated the chants into English. He has also written many books in English presenting the basis of Geluk teaching. In 1999, the school had over 200 centres in Britain and was quickly establishing centres in North America.

FRIENDS OF THE WESTERN BUDDHIST ORDER

Another new Buddhist movement that commenced in the twentieth century is the Friends of the Western Buddhist Order, founded in 1967 by the Venerable Sangharakshita. What makes this movement interesting is that it began in Britain with the aim of making Buddhism relevant to the West. Sangharakshita was born on 26 August 1925 into an ordinary family living in East Anglia and was named Dennis Philip Edward Lingwood. After an unfortunate childhood he was drafted into the Royal Signal Corps in 1943. This gave him the opportunity to visit the Buddhist Society and meet the Founder-President Christmas Humphreys. At the *Wesak* celebration of May 1944 he recited the Refuges and Precepts after a Burmese monk who was resident in Britain, and so formally adopted Buddhism. After serving in Asia, he was eventually ordained a Buddhist monk in 1950. For the next fifteen years he stayed in India studying, meditating, teaching and writing about aspects of Buddhism. During this time he met many exponents of the main traditions of Buddhism and received initiation and teaching from some of the leading Tibetan lamas.

From the foundation of the movement its aim was to be more than a mere society of people interested in Buddhist philosophy. Sangharakshita intended it to be a spiritual brotherhood, founded on a common commitment to the Buddha, *Dharma* and the *Sangha*. It was at this time that it was decided to change the name from *Sangha* to Order because *Sangha* sounded foreign. The name of the new movement then became 'Friends of the Western Buddhist Order' (FWBO).

The FWBO has a number of distinctive features that make it stand out from other Buddhist movements in Britain. Its primary aim is to present Buddhism in a way that is relevant to the modern West. FWBO therefore does not follow one particular Buddhist tradition, but draws upon any useful practice from whatever tradition. The FWBO is adamant that although it draws upon the Buddhist tradition as a whole, it does not mix Buddhism with other religious or spiritual traditions. Its second distinctive arises from the first, in that Western secular society is considered to be a very difficult context in which to develop one's own, true personality. The solution offered is the experience of living in single-sex residential communities. Such communities are seen as supportive environments for spiritual practice and provide opportunities for friendship with others who share the same interests.

Like most Buddhist traditions, the FWBO sees meditation as 'the royal road' to personal development. It teaches two types of meditation: calm and wisdom. The first consists of those practices which calm the mind, so that a person is able to come into touch with the deeper aspects of consciousness. The second group of practices comprises those that aim at developing wisdom and is sometimes called 'Insight into Reality'.

Buddhist movements have generally been imported into the West by Westerners who have first contacted the traditions whilst in the East. These Asian traditions have had to adapt to the different social context of the West. This process of adaptation has been taken to an extreme by the FWBO in its attempt to develop a tradition specifically relevant to the urbanized West. Buddhist ideas have also had a major influence upon the New Age movement, from which Buddhists now seek to keep a marked distance. In such a dynamic situation it is difficult to predict how these movements will develop in the coming years.

BIBLIOGRAPHY

S. Batchelor, *The Awakening of the West* (Berkeley, CA, 1994); D. G. Burnett,

Buddhism Comes West (forthcoming); D. Cush, *Buddhists in Britain Today* (London, 1990); C. S. Prebish and K. K. Tanaka, *The Faces of Buddhism in America* (Berkeley, CA, 1998); Subhuti, *Bringing Buddhism to the West: A life of Sangharakshita* (Birmingham, 1995); Sumedho, *Cittaviveka: Teachings from the Silent Mind* (Hemel Hempstead, 1992).

D. G. Burnett

NEW RELIGIOUS MOVEMENTS IN CHRISTIANITY

New religious movements (NRMs) within Christianity have always existed and are not merely a contemporary phenomenon. Church history has many examples of unorthodox new movements that have appeared to challenge orthodox Christianity. The Gnostics, Montanists and Marcionists in the early church, the Albigenses (Cathari), Waldenses and Flagellants in the Middle Ages, and the Reformers and 'Radical Reformers' (Anabaptists) in the sixteenth and seventeenth centuries are just a few examples. From the eighteenth century onwards, Britain and North America had Baptists, Quakers, Methodists, Ranters, Shakers, Irvingites, Mormons, Christadelphians, Adventists and Pentecostals, all characterized by conflict with established Christianity.

These movements were the forerunners of hundreds of new movements in Western Christianity arising in the nineteenth and twentieth centuries. Increasing religious toleration and the multiplicity of Christian denominations, especially in North America (among many other factors), assisted in the rise and proliferation of these new movements. Some, like the Baptists and the Methodists, became major denominations, and two of the more recent ones (Mormonism and Jehovah's Witnesses) have become major alternative forms of Christianity of international proportions. Pentecostalism, which only a century ago emerged out of the Holiness movement, has become the second largest expression of Christianity after Roman Catholicism, now with more adherents than historic Protestantism itself.

The latter half of the twentieth century has also seen a proliferation of movements originating in Asia that have challenged Christianity's monopoly in Western societies. This has resulted in what has been called 'the great American cult scare', in which many in the USA have been 'preoccupied with one of the bitterest and most significant religious conflicts of the twentieth century' (Bromley and Shupe, *Strange Gods*). The anti-cult movement has so dominated the agenda that all NRMs have been evaluated according to its criteria and, according to Bromley and Shupe, 'the question of what, if any, positive or redeeming qualities the new religions may have has been largely ignored.' Some Christian apologists even attack as satanic all religions (including some Christian movements) other than their particular brand of

Christianity. Such an approach generates antagonism and makes mutual understanding impossible. It fails to find points of contact and similarities that will encourage communication, and therefore often fails in genuine Christian love and outreach.

DEFINITIONS AND APPROACHES

The different kinds of new movements arising in Christianity can no longer be regarded in isolation from each other. They exist together as significant phenomena posing great challenges to orthodox and 'status quo' Christianity. Because of the strong feelings that these NRMs evoke, the terms used to designate them should be neutral and non-judgmental. They have been called 'sects', 'cults' and even 'heresies', and in the past their followers might have been burnt at the stake. Every section of Christianity was once regarded by other, usually older, Christian traditions in this antagonistic way; in fact, Jesus himself was so regarded by established Judaism. Many of these movements are Christian churches, in that they are communities who believe in Jesus Christ as Lord and Saviour, even though their Christology often differs from that of mainstream Christianity.

The new movements in Christianity exhibit many similarities with NRMs in general. In the first place, what we call NRMs are *new* in that they are comparatively recent, in most cases originating in the nineteenth and twentieth centuries. They are also new in that they often offer something different, meeting felt needs apparently not being met by conventional and older Christian traditions. They often present a 'new truth' taught by an innovative charismatic leader, or a new way of doing things, such as new ways of praying, singing, healing or worshipping. But, paradoxically, in some NRMs very old phenomena reappear. Secondly, NRMs are primarily *religious* in orientation and purpose, and in the case of the movements we are discussing, they consider themselves 'Christian' churches – facts that must be borne in mind when discussing their causes. Thirdly, these are *movements*, continually moving organisms offering people new experiences of God and the meeting of felt needs. Furthermore, they are growing in remarkable ways, in some cases to the detriment of more established Christian organizations.

Many different reasons have been put forward by anthropologists, sociologists, theologians and other scholars for the rise and proliferation of these movements, particularly in Western Christianity. Popular explanations include accusations of brainwashing and 'sheep stealing', which tend to shift the responsibility for alleged misconduct to the new movements themselves. This approach refuses to admit that the reasons people join these movements might lie elsewhere, not least of all in the failures of existing, older churches adequately to meet human needs in a modern and postmodern context. Generally speaking, the adherents of NRMs join them for religious reasons, often pointing to a spiritual experience that they did not find anywhere else or to other factors less esoteric but equally important, like healing from prolonged illness, provision of a family or a community, a job or even a marriage partner, and a sense of dignity and destiny, or of a new ability to cope with life's stresses and hardships. These experiences are often found in NRMs, and those who find them sometimes point to the lack of them in the more traditional forms of Christianity from which they came.

NRMs within Christianity include movements as diverse as the many different expressions of worldwide Pentecostalism or the thousands of African-initiated (independent) churches, including Aladura and Harrist churches in West Africa, Kimbanguists in Central Africa, and Zionist and Apostolic churches in Southern Africa. These African churches have come to the West with the migration of African peoples, and they often provide a creative interface between Christianity and African cultural and religious values. Movements such as the Unification Church (Moonies) from Korea, the Ratana movement among New Zealand Maoris and the 'cargo' movements of Melanesia provide examples of syncretism between Christianity and other religions. Movements with origins in the West, such as Seventh-Day Adventists, classical Pentecostals and Neo-Pentecostal independent churches, are increasingly recognized as part of the ecumenical Christian church. Other groups regarding themselves as Christian, such as Mormons, Jehovah's Witnesses and Christian Science, are not so recognized by older churches. More exotic Christian groups, like the Family of Love (formerly the Children of God), The Way International, and Caribbean movements like Mita, Revival Zion and Spiritual Baptists, have departed in several ways from orthodoxy. In this category could be included infamous but unique movements such as the People's Temple (Jim Jones) and the Branch Davidians (David Koresh), both of which caused the abuse and death of many people. Fundamentalist groups with a fairly orthodox theology with respect to Christian essentials, but whose practices often create conflict with most other Christian churches, include the (Boston) International Church of Christ, the Jesus Army in Britain, and some new Pentecostal groups that promote a 'health and wealth' gospel.

ENCOUNTERING CONTEMPORARY CULTURE

One of the effects of modernity has been the rejection of uniformity and the traditional and a search for new ideas. NRMs both within and outside Christianity are a direct result and a manifestation of this. Sociologists have demonstrated how 'revitalization movements' emerge and interact with their socio-cultural environment and are evidence of a modernization or secularization process leading to the privatization of religion. The rise of postmodernity in the late twentieth century has suited some NRMs well, especially those that have implicitly rejected both modernity's scientific objectivity and premodernity's traditions and have emphasized the validity of subjective religious experiences. Those new Christian movements that have survived and flourished in Western societies have often done so because they have adapted to a changing context. Some have made considerable changes to become more conventional and acceptable to society at large, such as Seventh-Day Adventists, Mormons and some African movements (e.g. the Kimbanguist church). The Worldwide Church of God, founded by Herbert W. Armstrong, was long considered a cult by evangelical Christians, but some time after Armstrong's death in 1986 its new leader Joseph Tkach repudiated its most offending teachings. Other movements, such as the Jehovah's Witnesses, have steadfastly refused to change in the face of opposition and yet have continued to attract some of those who are prepared to give their total allegiance to such radical causes, at least partly because of their emphasis on their discontinuity with all other forms of Christianity. Few NRMs grow to become world religions, but when they do, they offer spiritual alternatives not always offered by existing, older traditions. At the same time, they challenge older churches to re-examine their own beliefs and ethics.

We should assume that both followers and leaders of the various Christian NRMs have a genuine and serious belief in the truthfulness of their claims and the usefulness of their practices, and that they are not charlatans. As fellow human beings on a religious quest, they deserve respect and should be studied from their own perspective. This does not mean that every human response to divine reality should be regarded as equally acceptable, particularly when it appears to conflict with more traditional understandings of biblical revelation. Nevertheless, in our approach to these NRMs we should avoid hasty judgments and irresponsible generalizations from the perspective of the outsider. Fanatical NRMs suspected of ritual suicide or exhibiting antisocial behaviour might make front page news, but the vast majority of NRMs are not sinister or subversive movements heading in the same direction as the People's Temple in Guyana or the Branch Davidian cult in Waco, Texas. Of course, concerned Christians inevitably must make evaluations, particularly when a NRM proposes a different belief system and lifestyle, and openly attacks accepted Christian values. Unfortunately, when a NRM actively promotes a confrontational attitude towards other churches and aims at the conversion of people from these traditions, churches feel threatened. To a certain extent, NRMs are protest movements against conventional Christianity and society and sometimes evidence of major changes in both. To study them is to increase our understanding of those changes. Furthermore, if we have not studied NRMs, we cannot expect to help or understand people who get involved in them.

A common view among some Christians is that 'cults' are unorthodox, pseudo-Christian or heretical groups needing to be refuted theologically according to previously assumed criteria. This view may seem reasonable for members of orthodox Christian traditions, but it lacks theological depth and leaves many unanswered questions. Although some alternative Christian movements definitely fall outside the parameters of orthodox Christianity, the problem of *who* decides what is orthodox and the fact that different movements might be more 'Christian' (and therefore less heretical) than others are seldom acknowledged. This polemical approach does not usually facilitate an understanding of the reasons for the existence of NRMs, nor answer wider questions concerning the variety of different beliefs and practices and the even more fundamental questions relating to religious pluralism. NRMs challenge older churches seriously to rethink their own beliefs and moral standards, as well as their commitment to 'truth'. To say all this is not to suggest that the differences between newer and older Christian churches should not be examined carefully, or that errors should not be refuted theologically. But even those movements judged most heretical have lessons to teach us. Older churches may be challenged to consider whether the example of the newer movements does not judge the complacency and lack of devotion and enthusiasm shown by their own adherents, who have fallen into a trap of dead formalism and orthodoxy from which it is difficult to escape. Young people in particular are voting with their feet and rejecting old traditions for new ones. Religious pluralism is a fact of the Western world and has many manifestations. To understand religion in the West today, the contribution of these new movements to Christianity and what they are saying to modern and postmodern society must be taken seriously.

BIBLIOGRAPHY

D. G. Bromley and A. D. Shupe, *Strange Gods: The Great American Cult Scare* (Boston, 1981); M. Burrell, *The 'Christian' Fringe: A Critical Assessment of Seven Religious Alternatives to Mainstream Christianity – with a Christian Response* (Norwich, 1996); H. Cox, *Fire from Heaven: The Rise of Pentecostal Spirituality and the Reshaping of Religion in the Twenty-First Century* (London, 1996); I. Hexham and K. Poewe, *New Religions as Global Cultures: Making the Human Sacred* (Boulder, CO, 1997); J. A. Saliba, *Perspectives on New Religious Movements* (London, 1995).

A. H. Anderson

NEW RELIGIOUS MOVEMENTS IN HINDUISM

Mention of Hindu-inspired new religions usually causes people to think of saffron-robed young people chanting 'Hare Krishna' in Oxford Street, London, or the Beatles sitting down with Maharishi Mahesh Yogi in a room full of flowers. Such events were certainly characteristic of the 1960s, when Indian religious movements exploded into Western society amidst a wave of controversy. These movements were an expression of the counter-culture movement of the time and expressed its quest for an alternative way of life. The motives that led people to join such movements were various. Some were looking for answers to ultimate questions of life; others wanted a spiritual experience without the after-effects of drugs; others sought to develop their full human potential; and some wanted to establish a radically new society.

It is not possible to consider new religious movements in the Hindu tradition in the same way as those in Western religions for a number of reasons. First, there is no organization within Hinduism that sets statements of orthodoxy, and Hinduism is therefore more tolerant of different views. Second, Hinduism embraces a wide range of religious expressions that have continually been redefined by gurus, teachers and poets. Each of these is associated with the richness of the Hindu religious tradition and a particular line of teachers. Third, although these movements may be associated with ancient traditions they have only recently appeared in the West. The word 'new' is therefore used here in a relative sense, as applying to those religious movements drawing upon the Hindu tradition that have emerged and grown in the Western world within the last few decades.

ISKCON

The best-known movement is the International Society for Krishna Consciousness (ISKCON), or as it is more popularly known, Hare Krishna. It was founded by A. C. Bhaktivedanta Swami Prabhupada (1896–1977), who was born in Calcutta. He became a follower of the Gaudiya Mission, a Hindu revivalist group, and in 1933 he was charged by the leader to take Krishna Consciousness to the West. During the next thirty years he worked for a pharmaceutical company and translated Hindu scriptures into English. In 1959, he finally renounced his possessions and family to seek a new spiritual life. He went to the USA in 1965, where he was accepted among the hippies of New York and San Francisco, and in 1965 ISKCON was established.

Six American members came to Britain in 1968 when Beatle George Harrison recorded 'My Sweet Lord', which was based upon the Hare Krishna chant. The song brought the new movement immediate publicity. Over the next few years the movement grew rapidly and particularly attracted ex-hippies and drug-takers, who seemed to find fulfilment in its alternative lifestyle. Before his death, Prabhupada set up an international body to run ISKCON with eleven leading gurus. However, the movement failed to deal with the many social problems that emerged, and ISKCON had to undergo many changes in order to deal with its internal problems.

As the name of the movement suggests, Krishna Consciousness teaches a particular relationship between an individual and the god Krishna. Krishna is considered the eighth incarnation (*avatara*) of Vishnu and is presented as the Supreme Godhead in the

Bhagavad-Gita. In this text Krishna is portrayed as a personal deity who is omniscient, omnipresent, omnipotent and eternal. He requires loving devotion that expresses itself in continual mindfulness of Krishna and is assisted through the chanting of the name of Krishna.

The daily life of a devotee is rigorous. Those who live in *ashrams* get up at 4.00 am for worship. They must chant the Hare Krishna *mantra* 1,728 times – once per bead for sixteen rounds of the 108 beads on the string. This usually takes two hours and is believed to clear the consciousness. All members give up eating meat, fish and eggs. Drugs including tobacco, tea and coffee are not allowed and sex is allowed only occasionally for procreation. All shave their heads except for a small pigtail, and they usually wear a white stripe of clay on their foreheads. The movement has matured; it is now far more oriented towards study than in the past, and temples have become centres for teaching devotional Hinduism. It is now much more acceptable to the Asian community, and its festivals attract thousands of Asian Hindus.

RAJNEESHISM

ISKCON was not the only movement to attract Western followers in the 1960s. Guru Rajneesh (1931–90) began teaching in India in 1966, promoting meditation and free love. He first had an *ashram* in Bombay, and then in 1974 moved to Poona, as he continued to attract many Western backpackers. In 1981 he moved to a ranch in Oregon, USA, where he endeavoured to build the city of Rajneeshpuram.

The teachings of Rajneesh were confusing, but were essentially a form of neo-Tantrism. His followers practised Dynamic Meditation, which involves the total shaking of the body to dissipate tensions; this is followed by periods of silence. Tax irregularities and the emphasis upon free sex resulted in growing criticism that made the movement conscious of outside pressures. The leaders fled, and Rajneesh himself was detained, given a suspended jail sentence and deported. He returned to India suffering from failing health and died in 1990. However, shortly before he died he changed his name to Osho. Since his death, Osho International has been established at the original commune in Poona, with the aim of propagating his teachings. The movement seems more disciplined than in previous decades.

ELAN VITAL

A different figure was Guru Maharaj Ji (b. 1957), the son of Shri Hans Ji Maharaj, who founded the Divine Light Mission in India in 1960. This mission was based upon the teaching that enlightenment comes through knowledge. When his father died in 1966, the 8-year-old son proclaimed himself the new guru and started teaching. In 1971, he went on a world tour and quickly established a following in Britain and America. In 1973 he attempted to hold a huge event in Houston, but this was a failure. Then, when only 16, he married his 24-year-old secretary to the shock of many. About this time he had a disagreement with his mother, who disapproved of his luxurious lifestyle. As Maharaj Ji matured into an adult he made it increasingly clear that knowledge is not merely Indian teaching but is universal. The movement took the new name 'Elan Vital' and has now dropped all of its Indian religious practices. It now teaches that each individual should seek to know his or her own true self.

These three movements (ISKCON, Rajneeshism and Elan Vital) initially showed remarkable growth, but eventually declined before re-establishing themselves in a different form.

TRANSCENDENTAL MEDITATION

Maharishi Mahesh Yogi (b. 1911) graduated in physics from Allahabad University in 1940 before studying for thirteen years under Guru Dev. The latter claimed to have rediscovered from the ancient Hindu scriptures the technique that was to become known as Transcendental Mediation (TM). After Guru Dev's death in 1953, Mahesh became the leading teacher of TM; he went into seclusion for two years before presenting the teaching to the world. He took the title 'Maharishi' ('Great Seer') in 1958 when he launched the Spiritual Regeneration Movement in Madras. He first came to Britain in 1960, but it was in 1968 when the Beatles went to India to learn from him that he gained publicity. In 1971 he established the Maharishi International University in Iowa, and in 1972 announced his World Plan to create one teaching centre per million people in the world, with one TM teacher per thousand of population.

TM firmly states that it is not a religion, but a scientific technique. Even so, it includes elements typical of Hinduism, such as offerings of fruit and flowers and songs of gratitude to Guru Dev. During basic training people are given a *mantra*, selected on the basis of sex and age from a list of about sixteen. Every morning and evening practitioners meditate for about twenty minutes with the result, it is claimed, that they develop deep relaxation, inner potential and intelligence and become successful in life. Those who wish to study further can develop more advanced techniques such as the controversial yogic flying. The movement makes tremendous claims for the benefits of TM, including reduction of the crime rate in areas where a significant proportion of the population practises TM. Critics argue that it is merely a relaxation method, and its claims have not been statistically proven.

In the 1990s TM moved into British politics with the Natural Law Party, which put forward candidates in local, national and European elections. Its literature claims that the Natural Law Party 'was founded to bring the light of science into politics. It offers conflict-free politics and problem-free government'.

A comparison of TM with ISKCON shows two opposite responses by Hindu traditions to Western society. Whereas TM has aligned itself with scientific notions, ISKCON has rejected them. Similarly, ISKCON has withdrawn from Western society, whilst TM offers itself as an answer to the problems of modern societies.

SATYA SAI BABA SOCIETY

Indian religion has been characterized throughout the centuries by great gurus. In recent years Satya Sai Baba (b. 1926) has been worshipped by millions of devotees in India. From his youth he began to compose religious songs and supposedly was able to materialize objects out of thin air. At the age of 14 he fell into a deep trance, and when he finally awoke he claimed to be the reincarnation of a master guru who died in Bombay in 1918. In 1950, Sai Baba established an *ashram* in a village outside Puttaparthi in South India, and this has become the centre of pilgrimage for thousands of devotees. They come to experience 'Sai power', which is believed not only to manifest miracles but also to effect telepathy and spiritual surgery.

Sai Baba proclaims that he is the embodiment of all aspects of God that have been manifested on earth and also claims to be the reincarnation of Christ. He has millions of followers in India and amongst the Asian community in Britain and North America. Pictures of his smiling face and mass of dark hair are common in many homes. However, there have been reports of corruption, manipulation and homosexuality among the leaders of the movement.

SAHAJA YOGA

Sri Mataji Nirmala Devi, the founder of Sahaja Yoga, was born on 21 March 1923 in Chindwara, India. She enjoyed an affluent childhood in a Christian household, but her family knew poverty during the struggle for independence. After independence, Nirmala was married to a successful administrator and diplomat, and they had two daughters. It is said that by the 1960s she was troubled by the 'fake gurus' and began spending time with a number of them, including Rajneesh. She was disillusioned with what she saw and embarked on her own spiritual quest. On 5 May 1970 she claimed to have become 'fully realized', and began her mission as a faith healer. In London on 2 December 1979 she declared to her followers that she was divine. Since then, she has been understood by her followers to be the *Devi*, the goddess of Indian religious tradition who comes to save the world. The movement has grown slowly in Britain; by 1987 there were five small *ashrams* in the country, with some 220 members. Sri Mataji began to travel widely and teach her vision of Sahaja Yoga as a 'global religion'.

Sri Mataji teaches that at the base of the spine is the spiritual energy of *kundalini*, which is in a dormant state. The awakening of this force traditionally involves strenuous effort, but she claims to be able fully to awaken the force instantly. Once awakened, the *kundalini* rises through the *chakras* along the spine and emerges in the fontanelle area at the top of the head. The benefits of an activated *kundalini* are said to include increased good health, relief from stress and a more balanced outlook on life.

CONCLUSION

These movements illustrate key elements of Hindu religious thought that have provided an alternative worldview to that of Western materialism. These elements include reincarnation, meditation (yoga), development of inner potential, spiritual power and ancient wisdom. These movements are a visible expression of the wider influence of Hindu thought in the contemporary world, which is also expressed in the more diffuse New Age movement.

BIBLIOGRAPHY

E. Barker, *New Religious Movements: A Practical Introduction* (London, 1989); D. V. Barrett, *Sects, 'Cults' & Alternative Religions: A World Survey and Sourcebook* (London, 1998); J. Coney, *Sahaja Yoga* (London, 1999); M. Rothstein, *Belief Transformations* (Aarhus, 1996).

D. G. Burnett

NEW RELIGIOUS MOVEMENTS IN ISLAM

From the middle of the twentieth century until the present day, Islam has grown in Europe and North America from a virtually invisible religious expression to a flourishing and sizeable set of communities. In Europe the three states with the largest Muslim populations are France, Germany and the United Kingdom (in that order). Amongst the streams of modern Islam there is great diversity: intellectual, devotional, ethnic and cultural. There are revivalist, reformist, modernist and strictly Qur'anic movements.

Reformist or modernist groups aim to create a form of Islam that is compatible with life in a Western society. In contrast, amongst revivalist movements there are those who see Western secular ideas as threatening to an Islamic way of life. The second and third generations of Muslims, born in the West, are to be found in both kinds of group.

The Muslim communities in Europe are not only diverse but also swiftly changing. The first wave of (largely male) migrants seeking economic improvement were joined in the 1960s by wives and families; since then second and third generations have been born. In North America there is a similar diversity with the emergence of an African-American Islam (both orthodox Sunni and heterodox Nation of Islam) and the arrival of migrant Muslims from the Middle East seeking political asylum, work and higher education. The complexity and diversity of Islam in Europe and America manifest themselves in various new religious movements.

THE SIZE AND SPREAD OF THE NEW MOVEMENTS

Estimates of the sizes of the Muslim communities in the various European states and in North America vary. France's Muslim population is chiefly drawn from North Africa: Algerians 850,000; Moroccans 450,000; Tunisians 200,000; French Muslim repatriates from Algeria 400,000; French-born children of Arab migrant parents 450,000; Turks 200,000; and West African Muslims 100,000 (Clarke, *New Trends*, pp. 4–5). In Germany the Muslim communities are largely of Turkish background, originating from *gastarbeiter* ('guest workers') who arrived in the 1960s. They now make up some 75% of Germany's Muslims; smaller numbers come from North Africa, the Middle East, Iran and South Asia, and there are some German 'converts' to the faith. (Instead of the term 'convert' Muslims use the term 'revert', in accordance with their belief that Islam is the primordial faith from which other religions such as Judaism and Christianity are deviations. Thus to embrace Islam is to 'revert' to the original, pristine faith.) Britain's Muslim population is estimated at 1.5 million members (Nielsen, *Muslims in Western Europe*, p. 41), the majority of whom are of South Asian origin (750,000); other communities are drawn from the Middle East, North and West Africa and Turkey, and there is a small but growing number of British converts. Islam has a long history in Britain and its communities have an increasing influence on and involvement with wider UK society and government. Debates continue about the nature of Islamic education, dress, diet, marriage and the aspirations of the younger generation for education and higher standards of life commensurate with Muslim ideals. The Netherlands and Belgium also have significant Muslim expressions. Holland's communities (450,000) are drawn from Turkey, Morocco, South Asia and Indonesia. Belgium's Muslim population, estimated at 250,000, is extremely diverse, with forty-two countries represented; the predominant groups are of Moroccan and Turkish origin.

In North America, the arrival of Islam is dated to the entry of slaves of African origin into the United States. Some 14–20% of the slave population is estimated to have been from a Muslim African background (Austin, *African American Muslims*, pp. 29–36). There were further waves of migration, from the Middle East, between the two world wars, and substantial entries from Muslim majority states in the 1960s–1970s of those seeking higher education.

Additional to these developments is the rise of African-American Islam in 'the Nation of Islam', which drew upon an emergent self-assertiveness amongst African Americans who sought to discard

Christianity as a 'White' enslavement religion. After the death of its charismatic leader, Elijah Muhammad (1897–1975), his son Warith Muhammad (b. 1933) led part of the movement into an orthodox Sunni Islamic expression; another section of the Nation of Islam remained independent under the leadership of Louis Farrakhan (b. 1933). The Muslim population of the United States is estimated to number between 1.5 and 3 million adherents (Stone, 'Estimates', p. 25).

MOVEMENTS IN THE UK AND EUROPE

The reactions of new Muslim movements in the UK and Europe to wider society are varied, ranging from strict separationism to more positive dialogue and accommodation. Most of the new movements tend towards a sectarian rejectionist attitude (Bruce, *Religion in the Modern World*, pp. 82–83), aiming to maintain as distinctive an Islamic identity as possible in a largely secular context. These movements invariably have their roots in the homelands of their adherents and draw upon them for their ideals and worldviews.

The earliest movements to be established in the UK include the Deobandi stream, which emerged in North India after the British assumption of power in 1859. Firmly based on the Qur'an, *Hadith* and *Shari'a*, the movement is an intellectual form of Islam and, whilst opposed to populist shrine-based mystical cults, none the less favours Sufism (Islamic mysticism). The Barelwi tradition maintains the ideals of popular Sufism: devotion to and a high understanding of the Prophet Muhammad, and devotion to spiritual guides (*pirs* or *shaykhs*) as intercessors, including pilgrimages to their shrines or tombs. A third movement originating from the subcontinent is the Ahl I-Hadith, with its stress upon individual interpretation of the Qur'an and the *Hadith* of the Prophet.

Sufi movements have transplanted themselves and grown in the UK and elsewhere in Europe since the 1950s. Amongst the migrant workers who arrived at that time were Sufi leaders representing the Naqshbandi, Qadiri and Chisti *tariqas* ('orders') from South Asia, who began to gather *murids* ('disciples') around themselves and to establish mosques and Qur'an schools.

In contrast, the Jama'at I-Islami movement emerged from twentieth-century prepartition India. In Pakistan it functions as a political party advocating Islam as a complete cultural, economic, philosophical and educational pattern. The Islamic Foundation in Leicester is an offshoot of the Jama'at and emphasizes education and publishing; it influences the UK Islamic Mission, The Muslim Educational Trust and the Muslim Youth Educational Council.

The Tablighi Jama'at, founded in prepartition India in 1927, works in close alliance with the Deobandi tradition and has been active in both the UK and other European states since the 1960s as a missionary (*daw'a*) movement. Its founder Maulana Muhammad Ilyas (1886–1944) emphasized personal devotion drawn from Sufi sources, the recalling of lapsed Muslims to faith and an apolitical stance towards wider society. Dewsbury, West Yorkshire, with its mosque and college, is the focus for the movement in Britain. As a 'conversionist' movement it aims to hold adherents to the spiritual ideals of Islam (e.g. sound moral behaviour and personal piety).

A more recent movement is the Islamic Party of Great Britain (founded in 1989), in which the key figure is Sahib Mustaqim Blehr, a German convert to Islam. It combines a political agenda (seeking to represent Muslims in the political sphere) with a missionary purpose. Similarly, the Muslim Parliament, founded in 1992 by Dr Kalim Siddiqi (d. 1996), aims to provide a focus for an activist expression of Islam within British society.

Hizb ut Tahrir (the Islamic Liberation Party) has been active in the UK since the early 1990s. Originally founded in Palestine by Taqi Uddine Al Nabahani (1905–1978), it aims to establish an Islamic state under a restored caliphal system. It believes that Islam has suffered decline and disunity due to the abolition of the caliphate by Turkish secularism in 1924 and to the creation of the state of Israel in 1948. It is deeply committed to the establishment of an autonomous Palestine and is convinced that Western ideals are corrupt. The Al-Muhajiroun emerged from the Hizb ut Tahrir in Saudi Arabia in 1983 under Sheikh Omar Bakhri Muhammad (b. 1958), who introduced the movement to the UK in 1996. The group sees Islam as being in conflict with both Western secularism and nominally Islamic but faithless governments. Its policies therefore include separation from the world and preparation for the implementation of Islamic *Shar'iah* law. Similar to the Al-Muhajiroun is Supporters of Shari'ah, which functions as an oppositionalist group seeking a global implementation of *Shari'a* law.

In other European nations, Muslim movements also reflect the home roots of their communities. In France, groups such as the Amicale des Algériens, and the Amicale des Travailleurs et Commerçants Marocains have distinct national features and intentions regarding their religious commitment and devotion. An international element is found in Les Amis de l'Islam, a stream composed mainly of French converts to Islam and including the Muslim World League (based in Paris since 1976), and in numerous flourishing Sufi *tariqas* ('orders'; Nielsen, *Muslims in Western Europe*, pp. 18–19).

The German Muslim population, through movements such as the Avrupa Milli Gorus Teskilatlari (1976), has focused upon improving the status of Islam in Germany. The Islamische Kulturzentren is a major group which provides Qur'anic schools and religious instruction for the Islamic communities.

In Holland, the Sufi organization the Suleymanci is active alongside the Diyanet organization amongst people of Turkish origin, whilst other Sufi groups and the South Asian Tablighi Jama'at are found amongst communities of Moroccan origin.

Belgian Muslims have had a more disparate history resulting from their highly varied origins. Moreover, governments have been hesitant about meeting Muslim representatives.

MOVEMENTS IN NORTH AMERICA

Some two thirds of Muslims in the United States are immigrants. Their ancestors were both Sunni and Shi'a Muslims who initially arrived in waves from the Middle East during the late nineteenth century. The extended families of these migrants founded the first mosques in North America but lost much of their distinctive Muslim identity by assimilation into American society. A second wave of family groups arrived between 1947 and 1960 from a wider range of ethnic backgrounds: the Middle East, South Asia, Eastern Europe and the Soviet Union. A third wave (from 1967 to the present day) has come from some of the same homelands as the second wave, including Iran, Iraq, Afghanistan and the Gulf States. The second and third waves have arrived with firmer Muslim identities and self-consciousness. These groups have sought to adhere to traditional Muslim practices of religious and *shari'ah* observance, diet, dress and morality.

Most of the non-migrant Muslims in North America are African-American converts to Islam. This conversion phenomenon amongst African-Americans can be traced back to Timothy Drew/Noble Drew Ali (1886–1929) and the Moorish American Science Temple (Newark, New Jersey), and to Elijah Muhammad and the Nation of Islam. One of the best known converts to the Nation was Malcolm X (1925–1965), who eventually, after an experience of *Hajj* (pilgrimage) to Mecca in 1963, broke with Elijah Muhammad and embraced orthodox Sunni Islam, taking many African-American Muslims with him. After Elijah Muhammad's death, his son and successor Warith Deen Muhammad also moved into orthodox Sunni Islam, establishing the American Muslim Mission. The Nation of Islam continues as a distinct movement. There are also several Muslim organizations active alongside mosque communities, including the Muslim Student Association, which coordinates university activities, and the Islamic Society of North America, which links service and professional groups.

ONE ISLAM AND MANY 'ISLAMS'

All orthodox Muslims will subscribe to key and basic beliefs of the faith. There is, however, a considerable diversity within modern Islam, particularly in its responses to Western, postmodern society and culture. Islam is a global faith, which has embraced many cultures and has both adopted and adapted the cultures within which it has settled. When the first Muslim migrants arrived in Europe and in the Americas they formed close-knit communities for whom faith and its expression were cast in the traditional forms of the homeland. For the subsequent generations born in these new environments there is a greater need to re-examine the received tradition and patterns of Muslim expression. New Muslim movements reflect this process of adaptation. Many maintain conservative attitudes and seek to distinguish themselves from the surrounding culture. Others represent innovative moves towards the creation of indigenous European, British and American Islams.

BIBLIOGRAPHY

A. Austin, *African American Muslims in Ante Bellum Americas: A Sourcebook* (New York, 1984); S. Bruce, *Religion in the Modern World. From Cathedrals to Cults* (Oxford 1996); P. Clarke (ed.), *New Trends and Developments in the World of Islam* (London, 1998); J. Nielsen, *Muslims in Western Europe* (Edinburgh, 1995); C. Stone, 'Estimates of Muslims Living in America', in Y. Y. Haddad, *The Muslims of America* (Oxford, 1991).

I. G. Williams

NEW RELIGIOUS MOVEMENTS IN JAPAN

Japan's long and fascinating religious history grows out of the complex interplay of various traditions (Buddhism, Confucianism, Daoism and, much later, Christianity) with Shinto, the indigenous animistic folk religion predating the sixth century AD arrival of Buddhism. Various traditions have been dominant at different times, depending in part upon shifting social and political forces, but throughout there has evolved a kind of mutual accommodation which recognizes distinctive religious traditions as each having its own place and contribution to make within the broader Japanese cultural setting. Buddhism and Shinto have been the dominant religions, and in spite of times of open hostility in the past, the two have developed a rather uneasy sense of mutual acceptance, each finding ways to interpret and accommodate the other within its own framework. Popular religiosity has found ways to embrace both traditions through careful task differentiation: Shinto is associated with ritual purity, birth, weddings and the ubiquitous *kami* (deities), whereas Buddhism is linked to death and the cult of the ancestors.

In the 1860s, after two hundred years of feudalism and self-imposed isolation from the outside world, Japan embarked upon an ambitious programme of modernization. Today Japan is one of the most modernized, technologically advanced and affluent nations in the world. Globalization has relativized the older distinctions between the West and the East, so that in many ways Japan today has as much in common culturally with Europe and North America as it has with other Asian nations. The profound social and cultural changes accompanying modernization have stimulated new religious movements which, while rooted in the older traditional religions, have taken on distinctively modern elements. Since the early nineteenth century several hundred Japanese new religious movements have emerged, some of which have gone on to become well established and accepted not only in Japan but also in parts of South America, North America and Europe. Japan thus provides a fascinating case study in how religious traditions rooted in ancient, well-established institutions and practices fare when confronted by rapid modernization and globalization.

EARLY NEW RELIGIOUS MOVEMENTS

The new religions are generally divided into several broad groups, the first of which comprises those new religions which appeared prior to the Meiji Restoration of 1868 and full-scale modernization. The 1830s and 1840s were times of social and political unrest, and from this discontent arose a number of highly charismatic religious figures claiming special revelations, visions and/or powers. Although the earliest new religions had close affiliations with Shinto belief and practice, which was polytheistic, many of them focused upon one major *kami* or deity.

Perhaps the most significant new religion from this era is Tenrikyo ('religion of heavenly wisdom'), which began in 1838 when Nakayama Miki (d. 1887), a farmer's wife, was supposedly possessed during a shamanistic ritual by a deity identified as the true and original God, Tenri Ono Mikoto, the creator of the world. Tenrikyo teaches that this one true God revealed himself through Nakayama in order to rescue humankind from suffering and social evils and to lead the way to the 'perfect divine kingdom', in which people will enjoy *yokigurashi* ('joyous and blissful life'). Long regarded as a sect of Shinto, in 1970 Tenrikyo withdrew from the Association of Shinto Sects and now projects itself as a global religion with a universal message, the culmination of all previous divine revelations. Tenrikyo missions were first established in the United States in 1896, and it claims some three million followers (one million outside Japan), with over 16,000 churches worldwide.

THE OMOTO GROUP OF NEW RELIGIONS

A second distinct group of new religions emerged in the late nineteenth and early twentieth centuries, many of which were influenced by the Omoto-kyo ('Teaching of the Great Origin') movement of Deguchi Nao (d. 1918). Omoto-kyo was based upon a series of divine oracles which spoke of one God; a spiritual world behind the physical world; the temporary descent of spirits into the material world; and the coming of a new messianic age. Persecuted by the Japanese government in the 1930s, Omoto-kyo has not been a numerically large movement, but it has exerted significant influence upon many other new movements, including Sekai Kyuseikyo ('The Religion for World Salvation'). Sekai Kyuseikyo was founded by Okada Mokichi (d. 1955), a follower of the Omoto movement who, it is claimed, while in a state of divine possession, was told that he was the messiah for the present age. The movement emphasizes the coming of a paradise on earth (centred in Atami, Japan), and to prepare the way for this it promotes the practice of *jorei* (channelling divine healing light through cupped hands), as well as the cultivation of art and beauty.

Yet another new religion influenced by Omoto is the Perfect Liberty (or PL) Kyodan, founded by Miki Tokuharu (d. 1938) and his son Tokuchika (b. 1900). PL Kyodan is monotheistic and is well known for its view that 'life is art' and should be lived in a balanced, creative, harmonious manner.

NICHIREN BUDDHIST NEW RELIGIONS

A cluster of new religious movements have grown out of the thought of the thirteenth-century Japanese Buddhist Nichiren. The most famous of these is the Sōka Gakkai ('Association for Creating Values'), founded in 1937 by Makiguchi Tsunesaburo (d. 1944) and Toda Josei (d. 1958). Although it initially held strongly exclusivistic views, regarding other religions as false and other Buddhist sects as heretical, Sōka Gakkai has moderated somewhat since the 1970s. Employing aggressive proselytization techniques, Sōka Gakkai experienced remarkable growth through the 1960s. Today it claims over 16 million adherents. Under the leadership of Ikeda Daisaku (b. 1928) the movement has emphasized cultural and social improvements, seeking to advance the coming of the 'Third Civilization', when, it is believed, true faith worldwide will result in an era of peace and plenty. Sōka Gakkai is active worldwide, although in the West it generally adopts the name Nichiren Shō-shu Sōka Gakkai. In the United States the Nichiren Shō-shu of America claims over 340,000 adherents, most of whom are of non-Japanese descent. Reiyukai ('Friends of the Spirit Association'), founded by Kubo Kakutaro (d. 1944), combines a focus upon the *Lotus Sutra* and Nichiren Buddhism with traditional Japanese ancestral practices, quasi-shamanistic faith healing and a unique form of group counselling called *hoza* ('*dharma* circle'). Similar in emphasis is Rissho Koseikai, founded by Niwano Nikkyo (b. 1906) and Naganuma Myoko (d. 1957).

THE 'NEW' NEW RELIGIONS

In the 1980s a significantly different stream of new religious movements emerged, which were called 'new new religions' (*shin shinshukyo*) to distinguish them from earlier movements. These movements have experienced rapid growth and combine themes from earlier traditions with the realities of technologically advanced, highly modernized, urbanized life. It is estimated that between 10% and 30% of Japanese today are involved in the 'new' or 'new new religions'.

One such new new religion is Mahikari, which was founded in 1959 by Okada Kotama (d. 1974). Okada claimed to have had a revelation from Su-God (full name: Reverend-Parent Origin-Lord True-Light Great-God), the central deity in Mahikari's pantheon, who informed Okada that he was to be the 'saviour' of the world by passing on the teachings through which the influence of lesser deities and evil spirits can be overcome. Mahikari includes exorcistic purification rites (*okiyome*) to dispel evil as well as the toxins produced by modern life which result in illness and death.

One of the more remarkable new new

religions is Agonshu, founded by Kiriyama Seiyu (b. 1921) in 1978. Agonshu is a kind of revitalization movement within Buddhism, for it claims that it has discovered the hidden meanings of the ancient *Agama Sutras* of early Buddhism, through which people can 'cut the *karma*' binding them and thus find salvation and fulfilment in the present life. According to Agonshu, all problems and misfortunes are the product of spiritual factors caused by the unhappy spirits of those who have not achieved liberation after death due to the failure of those still living to perform proper memorial services for them. Agonshu claims that it alone, because of its mastery of the esoteric truths of the *Agamas Sutras*, is able to perform the correct rites to liberate the souls of the dead, and in this way to ensure the prosperity and happiness of the living.

A radical movement which gained worldwide notoriety far disproportionate to its size is Aum Shinrikyo, founded by Asahara Shoko (b. 1955). Asahara combined a bizarre mixture of Hindu, Buddhist, Christian and occult practices with an obsession with violence and doomsday scenarios, culminating in the March 1995 sarin gas attack on the Tokyo underground system, in which twelve people were killed and over 6,000 injured.

Japanese new religious movements manifest certain patterns which might be significant for the study of religion and modernization in other contexts. First, the rapid growth and popularity of the new movements tends to be linked to periods of widespread change and social unrest. In particular, the challenges of technology, modernity and urbanization stimulate revitalization movements which accommodate earlier cosmology and practices within a modern, technologized social setting.

Second, although they are identifiably different from institutional Buddhism or Shinto, the new religious movements are very much in continuity with basic themes in traditional Japanese religion. For example, Japanese religiosity has traditionally been highly eclectic and syncretistic, mixing together elements from various religions. Although many of the new religions focus upon one major deity or revelation as definitive, they also embrace teachings, practices and symbols from many different traditions. The influence of Christianity, for example, can be seen in the way many of the new religions incorporate Christian symbols and motifs, assimilating Jesus and Moses into their respective cosmologies. Mahikari claims that Jesus came to Japan for religious training prior to his public preaching, and the Omoto movement transformed Jesus and Moses into Shinto *kami*. Numerous charismatic leaders of new movements claim either to be reincarnations of Christ or to be inspired by Christ.

Similarly, the heavy emphasis in the new religions upon miracles and healings, the ancestral cult, prosperity and tangible, 'this-worldly' benefits echoes themes which have been dominant in traditional Japanese religions. Reports of miraculous healings abound, suggesting that although modern medicine and science can be helpful, ultimately the root causes of illness and misfortune are spiritual and thus must be addressed on that level. Thus it would seem the new religions are not a rejection of traditional religious themes so much as a fresh, modernized expression of older motifs.

There is also often a combination of universalism, or a sense of global mission, with a particularized focus upon Japan as the unique vehicle for universal well-being. Many groups (Tenrikyo, Rissho Kosei Kai, Soka Gakkai, Sekai Kyuseikyo, Agonshu) view themselves as having a global mission for world peace and prosperity and thus are active in various global cultural and peace initiatives. Yet frequently, as with Agonshu, this is combined with a strong sense of nationalism, emphasizing Japan's special role in mediating world peace and internationalism. In this, as in so many ways, the new religions combine elements of modernity and globalization with ancient values and beliefs.

BIBLIOGRAPHY

R. S. Elwood, 'New Religions in Japan', in *ER* 10, pp. 410–414; S. Murakami, *Japanese Religion in the Modern Century* (Tokyo, 1980); I. Reader, *Religion in Contemporary Japan* (London, 1991); I. Reader and G. Tanabe, *Practically Religious: Worldly Benefits and the Common Religion of Japan* (Honolulu, 1998); S. Shimazono, 'The Expansion of Japan's New Religions into Foreign Cultures', in M. Mullins et al. (eds.), *Religion and Society in Modern Japan: Selected Readings* (Berkeley, CA, 1993), pp. 273–300; R. F. Young, 'The "Christ" of the Japanese New Religions', *JCQ* 57:1 (1991), pp. 18–28.

H. A. Netland

NEW RELIGIOUS MOVEMENTS IN JUDAISM

Contemporary Judaism displays an unprecedented diversity. In part this represents an outworking of the changes brought by emancipation and the consequent exposure of Jewish communities to wider culture. In part it reflects the lack of any central authority to legislate on the many important and controversial issues arising in Jewish communities. Even Orthodox Jews, who find the greatest difficulty with Jewish diversity, do not recognize any common human authority and have failed to create one national or international body in which all Orthodox groups could speak as one. As so much store is laid on personal choice in religion at the end of the twentieth century, it is difficult to foresee any significant change in this position, despite the considerable practical problems it raises. Thus we find different groups of Jews disagreeing on such fundamental matters as who is to be counted as a Jew or what validity is to be given to the religious rites in different Jewish denominations.

TRENDS TOWARD ORTHODOXY

Nevertheless, some trends are apparent among modern Jews. The last part of the twentieth century saw most growth at both ends of the Jewish spectrum, among the Orthodox and among avowedly secular Jews. The *teshuvah* movement – the return of Jews from a secularized or non-observant position to a more wholehearted religious commitment – has benefited Orthodoxy especially. Indeed, the movement was encouraged by the Lubavitch, hitherto a smaller Hasidic movement, under Rabbi Menachem Mendel Schneerson, who promoted a vigorous proselytizing programme among loosely committed Jews. This programme took off in the 1960s, the hippie era and the period of the Six Day War, which had a profound impact in inculcating Jewish national consciousness among Jews throughout the world. At that time it was considered counter-cultural to become Orthodox, since to do so meant setting aside secular modes of American life and adopting the beliefs and practices of some Orthodox group. Though the hippie era ended, the phenomenon of *teshuvah* did not; instead, it began to attract yuppie sections of American society. A similar movement appeared with the demise of communism in the old Soviet Union. There, most of the Jews who wished to take up a religious commitment chose to be schooled in Orthodoxy, presumably because they considered this premodern expression of Jewish faith offered the best antidote to the evils of modernity and secularism that they most detested.

The same phenomenon has been found in the state of Israel, where a number of *yeshivot* have been established to help Jews to return to the roots of their religion. Moreover, the nature of coalition politics in Israel has allowed Orthodox Jews more power than their numbers (no more than 20% of the population) would suggest. They have acquired a reputation for being aggressive and intolerant defenders of the Jewish tradition as they see it. But they have not had things all their own way. There has been something of a secular backlash, not least after the assassination of Prime Minister Rabin in 1995 by an Orthodox student. Moreover, the Haredim have been criticized for being exempt from military service and from the nation's workforce, despite benefiting through their educational institutions from the nation's taxes. To counter Orthodox influence, secular Jews, in conjunction with Reform and Conservative Jews, have advocated a definition of Jewishness relying more on ethnic ties than on religion.

TRENDS TOWARD SECULARISM

The secularist end of the spectrum is represented by both Reconstructionist Judaism and Humanistic Judaism. Of these, Humanistic Judaism is the more consistently secular in orientation, with few differences from humanist societies in Western countries. Reconstructionist Judaism, however, highly values Jewish religious practices in their traditional form as a way to preserve Jewish identity. This movement was the creation of an American rabbi, Mordecai Kaplan (1881–1983), who first hoped to revitalize the Orthodox, Conservative and Reform movements from within, but who from the 1960s began to establish a separate denomination. His system is secular to the extent that he dismissed the idea of a supernatural God who had created the Jewish people and given it the Torah. Instead, he conceived of God as the highest possible fulfilment of human beings. The Torah, for its part, was the creation of the Jewish people in its search for divine illumination and as a mark of its distinct identity. At the same time, however, Kaplan believed that all Jewish traditions, including religious practices, were to be carefully studied and appreciated because they represented the most durable and compelling insights revealed by preceding generations about the ultimate meaning and sanctity of life. However, contemporary Jews should not be slavishly bound by them. On the contrary, Judaism was an 'evolving religious civilization', whose members were to play an active and informed part in the process of evolution. To further this process, Kaplan advocated the establishment of a network of organic Jewish communities that would decide on a democratic basis what the Judaism of the future would be like. Yet membership of these groups would be voluntary and there would be respect for private religious opinions. With his strong sense of a distinct Jewish people and civilization, Kaplan was confident that the majority of Jews would light upon a suitable path forward into the future. Certainly he was realistic enough to see that this process would be greatly assisted if the Jewish people acquired a land of their own. Hence the Reconstructionist movement was from the outset strongly Zionist. The state of Israel was envisaged as a centre for the cultural rejuvenation of Judaism, which would in turn benefit the communities in the diaspora. In practice, however, Reconstructionism has remained an American rather than an Israeli movement.

Humanistic Judaism, like its Reconstructionist cousin, views Judaism in non-theological terms as the cultural creation of the Jewish people. It also values Jewish ceremonies as a means of fostering Jewish identity. But it differs from Reconstructionism in that it follows traditional practices only insofar as they promote humanistic values. Indeed, it has even jettisoned some practices, such as male circumcision, as contrary to the principle of sexual equality, and has replaced it with a birth rite equally applicable to male and female. It is also a more ideological movement than Reconstructionism, with a thoroughly modernist stress on human reason as a sure guide in all spheres of life. It decries other modern Judaisms as inconsistently trying to combine a rational acceptance of a secular world with aspects of an irrational Jewish faith. In other words, it shares the worldview of Ultra-Orthodoxy that premodern Judaism is incompatible with modern patterns of life, but of course makes the opposite choice from that of Ultra-Orthodoxy.

Beginning on a small scale in the USA in the mid-1960s, Humanistic Judaism has expanded to become an international movement (International Federation of Secular Humanistic Jews) with nine separate national organizations. Its expansion has resulted, at least in part, from debates within the Jewish community. In particular, it has reacted against some Orthodox attempts to insist on a religious definition for a Jew. Humanistic Jews, relishing pluralism, have seen this definition as a potential threat to the existence of the Jewish community. By contrast, they advocate a broad view of Judaism as essential to the survival of Jewish identity. Hence they welcome as a Jew any 'person of Jewish descent or any person who declares herself or himself a Jew and who identifies with the history, ethical values, culture, civilization, community and fate of the Jewish people'. This is the point at which Humanistic Judaism has made its greatest impact. Its open, pluralistic approach to the Jewish community has impressed some other Jews with more theistic leanings.

The issue of Jewish identity had already been posed by the most successful of recent secular Judaisms, Zionism. For Zionism challenged the idea undergirding premodern Judaism ('The Jewish people is a people only for the sake of its Torah') because it had allowed the Jewish people to become satisfied with life in exile. By contrast, the Zionists located Jewish unity in a common historical experience, interpreted not in the categories of Jewish faith but in largely secular terms. In particular, Jewish history was characterized both by periods of anti-Semitism and by times when heroic initiatives had brought a flowering of Jewish life. Jews could, the Zionists believed, break free of the cramping conditions of exile and establish their own state, where they would be left unhindered to work out a more satisfying destiny. This conviction encouraged a view of Jewish identity as participation in a common history and the willingness to continue into the future in pursuit of a common destiny. It would not be an exaggeration to say that in Zionist ideology the state of Israel took the place of God himself, not least because this state was supposed to ensure for Jews protection from their enemies. However, the state of Israel has not been constituted on entirely secular lines. On the vital question of who counts as a Jew with the right to return to Israel, its political leaders have had to look to more traditional religious definitions, though they have not found that every problem can be solved by these means.

MESSIANIC JUDAISM

The question of Jewish identity is a sore point with the Messianic Jews, another group that emerged in the USA out of the counter-culture of the 1960s. These are Jews who have recognized in Jesus their Messiah, but who have preferred to link with Jews of the same persuasion in formal or informal structures rather than to associate with Gentile churches. They have rejected the latter course as a sure path to assimilation. They believe that by maintaining a distinct Jewish identity and by following Jewish practices and festivals they can more effectively evangelize their fellow Jews as well as express their Jewishness. Yet they have been dismissed, even vilified as deceptive Christians, by most Jewish authorities. Ironically, the few Jews who have been prepared to accept them as genuine Jews have been those liberals who have endorsed the pluralist, open definition of a Jew.

NEW AGE JUDAISM

Another movement from the counterculture of the 1960s further exemplifies the trend away from the traditional religious authority of the rabbis towards the assertion of personal autonomy. This is the Havurah Movement, in which informal groups of Jews, typically numbering from ten to fifty people, began meeting for Torah study, worship and doing *mitzvot*. These groups operated on a democratic basis, with all members making a contribution and with a particular emphasis on spontaneity and creativity. The *havurot* were trans-denominational and often profited by bringing together Jews from very different backgrounds. Essentially they engaged in do-it-yourself Judaism. If rabbis were involved at all, they were used as resource people rather than as leaders.

At first *havurot* were alternatives to the synagogues, which were seen as uninspiring and monopolized by a religious hierarchy. In time, however, they did influence the synagogues to embrace a greater degree of informality and democracy. The Havurah Movement has its own institutional successor, the Jewish Renewal Movement, based at Elat Chayyim near Woodstock, New York. It has emphasized an experience-centred spirituality that has been criticized as anti-intellectual and antinomian. It is open to influences from other religions, especially eastern religions. Techniques such as chant, meditation and yoga have become part of its worship. In short, it has imbibed a New Age spirituality. While some will fault its loose grasp on the Jewish tradition, it has maintained a Jewish identity for people at the periphery of the Jewish religious community who would be alienated by more traditional forms of Judaism.

CONCLUSION

In the current climate the desire of Jewish secularists and pluralists for a wide definition of Jewishness is understandable. However, a Jewish identity without a firm religious base seems fragile. Jewish culture, civilization and history all make poor substitutes. The Jewish community will continue to wrestle with its identity problem as long as there remains a wide mismatch between its religious inheritance and the beliefs of contemporary Jews.

BIBLIOGRAPHY

D. Cohn-Sherbok, *Messianic Judaism* (London and New York, 2000); D. Cohn-Sherbok, *Modern Judaism* (Basingstoke and New York, 1996); J. Neusner, *Judaism in Modern Times* (Oxford and Cambridge, MA, 1995); J. Neusner and A. J. Avery-Peck (eds.), *The Blackwell Companion to Judaism* (Oxford and Malden, MA, 2000), pp. 334–511; J. Neusner and A. J. Avery-Peck (eds.), *The Blackwell Reader in Judaism* (Oxford and Malden, MA, 2001), pp. 256–431; A. Ravitzky, *Messianism, Zionism and Jewish Religious Radicalism* (ET London and Chicago, 1996).

G. A. Keith

NEW RELIGIOUS MOVEMENTS IN PRIMAL SOCIETIES

The term 'New Religious Movements in Primal Societies' was coined in the 1960s by the New Zealand scholar Harold W. Turner to denote 'a historically new development arising in the interaction between a primal (i.e. traditional or tribal) society and its religion, and one of the higher cultures and its major religion, and involving some substantial departure from the classical religious traditions of both the cultures concerned, in order to find renewal by reworking the rejected religious traditions into a different religious system.'

By 'historically new' Turner meant that these movements are essentially modern phenomena, first visible in the seventeenth century and most noticeable in the twentieth century. They are also *religious* movements, concerned with human relationships with the transcendent world of spirit, and not reducible to purely political or economic terms. They are movements of interaction between, on the one hand, 'primal' or 'tribal' host societies, with their own traditional religions, and, on the other, cultural and religious influences foreign to those societies. They mobilize people who are no longer satisfied with traditional ways, but who find the alternatives offered by the foreign influences unacceptable, at least in the forms they see before them. The outcome is a process in which old ideas and practices are reworked together with new ideas and practices, each being reconceived in the light of the other. The term comprehends many movements formerly classified as 'nativistic', 'revitalization', 'millennial', 'messianic' or (by Marxist commentators) 'religions of the oppressed'.

Turner identified thousands of such movements in all six continents; they are particularly prolific in sub-Saharan Africa and in Oceania. Although in principle they may arise in relation to any major religion, historically the overwhelming majority have arisen in relation to Christianity, and hardly any in relation to Islam.

The nature of the relationship between these movements and historical Christianity differs widely. Turner identified four main categories of movement.

In *Neo-Primal movements* the structure and content of the traditional religion is substantially retained, but incidental features are introduced from Christian teaching, worship or activities. These are 'modernizing' features that promote efficiency, relevance or an appeal beyond the original ethnic group.

Synthetist movements combine traditional and Christian elements to make an altogether new religion.

Hebraist movements are marked by a call to allegiance to God and a rejection of alternative or lesser spirit powers, but without a correspondingly clear assertion of the ultimacy of Christ. In effect these are 'Old Testament' or 'John the Baptist' movements.

Independent churches are indigenous appropriations of the Christian message, translating traditional religious institutions and concerns into biblical terms, and often using models of church life quite different from those of churches that arise out of the work of Western missions.

The four categories are not rigidly self-contained, but represent a spectrum. The movements, being dynamic, may shift along the spectrum in either direction. Hebraist movements may shade into independent churches as the significance of Christ is clarified, or the significance of

Christ may become overshadowed by the prominence of the founding prophet.

Synthetist movements have been especially characteristic of Melanesia, and independent churches of sub-Saharan Africa and the New Zealand Maori. The troubled history of Native American religion has generated movements in all four categories; Hebraist movements led by indigenous prophets have been especially prominent.

Despite Turner's huge resource collection (now at the University of Birmingham, England), few subsequent scholars have viewed the movements as a whole, concentrating rather on particular movements or regions, and especially on those in the category of African independent churches, now often called 'African instituted', or 'spiritual' churches. It is now clear that the worldviews and religious concerns once thought characteristic of these churches are shared by large numbers of other African Christians. Further, a plethora of new churches, associations and organizations has emerged in urban areas of Africa since the 1970s, as part of the charismatic movement. These share many features of the African independent or spiritual churches, in particular their keen apprehension of the nearness of the spirit world as a theatre of combat, but they generally oppose these older bodies, and their own models of church life resemble those of the Western church much more closely.

BACKGROUND AND ORIGINS

The background for most movements is the disruption of traditional patterns of life by the invasive influences of modernity, accompanied by Christianity mediated by Western missions. Many movements emerged during the period of colonial rule, when indigenous people lost a large measure of control over their lives. War and disaster have also been catalysts; the First World War and the influenza epidemic which followed caused unprecedented events in Africa, while the Second World War was cataclysmic in its effects on many Pacific peoples. The Native American history of recurrent displacement is marked by the appearance of many new religious movements. The religious effects of the Nigerian Civil War (1966–70) and the Zimbabwean War of Independence are still being measured.

At such times established social relationships and local patterns of leadership break up. People are forced into association with other people and groups with whom they previously had nothing to do and may find themselves caught up in a new type of economy or method of subsistence. Accepted standards of behaviour and patterns of mutual responsibility lose their hold, so moral confusion, insecurity and a sense of moral breakdown follow.

In such situations there has often been a large-scale movement towards Christianity. Christian teaching, especially when accompanied, as in the work of many Western missions, by education and healthcare, offered ways of adjusting to or coping with change. But the version of Christianity offered by the missions did not always seem adequate: too much was alien or unintelligible; too much of life was left unexplained. Some decided that there was truth in Christianity, and power in the Bible, of which Westerners did not know, or which they perhaps deliberately withheld, and new religious movements emerged, based on this conviction.

Some neo-primal movements embody resistance to change, and some post-Christian movements try to nourish cultural roots by reviving traditional religion. Some Native American movements have sought to renew their broken culture by reviving religious practices, such as the 'vision quest' and the 'sweat lodge', that had almost ceased, and by developing a spirituality incorporating elements from diverse Native American ethnic groups. The Native American Church, which has various manifestations across North America, exemplifies this approach. Similarly, some African Americans have been asserting their African identity by obtaining a shrine name from Africa. African intellectuals have sometimes attempted to formulate universalized (rather than localized) African traditional religions; among such developments are Godianism and the National Church of Nigeria and, in Ghana, the Afrikania movement (which was founded by a former Catholic priest and enjoyed official favour for a time).

Many synthetist movements have arisen in Melanesia, where the impact of the outside world on traditional communities has been particularly drastic and the need for adjustment correspondingly great (hence the commonly adopted term 'adjustment movements'). Melanesian movements tend to have a strong eschatological element, offering a prosperous trouble-free future, often with rich material blessings. (The latter feature, which has occasioned the misleading label 'cargo cults', has to be understood in the context of fragile, vulnerable economies in encounter with the West and its flood of consumer goods.) Old myths about the origin of the local people group are reinterpreted in the light of themes from the Bible and the group's experiences of the wider world, and especially of white people. Salvation is presented in corporate terms, with the ancestors returning to rejoin their descendants (whereas Christian preaching often offered salvation in a highly individualized form). The movements commonly demand moral renewal to prepare for the new age, sometimes urging a return to neglected traditional ways, sometimes demanding the abandonment of tradition, sometimes combining old and new in a new customary law. Some movements localize the biblical narratives, so that the topography of Papua merges with that of Palestine; others present a direct alternative to Christianity. (In the island of Tanna, in Vanuatu, one such post-Christian movement has gone far towards replacing a long-established Reformed Christianity).

But the most widely influential movements are those, originating among Christians, that represent an appropriation of the Christian message based on a new and localized reading of Scripture, and influenced by the vision and worldview of local people. These movements are best distinguished from the so-called 'Ethiopian' movements, which first arose late in the nineteenth century to challenge missionary domination in African churches and promote African leadership. The resulting 'Ethiopian' churches left the worship, doctrine and polity of the missions virtually unchanged.

But in the period just before the First World War and for a decade or so thereafter, a succession of charismatic figures appeared in different parts of West, Central and Southern Africa. Some, such as the most famous, the Liberian William Wade Harris, and Sampson Oppong in Ashanti, emerged quite independently of ecclesiastical structures; others, such as Simon Kimbangu in Congo and Garrick Braide in the Niger Delta, belonged to the junior ranks of the mission hierarchy. But all attributed their commission to preach, heal, confront evil powers and destroy fetish to a direct call from God. Sometimes, the call had accompaniments (a dream, a trance, a grave illness that vanished when the divine commission was accepted) typical of the calling of traditional priests or diviners, but these preachers could point to similar phenomena in the Scriptures.

The response to these figures was immense; Harris, for instance, is the single most important figure in Ivory Coast Christianity. They were not generally opposed to the missions as such, but tensions often arose in their relationships with them. When these occurred, the prophets left a double legacy: congregations owing their origin to their ministry but in the pastoral care of the missions, and congregations unconnected with the missions. (In Ivory Coast, for instance, the mission-related churches owe much to Harris, but there are also independent 'Harrist' churches). The independent congregations maintained and sometimes developed the tradition of the founding prophet, and became more distinct from the mission churches. Thus in colonial Congo the brief ministry of Simon Kimbangu, originally a Baptist catechist, produced a powerful underground movement. At independence this emerged as a major church, the Eglise de Jésus-Christ sur la Terre par le prophète Simon Kimbangu (EJCSK).

The term 'new religious movement' is used both for the movements surrounding these charismatic figures and for the resulting churches outside the mission structures. It also applies to churches that originated in religious movements inside mission-related churches. Thus the influenza epidemic of 1918, which appeared to show Western medicine to be powerless, induced a group of Anglican Christians in Ijebu-Ode, Western Nigeria, to turn to fasting and prayer. The resulting Precious Stone Society in turn generated a separate church that regarded dreams as a channel of God's activity and engaged in prophecy and healing in the name of Christ. A whole succession of such 'prophet-healing' groups emerged and spread, many taking the name 'aladura' (Yoruba for 'praying people'). In South Africa a different chain of events led to the appearance of many 'Zionist' churches with analogous features, and parallel movements arose in East Africa.

The worldwide influenza epidemic was also the catalyst for a movement of healing and prophecy among the New Zealand Maori. Following a vision and other remarkable signs, T. W. Ratana was hailed as the *Mangai* (or mouthpiece) of God. The movement of religious and moral revival which followed, in a demoralized and alcohol-damaged community, issued in a new church. The associated social consciousness produced a campaign for land reform and Maori rights. ('First let us unite in the Lord', said Ratana, 'and then we will unite in the land.') For many years, most Maori Members of the New Zealand Parliament were Ratana followers.

AFRICAN INDEPENDENT CHURCHES

The African independent churches addressed a worldview in which a variety of active spiritual forces were at work, witchcraft and sorcery could have devastating effects, and illness was seen as due to personal wrongdoing, neglect of social or family duty, or someone else's malice. To this they brought certain features they found in Scripture but not in mission Christianity: the immediate revelation of prophecy, and healing by the power of Christ or the Spirit. Parts of the Old Testament addressed concerns about ritual purification to which mission Christianity had nothing to say. The new movements brought a sense of liberation, even if the charismatic founder became domineering or divisions appeared.

The initial reaction of missions and their churches was usually hostile. The new churches were seen as separatist, and also as syncretistic, because of their debt to African worldviews, their use of divinatory practices (again often justified by biblical precedents), the drumming and dancing that many practised, and their use of white robes and uniforms. The fact that many did not insist on monogamy (others, including the EJCSK, did) provoked accusations of sexual laxity.

Western Pentecostals responded differently. White charismatics played a part in the emergence of the South African Zionists; in Nigeria and Ghana Western Pentecostal missionaries and indigenous charismatics delightedly recognized one another. But tensions and ruptures often followed over leadership, priorities or practices.

A series of bridge-building efforts in the 1960s and 1970s, in which American Mennonites played a significant part, helped to effect better understanding between the independent and the mission churches. Some of the former, notably the EJCSK, have even become members of the

World Council of Churches. In New Zealand, the Ratana Church has long been an associate member of the Council of Churches.

NEW RELIGIOUS MOVEMENTS IN THE WEST

The African diaspora has brought many of the African independent churches to the cities of Europe and North America. Among the most prominent are various branches of the Cherubim and Seraphim, the Church of the Lord (Aladura) and the Celestial Church of Christ. All of these are originally of Nigerian Yoruba (or related) origin, but they have found a ready response among other immigrants from Africa and now have some impact on the wider community in the West. They operate side by side with the older churches from Africa, with the newer African charismatics such as Deeper Life, and with churches of Caribbean origin to form an important part of the urban religious scene.

BIBLIOGRAPHY

D. B. Barrett, *Schism and Renewal: An Analysis of Six Thousand Contemporary Religious Movements* (Nairobi and Oxford, 1968); H. W. Turner, *African Independent Church*, 2 vols. (Oxford, 1967); H. W. Turner, *Religious Innovation in Africa* (Boston, 1979); H. W. Turner, 'Tribal Religious Movements, New', in *Encyclopaedia Britannica* (London, [17]1974); A. F. Walls and W. R. Shenk (eds.), *Exploring New Religious Movements: Essays in Honour of Harold W. Turner* (1990); P. Worsley, *The Trumpet Shall Sound: A Study of 'Cargo' Cults in Melanesia* (London[2]1968).

A. F. Walls

PAGANISM

The word 'pagan', derived from the Latin term *paganus* (lit. 'from the countryside' (*pagus*) or 'rural'), has over the years been used pejoratively by Christians to mean 'uncivilized', 'non-Christian' and even 'Satanic'. Indeed, the term 'pagan' was first used in a general religious sense by the early Christians to describe the non-Christian Gentile religions.

Although some Christians still use the term 'pagan' (lower-case 'p') in a pejorative sense, it is now generally used to refer to a growing and increasingly prominent contemporary religious tradition. Just as the term 'Hinduism' refers not to a single religion, but to a diverse and complex network of traditions of Indian origin, so 'Paganism' refers to a broad range of nature-venerating religious traditions. Whilst the term 'Neo-Paganism' is sometimes used by academics and even by some devotees, particularly in the USA (e.g. the Church of All Worlds), practitioners generally prefer the simpler term 'Paganism'.

PAGANS, SATANISTS AND NEW AGERS

It is common in some circles, particularly conservative Christian and media circles, (a) to include Paganism under the umbrella term 'New Age' and/or (b) to understand the term 'Paganism' as a synonym for 'Satanism'. Although it is always difficult to generalize about such diverse and eclectic spiritualities as the New Age and Paganism, on the whole it is true to say that Pagans are right to deny both of these interpretations.

Firstly, most contemporary Pagans will insist that, because Satan does not feature in the Pagan worldview, and because Satanists work with a perverted understanding of the Christian worldview, they are not Pagans, but rather Christian heretics. Indeed, many Pagans will actively distance themselves from Satanists and Satanism. The Paganism–Satanism confusion, which probably stretches back to the Christian denunciation of Pagans as devil worshippers, has been exacerbated in recent years by misrepresentations in films, horror novels and popular books dealing with the occult. Moreover, because Satanists themselves will use the names of Pagan gods (as well as the names of the gods of other faiths, e.g. Kali) to refer to Satan and the demonic pantheon, some have wrongly concluded that when genuine Pagans refer to gods such as Hecate, Lilith, Pan and Set they are actually worshipping Satan. However, 'Paganism is not Satanism, it has no place for a devil, or for belief in ontological evil. Its cosmology has no room for a battle between forces of "good" and "evil" fought over the "souls" of humans who might be enticed towards heaven or hell' (Harvey, *Listening People, Speaking Earth*, p. 218). Hence, although there has been debate amongst some Pagans over the significance of the figure of Satan (e.g. can the name be divested of its Christian content and usefully used in a Pagan context?), and although some Satanists do consider themselves to be Pagan, generally speaking Paganism and Satanism are distinct and should not be confused, and such confusion will cause offence to many Pagans.

Secondly, although (principally because of the eclectic nature of the New Age) there are areas of overlap (sometimes considerable) between the New Age and Paganism, they are distinct. For example, (1) Pagans are critical of what they understand to be the New Age's overly sanguine, saccharine, light-emphasizing view of reality. Paganism emphasizes both the beauty of nature and the fact that it is 'red in tooth and claw'; inspired by the polarities of the natural world, Pagan thinking incorporates spring and autumn, life and death, light and darkness, the dark being understood not as evil, but, like the winter and the night, simply another side of the natural world. (2) Paganism is more ritualistic than the New Age. Some of its traditions have a priesthood; it works with particular rites and symbols and has a religious calendar of festivals (followed by some New Agers). (3) Whereas much in the New Age is aimed at enabling the individual to 'go within' and discover the 'higher self', in Paganism there is a greater emphasis on the other, that which is external to the self: the planet, the deities and the community. Most Pagans, for example, are polytheists who will look to gods and goddesses for help and guidance. Again, there is a great emphasis on one's responsibility towards other creatures (human and non-human) and the environment. And whilst there are solitary practitioners, generally speaking the Pagan community is valued by individual Pagans as a source of spiritual guidance and support. (4) Regarding the local group to which a person belongs (e.g. one's coven in the Wicca tradition), often the initiation process and the high level of commitment required is quite distinct from what would normally be found in the New Age.

GODS AND GODDESSES

Paganism rejects patriarchal monotheisms and the depiction of God as solely male.

Although some place the emphasis very firmly on 'the Great Goddess' and the feminine, generally speaking Paganism seeks balance, teaching that the God and the Goddess are of equal importance. Many Pagans (not all) would insist that, however the divine is conceived, it must be conceived in such a way that both the masculine and the feminine are embraced.

A further variation of this inclusive understanding of deity is that of the Triple Goddess: 'the virgin', 'the mother' and 'the crone' (old woman). Often symbolized as the waxing moon (early life), the full moon (prime of life) and the waning moon (later life), the Triple Goddess affirms the equality of all the stages of womanhood. Moreover, this understanding of the divine also affirms, not just virginity, but also the sexual and the bodily; not just the young, but also the aged. Again, the Earth is identified as 'the Great Mother' or as Gaia, and humans are understood to be her children. Mother Nature provides for her offspring and receives them back when they pass away. Similarly, as 'the crone' or wise woman, the Goddess is understood to be a guardian and teacher of secret knowledge.

The God of Paganism is principally understood in terms of fertility (e.g. the Green Man) and protection (e.g. Thor). Having said that, like the Goddess he is also a caring parent (e.g. Dagda) and a wise counsellor (e.g. Odin).

The many minor 'gods' and 'goddesses' of Paganism are often understood to be manifestations or representations of 'the Goddess' and 'the God' (or simply 'the Divine'). Hence, for some Pagans, these deities represent different facets of the divine. There are warrior gods, fatherly gods, gods of fertility, virgin goddesses (e.g. Aradia), mother goddesses (e.g. Isis) and crone goddeses (e.g. Cerridwen).

Finally, many Pagans are essentially pantheistic, in that the divine is believed, in some sense, to be absolutely identical with nature. The Goddess or God is the force which animates all living things. Having said that, some Pagans are more accurately defined as panentheist because, strictly speaking, they do not understand the divine and the universe to be one. Whilst the divine indwells nature, is immanent within nature, is inseparable from nature, there is also a sense in which the Goddess or God transcends, guides and cares for the natural world.

THE WHEEL OF THE YEAR

Because Paganism is a nature religion, seasonal festivals are important. In the Pagan calendar there are eight major festivals which together make up 'the Wheel of the Year'. *Samhain* is generally understood to be the beginning of the Wheel of the Year and is celebrated by many as the Celtic New Year (Hallowe'en or All Hallows Eve). *Midwinter* (also Yule or Winter solstice) is celebrated by all Pagans (as are Midsummer and both equinoxes). Many Heathens (see 'The Northern Tradition', below) will celebrate Yule as the New Year. *Imbolc* (also Oimelc or Candlemas) welcomes the return of the bright sun and celebrates the emergence of new life. Many of the Imbolc rituals depict the emergence of the Goddess (the Virgin of Light) from the underworld. The *Spring Equinox*, the point in the calendar when the hours of darkness are equal to those of light, is the time when Pagans celebrate fertility and the power of the life force. This is often done with painted eggs (usually green as this colour depicts the fertility of the Spring). Traditionally the time for May queens and May poles (which are sometimes reinvested with religious significance by Pagans, the May queen symbolizing the Goddess and the May pole symbolising the God), *Beltane* celebrates the emergence out of Spring into the full bloom of Summer. Often the night will be spent around a bonfire. *Midsummer* (also Summer solstice) celebrates the power of the sun and often focuses on a solar deity. Many Pagans will gather to observe the sunrise. *Lammas* (or Lughnasadh) is the

Old English term for 'loaf mass' or 'low feast', the celebration of the first loaf baked from the newly harvested corn. Lammas is a first-fruits festival that is traditionally celebrated by fairs and games. Particular deities are thanked for their bounty. Moreover, for many Pagans the Lammas festival teaches an important truth regarding the two sides of nature, namely that the brutality and death of harvesting is necessary for the sustenance and continuance of life. At the *Autumn Equinox* the Wheel of the Year has turned full circle and Pagans reflect on the previous year.

Because the Wheel of the Year and the nature of the festivals are determined by the seasonal cycle, there are of course regional variations. For example, whereas in Britain Pagans tend to celebrate seed sowing at the Spring Equinox, this is not the case in the cold northerly parts of Canada, where this celebration happens later in the year.

PAGAN TRADITIONS

Whilst Paganism prides itself on being a non-dogmatic spirituality which encourages people to pursue their own religious path as directed by personal experience, many Pagans choose to belong to a particular tradition with particular deities and particular rituals. Hence within contemporary Paganism there are a variety of clearly defined traditions, and the relationships between some of them are fairly complex. The following are three of the major paths followed by Western Pagans.

WICCA

Also called the Old Religion, Witchcraft, Wisecraft or simply the Craft, Wicca (from the Anglo-Saxon *Wicce* meaning 'witch') is possibly the most influential and (largely because of the media) certainly the most well-known form of Paganism. Needless to say, the popular media-perpetuated image of the Witch (i.e. the spooky old hags portrayed in William Shakespeare's *Macbeth* or Roald Dahl's children's book *The Witches*) is inaccurate. As with all types of Pagan, many of them are very normal, unassuming people with ordinary lives (academics, unemployed persons, lawyers, shop assistants, accountants, etc.).

Wiccans meet regularly in small groups or 'covens' of like-minded people for social, religious and educational purposes. Sometimes during these meetings (and sometimes solitarily) they seek to practise magic, of which there are the two forms: 'natural magic' and 'high magic', both of which, it is stressed, should be directed toward good and healthy ends. Involving initiation and rituals, high magic (often spelled 'magick') aims at personal transformation through contact with the divine. Natural magic, on the other hand, is more materialistic in that, by means of herbs, crystals or other natural materials, it aims to harness what are believed to be natural (or sometimes supernatural) forces in order to effect changes in the physical world, from healing of sick minds and bodies to changes in the weather. Needless to say, whilst some people become Wiccans out of a spiritual concern for the environment, or because they seek a radically feminist spirituality, or because they are attracted by non-dogmatic faith, many are drawn by the desire to practise magic(k). Magic(k) is enormously attractive, not only because of the sense of power that it brings, but also because, particularly in high magick, there is a Gnostic-like sense of being initiated into a secret tradition with secret knowledge and secret symbols.

Although there are many Wiccan traditions, there are four principal ones, from which many of the others have evolved: Gardnerian Wicca, Alexandrian Wicca, Hereditary Craft and Traditional Craft. Gardnerians base their religion on the techniques taught by Gerald Gardner. Arguably the most important figure in modern Wicca, Gardner zealously sought to make pre-Christian Paganism ('Wicca', as he called it) available and accessible to the public. Following the 1951 repeal of the 1735 Witchcraft Act (which had forbidden

Witchcraft in England), in 1954 Gardner published his influential *Witchcraft Today*. One of the most important Pagan figures to be initiated into Wicca by Gardner was Doreen Valiente who, although far more private than Gardner, has remained an influential and revered figure, particularly in British Wicca (she died in September 1999). Another influential publicity-conscious Wiccan theoretician, who developed Gardner's ideas, was Alex Sanders, the leader of a coven near Manchester, England. Giving himself the title 'King of Witches', he established a rival form of 'Alexandrian' Wicca.

Hereditaries and Traditionalists argue that their beliefs and practices pre-date modern manifestations of the Craft and have been carefully preserved and passed down through the generations. The Hereditaries make the more specific claim that this knowledge has been handed down within particular families.

Finally, an increasingly popular Wiccan tendency should be mentioned, namely Hedge Witchcraft. 'Hedge Witch' is a term used by those practitioners who prefer to work on their own, rather than as a member of an organized coven.

DRUIDRY

Whilst Druidry was clearly a pre-Christian Celtic religion, the continuity between this ancient faith, of which little is known, and contemporary Druidry is questionable. Moreover, the history of contemporary Druidry, which stretches back to the eighteenth-century revival of the tradition, is not the history of a Pagan tradition as such, in that many of the early Druids considered themselves and their beliefs to be fully compatible with traditional Christianity. Indeed, many continued to worship as Christians and hold offices in their local churches. Although Pagans have been involved in Druidry for many years, and increasingly so since the 1960s, explicitly Pagan Druid orders did not emerge until the late 1970s.

Druidry is more structured than Wicca. Individual Druid groups belong to a particular Druid Order which is overseen by an elected 'Archdruid' (different orders use different titles). In Britain most of these orders belong to an umbrella organization, the Council of British Druid Orders. Although no such council exists in the USA, there are two main bodies to which most Druids belong, Ar nDraiocht Fein (meaning 'Our Own Druidism') and Keltria.

Whilst there is no Druid orthodoxy as such, generally speaking contemporary *Pagan* Druids (there are still many Druids who very clearly identify themselves as Christian and *not* Pagan) have what might be described as a neo-Celtic Pagan faith, in that it is an eclectic mixture of general Pagan beliefs constructed around what is known of Celtic belief and culture. It is Paganism with a Celtic bias. For example, Celtic gods and goddesses are worshipped, ley lines (a network of natural energy lines believed to criss-cross the planet) are important and prehistoric sites (e.g. Stonehenge and Avebury) are revered as sacred spaces. Smaller Druid orders which are focused on particular mythologies and narratives have emerged in recent years. For example, the Glastonbury Order of Bards focuses on the mythology of the town of Glastonbury, Somerset, UK.

THE NORTHERN TRADITION

Those who belong within the Northern Tradition often prefer the term 'Heathen' to 'Pagan'. 'Heathen' means roughly the same as 'Pagan', but is derived from Germanic languages rather than Latin; it is also a term that has been used pejoratively by Christians. The Northern Tradition or Heathenism draws inspiration principally from Anglo-Saxon, Norse and Icelandic pre-Christian mythology, religion and culture.

Whilst, as with all Paganism, there is great variety in Heathenism, and whilst there are particular local traditions, generally speaking they have a common cosmology and theology. There are believed to be nine worlds, of which ours is the middle (Midgard or Middle Earth). These worlds are connected by Yggdrasil (the World Tree). The worlds are populated by different beings (deities, humans, giants, dwarves, elves etc.), some of which can travel between worlds.

The Northern Tradition recognizes two distinct groups of deities: namely, the Aesir and the Vanir. The Aesir, the sky gods and goddesses of Norse mythology, are the sovereign deities of warfare and magic. Generally understood to be the High God, the most important deity in contemporary Heathenism is Odin. His significance is reflected in the names of some of the Heathen groups: the Odinist Fellowship, the Odinic Rite, Odinshof. However, because Odinists often worship other deities as well as Odin, sometimes the name Asatrú ('loyalty to the Aesir') is preferred. Other deities among the Aesir include Frigga, Thor and Tyr. The Vanir, who include Freyja, Frigg, Freyr and Njord, are basically the deities of the Earth associated with agriculture and fertility.

One of the most well-known aspects of Heathenism, which has been popularized by New Agers as a form of 'fortune-telling', is the use of runes. Runes are symbols (often painted on small, smooth stones) which, for Heathens, are more than simply tools for 'fortune-telling' in the modern sense of that term. That is to say, using the runes is more about spiritual guidance, achieving wholeness, communicating with non-human beings and listening to the deities, and less about finding out what a person's future might hold. The chanting of runes is common during Heathen rituals.

PAGANISM AND CONTEMPORARY WESTERN CULTURE

There is little doubt that Western Paganism has grown rapidly in the last couple of decades and will continue to grow in the twenty-first century. Whilst there are many reasons for this growth, the following would seem to be some of the more obvious.

Although there are always exceptions to the rule, generally speaking contemporary Paganism *eschews masculine images* of power and authority. Many contemporary Westerners have thus found the Pagan emphasis on the priestess, the Goddess and the feminine per se to be liberating and enlightened. Those considering some form of Pagan spirituality will cite this aspect of Paganism as a welcome alternative to the attitudes of the principal monotheistic faiths, particularly Christianity.

Not only is Paganism feminist, it is also 'ecofeminist'. Paganism is an *ecological* faith tradition, a nature-centric spirituality that seeks to break down hierarchies. As such, in the contemporary Western world, its attitudes to animals or non-humans and to the Earth is felt by many to be healthy, even if rather naïve at times. In an eco-conscious culture an eco-conscious spirituality is understandably attractive.

Regardless of whether this is always the case or not (and sometimes it is not), Paganism certainly advertises itself as being *non-dogmatic*. In a culture which is uncomfortable with exclusive truth claims, such as those made by Christ and Christianity, it is not difficult to see the attraction of a religion which demands only a reverence for 'the Life force', an honouring of 'the Divine' (however that might be understood) and the single ethical injunction: 'If it harms none do what thou wilt.'

For the above reasons, Paganism is obviously very attractive to spiritually and ecologically minded young people. Moreover, it is a matter of observable fact that the Pagan worldview is both *consciously and unconsciously promoted* by popular fantasy literature, contemporary rock and dance music, films and computer games. For example, the cosmology of J. R. R. Tolkien's wonderful stories about Middle Earth and strange non-human beings and powers is not entirely different from contemporary Heathen cosmology. Whilst conspiracy theories (for many of which there is no substantial evidence) should be avoided, it does seem clear that, for a variety of cultural, philosophical and social reasons, areas of contemporary Western popular culture have both been moulded by and helped to mould the Pagan worldview. Thus, although there is still a great deal of misunderstanding and antipathy regarding Paganism, its future as a popular Western spirituality looks assured. Obscure and alien though it may seem to many Westerners, increasing numbers of people are finding it more acceptable than Christianity as a contemporary spirituality.

As mentioned above, *the appeal* of ancient, secret or occult knowledge, power and ritual is perennial. Particularly in an individualistic and selfish culture which engenders feelings of powerlessness and insignificance, the attraction of a small, closely knit group of people who claim to have access to such ancient power and knowledge is hard to overestimate.

Finally, the repeal of the Witchcraft Act in 1951, the founding, in Britain, of the Pagan Federation twenty years later in 1971 and the emergence of the Internet have done a great deal *to raise the public profile* of Paganism as an acceptable spiritual path.

BIBLIOGRAPHY

V. Crowley, *Principles of Paganism* (London, 1996); G. Harvey, *Listening People, Speaking Earth: Contemporary Paganism* (London, 1997); G. Harvey and C. Hardman (eds.), *Paganism Today* (London, 1995); P. Jones and N. Pennick, *A History of Pagan Europe* (London, 1995); J. R. Lewis (ed.), *Magical Religion and Modern Witchcraft* (New York, 1996); J. Pearson, R. H. Roberts and G. Samuel (eds.), *Nature Religion Today: Paganism in the Modern World* (Edinburgh, 1998).

C. H. Partridge

PARAPSYCHOLOGY

Psychic events have been recorded since ancient times and have been incorporated within the beliefs of both primitive and more sophisticated religions. They have been central to spiritualism since its foundation as a religion in 1848, but psychical investigation as a scientific subject began only when the Society for Psychical Research (SPR) was founded in 1882 and the American SPR in 1885. Parapsychology is now studied in a number of universities, notably under the auspices of the Koestler chair at Edinburgh. Its professional body, the Parapsychological Association, was recognized by the American Association for the Advancement of Science in 1969.

The paranormal is defined by the *New Shorter Oxford English Dictionary* as 'phenomena or powers ... whose operation is outside the scope of the known laws of nature or normal objective investigation' and by the SPR as 'those faculties of man, real or supposed, which appear to be inexplicable on any generally recognised hypothesis'. It includes such phenomena or alleged phenomena as telepathy, clairvoyance, precognition, psychokinesis and communication with discarnate (human or non-human) beings.

Parapsychological findings are disputed, although the SPR (which long prided itself on having no corporate opinions but on simply investigating phenomena 'without prejudice or prepossession') now claims that 'it has for over a century published an impressive body of evidence for the existence of such faculties and the occurrence of paranormal phenomena'. Some investigators find it easier to believe in mental phenomena such as telepathy than in physical phenomena such as levitation or dowsing or psychokinesis and have great difficulty in reconciling the idea of precognition with either causality or human free will; and people whose beliefs cannot include survival of death or reincarnation find ways of interpreting the evidence which allow them to remain agnostic or unbelieving. The late Renée Haynes coined the term 'boggle threshold' to denote the point beyond which people felt they were being asked to believe in impossible things.

Equally disputed is the relevance of parapsychology to philosophical questions such as the mind–body problem or such religious questions as the debate between materialism and a more spiritual interpretation of the world. The data are there, but their interpretation is debated. When a medium (or, as usually termed in a New Age setting, 'channeller') goes into an altered state of consciousness and speaks when entranced or writes automatically, is s/he simply objectifying unconscious fantasies, or engaging in telepathy with someone on this earth, or genuinely bringing communications from another world? When a patient is rescued after a cardiac arrest and speaks of seeing the body from outside and having a near-death experience, is s/he describing the beginnings of an after-death existence, or misinterpreting the wild paroxysms of a brain starved of oxygen? For that matter, when a Christian speaks of having an ineffable religious experience, is it no more than an emotional by-product of hormonal imbalance? The experience may be undoubted, but it can have more than one interpretation.

Telepathic powers are mentioned in Scripture. Joseph used his goblet for divination (Gen. 44:5); Elisha was able to tell what the king of Aram said in his bedchamber (2 Kgs. 6:21); and Jesus knew what Nathanael was thinking when he sat under the fig-tree (John 1:48); but the biblical attitude to psychic powers is at best ambivalent. Their use could be seen as relapse into Canaanite practices and disloyalty to Yahweh (Is. 8:19–20); they could become an obsessive nuisance (Acts 16:18); and Saul consulted a medium at En-Dor with disastrous results (1 Sam. 28).

Eastern religions hold that psychic phenomena often attach themselves to holy people; but they regard them as distracting *siddhis* which are irrelevant to the search for spiritual progress. The biblical miracles are better interpreted as unusual signs of God's activity than as data for a thesis on 'the paranormal in holy Scripture'.

According to the practitioners, the Christian deliverance ministry is directed at people who have been subjected to unwanted psychic happenings (usually poltergeists, hauntings such as place memories, or the attentions of departed human spirits who have remained earthbound). This ministry is often known as 'exorcism', but this term is better reserved for those rare occasions on which it is necessary, in the name of Jesus, to command a non-human evil spirit which is causing trouble on earth to go to its own place, harming no-one, and there remain until the Day of the Lord. Deliverance is more usually a pastoral activity directed towards helping humans who are disturbed by psychic events that they fear because they are unable to understand them, or who have been experimenting unwisely in the psychic field, or who have departed this earth and are not at rest.

The Churches' Fellowship for Psychical and Spiritual Studies (CFPSS) is an ecumenical organization founded in 1953 to help Christians who have (or believe they have) psychic ability to exercise it in a responsible and Christian way. Full membership is restricted to those who belong to one of the mainstream Christian churches or who can declare their belief in Jesus Christ as Lord and Saviour of the world. Spiritual Frontiers Fellowship International (SFFI) is an American organization which began with a similar aim, but has since broadened out into a more New Age and interfaith stance. CFPSS publishes *The Christian Parapsychologist* (1975–), whilst SFFI has an 'Academic Affiliate', the Academy of Religion and Psychical Research, which publishes the *Journal of Religion and Psychical Research* (1978–).

BIBLIOGRAPHY

The Christian Deliverance Study Group (ed. M. Perry), *Deliverance* (London, [2]1996); A. H. Haddow, 'The Churches and Psychical Research: a review of some twentieth-century official documents', *TCP* 3, 1980, pp. 291–303; M. Mitton and R. Parker, *Requiem Healing: A Christian Understanding of the Dead* (London, 1991); E. G. Moore, *Believe it or Not: Christianity and Psychical Research* (London and Oxford, 1977); in the USA as *Try the Spirits* (New York, 1978); M. Perry *Psychic Studies: A Christian's View* (Wellingborough, Northants., 1984).

M. C. Perry

PSYCHEDELIC SPIRITUALITY

Psychedelic spirituality is a form of spirituality in which hallucinogens are central. Hallucinogens are substances which, when taken in small doses, cause a chemical reaction in the brain, the effect of which is an alteration in the user's perception, mood and thought processes. However, unlike with some drugs, people under the influence of hallucinogens will often (not always) be aware of what is happening and will be able to reflect, usually in detail, on the experience after it has passed. Generally speaking, there is a heightened sense of awareness, a belief that one's perception is sharper, deeper and more responsive to the material and spiritual environment. In other words, along with exaggerated sense perception, users report a feeling of transcending the mundane and a consequent belief that the scales have fallen from their eyes. Hence, in recognition of this spiritual feeling, psychedelic drugs are sometimes termed 'entheogens' because they are thought to engender a sense of 'god within'.

Throughout religious history there are examples of psychedelic spirituality. Perhaps the most obvious early mention of hallucinogens in the world's sacred writings appears in the earliest sacred text of Hinduism, the *Rig Veda* (c.1200–900 BC). Of its 1,028 hymns, 120 are devoted to *soma*, a psychoactive plant which was also visualized as a deity. *Soma* seems to have been given its privileged position in Vedic spirituality because of its powerful hallucinogenic properties. However, whether one thinks of the use of *soma* by the early nomads who entered the Indus valley or the peyote-induced 'flowery dreams' of the Aztecs, it is not difficult to find evidence of this attitude to drugs in many human societies.

ALDOUS HUXLEY AND THE DAWN OF THE PSYCHEDELIC REVOLUTION

Although drug-related spirituality has a long history, and although the modern Western psychedelic story can be said to have begun in 1938 when Albert Hofmann, a research chemist working for Sandoz Pharmaceutical Laboratories in Switzerland, produced LSD–25, arguably the roots of contemporary Western psychedelic spirituality are to be found in the 1950s. Humphrey Osmond, a British psychiatrist working in Canada who had used LSD to treat alcoholics, introduced Aldous Huxley (1894–1963) to the use of mescaline. During this decade, several other key figures, such as Huxley's friend Gerald Heard (1889–1971), began exploring, not merely the psychological and psychiatric potential of hallucinogens, particularly LSD (the study of which had been going on for some time), but also their spiritual potential. They became convinced that the altered states of consciousness produced were in fact mystical states and that drugs provided a gateway to a larger, truer grasp of reality. Indeed, the term 'psychedelic' (which means 'soul- or mind-manifesting') was coined by Osmond to denote the mystical and visionary potential of hallucinogens. (Huxley's term 'phanerothyme', meaning 'to make the soul visible', proved less popular.)

However, if Osmond coined the key term, Huxley produced the most influential text of psychedelia, *The Doors of Perception* (1954). The revealing title of the book is taken from William Blake's *Marriage of Heaven and Hell*: 'If the doors of perception were cleansed, everything would appear to man as it really is – infinite.' When the doors of perception were cleansed for Huxley in Los Angeles, on the morning of 6 May 1953 after he had ingested 300 milligrams of mescaline, he was literally lost for words and awed by what he felt and saw. He was not simply struck by the rainbow brilliance of the world he had entered, but also, more profoundly, moved by his sense of oneness with reality, a reality which, he perceived, was essentially divine. That he perceived this is not coincidental in that, arguably, mescaline simply allowed him to experience the type of Indian-influenced mysticism explored in his earlier book *The Perennial Philosophy* (1946).

One of Huxley's principal claims was that psychedelic experience is directly analogous to those experiences claimed by mystics in the world's religions. However, psychedelics provide experiences instantly: 'Training in mysticism can be speeded up and made more effective by a judicious use of the physically harmless psychedelics now available'. Indeed, he believed that mescaline had introduced him to the Beatific Vision, which, he argued, was to be identified with the experience of 'Being-Awareness-Bliss' found in Indian religious tradition. However, not only are there problems with this identification, but also R. C. Zaehner has argued that it betrays muddled thinking rather than any profound mystical experience. Nevertheless, similar claims are regularly made by those people who practise psychedelic spirituality.

It is difficult to overestimate the significance of Huxley for the development of psychedelic spirituality in the West. Certainly psychedelic religious experience gained a kudos that would have been denied if it had it not been for Huxley. His ideas, which were set forth in eloquent and informed prose, found their way into the minds of those who would not normally have considered psychedelic spirituality worthy of critical scrutiny.

THE EMERGENCE OF POPULAR PSYCHEDELIC SPIRITUALITY

The psychedelia of the 1950s tended to be the elitist philosophy of several prominent intellectuals who wanted to avoid damaging publicity, stress respectable research and develop esoteric psychedelic thought. Elitism was hardly a characteristic of the man Allen Ginsberg called 'a hero of American consciousness ... faced with the task of a Messiah': namely, Timothy Leary (1920–1996).

Motivated by Leary's drive and charismatic personality, the 1960s psychedelic revolution quickly became a large and influential subculture. The term 'psychedelic' rapidly expanded to include all forms of culture which were thought to inspire, or to be inspired by, the use of hallucinogens. A great deal of time and creative energy was invested in the production of (particularly) music and art which would encourage successful psychedelic 'spiritual' experiences, much of which reflected the impact of Huxley's and Leary's thought. As is evident in the writings from the period, it was clearly believed that humanity was on the verge of a new age of drug-provoked, Indian-influenced, expanded consciousness. Beatnik culture in the 1960s turned East, enthusiastically converted to psychedelia and, for the most part, accepted Leary's philosophy of 'turn on, tune in, and drop out'; the new psychedelic *mantra*.

CONTEMPORARY PSYCHEDELIC SPIRITUALITY

Moving up to what might be described as the third phase of the psychedelic revolution (the 1950s being the first and the 1960s the second), it is not difficult to trace the continuity between the psychedelic hippy culture of the 1960s and the rave culture of the 1980s and 1990s. Indeed, not only have the words of Leary been set to contemporary ambient and 'trance' music, but there is much in contemporary rave culture that betrays the influence of the psychedelic subcultures of the 1960s.

However, whilst Buddhist and Hindu beliefs were central to much earlier psychedelic mystical experience, and although their influence is still important, arguably contemporary psychedelia tends to be more eclectic and certainly more Pagan in orientation. A good example of this type of essentially Neo-Pagan psychedelia is that developed by Terence McKenna, probably the most important contemporary exponent of psychedelics. Essentially McKenna's spirituality is based on the belief that the evolution of human spirituality and rationality was kick-started by the ingestion of hallucinogenic mushrooms. Indeed, he claims that humans have a very basic and important relationship with mushrooms. We are rational, spiritual beings, not because of evolution or because we are made in the image of God, but because our early ancestors ate hallucinogenic mushrooms. McKenna's basic thesis is simply that psychedelic mysticism takes us back to our roots. Hence the drug-induced feeling of oneness with nature is by no means coincidental. Hallucinogenic plants encourage the re-emergence of a Gaia consciousness, which is, he argues, the archaic consciousness of primal peoples who recognize humanity's connectedness to the planet.

As in the 1960s, contemporary psychedelic spirituality has been propagated through music. Within rave culture an eclectic psychedelic spirituality is emerging. Indeed, psychedelicists such as McKenna and Fraser Clark believe rave culture to be extremely important for the future of human spirituality.

CONCLUDING COMMENTS

First, the increasing desire in Western consumer culture for instant experience makes psychedelic spirituality particularly appealing. Secondly, the ingestion of natural hallucinogens (psilocybin mushrooms etc.) which increase the user's perception of oneness with the Earth is attractive in a culture with a heightening sensitivity to environmental issues and a consequent emphasis on humanity's interdependence with the natural world. Thirdly, the current appeal of primal cultures, which are considered to be more in tune with the Earth, has led to increased interest in the religious use of hallucinogens in these cultures as an aid to a more nature-centric spirituality. Fourthly, because hallucinogens tend to engender experiences of a monistic or pantheistic nature, psychedelic spirituality is attractive to the increasing numbers of Westerners sympathetic to Buddhist, Hindu and Daoist worldviews. Finally, it should be noted that many psychedelics and 'dance drugs' such as 'ecstasy' (MDMA) are now illegal in Western countries, because they have proved not to be as harmless as Huxley and others believed them to be.

BIBLIOGRAPHY

P. Devereux, *The Long Trip: A Prehistory of Psychedelia* (London, 1997); A. Huxley, *The Doors of Perception* and *Heaven and Hell* (London, 1994); T. Leary, *The Politics of Ecstasy* (London, 1970); T. Leary et al. (eds.), *The Psychedelic Reader* (New York, 1993); R. E. L. Masters and J. Houston, *The Varieties of Psychedelic Experience* (London, 1966); A. Melechi (ed.), *Psychedelica Britannica: Hallucinogenic Drugs in Britain* (London, 1997); S. Redhead (ed.), *Rave Off: Politics and Deviance in Contemporary Youth Culture* (Aldershot, 1993); J. Stevens, *Storming Heaven* (London, 1993); R. C. Zaehner, *Mysticism, Sacred and Profane* (Oxford, 1961).

C. H. Partridge

RASTAFARIANISM

Rastafarianism may be only a minor new religious movement in the West, but such is its impact on popular Western culture, particularly Caribbean and British culture, and such is the ignorance regarding the movement, that it deserves a separate entry. Not only is much reggae (from Bob Marley to the more ambient and ethereal dub reggae) essentially religious music, but also there are some forms of contemporary dance/trance music which betray Rastafarian influence, as do certain aspects of popular fashion, particularly the cultivation of 'dreadlocks' (long, tightly curled, often matted hair). Again, fairly common subcultural terms such as 'dread' (a broad term meaning, variously, 'rebellion' or 'rebel', 'inspired self-understanding', 'commitment' to Jah and his cause), 'Jah' (God) and 'Babylon' (oppressive white society) are all central to Rastafarian theology. Hence, whilst the numbers of committed Rastafarians are relatively small (there are, for example, an estimated 5,000 in Britain), Rastafarianism has, particularly through its music, touched the lives of millions.

Originating as a black liberation movement in the ghettos of Kingston, Jamaica, Rastafarianism can be found throughout the Caribbean, Western Europe, North

America and, in smaller numbers, in certain parts of Africa, Australia and New Zealand, where the Maori have been particularly receptive. However, the movement has grown most rapidly and has had its greatest cultural impact in Jamaica and Britain.

BACK-TO-AFRICA

It is not surprising that many Africans who were forcibly transported to the Caribbean, the Americas and Europe by white slave-traders longed to return to their homeland. Over time, this longing had a sacralizing effect, in the sense that, as in Rastafarian theology, Africa came to be understood in terms of a sacred, promised land of peace and goodness. This in turn led to the emergence of Back-to-Africa movements from the late eighteenth century onwards. That said, it should be pointed out that many of those who initially returned to Africa were black Christian converts motivated by a negative understanding of Africa as a spiritually dark continent.

One of the first key figures in the Back-to-Africa movement who eventually rejected a negative view of Africa was the Christian clergyman Edward Wilmot Blyden (1832–1912). Acutely aware of both the problems caused for Africans by Western society and the great cultural and historical riches of Africa, he sought to inspire pride in Africa and blackness. Like the Rastas, he also claimed that Western Christianity had hindered the development of the African personality.

Following Blyden, one of the greatest influences on Rastafarianism (and indeed on Islamic movements such as the Nation of Islam) was the Jamaican Marcus Garvey (1887–1940), the leader of the first genuine large-scale black movement in America and Europe. Central to Garvey's teaching and to his militant Universal Negro Improvement Association was the return of Africans to Africa, the only place, he believed, where black people would feel at home and be respected as a race. Africans should be proud of their blackness, return to their homeland, lay the foundations for a new superior African civilization, correct the prejudiced white histories of Africa and worship a black God 'through the spectacles of Ethiopia' (Garvey). Although physical repatriation did not take place, and although Garveyism eventually died out in the 1920s, Garvey did succeed in focusing the minds of Africans on these issues which were to become central to the emerging Rastafarian movement.

RAS TAFARI

It was widely believed that Garvey made this prophecy: 'Look to Africa for the crowning of a Black King; he shall be the Redeemer.' In November 1930, Ras (meaning 'Prince') Tafari (meaning 'Creator') Makonnen (1891–1975), the great-grandson of King Saheka Selassie of Shoa, was crowned Negus of Ethiopia. He declared himself to be in the line of King Solomon and took the name Haile Selassie I ('Might of the Trinity'), as well as 'King of Kings' and 'Lion of the Tribe of Judah'. It is not surprising that, when he was crowned in St George's Cathedral in Addis Ababa in front of representatives from many nations, those who had been inspired by Garvey's teaching saw more than the accession of another Ethiopian ruler. In Haile Selassie I or Ras Tafari many saw the Messiah, Christ returned, the fulfilment of biblical prophecy, God incarnate. This was taught particularly by Leonard Howell, a clergyman who came to believe that Ras Tafari had been prophesied in the Bible (e.g. in Rev. 5:5; 19:16) and would lead Africans out of white society and back to the promised land of Ethiopia (often used as a synonym for Africa).

CONTEMPORARY DOCTRINE AND PRACTICE

Although initially a very small Jamaican movement, in the 1950s Rastafarianism began to grow rapidly, particularly amongst the poor and disaffected, who were inspired by its teachings regarding black superiority, the destruction of white oppressors and the imminent return of Africans to the promised land of peace and justice. Indeed, Rastafarianism is a millennial religious movement which teaches the apocalyptic end of the present era, the judgment of Babylon (oppressive white society and religion) and the dawning of a new age of peace and love.

Whilst there are several branches of Rastafarianism, in the West (particularly in Britain) perhaps the two most important are the Twelve Tribes of Israel (founded in 1968 by Vernon Carrington), which is the most visible expression of Rastafarianism, and the Ethiopian Orthodox Church, a Christian church which denies the deity of Ras Tafari. Indeed, whilst many Rastafarians will attend its meetings and declare allegiance to it, there is a question as to whether the Ethiopian Orthodox Church can, strictly speaking, be considered Rastafarian. It is perhaps better thought of as a form of, to use William David Spencer's term, 'Rastafarianity'. Whereas many Rastafarians reject traditional Christologies because of their connection with white, European history, Spencer points out that, particularly in Africa, 'Rastafari and Christianity are being wed into a hybrid "Rastafarianity", exalting the emperor but rejecting his divinity. Jesus too has taken on a new significance, freed from his blond-haired, blue-eyed western captivity and wedded to African images of a black liberating Christ.'

Although Rastas seek to be biblical, Rastafarianism has developed certain key beliefs which differ significantly from traditional Judeo-Christian belief (e.g. reincarnation) and, like much New Age spirituality, emphasizes the primacy of 'the self' in determining truth and lacks any formal creed. As such it is very attractive to those (particularly of African origin) looking for a spirituality which fits in with the contemporary penchant for a non-dogmatic, experience-based spirituality.

Whilst the Bible is important in Rastafarianism, in the final analysis biblical authority must submit to the authority of 'the self'. Biblical truths and their correct interpretation must be personally verified by privately 'head resting' (meditating) with Jah and/or by communally 'reasoning' at 'groundings' (religious discussion sessions). Suspicious of much biblical interpretation, particularly that of traditional Christianity, Rastas seek only the guidance of Jah and thus will not accept any doctrine until it has been internally validated. This, it is claimed, leads to spiritual 'knowledge' rather than simply 'belief'. Moreover, trust in the judgment of 'the self' is supported by a strong immanentist theology which understands the divine to be *within* 'the self'; to 'know' the will of Jah and to know 'truth' one must turn within. (For some Rastas the understanding of the divine within has led to a theology in which the divine–human dualism has collapsed; there is little or no distinction between the self and the divine.)

According to Rastafarianism, the Bible, when properly interpreted, speaks of the ancient history of the black race, God's chosen people. Understanding Israelites and Ethiopians to be the same holy people, they believe that the Israelites/Ethiopians/Africans have been scattered across the globe by means of the slave-trade as a punishment for sin, sin which has long since been forgiven. They should now throw off the yoke of slavery, which is increasingly psychological rather than physical, and return to Ethiopia. That said, in recent years, since the death of Ras Tafari and the beginning of problems in Ethiopia, there has been a marked spiritualization of the notion of a return to Africa, in that increasingly Rastas understand an intellectual and spiritual return to be more important than literal repatriation. One needs to cultivate an African way of thinking and an African spirituality and in so doing leave white thinking and Western ways behind. Indeed, there has been a spiritualization of blackness in some quarters, in that some Rastas are less concerned about the colour of a person's skin, and more concerned about a person's worldview. This has paved the way to greater involvement in the movement by white Rastafarians.

Often the Rastafarian identification with Israel is underpinned by a doctrine of reincarnation; this is particularly true of those belonging to, or sympathetic to, the Twelve Tribes of Israel sect. Not only are black people understood to be reincarnations of the Israelites, but also, as in the Hindu doctrine of *avataras*, God is supposed to have appeared at key points in history, as Moses, Elijah, Jesus and finally Ras Tafari.

In accordance with Numbers 6, and recalling Samson's strength, many Rastas (except those of the Ethiopian Orthodox Church) take the Nazirite vow and do not cut their hair. The consequent dreadlocks are believed to resemble the mane of the lion. This is significant not only because Ras Tafari is 'the Lion of the Tribe of Judah', but also because the lion symbolizes strength, vitality, superiority and royalty. As with fashion in many subcultures, dreadlocks are also a symbolic way of confronting and standing apart from society.

One of the most controversial Rastafarian religious practices is the sacramental smoking of 'ganja' (marijuana). Although not all Rastas smoke ganja, there are a great many who do take 'the chalice' (large pipe) or 'spliff' (long cigarette). Drawing on biblical passages such as Revelation 22:2 ('And the leaves of the tree [of life] are for the healing of the nations'), they argue that not only does this smoking have biblical support, but also it is good for physical and spiritual healing. They claim not only that it relaxes, but also, in a similar way to psychedelic religionists, that 'the herb' is a source of inspiration, in that its use makes one more receptive to the divine within.

Ganja smoking is also in accordance with the Rastafarian concern to live naturally, to live in obedience to the laws of Nature (central to Rastafarian ethics). Many devout Rastas will thus eat only organic food, much of which they seek to grow themselves. Indeed, not only are many Rastas vegetarian, but also many observe strict dietary rules which require, for example, abstinence from pork, alcohol and any food which has come from an unknown source.

Finally, although there are still many Rastas who seek some form of separation from white society, and although it is not difficult to find contemporary reggae songs which call for the elimination of the dominant culture or the burning of Babylon, increasingly the emphasis is on the development of black culture rather than the end of white culture. The move is towards pluralism and dialogue rather than separation from white society.

BIBLIOGRAPHY

L. E. Barrett, *The Rastafarians: the Dreadlocks of Jamaica* (Kingston, Jamaica, and London, 1977); D. Bishton, *Blackheart Man: A Journey Into Rasta* (London, 1986); E. Cashmore, '"Get Up, Stand Up": The Rastafarian Movement', in J. Obelkevich, L. Roper and R. Samuel (eds.), *Disciplines of the Faith: Studies in Religion, Politics and Patriarchy* (London, 1987), pp. 422–431; E. Cashmore, *Rastaman: The Rastafarian Movement in England* (London, 1983); P. B. Clarke, *Black Paradise: the Rastafarian Movement*, Black Political Studies No. 5 (San Bernardino, CA, 1994); B. L. Petry, 'A Bibliography on the Rastafarians', in P. B. Clarke, op. cit.; N. Redington, 'A Sketch of Rastafari History': http://24.93.2.2/rastafari; W. D. Spencer, *Dread Jesus* (London, 1999).

C. H. Partridge

SATANISM

Satanism, sometimes called 'Devil-worship', is often understood to be 'a cult of opposition', in that its *raison d'être* is to stand in opposition to and rebel against an established culture or religious tradition. As such, Satanism is essentially parasitic upon Christian culture, being dependent upon Christian symbolism and theology. Having said that, many Satanists would reject this definition of their belief system. Rather, it is claimed that Satanism is not simply an inversion of Christianity, but a self-religion which encourages egocentricity and personal development and has little interest in actively opposing Christian doctrine and practice. Nevertheless, it is hard to avoid the view that, for whatever reason, 'Satanists' do explicitly encourage blasphemy and vehemently oppose Christian doctrine, symbolism and practice, judging Christian civilization to be corrupt and hypocritical.

SATAN IN SATANISM

Some Satanists will not use the term 'Satan', preferring, for example, the name 'Set'. Such 'Setians' will claim that the concept of Satan was simply invented by the Christian church in order to frighten followers into submission and to justify Christianity's existence; this is not the deity they follow. However, generally speaking, most Satanists are happy to work with the concept of Satan. (Hence, as many Pagans are keen to point out, Satanism should not be confused with Paganism, which is essentially a nature religion, the theology of which has no concept of Satan.)

According to a 1995 survey by Graham Harvey, Set or Satan is variously understood by contemporary Satanists: 'Some say that Set is a "real being", "an incorporeal entity", "a metaphysical reality" ... "Lord of this world" ... Others consider Set to be "the archetypal rebel", "the ultimate male principle", "a figure representing pride, self-interest, and self-gratification" ... "the driving force in human evolution".' However, although some view Set or Satan as a rebellious, self-serving being, rather paradoxically, they rarely view him in the sinister way that Christians do, believing him to be a deity who can be 'approached as a friend' and who (sometimes with reference to the serpent in Gen. 3) dispenses knowledge (the Black Flame) to those who strive for it.

Other Satanist groups, whilst they sometimes speak in terms of a personal being called Satan, do not require belief in such an entity. Satan is understood more in terms of a useful icon which encourages self-interest and individualism and promotes opposition to institutional religion and the dominant culture. Indeed, in this sense, Satanism is essentially a self-religion or human potential movement which utilizes the rebellious, offensive and provocative symbolism the figure of Satan provides.

Although it may be true that few of the Satanists who belong to organized groups would claim actually to worship the devil of the Bible, there are a growing number of individuals (usually adolescents) inspired by, for example, gothic imagery, horror films and certain rock musicians (e.g. Deicide and Marilyn Manson) who, because they very clearly define themselves by opposition to Christianity (symbolized by the wearing of inverted crucifixes), do claim to worship the devil. Although in many cases this may be little more than youth rebellion, it has led to, for example, the desecration of churches and criminal activity.

PROMINENT SATANIST GROUPS

Because of the small numbers involved, several Satanist groups have proved to be short-lived (e.g. the Process-Church of the Final Judgment). Nevertheless, there are several active Satanist groups in the West (e.g. Dark Lily, the Order of the Nine Angles and the Church of Satanic Liberation), some of which are very secretive and about which little is known. However, within contemporary Satanism, the following two rival groups are clearly the most important.

THE CHURCH OF SATAN

On the evening of 30 April 1966, Anton Szandor LaVey (d. October 1997) declared the arrival of 'the Age of Satan'. Declaring himself to be 'the Black Pope', in that year he founded in California the Church of Satan, perhaps the most well-known and influential Satanist organization. It was not long before the charismatic LaVey was gaining considerable publicity by performing Satanic weddings for famous people and the Satanic baptisms of children.

LaVey's *The Satanic Bible* (1969) – which has been translated into Swedish, Danish and Spanish – and *The Satanic Rituals* (1972) remain key texts for many Satanists (whether they belong to the Church of Satan or not), as does the Church's magazine, *The Black Flame* (published in New York).

Central to the beliefs of the Church of Satan is an emphasis on the 'animal' or physical appetites of humans, which are to be indulged rather than denied. LaVey is particularly critical of Christianity for suppressing this side of humanity by labelling it 'sinful'. Indeed, *The Satanic Bible* contains an assault upon Christianity and, whilst LaVey denies that he worships an actual entity called Satan (the Satanist's object of worship being 'the self'), he argues that Satan is nevertheless a powerful symbol of opposition to Christianity, and in fact to all authority. That said, LaVey was, according to Jean La Fontaine, 'a firm believer in order and observing the rule of law, which appears somewhat inconsistent with rebellion against authority.' Indeed, although some Satanists will (following Aleister Crowley [1875–1947], a notorious and influential British occultist) use drugs in their rituals, the Church of Satan has maintained a strong opposition to the use of drugs (apart from alcohol). Also inconsistent with their stance against authority was the centralized, hierarchical ordering of the Church into local 'grottoes', overseen by the 'central grotto' run by LaVey. However, in 1975 the Church was decentralized. The hierarchy was dismantled and individual grottoes were given independence. As a result many small groups have emerged with different names, some with little connection to the Church of Satan.

As with many forms of Satanism, the implications of LaVey's social Darwinism are brutal. For the Church of Satan, a principal law by which life should be lived is survival of the fittest. The human is understood to be an animal which should strive to overcome the weak. Such 'human garbage' should be pushed aside in the interests of attaining one's own potential. Indeed, Satanists are encouraged to distance themselves from 'the common herd'.

THE TEMPLE OF SET

According to La Fontaine, there has been 'only one defection from the Church: it became Michael Aquino's Temple of Set, which, although much smaller, is the Church of Satan's main rival and is never mentioned by name'. Michael Aquino (a former US army officer) left the Church in 1975 and founded the Temple of Set. Although it shares some beliefs with the Church of Satan, the Temple of Set is arguably a more intellectual form of Satanism. Whereas the Church of Satan stresses the continuity between animals and humans and emphasizes evolutionary development, the Temple of Set insists that humans are distinct from animals by virtue of their intellect and that this enquiring intellect is not simply the result of evolution, but is rather the gift of Set/Satan to humanity. The Temple of Set seeks to exercise this gift, symbolized as the Black Flame: 'the symbol of knowledge and scepticism towards the received wisdom of established religions' (La Fontaine). The increase in knowledge leads, in a Gnostic-like way, to self-development and spiritual progress: 'As Set was, we are; as Set is, we will be.' The aim is, therefore, not to worship Set, but rather to learn from him and eventually become like him. As noted above, the Temple of Set seems to take the figure of Satan far more seriously than the Church of Satan, in that he is understood to be a real personal being.

As with many Satanists (who, in many respects, follow the practices and theories of Crowley), there is an emphasis on ritual and ceremonial magick (spelt with a 'k' to distinguish it from conjuring trickery). Of particular note is the distinction made between 'an "objective universe", the natural world, and the "subjective universe", which is the individual's personal perspective' (La Fontaine). Essentially, one is able to effect changes in the objective universe by the application of the will. Ceremonial magick, particularly 'Black Magick', as described in Aquino's book, *Black Magic in Theory and Practice* (1992), has an impact upon the subjective universe, 'raising power' within the individual, and thereby increasing the effect of the will upon the 'objective universe'.

The Temple of Set is hierarchically ordered: the ruling body is called 'the Council of Nine' and the smaller groups are known as 'pylons' (of which there are several in Britain). As in Gnostic initiation, there are various 'degrees' (levels) of members. Beginning with the lowest, these are: Setian; Adept (the status of most members); Priest/Priestess; Magister/Magistra Templi; Magus/Maga; and Ipsissimus/Ipsissima.

CONCLUDING COMMENTS

Partly because of the secretive nature of some of the groups and partly because there is a paucity of serious academic research in this area, there is no consensus regarding the numbers involved in Satanism. Whilst those who are convinced of the existence of a massive underground network of organized Satanic groups permeating all levels of society are almost certainly mistaken, it does seem clear that Satanism is a growing phenomenon. Even if those who belong to particular groups such as the Church of Satan and the Temple of Set are still relatively small (Harvey, for example, estimates that, in Britain, 'There are six groups who between them have less than 100 members'), there are larger and increasing numbers of solitary practitioners who consider themselves Satanist, subscribe to *The Black Flame* and make use of the writings of LaVey and Aquino.

As to why people might be attracted to Satanism, the appeal of promised power, elitism, occult knowledge and esoteric rituals and rites, and the sense of belonging within a small group, are clearly significant. Moreover, the rebellious and provocative stance taken against what is seen to be an authoritarian and freedom-stifling Christian-based culture is also a powerful incentive for certain people, particularly young people. For such individuals, Satanism is, at least initially, quite clearly a cult of opposition in which rebellion against particular cultural and religious values is the motivating factor. Finally, although Satanism sometimes involves a high level of commitment (particularly in the Temple of Set), the Satanist emphasis on self-development, even self-deification, has a strong attraction in the hedonistic and egocentric Western world.

BIBLIOGRAPHY

J. C. Cooper, *The Black Mask: Satanism in America Today* (Old Tappan, NJ, 1990); G. Harvey, 'Satanism in Britain Today', *JCR* 10 (1995), pp. 283–296; J. La Fontaine, 'Satanism and Satanic Mythology', in B. Ankarloo and S. Clark (eds), *Witchcraft and Magic in Europe: the Twentieth Century* (London and Philadelphia, PA, 1999), pp. 81–140; C. Raschke, *Painted Black* (San Francisco, 1990); J. Russell, *The Prince of Darkness* (Ithaca, NY, 1988).

C. H. Partridge

SEVENTH-DAY ADVENTIST CHURCH, THE

The Seventh-Day Adventist (SDA) Church was founded on the doctrine of the interdenominational millennial revivalist, William Miller (1782–1849), who never intended to start a new Christian movement. Miller was a farmer who became a full-time Baptist evangelist in rural New York and taught that Christ would return in 1843–4, on the basis of the 2,300-day prophecies of Daniel 8:14, which he took to refer to a period of 2,300 years. He became a nationally known preacher. After several mistaken predictions of the date, a final day was set: 22 October 1844. When this date arrived there were an estimated 100,000 Millerites or Adventists, but as the second coming did not occur (the 'Great Disappointment'), thousands then left the movement. Miller acknowledged his mistake, although he continued to believe in the imminence of Christ's return until his death five years later. Other Adventists retained Miller's original teachings and said that Christ had returned to purify the 'sanctuary' in heaven in 1844, an event that was later to be called the 'investigative judgment'. Many Adventists were expelled from their churches for their views and they began to group together.

Three Millerites, Ellen White (1827–1915), James White (1821–81) and Joseph Bates (1792–1872), organized the SDA Church in 1863 with 3,500 founding members. Bates, a retired sea captain, taught that the Sabbath for Christians was on the seventh day, and his pamphlet on the subject persuaded Ellen and James White. By 1850, many of the basic beliefs of the SDA movement had begun to emerge, encouraged by regular Bible conferences and including the observance of Saturday as the Sabbath, Old Testament dietary laws and the 'investigative judgment' of 1844. It was Ellen White, however, who emerged as the charismatic leader of the new movement. Her visions formed the basis of her many writings, and the SDA movement accepted her as a prophet. Her writings are accepted by SDAs as divinely inspired, although they are not given the same authority as the Bible, which is regarded as the divine authority for all SDA teaching. The SDA headquarters was situated in Battle Creek, Michigan until 1903, when it moved to Washington, DC. Since 1988 it has been at Silver Spring, Maryland.

Charles Russell, founder of the Watchtower (Jehovah's Witnesses) movement, was influenced by Adventist teaching in the 1870s before his beliefs led him in different directions. The Branch Davidians, also known as the Shepherd's Rod and the Davidian Seventh-Day Adventists, separated from the SDA church in 1929 under their founder Victor Houteff and drew their members only from SDA members. Their leader from 1987, David Koresh (real name Vernon Howell), espoused many SDA views but added that he was the messiah and spiritual successor to King David who would renew humanity, and viewed his followers as the 'remnant church'. When the siege of their compound in Waco, Texas, began in February 1993, the SDA General Conference distanced itself from the Davidian movement. A larger Davidian movement unrelated to Koresh, called the Davidian Seventh-Day Adventist Association, continues today; its teachings are closer to standard SDA doctrine.

PRINCIPAL BELIEFS AND PRACTICES

The core of SDA beliefs is conservative evangelical, perhaps even fundamentalist, but SDAs also have teachings which set them apart from most other evangelicals. Their eschatology includes the 'investigative judgment' in 1844 and the personal, literal and imminent return of Christ. They declare that Christ entered the heavenly sanctuary in 1844 for the investigative judgment that reveals those who will be worthy of resurrection or translation at the second coming of Christ. The Old Testament cleansing of the sanctuary on the Day of Atonement typified this event.

The keeping of the Sabbath from Friday evening to Saturday evening and other Old Testament laws, especially the dietary laws of the Pentateuch, are stressed. Joseph Bates taught that keeping Sunday as the Sabbath was the 'mark of the beast' and that people who did not observe the Saturday Sabbath would be excluded from heaven. This seems also to have been White's, but is no longer official SDA teaching.

SDAs are also distinctive in their belief in 'soul sleep', the unconscious state of death, and the 'conditional immortality of the soul'. They abstain from tea, coffee, alcohol, tobacco and 'unclean meats' like pork and seafood without scales and fins. They practise feet washing as an ordinance before the Lord's Supper, and baptism of adult believers by immersion.

The role of Ellen White has also been a source of controversy. SDAs believe that her writings are evidence of the 'Spirit of prophecy' that was to identify the 'remnant church' and continue beyond the biblical canon. The term 'remnant church' seems to have exclusive reference to the SDAs, those who keep the commandments and have the testimony of Jesus (Rev. 12:17), although all believers in Christ constitute the 'universal church'. But because of their agreement with cardinal doctrines like the Trinity and the atonement of Christ, SDAs have been accepted into the mainstream of North American Protestantism.

Like many Christian fundamentalists, SDAs are opposed to the theory of evolution and teach creationism in hundreds of publications and in higher education institutions.

A recent theological controversy related to a leading Australian SDA theologian, Desmond Ford, who questioned the status of Ellen White's writings and the doctrine of 'investigative judgment'. Ford was disciplined in 1980 for casting doubt on these cherished SDA beliefs. Prominent SDA pastors withdrew from the movement in support of Ford's views.

ENCOUNTERING CONTEMPORARY CULTURE

Through their extensive missionary outreach, the SDAs have become a worldwide movement with more than nine million members (of whom over 75% live in the

Third World), a major force in world Christianity today and one of the fastest-growing movements within Christianity. Their church is one of the most integrated in the UK, mainly because of large numbers of members of African-Caribbean descent.

The SDAs maintain the largest Protestant school system in the world with over 5,000 schools, higher education colleges and universities, extensive welfare programmes, hospitals, publishing houses and radio and television networks. The Adventist Loma Linda University and Medical Center has pioneered medical research into infant heart transplants and proton radiation therapy for cancer. The Adventist Development and Relief Agency is a major agency for international development and disaster relief.

SDAs are also renowned for health food products. Many SDA health care practices have their origins in the writings of Ellen White, who was remarkably ahead of her time in her views on nutrition and preventative medicine. John Kellogg was an early SDA surgeon and author who invented breakfast cereals in order to demonstrate that attractive, healthy foods were available for vegetarians. His Kellogg Cereal Corporation is now a household name. As a result of their strong promotion of a healthy lifestyle, the contribution of SDAs to health care has been considerable. SDA literature discussed the problems of cholesterol and eating red meat decades before these topics became common in medical journals. Their five-day programmes to stop smoking have been hugely successful. Their views on low-fat diets and tobacco have recently become mainstream views in the West. Many SDAs are vegetarians, although this is not mandatory for members.

SDAs were formerly pacifists, like Jehovah's Witnesses, declining all forms of military service, though they later declared this to be a matter of individual conscience and encouraged obedience to civil government. Most recent legal difficulties encountered by Adventists relate to their Sabbath observance, as their refusal to work on Saturdays has brought conflict with employers and cases of religious discrimination to the courts. The many activities and achievements of SDAs have had the effect of reducing the high level of tension between church and society that has been characteristic of the Jehovah's Witnesses' relationship with others, and have increased the SDA Church's participation in society and the upward social mobility of its members.

BIBLIOGRAPHY

J. Bergman, 'The Adventist and Jehovah's Witness branch of Protestantism', in T. Miller (ed.), *America's Alternative Religions* (Albany, NY, 1995), pp. 33–46; D. G. Bromley and E. D. Silver, 'The Branch Davidians: A Social Profille and Organizational History', in T. Miller (ed.), *America's Alternative Religions* (Albany, NY, 1995), pp. 149–157; G. Land (ed.), *Adventism in America: A History* (Grand Rapids, MI, 1986); M. Pearson, *Millennial Dreams and Moral Dilemmas: Seventh-Day Adventism and Contemporary Ethics* (Cambridge, 1990); *Seventh-Day Adventist Enclyclopedia* (Hagerstown, MD, 1996); *Seventh-Day Adventists Believe: A Biblical Exposition of 27 Fundamental Doctrines* (Hagerstown, MD, 1988).

A. H. Anderson

SHAMANISM

The term 'shamanism' is used with a range of meanings. It is best understood by considering the practice of ecstasy by religious specialists among certain Siberian peoples, practices which have analogies in other parts of the world. The word 'shamanism' is sometimes used to designate the religion, past or present, of peoples among whom the practice is present, but this usage is unsatisfactory since these religions contain many other elements. Shamanism is a religious institution rather than a religion. The term is also applied to the practice of spirit possession or spirit mediumship, but this usage too is loose and misleading. Spirit possession may, and does, occur where shamanism operates, but shamanic ecstasy and soul flight are to be clearly distinguished from possession or mediumship.

The new interest in shamanism has three sources: Native American concern to reconstitute a broken identity and reclaim elements from a damaged past; Western post-Christian interest in aspects of Tibetan Buddhism (not considered here, since it belongs to the Buddhist realm of discourse); and post-Christian (and post-Enlightenment) endeavours to apprehend spiritual realities. These efforts break the link with the surrounding society that originally gave shamanism meaning and the shaman significance.

THE SIBERIAN SHAMAN

The word 'shaman' derives from the *samen* of the Tungus people of Siberia, so it is best to begin this analysis with its significance among the Tungus and their neighbours. Siberian shamans are believed to have three main functions. They heal the sick, replacing displaced souls; they conduct the souls of animals after sacrifice to their heavenly destination; and they lead the souls of dead people to the world of the dead, and away from the vicinity of their corpses (where they might trouble the living).

These functions require shamans to force a way into realms which most mortals cannot enter. In ecstasy (conditioned by the beating of a drum) the shaman's soul flies through these worlds on a drum, conducting souls from earth or recovering those who may be lost there. Before the shaman enters a trance the noise of birds and animals declares that their spirits are present, and the shaman speaks with bird or animal voices. While in ecstasy the shaman performs feats of extraordinary strength, and (as many independent witnesses attest) strange phenomena occur: a heavy tent shakes furiously; fire appears from nowhere; a rope dangles from the sky; unearthly noises come from all directions. Successful soul flight, however, is followed by the healing of the sick and by the assurance that sacrifices, often offered to ensure a continued food supply, have been accepted (or, it may be, that more are needed) and that a person who has died has now safely reached the home of the dead.

The shaman's dress is distinctive: cap and mask, with a tunic covered with pictures of animals and reaching to the knees in front and to the ground behind.

SHAMANISM WORLDWIDE

The features characteristic of the Siberian shaman, including the dress, are to be found not only in Alaska but among most of the northern Native American peoples, and also among the Inuit of the Arctic. Most of them were also characteristic of the indigenous peoples of Greenland, the Sami (Lapps) of northern Europe and the Finns before their conversion to Christianity.

Similar phenomena in Tierra del Fuego, and in more attenuated form among some Australian Aboriginal groups, suggest that shamanism existed in far southern as well as far northern latitudes.

A third belt extends across East and Central Asia, including Korea, parts of China, tribal peoples in northeast India and Myanmar, and forest peoples of southeast Asia and Tibet. Among the last of these groups shamanism merged with ancient Indian and Buddhist elements to form a unique religious compound. In many of the other areas Buddhism or Christianity or both have subsumed or replaced the shamanistic elements in the culture.

Other parts of the world, however, also exhibit (qualified by environmental differences) the leading features of the shaman's activity: they are found among the Nilotic peoples of south Sudan, for instance, and among the indigenous peoples in many parts of Latin America. Some have claimed though speculatively) that prehistoric cave paintings of human figures with animals at Lascaux and elsewhere depict the shaman at work. Mircea Eliade, indeed, argues that shamanism is 'primordial', in that it arises independently of cultural diffusion. However, most of the contexts in which shamans play a central part in religion have certain common elements. They are cultures where a 'High God' is known and worshipped; they are harsh environments where life is particularly fragile and uncertain; and if no longer hunting societies, they are societies where animals are of vital importance. The services of the shaman help the group, and its associated animals, to survive in a perilous terrain. They also help to counteract 'bad shamans' who use their power destructively.

SHAMANIC VOCATION

Shamans are instituted in various ways; even among the Siberian peoples there is no uniformity of method. Sometimes dramatic events are seen as indicating the divine choice of an instrument. Some shamanates are hereditary, some elective, but it is usual for predisposing signs to appear: unusual physical features or conditions; powerful dreams and visions; an illness, physical or psychic, that nothing will cure but response to the shamanic vocation. A substantial initiation period with a recognized shaman follows, then acceptance by the group.

The shaman is thus a sacred person, set apart from others but with a role on behalf of others. The 'otherness' is sometimes reflected in the assumption that shamans have bisexual, or transsexual, or asexual characteristics. Female shamans are common in Korea, northeast India and some Siberian societies. That the shamanic vocation is potentially open is suggested by the fact that in some Siberian societies each family has its own drum. It is analogous to the shamanic experience in those Native American societies where young warriors voluntarily undertook arduous feats of endurance and deprivation to achieve a special vision from the transcendent world. The whole group would know when this self-imposed 'vision quest' had been successfully completed; as with the shaman, the dislocation of the quest was succeeded by the demonstrable assurance and strength of an integrated personality. Nevertheless the functions of the shaman are essentially exercised on behalf of the community. It is the 'bad shaman', the destructive agent, who works privately.

FUNCTIONS OF THE SHAMAN

The ideological premise of shamanism is the existence of a supernatural world that humans may enter. The shaman is thus a sacred geographer, who explores and makes known that world. Shamans are diagnosticians, searching for the underlying causes of illness, and healers, who seek to catch the drifting souls of those in coma or, with the aid of the spirits, to expel (typically by sucking, blowing or sweeping) alien substances that have intruded into the body. The shaman is also a diviner, in relation both to past and to future events, and the leader of souls through the territory of the spirits. Though an intermediary, the shaman is not usually a priest; someone else performs sacrifice and other cultic acts. And the shamanic experience, though manifesting the power of the spirit world, is in no way mystical; there is no quest for union with the divine.

SHAMANISM AND CHRISTIANITY

Shamanism in East and Central Asia has commonly achieved a symbiosis with Buddhism. In societies that have become Christian, in North America, Greenland, Northern Europe, Korea and northeast India, the institution has in most cases disappeared, and in many cases the situations it addressed have also disappeared in the process of social change. Some have detected the continuing influence of shamanism in the attributes of some Korean Christian leaders, in particular their devotional practices, and others have seen its legacy in revival movements (many with outstanding women leaders) in parts of northeast India.

Russian Orthodox missions in Siberia and Alaska left a place for shamanic practices in Christian communities, as gifts of insight and healing to be consecrated to God; and in Latin America shamanic practice has continued alongside popular Roman Catholic Christianity.

NEO-SHAMANISM IN THE WEST

Western popular interest in shamanism has grown since the 1960s. One source was the attraction of Native American culture that followed the cultural renaissance among Native Americans in the USA. A feature of the renaissance was the revival of neglected or abandoned practices such as shamanic ecstasy and the vision quest. Another feature was the emergence of a 'pan-Indian' culture that incorporated elements of widely separated ethnic origins. Thus the drug peyote, formerly used only among peoples of the Rio Grande area, was adopted in other places where the vision quest was being revived. Shamanic practices thus reappeared with new accompaniments and under the constrictive conditions of modern life, but as much as a statement of cultural identity as for practical use. Many young people, sympathetic to that identity but not sharing it, came to know these practices in a form less arduous than the traditional ones.

The books of Carlos Castaneda, which purported (though doubts have been raised as to whether they represent actual fieldwork) to relate the initiation of a young anthropologist by a Mexican shaman, increased the interest. But the main spur to popular shamanism in the West has been the postmodern and post-Christian search for spiritual reality frequently designated 'New Age', with its eclectic approach to religion and its archaizing appropriation (not always with historical justification) of ancient traditions.

Another academic anthropologist with experience of Latin America, Michael Harner, has given structure to the movement and has set out the features of traditional shamanism that can be practised in the modern Western world. The new ecological awareness is also hospitable to ideas of harmony with nature and animals. The result has been 'neo-shamanism', sometimes called 'urban shamanism' or, especially by its followers, 'core-shamanism'. It is supported by courses and seminars drawing upon Nordic, Celtic or Native American traditions and by a vast literature.

The environment of neo-shamanism differs from that of the traditional form. Typically, shamanistic cultures reflect harsh, insecure or difficult physical conditions. Neo-shamanism also has a different cosmology. The terrific aspects of traditional shamanism are not usually found in it. The urban shaman, like the traditional one, has helping spirits, but whereas traditionally the shaman had to strive for mastery in hostile or at least alien spiritual surroundings, the assumption underlying neo-shamanism is that the spirits are benevolent and cooperative. Mastery is not required. No religious structure is implied, but typically adherents are dissatisfied with positivist views of the world and disillusioned with contemporary psychology and psychiatry; some have had striking spiritual or psychic experiences.

The key difference lies in the relationship of shamans to the wider community. Traditionally, community and shaman were interdependent. A shaman working as an individual could be anti-social, and the community needed protection accordingly. Urban shamans pursue their path as individuals, perhaps with support from a drumming group, perhaps using tapes, and starting and ceasing at will. Testimonies, however, suggest that neo-shamanism has attracted people in the teaching and caring professions who desire to use the path for healing and harmony, perhaps reflecting a sense of failure by the secularized professions to cope with the spiritual realities underlying society.

BIBLIOGRAPHY

G. Doore (ed.), *The Shaman's Path: Healing, Personal Growth and Empower-ment* (London, 1988); M. Eliade, *Shamanism: Archaic Techniques of Ecstasy* (London, 1951, 1989); M. Harner, *The Way of the Shaman* (San Francisco, 1980, 1990); S. M. Shirokogoroff, *Psychomental Complex of the Tungus* (London, 1935, 1982).

A. F. Walls

SHINTO

Shinto is the indigenous faith of Japan. It arose out of the variety of religious practices of early Japanese communities which adhered to a particular, localized deity, a *kami*. This deity was supposed to provide protection for the village and prosperity in the harvest. 'Shinto' has frequently been translated as 'the way of the gods', but in Japanese thinking *kami* suggests something different from the Western concept of 'god'. *Kami* was used originally to refer to anything awe-inspiring in nature, and so trees, mountains, rivers and oceans may all be regarded as *kami*. It is very common throughout Japan, in any place of natural beauty, to find a small shrine dedicated to the *kami* of that particular locality. Certain humans may also come to be regarded as *kami*, usually after they have died. Sugawara Michizane, who came to be sacralized as Tenjin, the *kami* with a particular concern for education, is one such example. Perhaps the most important aspect of the *kami* is the fact that there is no essential discontinuity between them and the natural world.

SHINTO IN ANTIQUITY AND HISTORY

Shinto has no founder, nor does it have any sacred texts as such, although the writings in the *Nihongi* and the *Kojiki* contain many legends concerning the formation of Japan and the establishment of the Imperial line through the sun goddess Amaterasu. These two ideas, that the islands and people of Japan are creations of the *kami* and that the Imperial line is divine, were used in the late nineteenth and early twentieth centuries to help provide a focus for national unity.

When Buddhism was introduced into Japan in the sixth century it did not replace Shinto; the two existed side by side. Even today, surveys of religious affiliation show that over 95% of the population claim to practise Shinto, while 75% claim to be Buddhist. It is quite common for Buddhist temples and Shinto shrines to exist within the same complex.

It was only during the period of intense Japanese nationalism, from the late nineteenth century until the end of the Second World War, that Shinto effectively became the state religion and the Emperor came to be regarded as a living *kami*. After the war, the link between Shinto and the state was broken, and the Emperor is no longer held to be divine by the vast majority of Japanese. The concept of *ikigami* (living *kami*) does, however, still occur within some of the new religious movements which have their origin in Shinto.

SHINTO IN PRACTICE

Shinto for most Japanese is a religion of praxis. This partly explains why many follow both Buddhist and Shinto practices. Shrines are usually the focus for activity. At New Year over 80% of the population will visit a local shrine for *hatsumode*, the first prayer of the year. At that time people pray for good health, success in business or studies and in general for a happy and prosperous year. Before high school and university entrance exams many students will visit shrines dedicated to Tenjin (see above) to pray for academic success. While on holiday, many Japanese will take a moment to pray at the shrine which is invariably present at the nation's places of natural beauty. Some families will have a *kamidana*, a miniature shrine, within their own home, and will pray regularly for the protection of the *kami* on the household.

A Shinto shrine is entered by passing under the archway known as the *torii*. The shrine precincts have a sense of being sacred space, and before praying there is a need for purification. This consists of washing out the mouth and rinsing the hands. One then approaches the shrine itself. The act of prayer is very simple. First a small financial offering is placed in the offering box by the shrine. Then one claps twice to inform the *kami* of one's presence, bows twice to show respect, utters a short silent prayer, bows again, and withdraws.

Many worshippers at a shrine leave a record of their prayer by writing down their request on a small tablet known as an *ema*. These are then hung up within the shrine. The majority of them focus on success in education or business, or on family safety. The exceptions are those addressed to the spirit of a child who has been aborted, and are usually expressions of regret to the child. All, however, indicate the focus of Shinto on 'worldly benefits' (see Reader and Tanabe, *Practically Religious*). These benefits may be material, or a sense of solace, comfort or well-being. Shinto is generally unconcerned with the afterlife, one reason why most Japanese will have a Buddhist funeral.

Prayer offered at the shrine is a personal act of piety. Communal worship, or activity, is expressed in the shrine festivals. Many larger shrines have such festivals annually. They have both a religious and a social function within villages, small towns, or districts within larger cities. These festivals have certain common features. A procession, in which many people from the local community take part, leaves from the shrine and follows a route through the neighbourhood. At the heart of the procession is a portable shrine, usually carried by the younger men of the community. This symbolic tour of the neighbourhood helps to solidify the sense of community consciousness, and is intended to show that the *kami* provide spiritual and physical protection to the area.

SHINTO AS A CONTEMPORARY RELIGION

Modern Japan is frequently referred to as a secular society, and this process of secularization has accompanied the process, on the surface at least, of Westernization. This began in the mid-nineteenth century and accelerated after the Second World War, as Japan rebuilt itself, industrialized and transformed itself from a predominantly rural society into an urban one, modelled on the societies of the Western world.

One result of this secularization is that now few Japanese claim to believe in the *kami*. Significantly, however, far more still practise Shinto. It is clear, then, that Shinto has as much a cultural as a religious significance. It is in the practice of prayer at the shrine or in participating in festivals that people express and confirm their identity as Japanese.

Nevertheless, Shinto practice cannot be dismissed as a form of superstition or a traditional hangover from the past. Shinto has adapted remarkably well to contemporary 'secular' Japan. The majority of those who leave *ema* at a shrine, for example, are young people. Companies often have a small shrine on the roof of their building. Construction projects begin with a Shinto ground-breaking ceremony. Many of the larger shrines even offer ceremonies of exorcism for the protection of newly purchased cars.

How and why has Shinto managed to adapt itself to a secular society which has much in common with contemporary Western society? First, it is not a religion which makes great demands on practitioners, either in terms of time committed to it, or in terms of confessions of faith. Secondly, its focus on this-worldly benefits has enabled it to adjust from its origins as a rural religion concerned with harvest to encompass all the concerns of contemporary society, including the spheres of education and business as well as the continuing concerns of health and family. Thirdly, it has become intertwined with the national and cultural identity of Japan. In a nation which prides itself on its traditions and its sense of uniqueness in the world, Shinto still gives expression and focus to that feeling.

SHINTO IN THE WESTERN WORLD

Because of its close identification not just with the Japanese people but with Japan, Shinto has not exported itself to any great degree. When Japanese emigrated to Hawaii and the USA at the end of the nineteenth century, Shinto shrines were built to provide a focus for these communities. It is not, however, a missionary religion.

The presence of Shinto is felt indirectly through the 'new religions' of Japan. The 'old' new religions often drew on Shinto teaching, and were described as sects of Shinto. These groups, such as Tenrikyo and Omotokyo, have not attracted many converts in the West from outside the Japanese communities. Some of the 'new' new religions which have attracted Western converts, such as Sekai Kyusei Kyo ('The Church of World Messianity') and Mahikari ('True Light'), contain Shinto ideas or use Shinto forms. The hall of a branch of Mahikari in London, for example, bears a close resemblance to a Shinto shrine (cf. Clarke and Somers, *Japanese New Religions in the West*, pp. 56ff.). Few Japanese people in the West practise pure Shinto; there is usually no shrine to provide a focus for their activities and few possess a *kamidana*. Strictly speaking, then, Shinto is not a religious movement in the Western world. Nevertheless, within the Japanese context, it is a clear example of a religious tradition successfully adapting itself to a contemporary society significantly influenced by the West.

BIBLIOGRAPHY

P. B. Clarke and J. Somers (eds.), *Japanese New Religions in the West* (Sandgate, 1994); J. Nelson, *Enduring Identities: The Guise of Shinto In Contemporary Japan* (Honolulu, HI, 2000); S. Ono, *Shinto: The Kami Way* (Rutland, VT and Tokyo, 1962); I. Reader, *Religion in Contemporary Japan* (London, 1991); I. Reader and G. J. Tanabe, *Practically Religious: Worldly Benefits and the Common Religion of Japan* (Honolulu, HI, 1998); N. Tamaru and D. Reid (eds.), *Religion in Japanese Culture* (Tokyo, 1996).

D. Miller

SIKHISM

BRIEF HISTORICAL OVERVIEW

Sikhs revere Guru Nanak (1469–1539) as the founder of their faith. Born in Punjab of Hindu parents, he was a reformer, attacking ritualism, idolatry and the caste system and teaching the inwardness of true spirituality. He was followed by nine gurus, the tenth being Guru Gobind Singh (1666–1708). Gobind Singh gave Sikhism its definitive character and organization. In 1699 he established the *Khalsa* (the Sikh religious order) and required all his followers to accept a rite of initiation. Males were given the name 'Singh' ('lion') and females had 'Kaur' ('princess') added to their name. Each man was to wear the same highly visible uniform including uncut hair, turban and sword.

It was not until the late nineteenth century that Sikhism clearly distinguished itself from Hinduism as a religion in its own right. In recent times some Sikhs have asserted their claim to an independent territory of their own, known as Khalistan, which would ideally consist of the whole of Punjab, in both India and Pakistan and independent of both. During the past hundred years Sikhs have spread into many parts of the world, including Europe and North America. Recent estimates suggest that there are about 20 million Sikhs worldwide, of whom about a million live in Europe and North America, including approximately 500,000 in the UK, 100,000 in the USA and 250,000 in Canada.

SCRIPTURES

The Sikh holy book is known as the *Guru Granth Sahib* or the *Adi Granth*. Written in the Gurmukhi script, it consists mostly of hymns written by the gurus with devotional hymns from Hindu and Muslim saints. The tenth guru declared that there would be no guru after him, but henceforth the *Granth Sahib* would be for Sikhs their guru. The *Dasam Granth* containing the writings of Guru Gobind Singh, is also important.

BELIEFS

Sikhs are monotheistic. There is but one God, though he may be given many names. The *Mul Mantra*, which is repeated at the beginning of every section of the *Guru Granth Sahib*, defines Sikh belief: 'There is but One God, the Eternal Truth, the Creator, without fear, without enmity, timeless, immanent, beyond birth and death, self existent; by the grace of the Guru, made known.' Because God is formless he can never be incarnated in human form.

Like Hindus, Sikhs believe in transmigration and the cycle of birth, death and rebirth. A person's present status (good or bad) is determined by his or her past deeds. The gurus taught that there is an almost endless round of 8,400,000 rebirths. But being born as a human gives the soul the opportunity to break that cycle through the grace of the guru and meditation on the divine name. The soul must pass through five stages of development to reach the realm of bliss.

PRACTICES

Orthodox Sikh males are expected to wear the Five Ks. These are five things the names of which all begin (in Punjabi) with 'k'. They are the *kesh* (uncut hair tied with a turban), the *kangha* (a small comb worn in the hair), the *kara* (a steel bracelet), the *kachha* (shorts) and the *kirpan* (a ceremonial sword).

Community life revolves round the *gurdwara* or Sikh place of worship. Here congregational prayers and reading of the scriptures take place morning and evening. Large *gurdwaras* are open all day for individual prayer and meditation. Worshippers are given *karah prasad* (sacramental sweet food) at the conclusion of worship. Every *gurdwara* has a *langar* (community kitchen), where food is served to all, free of charge. Educational and social activities also take place in the *gurdwara* and temporary accommodation is provided for visitors.

The *gurdwara* is above all the place where the *Guru Granth Sahib* is the focus of worship and attention. Sikhs display their reverence for their scriptures on entering the prayer hall by touching the floor with their foreheads. The *Guru Granth Sahib* is placed upon a dais and nothing must be elevated above it. The scriptures are read and expounded every day. Some Sikhs keep a copy of the *Guru Granth Sahib* at home in a separate room, but this entails the responsibility of daily ceremonial, which many feel unable to undertake. Continuous readings of the *Adi Granth* may take place on special occasions in the *gurdwara* or the home, when the entire book is read in a forty-eight-hour period.

Prayers may be said at home as well as in the *gurdwara*. In the morning the *Japji Sahib* of Guru Nanak is recited. This long hymn of praise to God forms the first eight pages of the *Guru Granth Sahib*. Some will also say the *Jaap* of Guru Gobind Singh, consisting of 199 short verses in praise of God. In the evening the *Rehras* is recited. This mostly consists of nine hymns, which follow the *Japji Sahib* in the *Guru Granth*, pages 9–12. Before going to sleep, devout Sikhs will also recite the five hymns of *Kirtan Sohila*.

Initiation into the Sikh brotherhood, the *Khalsa*, is open to those who are willing to vow to follow the teaching of the gurus. The word *khalsa* (derived from a Persian word) means 'pure'. Entry into the *Khalsa* is made by a ceremony known as *Amrit Sanskar* or the *amrit* initiation. The initiated drink the nectar (*amrit*) of sweetened water and vow to wear the Five Ks and keep a strict code of conduct. Only a small percentage of Sikhs undergo initiation, but those who do are regarded as fully fledged Sikhs and are known as *Amritdharis*. Strictly speaking, only those who have undergone the *amrit* initiation constitute the *Khalsa*, but in practice those Sikhs who keep the Five Ks (Kesdhari Sikhs) are usually included. The Sikh community as a whole is known as the *Panth*, just as the community of Christians is the church.

The chief festivals of the Sikh calendar are *Baisakhi*, *Diwali* and *Gurpurbs*. *Baisakhi* is the New Year festival in March/April. It was on this day in 1699 that Guru Gobind Singh is said to have inaugurated the *Khalsa*. It is also the day for the devout to be initiated into the *Khalsa*. *Diwali*, the festival of light, is celebrated by Sikhs and Hindus. Sikhs commemorate the release of Guru Hargobind from prison on this day. *Gurpurbs* are birth or death anniversaries associated with the gurus. The best known are the birthdays of Guru Nanak (November 2) and Guru Gobind Singh (December/January).

SECTS

The Sikh community is divided not only by caste distinctions, but also into sects. Some of the better known are Namdharis, Nirankaris, Sant Nirankaris, Nihangs and the Nanaksar movement. A sect of a different kind, whose members are numerous in Britain and North America, are the Radha Soamis of Satsang Beas. This group, though led by a Sikh, has a majority of Hindu devotees. It is syncretistic, drawing on the teachings of other religions, including the Christian, Hindu, Buddhist and Muslim scriptures. It is not regarded as a Sikh sect in the strict sense, because it does not install the *Adi Granth* at its places of worship. Devotees are dependent on the teachings of their guru, listening to his lectures on video and being expected to adhere zealously to his doctrines and directions. However, not all Radha Soamis look to the guru at Beas as their authority.

THE IMPACT OF WESTERN CULTURE ON SIKHISM

Unquestionably the single most important question that diaspora Sikhs have to face is one of identity: who is a Sikh? This is not a new question in the history of Sikhism, but for Western Sikhs it has a new context and an added urgency. Are those who have cut their hair and abandoned their turbans still Sikhs? To what extent are Sikhs tied to Punjab and Punjabi culture? Can white Westerners become real Sikhs? Is Sikhism a global religion in the sense that it welcomes disciples from any country provided they adhere to the core beliefs and practices of the gurus? Is there a consensus regarding core beliefs and practices?

The phenomenon of Gora (white) Sikhs in North America has highlighted the question of identity. White North Americans first entered the Sikh *Panth* as disciples of Harbhajan Singh Puri, also known as Yogi Bhajan, and became members of his Healthy, Happy, Holy Organization (3HO) in the 1970s. As zealous converts they adhere to a strict interpretation of the standard manual of doctrine and practice called the *Sikh Rahit Maryada*, published in Punjab in 1950. They challenged the right of those who do not wear turbans to call themselves Sikhs, whilst demanding that they themselves be accepted as full members of the *Panth*. Thus they exposed the rift between Amritdhari, Kesdhari and Sahajdhari Sikhs. The Amritdharis (approximately 10–15% of Sikhs) have undergone the *amrit* initiation ceremony for admission into the *Khalsa* and observe strict vows; the Kesdharis wear the Five Ks without taking the vows of initiation; and the Sahajdharis have cut their hair and do not wear turbans. All claim to be Sikhs.

Caste distinctions within society continue to be important. The gurus were against caste, but nevertheless every Sikh is aware of his or her caste. The divisions between Jats, Ramgharias, Ravidasis and Valmikis have not disappeared in the West. In one respect they have even been reinforced, because each caste has enough money to build its own *gurdwaras*, even lavish ones. The low-caste Ravidasis and Valmikis, having prospered economically in the West, have been able to establish themselves in much better buildings than they can afford in Punjab. Caste also affects the status of white Sikhs. Since they have no known caste, where do they fit into the *Panth*? If caste distinctions were of no significance, the Gora Sikhs would be accepted on equal terms, but since caste determines marriage arrangements and leadership of *gurdwaras*, whites are not accepted as completely as those who are Punjabi Sikhs by birth.

The impact of the West varies enormously, depending largely on which generation is in view. The older generation who migrated from Punjab have retained their practices, and religious activity in UK *gurdwaras* is more intense than in most Punjabi villages. Visiting *sants* (Sikh holy men) have influenced all generations, keeping the traditions of Punjab alive among the diaspora. Subsequent generations, whilst remaining loyal to their Sikh identity, have adopted Western ways, and children at school are trained to question traditional rituals. Those who have undergone multiple migrations (e.g. from India to East Africa to the UK to the USA) have changed culturally and socially more than religiously. We have yet to see what will happen when more Western-born Sikhs take over as presidents of important *gurdwaras* and whether *gyanis* (traditional Sikh scholars) will be trained in the West to communicate to the young in English.

One very obvious characteristic of Sikh practice in Europe and America is that Sunday has become the weekly holy day, when large numbers go to the *gurdwara* and weddings take place. Because of the wealth generated in the West the number of *gurdwaras* continues to grow: there are more than 200 in the USA and Canada and well over 150 in the UK. An increasing proportion of these are purpose-built structures with lavish adornments. In 1999 a ruling from Amritsar banned the use of chairs and tables in the worship hall and *langar* of *gurdwaras*. This unprecedented action is an attempt to keep diaspora Sikhs under the control of Amritsar's Golden Temple authorities. Festivals are of great importance to the community, especially those that are recognized by schools and civic authorities. On these occasions *gurdwaras* in the same city work together more than they did and may make joint processions.

Marriage practice has been affected not only by changes to procedures for arranged marriages, but also by the incidence of divorce and mixed marriages. Whether this will undermine the cohesion of family life has yet to be seen. Feminism also affects marriage relationships. The Western emphasis on women's rights, equal opportunities and working wives has already had an impact. On the intellectual front, there are feminist writers who claim support from the writings of the Gurus for a feminist understanding of the divine and for equality of the sexes in all matters religious (e.g. Nikki-Guninder Kaur Singh, *The Feminine Principle in the Sikh Vision of the Transcendent* [Cambridge, 1993]). In 1976 a woman took part as an officiant at the *amrit* ceremony in Vancouver for the first time (though this is allowed by the Sikh manual), and more women *granthis* (those authorized to read the *Granth Sahib* in worship) can be expected to officiate in *gurdwara* services.

Though predominantly political in motivation, the Khalistan movement is also of religious significance in that it represents the desire for some form of theocracy. But this movement affirms the view that Sikhs belong both to a religion and to one racial group; they claim a homeland for Punjabis who are born Sikhs, rather than proclaiming a faith that non-Punjabis can join and in which they can feel at home. Many Jat *gurdwaras* have been taken over by supporters of Khalistan, and their *langar* walls are covered with pictures of martyrs for Sikh independence.

On the intellectual front, much good has

been done for the Sikh cause by the inclusion of Sikh studies in Western universities. However, much damage has been done by the clash between Sikh traditionalists and academic scholars. The subjection of the *Guru Granth Sahib* to critical methodology has not been appreciated, and even champions of Sikh history such as W. H. McLeod have been vilified. This clash will be damaging to the community if it inhibits young Sikh scholars from taking up academic research and working out a new synthesis of tradition and Western thought.

THE IMPACT OF SIKHISM ON THE WEST

The court cases in the West over Sikh insistence on wearing turbans and carrying swords, even miniature ones, have led to the recognition that ethnic minorities have legitimate rights to diverge from majority norms, especially when their practices are dictated by religion.

Sikh men with their distinctive turbans are highly visible in any society. In Britain the high percentage of Sikhs in the Asian community has added to their influence. Though only 1.5% of India's population, Sikhs in Britain are said to outnumber Hindus; for this reason they have a much higher profile in Britain than they enjoy in their homeland. The presence of Sikhs in such large numbers in the West has resulted in Sikhism being accepted as a world religion in its own right, distinct from Hinduism.

BIBLIOGRAPHY

W. O. Cole and P. S. Sambhi, *The Sikhs: Their Religious Beliefs and Practices* (London, 1978); R. Gidoomal and M. Wardell, *Lions, Princesses, Gurus* (Godalming, 1996); J. S. Grewal, *The Sikhs of the Punjab* (Cambridge, 1990); W. H. McLeod, *Sikhism* (London, 1997); J. T. O'Connell, M. Israel and W. G. Oxtoby (eds.), *Sikh History and Religion in the Twentieth Century* (Toronto, 1988); H. S. Rahi, *Sri Guru Granth Sahib Discovered* (Delhi, 1999).

B. J. M. Scott

SPIRITUALISM

From time immemorial, human cultures have attempted to contact the spirits of the dead, a practice of which the biblical writers always take a dim view (Is. 8:19–22; Deut. 18:10–11). But the effective beginning of modern Western spiritualism came with Emanuel Swedenborg (1688–1772), a Swedish scientist and mystic who aroused international astonishment by claiming, 'Of the Lord's Divine mercy it has been granted me now for several years, to be constantly and uninterruptedly in company with spirits and angels, hearing them converse with each other, and conversing with them.' After Swedenborg's death his followers founded the Church of the New

Jerusalem, which still exists, and laid the foundation upon which later spiritualists would build.

The idea that we are surrounded by invisible spirits, with whom contact can be made, was encouraged by the growth of mesmerism in the same period. Franz Anton Mesmer (1734–1815) and his disciples produced hypnotic phenomena which looked very like possession by alien spirits. The trance state, in which mediums typically received messages, was one of mesmerism's legacies to spiritualism.

In 1844, the semi-illiterate Andrew Jackson Davis (1826–1910) had a mesmeric experience which led to his writing *The Principles of Nature*, in which he forecast that the barrier between the visible and invisible worlds was soon to be opened. Then on 31 March 1848, in a cabin in Hydesville, New York State, two young sisters of the Fox family thought they communicated with a poltergeist who informed them he was the spirit of a murdered pedlar, buried in their cellar. Interest was immediate, worldwide and lucrative; the girls turned professional and made a great deal of money; and by 1851 there were over a hundred mediums in New York alone.

Spiritualism fascinated the people of the mid-nineteenth century, for it seemed to provide factual evidence about one of the most obsessive riddles of Victorian times: the possibility of survival beyond death. Spiritualist circles and churches formed everywhere; scientists and men of letters devoted themselves to investigating the phenomena. 'Table-tilting' became a popular society hobby; in 1853 Sir David Brewster estimated that 'there are thousands of tables turning every night in London, so great is the excitement on the subject'. Baltimore cabinet-maker Isaac Faulds invented the 'ouija board' in 1869 and stimulated massive growth in 'do-it-yourself' spiritualism. French philosopher H. Leon Denizard Rivail (1804–69) became a reluctant convert to the movement and wrote *The Spirits' Book*, under the pen name 'Allan Kardec', to share the information he believed the spirits had given him. Kardec's brand of 'spiritism' (which stresses reincarnation and the endless progression of souls towards perfection) became the classic form of spiritualist belief in South America.

There are 'spiritists' in America and Europe too, but the more influential non-Kardecian variety is usually called 'spiritualism'. In Britain it is promoted primarily by the Spiritualist Association of Great Britain (founded in London in 1872) and the Spiritualist National Union (Manchester, 1890). After its heyday in the nineteenth century, spiritualism settled down to become a sizeable minority faith in most Western countries, though there have been occasional flurries of exceptional interest (not least following both World Wars).

Spiritualism does not see itself as a continuation of Christianity (unlike spiritism; Kardec wrote, 'The Law of the Old Testament was personified in Moses: that of the New Testament in Christ. Spiritism is then the third revelation of God's law'). But in 1931 a 'Christianized' version arrived. The Greater World Christian Spiritualist League started when Winifred Moyes in South London claimed to have received communications from one Zodiac, a temple scribe in the time of Christ. Christian spiritualists regard Christ 'as the only means by which we can get to know what God is like'. They believe in prayer, water baptism, nine gifts of the Spirit and (often) breaking of bread.

BELIEFS AND PRACTICES TODAY

Spiritualists base their faith on seven principles supposedly received from the world beyond: the fatherhood of God; the brotherhood of humanity; continuous existence; communion of spirits and ministry of angels; personal responsibility; compensation and retribution hereafter for good or evil done on earth; a path of endless progression. Although there have been attempts to dispense with the principles (particularly amongst younger spiritualists who have come to share Kardec's views on reincarnation), in practice spiritualism places more emphasis on experimental practice than on subscription to a creed.

'Compensation and retribution' refer to *karma*, not heaven and hell; Christian ideas of vicarious atonement through Christ are energetically rejected; Jesus is seen primarily as an outstandingly gifted medium. Christian spiritualists, however, 'accept the leadership of Jesus Christ' and give him a role in human forgiveness ('sins committed can only be rectified by the sinner himself, through the redemptive power of Jesus Christ, by repentance and service to others'), but ultimately the gospel of spiritualism is one of salvation by human effort. 'All forms of life created by God ... evolve until perfection is attained.' Christian spiritualists emphasize that it is the love of Christ, and the example he showed, which draws people to God; his death has no redemptive power in itself.

The Swedenborgian Church, similarly, operating with a reduced Bible from which 33 books have been censored, believes that the idea of vicarious atonement is 'a mere human invention'. There is no Trinity; Christ is the Father; and the only 'resurrection' is our progression beyond death. All religious systems, not just Christianity, have a divine duty and purpose. The spirit world exists as a number of concentric spheres, each with its own inhabitants; they live in houses, build churches and run schools. Swedenborg alone is able to interpret the Bible properly.

The spiritualist view of human life is that through the processes of evolution we have gained 'the higher moral and spiritual faculties, which survive, unaffected, the decomposition of the human body'. We are all children of God from birth, and need only to progress from one sphere of existence to other, higher realms. This progress can continue after death, but is more easy to begin during life on earth. Evil spirits are not 'demons', but simply people who have not yet learned to desire growth and progression and who are bound in selfish destructiveness.

Spiritualist churches have some of the trappings of orthodox churches (hymns, prayers and talks), but the emphasis is primarily upon the development of mediumistic gifts and public demonstrations of spirit communication. Those with the ability to learn mediumship are shown how to enter a state in which they are receptive to messages supposedly coming from beyond themselves and can transmit them to onlookers.

'Physical' mediumship, in which heavy objects levitate and musical instruments play spontaneously, has declined a great deal this century. However, there has been a growing interest in spiritual healing, promoted by the renowned Harry Edwards, and fanned into flame by the 1970s vogue for Filipino spirit healers, who claimed to carry out operations simply by pummelling the body, without making an incision, and to remove cancerous growths while leaving no scar behind. After numerous exposures, the spirit healers are no longer so popular, but healing remains one of the most enticing possibilities which spiritualism offers.

SPIRITUALISM IN THE MODERN WORLD

Spiritualism has been both helped and hindered by the modern explosion of interest in all things supernatural and bizarre. It has been helped by the public's willingness to look in unorthodox directions for advice, help, counselling and physical remedies, and some spiritualist 'stars' (such as the late medium Doris Stokes) have achieved considerable celebrity. But spiritualism has also been hindered by its nineteenth-century shape; committed to the style of a 'church', with a definable creed (however sketchy), it has been rejected by many psychic investigators as too rigid a framework for the uncommitted stance they wish to take. New

Age 'channellers' produce communications which are very like those of spiritualist mediumship, but they claim to be in contact with 'ascended masters' rather than the dead relatives of sitters.

Spiritualism has also been undermined by a century of investigation, which has proposed alternative explanations for the phenomena (there is plenty of evidence to suggest, for example, that some of the information produced comes from unconscious telepathy), and by repeated exposures of leading mediums who have been shown to have produced results by fraud. (Mediums themselves have testified that the spirits deceive; the famous Eusapia Palladino warned one investigator, 'Watch me or I'll cheat; John King makes me cheat.' 'John King' was the name of her control spirit.) Although it would be far too sweeping to claim that all spiritualist practice is based on deception, the movement's well-documented, unremitting history of trickery has made observers extremely cautious about paying too rapid credence to spiritualist claims.

BIBLIOGRAPHY

A. Ford, *The Life Beyond Death* (London, 1972); R. Gasson, *The Challenging Counterfeit* (Plainfield, NJ, 1966); A. Gauld, *Mediumship and Survival: A Century of Investigations* (London, 1982); J. A. Pike, *If This be Heresy* (New York, 1967); E. Twigg, *Medium* (London, 1973); J. Stafford Wright, *Mind, Man and the Spirits* (Exeter, 1972).

J. D. Allan

TRANSPERSONAL PSYCHOLOGY

Transpersonal psychology is the title of an emerging (fourth) 'force' in the psychology field. It is led by a group of psychologists and professional men and women from other fields who are interested in those ultimate human capacities and potentialities that have not had a place in classical psychoanalytical theory of the Freudian type ('first force'), or in behaviourist theory ('second force'), or in humanistic psychology ('third force'). Transpersonal psychology is known as the 'fourth force' and is concerned with the exploration of transcendent and altered states of consciousness, including mystical experience.

Humanistic psychology is most closely identified with the experimental psychologist Abraham H. Maslow (1908–70). It is known as 'third force' psychology to differentiate it from the first and second force psychologies of Freudianism and behaviourism. It was a post-Second World War creation of psychologists interested in studying psychology scientifically from the perspective of healthy individuals. It sought to discard behaviouristic models based on observations of animal behaviour. Maslow believed that all human beings have an innate spiritual yearning to experience the sacred and fulfil their maximum potential for goodness. Humanistic psychology had barely been organized when Maslow recognized a 'fourth force' emerging from it, which overlapped with humanistic psychology, but which went beyond it. In 1967 he called this force 'transhumanistic psychology'.

Transpersonal psychology (a term which was coined by Stanislav Grof and subsequently used by Maslow) has developed since 1976 as that branch of psychological theory which takes religious and mystical experiences seriously. It refuses to follow the reductionistic interpretations widely accepted in other psychological schools. In doing so, it claims well-known authorities like William James (1842–1910) and Carl Gustav Jung (1875–1961) as predecessors. G. I. Gurdjieff (1877–1949) had some influence on the movement with his emphasis on the 'fourth way' or necessary spiritual resources.

William James believed that the unconscious depths of the human personality are at once psychological and spiritual. This view made it possible for modern people to view self-exploration as spiritually significant and religious experience as psychologically profound. Carl Jung also is seen as a forerunner of transpersonal psychology because he held that the world of the psyche and the world of 'outer' reality were simply different reflections of the one world. He was concerned to decipher the 'primal' or archetypal images and symbols that rise up in a person as landmarks on the inner way towards the maturing of the soul (individuation). The Jungian way to individuation, which leads to the formation and knowledge of the human self, guides both Christians and non-Christians, religious and non-religious, to maturity of the soul and the spirit. Thus, like transpersonal psychology, Jung embraced spirituality as a vital component of personality. In Jungian psychology there was room for religious thought and mystical experience.

Transpersonal psychologists have devised what they call 'cartographies of consciousness' which distinguish a hierarchy of levels in the psyche. Their premise is that the traditional psychological schools address the lower levels of the psyche, but are largely inadequate for dealing with the higher or transpersonal levels. The transpersonal levels are seen as the proper domain of spiritual traditions, especially those of oriental origin. Transpersonal psychology thus aims at providing a theoretical synthesis of Western psychology and oriental spiritual systems and technologies. The union with the 'more' in the universe that religion effects helps us to overcome our sense of 'wrongness' and thus fosters true ethical life.

This attempt to integrate religiously based theories into secular psychology has brought transpersonal psychologists into conflict with what they consider to be an outdated 'Cartesian-Newtonian' or scientific framework. Most transpersonalists go beyond the basically empirical approach to transpersonal experiences in the manner exemplified by William James and Carl Jung. This has resulted in an openly 'spiritual' form of psychology, the influence of which has spread beyond the strictly psychological domain to the fields of religious studies and New Age therapy and beyond. It has, for example, influenced the well-known religious studies scholar Huston Smith.

It should be noted that the idea of shamanic consciousness (of which much is made by New Agers and Neo-Pagans) is closely connected to the transpersonal movement. It is based on the view of the shaman as the specialist in the field of altered states of consciousness. The shaman claims to mediate between the transpersonal realm of spirits and gods and the world of humans. Also related to transpersonal psychology is the holistic health movement. This movement affirms that every human being is a unique holistic, interdependent relationship of body, mind, emotions and spirit. In this context, healing is a process in which a person becomes whole physically, emotionally, mentally and at deeper levels, resulting ideally in an integration with the underlying inward power of the universe.

With its emphasis on the ability of each individual to achieve a higher consciousness, the transpersonal approach requires therapists to lay an experiential foundation. They do so using both Eastern and Western methods such as dream analysis, meditation, yoga; behavioural medicine; bodywork; and the transpersonal experience of altered states of consciousness as a means of achieving higher states. Transpersonal psychology is still in its infancy and is still controversial. Critics argue that it is not sufficiently defined and trespasses too much upon the province of religion.

Transpersonal ideas have been made popular by psychologist Gerald Janpolsky in his book *Love Is Letting Go of Fear*. Ken Wilber is regarded as the foremost theoretician in the transpersonal movement. He states that the different Western psychological schools are not mutually exclusive but complementary. They address different levels of consciousness and each approach is valid as long as it remains within its proper domain and does not claim to be able to explain other, particularly higher, levels.

According to Wilber, whereas the higher levels have been largely ignored by Western psychology, this has generally not been the case in the East. Oriental spiritual schools, it is argued, have developed psychological systems addressing these higher levels of consciousness. Stanislav Grof, a leading empirical researcher in transpersonal psychology, has produced a cartography of the unconscious, embodying a non-reductionistic approach to the 'higher' levels of experience. This has become one of the pillars of transpersonal psychology. Grof's work can be seen as an example of trends evident since the early 1960s which have enabled psychologists and psychiatrists of various backgrounds to take a new look at mystical states of consciousness as part of a broad concern to investigate alternatives to mechanistic and deterministic views of human life.

As individual interests in the field of transpersonal psychology became more diverse, some of them were classified under the rubric 'New Age'. The New Age movement can be understood as developing broader, more applied versions of transpersonal psychology. Even though transpersonal psychologists have made a careful effort to remain academically respectable, they have attained only a modest acceptance in academic and psychological circles.

In an almost paradoxical way, transpersonal psychology postulates a source of outside power without giving up the centrality of the individual self. Universal wisdom is greater than the self, yet is contained within the self. By accepting a 'divine within' (although it is not always articulated in these terms), transpersonal psychology has tended to silence the question of God.

In transpersonal psychology the ground of all being is consciousness. We gain experience of reality only when all the barriers are broken down. We then move toward higher consciousness, which can be induced by meditation or peak experiences (e.g. mystical experience, altered states of consciousness, even drug-induced hallucinations). The goal is the return of consciousness to its original state. The conclusion that consciousness is all-pervading entails a particular view of the divine, which is not seen (as in Christianity) as the transcendent Other searching for humanity's renewal and communicating to humans.

Transpersonal psychology has made a significant impact on Western culture. Certainly the New Age movement has embraced one of its basic tenets: one has infinite potential and can realize it, become enlightened, because personal experience equals reality, and reality can thus be created by focusing on the experiences of the self. This is also the reason why transpersonal psychology has been closely associated with the human potential movement, 'est' (Erhard Seminars Training), and such groups as Lifespring and Forum.

BIBLIOGRAPHY

R. Chandler, *Understanding the New Age* (Dallas, TX, 1991); A. Faivre and J. Needleman (eds.), *Modern Esoteric Spirituality* (New York, 1992); W. J. Hanegraaff, *New Age Religion and Western Culture: Esotericism in the Mirror of Secular Thought* (Leiden and New York, 1996); J. P. Newport, *The New Age Movement and the Biblical Worldview: Conflict and Dialogue* (Cambridge and Grand Rapids, MI, 1998); C. Tort (ed.), *Transpersonal Psychologies* (London, 1975).

J. P. Newport

UFO RELIGION

The UFO movement, which began in the 1940s, can be divided into two categories: the scientific and the religious. Some ufologists believe that flying saucers are real and that the political establishments have suppressed evidence proving their existence. But, the scientific proof being meagre, what began as science has often turned into religion. In fact, the religious interpretation of UFOs has tended to overwhelm the scientific in the minds of both its believers and the general public.

Though unidentified flying objects (UFOs) are a new phenomenon, there is some precedent for them. In the eighteenth century, Emanuel Swedenborg reported conversations with beings from outside the solar system. During the nineteenth and twentieth centuries some people, primarily psychics, claimed to have met visitors from other planets. UFO movements have particular roots in the theosophical and spiritualist traditions. Along with contemporary UFO phenomena, these claims of earlier contacts with extraterrestrial beings provide a background for the modern UFO cults.

The modern history of UFOs began on 24 June 1947. On that day, in the state of Washington, Kenneth Arnold saw nine bright disks moving like 'saucers' in front of his plane. Since that time, tens of thousands of people around the globe claim to have seen UFOs. Most of the reports have admitted of 'conventional' explanations, but approximately 10% of them have not been explained by scientific analysis and traditional reasoning. These mysterious sightings have been the subjects of scientific controversy and have prompted occult explanations.

In the early years, even UFO proponents rejected occult explanations and instead appealed to the laws of physics. But in 1952, UFO sightings took on another dimension when George Adamski claimed that a UFO occupant had met and talked with him. He wrote several books on the subject, and many other reports of contacts with visitors from other planets followed.

Some of the people who claimed to have been contacted by UFO occupants sought to explain the nature of UFO visitors in scientific terms. But a second group viewed the UFOs from an occult perspective. Having made contact with what they claimed to be extraterrestrial beings, they committed themselves to telling others the message of the space people. The movement had acquired a religious dimension.

While the message articulated by the space people varied in specifics, the general thrust was usually the same. The space people were more highly evolved beings who were coming to aid the occupants of Earth. They brought a message of concern about the course of humanity, whose materialism was leading them to destruction. But the space people also offered a means of salvation: humankind could avoid the coming destruction by following the message of love.

On the whole, the UFO movement must be regarded as a world-affirming religion. The message coming from the space aliens is essentially redemptive. They will cure all diseases, deliver humanity from nuclear holocaust and even provide transportation to another planet where there is happiness and security. In sum, salvation is to come through the intervention of the space beings, who will lead humanity to a higher stage of evolution.

Examples of world-affirming groups are Unarius, the Raelian movement, Understanding, Inc., and the Amalgamated Flying Saucer Clubs of America. Begun by Ruth and Ernest Norman, Unarius awaits the landing of starships in 2001. Each space ship will bring 1,000 scientists to earth. They will bring us a new science to heal most mental and physical diseases. But most important, they will train earth people to live together in love and peace. Founded in 1973 by 'Rael', the Raelian movement is a non-communal millenarian group. Rael allegedly had an encounter with a space being and since then he has been proclaiming that earthlings have entered the 'Age of the Apocalypse' and have the choice of destroying themselves with nuclear weapons or leaping into a planetary consciousness. But immortal space prophets will descend and help humanity to choose the path of immortality through science. Understanding, Inc., is an eclectic group allegedly in contact with space beings. These saucer people (a remnant of a super-civilization on earth) offer us a 'true' and 'spiritual' science that will enable humanity to live in harmony. The Amalgamated Flying Saucer Clubs of America (AFSCA) claim that with the help of the space beings humankind can liberate itself from its current mental, physical, spiritual and economic problems.

However, some UFO messages are starkly apocalyptic, predicting catastrophes that will bring an end to history. Some speak of an economic collapse; others point to natural disasters, perhaps a depletion of the ozone or pollution of the oceans. Yet some insist that humanity will survive, either by being transplanted to some safe planet to live with the aliens or, in some cases, to become one with the aliens through the process of hybridization. Hybridization refers to the union of a space being with a human, a process through which the superior knowledge and moral strength of the alien raises humankind to a higher level.

Examples of the UFO apocalyptic strand are the Aetherius Society and Heaven's Gate. Influenced by theosophy, the Aetherius Society claims that earth is at a crisis point as it enters the Aquarian Age. On the one hand, evil magicians from the lower astral realms are attempting to enslave humanity, whilst on the other hand, Interplanetary Adepts will come to Earth to battle the forces of darkness and free humankind. In March 1997 UFO apocalypticism took a deadly twist: 39 members of the Heaven's Gate cult committed mass suicide. Its leaders, Marshall Applewhite and Bonnie Nettles (at times called Bo and Peep), had proclaimed their UFO gospel for years. They argued that only by escaping from our doomed planet could the human race be saved. Salvation meant being taken up by a flying saucer. By the 1990s this UFO gospel had acquired a more drastic apocalyptic tone: people could be beamed up by a flying saucer only if they left their human containers (physical bodies); that is, committed suicide.

As noted, religious ufologists can be divided into those who bring a positive message and those who bring a negative one. But they may be classified in another way. Some regard alien encounters as psychic contacts with superior beings. Others attempt to interpret UFO appearances within the broad framework of Christian apocalyptic theology. But both of these groups embrace an occult outlook.

Those regarding alien visitations as psychic encounters maintain that space creatures from UFOs have contacted human beings and conveyed information pertaining to the future of planet Earth or the human race. These messages come through supernatural, psychic or paranormal manifestations and they deal with the urgent needs of this planet. Such UFO encounters can be compared to traditional religious or mystical experiences. The contactees function as mediums and become the prophetic bearers of information from alien creatures.

This 'psychic contact' category can in turn be subdivided into at least two major types. There are those who have modelled themselves after the theosophical tradition, notably the 'I AM' branch. They believe that their leaders are in touch with the space beings, who are, for the most part, the Ascended Masters of the Theosophical Society. The second and more common group has its roots in the spiritualist tradition and believes that superior beings in UFOs contact humans through selected mediums. Those embracing this position believe that they are in direct contact with space beings. Thus their beliefs and practices do not hinge on the existence of flying saucers.

The second broad category consists of those who view UFOs from a broad but often twisted Christian perspective. They attempt to interpret their flying saucer experiences within the context of Christian teachings. Some in this group do not abandon their Christian faith, but ask serious questions; for example, how do UFOs fit into a Christian worldview? Others travel far from the Christian faith, infusing occult teaching into a vaguely Christian framework. For example, they believe they will be 'beamed up' by a flying saucer and transformed, in what is a superficial imitation of the Christian rapture. Others see the space beings as God's agents in the world, akin to angels. Still other ufologists regard the space beings as demonic intruders whose goal is to subdue the Earth.

BIBLIOGRAPHY

W. M. Alnor, *UFO Cults and the New Millennium* (Grand Rapids, MI, 1988); J. Dean, *Aliens in America* (Ithaca, NY, 1999); J. R. Lewis (ed.), *The Gods Have Landed* (Albany, NY, 1995); R. Story (ed.), *UFOs* (New York, 1980).

R. Kyle

UNIFICATION CHURCH

One of the most interesting religious groups to emerge in the second half of the twentieth century is the Holy Spirit Association for the Unification of World Christianity, called 'Tong-il-Kyo' in Korea and better known as the 'Unification Church' in the West. The news media frequently featured the face of its founder, Sun Myung Moon, in their broadcasts, newspapers and periodicals during the 1970s and 1980s.

THE BIRTH AND GROWTH OF THE UNIFICATION CHURCH

The genesis of the Unification Church can be traced back to a Korean mountainside in 1936. Sun Myung Moon was 16 at the time and deep in prayer. He later claimed that Jesus then appeared to him and pleaded with him to complete the mission he had left unfulfilled more than nineteen centuries ago. Despite knowing that the hardships and challenges would be greater than those any normal man could endure and overcome, he accepted the call to be the Lord of the Second Advent, or the second Messiah, because he believed the salvation of all of humanity depended upon him.

After several years of collecting and processing doctrinal insights from other religious thinkers, Moon gathered a small band of devoted followers and officially established his church in 1954. Three years later he produced the first version of the *Divine Principle*, which Unificationists regard as the third testament of the Bible, or the 'Completed Testament', because it reveals the hidden truths of the Old and New Testaments.

Western news agencies first became fascinated with Moon during his 'Day of Hope' tour in the United States in 1971 and 1972, when he called upon Americans to turn to God and become a more godly nation. He drew increased attention to himself while on his next tour in November 1973, when he announced that God had chosen Richard Nixon to be president and did not want him to be removed from office during the Watergate hearings. At a single wedding ceremony, Moon married 1,800 couples, including seventy couples from the United States, in February 1975, which confirmed in the minds of many Americans that he and his church were brainwashing unsuspecting American college students.

After Moon and his family took up permanent residence in a suburb of New York City, he continued to expand his financial empire. One consequence of his notoriety and economic success was a lengthy legal struggle with the Internal Revenue Service, which resulted in his indictment and conviction for tax evasion. He served thirteen months at the federal prison in Danbury, Connecticut, from 1984 to 1985. Although this setback further tarnished his public image, his followers within the Unification Church viewed him as a victim of religious persecution and a martyr for his remarkable faith in God.

UNIFICATION DOCTRINES AND SACRAMENT

Sun Myung Moon and the *Divine Principle* offer a quite different interpretation of Genesis 3 from the traditional, orthodox view of the fall of humankind. Though not entirely original, the Unificationists' teaching is both curious and involved. They assert that Adam and Eve did not literally eat from the fruit of the tree of knowledge of good and evil, but that the fruit symbolized ungodly sexual relations: the first act of disobedience was the sexual union between Eve and Lucifer, which constituted the physical fall of humanity; and the second act of disobedience was the sexual union between Eve and Adam, which was unlawful because of Eve's prior sin with Lucifer and which constituted the spiritual fall of humanity.

Unification doctrine teaches that God tried many times to redeem humankind through various people, such as Abraham, Moses and David, but that each failed. Finally, God called Jesus to be the Messiah by redeeming humanity both physically and spiritually. It was God's intention for Jesus to perfect himself by defeating Lucifer (who had become Satan when he seduced Eve), then marry the perfect woman and have sinless children, and thus establish the kingdom of heaven on earth, which had been God's original plan with Adam and Eve, but which Lucifer had foiled because of his jealousy of their intimacy with God and his physical lust for Eve.

Despite Jesus' unparalleled faith in God, the Jews failed to accept Jesus as the Messiah, largely because John the Baptist, whom the Jews revered, refused to become one of Jesus' apostles. Therefore, Jesus had to take a secondary path during his earthly ministry, which led him to death on the cross, thereby enabling him to redeem humankind spiritually, but not physically. Thus a second Messiah must complete the mission Jesus left unfulfilled. Incidentally, Unificationists believe Jesus is not God in the sense of being equal with God the Father; that is, they dispute the notion of a triune Godhead in which Jesus is the second person of the Trinity.

Moreover, their understanding of the Messiah diverges from orthodox teaching. In order for one to be the Messiah, he must perfect himself, his family, his nation (or people) and the world (or creation, including all of humanity, past, present and future). Unificationists believe that Sun Myung Moon has accomplished the first two requirements and is well on his way to fulfilling the last two. After Moon accepted Jesus' call in 1936, he fought Satan spiritually for nine years until he subjugated the devil, thus attaining self-perfection. Subsequently, he married Hak Ja Han, and they produced twelve children to represent the twelve tribes of Israel, thereby establishing God's heavenly family on earth.

When communism, the culmination of Satan's evil lies, is thoroughly obliterated and Korea is finally unified under a godly democracy, the third requirement will be achieved. When all religions and other human pursuits are united under the single banner of the Unification Church and all dominions, both earthly and heavenly, including the spirits of deceased individuals, are devoted to Sun Myung Moon, then the last requirement will be realized. The Unificationists believe these two requirements will ultimately be attained even if Moon passes into the heavenly realm beforehand. What he has accomplished has ensured that God's plan will be entirely fulfilled.

This understanding of Unification doctrine reveals a deeper significance to the mass marriages Moon conducts. Indeed, Unificationists regard their weddings as sacraments, displacing baptism and communion which were the sacred institutions of the previous dispensation. In fact, they believe that we have passed from the Old Testament period and the New Testament period into the Completed Testament period, and that when Moon dies he will open the way into the highest realm of heaven, never attained before even by Jesus.

THE ATTEMPT TO ASSIMILATE

Although Western society in general and many voices within the Christian church in particular have been strongly critical of Moon and his movement, a high priority of the Unification Church has been and continues to be joined to the mainstream of religious life in North America. Constant attempts to find common ground with Christians have succeeded in erasing much of the hysteria of the 1970s and 1980s regarding Moon's movement. Now it is no longer viewed with the same suspicion with which many view, for example, the People's Temple and Branch Davidians, but rather as an offshoot of the Christian tradition with aberrant doctrines and practices.

Meanwhile, Unificationists are still aggressive in recruiting new members, increasing their political influence and economic wealth and, most importantly, propagating Moon's teachings. Their success in achieving these goals is difficult to determine, particularly because the Unification Church is reluctant publicly to release membership figures for its main organization and affiliates. Nevertheless, it is estimated that the number of North American Unificationists has never exceeded 30,000 and is probably closer to 10,000 at present. Most of the one or two million followers of Moon are Korean and Japanese.

PROMINENT RELATED ORGANIZATIONS

Family Federation for World Peace and Unification is the official modern form of the Unification Church. News World Communications own the *Washington Times* and the United Press International news service.

The Unification Theological Seminary in Barrytown, New York, is a theological training centre which has produced current leaders and theologians of the Unification Church. For decades the Collegiate Association for the Research of Principles has been active on college campuses throughout North America, enlisting new recruits to the church and promoting conservative social and political values. The United Federation of Churches sponsors forums and conferences, promoting interfaith and ecumenical dialogue.

Meanwhile, Unificationists have launched countless business ventures, associations for the arts and sports, and evangelistic campaigns. Although the Unification Church may not be as visible as it once was, its presence in Western society still warrants its serious consideration as a unique alternative to traditional Christianity.

BIBLIOGRAPHY

E. Barker, *The Making of a Moonie: Choice or Brainwashing?* (New York, 1984); W. Martin, *The Kingdom of the Cults* (Minneapolis, rev. edn., 1985), ch. 13; S. M. Moon, *Divine Principle*, (Washington, DC, ^{2}1973); R. A. Tucker, *Another Gospel: Alternative Religions and the New Age Movement* (Grand Rapids, MI, 1989), ch. 11; J. I. Yamamoto, *The Puppet Master: An Inquiry into Sun Myung Moon and the Unification Church* (Downers Grove, IL, 1977); J. I. Yamamoto, *Unification Church* (Grand Rapids, MI, 1995).

J. I. Yamamoto

ZOROASTRIANISM

The influence of Zoroastrianism before the advent of both Christianity and Islam was so great and widespread that no modern religion has been untouched by it. During the second millennium BC Aryan peoples living to the northwest of India began to move south. One group (amongst whom Hinduism developed) entered India; another entered present-day Armenia, Azerbaijan and the Iranian plateau region. In this area Zoroastrianism was to evolve.

When Cyrus the Great established the Persian Empire in the sixth century BC, Zoroastrianism became the official religion of the then largest world empire. Alexander (known in the West as 'the Great', but in Iran as the 'accursed') overthrew this empire in the fourth century. In the second century BC Iranian religious traditions re-emerged with the Parthians, who established a new empire which challenged Rome, and represented a powerful world faith in the lifetime of Jesus of Nazareth. From the fourth century until the seventh, the Sasanian Empire dominated Iran; then it fell to Islam, which gradually suppressed Zoroastrianism until it was a minute remnant.

The indications are that the religion of ancient Persia was similar to the Vedic religious culture and practices of India. There are parallels between their pantheons of nature gods.

The main ritual practice of the ancient Persian religion consisted of various forms of sacrifice: animal, libation and fire. The first two forms seem to have been combined into one ceremony, and the evidence suggests that the ritual became orgiastic. Zoroaster was later to condemn the priests for their drunkenness and their attempts to deceive the people.

The fire sacrifice, however, is significant because of its parallels to the Vedic fire sacrifice recorded in the ancient Hindu texts (e.g. *Rig Veda*) and also its continuance as the most important ceremony in Zoroastrianism to modern times.

On this religious scene the figure of Zarathustra (known to us through the Greeks as Zoroaster) appeared. A monotheist teaching ethical dualism, Zoroaster reformed the existing religion so forcefully that it has carried his name ever since.

ZOROASTER AND THE AVESTA

It is difficult to identify the historical figure of Zoroaster. Whilst some scholars assert that he is a mythical figure created to account for the religious reform movement in Persia, most accept the claim of the Zoroastrian scriptures, the *Avesta*, that such a person did exist.

The *Avesta* comprises writings composed over a period of thousand years, from the sixth century BC to the fourth century AD. According to tradition, the *Avesta* is a surviving remnant of a once vast literature. The main texts are: the *Yasna*, a collection of prayers and liturgies within which are the *Gathas*, seventeen chapters of hymns attributed to Zoroaster; the *Yasht*, a collection of sacrificial hymns; the *Videvdat*, literally 'Law (*Dat*) against (*vi*) the demons (*dev*)', writings concerned mainly with ritual purification.

Whilst the generally accepted view is that the *Gathas* represent the work of Zoroaster, there are contrasting perspectives on the other texts. Some modern scholars argue that there is a large degree of continuity between the *Gathas* and the later writings. These academic debates reflect contemporary conservative and liberal discussions within Zoroastrianism about the authority of priests and that of the *Gathas*, which are understood to be the source of authority.

ZOROASTER

There is considerable discussion over his dates. Early scholarship placed him in the seventh to sixth centuries BC, but more recent research has placed him around 1200 BC. His lineage was traced back to Gayomart, the first man in Persian mythology, through forty-five generations. It is related that his mother, Drughdhova, conceived him by a shaft of heavenly light. In parallel to the birth narratives of other significant religious figures, the accounts relate how miraculous events surrounded Zoroaster's birth and demonic assaults were made upon his life. At the age of seven, Zoroaster was placed with a teacher for some eight years before returning home at fifteen to assume the responsibilities of adulthood.

Like Siddartha Gautama a century later, Zoroaster was distressed by human suffering. For some fifteen years he withdrew into isolation before enlightenment came; in an instant, he identified all the evils and pain of creation with the sunset that divided day from night, light from darkness. In Zoroaster's perception, there is day and night, light and darkness, so human life embraces good and evil. In the same way as day and night cannot be altered, so good cannot become evil and evil cannot become goodness. Zoroaster concluded that two forces ruled the world: Good, which he called Ahura Mazdah (Wise Lord) and Evil, called Angra Mainyu (Lie, or Demon).

On the day following his enlightenment, Zoroaster is said to have been standing by the sacred river Daiti and there to have received a vision of Ahura Mazdah. Later generations, seeing the importance of Zoroaster's experience, probably embellished and elaborated the account with further details. The central feature of the event was Zoroaster's being taken into the presence of Ahura Mazdah, where he learned the principles of true religion. Zoroastrian calendars begin with the date of Zoroaster's vision, 5 May 630 BC, which is termed the first 'Year of Religion' (1 AR). From Zoroaster's insight at sunset developed his belief in the dualism of the universe, of the two forces of good and evil in continual struggle. Zoroastrianism is a teleological religion: its churches believe that Ahura Mazdah, the Lord of goodness, wisdom, truth and light will finally defeat Angra Mainyu, the Lord of evil, lies and darkness.

Ten years passed before Zoroaster gained converts; these included the King of Bactria, with whose royal support further missions were commissioned. Zoroaster died at the age of seventy-seven. Although he had three wives and several sons and daughters, he seems to have spent most of his life as a solitary.

ZOROASTER'S TEACHINGS

Zoroaster was repelled by what he saw as the religious corruption of his time. He condemned the religious leaders as enemies of Ahura Mazdah and his law. However, he did not abolish every aspect of the ancient religion; some he proceeded to adapt.

MONOTHEISM

The established worship of Atar (the God of Fire) was refocused upon Ahura Mazdah, with Atar becoming the symbol of Ahura Mazdah's righteousness and light. The ancient Persian religion had embraced a pantheon of both benign and malevolent deities; Zoroaster affirmed that Ahura Mazdah was dominant over them. This affirmation explains Zoroaster's tendency to monotheism and his gathering of varied myths and symbols into a picture of a single universal conflict between good and evil.

HUMAN CHOICE

Humankind is divided into two opposing groups: *ashavants* (followers of truth) and *dregvants* (followers of evil). The dualism which Zoroaster saw in human life and the creation is found throughout the whole cosmos and in every aspect of it, material and spiritual. Between every pair of opposites humankind has to make a choice, for good or evil. In the *Gatha* writings humans become the arbiters between these two forces. The choices are made in the three areas of thought, word and action and determine a person's final destiny. This constant conflict between Ahura Mazdah, representing light, truth and life, and Angra Mainyu, representing darkness, lies and death, raises the issue of the origin of the universe. According to Zoroaster, Ahura Mazdah is the creator: 'He [Ahura Mazdah] who, through His holy mind, thought: "Let the blessed expanses be filled with light." He Himself [Ahura Mazdah], in His wisdom ... created ... Physical bodies, consciences and wills ...' (*Yasna* 31:7–11).

Whilst Ahura Mazdah is the creator, he is also the model of freedom of choice and he gives this capacity to every person. Consequently, every human being has the freedom to choose good or evil, and (without overriding this freedom) he desires all humanity to believe and trust in him freely.

HUMAN DESTINY

Zoroaster is portrayed as believing that Ahura Mazdah will triumph over evil in a final judgment at the end of the world. For the 'followers of truth' this judgment will seem like passing through warm milk. To the 'followers of the lie' the experience will be an ordeal of fire. In subsequent developments of this teaching the individual soul is seen as being judged at the *Chinvat* bridge, which crosses hell and leads to paradise on the other side. As the soul traverses the bridge, its record of good and evil actions will be opened and read. If the good outweighs the evil then the soul continues on to paradise; however, if evil outweighs good then the soul moves no further than the middle of the bridge and falls into hell beneath.

LATER DEVELOPMENTS IN ZOROASTRIANISM

The dualism between the protagonists Ahura Mazdah and Angra Mainyu created problems for later Zoroastrian thought. If Ahura Mazdah were to triumph over evil, then Angra Mainyu had to be seen to exist by the permission of Ahura Mazdah. Moreover, if Angra Mainyu is an eternal force then Ahura Mazdah cannot be seen as the sole creator. Disputes on such matters led eventually to the formation of submovements within the religion, such as Mazdaeism, Zurvanism and Mithraism.

The *magi* of Matthew 2:1–2 may have belonged to a group, probably from Media, who had adopted Zoroaster's religion and supplied its priests. Known for their abilities in astrology, divination and 'magic', they became expert exponents of Zoroaster's doctrines.

In modern Zoroastrianism two buildings are significant. The Fire Temple, as the focus of ritual, will be visited by the devout daily and by most adherents at least four times a month. In the Tower of Silence the bodies of the dead are exposed and, according to ancient custom, vultures strip the remains bare. This is to protect the sacred elements of earth, fire and water from pollution.

A child is initiated into the faith by the *naojote* ceremony (*nao*, 'new'; *zote*, 'to offer prayers'; so *naojote*, 'new initiate to offer prayers'). After this a child is considered responsible for prayer and observance of the ritual customs. Integral to the initiation is dressing with the *sudrah* (sacred shirt) and *kushti* (sacred thread), which a Zoroastrian will wear as the signs and symbols of his or her faith.

ZOROASTRIANISM IN DIASPORA

As circumstances for Zoroastrians in Iran worsened after the Islamic invasion, migrants finally formed a base in India within the Gujarat. Known as the 'people from Pars' (Persia), or the Parsees, they lived in obscurity and peace before flourishing under British colonial rule in the nineteenth century. This process has continued since Indian independence with their entrepreneurial skills taking them further afield to found communities in Hong Kong and Pakistan, through East Africa to the UK, Canada and the USA in the early 1970s, and in the next decade to Australia. Today Zoroastrians are more widely dispersed than at any time in their history. Having said that, numerically they are in decline, due to an ageing population, late and low marriage rates, small or no families and a non-proselytization policy.

ISSUES FACING MODERN ZOROASTRIANS

Identity: Asian Zoroastrians resent being grouped with adherents of other Asian religions and prefer to identify with the homeland of Zoroastrianism in Iran, whilst acknowledging their homes are now in the UK or elsewhere.

Language: English has now become the stepmother language of Zoroastrians in the UK, the USA and other English-speaking contexts. Fluency in English is a sign of the community's increased prosperity.

Prejudice: both Asian and Iranian Zoroastrians object to being identified as 'Indian', 'Pakistani' or 'Arab', asserting their distinctness from these ethnic groups.

Intermarriage: the community in the West has to face exogamous marriages, which lead to a decline in observance of its rituals and the consequent redrawing of its boundaries.

Conversion: there are divisions in the community on the initiation of outsiders into the faith. The place of non-Zoroastrian spouses and their debarment from attendance at rituals is also contentious.

BIBLIOGRAPHY

J. K. Amighi, *The Zoroastrians of Iran: Conversion, Assimilation, or Persistence* (New York, 1990); M. Boyce, *A History of Zoroastrianism: Zoroastrianism under Macedonian and Roman Rule* (Leiden, 1991); M. Boyce, *Zoroastrianism: Its Antiquity and Constant Vigour* (Costa Mesa, CA, 1993); M. Boyce, *Zoroastrians: Their Religious Beliefs and Practices* (London, 1988); P. Clark, *Zoroastrianism: An Introduction to an Ancient Faith* (Brighton, 1999); J. R. Hinnells, *Zoroastrians in Britain* (Oxford, 1996); R. Writer, *Contemporary Zoroastrians: An Unstructured Nation* (New York, 1994).

I. G. Williams

INDEX OF NAMES

INDEX OF SUBJECTS

INDEX OF ARTICLES